P·A·R·S·E·D
VERGIL

COMPLETELY SCANNED-PARSED
VERGIL'S *AENEID* BOOK 1
WITH
INTERLINEAR AND MARGINAL TRANSLATIONS

ARCHIBALD A. MACLARDY

Bolchazy-Carducci Publishers, Inc.
Wauconda, Illinois USA

Cover Design
Adam Phillip Velez

Parsed Vergil
Completely Scanned-Parsed Vergil's Aeneid Book 1
with Interlinear and Marginal Translations

Archibald A. Maclardy

© 2005 Bolchazy-Carducci Publishers, Inc.
(1899, 1901, by Hinds & Noble)
All rights reserved.

Bolchazy-Carducci Publishers, Inc.
1000 Brown Street
Wauconda, IL 60084 USA
www.bolchazy.com

Printed in the United States of America
2005
by United Graphics

ISBN-13: 978-0-86516-630-1
ISBN-10: 0-86516-630-7

Library of Congress Cataloging-in-Publication Data

Virgil.
 [Aeneis. Liber 1. English & Latin]
 Parsed Vergil : completely scanned-parsed Vergil's Aeneid Book 1 with interlinear and marginal translations / Archibald A. Maclardy.
  p. cm.
 ISBN-13: 978-0-86516-630-1 (pbk. : alk. paper)
 ISBN-10: 0-86516-630-7 (pbk. : alk. paper)
 1. Aeneas (Legendary character)--Poetry. 2. Legends--Rome--Poetry. 3. Latin
language--Readers. I. Maclardy, Archibald A. II. Title.

PA6807.A5M224 2005
873'.01--dc22

2005029460

PREFACE.

WITH this book *anyone* can learn not only *about* the Latin language, but can learn *the language itself*.

The editor has designed it as an aid to three classes of learners, and it is his confident belief that *they* will find it in practice to be of really invaluable service — first, *teachers*, both those rusty in Latin who nevertheless find themselves called upon to teach Vergil without much time for preparation ; and also those who are "up" in Vergil, but still may benefit greatly, at the first, by having at their elbow a model for teaching and drilling which, like this, sets forth to the most minute detail each step in the parsing and the translation of every word in the text, and indicates to the eye clearly and correctly the scansion of every line — then *clergymen*, whose opportunities may not have permitted the acquisition of Latin, but who yet desire to possess themselves rapidly of so much of this language as a minister really needs for etymological, philological, and literary purposes, as well as for the simple satisfaction of emerging from a state of ignorance regarding a language so familiar to the educated — then *students*, both those who are not so situated as to have an instructor, but are still ambitious enough to study Latin without a teacher, and also students who, though members of a class, yet need the help of a complete model for translation and analysis and scansion, to be used, of course, under wise guidance. Again, it is not wholly unlikely that the perfectly competent teacher of Latin will find this book of service — not because of any need for assistance, but because of the advantage of comparing one's

own ways and opinions with the methods and views of another
competent teacher, particularly if that other's ideas are not always
in accord with one's own.

The following suggestions are made to aid any learner who
may wish to use this book as a BEGINNER'S LATIN BOOK: Take
any one of the Latin grammars referred to farther on in this
preface; learn from it to distinguish and to decline the five Latin
declensions of nouns; the first and second and the third declen-
sion of adjectives; learn also how to distinguish the four conju-
gations of the verbs and how to inflect the verbs; read attentively
Latin Syntax, especially the coarse print portion of it. With this
equipment, turn to any nude text of the First Book of Vergil's
Aeneid — the TUTORIAL, for instance, or any other. Read a line
or sentence or paragraph, noting carefully the cases and numbers
of the nouns and adjectives, and the persons and numbers of the
verbs. If without knowledge of the *meaning* of the words, turn
to the interlined translation in this volume, using it *now* as a
vocabulary; and then turning from this back to the nude text,
translate the line, sentence, or paragraph — always in the Latin
order of the words. Compare your version with the interlinear
translation. After this transpose your line, sentence, or para-
graph into the English order of the words, making as good
English as possible, and then, not till then, compare your per-
fected whole with the English *translation in the margin*. Finally,
look up the grammatical references as given in the footnotes, and
examine the synonyms carefully, and thus develop a critical schol-
arship. Not only will rapid progress be made in the facility to
translate Latin, but a certain degree of culture will be attained
as the outcome of the process.

The text of this FIRST BOOK OF THE AENEID is based upon
Papillon and Haigh's revision of the text of Ribbeck, with a few

orthographical and lectional modifications where the common acceptance of a form of spelling and superior MS. or editorial sanction of a reading in the text appear to justify the change. Instances of the latter kind are comparatively few, as the text of Vergil may be regarded as almost fixed, but when the chief Vergilian commentators disagree, reference is made to the fact in the footnotes, which discuss the grounds and estimate the value of the most noteworthy variations.

Every verse of the text is fully scanned, being divided off into its several feet (*e.g.* the first foot of verse 1, *Árma vi-*) with the first syllable of each foot accented like *arma* above; the principal *caesura* or break of every verse is indicated by the sign ,, as after *cano* in the first verse of the text. Syllables or vowels which are elided by *Elision* or *Ecthlipsis* (which, with other matters relative to the hexameter, are explained in the footnotes) are printed in *italics*. It is necessary, in order to acquire a knowledge of the internal construction of hexameter verse and thereafter an appre-. ciation of Vergil's unexampled mastery of this metre, — the metre of the Iliad and the Odyssey — that the learner should closely study in one of the grammars named later in this preface such of the final sections or chapters as are devoted to the rules governing the quantity of vowels and syllables, as well as those that treat of the Dactylic Hexameter in particular. Then he would do well to write out a few lines of the text and endeavor to mark off the feet, together with one or more (if there are more) of the *caesurae;* after a little practice of this kind and a comparison of the result with the scansional marking of the text, a good working grasp of the metre will probably be obtained.

The text is accompanied by a rigidly literal interlinear translation according to the Latin order of the words, and a passably literal translation in the order of English idiom in the margin;

the author has tried to perform the difficult task of keeping the latter from extremes of over-freedom or paraphrase on the one hand and baldness on the other.

The footnotes are both explanatory and critical. Every word of the text is parsed; and when the construction or metre seems to require it, reference is made to the Latin grammars of Allen and Greenough's Revised Edition, Bennett, Gildersleeve revised by Lodge, and Harkness's Revised Standard Edition. Mythological and historical allusions are treated at sufficient length for a correct understanding of the subject matter of the text.

Latin synonyms have been noted wherever they occur, and hints as to critical word study are given on almost every page. Grammatical references, and occasionally the synonyms, are repeated, especially in the first part of the book, in order that principles, grammatical and philological, may be kept continually before the reader's eye.

At the end of this volume is added a complete and continuous scanned Latin text, which will assist student and teacher alike, — the *former* in testing his grasp of the constructions and the interdependence of clauses, and his facility in translating; the *latter* in orally conducting a class whose members have prepared their work from the pages wherein text, translation, and footnotes are all found together. Moreover, this text will afford an opportunity for occasionally undergoing that best of disciplines, translation at sight. A further advantage it has is that it enables a student to obtain a bird's-eye view, so to speak, of the scansion of whole verses and whole paragraphs, thereafter to appreciate the melody and artistic beauty of the rhythm, and finally to commit passages to memory not only with ease, but with enjoyment.

ARCHIBALD A. MACLARDY.

ABBREVIATIONS.

abl.	= ablative.	*ind.*	= indicative.
abs. or *absol.*	= absolute.	*indecl.*	= indeclinable.
acc.	= accusative.	*indef.*	= indefinite.
act.	= active.	*infin.* or *inf.*	= infinitive.
adj.	= adjective.	*interrog.*	= interrogative.
adv.	= adverb.	*intrans.*	= intransitive.
appos.	= apposition.	*l.*	= line.
A. & G.	= Allen & Green-	*ll.*	= lines.
	ough's Latin	*m.*	= masculine.
	Grammar, Re-	*n.* or *neut.*	= neuter.
	vised Ed.	*neg.*	= negative.
B.	= Bennett's Latin	*nom.*	= nominative.
	Grammar.	*num.*	= numeral.
cf. (*cōnfer*)	= compare.	*obj.*	= object.
comp.	= compound.	*p.*	= page.
conj.	= conjunction.	*pp.*	= pages.
cop.	= copulative.	*part.*	= participle.
dat.	= dative.	*pass.*	= passive.
decl.	= declension.	*perf.*	= perfect.
dem.	= demonstrative.	*pers.*	= personal.
dep.	= deponent.	*pluperf.*	= pluperfect.
disc.	= discourse.	*plur.*	= plural.
distrib.	= distributive.	*poss.*	= possessive.
=	= *equals, equivalent*	*pred.*	= predicate.
	to, or *denotes.*	*prep.*	= preposition.
e.g. (*exemplī*		*pres.*	= present.
grātiā)	= for example.	*pron.*	= pronoun.
etc. (*et caetera*)	= and so forth.	*rel.*	= relative.
f. or *fem.*	= feminine.	*sc.* (*scīlicet*)	= that is to say;
ff.	= following.		sometimes =
fr.	= from.		supply.
fut.	= future.		
G.	= Gildersleeve's	*sing.*	= singular.
	Latin Gram.,	*subj.*	= subject.
	Revised Ed.	*subjunct.*	= subjunctive.
gen.	= genitive.	*subst.*	= substantive.
gov.	= governs; some-	*superl.*	= superlative.
	times = gov-	*trans.*	= transitive.
	erned.	*viz.* (*vidēlicet*)	= namely.
H.	= Harkness's Latin	*1, 2, 3, 4*	
	Grammar, Rev.	with verbs	= 1st, 2d, 3d, 4th,
	Stand. Ed.		conjugation.
i.e. (*id est*)	= that is.	*1st, 2d, 3d, 4th,*	
imperf.	= imperfect.	*5th.*	= 1st, 2d, 3d, 4th,
impers.	= impersonal.		5th, declension.

1   Arma vi,rúmque ca,nó „ Tro,iae qui,prímus ab,| I sing of arms and
                                                  | the hero who first
    Arms   and the man I sing   of Troy who   first   from | from the coasts of

LINE I. **Arma,** acc. plur., gen. *armōrum,* n., 2d (no sing.); direct obj. of *cano.*
The term includes all kinds of warlike accoutrements, weapons and armor. In the
Aeneid Vergil combines the warlike deeds such as Homer describes in the Iliad
with the personal adventure of the Odyssey; see *virum* below. —— **virum,** acc.
sing. of *vir, virī,* m., 2d; direct obj. of *cano.* *Vir* is used for (1) *man,* as
distinguished from woman; *homo* distinguishes *man* from other animals; (2) *hero,* as
here. The reference is to Aeneas, whom Vergil represents as the ancestor to
Romulus and the national hero of Rome. —— **que,** enclitic conj., joining *arma* and
virum. Observe, with regard to the copulative conjunctions, that: *et* simply
connects; *que* closely joins together two members internally connected, and is
appended to the second word so joined; *atque* (written *ac* before consonants, except
c, g, qu) adds emphasis to the second of the words it connects, and is sometimes
used specially to join a third member of a series.   A. & G. 156, *a*; B. 341;
G. 475, 476, 477, and NOTE to 481; H. 554, I. —— **canō,** 1st pers. sing. pres. ind.
act. of *canō, -ere, cecinī,* no supine, 3; its subject is *ego* understood. A pers. pron.,
when standing as subj. in a sentence, is not expressed except for purposes of
distinction or emphasis.   A. & G. 206; B. 166, 2; G. 207; H. 446.   There is a
caesura after *cano,* i.e. a pause made by a word ending within a foot. A *caesura*
occurs in each line always once and sometimes twice, most frequently, as here, after
the 1st (rarely the 2d) syllable of the 3d foot; it is also common after the 1st
(rarely the 2d) syllable of the 4th foot, as after *profugus,* l. 2, when it is usually
accompanied by an earlier *caesura* in the 2d foot, as after *Italiam,* l. 2.   A. & G.
362, *b, c*; B. 368, 3; G. 784, and NOTES 1, 2, 3; H. 611. —— **Trōiae,** gen. sing.
of *Trōia, -ae,* f., 1st; poss. gen. limiting *oris.*   A city of Phrygia which the
Greeks besieged for 10 years in order to: (*a*) recover Helen, wife of Menelaus,
whom Paris, son of Priam, king of Troy, had abducted from her home; (*b*) exact
vengeance for violated hospitality. —— **quī,** nom. sing. m. of the rel. pron. *quī,*
quae, quod, gen. *cūius,* dat. *cui,* abl. *quō, quā, quō,* acc. *quem, quam, quod;* subj. of
venit, and in agreement with its antecedent *virum.* A rel. pron. agrees with its
antecedent in gender, number, and person, but its case is determined by its own
clause. A. & G. 198; B. 250, 1 and 2; G. 614; H. 453. As rel. clauses limit a noun
or pron. which has gone before, they are adjectival in force. The rel. pron.
usually stands first in its own sentence. —— **prīmus,** nom. sing. m. of the ordinal
adj. *prīmus, -a, -um;* agrees with *qui,* and qualifies *venit* with adverbial force.
A. & G. 191; B. 241, 2; G. 325, REM. 6; H. 443. Some commentators translate
primus as *of old,* but it should probably be taken literally as *first;* Antenor (see
l. 242) settled near the modern Venice, in Cisalpine Gaul, and *not* within the limits
of ancient Italy. —— **ab,** prep. with the abl., here marking *place from which.* It is
written *ab* before words beginning with a vowel or *h,* and *a* or *ab* before words
whose initial letter is a consonant.   A. & G. 152, *b,* and 153; B. 142, 1;
G. 417, 1; H. 434.   *A* or *ab* is used to point out (1) agent, (2) place whence,
(3) cause, (4) origin, (5) separation in time. —— **ōrīs,** abl. plur. of *ōra, -ae,* f., 1st;
governed by *ab.* *Ora* lit. means a *border limit,* hence *coast;* it is used more widely
to signify *region, country.*

Troy came, an exile of fate, to Italy and the shores of La-	óris	Itali,ám, „	fa,tó	profu,gús, „	La,víniaque, 2
	the shores	*to Italy*	*by fate*	*exiled*	*and Lavinian*
vinium, having been much buffeted both on land and on the	vénit	Lítora,, múltum	il,le ét	ter,rís „	iac,tátus 3
	came	*shores*	*much*	*he both*	*on lands tossed about*

LINE 2. **Italiam**, acc. sing. of *Italia, -ae*, f., 1st; marks *limit of motion* without a prep. In prose the prep. *ad* or *in* would be required, but here the ordinary rule, that *motion towards* a town or small island is expressed by the acc. without a prep., is poetically extended to include countries. A. & G. 258, *b*, NOTE 5; B. 182, 4; G. 337; H. 380, I and II, and esp. NOTE 3. There is a *caesura* before *fato;* a *caesura* in the 2d foot frequently accompanies a principal *caesura* in the 4th foot, but that in the 2d foot is sometimes the principal one. See the note on *cano,* l. 1, and A. & G. 362, *b*, *c*; B. 368, 3; G. 784, and NOTES 1, 2, 3; H. 611. —— **fātō, abl.** sing. of *fātum, -ī*, n., 2d; abl. of cause, closely dependent on *profugus*. A. & G. 245; B. 219; G. 408; H. 413. —— **profugus**, nom. sing. m. of the verbal adj. *profugus, -a, -um*, limiting *qui*. The reference is to the flight of Aeneas after the fall of Troy. The main *caesura* or break in the sentence follows *profugus*. See note on *Italiam* above, and esp. the references there given. —— **Lāvīnia**, acc. plur. n. of *Lāvīnius, -a, -um*, qualifying *litora*. Lavinium was a town of Latium afterwards founded by Aeneas and called in honor of his wife Lavinia. In scanning, note that the two syllables *ia* are united to form one single syllable; the *i* must be slurred and given a *y* sound, i.e. *Lavinya*, in accordance with the rule for *synizesis* or *synaeresis*. A. & G. 347, *c*, and REM. on *d*; B. 367, 4; G. 727; H. 608, III, NOTE 2. Many who think Vergil would not at the outset have allowed himself such a licence read *Lavinia*, for which there is much MS. support. —— **que**, conj., connecting *Italiam* and *Lavinia litora*. See note on *que*, l. 1. —— **vēnit**, 3d pers. sing. perf. ind. act. of *veniō, -īre, vēnī, ventum*, 4.

LINE 3. **Lītora**, acc. plur. of *lītus, lītoris*, n., 3d; marks *limit of motion* without a prep. *Lavinia litora* = the single idea *Lavinium*. See note on *Italiam* above. The phrase defines Italy in an epexegetical or restrictive manner; the *whole* is first stated, and then the *part*. —— **multum**, acc. sing. n. of *multus, -a, -um*, qualifying *iactatus* adverbially. A. & G. 238, *b*; B. 366, 7; G. 91, I, *c*; H. 304, I. The final *um* is suppressed before the vowel *i* of *ille:* the rule is that final *m*, with the vowel preceding it, is suppressed or *squeezed out* (*ecthlipsis*) before a word beginning with a vowel or *h*. A. & G. 359, *d*; B. 366, 7; G. 719, 2; H. 608, I. —— **ille**, nom. sing. m. of *ille, illa, illud*, gen. *illīus*, the demonstr. pron. of the 3d pers.; in appos. to *qui* which it vividly recalls; grammatically it is superfluous. The final *e* is suppressed by elision before the initial vowel in *et*. A. & G. 359, *c*; B. 366, 7; G. 719, 1; H. 608, I. —— **et**, cop. conj. used correlatively. See *et* below, and A. & G. 156, *h*; B. 341, 3; G. 476, NOTE 5; H. 554, I, NOTE 5. —— **terrīs**, abl. plur. of *terra, -ae*, f., 1st; locative abl., denoting place where. A. & G. 258, *f*; B. 228, 1, *d*; G. 385; H. 425, II, NOTE 3. The plur. is used poetically for the sing.; but perhaps Vergil hints at the wanderings of Aeneas to Thrace, Crete, Sicily and Africa. —— **iactātus**, nom. sing. m. of perf. part. pass. of *iactō, -āre, -āvī, -ātum*, 1: agreeing with *ille*. *Iacto* is the frequentative of *iacio, I throw;* cf. *canto*, frequentative of *cano*. *Iactatus* is used more correctly with *alto* than with *terris*, but there is a figurative allusion to *storm-tossings* on both elements. —— **et**, cop. conj. used correlatively. See note on *et* above. —— **altō**, abl. sing. of *altum, -ī*, n., 2d; strictly it is the neut. of the adj. *altus, -a, -um*, corresponding exactly to *the deep* instead of *the deep sea*. For the case of *alto*, see the note on *terris* above.

4 et , álto   **Ví**   supe,rúm sae,vae „ memo,rém
and on the deep by might of the gods above cruel   mindful

5 Iu,nónis   ob , íram,   **Múlta** quo,que ét
of Juno   on account of   the wrath   many things   also   too

deep by the vio-
lence of the gods
above for the sake
of cruel Juno's un-
forgetful anger; hav-
ing, moreover, suf-

LINE 4. **vī**, abl. sing. of *vīs*, f., 3d; acc. *vim;* gen. and dat. very rare; plur. *vīrĕs*, *-ium = strength;* may be considered either as an abl. of cause, or as an abl. of means. A. & G. 245, 248, *c*; B. 218, 219; G. 401, 408; H. 416, 420. —— **superūm**, gen. plur. of plur. noun *superī*, gen. *superōrum* or in contracted form *superūm;* gen. after *vi*. The masc. of the adj. *superus, -a, -um* (comp. *superior;* superl. *supremus* or *summus*) is used substantively; cf. *vicinus, neighboring*, as adj., *a neighbor*, as noun. With *superum* cf. *deum* for *deorum*, *virum* for *virorum*, and consult A. & G. 40, *e*; B. 25, 6; G. 33, REM. 4; H. 52, 3. Jupiter, Venus, Neptune, and other *superi* took an active interest in Aeneas. —— **saevae**, gen. sing. f. of *saevus, -a, -um,* agreeing with *Iunonis*. —— **memorem**, acc. sing. f. of *memor, memoris*, no neut. plur.; agrees with *iram*. Though strictly personal, this adj. is applied figuratively by poets to emotions and things. Note that the final *em* is not elided before *Iunonis* as the initial *i* is equivalent to *j;* cf. *iacio* and *jacio*. —— **Iūnōnis**, gen. f. of *Iūnō:* subjective poss. gen. A. & G. 214, I; B. 199; G. 362, 363, 1; H. 396, II. Juno (in Greek, *Hera*) was the daughter of Saturn, and the sister and wife of Jupiter. —— **ob**, prep. gov. acc. —— **iram**, acc. sing. of *ira, -ae*, f. Juno's resentment, which was directed against Trojans in general during the siege of Troy, and after its fall against Aeneas and his followers, had its origin in the slight put upon her by Paris, son of Priam, king of Troy, in assigning the prize of beauty over her head to Venus; cf. l. 27.

LINE 5. **multa**, acc. plur. n. of *multus, -a, -um;* gov. by *passus*. —— **quoque**, conj., but generally classed as an adverb; not quite so strong in force as *etiam*. Observe that it never stands first in a sentence, but usually second, or even third if the second word is emphatic. A. & G. 151, *a*; 345, *b*; B. 347, 1; G. 479; H. 554, I, 4. The final syllable *que* is elided before the *e* of *et*, in accordance with the rule that final vowels and diphthongs, except interjections, are suppressed before words commencing with a vowel or *h*. See *ille*, l. 3, and A. & G. 359, *c*; B. 366, 7; G. 719, 1; H. 608, I. —— **et**, conj. with the force of *etiam;* it is redundant after *quoque*, but has an intensifying effect; cf. the Greek ἔτι δὲ καί. —— **bello**, abl. sing. of *bellum, -i,* n.; abl. of *specification*. Note that *bellum* is another form of *duellum*, a struggle between two (*duo*) adversaries. —— **passus**, nom. sing. m. of the perf. part. of the deponent verb *patior, patī, passus sum*, 3: agreeing with *ille*, like *iactatus* with which it is connected by *quoque*, and governing *multa*. Deponent verbs are passive in form, but *active* in meaning. A. & G. 135; B. 112; G. 113, 220; H. 231. The reader should note that *iactatus* and *passus* are participles referring back to *qui*, and that *dum . . . Romae* is dependent on *passus*. Thus the relative clause to which *virum* is antecedent extends from *Troiae qui*, l. 1, to *Romae*, l. 7. It is quite unnecessary to construe *passus* as *passus est* with the *est* suppressed. —— **dum**, temporal conj. It has two common meanings: (1) *while*, (2) *until*. With the subjunct. *conderet* it implies purpose or aim, and hints at the difficulties which preceded the founding of the city. *Dum* meaning *while* takes the pres. ind., even in reference to the past, and also in *oratio obliqua;* meaning *until*, it takes the ind. usually, but when purpose or doubt is implied, the subjunct. A. & G. 328; B. 293, UI; G. 572; H. 519, II, NOTE I. —— **conderet**, 3d pers. sing. imperf. subjunct. act. *condō, -ere, condidī, conditum*, 3; gov. by *dum;* the subjunct. indicates purpose.

fered much in war too, till he should found his city and bear his gods to Latium — whence arose the Latin race, the Alban fathers, and the walls of lofty Rome.	bel,ló pas,sús „ dum , cónderet , úrbem, *in war having suffered until he should found the city* Ínfer,rétque de,ós Lati,ó, „ genus, únde La,tínum 6 *and should bring gods to Latium the race whence Latin* Alba,níque pa,trés „ at,que áltae, moénia, Rómae. 7 *and Alban the fathers and lofty the walls of Rome.*

See note on *dum*. —— **urbem**, acc. sing. of *urbs, urbis,* f., 3d; direct obj. of *conderet.* The city meant is Lavinium.

LINE 6. **Inferret**, 3d pers. sing. imperf. subjunct. act. of *inferō, inferre, intulī, illātum*, 3; gov. by *dum*. —— **que**, enclitic conj., joining *conderet* and *inferret.* See note on *que*, l. 1. —— **deos**, acc. sing. of *deus, -ī.,* m., 2d (voc. sing. *deus;* plur. irreg.: nom. *deī, diī,* or *dī;* gen. *deōrum* or *deūm;* dat. and abl. *deīs, diīs, dīs*); direct obj. of *inferret.* The Penates, i.e. household gods, included deified ancestors, whose statues were carefully preserved, as well as certain of the recognized gods. States, as well as families, had their Penates. —— **Latiō**, dat. sing. of *Latium, -ī,* n.; poetically used to express *end of motion,* instead of the acc. with a prep.; cf. the stock example *it clamor coelo,* Aen. V. 451, and see A. & G. 258, NOTE 3; B. 193 (specially); G. 358; H. 380, II, 4. Latium was a country of Italy near the Tiber, whose inhabitants, the Aborigines, were called Latini after their king Latinus. —— **genus**, nom. sing. of *genus, generis,* n., 3d; subj. of *est* understood. The order may be simplified thus: *unde (est) genus Latinum, patresque Albani, atque moenia altae Romae.* —— **unde**, conjunctive adv.; it is purposely vague, referring (1) to Aeneas (= *a quo*), (2) to his followers, (3) to circumstances already mentioned, e.g. *inferret deos* (= *ex qua re*). *Unde* has three common meanings: (*a*) *whence?* interrog.; (*b*) *whence,* relative to an antecedent *inde* expressed or implied; (*c*) as here, denoting origin, *whence, from which*. —— **Latīnum**, nom. sing. n. of adj. *Latīnus, -a, -um;* agrees with *genus.* Aeneas united the Latin races of Latium and his Trojan followers under the name *Latini.* The reader should refer to ll. 265, *seq.;* we there learn that Aeneas reigned three years in Latium.

LINE 7. **Albānī**, nom. plur. m. of *Albānus, -a, -um*, agreeing with *patres.* Alba, or, as it is usually called, Alba Longa was a city of Latium; it was destroyed by the Romans in 665 B.C., and its inhabitants were carried to Rome. —— **que**, enclitic conj. See note on l. 1. —— **patrēs**, nom. plur. of *pater, patris,* m., 3d; connected with *genus* by *que. Patres* often means *senators;* here it suggests that the Albans were nobles or *patricians,* the *plebs* springing into being later on. —— **atque**, cop. conj., throwing emphasis on *moenia Romae.* For the distinctions between *et, que,* and *atque,* refer to the note on *que,* l. 1. The final *ue* is elided before *altae.* See note on *ille,* l. 3, and references. —— **altae**, gen. sing. f. of *altus, -a, -um;* qualifies *Romae. Altus = high,* looked at from below; *deep,* looked at from above. The city of Rome was built upon the Palatine hill originally, and afterwards extended to cover six other hills, Capitoline, Esquiline, Quirinal, etc. —— **moenia**, nom. plur. of *moenia, -ium,* n., 3d; no sing.; joined to *patres* by *atque. Moenia* is specially used of defensive walls, or battlements; *murus,* the general word for *wall,* is also used for *city wall; paries,* as distinguished from *murus,* means the *wall of a house.* —— **Rōmae**, gen. sing. of *Rōma,* f., 1st; poss. gen. limiting *moenia.* See note

8 **Mūsa,** mi,hí cau,sás memo,rá, „ quo , nūmine,

   O muse,   *to me*   *the causes*   *narrate*   *what*   *divinity*

9 laéso,   Quídve do,léns, re,gína de,úm „ tot ,

   being offended or what grieving for the queen of the gods so many

O Muse, recount to me the reasons — how was her divinity insulted, or feeling what grudge did the queen of the gods force a hero

---

on *Troiae*, l. 1. Tradition has it that Romulus founded Rome on April 20th, 753 B.C.

LINE 8. **Mūsa,** voc. sing. of *mūsa, -ae,* f., 1st. There were nine Muses; the one addressed is Calliope, daughter of Jupiter and Mnemosyne, the special patron goddess of heroic poetry. —— **mihī,** dat. sing. of the 1st pers. pron. *ego,* acc. *mĕ,* gen. *meī,* abl. *mĕ* (plural nom. and acc. *nōs,* gen. *nostrum* or *nostrī,* dat. and abl. *nostrīs*); dat. of remoter obj. The personality of Vergil as the author here appears; the invocation is in imitation of Homer's in the opening of the Iliad and the Odyssey. —— **causas,** acc. plur. of *causa, -ae,* f., 1st (some write *caussa, -ae*); direct obj. of *memora.* The motives are suggested by *quo numine laeso,* and given in ll. 25-28. —— **memorā,** 2d pers. sing. imperat. mood act. of *memorō, -āre, -āvī, -ātum,* 1, trans. and intrans. (*memor,* mindful). —— **quō,** abl. sing. n. of the interrog. adj. *quī, quae, quod,* gen. *cūius,* dat. *cuī,* abl. *quō, quā, quō;* here agreeing with *numine.* Do not confuse this, the interrog. pron. adj., with the interrog. pron. *quis, quae, quid.* —— **nūmine,** abl. sing. of *nūmen, nūminis,* n., 3d (*nuō,* I nod); goes closely with *laeso* in the abl. abs. construction. It has a variety of meanings: (1) *nod,* (2) *wish* or *command,* (3) *godhead,* in the abstract, (4) *god, deity.* As to which particular meaning is suitable in this passage, see the special note appended below. —— **laesō,** abl. sing. n. of *laesus, -a, -um,* perf. part. pass. of *laedō, -ere, laesī, laesum,* 3. *Quo numine laeso* stands in the abl. abs. construction, which is used in Latin where we should in English employ a subordinate clause. The abl. abs. is grammatically independent of the rest of the sentence, a noun or pronoun being put in the abl., with a participle in agreement, to mark the time, the circumstances, or the cause of an action. Thus the abl. abs. may take the place of a temporal, causal, conditional, or concessive clause. Read carefully A. & G. 255; B. 227; G. 409, 410; H. 431.— NOTE. *quo numine laeso.* This difficult passage is variously explained: (1) *"What god being injured?"* But Juno is clearly indicated, so this may be ignored. (2) *"What wish being frustrated?"* This is taken to mean that Juno knew that Rome would one day crush Carthage. (3) *"Her godhead being insulted in what?"* *Quo,* the adj., must be regarded as virtually adverbial; cf. line 181, *Anthea si quem videat* = "if he can ANYWHERE see Antheus," where *quem* is used adverbially. A. & G. 191; B. 239; G. 325, 6; H. 443, for the common form of this idiom. Most commentators prefer (3), though many support (2).

LINE 9. **Quid,** acc. sing. n. of interrog. pron. *quis, quae, quid* (other cases like *qui*); acc. after *dolens,* for verbs expressing *emotion,* though intransitive generally, may sometimes govern an object. A. & G. 237, *b*; B. 175, 2, *b*; G. 333, 1, REM. 2; H. 371, III. Some scholars prefer to consider it an acc. of respect = *in respect to what;* others regard it as the adverbial use of the neut. = *why? how?* —— **ve,** enclitic disjunctive conj., joining *quid dolens* and *quo numine laeso. Ve* and *vel* (*vel* being probably the imperative of *volo,* and *ve* a weaker form of it) offer a choice between two alternatives: *aut* is employed when each alternative excludes

distinguished for his sense of right to endure so many misfortunes, to cope with so many hardships? Are there passions so strong in heavenly minds?

vólvere , cásus Ínsig,ném pie,táte vi,rúm, „ tot 10
to undergo calamities remarkable for piety a man so many

ad,íre la,bóres Ímpule,rít. Tan,taéne „ ani,mís 11
to enter on labors drove. (Are there) so great in minds

coe,léstibus , írae?
celestial angers?

---

the other; *sive* gives a choice between two names of the same thing; the correlatives are *aut — aut, vel — vel, sive — sive.*. A. & G. 156, *c*; B. 342; G. 494; H. 554, II, 2. —— **dolēns**, nom. sing. of *dolēns, -entis*, pres. part. act. of *doleō, -ere, doluī*, no supine, 2; agreeing with *regina*. This verb is ordinarily intrans. See note on *quid* above. There is a *caesura* after this word, and it is as strong as that after *deum*, but for the sake of uniformity the latter is marked in the text. See note on *Italiam*, l. 2. —— **rēgīna**, nom. sing. f., 1st; subj. of *impulerit*. Juno, the wife of Jupiter, is referred to. —— **deūm**, contracted gen. plur. of *deus, -ī*, m., 2d; gen. after *regina*. For peculiarities in the declension of *deus*, see note on *deos*, l. 6. *Deum* is shortened from *deorum*, and is common in poetry; cf. *virum* for *virorum*, and specially l. 4, *superum* for *superorum*, and consult A. & G. 40, *e*; B. 25, 6; G. 33, REM. 4; H. 52, 3. —— **tot**, indecl. num. adj., qualifying *casus*. *Tot* is the demonstr. correlative of the interrog. *quot*; cf. *tantus*, correl. of *quantus; talis* of *qualis*, etc. ——**volvere**, pres. inf. act. of *volvō, -ere, volvī, volūtum*, 3; dependent on *impulerit; volvo*, which here means *to run the round of*, has several other meanings: (1) *roll*, (2) *ordain*, see l. 22, (3) *unroll*, (4) *roll over in the mind, ponder*. The inf. is used prolatively, i.e. to extend the meaning of the verb; in prose *ut* with the subjunct. would be required. The *prolative* inf. is borrowed by the poets from the Greek, and is also used after adjectives. A. & G. 331, *g*; B. 326; G. 423, NOTE 1; H. 533, and cf. *contendunt petere*, l. 158. —— **cāsūs**, acc. plur. of *cāsus, casūs*, m., 4th (*cadō*, I fall); direct obj. of *volvere*. *Casus*, literally a *falling out*, means *chance* or *fortune* whether good or bad, but it is usually employed for *bad fortune*.

LINE 10. **Insignem**, acc. sing. m. of *insignis, insigne*, adj., 3d (*signum, a mark;* hence *insignis, marked*); qualifies *virum*. —— **pietāte**, abl. sing. of *pietās, pietātis*, f., 3d; abl. of cause, taking the place of *propter* with the acc. A. & G. 245; B. 219; G. 408; H. 416. *Pietas* does not mean *piety*, but rather *dutiful reverence*, that respect which a man owes to his parents, country, and gods. Similarly *pius*, the common epithet of Aeneas, means *dutiful* or *loyal*. —— **virum**, acc. sing. of *vir, -ī*, m., 2d; obj. of *impulerit*. —— **tot**, indecl. num. adj.; qualifying *labores*. See *tot*, l. 9. —— **adīre**, pres. inf. of *adeō, adīre, adīvī* or *adiī* (latter more frequent), *aditum*, irreg.; prolative or explanatory inf. after *impulerit;* cf. *volvere*, l. 9, and see note. This transitive use of *adeo* is poetical. By *asyndeton, tot volvere casus* and *tot adire labores* are not joined by a conj.; cf. the stock example "*veni, vidi, vici*," and see A. & G. 208, *b*; B. 346; G. 473, REM.; H. 636, I, 1. —— **labōrēs**, acc. plur. of *labor, labōris*, m., 3d; obj. of *adire*. Observe the contrast between *casus*, misfortunes to be met as they occur, and *labores*, tasks requiring personal initiation and calling for firmness and courage in their fulfilment.

LINE 11. **Impulerit**, 3d pers. sing. perf. subjunct. act. of *impellō, -ere, impulī, impulsum*, 3 (*in* and *pellō* compounded): its subj. is *regina*. The verb is in the

12 Úrbs an,tíqua fu,ít, „ Tyri,í tenu,ére co,lóni,
   A city   ancient   there was   Tyrian   held (it)   settlers

13 Cártha,go, Ítali,ám con,trá „ Tibe,rínaque , lónge
   Carthage   Italy   opposite   and Tiber's   far away

There was an an-cient city — Tyrian settlers held it—Car-thage, fronting Italy from afar and the mouths of the Tiber,

---

subjunct., as it is the principal verb in the indirect question introduced by *quo nu-mine laeso* (l. 8) which practically = *cur*. An indirect question is one introduced by an interrog. pron. or adv., and contained within a principal sentence; the verb of the contained interrog. sentence must be in the subjunct., and follows the rule as regards sequence of tenses. A. & G. 334; B. 300; G. 467; H. 528, 2, 529, I. —— **tantae**, nom. plur. f. of *tantus, -a, -um;* agrees with *irae*. *Tantus* is correl. to *quantus*, as *talis* to *qualis*. —— **ne**, enclitic interrog. particle; it is used to introduce a question, and is appended to the emphatic word, as here to *tantae*. *Ne* simply asks for information; *nonne* introduces questions to which an affirmative answer is expected; *num*, questions suggested in the negative answer. A. & G. 210, *a–d;* B. 162, 2, *c*; G. 454; H. 351, 1 and 2. In scansion, the final *e* is elided before the commencing vowel of *animis*. See note on *ille*, l. 3, and references. —— **animīs**, dat. plur. of *animus, -ī*, m., 2d; dat. of possession, with *sunt* understood. A. & G. 231; B. 190; G. 349; H. 387. *Animus* (as distinguished from *mens* = *mind, intellect*) means (1) *mind*, as the seat of the *will*, (2) *mind* or *heart*, as seat of emotions, (3) *mind*, in same sense as *mens*, (4) *passion*. It is here used with the meaning of (2). —— **coelestibus**, dat. plur. m. of adj. *coelestis, -e* (pertaining to *coelum*); in agreement with *animis*. —— **īrae**, nom. plur. of *īra, -ae*, f., 1st; subj. of *sunt* under-stood. Nouns expressing emotion are frequently used in the plur. instead of the sing. in poetry. The copula *sum* is often omitted, esp. in the ind. and inf. moods. A. & G. 206, *c*, 2; B. 166, 3; G. 209; H. 368, 3. Such omissions of the verb are allowable with some other verbs in well-known sayings and where the context makes it obvious what is to be supplied.

LINE 12. **Urbs**, nom. sing. f., 3d, gen. *urbis;* subj. of *fuit*. —— **antīqua**, nom. sing. f. of *antīquus, -a, -um;* qualifies *urbs*, and is used with reference to the time of Vergil, not of Aeneas; for cf. ll. 423 *seq.* where Aeneas lands in Africa and finds it just being built. —— **fuit**, 3d pers. sing. perf. ind. of *sum, esse, fuī* and *futūrus*, no supine. It is here used in the sense of *to be, to exist*, and forms a com-plete predicate; the most common use of *sum* and its parts is as the copula, when it requires a *complement* in the form of a subst., an adj., or equivalent to complete the predication. The *caesura* after *fuit* is very decided.—— **Tyriī**, nom. plur. m. of *Tyrius, -a, -um* (pertaining to *Tyros* or *Tyrus, -ī*, f., *Tyre*, chief town of Phoenicia); agrees with *coloni*. Similarly the adjectives *Phoenicius, -a, -um* and *Sidonius, -a, -um* are applied to Carthage and Carthaginians. *Tyrii ... coloni* occurs here parenthetically, as often in explanations; cf. l. 150. —— **tenuēre**, 3d pers. plur. perf. ind. act. of *teneō, -ēre, tenuī, tentum*, 2; its subj. is *coloni*. The perf. act. has two endings in 3d pers. plur. from early times, viz. *erunt* and *ere; erunt* is the usual form of classical prose; *ere* was a popular form, and was much used by poets, as it easily conforms to most metres in common use. —— **colōnī**, nom plur. of *colōnus. -ī*, m., 2d; subj. of *tenuere*. *Colonus* means (1) *a tiller, one who cultivates* (*colo*, 3), (2) *a settler;* cf. *colonia* (*colo, I inhabit*).

LINE 13. **Carthāgō**, *-inis*, f., 3d; nom. sing. in apposition to *urbs*. A city in N. Africa, founded by Phoenicians under Dido; cf. l. 338. In wealth and power it became a formidable rival of Rome, with which it waged the three famous Punic

rich of store and | Óstia,, díves o,púm „ studi,ísque as,pérrima , bélli; 14
most fierce in war-
like pursuits, which | *mouths   rich of means and in the pursuits very fierce   of war*
particularly, in pref-
erence to all lands, | Quám Iu,nó fer,túr „ ter,rís magis, ómnibus, únam 15
Juno is said to have | *which   Juno   is said   than lands more   all   alone*

Wars; it was destroyed by P. Cornelius Scipio Africanus Minor in 146 B.C. The
final vowel is elided before *Italiam;* cf. *ille*, l. 3. —— **Italiam**, acc. of *Italia, -ae,* f.,
1st; obj. of the prep. *contra.* —— **contrā**, prep. with the acc. *Contra* and certain
other prepositions occasionall· follow their nouns. A. & G. 263, NOTE; B. 144, 3;
G. 413, REM. 1; H. 569, II, 1. *Contra, infra,* and other prepositions ending in *a,* were
originally ablatives, and therefore the final vowel is by nature long. Observe that
contra hints here at the rivalry of Rome and Carthage.—— **Tiberīna**, acc. plur. n. of
Tiberīnus, -a, -um (belonging to *Tiberis,* gen. *Tiberis,* m., 3d, = *Tiber*); agrees with
ostia. The Tiber is a river of Italy, rising in the Apennines and flowing into the
Etruscan Sea; Rome was built on its left bank. —— **que**, enclitic conj. joining
Italiam and *ostia;* cf. *que*, l. 1. —— **longē**, adv. of place; here used to qualify *Italiam*
contra Tiberinaque ostia, as if it stood in a participial clause with the part. sup-
pressed, such as *Carthago longe distans;* Carthage is described as *fronting Italy,* but
from a great distance, viz. across the Mediterranean.

LINE 14. **Ostia**, acc. plur. of *ostium, -ī,* n., 2d (*ōs, ōris,* n., 3d, a *mouth*); obj. of
contra. The *whole,* Italy, is restricted by *ostia,* the *part;* cf. *Lavinia litora,* l. 3.
The town called Ostia, at the Tiber's mouth, afterwards became the sea-port of
Rome. —— **dīves**, nom. sing. f. of adj. *dīves, divitis,* 3d; qualifies *Carthago.* Its
case-forms are irreg., e.g. abl. sing. *divite;* gen. plur. *divitum.* The comp. degree is
divitior or *ditior,* the superl. *divitissimus* or *ditissimus.* —— **opum**, gen. plur. after
dives; from *opēs, opum,* f., 3d, meaning *resources* or *wealth.* The nom. sing. *ops* only
occurs **as** the name of a goddess; the other sing. cases, acc. *opem,* gen. *opis,* dat. *opī,*
abl. *ope* are used with the meaning of *help, aid;* cf. *fruges* for like defectiveness, and
see A. & G. 46; B. 57, 6, and 61; G. 70, *d;* H. 133, 1. *Opum* is a poetic gen. of speci-
fication, common after words expressing want or fulness. A. & G. 218, *c;* B. 204, 4;
G. 374, NOTE 1; H. 399, III, 1. —— **studiis**, abl. plur. after *asperrima;* from
studium, -ī, n., 2d (*studeō = I apply myself to*); abl. of specification. A. & G. 253;
B. 226; G. 397; H. 424. —— **que**, enclitic conj. joining the adjectival phrases *dives*
opum and *asperrima studiis.* In scansion the diphthong *ue* is elided before *asperrima;*
see *quoque*, l. 5. —— **asperrima**, nom. sing. f. of *asperrimus, -a, -um,* superl. of *asper,*
aspera, asperum (comp. *asperior*); qualifies *Carthago.* Asper (*ab, spes*) means literally
without hope; hence *fierce* or *harsh* of moral, and *rough* of physical qualities. Ad-
jectives in *er* form the comp. by adding *ior* to the stem of the positive, and the
superl. by adding *rimus* to the nom. m. of the positive. A. & G. 89, *a;* B. 71, 3;
G. 87, 1; H. 163, 1. —— **bellī**, gen. sing. of *bellum,* n., 2d; poss. gen. limiting *studiis.*

LINE 15. **Quam**, acc. sing. f. of the rel. pron. *quī, quae, quod;* agrees in gender
and number with its antecedent *urbs,* and in the acc. case because governed by
coluisse. A. & G. 198; B. 250, 1; G. 614; H. 445. *Quam* is not elided before *Iuno,*
the *i* of which is equivalent to *j;* see *memorem*, l. 4. —— **Iūnō**, gen. *Iūnōnis,* f., 3d;
nom. case subj. to *fertur.* See note on *Iunonem*, l. 4. —— **fertur**, 3d pers. sing.
pres. ind. pass. of *ferō, ferre, tulī, lātum,* irreg., in agreement with its subj.
nom. *Iuno. Fero* in its original sense means *I carry* or *I bring;* this meaning is
sometimes extended, as *I bear news,* hence *I tell* or *narrate.* The latter meaning
occurs most frequently in the indef. *ferunt, they say* (French, *on dit*), and the impers.
pass. *fertur, it is said.* For the conjugation of *fero,* consult A. & G. 139; B. 129;

16 Pósthabi,tá   coluísse   Sa,mó; „ hic , íllius ,| made her home,
                                                           | prizing Samos less;
being less esteemed to have cherished Samos   here   of her | here was her armor,

G. 171; H. 292. —— **terrīs**, abl. plur. of *terra, -ae,* f., 1st; abl. of comparison after *magis* instead of the more common *quam* (*than*) *terras omnes.* The rule for comparisons is that when *quam* is employed, the thing compared has the same case as that of the thing with which it is compared; when *quam* is omitted, the object compared goes into the abl. case. The abl. of comparison seems to be a branch of the abl. of separation. A. & G. 247, and NOTE; B. 217; G. 296; H. 417. —— **magis**, adv. of comparative degree; used in close connection with *terris* in the abbreviated construction; see *terris* above. *Magis* (akin to *magnus*) has no regular positive, but *magnopere* supplies the deficiency; the superl. is *maxime. Magis* and *maxime* are used with certain adjectives which do not form the comp. and superl. in the regular way, and specially with those in *us* preceded by any other vowel than *u,* e.g. positive *idoneus,* comp. *magis idoneus,* superl. *maxime idoneus.* —— **omnibus**, abl. plur. f. of *omnis, -e;* qualifies *terris.* The uses of *omnis* are (1) *all, every;* very often substantially, e.g. *omnes, all men; omnia, all things;* (2) *the whole.* —— **ūnam**, acc. sing. f. of the num. adj. *ūnus, -a, -um* (gen. *ūnīus,* dat. *ūnī*); qualifies *quam. Unus* means *one,* but often, as here, *alone;* it is frequently used with superlatives to emphasize their force, but its use with the comparative degree is rare. In this passage note that *magis omnibus* is practically equivalent to the superl. *maxime.*

LINE 16. **Posthabitā**, abl. sing. f. of *posthabitus, -a, -um,* perf. part. pass. of *posthabeō, -ēre, -uī, -itum,* 2; agreeing with *Samo* in the abl. abs. construction. The abl. abs. in point of grammar is independent of the rest of the sentence, and is used where in English a temporal, causal, or some other clause would be employed; it consists of a noun or pron. in the abl., limited by a participle or adjective. The abl. abs. may be variously translated, e.g. *hoc facto,* lit. *this having been done, when this was done, although this was done,* etc. See notes on *numine* and *laeso,* l. 8, and consult A. & G. 255; B. 227; G. 409, 410; H. 431. —— **coluisse**, perf. inf. act. of *colō, -ere, coluī, cultum,* 3, irreg.; used prolatively after *fertur.* This inf. is what is variously called *prolative, epexegetic, complementary,* and *explanatory.* A. & G. 271; B. 326; G. 423; H. 533. —— **Samō**, abl. sing. of *Samus, -ī,* f., 2d (nom. sometimes written in Greek form *Samos*)*;* abl. abs. with *posthabita;* the names of islands are in fem. gender. Samos is an island of considerable size off the coast of Asia Minor, south of Chios; it possessed one of the wonders of the ancient world, the *Heraeum,* i.e. temple of *Hera* (Greek goddess equivalent to the Latin *Iuno*). Note that there is a *hiatus* in scansion, i.e. the final *o* of *Samo* is not elided before *hic.* Hiatus is not often resorted to, but it may be explained here by the long caesural pause after *Samo* occasioned by the change in the construction, and also by the fact that the termination is Greek and some licence is therefore allowable. On *hiatus,* consult A. & G. 359, *e;* B. 366, 7, *a;* G. 720, 784, NOTE 6; H. 608, II. Hiatus is defined as the meeting of two vowels in separate syllables without any elision, thus creating a long pause (*hiatus = yawning*)*;* it is most common in the chief *caesura,* and after long monosyllables; it may be partly avoided by *semi-hiatus,* i.e. shortening the long final vowel. —— **hīc**, adv. of place; referring to Carthage, *not* to Samos. —— **illius**, gen. sing. f. of *ille, illa, illud* (see *ille,* l. 3); poss. gen., the pron. recalling the noun *Iuno. Ille* as a pron. means *he;* as an adj. *that.* Observe that the second syllable *i,* which is usually long in quantity, is short here. A. & G. 347, *a,* EXCEPTION; B. 362, 1, *a;* G. 706, EXCEPTION 4; H. 577, I, 3, (3). The penultimate *i* of *alterius* is always short. —— **arma**, nom. case plur., gen. *armōrum,* 2d; subj. to *fuerunt* understood. See *arma,* l. 1.

here her chariot;	árma, Híc cur,rús fuit; , hóc „ reg,núm dea , 17
that this should be	
the seat of empire	*the arms here the chariot was this the kingdom the goddess*
for the nations, if	
haply the fates per-	géntibus , ésse, Sí qua , fáta si,nánt, „ iam , 18
mit it, even thus	*for the nations to be if in any way the fates allow even*

LINE 17. **Hĭc,** adv. of place. The repetition of *hic* is rhetorical and emphatic, an example of *anaphora*. See A. & G. 344,*f*; B. 350, 11, *b*; G. 682 and 636, NOTE 4, for repetition of a single word; H. 636, III, 3. —— **currus,** nom. sing. of *currus, -ūs,* m., 4th (*currō, I run;* hence *currus, that which runs*); subj. of *fuit.* Vergil imitates Homer in representing gods as having a particular place wherein they kept their chariots and armour after wars. —— **fuit,** 3d pers. sing. perf. ind. of *sum, esse, fuī;* its subj. is *currus.* See note on *fuit,* l. 12. Observe that with *fuit* the ending of the word is coincident with that of the foot; this is called *diaeresis.* A. & G. 358, *c*; B. 366, 8; G. 753; H. 602, 2. It is an useful device for avoiding monotony in rhythm. —— **hōc;** acc. sing. n. of demonstr. pron. *hĭc, haec, hōc,* gen. *hūius,* dat. *huĭc;* subj. of *esse,* agreeing in gender and number with *regnum.* On the declension of *hic,* consult A. & G. 101; B. 87; G. 104; H. 186. *Hic* (*this here*) denotes something near the speaker in place, thought, or time, and is therefore called the demonstr. of the 1st person; *iste* denotes something near the person addressed, and is demonstr. of 2d person (*that of yours*); *ille* (*that yonder*) refers to something remote, and is demonstr. of 3d person. *Hoc* refers to *urbs,* l. 12, but agrees with *regnum,* because adjectival pronouns are usually attracted into agreement with an appositive or a noun in the predicate. A. & G. 195, *d*; B. 246, 5; G. 211, 5; H. 445, 4. In spite of the pause after *fuit,* the *caesura* follows *hoc.* —— **regnum,** acc. sing. of *regnum, -ī,* n., 2d (*regō, I rule*); complement to *esse,* in conjunction with which it forms the predicate to *hoc. Regnum* = (1) *rule, authority,* (2) *a kingdom.* Here the two ideas are mixed, and *regnum* signifies a concrete place whence the abstract power radiates as from a centre. —— **dea,** gen. *deae,* f., 1st; nom. sing. subj. of *tendit fovetque; dea* means Juno. Observe that the dat. and abl. plur. of *dea, filia,* and a few other words of 1st decl. with corresponding masc. nouns in the 2d, terminate in *abus;* so also with the f. plur. of *ambo* and *duo.* A. & G. 36, *e*; B. 21, *e*; G. 29, REM. 4; H. 49, 4. —— **gentibus,** dat. plur. of *gens, gentis,* f., 3d (*genō, I beget*); dat. of indirect obj. after *regnum esse.* A. & G. 226, *a*; B. 187; G. 350, DATIVE OF PERSONAL INTEREST; H. 382. *Gens* here means *nation;* other meanings are *race; offspring; house,* made up of families, such as the *gens.Iulia* at Rome. —— **esse,** pres. inf. of *sum,* perf. *fuī* (see note on *fuit,* l. 12); prolative inf. connecting *hoc* and *regnum. Hoc esse regnum* stands as obj. to the idea of *wishing* contained in the verbs *tendit, fovetque;* otherwise it would have to be considered a poetical inf., instead of *ut* with the subjunct., such as *adire,* l. 10; see note on *adire.*

LINE 18. **Sĭ,** conditional conj.; with *sinant.* A conditional sentence consists of a hypothetical clause, called the *protasis,* introduced by *si, sin,* or *nisi,* and a conclusion, which is called the *apodosis.* The *apodosis* to *si* . . *sinant* is suppressed. It is important to remember that *si* takes the ind. when the *apodosis* is ind. or imperat., and the subjunct. when the *apodosis* is a natural subjunct.: thus cases of pure fact belong to the ind., while contingencies and supposed cases which are contrary to the fact belong to the subjunct. For examples and fuller explanation, see A. & G. 304-309; B. 301-304; G. 589, 594 *seq.;* H. 507-512. —— **quā,** adv.; originally abl. sing. f. of rel. pron. *quī, quae, quod;* here it denotes *manner.*

19 túm   ten,dítque   fo,vétque.   Prógeni,ém   sed | early is her design
                                                          | and dear desire. Nay
then   she both designs   and nurses hope.   *A race*   *but* | but she had heard

After *si*, *if*, and *ne*, *lest*, *qua* is indefinite, = *in any way;* other uses are (1) inter-
rog., *how?* (2) rel., *where*, (3) indef. of place, *wherever.* —— **fāta**, nom. plur. of
fātum, *-ī*, n., 2d; subj. to *sinant.* *Fatum*, derived from *for*, *fārī*, *to speak*,
means *that which has been spoken*, and so *destiny*. The plural is personified, and
practically the same as *Parcae*, which see on l. 22. The notion of a deity being
bound by a higher power than itself is strange to modern minds, but it was general
among cultured Greeks and Romans, finding its most powerful expression in the
tragedies of Aeschylus. —— **sinant**, 3d pers. plur. pres. subjunct. act. of *sinō*, *-ere*,
sīvī, *situm*, 3, irreg.; pred. of *fata*, dependent on *si*. The pres. subjunct. is potential,
expressing a contingency which may be realized in the future. A. & G. 307, *b*;
B. 303; G. 596; H. 509. —— **iam**, adv. of time; its force is increased in *iam tum*,
even then. —— **tum**, adv. of time. *Iam tum* here refers to the early period when
Carthage was being founded; cf. note on *antiqua*, l. 12. —— **tendit**, 3d pers. sing.
pres. ind. act. of *tendō*, *-ere*, *tetendī*, *tensum* and *tentum*, 3, irreg., trans. and intrans.;
subj. is *dea*. The historic present is used instead of the aorist to express strong
emotion or make a narrative vivid. A. & G. 276, *d*; B. 259, 3; G. 229; H. 467, III.
In prose *ut* with the subjunct. would follow, but see note on *esse*, l. 17. —— **que**,
enclitic conj., used correlatively. See *que*, l. 1, and note on *et*, l. 3. —— **fovet**, 3d
pers. sing. pres. ind. act. of *foveō*, *-ēre*, *fōvī*, *fōtum*, 2; subj. is *dea*. Historic present,
as in *tendit* above. *Foveo* is trans., and means *I cherish*, and, by poetic extension, *I
eagerly desire:* Juno *nurses* her design, as a mother might her child. This verb,
being trans., may take an inf. clause as object. —— **que**, enclitic conj., used correl-
atively; see *que* above.

    LINE 19.   **Prōgeniem**, acc. sing. of *prōgeniēs*, *prōgeniēī*, f., 5th; acc. and inf.
construction, *progeniem* being subj. of *duci;* see note on *duci*. The reference is gen-
erally understood to be to the Roman nation, but some commentators think *progeniem*
means Scipio Aemilianus, the destroyer of Carthage, as the *gens Aemilia* traced
its descent to Aemilius, whose father Ascanius was the son of Aeneas. —— **sed**,
adversative conj., joining sentences together, but introducing something in opposi-
tion to what has gone before; it is weaker than *verum;* *at* and *ast* are used like *sed*,
but often introduce a new point; *autem*, post-positive, has only slight adversative
force. A. & G. 156, *b*; B. 343, 1; G. 485; H. 554, III. In poetry, *sed* and other
conjunctions, such as *et*, *nec*, etc., are often *post-positive*, i.e. do not stand first word in
a sentence. *Sed enim* is elliptical, corresponding to the Greek ἀλλὰ γάρ, the context
suggesting what is to be supplied; so here *but* (*she feared for the future*) *for* . . . ; it
can be translated *however*. —— **enim**, causal conj., standing post-positive, and ex-
plaining what has preceded: *nam* is prae-positive, i.e. first word in the sentence. ——
Trōiānō, abl. sing. m. of *Trōiānus*, *-a*, *-um* (of *Trōia*, *Troy*); qualifies *sanguine*. The
allusion is of course to the descendants of Aeneas; see *progeniem* above. The final *o*
is elided before *a;* see note on *ille*, l. 3. —— **ā**, prep. with the abl., here denoting
separation or *source from which;* written *ab* before vowels and *h*. A. & G. 153 under *Ab;*
B. 142, 1; G. 417, 1; H. 434. See *ab*, l. 1. —— **sanguine**, abl. sing. of *sanguĭs*, *-inis*, m.,
3d; governed by *a*. —— **dūcī**, pres. inf. pass. of *dūcō*, *-ere*, *dūxī*, *ductum*, 3; acc. and
inf. construction after *audierat*. — NOTE. In indirect statements (*oratio obliqua*) after
verba sentiendi et declarandi (*feeling*, *hearing*, *saying*, *knowing*, etc.) the subj. goes
into the acc., and the verb of the predicate into the inf.; the verbs of all subordinate
clauses are put in the subjunct. In English the indirect statement is introduced

that from Trojan stock a race was springing which would overthrow in time to come the citadels of Tyre;	e͵ním „ Tro͵iáno a , sánguine , dúci Aúdie͵rát, 20
	for *Trojan from* *blood* *to be derived* *she had heard*
	Tyri͵ás „ o͵lím quae , vérteret , árces; Hínc 21
	Tyrian in time to come which would overthrow the citadels hence

by *that*, or *that* is understood; e.g. I know *that* he is here, I know (*that*) he is here. In this passage the *oratio recta*, i.e. direct statement, would be *Progenies sed enim Troiano a sanguine ducitur*. With respect to the tenses of the inf., observe that when the time of the action of the verb in the indirect statement is prior to that of the verb *sentiendi* or *declarandi*, the perf. inf. is used; when it is subsequent, the future inf.; when the time of both verbs is the same, the inf. is always present. So here the action of *duci* is contemporaneous with that of *audierat*. Consult carefully A. & G. 336; B. 313-318; G. 508, 526, 531; H. 522, 523, I, 524 and 525.

LINE 20. **Audierat**, 3d pers. sing. pluperf. ind. act. of *audiō, -īre, -īvī, -ītum*, 4; syncopated form of *audīverat*. A. & G. 128, *a*, 1, 2; B. 367, 8, and 7, 2; G. 131, 1; H. 235. The subj. of *audierat* is Juno or a pron. unexpressed; the obj. is the acc. and inf. clause *progeniem . . . duci*, and similar clauses down to *Parcas*, l. 22. —— **Tyriās**, acc. plur. f. of *Tyrius, -a, -um* (*Tyrus, -ī*, f., 2d); agrees with *arces*. See l. 12. —— **ōlim**, adv. of time (originally *ollim*, from *olle*, old form of *ille*); qualifies *verteret*. *Olim* more often refers to past time, *formerly, once upon a time*; but for its future use, compare l. 289. Its derivation from *ille* marks *remoteness*, whether past or future. Vergil is hinting at the great Punic Wars, and the final overthrow of Carthage by Rome in 146 B.C. —— **quae**, nom. sing. f. of rel. pron. *quī, quae, quod* (see note on *quī*, l. 1); agrees in gender and number with its antecedent *progeniem*, and stands subj. to *verteret*. This clause is a relative clause of purpose, *quae* being equivalent to *ut ea*; see note on *verteret*. —— **verteret**, 3d pers. sing. imperf. subjunct. act. of *vertō, -ere, vĕrtī, versum*, 3; final subjunct., i.e. subjunct. in purpose clause, after *quae*. *Verteret* instead of the usual *everteret*. Pure final clauses are introduced by *ut* (negative *ne*), but purpose may be expressed by the subjunct. after the rel. pron. *qui*, or rel. adverbs such as *ubi*, etc. A. & G. 317; B. 282; G. 545; H. 497. Note that in indirect discourse the tense of the subjunct. in subordinate clauses follows that of the verb *sentiendi vel declarandi*, the ordinary rule of tense-sequence being observed, viz. primary tenses follow primary (pres., perf., fut., fut. perf. are primary), and historic tenses follow historic (imperf., aorist, pluperf.). Thus *verteret*, in spite of *duci*, is imperf. subjunct., because it follows the historic *audierat* in the main part of the sentence. On sequence of tenses consult A. & G. 286; B. 267, 268; G. 509; H. 491; on tenses of the subjunct. in *oratio obliqua*, see A. & G. 336; B. 318; G. 517, 518; H. 525. The *oratio recta* would be *progenies . . . ducitur quae olim vertat arces, vertat* being subjunct. of purpose. —— **arcēs**, acc. plur. of *arx, arcis* f., 3d (root *arc* in *arceō, I enclose; cf.* Greek εἴργειν; hence *that which encloses, a castle*); obj. of *verteret*.

LINE 21. **Hinc**, adv. (derived from *hīc*, demonstr. of 1st person); limiting *venturum*, and signifying source or origin with reference to persons and things; practically equals *ex hac progenie; cf.* use of *unde* in l. 6. It is more widely found as adv. of place, *hence, from this place*; and as adv. of time, *after this, from this time.* Note the absence of a connecting conj., by *asyndeton*. A. & G. 346, *c*; B. 346; G. 473, REM.; H. 636, I, 1. —— **populum**, acc. sing. of *populus, -ī*, m., 2d (probably akin to Greek πολύς, *much;* in m. plur. *the many*); acc. after *audierat* in indirect discourse, standing subj. to *venturum* (*esse*), l. 22. See notes on *progeniem* and *duci*, l. 19. —— **lātē**, adv. (*lātus, wide*); qualifies *regem*, which is used almost adjectivally.

popu,lúm la,té re,gém „ bel,lóque su,pérbum	that thence a people, holding wide domin- ion and of proud fame in war, would come to work the destruction of Libya;
a people *widely ruling* (king) *and in war* *arrogant*	
22 **Véntu,***rum* éxcidi,ó Lib,ya'e; „ sic ,	
(she had heard) to be about to come for the ruin of Libya *thus*	

Adverbs are formed from 2d-declension adjectives by changing the vowel of the stem to *e*. A. & G. 148, *a, b, c, d*; B. 76; G. 91-93; H. 304. In prosody the quantity of the final *e* of 2d-declension adverbs is long. —— **rēgem**, acc. sing. of *rēx, rēgis*, m., 3d; qualifies *populum* with adjectival force. Certain nouns of verbal origin, particularly those ending in *tor*, e.g. *victor*, are sometimes employed appos- itively to limit another noun. Thus *late regem* is equivalent to *late regnantem;* com- pare the well-known example from Horace, *late tyrannus.* Rome, as a republic, extended her authority gradually over Italy, Spain, Carthage, Greece, Asia Minor, and Gaul; under the empire this process of absorption was continued until the Roman Empire embraced the whole world as known to the Ancients. —— **bellō,** abl. sing. of *bellum, -ī*, n., 2d; abl. of specification enlarging *superbum;* see note on *studiis*, l. 14. —— **que**, enclitic conj., connecting *regem* and *superbum;* see *que*, l. 1. —— **superbum**, acc. sing. m. of *superbus, -a, -um* (*super, above;* hence *superior to);* qualifying *populum. Superbus* is used in two ways, (1) complimentary, as *proud, excellent, of tried metal,* (2) uncomplimentary, *insolent, arrogant;* here it bears the former meaning.

LINE 22. **Ventūrum,** acc. sing. m. of *ventūrus, -a, -um*, fut. part. act. of *venio, -īre, vēnī, ventum*, 4, irreg.; agrees with *populum. Esse* is to be supplied with *ven- turum*, thus forming the *periphrastic* fut. inf. *venturum esse* to which *populum* is subj. in indirect discourse; the omission of *esse* is common in poetry. Note that all verbs form the fut inf. act. by adding *esse* to the fut. part. owing to the absence of any inflectional form; the fut. inf. pass. is also *periphrastic*, the supine in *um* being used with *iri* following A. &. G. 110, *d*; B. 115; G. 246 *seq.;* H. 248. The final *um* is suppressed (*ecthlipsis*) before *excidio;* cf. *multum*, l. 3. —— **excidiō,** dat. sing. of *excidium, -ī*, n., 2d; dat. of purpose or service. A. & G. 233, *a*; B. 191; G. 356; H. 390. This dat. is often accompanied by another dat. of the `person or thing interested; but see note on *Libyae.* —— **Libyae,** dat. sing. of *Libya, -ae*, f., 1st; dat. of the obj. affected; see references to *excidio.* Many scholars, however, prefer to consider *Libyae* as poss. gen. limiting *excidio.* Libya is the name given to the north coast of Africa west of Egypt; the *whole* stands for Carthage the *part.* Note that *Libyae* is dissyllabic, i.e. the *y* is slurred, as often with *i* equivalent to *j*: this is called *synaeresis.* A. & G. 347, *d*; B. 467, 1; G. 723, under HARDENING; H. 608, III, NOTE 2. —— **sīc**, adv. of manner, limiting *volvere. Sic* (locative originally from a root akin to the demonstr. *is*) is frequently used with *ut* in comparisons; also as the correlative of *si* in conditions. See *hinc*, l. 21, on *asyndeton.* —— **volvere,** pres. inf. act. of *volvō, -ere, volvī, volūtum*, 3; pred. in acc. and inf. construction after *Parcas.* See *volvere*, l. 9; here the metaphor seems to be taken from the turning of a wheel, or from the unwinding of a scroll. For note on the present tense in *oratio obliqua*, see *duci*, l. 19. —— **Parcās,** acc. plur. of *Parca, -ae*, f., 1st (root *par*, cf. *parō, I prepare*, i.e. one's destiny); subj. of *volvere* in acc. and inf. after *audierat.* The sing. is seldom found. *Parcae*, the Fates, were three in number, being called in Latin Nona, Decuma, Morta; in Greek Clotho, Lachesis, Atropos; they had absolute control over the lives of mortals, and even the gods were powerless against their decree. Clotho is represented as holding the thread of destiny, Lachesis as weaving, and Atropos as cutting it. *Fata* personified is identical with *Parcae.*

that thus the Fates ordained it. The daughter of Saturn, fearing that and mindful of the ancient war which she had erstwhile waged	vólvere, Párcas. Íd metu,éns vete,rísque me,mór „ 23
	to ordain the Fates. That fearing and old mindful
	Sa,túrnia , bélli, Príma quod, ád Tro,iám „ 24
	Saturn's (daughter) of the war first which at Troy

LINE 23. **Id**, acc. sing. n. of *is, ea, id,* demonstr. pron. of the 3d pers. (gen. *ēius,* dat. *eī,* abl. *eō, eā, eō);* direct obj. to *metuens,* and referring to the whole substance of the indirect statements introduced by *audierat,* l. 20. *Id* is a weak demonstr., frequently employed, as here, with regard to what has preceded, and may be used as pron. or adj.; it is the regular antecedent to the rel. *qui.* A. & G. 101; B. 87; G. 103, 1; H. 186, IV. —— **mctuēns** (gen. *metuentis*), nom. sing. f. part. act. of *metuō, -ere, metuī, metūtum;* agrees appositively with *Saturnia.* This verb expresses a vaguer kind of dread than *timeo.* —— **veteris**, gen. sing. m. of *vetus, veteris,* adj. of one termination; limiting *belli. Vetus* forms its comp. *vetustior* (from *vetustus*), and its superl. *veterrimus.* It means not so much that the war was an *ancient* one (*antiquus*) as *long protracted:* the war continued ten years. —— **que**, enclitic conj., joining *metuens* and *memor;* see *que,* l. 1. —— **memor**, nom. sing. f. (gen. *memoris,* gen. plur. *memorum;* no neut. plur.), agreeing with *Saturnia,* and used subjectively, *mindful of;* cf. *memorem,* l. 4. —— **Sāturnia**, nom. sing. f. of *Sāturnius, -a, -um;* it probably agrees with *filia* understood, but it is used by Vergil as a noun. Saturn was the father of Juno, Jupiter, Neptune, and others of the older gods. Observe that *Saturnia* has no apparent predicate, for the construction is broken off after *Argis,* l. 24, and the subj. changed; such an irregularity of construction is termed *anacoluthon.* A. & G. 385; B. 374, 6; G. 697; H. 636, IV, 6. But the difficulty may be met by taking ll. 25-28 as a parenthesis, and considering the construction resumed in l. 29; thus *accensa,* l. 29, is a part. summing up the parenthesis, and the pred. of *Saturnia* is *arcebat,* l. 31. —— **bellī**, gen. sing. n. of *bellum,* 2; objective gen. dependent on *memor.* A. & G. 218, *a;* B. 204, 1; G. 374; H. 399, I, 2.

LINE 24. **Prīma**, nom. sing. f. of *prīmus, -a, -um;* agrees with the subj. of *gesserat,* i.e. *Saturnia;* its force is adverbial, and limits *gesserat* rather than the subj.; cf. *primus,* l. 1, and note. Obviously it does not mean *first* in this instance; a choice is left between (1) *of yore,* (2) *beyond all others,* and on the whole (1) seems the simpler. —— **quod**, acc. sing. n. of the rel. pron. *quī, quae, quod* (cf *qui,* l. 1); agrees in gender and number with its antecedent *belli,* and is obj. of *gesserat;* see note on *qui,* l. 1, for the rule respecting the agreement of the rel. —— **ad**, prep. with the acc.; gov. *Troiam.* Its most common use is after verbs of motion, with the meaning *to, towards;* here it means *at.* A. & G. 153, under *Ad;* B. 182, 3; G. 416, 1; H. 433, I, under *Ad.* —— **Trōiam**, acc. sing. f. of *Trōia, -ae,* 1st; acc. after *ad;* see *Troiae,* l. 1. —— **prō**, prep. with the abl.; gov. *Argis.* A. & G. 153, under *Pro;* B. 142; G. 417, 10; H. 434, I, under *Pro.* Originally a prep. of place, it is (like the Greek πρό) used idiomatically as (1) *on behalf of,* as here; (2) *instead of;* the elastic prep. *for* embraces both. —— **cāris**, abl. plur. m. of *cārus, -a, -um (ca[m]rus;* Sanskrit root *kam = to love);* agrees with. *Argis.* Juno (Hera) was worshipped with particular reverence at Argos, where she had a far-famed temple. —— **gesserat**, 3d pers. sing. pluperf. ind. act. of *gerō, -ere, gessi, gestum,* 3; its subj. is Juno unexpressed. The Trojan War was in a sense Juno's war, for her hatred of Paris led her to incite the Greeks to vengeance and even to intervene in

25 pro , cáris , gésserat , Argis: Nécdum eti,ám | at Troy for the sak*
  for   dear   she had waged Argos   nor yet   also | of her beloved Argos
26 cau,sae íra,rúm „ sae,víque do,lóres Éxcide,ránt | —nor yet even had
  the causes of angers   and fierce the griefs   had fallen | the causes of her
                                                              | wrath or her savage
                                                              | resentment passed

the Greek interest on the battlefield. —— **Argīs**, abl. plur. m. of *Argī, -ōrum*, 2d
(*Argos*, n., sing. only in the nom. and acc. cases; Greek Αργος); obj. of *pro*. Argos
was the capital of Argolis in the Peloponnese; the inhabitants were called *Argivi*
or *Argolici*, terms often employed as representative of all the Greeks.

LINE 25. **Necdum**, co-ordinate disjunctive conj., introducing the parenthesis
of ll. 25-28. *Necdum* is short for *nequedum*, *dum* being an adv. enclitic meaning
then; neque (*ne* + *que*) = *and not*, but when used correlatively *neque . . . neque*, or
nec . . . nec, neither . . . nor. *Necdum* is sometimes written *nec dum*; cf. *necnon* and
nec non, lit. *and not not*, i.e. *and also*. The final *um* is suppressed in scansion; see
note on *multum*, l. 3. Observe that the following parenthesis, though it checks the con-
struction, carries the sense on quite naturally; it is practically = to a participial or
adjectival clause such as *metuens* and *memor*, l. 23, and the sense = *and still re-
membering the causes of her wrath*, etc. —— **etiam** (*et* + *iam*), cop. conj., intensify-
ing *necdum*, = nor yet *even*. It is also used, (1) as a conj. introducing something
new, = *also*, (2) as a temporal adv. = *still*. —— **causae**, nom. plur. of *causa, -ae*,
f., 1st; subj. nom. of *exciderant*. The final diphthong *ae* is elided before *irarum;*
cf. *quoque*, l. 5, and note. The causes are given in ll. 27 and 28. —— **īrārum**, gen.
plur. of *īra, -ae*, f., 1st; poss. gen. limiting *causae*. The plural is used poetically
for the singular; cf. *irae*, l. 11. —— **saevī**, nom. plur. m. of *saevus, -a, -um;* agrees
with *dolores*. Adjectives expressing personal qualities are often applied to feelings
and things in poetry. —— **que**, cop. conj., connecting *causae* and *dolores;* see *que*,
l. 1. —— **dolōrēs**, nom. plur. of *dolor, dolōris*, m., 3d (*doleō* = *I grieve*); goes with
causae as subj. nom. of *exciderant*. *Dolor* may mean *pain of body* or *pain of mind;*
luctus means *grief for one dead;* *moeror* means *great grief*, such as shows itself
visibly in the countenance.

LINE 26. **Exciderant**, 3d pers. plur. pluperf. ind. of *excĭdō, -ere, excĭdī, no
supine*, 3, intrans. (*ex* + *cadō*). Carefully distinguish this *excĭdo* from *excīdo* (*ex*
+ *caedo*), *-ere, excidi, excisum* = *I cut out*. —— **animō**, abl. sing. of *animus, -ī*, m.,
2d; abl. of separation after *exciderant*. Separation is usually expressed by the abl.
with a prep. in conjunction with a verb compounded with that prep., but when used
figuratively, the prep. is omitted; *exciderant animo* is a figurative expression. A.
& G. 243, *b*; B. 214; G. 390, 1, and also 390, 2, NOTES 1-3; H. 413, and esp. NOTE 3.
For distinctions of meaning, see note on *animis*, l. 11. —— **manet**, 3d pers. sing.
pres. ind. act. of *maneō, -ēre, mansī, mansum*, 2, intrans.; pred. to *iudicium*. Take
notice, (1) that *manet* is not connected by any conj. with *exciderant*, an instance of
asyndeton, for which see note on *adire*, l. 10; (2) that *manet* is a *historic present*,
used in vivid narrative instead of a past tense; cf. *tendit*, l. 18, and reference. ——
altā, abl. sing. f. of *altus, -a, -um ;* agrees with *mente*. It is used *partitively*, to point
out not what kind of object, but *what part* of it, is meant; thus *alta mente* = *in the
depths* of her mind. This use is most common with superlatives marking order or
sequence, e.g. *summus, imus, ultimus, medius; summus mons* = *the top of the moun-
tain*. A. & G. 193; B. 241; G. 291, REM. 2; H. 440, 2, NOTE 1. —— **mente**, abl.
sing. of *mens, mentis*, f., 3d; abl. of *place where*, or locative ablative, most common
when the noun is qualified by an adjective, but in poetry loosely used with nouns

| out of her soul; hidden away in the depths of her mind abides the judgment of Paris and the insult of beauty | ani,mó:
from her mind;

Iúdici,úm
the judgment | „
remains

Pari,dís
of Paris | manet ,
deep

„ | álta ,
in mind

spre,taéeque
and despised | ménte

 | re,póstum
laid up

in,iúria , 27
the injury |

alone. A. & G. 258, 4, under *f*, 2 and 3; B. 228; G. 385; H. 425, II, 1, 2). *Mens* here is almost = to *memoria;* cf. *in mentem venire* + the gen.; for its difference from *animus*, see note on *animis*, l. 11. —— **repōstum** (syncopated for *repositum*), nom. sing. n. of *repōstus, -a, -um,* perf. part. pass. of *repōnō, -ere, reposui, repositum,* 3 (*re = back + pōnō*); agrees with *iudicium.* *Re* is a form of *red*, which drops the *d* before consonants as a rule, and takes sometimes a long quantity in compensation; here the quantity is short. Observe the force of *red* and *re* in composition; (1) = *back,* e.g. *redeo, I go back, I return,* (2) = *again,* e.g. *repeto, I seek again,* (3) = *in return,* e.g. *respondeo,* lit. *I promise in return,* (4) = *away,* denoting reversal, e.g. *retego, I cover away,* i.e. *I uncover,* (5) intensive, e.g. *re-supinus,* lying *full* on the back. For *syncopation,* cf. l. 249, *compostus,* and see A. & G. 128, I, 2; B. 367, 8; G. 131, 1; H. 235.

LINE 27. **Iūdicium,** *-ī,* n., 2d; nom. sing., subj. of *manet* above. This refers to the myth that Discord intervened at a feast of the gods and threw a golden apple as a prize to the most beautiful; several claimed it, and chief of these Venus, Juno, and Minerva, and Paris, being selected as arbitrator, awarded it to Venus. —— **Paridis** (also *Paridos*), gen. sing. of *Paris,* Greek 3d-declension noun, m., poss. gen. after *iudicium.* *Paris* is declined in other cases:—acc. *Paridem, Parida, Parim,* and *Parin,* voc. *Paris* and *Pari,* dat. *Paridī,* abl. *Paride.* On Greek nouns of 3d decl. consult A. & G. 63, 64; B. 47; G. 65; H. 68. Paris, also called Alexander, was the son of Priam, king of Troy, who exposed him on a mountain in consequence of an omen at his birth prefiguring the destruction of Troy. He was saved by shepherds, and as a shepherd won by his decision the favor of Venus, who promised him Helen, fairest of women, as his wife; his abduction of Helen caused the Trojan War. —— **sprētae,** gen. sing. f. of *sprētus, -a, -um,* perf. part. pass. of *spernō, -ere, sprēvī, sprētum,* 3; qualifying *formae.* Observe that in this conjunction of noun and participle, the latter conveys the principal idea; this is one of the predicate uses of the participle; cf. *ante urbem conditam, before* (lit. *the city founded) the founding* of the city. A. & G. 292, *a;* B. 337, 5; G. 437, NOTE 2; ·H. 549, 5, NOTE 2. In such cases, the participle = an abstract noun followed by the gen. case, as *of the slighting of her beauty;* or it has the strength of a dependent clause, as *her beauty, which* (or *because it) was scorned. Spretae formae* explains *iudicium* above; Paris slighted Juno and Minerva by pronouncing Venus the fairest. —— **que,** enclitic conj., joining *iudicium* and *iniuria;* here, as frequently, it is used *expletively,* i.e. not to bring in something new, but to modify something already given. In scansion, *ue* is elided before *iniuria;* cf. *quoque,* l. 5. —— **iniūria,** *-ae,* f., 1st; nom. sing. joined by *que* to *iudicium,* the subj. nom. of *manet* above. Note that the 2d *i* is consonantal. —— **formae,** gen. sing. of *forma,* f., 1st (*ferō,* hence *that which is borne, form);* objective gen., modifying *iniuria.* The objective gen. is frequent after nouns expressing action or feeling. A. & G. 217; B. 200; G. 363, 2; H. 396, III. Often the context alone can guide the reader; thus *odium consulis* might be (1) subjective, = the hate *felt by* the consul, or (2) objective, = the hate *felt towards* the consul. *Forma,* lit. *form, shape,* then *beauty;* synonyms are *figura = figure, deportment; pulchritudo* = general *beauty* of features, symmetry, color, etc.

28 fórmae, Ét genus , ínvi,*sum*, „ ét rap,tí
of her beauty *and* *the race* *hated* *and* *carried away*

29 Gany,médis ho,nóres: Hís ac,cénsa su,pér „
of Ganymede *the honors:* *by these things* *fired* *in addition*

slighted, and the race of her hatred, and the honors bestowed upon ravished Ganymede — further enkindled

---

LINE 28. **Et**, cop. conj., connecting *genus* and *iudicium ;* see note and references under *que*, l. 1. —— **genus**, gen. *generis*, n., 3d; nom. sing., joined by *et* to *iudicium*. The reference is to the Trojan race, whose founder, Dardanus, was the son of Jupiter and Electra, daughter of Atlas. —— **invīsum**, nom. sing. n. of *invīsus, -a, -um*, perf. part. pass. of *invideō, -ere, invīdī, invīsum*, 2; used as an adj., and qualifying *genus*. Juno was naturally incensed at Jupiter's amours with other goddesses and mortal women. The final *um*, by *ecthlipsis*, is not scanned; cf. *multum*, l. 3. The *caesura* falls naturally after this word, where there is a distinct pause, rather than after the next word, *et*. —— **et**, cop. conj. —— **raptī**, gen. sing. m. of *raptus, -a, -um*, perf. part. pass. of *rapiō, rapere, rapuī, raptum*, 3; agrees with *Ganymedis*; it is equivalent to a rel. clause, as *Ganymede, who was seized*. —— **Ganymēdis**, gen. sing. of *Ganymēdēs*, m., 3d (Greek Γανυμήδης = *one who gladdens*); objective gen. after *honores*; cf. note on *formae*, l. 27 above. Ganymede, a beautiful youth of Phrygia, was, according to Homer, the son of Tros, king of Troy ; Lucan calls him son of Dardanus. For his beauty's sake the shepherd-boy was carried from Mount Ida by Jove's eagle and became the gods' cup-bearer in place of Hebe, Juno's daughter. This mark of Jupiter's favor aroused the jealousy of Juno. —— **honōrēs**, nom. plur. of *honor* (written *honōs* as well), *honōris*, m., 3d; joined by *et* to *genus*, as *genus* to *iniuria*, and that again to subj. nom. *iudicium ;* when a verb refers to each of a number of subjects, it is frequently expressed in agreement with one only and understood with the rest, even if one of the subjects is plural and the verb singular, as in this case. A. & G. 205, *d*; B. 255, 3; G. 285, EXCEPTION 1; H. 463, 1. *Honos* is properly used in two senses, (1) *esteem*, (2) *post* or *office;* but its use was extended to cover (3) *an offering*, as a mark of respect, cf. l, 49, *honorem*, (4) *beauty*, as often in Vergil. Here *honores* covers (2) and (3).

LINE 29. **Hīs**, abl. plur. n. of *hic, haec, hōc* (see *hōc*, l. 17); abl. of cause, embracing all the reasons for resentment in the parenthesis of ll. 25 to 28. A. & G. 245, and 2 *b*; B. 219; G. 408, and NOTE 2; H. 416, and NOTE 1. Some few regard *super* (see below) as a prep. governing *his*, but Vergil never separates a prep. from its obj. except in such ordinary cases as joining the prep. to a modifying adj. or a modifying gen. —— **accensa**, nom. sing. f. of *accensus, -a, -um*, perf. part. pass. of *accendō, -ere, accendī, accensum*, 3 (augmentative *ad* + root *can*, Greek καίω, *I burn*); agrees with *Saturnia*, l. 23, and resumes the construction as originally begun in l. 23. *Accendo* means *I set on fire, I kindle*, both literally and, as here, figuratively. —— **super** = *insuper*, adv., modifying *accensa*. It means *in addition*, rather than *exceedingly*. *Super* is rarely used as an adv., but see *his* above for the reason why it should not here be considered a prep. If it were a prep. here, it would mean *about, concerning* (Greek ὑπέρ). The prep. *super* is used with the acc. = *over*, of space and time, denoting *motion;* it is used with the abl. = (1) *over*, denoting *rest at*, and (2) *about*. A. & G. 153 and 260, each under *Super;* B. 143; G. 418, 4; H. 435. —— **iactātōs**, acc. plur. m. of *iactātus, -a, -um*, perf. part. pass. of *iactō, -āre, -āvī, -ātum*, 1; agrees with *Troas*, l. 30. In this and the next two lines *iactatos . . . Troas . . . arcebat* = *iactabat et arcebat*, the part. being used in a predicate way to compress into a single sentence two co-ordinate predications; this is a common Latin idiom worth remembering for prose composition. A. & G. *292,*

by this, all ocean	iac,tátos	,	aéquore	,	tóto	Tróas, , 30
over she tossed the Trojans, the remnant	*having been tossed about*	*on the sea-surface*		*whole*	*the Trojans*
left *unscathed* by the	réliqui,ás „	Dana,*um*	átque	im,mítis	A,chílli,
Greeks and merci-	*the leavings*	*of the Danai*	*and*	*harsh*	*Achilles*

REM.; B. 337, 2; G. 437; H. 549, 5. See *iactatus*, l. 3. —— **aequore**, abl. sing. of *aequor*, *-is*, n., 3d (*aequō, I make level*); locative abl., employed regularly when the noun is modified by *totus*, and loosely in other cases and in poetry; cf. *terris*, l. 3, where references are given. *Aequor* means *sea*, with special allusion to its *level surface;* synonyms are *mare*, the general word for sea; *altum* and *pelagus* = *the deep sea; fretum* = *a narrow sea, a strait; pontus* (Greek πόντος) = *sea* and also *sea-wave; oceanus* = *sea, ocean,* with a suggestion of its vast and interminable extent. —— **tōtō**, abl. sing. n. of *tōtus, -a, -um,* 2d, gen. *tōtīus,* dat. *tōtī,* otherwise regular; abl. in agreement with *aequore.* Quintilian has defined *totus,* as distinguished from *omnis,* as *the whole collectively, omnis* indicating the *particulars.*

LINE 30. **Trōās** (Greek Τρῶας), acc. plur. m. of adj. *Trōs,* gen. *Trōis,* dat. *Trōi,* etc., nom. plur. *Trōes,* gen. *Trōum;* direct obj. of *arcebat,* l. 31. *Tros* and *Troes* are generally nouns; the usual adjectives are *Trōiānus, Trōius, Trōus* and *Trōicus; Trōiades, -um,* f., 3d, = *Trojan women.* These words and Troy itself (*Troia*) derived their name from Tros, grandson of the founder of the Trojan race, Dardanus. For decl., cf. *heros,* and consult A. & G. 63, *f,* 64, *Heros;* B. 47, 2, 3; G. 65, *Heros;* H. 68, *Heros.* The vowel *o* of *Troas* is long by nature, and is not affected by its position before another vowel; cf. the Greek form above. —— **rēliquiās,** acc. plur. of *rēliquiae, -ārum,* f., 1st, no sing. (*relinquō, I leave*); acc. in apposition to *Troas,* which it modifies; *Troas reliquias Danaum* = *Troas qui a Danais relicti erant.* Observe in scansion that, to meet the needs of hexameter verse, the 1st syllable *re,* originally short (see note on *repostum,* l. 26), has been lengthened; in Plautus the *re* is short. The form *relliquiae* is a latter growth. —— **Danaūm,** gen. plur. of *Danaī, -ōrum,* m., 2d (plur. of adj. *Danaus, -a, -um* used as a noun); subjective gen. after *reliquias.* A. & G. 213, 1; B. 199; G. 363, 1; H. 396, II. Contrast this gen. with that in *formae,* l. 27, and study the note given there. *Danaum* is a contracted form of *Danaorum;* cf. *superum,* l. 4. The Greeks are alluded to in Vergil as *Graii, Argivi, Achivi, Danai,* etc., adjectives borrowed from Homer, who specially connects the army before Troy with Argolis and Achaea. The name *Danai* is derived from Danaus, a king of Argos. By *ecthlipsis,* the final *um* is not scanned; cf. *multum,* l. 3. —— **atque,** cop. conj., joining *Danaum* and *Achille;* see under *que,* l. 1, for use of *atque.* The final *ue* is elided; cf. *quoque,* l. 5. —— **immītis,** gen. sing. m. of *immītis, -e,* adj., 3d (*in* = *not* + *mītis, mild*); qualifies *Achilli.* An allusion to the merciless way in which Achilles treated his Trojan foes and especially Hector after the death of Patroclus, Achilles' bosom friend. —— **Achillī,** gen. sing. of *Achilleus;* subjective gen. after *reliquias,* like *Danaum* above. Observe that the most notable *particular* warrior is mentioned epexegetically to restrict the general notion contained in the *whole, Danaum;* cf. *litora,* l. 3, and note. *Achillēs* or *Achilleus* is a noun of mixed 2d and 3d declension; the acc. is *Achill-em, -ēn, -ea* (which last Vergil avoids); gen. *Achill-is, -eōs, -ī* (contracted from *Achilleī,* which Vergil does not use); dat. *Achillī;* abl. *Achill-ī* or *-ē.* A. & G. 43, *Orpheus,* and *a,* and 63, *f, i;* B. 27, 47, 6, 7; G. 65, *Achilles;* H. 68, *Orpheus, Pericles,* and 1. Greek nouns in -ης may form the gen. in *i* (Greek -ον), or in the regular Latin way, e.g. like *nubes, nubis;* Greek nouns in -ευς may form the gen. either in the Greek way, e.g. -έος, or like Latin nouns in -ĕus, e.g. -ĕi, commonly in the contracted form -ī or -ēī; cf. *Oili,* l. 41. Achilles was the son of

31 **Árce,bát**   lon,gé Lati,ó, „ mul,tósque per,
she was keeping away far from Latium   and many through
32 ánnos   **Érra,bánt**   ac,tí   fatís „ mari,ā ómnia,
years they were wandering driven by the fates seas   all

less Achilles, and
kept them far from
Latium; and many
a year were they
wandering, driven by

Peleus and Thetis. While, in his anger against Agamemnon, he ceased fighting,
the Greeks met reverses; but these were more than compensated for when, after the
death of Patroclus, Achilles again helped the Greeks. He was shot in the heel,
where alone he was vulnerable, by Paris, and died of the wound.

LINE 31. **Arcēbat**, 3d pers. sing. imperf. ind. act. of *arceō, -ēre, arcuī*, supine
arcitum rare, 2 (Greek ἀρκέω = *I ward off*); its subj. nom. is *Saturnia*, l. 23. The
imperf. tense denotes continued action in past time. —— **longē**, . adv. of space,
modifying *arcebat;* cf. *longe*, l. 13. The force of *longe* is apparent from the fact that
Aeneas had already visited Thrace, Delos, and Crete; from Crete he sailed to
Sicily, where he buried his father Anchises. —— **Latiō**, abl. sing of *Latium, -ī*, n.,
2d; abl. of separation after *arcebat*. Verbs signifying *to remove, set free, deprive,*
etc., take the abl. regularly without a prep., and *arceo* actually or very nearly
belongs to this class; it is at least certain that in good prose verbs like *arceo*, e.g.
prohibeo, interdico, are used with the abl., sometimes with a prep., and sometimes
without. A. & G. 243, *a*; B. 214, esp. 2; G. 390, 2, and NOTE 2; H. 413. This abl.
is slightly different from *animo*, l. 26, on which see note. For the country Latium,
see note on *Latio*, l. 6. —— **multōs**, acc. plur. m. of *multus, -a, -um;* an attribute of
annos. The actual number was *seven;* cf. l. 755, *nam te iam septima portat . . .
aestas.* —— **que**, enclitic conj., connecting the sentence in which it stands with the
preceding one. Notice that the subj. of *errabant* in this sentence is the Trojans,
who were the object in the one before (*Troas*, l. 30); the effect of this change of
subj. is to make *multosque . . . circum* almost an explanatory parenthesis. See
references to *que*, l. 1. —— **per**, prep. with the acc.; governs *annos*. It marks here
duration of time; other uses are *through*, (1) of *place*, (2) of *agent*, (3) of *motive*, (4) of
entreaty. A. & G. 153, *Per;* B. 181, 2; G. 416, 18; H. 433, *Per.* —— **annōs**, acc.
plur. of *annus, -ī*, m., 2d; obj. of *per*.

LINE 32. **Errābant**, 3d pers. plur. imperf. ind. act. of *errō, -āre, -āvī, -ātum*, 1 ;
its subj. is *illi* understood, referring to the Trojans; see *que* above. —— **actī**,
nom. plur. m. of *actus, -a, -um*, perf. part. pass. of *agō, -ere, ēgī, actum*, 3 ; agreeing
with and in appos. to *illi*, the understood subj. of *errabant*. The verb *ago* is used in
a large variety of senses; its original meaning is *to put in motion*, hence *to move,*
and as here *to drive.* —— **fātīs**, abl. plur. of *fātum, -ī*, n., 2d (see *fāta*, l. 16); abl. of
instrument or means. *Fata* in this passage is not strictly personified so as to =
Parcae, for then the abl. would be abl. of the agent, requiring the prep. *a* or *ab;* nor
yet does it mean *evil fates* or *disasters* caused by Juno, but rather it = the *decree* of
the Fates or, in other words, *the destiny* of the Trojans which the gods might defer
but not avert. For abl. of means, see A. & G. 248, *c*; B. 218; G. 401; H. 420. ——
maria, acc. plur. of *mare, maris*, n., 3d; obj. of *circum*. For synonyms, see *aequore*,
l. 29. Final *a* is elided before the *o* of *omnia;* cf. *ille*, l. 3. —— **omnia**, acc. plur. n.
of adj. *omnis, -e*, 3d; qualifies *maria*. *Omnis*, as distinguished from *totus*, draws
attention to the *parts;* so *maria omnia* = *every sea* of the ocean, i.e. every part of
the Mediterranean. —— **circum**, prep. with the acc., governing *maria*. *Circum* was
originally an adverbial acc. of *circus* (*in a ring*), and from its association with
nouns became a prep. Except in one instance, *circum* is used only of place.
A. & G. 153; B. 141; G. 416, 5; H. 433. Note that *circum* occasionally follows its
noun; cf. *contra*, l. 13, and see references.

| destiny over all seas. So great a task it was to found the Roman people. Scarcely out of sight of the land of Sicily | círcum. *around.* | Tántae , *So great* | mólis *of labor* | e͵rát *it was* | „ | Ro͵mánam *Roman* | , 33 |
| | cóndere , *to establish* | géntem. *the race.* | Víx *Hardly* | e , *out of* | cónspec͵tú *sight* | „ Sicu͵lae *Sicilian* | 34 |

LINE 33. **Tāntae,** gen. sing. f. of *tantus,-a,-um;* agrees with *molis.* Its correlative is *quantus;* cf. *talis* and *qualis.* —— **mōlis,** gen. sing. of *mōles, mōlis,* f., 3d; poss. gen. standing with *erat* in the pred., and frequent when the subj. is an inf. or a clause used as a subst. Remember that the verb *sum* does not form a complete pred., except in the sense of *existing.* A. & G. 214, *d;* B. 198, 3; G. 366, esp. REM. 2; H. 401-403. This pred. gen. is most common with adjectives, e.g. *stulti est . . ., it is (the part) of a foolish man to . . .;* it is then = to *stultum est.* So here *tantae molis erat = tam difficile erat.* The primary meaning of *moles* is *a mass,* or *bulk,* and it has this sense in l. 61, *molem;* here *molis* has the derived meaning of *difficulty, labor.* —— **erat,** 3d pers. sing. imperf. ind. of *sum, esse, fuī;* its subj. nom. is *condere* which, as the copula, it connects with *tantae molis,* thus forming the pred. See note on *fuit,* l. 12. —— **Rōmānam,** acc. sing. f. of *Rōmānus, -a, -um* (of *Roma, -ae,* f., 1st); qualifies *gentem.* In this line the purpose of the Aeneid is clearly indicated — viz., to glorify Rome and its emperor Augustus by tracing the former's foundation to the Trojans and the latter's ancestry to Aeneas, son of the goddess Venus. —— **condere,** pres. inf. act. of *condō, -ere, condidī, conditum,* 3; subj. of *molis erat.* The inf. mood was originally the dat. case of a verbal noun (*e* being the sign of the dat.); as a verbal noun it may be subj. or obj. of a sentence, and as a verb it has voice, tense, is often modified by adverbs, and can govern oblique cases. A. & G. 270; B. 326-328; G. 280; H. 532, 538. —— **gentem,** acc. sing. of *gens, gentis,* f., 3d (cf. *gentibus,* l. 17); gov. by *condere,* which, in so far as it is a verb, can take an object; thus the full subject is the phrase *condere Romanam gentem.* At this point the introduction, as it were, to the Aeneid comes to an end, and the narrative begins with l. 34.

LINE 34. **Vīx,** adv., qualifying the adverbial phrase *e conspectu Siculae telluris. Vix* is used as a quasi-negative adverb with reference to *degree* or *time;* here the latter use predominates. Note how Vergil plunges into his subject without any preliminary description of the fortunes of Aeneas after the fall of Troy; all these details are artistically introduced in Books II and III, when Aeneas tells his story to Dido at Carthage. —— **ē,** prep. with the abl.; gov. *conspectu.* It is written *ex* before vowels and *h, e* or *ex* before consonants; it means *from, out of* applied to *place, time, cause, origin* and in phraseological expressions A. & G. 152, *b;* B. 142, 2; G. 417; H. 434. —— **conspectū,** abl. sing. of *conspectus, -ūs,* m., 4th (*conspicio = I see;* root *conspec*); gov. by prep. *e.* —— **Siculae,** gen. sing. f. of *Siculus, -a, -um* (pertaining to the *Siculi = Sicilians*); qualifies *telluris.* Vergil elsewhere alludes to Sicily as *Trinacria* and *Triquetra,* terms suggesting its triangular shape with a headland at each angle. In l. 557 he calls it *Sicania* (pertaining to the *Sicani = Sicilians*), thus making no distinction between the two races, the *Sicani* and the *Siculi,* though Thucydides in his history describes them as two ancient and distinct bodies of settlers. It will be remembered that Aeneas is leaving Sicily after burying his father Anchises there. —— **tellūris,** gen. sing. of *tellūs,* f., 3d; objective gen. after *conspectu.* A. & G. 217; B. 200; G. 363, 2; H. 396, III. *Tellus =* the *earth* when used alone, but when limited by an adj., such as *Siculae* above, it is equivalent to *terra;* it is a purely poetical word. —— **in,** prep. with the acc. and abl.; gov. *altum.* With the acc. it denotes *motion,* and means *into, towards,*

35 tel,lúris	in	,	áltum	Véla	da,bánt	lae,tí	„	ét
of the land	*into*		*the deep*	*sails*	*they were giving*	*glad*		*and*

they were merrily setting sail towards the open sea and

36 spu,más salis	,	aére	ru,ébant,	Cúm	Iu,no
the foams	*of salt*	*with bronze*	*were casting up*	*when*	*Juno*

tossing the salt sea-foam with prow of bronze, when Juno,

aéter,núm	„	ser,váns	sub	,	péctore	,	vúlnus
eternal		*guarding*	*under*		*her breast*		*the wound*

nursing deep in her heart her undying wound, thus com

---

against, etc.; with the abl. it denotes *rest at,* and means *in, on, at,* etc.   A. & G. 153, under *In;* B. 143; G. 418, 1; H. 435, 1. —— **altum,** acc. sing. of the neut. of *altus, -a, -um,* used as a noun; obj. of the prep. *in;* cf. *alto,* l. 3, and for synonyms see note on *aequore,* l. 29.

LINE 35. **Véla,** acc. plur. of *velum, -ī,* n., 2d (probably connected with *veho = I carry);* direct obj. of *dabant.* The plural is most common; the sing. usually = a *covering* or *awning.* —— **dabānt,** 3d pers. plur. imperf. ind. act. of *dō, dare, dedī, datum,* 1, irreg.; its subj.-nom. is the same as that of *errabant,* l. 32, viz. either *Troes* or a pron. representing the Trojans. The verb *do* is used with the acc. of the thing given and the dat. of the indirect obj., i.e. the person to whom it is given. Here the dat. *ventis, to the winds,* is understood; the full phrase is *dare vela ventis, to give the sails to the winds,* i.e. *to set sail.* *Do* is used in many similar phrases, e.g. *dare amplexus = to give embraces,* i.e. *to embrace.* —— **laetī,** nom. plur. m. of *laetus, -a, -um,* agreeing with the unexpressed subj. of *dabant.* *Laeti* is used, like *primus,* l. 1, to limit the action of the verb, and has the force of an adverb. A. & G. 191; B. 239; G. 325, REM. 6; H. 443. The final *i* is elided before *et;* the *caesural* pause follows *laeti,* not *et.* —— **et,** cop. conj., joining *dabant* and *ruebant.* —— **spūmas,** acc. plur. of *spūma, -ae,* f., 1st (*spuo = I spit);* poetic plur., direct obj. of *ruebant.* *Spuma* denotes *foam* or *frothing,* whether of water boiling, the sea tossing, or of human rage or frenzy. —— **salis,** gen. sing. of *sāl,* m., 3d; gen. after *spumas.* *Sal* is used here as a synonym of *mare,* like the corresponding Greek word ἅλς, gen. ἅλος; in this case the gen. is purely poss. It is possible to regard *salis* as = *of salt,* in which case the gen. takes the place of an adj., qualifying *spumas.* —— **aere,** abl. sing. of *aes, aeris,* n., 3d; abl. of means or instrument; see references under *fatis,* l. 32. *Aere* here stands for *aerata prora = with prow* of bronze. *Aes* does not mean *brass,* which was probably little used, if at all, by the ancients; it = *copper* or *bronze,* hence occurring in many phrases relating to money; *statua ex aere* = a *bronze* statue. —— **ruēbant,** 3d pers. plur. imperf. ind. act. of *ruō, -ere, ruī, rutum;* co-ordinate with *dabant.* *Ruo* is only transitive in poetry, and is found in Virgil in many connections whose only common idea is that of violent movement; hence it may be rendered freely. It is used here instead of *eruo;* cf. *verteret* for *everteret,* l. 20.

LINE 36. **Cum,** conj., indicating a point of time; also written *quum, quom,* and rarely *qum* (an adverbial acc. of the rel. *qui*). The conj. *cum* can only be discriminated from the prep. *cum* by careful observance of the construction. It is often a correlative of *tum = then,* and this relation is perceptible here, for the sense is practically *they were just then out of sight . . . when Juno,* etc. *Cum* temporal takes the subjunct. in the imperf. and pluperf. tenses, and the ind. in others; but when the clause it introduces is simply explanatory of *tum* or 'a previous temporal phrase, it may take the imperf. and pluperf. indicative. *Cum* is also used to introduce, (1) a *causal* clause, *cum = since, as,* (2) a *concessive* clause, *cum = although:*

muned with herself:	Haec	se,cúm:	"Me,ne	íncep,tó „ 37
"Must I retire from my purpose baffled,	*these things*	*with herself* (*pondered*):	*Me*(=*am I*)	*from my design*
and in no wise	de,sístere ,	víctam,	**Néc** pos,se	Ítali,á „ 38
avail to turn the	*to desist*	*conquered*	*and not to be able*	*from Italy*

in both cases its verb is in the subjunct. mood, whatever the tense. A. & G. 325, 326; B. 286, 2, 288, 289, and 309, 3; G. 581-587; H. 515, III, 517, and 521. —— **Iūnō**, nom. sing. (see l. 4); subj. of an understood verb *dixit* or *collocuta est.* Verbs of *saying* are frequently omitted before speeches in Vergil; cf. ll. 76, 335 and 559. Observe the elision of the final *o*. —— **aeternum**, acc. sing. n. of *aeternus, -a, um* (from same root as *aevum, an age,* and *aetas, age*); qualifies *vulnus*. *Aeternus* is an adj. only properly used with objects or states which are super-human. —— **servāns**, nom. sing. f. of the pres. part. act. (gen. *servantis*) of *servō, -āre, -āvi, -ātum,* 1; agrees with *Iuno*. The implication is that Juno *kept alive* her anger so as not to forego vengeance. —— **sub**, prep. with the abl. *pectore*. *Under her breast* = *deep in her breast*. *Sub*, like *in, super* and *subter*, is used with the acc. denoting *motion* in space or time; with the abl., denoting *rest* or *state*. A. & G. 153, 260; B. 143; G. 418; H. 435. —— **pectore**, abl. sing. of *pectus, pectoris,* n., 3d; gov. by *sub*. —— **vūlnus**, gen. *vūlneris,* n., 3d; acc. sing., object of *servans*. Often written *volnus*. It refers to *saevi dolores,* l. 25.

LINE 37. **Haec,** acc. plur. n. of *hīc, haec, hōc* (see *hoc,* l. 17); obj. of the verb of *saying* understood after *cum;* see note on *Iuno* above. *Haec* refers to what follows. —— **sēcum** (*sē* + *cum*), abl. sing. of the reflexive pron. of the 3d person; gov. by *cum,* and refers to *Iuno*. No nom., acc. *sē* or *sēsē,* gen. *suī,* abl. *sē* or *sēsē;* the forms of the sing. and the plur. are the same. When reference is made in the oblique cases to the subject of the sentence, this pronoun is regularly used. A. & G. 196; B. 85; G. 309; H. 448. The prep. *cum* takes the abl., and is only enclitic (i.e. appended to its object) when used with a personal or reflexive pron., or the rel. pronoun. A. & G. 99, *e,* and 104, *e;* B. 142, 4; G. 413, REM. 1; H. 184, 6, and 187, 2. —— **Mēne** (*mē* + *ne*); *me* is the acc. sing. of the 1st personal pron. *ego* (see *mihi,* l. 8), subj. of the inf. *desistere; ne* is an enclitic interrog. particle, for the use of which refer to note on *ne,* l. 11. The acc. and inf. are used to express surprise or strong emotion in exclamatory fashion, a construction which, like the exclamatory acc., e.g. *me miserum* = *unhappy me!* is mainly colloquial. The idiom is probably explained by supposing the acc. and inf. to be the object of a verb understood, as in English (*to think that*) *I must desist,* etc. A. & G. 274; B. 334; G. 534; H. 539, III. The addition of *ne* heightens the effect of the speaker's emotion; cf. l. 97. Notice the elision of the final *e* in *mene.* —— **inceptō**, abl. sing. of *inceptum, -ī,* n., 2d (*incipio* = *I begin;* hence a *thing begun,* an *enterprise*); abl. of separation, partly gov. by *de* in *desistere.* A. & G. 243, *b;* B. 214; G. 390, 1 and 2, NOTE 3; H. 413, esp. NOTE 3. *Incepto* signifies Juno's revenge. —— **dēsistere,** pres. inf. act. of *dēsistō, -ere, dēstitī, dēstitum,* 3 (*dē* + *sistō, I make to stand*); its subj. is *me* in indignant exclamation. —— **victam,** acc. sing. f. of *victus, -a, -um,* perf. part. pass. of *vincō, -ere, vīcī, victum,* 3, irreg.; agrees with *me,* but qualifies the pred. expressing manner or cause. A. & G. 292, *a;* B. 337, 2; G. 437; H. 549, 5. Synonyms: *vincere* = *to conquer* decisively, and implies exertion; *superare* = *to overcome,* and does not imply so marked or permanent a superiority as *vincere;* but both verbs are commonly used indifferently to express mastery.

LINE 38. **Nec,** disjunctive conj., abbreviated from *neque* (*ne* + *que*) = *and not; neque* (*nec*) ... *neque* (*nec*) = *neither* ... *nor;* cf. *necdum,* l. 25. —— **posse,**

39 Teu‚crór*um* a‚vért*e*re ‚ rég*e*m? Qúippe ve‚tór | Teucrian king away from Italy? because

of the Teucri   to turn away   the king   because I am forbidden | I am forbidden of

pres. inf. of *possum*, perf. *potuī*, no supine, irreg.; joined by *nec* to *desistere*, and like *desistere* is gov. by the acc. *me* in indignant exclamation. *Possum* is compounded of *potis* = *able*, and *sum* = *I am*; *potsum* was the next step, and finally the *t* was assimilated, becoming *s* in *possum*. A. & G. 137, *b*; B. 126; G. 119; H. 290. The final *e* is elided before *Italia*. —— Italiā, abl. sing. of *Italia*, -*ae*, f., 1st; abl. of separation, figuratively dependent on the prep. *a* in the compound verb *avertere;* consult references given under *desistere*, l. 37 above. Strictly a prep. denoting separation is required with *Italia*. —— Teucrōrum, gen. plur. of *Teucrī*, m., 2d (adj. *Teucrus* or *Teucrius* = lit. *belonging to Teucer*); poss. gen. limiting *regem*. The *Teucri* (Trojans) derived their name from *Teucer* (sometimes written *Teucrus*), the first king of Troy (so *Teucria*, -*ae*, f., 1st = *Trojan land*); he was a son of the river-god Scamander (in the Troad) and a nymph, but later accounts represent him as son of a Cretan noble, Scamander. This Teucer must be distinguished from Teucer, son of Telamon, who founded Salamis in Cyprus. By *ecthlipsis*, the final *um* is suppressed; cf. *multum*, l. 3. —— āvertere, pres. inf. act. of *āvertō*, -*ere*, *āvertī, āversum*, 3 (*ā* = *from*, + *vertō*); *prolative* or *complementary* inf., explaining *posse*. A. & G. 271; B. 326; G. 423; H. 533. Note that the initial vowel is not rendered short by its position before a single consonant, though such is the general rule; it is long by nature. —— rēgem, acc. sing. of *rēx, rēgis*, m., 3d; direct obj. of *avertere*. *Regem* is used loosely for *ducem* = *leader*, though Aeneas, as leader of the *reliquiae Danaum*, l. 30, might have claimed that royal authority had passed to him.

LINE 39. **Quippe**, conj.; it is compounded of *qui*, an old locative or abl. of the rel. pron. *qui*, and the suffix *he;* cf. *quin* = *qui* + *ne, by which not*. *Quippe* was originally used interrogatively, and for that reason some editors put a question stop after *fatis;* but its interrog. character very early disappeared, and we find it, as in this instance, conveying a reason for something and emphasizing it. Here *quippe* states the reason *vetor fatis* with indignant scorn; it must be taken as an exclamation, i.e. *because, forsooth, I am forbidden by the fates!* *Quippe* is often used with the rel. *qui*, e.g. *quippe qui* = *since he*, etc. —— **vetor**, 1st pers. sing. pres. ind. pass. of *vetō*, -*āre, vetuī, vetitum*, 1, irreg.; its subj. is *ego* (i.e. Juno) understood. The student will remember that the Tribunes of the Plebs had the right of saying *Veto* (= *I forbid*) and thereby stopping any law or proposal that did not please them. —— fātīs, abl. plur. of *fātum*, -*ī*, n., 2d; abl. of means or instrument; see *fatis*, l. 32. —— **Pallasne** (*Pallas + ne*); *Pallas* is nom. sing., gen. *Palladis* or *Pallados*, f., 3d; subj.-nom. of *potuit*. *Ne* is an enclitic interrog. particle; cf. *tantaene*, l. 11. *Pallas* is emphatic in position, and *ne* is used for *nonne* to express the greater surprise; observe the elision of *ne*. The Greek goddess Pallas (Pallas Athene) corresponds to the Roman Minerva; she was born from the head of Jupiter (Zeus), and was the goddess of war, weaving, and wisdom. Athens was her favorite city, and there her sacred olive-tree was greatly reverenced. —— exūrere, pres. inf. act. of *exūrō*, -*ere, exussī, exūstum* (*ex*, intensive, + *uro*); *prolative* inf. after *potuit;* see note on *coluisse*, l. 16. Juno displays jealousy of Pallas' power to destroy her enemies by fire and water. The allusion is to the story that Ajax Oïleus tried to abduct Cassandra, daughter of Priam, from the very temple of Pallas, and the goddess in her anger wrecked the Greek fleet and burnt it by lightning at Caphereus in Euboea, and caused Ajax to be impaled on a sharp rock. —— **classem**, acc. sing. of *classis*, -*is*, f., 3d; obj. of *exurere*. *Classis* in good Latin = a *fleet;* rarely it stands

| the fates! Could Pallas consume with fire the Argive fleet and sink the Argives too beneath the sea, for the guilt of one alone, even the frenzy of Ajax, son | fa,tís. „ Pal,lásne ex,úrere , clássem Árgi,vum 40
by the fates! Pallas to burn up the fleet of the Argives
átque iṇ,sós „ potu,ít sub,mérgere , pónto,
and them themselves was she able to sink in the sea
Únius , ób no,xam ét furi,ás „ A,iácis 41
of one man on account of the crime and the rages of Ajax |

for *class, division,* as the old class-divisions of the Roman people; the meaning *forces* was obsolete in Vergil's time.

LINE 40. **Argīvum** (sometimes written *om* for *um* when *v* precedes), gen. plur., contracted for *Argīvōrum*, from *Argīvī*, 2d, *the Greeks;* poss. gen. limiting *classem.* For the contraction, see note on *Danaum*, l. 30; final *um* is suppressed by *ecthlipsis.* *Argīvi* is used as representative of the Greeks in general; the *Argīvi* mentioned were Locrians. —— **atque,** co-ordinate cop. conj., connecting *exurere* and *submergere;* see under *que,* l. 1. Observe the elision of the final *ue*, and see *quoque,* l. 5. —— **ipsōs,** acc. plur. m. of *ipse, -a, -um* (perhaps *is* + *pse*), gen. *ipsīus,* dat. *ipsī,* abl. and acc. sing. and the plural are declined like *bonus; ipsos* is obj. of *submergere.* *Ipse* is a determinative pronoun, and may be used, (1) as intensive adj. in agreement with a noun or another pronoun, e.g. *Caesar himself* is *Caesar ipse; I myself* is *ego ipse;* (2) independently, in which case the particular pronoun intensified is suggested by the verb, or the context; e.g. *ipse feci, I did it myself.* *Ipsos* here means *the Argives themselves,* in contrast to the *fleet* mentioned before. A. & G. 102, *e;* B. 88; G. 103, 3; H. 186 and 452. Beware of confusing *ipse* with the reflexive pron. of the 3d pers. *se.* —— **potuit,** 3d pers. sing. perf. ind. of *possum, posse, potuī,* no supine (see note on *posse,* l. 38); pred. of subj.-nom. *Pallas,* l. 39. The order may be simplified thus: *Pallasne potuit exurere classem Argivum atque submergere ipsos ponto,* etc. —— **submergere,** pres. inf. act. of *submergō, -ere, submersī, submersum,* 3; *prolative* inf., like *exurere* above. —— **pontō,** abl. sing. of *pontus, -ī,* m., 2d; locative abl.; cf. *mente,* l. 26. For synonyms, see *aequore,* l. 29.

LINE 41. **Ūnius,** gen. sing. m. of *ūnus, -a, -um* (see *unam,* l. 15); poss. gen. limiting *noxam. Unius* by its emphatic position in the sentence points a strong contrast: Pallas was offended by *one* man Ajax, yet could destroy a whole fleet; Juno was incensed at the *whole race* of the Trojans, but her vengeance was being impeded by fate. Observe that *unius* is a *dactyl,* the *i* being short in quantity; as a rule, the *i* is long; cf. *illius,* l. 16, and consult the note. —— **ob,** prep. with the acc., gov. *noxam;* see *ob,* l. 4. —— **nōxam,** acc. sing. of *nōxa, -ae,* f., 1st (*noceo = I injure);* gov. by *ob.* The crime indicated is stated in the note to *exurere,* l. 39 above. By derivation *noxa = injury,* but it is frequently used in good Latin = (1) *guilt, crime,* (2) *punishment* for crime. Grammarians insist that *noxa =* *punishment,* and that the word for *crime* is *noxia.* The final *am* is suppressed (*ecthlipsis*). —— **et,** conj., joining *noxam* and *furias.* —— **furiās,** acc. plur. of *furiae, -ārum,* f., 1st, sing. very rare (*furo = I rage); acc.* after *ob. Furias = furorem,* i.e. *madness* (Greek ἄτη) inspired by the Furies, whose names were Alecto, Megaera, Tisiphone. *Guilt and madness* is an instance of *hendiadys* (ἓν διὰ δυοῖν), viz. the expression of a single idea by two nouns connected by a conjunction; here the idea is *mad guilt;* cf. the stock Vergilian example *pateris libamus et auro = we make libation with bowls and gold* (= *golden bowls*). A. & G. 385; B. 374, 4; G. 698; H. 636, III, 2. —— **Aiācis,** gen. sing. of *Aiāx,* m., 3d (Greek ᾿Αίας); poss. gen. limiting *furias.* This Ajax must not be confused with Ajax, son of Telamon, who

42 O,íli?   Ípsa,   Io,vís rapi,dúm „ iacu,láta | of Oileus? With
(son) of Oīleus She herself of Jupiter   swift   having hurled | her own hand she
                                                                   | launched forth from
43 e , núbibus , ígnem,   Dísie,cítque ra,tés „ | the clouds Jove's
                                                     | flashing fire, scat-
from   the clouds   the fire   both dispersed   the vessels | tered the ships, and

committed suicide because the arms of Achilles were given to Odysseus, instead of
to himself. —— Oīlī, gen. sing. of Oīleus, m., Greek noun (for declension, see note
on Achilli, l. 30); patronymic gen., = son of Oileus (Greek ' Οϊλῆος); in origin it is
a poss. gen., limiting fili, the understood appositive of Aiacis. The noun limited,
when expressing relationship (e.g. filius, uxor, etc.), is often thus understood, and
sometimes other nouns also (e.g. ad Cereris = to the temple [aedem] of Ceres).
A. & G. 214, 1, b; B. 196; G. 362, NOTE 1; H. 398, 1, NOTES 1 and 2.   Otli is the
reading of the Medicean MS.; the Roman MS. reads Otlei; both MSS. have great
authority, and many editors prefer Otlei.

LINE 42. Ipsa, nom. sing. f. of ipse, -a, -um (see ipsos, l. 40); qualifies Pallas
understood, the subj. of disiecit. Ipsa, always intensive, is rendered more so by its
prominent position in the sentence; it conveys the idea that Juno usurped Jove's
right to use the thunderbolt, and also that she hurled it unaided by others. Ob-
serve how the rhythm of this line suits its subject — a succession of smooth dac-
tyls broken off short in the penultimate syllable of iaculata by a spondee, seeming to
represent the swinging of the bolt and the jerk with which it was cast. —— Iovis,
gen. sing. of Iupiter, acc. Iovem, dat. Iovī, abl. Iove, m., 3d, irreg.; poss. gen. limit-
ing ignem. Jupiter was the son of Saturn, whom he deposed from his sovereignty
over the gods, ruling in his stead. His worship was pure nature-worship, for
Jupiter was the lord of light, the sender of rain, snow, and the lightning. His name
= Diespiter (dies = day + pater = father); cf. the Greek Zεύς, gen. Διός, and the
Sanskrit dju = light, and dyu = heaven.—— rapidum, acc. sing. m. of rapidus, -a,
-um; qualifies ignem. —— iaculāta, nom. sing. f. of iaculātus, -a, -um, past part. of
the deponent iaculor, -āri, iaculātus sum, 1 (cf. iacio = I throw, and iaculum = a
javelin); agrees with ipsa, and the clause it introduces is an adjectival enlargement
of the subject. Deponent verbs are pass. in form, but act. in meaning; thus they
alone have past participles with active sense; Greek verbs do not labor under this
disability. A. & G. 111, b; B. 112; G. 220; H. 231. Final a is elided. —— ē, prep.
with the abl.; gov. nubibus; see e, l. 34, for references to grammars. —— nūbibus,
abl. plur. of nūbēs, -is, f., 3d (Greek νέφος); gov. by e. For decl., see A. & G. 52;
B. 40, 1, a; G. 56, 2; H. 62. —— ignem, acc. sing. of ignis,`-is, m., 3d; obj. of
iaculata. For decl., see A. & G. 57, b; B. 38; G. 57, REM. 2; H. 62. Ignis Iovis = the
lightning, or sometimes the thunderbolt.

LINE 43. Dīsiēcit, 3d pers. sing. perf. ind. act. of disiciō, disicere, disiēci, disiec-
tum, 3 (dis, denoting here severance, + iacio); its subj.-nom. is ipsa, i.e. Pallas.
The prefix dis marks separation in thought or in fact; cf. dissimilis = unlike. ——
que, conj., here correlative of que appended to evertit; see note on.et . . . et, l. 3. ——
ratēs, acc. plur. of ratis, -is, f., 3d; direct obj. of disiecit. Ratis in prose means raft,
but in poetry is used just as freely as the word bark (= ship) in English poetry.
Synonyms: navis, the generic word; puppis, lit. = stern, by synecdoche = ship; biremis
and triremis, which lit. = bireme and trireme (unknown in Homer's times), are now
and then used by Vergil, in each case purely as synonyms of navis; carina, lit. =
keel, by synecdoche = navis, the whole. —— ēvērtitque (ēvērtit + que), 3d pers.
sing. perf. ind. act. of ēvertō, -ere, ēvertī, ēversum, 3 (e + verto); joined by que to

with the winds up-turned the main; him, as he breathed the flames from his pierced breast, she seized in a whirl-wind and impaled upon a sharp rock;	e,vértit,que *and upward*	a'equora *the seas*	,	véntis; *with the winds*	Íllum 44 *him*
	ex,spíran,tém *breathing out*	„ trans,fíxo *pierced through*	,	péctore *from his breast*	, flámmas *flames*
	Túrbine *in a whirlwind*	, córripu,ít *she caught up*	„	scopu,lóque *and on a crag*	in,fíxit 45 *fixed*

disiecit above. *Everto* generally means *overthrow*, but here it is figurative, expressing violent agitation. For *elision* of *ne*, cf. *quoque*, l. 5. —— **aequora,** acc. plur. of *aequor, -is*, n., 3d (root in *aequ-us = level;* hence *smooth surface*); obj. of *evertit.* Vergil uses singular and plural of this word indiscriminately; cf. *aequore*, l. 29. —— **ventis,** abl. plur. of *ventus, -i*, m., 2d (Sanskrit root *va = to blow);* abl. of means or instrument. A. & G. 248, *c*; B. 218; G. 401; H. 420.

LINE 44. **Illum,** acc. sing. m. of *ille, illa, illud*, the dem. pron. of the 3d person; *illum* refers to Ajax mentioned in l. 41, and is in the acc. case as obj. of *corripuit.* For declension of *ille*, see A. & G. 101; B. 87; G. 104, III, and NOTES; H. 186, III. The contrast is so strongly pointed by the position of *illum* that there is no need for a conj. such as *sed;* the omission of a conj. is called *asyndeton.* A. & G. 346, *c*; B. 346; G. 483, NOTE; H. 636, I, 1. Homer's account in the Odyssey represents Ajax as being overwhelmed by a rock to which he had clung and which Poseidon had struck with his trident and cleft in twain. By *ecthlipsis* the final *um* is suppressed; cf. *multum*, l. 3. —— **exspīrāntem,** acc. sing. m. of *exspīrāns, -āntis*, pres. part. act. of *exspīrō, -āre, -āvī, -ātum*, 1; agrees with *illum*, the clause *exspirantem . . . flammas* being an enlargement of the object *illum.* —— **transfīxō,** abl. sing. n. of *transfīxus, -a, -um*, perf. part. pass. of *transfīgō, -ere, transfīxī, transfīxum*, 3; qualifies *pectore.* The breast of Ajax was apparently pierced by the thunderbolt. —— **pectore,** abl. sing. of *pectus, pectoris*, n., 3d; abl. of separation, partly dependent on the *ex* in *exspirantem;* cf. *exciderant animo*, l. 26, and note. —— **flammās,** acc. plur. of *flamma, -ae*, f., 1st (*flag-ma*, root *flag* or *fleg;* cf. Greek φλέγ-ω); gov. by *exspirantem.*

LINE 45. **Turbine,** abl. sing. of *turbō, turbinis*, m., 3d (another form is *turben, turbinis*, n., 3d); abl. of instrument or means, on which see *ventis* above. The root of the noun and of the verb *turbo* indicates rotatory motion; hence the noun = *whirlwind*, or sometimes *a top, a spindle*, or a *round* of duties. —— **corripuit,** 3d pers. sing. perf. ind. act. of *corripiō, corripere, corripuī, correptum*, 3 (*cum + rapiō);* its subj.-nom. is *Pallas* understood. This is one of many *onomatopœic* lines, wherein the rhythm corresponds closely to the sense; notice how the *spondaic* fourth foot checks the swift movement of the first three *dactyls*. A line purely *dactylic* (except for the 6th foot, of course), though common in Homer, is rare in Latin; but Vergil is fond of lines such as this one. —— **scopulōque** (*scopulō* + *que*), abl. sing. of *scopulus, -ī*, m., 2d (Greek σκόπελος = a *look-out* place); dat. of the indirect obj. after *infixit.* Verbs compounded with *in, ad, con, pro*, etc., take the dat. of the indirect obj., but those compounded with *in* frequently take the abl. or acc. preceded by the prep. *in.* A. & G. 228; B. 187, III; G. 347; H. 386. *Que*, cop. conj., connects the sentence in which *infixit* is the pred. with the preceding one whose pred. is *corripuit.* Observe the *elison* of *ue.* —— **infixit,** 3d pers. sing. perf. ind. act. of *infīgō, -ere, infīxī, infīxum*, 3 (*in + fīgo);* joined by *que* to *corripuit.* This is the reading of the best MSS. and is most suitable with *scopulo acuto*, but some MSS. have *inflixit* (of *infligo, -ere*, etc. = *to strike against*). —— **acūtō,** dat. sing. m. of *acūtus, -a, -um*, adj. (but by origin perf. part. pass. of *acuō, -ere, acuī, acūtum* = *I sharpen);* qualifies *scopulo.*

46 a,cúto;　　Ást ego, ,　quaé di,vum　„　ínce,dó | but I, who move
　　sharp　　　but　I　　who　of the gods　　　walk | the queen among
47 re,gína,　　Io,vísque　Ét soror , ét con,iúnx, „ | the gods, sister
　　(as) the queen　and of Jupiter　both　the sister and　　wife | and wife alike of
　　　　　　　　　　　　　　　　　　　　　　　　　　　　　| Jupiter, with a

LINE 46. **Ast** (archaic form of *at*), adversative conj., generally used when a new point is introduced into an argument, or when lively objection is intended; *sed* and *tamen* are more strictly adversative; consult the note and references under *sed*, l. 19. *Ast* here portrays indignant objection to the full power of vengeance being allowed Pallas, while the queen of the gods is thwarted in her own; moreover its archaism suits the marked dignity of the line. —— **ego**, nom. sing. of the 1st pers. pron., acc. *me*, gen. *mei*, dat. *mihi*, abl. *me;* subj. of *gero*, l. 48, signifying *Iuno*. The personal pronouns, when in the nom. case, are usually omitted, but are found when *emphasis* or (as here) *contrast* is desired. —— **quae**, nom. sing. f. of the rel. pron. *qui, quae, quod* (see *qui*, l. 1); subj. of *incedo*, and agrees with its antecedent *ego*. —— **divum**, contracted for *divorum* (cf. *deum*, l. 9), gen. plur. of *divus, -i*, m., 2d (strictly m. of the adj. *divus, -a, -um*); poss. gen. after *regina*. Some editors prefer the ancient form *divom* for the gen. plur.; cf. *Argivom* for *Argivum*, l. 40. Observe the *ecthlipsis* in scanning *divum*. —— **incēdō**, 1st pers. sing. pres. ind. act. of *incēdō, -ere, incēssī, incēssum*, 3; its subj. is *quae*, whose antecedent is *ego;* hence the 1st person. *Incedo* here is like *sum* (the copula), requiring a *complement* to make the predication perfect; the complement is *regina*. The clause = *who am the majestically-walking queen*. *Incedo* conveys the idea of majestic and dignified motion; cf. *incessit*, l. 497, and the noun *incessu*, l. 405. Synonym: *ambulo* = *I walk*, i.e. for amusement or exercise, but without any hint at manner. —— **rēgīna**, nom. sing. (see l. 9), subjective complement of *incedo*. Predicate adjectives and nouns are common with (1) the copula *sum*, (2) verbs meaning *to become, be called, be made*, e.g. *consul creatus est*, (3) intransitive verbs, e.g. *mortuus cecidit* = he fell *dead;* such nouns and adjectives agree with their subjects. A. & G. 176; B. 167, 168; G. 205, 206; H. 360-362. —— **Iovisque** (*Iovis* + *que*), gen. of *Iupiter* (cf. *Iovis*, l. 42); poss. gen. after *soror*, in the next line: *que* joins *soror* with *regina*.

LINE 47. **Et**, cop. conj., correlative of *et* below; cf. *et . . . et*, l. 3. —— **soror**, gen. *sorōris*, f., 3d; nom. sing. joined to the predicate noun *regina* by *que*, and closely connected with *coniunx* by *et . . . et*. Jupiter and Juno were both children of Saturn. —— **et**, conj. —— **cōniunx**, gen. *cōniugis*, m. or f., 3d (*cum* + *iungo*); nom. sing. feminine. It is usually f., = *wife;* but sometimes m., = *husband;* cf. *huic coniunx Sychaeus erat*, l. 343. Synonyms: *coniunx* = *wife*, considered as the husband's equal partner in life (cf. *consors*); *uxor* = *wife*, the common word for a married woman; *marita* is only met in poetry. —— **ūnā**, abl. sing. f. of *ūnus, -a, -um* (see *unam*, l. 15); agrees with *gente*. —— **cum**, prep. with the abl.; gov. *gente*. For the position of the monosyllabic prep. between a noun and an adjective modifying it, see A. & G. 345, *a*; B. 350, 7, *b*; G. 413, REM. 1; H. 569, II, 1. It is usual in such cases for the adj. to precede and the noun to follow the prep. See *cum*, l. 36, for the use of *cum* as a conj. in temporal, causal, and concessive clauses. —— **gente**, abl. sing. of *gens, gentis*, f., 3d (see l. 17); gov. by *cum*. —— **tot**, indeclinable num. adj., modifying *annos;* cf. *tot*, l. 9. —— **annōs**, acc. plur. (see l. 31) of *annus ;* acc. of duration of time. Duration of time (answering the question *how long?*) is expressed by the acc. alone, or by the acc. with the prep. *per* (cf. l. 31); extent of space is also put in the acc. A. & G. 256; B. 181; G. 336; H. 379. Juno had been persecuting Aeneas since the fall of Troy, seven years before; but her quarrel with Troy was many years older.

single people these many years have been waging war.	u,ná *one*	cum *with*	, génte *race*	tot *so many*	, ánnos *(for) years*	Bélla *wars*	ge,ro. 48 *am waging.*
And is there one who yet entreats the divinity of Juno, one	Ét *And*	quis,quám *(does) anyone*	„	nu,men *the godhead*	Iu,nónis *of Juno*	a,dórat *adore*
who with suppliant hands will lay an	Pra'etere,*a*, *after this*	aút *or*	sup,pléx *a suppliant*	„	a,rís *on her altars*	im,pónet 49 *will he place*

LINE 48. **Bella,** acc. plur. of *bellum, -ī,* n., 2d (see l. 5, *bello*); direct obj. of *gero.* The plural, marking long-continued warfare, is in contrast to the single and decisive blow of Pallas. —— **gerō,** 1st pers. sing. pres. ind. act. of *gerō, -ere, gessī, gestum,* 3; its subj. is *ego,* i.e. *Iuno,* understood. *Gero* illustrates one of the uses of the *historical present,* viz. in representing an act begun in past time and continued into the present; it is very common after *iam diu* or *iamdudum.* This present is best translated by *have* or *has been* + the pres. part. of the verb in the present, e.g. *gero = I have been waging.* A. & G. 276, *a*; B. 259, 4; G. 230; H. 467, III, 2. This idiom may be met with also in English; cf. Mr. Gildersleeve's apt quotation from Hamlet: *How does your honor for this many a day?* The final *o* is elided. —— **Et,** conj., here, like the Greek καὶ, employed to emphasize the indignation expressed in the question, and to hint at denial. —— **quisquam,** nom. sing. m. of *quisquam,* f. wanting, *quicquam (quidquam),* no plur., indefinite pron. = *anyone;* subj. of *adorat.* For decl., see A. & G. 105, *d*; B. 91; G. 107, 3, and NOTE 2; H. 190. In the oblique cases it is declined like *quis* + the suffix *quam*   *Quisquam* is rarely an adj., *ullus* being the common word; as a pron., it occurs chiefly in negative sentences, or in interrog. sentences implying a negative; sometimes in conditional sentences, with more emphasis than the usual *quis* and so suggesting a negative, e.g. *si quis = if anyone; si quisquam = if anyone* AT ALL (which is highly improbable!). Consult carefully A. & G. 105, *h*; B. 252, 4; G. 317, 1; H. 457. Of the indef. pronouns, the weakest is *quis; quidam = a certain one* (known, but not named); *aliquis = someone* (not known, but more definite than *quis*); *quisque = each; quivis* and *quilibet = anyone whatever.* The negative of *quis-quam* is *nemo = no one.* —— **nūmen,** acc. sing., gen. *nūminis,* n., 3d; obj. of *adorat. Numen* in this passage = *godhead, divinity;* for other meanings cf. *numine,* l. 8. As Juno is speaking, *numen Iunonis* is a periphrasis for the pers. pron. *me* and much more striking and emphatic. —— **Iūnōnis,** gen. sing. of *Iūnō,* limiting *numen.* —— **adōrat,** 3d pers. sing. pres. ind. act. of *adōrō, -āre, -āvī, -ātum,* 1 (*ad,* without particular force, + *oro*); gov. *numen.* The pres. tense is somewhat perplexing, for the meaning is scarcely *can it be possible that anyone is worshipping;* but *adorat,* taken with *praeterea, after this,* makes a virtual future corresponding to the fut. *imponet* in next line. This disagreement in tenses has caused various emendations, but *adorat* has the best MSS. support. Some, however, read *adoret,* pres. subjunct., the *deliberative* subj. implying (1) doubt, with indignation, (2) impossibility. A. & G. 268; B. 277; G. 259; H. 486, II. The literal sense is: *does anyone henceforth worship,* etc.? *will anyone place gifts?*

LINE 49. **Praetereā,** adv., modifying *adorat. Praeterea* is compounded of *praeter* and *ea;* cf. *post-ea, aut-ea,* etc.; *ea* is by some considered an abl., whose connection with the prep. dates from a time when *praeter, post,* etc., could be used with that case; Corssen, however, calls *ea* the neut. acc. plural of *is, ea, id.* The usual meaning of *praeterea* is *besides,* but here it has the rare sense of *after this, henceforth.* The final *a* is long in quantity, but is here elided before *aut.* —— **aut,** disjunctive conj., excluding the alternatives; often correlatively *aut ... aut.* For

50 ho,nórem?"	Tália ,	flámma,tó	„ se,cúm	offering upon her
a thank-offering?"	*Such things*	*inflamed*	*with herself*	altars?" Revolving such thoughts as
51 dea ,	córde	vo,lútans	Nímbo,*rum* ín	these to herself within her burning
the goddess	*in her heart*	*turning over*	*of storm-clouds* *into*	heart, the goddess

synonyms and distinctions, refer back to note on *ve*, l. 9. —— **supplēx**, gen. *supplicis*, 3d-declension adj. of one termination (*sub* = *under*, + *plico* = *I fold* or *bend*, i.e. the hands, or the knees, in submission); nom. sing. m. agreeing with *quisquam*, but qualifying with the force of an adv. the verb *imponet*. A. & G. 191; B. 239; G. 325, REM. 6; H. 443. —— **ārīs**, dat. plur. of *āra, -ae*, f., 1st; dat. of the remoter obj. after *imponet;* cf. *scopulo*, l. 45 and note. *Ara* (old form *asa*) = lit. *a raised place*, such as is devoted to religious purposes; with this lit. meaning it is easy to understand *Arae*, the plural, being the name of some rocks in the Mediterranean; cf. l. 109. —— **impōnet**, 3d pers. sing. fut. ind. act. of *impōnō, -ere, imposuī, impositum*, 3 (*in* + *pono*); subj.-nom. is *quisquam* above. The discrepancy in tense between *adorat* and *imponet* has been pointed out (cf. *adorat*), but *imponet* is read by the best MSS. The present *imponit* has some support, and corresponds to *adorat*. A third reading is *imponat*, the pres. subjunct., which corresponds to *adoret* (a *varia lectio* for *adorat*) and is of similar character in syntax; refer back to note on *adorat*. —— **honōrem**, acc. sing. of *honōs, -ōris*, m., 3d; direct obj. of *imponet*. For the various meanings of *honos*, cf. note on *honores*, l. 28.

LINE 50. **Tālia**, acc. n. plur. of *talis, -e;* obj. of *volutans*. The correlative of *talis* is *qualis;* cf. *tot . . . quot, tantus . . . quantus*, etc. —— **flammātō**, abl. sing. n. of *flammātus, -a, -um*, the perf. part. pass. of *flammō, -āre, -āvī, -ātum*, 1; agreeing with *corde*. *Flammatus* literally = *set on fire*, figuratively = *angered*. —— **sēcum** (*sē* + *cum*); *se* is the abl. sing. of the reflexive pron. *se*, gov. by the prep. *cum*. For *secum*, refer back to the note on *secum*, l. 37. —— **dea**, nom. sing. f., gen. *deae*, 1st; subj. of *venit*, l. 52. The dat. and abl. plur. of *dea* are sometimes *deabus;* cf. note on *dea*, l. 17. —— **corde**, abl. sing. of *cor, cordis*, n., 3d (Greek κῆρ, and καρδία) the abl. may be considered either abl. of the instrument, or abl. of place where. For abl. of instrument, consult A. & G. 248, *c;* B. 218; G. 401; H. 420. For the abl. of place where, consult A. & G. 258, 4, under *f*, 2 and 3; B. 228; G. 385; H. 425, II, 1, 2; and cf. *alta mente repostum*, l. 26. *Cor, the heart*, being the seat of the emotions, is often used instead of *mens*, when matters of strong emotional interest are being pondered or discussed. —— **volūtāns**, nom. sing. f. of *volūtāns, -āntis*, pres. part. act. of *volūtō, -āre, -āvī, -ātum*, 1 (intensive of *volvo*); agreeing with the subj. *dea*, of which *talia . . . volutans* is a participial enlargement.

LINE 51. **Nimbōrum**, gen. plur. of *nimbus, -ī*, m., 2d; poss. gen. limiting *patriam*. *Nimbus* originally = *rain-storm*, but has other derived meanings, e.g. *storm-cloud*, the bright *cloud* which encircled the gods when they made their presence visibly on earth, a *cloud* of dust, etc., and in Cicero a *calamity*. By *ecthlipsis*, the final *um* is not scanned. —— **in**, prep. with the acc. denoting motion to (with the abl. rest in or at); gov. the acc. *patriam*. *In* = *into*, signifying penetration into the centre or interior; *ad* = *to*, i.e. to the border of something. For *in*, see A. & G. 153; B. 143; G. 418, 1; H. 435, 1. —— **patriam**, acc. sing. of *patria, -ae*, f., 1st (properly *f*. of adj. *patrius, -a, -um* = *belonging to one's father*, and probably agreeing with an understood word, e.g. *terra*); obj. of prep. *in*. —— **loca**, acc. plur. of *locus, -ī*, m., 2d; appositive of *patriam*. *Locus* belongs to a class of heterogeneous nouns having a masc. form in *us*, and neut. in *um;* cf. *iocus* = *a jest*. The plural of *locus* may be (1) *loca* = *places*, properly speaking, (2) *loci* = *spots, topics*, in books or discourses.

comes to Aeolia, the home of storms, a region teeming with raging southern winds. Here in a wide cavern Aeolus, their king, subjects to his com-	patri,ám, *the native home*	„	loca *places*	,	féta *filled with*	fu,réntibus , *raging*	
	Aústris, *south winds*	A'eoli,ám *to Aeolia*	venit. *comes.*	,	Híc *Here*	„	vas,tó 52 *huge*
	rex , *king*	A'eolus *Aeolus*	,	ántro *in a cave*	Lúctan,tés *struggling*	ven,tós *the winds*	„ 53

A. & G. 78, 2, *b*; B. 60, 2; G. 67, 2; H. 141. An appositive is a noun describing another noun and standing in the same part of the sentence. A. &. G. 184; B. 169; G. 320, ff.; H. 359, NOTE 2. —— **féta**, acc. plur. n. of *fētus, -a, -um* (adj. from same root as *fecundus*, as if from an obsolete *feo*); qualifying *loca*. —— **furéntibus**, abl. plur. m. of *furēns, -tis*, pres. part. of *furō, -ere, furuī*, no supine, 3, intrans.; agreeing with *Austris*. —— **Austrīs**, abl. plur. of *Auster, Austrī*, m., 2d (αὔω = *I dry*); abl. of means, in its particular use after verbs or adjectives expressing fulness, abundance, and the like. A. & G. 248, *c*, 2; B. 218, 8; G. 405; H. 420. *Auster* = literally the hot, dry south wind, but here it is used loosely to picture any 'furious wind'; so *Zephyrus* is typical of winds that are light and gentle.

LINE 52. **Aeoliam**, acc. sing. of *Aeolia, -ae*, f., 1st; in apposition to *patriam*. With this passage should be compared the beginning of Book X of the Odyssey. Homer describes Aeolus as having his home in a floating island; Virgil, too, speaks of *one* island only, which he identifies with the volcanic island of Lipara on the north coast of Sicily. In fact there is a group of ten islands, called *Aeoliae, Aeolides*, or *Vulcaniae* (the last name being due to the story that Vulcan's forge was in one of them). The volcanic nature of these islands easily accounts for their being regarded as the home of storms. —— **venit**, 3d pers. sing. pres. ind. act. of *vĕniō, -īre, vēnī, ventum*, 4, irreg.; its subj. is *dea*, l. 50. The present tense is used to bring the scene vividly before the reader; that *venit* is the pres. and not the perf. is clear, because in the former tense the vowel *e* is short, in the latter long. —— **Híc**, adv. of place; qualifies *Aeolus premit*, and is emphatic in position. See note on *hīc*, l. 16. —— **vastō**, abl. sing. n. of *vastus, -a, -um*; qualifies *antro*. *Vastus* = empty, waste, hence *huge, immense*. —— **rēx** (*reg-s*), nom. sing. m., in apposition to *Aeolus*. —— **Aeolus**, gen. *Aeolī*, m., 2d (Greek Αἴολος = *the changeable one*); subj. of *premit*, l. 54. Aeolus, the son of Hippotas, was not called king of the winds till after Homer's time; he was ruler over Lipari, and his superior knowledge of the forces of nature afterwards gained him his sovereignty over the winds. —— **antrō**, abl. sing. of *antrum, -ī*, n., 2d (Greek ἄντρον); abl. of place where, loosely used in poetry. A. & G. 258, 4, under *f*, 2 and 3; B. 228; G. 385; H. 425, II, 1 and 2.

LINE 53. **Luctantēs**, acc. plur. m. of *luctāns, -tis*, pres. part. of the deponent *luctor, -ārī, luctātus sum*, 1; qualifying *ventos*. Homer does not represent the winds in Odyssey X as struggling; Vergil, however, does not merely imitate, but makes his themes, even when old, his own by using the imagery of later times. Observe the heavy, spondaic character of this line, wherein the sound is so cleverly adapted to the sense; *onomatopœia*, as this device is called, is common in Pope, the English poet and translator of Homer. A. & G. 386; B. 375, 4; G. 784, NOTES 11, 14, and 15; H. 637, XI, 5. —— **ventōs**, acc. plur. of *ventus, -ī*, m., 2d; obj. of *premit*. —— **tempestātēsque** (*tempestātēs + que*), acc. plur. of *tempestās, -ātis*, f., 3d (same root as *tempus*); joined by conj. *que* to *ventos*. —— **sonōrās**, acc. plur. f. of *sonōrus, -a, -um* (*sono = I sound*; hence *loud-sounding*); qualifies *tempestates*. This word, like the line. is itself *onomatopœic*.

54 tem,pésta,tésque   so,nóras   Ímperi;ó   premit, ,
and the storms   *loud-sounding* *by his command* *restrains*

55 ác   vin,clís „ et , cárcere , frénat.   Illí
and *by chains* *and* *prison* *curbs (them).* *They*

in,dígnan,tés „ mag,nó cum , múrmure ,   móntis
indignant   *great* *with* *a noise* *of the mountain*

mand the struggling
winds and echoing
storms, and curbs
them with his fet-
ters and his dun-
geon. They with
loud groaning rage
angrily round the

Line 54. **Imperiō**, abl. sing. of *imperium, -ī,* n., 2d (*impero = I command*);
abl. of manner, with the prep. *cum,* by poetical licence, omitted. A. & G. 248, at
the end; B. 220; G. 399, NOTE 2; H. 419, III. It is, however, possible to regard
the abl. as one of means, for which see references on *corde,* l. 50. The choice
depends on whether the question is "*How* did he control?" or "*With what* did he
control?" *Imperium =* (1) *a command;* (2) *authority;* (3) *sovereignty,* esp. in prose
in regard to the consul's military power; (4) *empire.* —— **premit,** 3d pers. sing. pres.
ind. act. of *premō, -ere, prèssī, prèssum,* 3; its subj. is *Aeolus.* —— **ác,** conj., abbre-
viated for *atque* (see note on *que,* l. 1); connects the two verbs *premit* and *frenat.*——
vinclīs, syncopated form of *vinculīs,* abl. plur. of *vinculum, -ī,* n., 2d (syncopated
vinclum); abl. of means or instrument. *Vinculum* (from *vincio = I bind*) = a *bond*
or *fetter,* but in the plural often *prison.* —— **et,** cop. conj., connecting *vinclis* and
carcere. —— **carcere,** abl. sing. of *carcer, carceris,* n., 3d (Sicilian κάρκαρον); abl. of
the instrument. *Carcer* in the sing. *= prison;* in the plur. it *= the barriers* or
starting-place on a race-ground. *Vinclis et carcere* present an instance of *hendiadys,*
two words expressing one main idea; cf. the note and references on *furias,* l. 41.——
frēnat, 3d pers. sing. pres. ind. act. of *frēnō, -āre, -āvī, -ātum,* 1 (*frenum = a bridle*);
joined by *ac* to *premit.*

Line 55. **Illī,** nom. plur. m. of the demonstr. pron. *ille, illa, illud* (see *ille,* l. 3);
illi = the winds, and is subj. of *fremunt.* The final *i* is *elided* before *indignantes.*
—— **indīgnantēs,** nom. plur. m. of *indīgnāns, -āntis,* pres. part. of the dep. verb
indignor, -ārī, -ātus sum, 1 (*in = not + dignor*); in agreement with *illi.* It should
be remembered that deponent verbs are of passive form, but active meaning, and
that they alone of Latin verbs have a past as well as a present participle. Like
l. 53, this is another spondaic line, and the artistic finish of it is increased by the
alliteration, i.e. the rhetorical figure of two or more words beginning with or con-
taining the same sound; in *illi indignantes,* the sound of the vowel *i* is noticed; in
magno cum murmure montis the succession of letters *m* is very marked. A. & G. 386;
B. 375, 3; G. no reference, but read 784, NOTE 15; H. 637, XI, 1. —— **magnō,** abl.
sing. n. of *magnus, -a, -um;* qualifies *murmure.* Comparison: positive, *magnus;*
comparative, *maior;* superlative, *maximus.* Observe that when a monosyllabic
prep. is used with a noun qualified by an adjective, the adj. usually stands first, and
the prep. between the adj. and the noun; cf. *una cum gente,* l. 47, and references. ——
cum, prep. with the abl., gov. *murmure.* *Cum* is used with the abl. (1) to express
accompaniment, (2) to express manner. Here manner is signified, and the rule is
that the noun must be in the abl. with *cum,* but when the noun is qualified by an ad-
jective, *cum* may be retained or omitted. A. & G. 248; B. 220; G. 399; H. 419, III.
—— **murmure,** abl. sing. of *murmur, murmuris,* n., 3d (*onomatopœic* word from sound
MUR); gov. by prep. *cum.* This word covers any muttering or roaring sound. ——
montis, gen. sing. of *mons,* m., 3d; poss. gen., limiting *murmure.* *Mons* (also *dens,
pons,* etc.) is an exception to the rule that words of 3d decl. ending in *s* preceded by
a consonant are feminine. A. & G. 67, *d;* B. 43, 2, and 45, 5, *a;* G. 55; H. 110.

mountain prison;	Círcum	,	cláustra	fre,múnt;	„	cel,sá	sedet	,56
in his lofty citadel	around		the barriers	rage		high	sits	
is Aeolus seated,								
holding his sceptre,	Áeolus	,	árce	Scéptra	te,néns,	mol,lítque 57		
and calms their	Aeolus		citadel	sceptres	holding	and soothes		

There is little doubt (as the alliteration alone proves) that *montis* limits *murmure*, not *claustra:* but the rendering in the margin of the text is similar to that of the best translator of Vergil. *Magno cum murmure montis* is rather harsh as a phrase, but the student may render it with *loud groaning of the mountain;* it = such a clause as *ita fremunt ut mons murmuret.*

LINE 56. **circum,** prep. with the acc.; gov. *claustra.* A. & G. 153; B. 141; G. 416, 5; H. 433. —— **claustra,** acc. plur. of *claustrum, -ī,* n., 2d (for *claud-trum,* from *claudo, I shut*); obj. of *circum.* The singular is very seldom found. The alliteration of the previous line is contained in this; observe the repetition of the letter *c.* —— **fremunt,** 3d pers. plur. pres. ind. act. of *fremō, -ere, fremuī, fremitum,* 3 (Greek βρέμω); its subj. is *illi,* l. 55. —— **celsā,** abl. sing. f. of *celsus, -a, -um* (from *cello,* so originally = *driven aloft*); qualifies *arce.* Notice the close juxtaposition of *s* in *celsa* and *sedet.* The absence of a conjunction (*asyndeton*) to connect the clause *celsa sedet Aeolus,* etc., with the previous one *illi . . . fremunt* is to be observed; the break in the sense at the *caesura* after *fremunt* partly covers the deficiency. A. & G. 208, *b*; B. 346; G. 473, REM.; H. 636, I, 1. —— **sedet,** 3d pers. sing. pres. ind. act. of *sedeō, -ēre, sēdī, sessum,* 2, intrans. (akin to Greek ἕζομαι; the initial *s,* perhaps the supplanter of an original *Digamma,* is lost in Greek, but compensation is made by the rough breathing); subj. is *Aeolus.* —— **Aeolus,** nom. sing., subj. of *sedet.* —— **arce,** abl. sing. of *arx, arcis,* f., 3d (for *arc-s,* from *arceo, I enclose*); abl. of place where. See note on *antro,* l. 52. — NOTE. *celsa arce.* These words have given rise to some disputation. It is generally admitted that *arx* (*a citadel*) is properly applied here as the seat of an absolute ruler, but it is not definite where or exactly what the *arx* was. Some consider it identical with *aula,* l. 140, i.e. the mountain-top. A scholar named Dr. Henry understands by *arx* an elevated seat or throne actually within the cavern, corresponding to the judges' seat on the race-course, to which the terms *carcere, frenat,* etc., also seem to refer in a metaphorical way. Conington and other Vergilian scholars, however, prefer avoiding a too minute study of the language, holding that it is a poet's province not to give too many facts, but to create an atmosphere, as it were, of reality. So the scene is simply that of Aeolus exercising from above absolute sway over his troublesome subjects, the winds.

LINE 57. **Scēptra,** acc. plur. of *scēptrum, -ī,* n., 2d; gov. by *tenens.* The poetic plural is merely for intensive effect, and is not intended literally; it is also metrically useful. —— **tenēns,** nom. sing. m. of the pres. part. act. of *teneō, -ēre, tenuī, tentum,* 2; enlarging the subj. *Aeolus.* —— **mollitque** (*mollit + que*); *mollit* is the 3d pers. sing. pres. ind. act. of *molliō, -īre, -īvī* or *-iī, -ītum,* 4 (*mollis = soft*; hence *to make soft*); the subj. is *Aeolus.* *Que* is a cop. conj., joining *mollit . . . iras* with the previous sentence, whose predicate is *sedet.* The final diphthong is *elided;* cf. *quoque,* l. 5. —— **animōs,** acc. plur. of *animus, -ī,* m., 2d (see *animis,* l. 11, for distinctions of meaning); obj. of *mollit.* —— **et,** cop. conj., joining *mollit* and *temperat.* —— **temperat,** 3d pers. sing. pres. ind. act. of *temperō, -āre, -āvī, -ātum,* 1 (probably for *tempor-o,* from *tempus, -oris, = a section;* hence to *divide,* and afterwards to *regulate*); joined by *et* to *mollit* above. —— **īrās,** acc. plur. of *īra, -ae,* f., 1st; obj. of *temperat,* and plur. as often in poetry.

58 ani,mós	„	et	,	témperat	,	íras:	Ní	passions and re-
their minds		*and*		*moderates*		*their anger:*	*Unless*	strains their wrath: if he did not so,
faci,át,		mari,*a*	ác	ter,rás	„	coe,lúmque		seas and lands and
he were to do (this)		*seas*	*and*	*lands*		*and heaven*		the deep heaven
59 pro,fúndum		Qúippe		fe,ránt		rapi,dí		they would certainly bear off swiftly with
deep		*because*		*they would carry*		*swift*		them, and sweep
se,cúm	„	ver,rántque		per	,	aúras:		them away through
with themselves		*and would sweep them*		*through*		*the air:*		the air: but, fearful

LINE 58. **Ní** (old form *nei*, so probably same as *ne*, though often regarded as a contraction of *nīsi*), conditional conj., gov. *faciat. Si* is used for affirmative conditions, *nīsi* (*ni*) and *si non* for negative. When *nīsi* (*ni*) is used, it usually = *unless*, and the *apodosis* is altogether true, except for the single condition mentioned; when *si non* is used, the *apodosis* is referred to as true only for the case in point. A. & G. 315, *a*; B. 306; G. 591; H. 507, and 3, NOTE 3. *Nīsi* and *ni* are most common when the *apodosis* or principal clause is negative; *si non* is the general negative conditional conjunction. For the general laws in hypothetical sentences, see A. & G. 304-309; B. 301-304; G. 589, and 594, ff.; H. 507-512. —— **faciat,** 3d pers. sing. pres. subjunct. act. of *faciō, -ĕre, fēcī, factum,* 3 (*fio, fiĕri, factus sum* is used as the passive); the obj. is understood, e.g. *hoc.* For the tense of *faciat,* consult A. & G. 308, *e*; B. 303; G. 596; H. 509, esp. NOTE 2. It will be seen that A. & G. and H. regard the hypothesis as one contrary to the fact and consider the pres. subjunct. as an exception to the usual imperf. subjunctive. In prose we should expect *ni faceret . . . ferrent,* but the present tense leaves the matter still one to be considered, and is at any rate more vivid. —— **maria,** acc. plur. of *mare, maris,* n., 3d; obj. of *ferant.* For synonyms, see *aequore,* l. 29. The final vowel is *elided.* —— **āc,** cop. conj., joining *maria* and *terras;* cf. *ac,* l. 54. —— **terrās,** acc. plur. of *terra, -ae,* f., 1st; obj. of *ferant,* and joined to *maria* by *ac.* The plural is used intentionally so as to be exhaustive. —— **coelumque** (*coelum + que*), acc. sing. n., obj. of *ferant,* and joined by the conj. *que* to *terras.* —— **profundum,** acc. sing. n. of *profundus, -a, -um;* agrees with *coelum.*

LINE 59. **Quippe,** conj. used to corroborate something; see note on *quippe,* l. 39. *Quippe,* here as in other passages, is not in its natural position. The order may be simplified thus: *Quippe, ni (hoc) faciat illi rapidi maria ac terras coelumque profundum secum ferant, (ea)que per auras verrant.* —— **ferant,** 3d pers. plur. subjunct. act. of *ferō, ferre, tulī, lātum,* irreg.; the subj. of *ferant* is the *winds* understood. The pres. subjunct. is used in the *apodosis* either as an exception of the rule (viz. imperf. subjunct. when the condition is at the time contrary to the fact), or because, following the rule, the condition is left open as an imaginary possibility in the future. See the references on *faciat,* l. 58 above. —— **rapidī,** nom. plur. m. of *rapidus, -a, -um;* agrees with *venti* understood, but really qualifies the action of the verb *ferant.* A. & G. 191; B. 239; G. 325, REM. 6; H. 443. *Rapidus = swift* and is an expressive word; its derivation is from *rapio = I snatch away.* It may be considered either as passive = *that which is carried off,* or as active = *that which carries off;* in l. 117, *rapidus vortex,* the adj. is certainly active in implication. Observe how well the metre of this line suits the sense; it hurries along from the start; contrast it with ll. 53 and 55. —— **sēcum** (*sē + cum*), abl. plur. of the reflexive pron. *sē,* recalling *venti,* the subj.; the abl. is gov. by the enclitic prep. *cum.* See

of this, the father all-powerful has hidden them in dark caverns, and set above them the	Séd	Pater,	ómnipo,téns	„	spe,lúncis,	ábdidit, 60
	but	the father	almighty		in caves	hid them
	átris,	Hóc	metu,éns,	„	mo,lémque	et, 61
	gloomy	this thing	fearing		and the mass	and

note on *secum*, l. 37. —— **verrantque;** *verrant* is 3d pers. plur. pres. subjunct. act. of *verrō, -ere, verrī, versum*, 3; joined by the enclitic conj. *que* to *ferant*, with which it is co-ordinate. —— **per,** prep. with the acc., gov. *auras;* see references on *per*, l. 31. —·— **aurās,** acc. plur. of *aura, -ae,* f., 1st (Greek αὔρα); obj. of *per*. *Aura* = (1) the *air*, in gentle motion; (2) *a breeze;* (3) *upper air*, as opposed to *aër;* (4) *daylight;* (5) *a gleam*, or *sheen;* (6) *a voice;* (7) *an odor;* the 1st and 2d meanings are most common, but nearly all are found in Vergil.

LINE 60. **Sed,** adversative conj.; for distinctions between *sed, verum, at,* etc., see note on *sed,* l. 19. —— **pater,** gen. *pătris,* m., 3d; nom. sing., subj. of *abdidit*. The reference is to Jupiter. —— **omnipotēns,** gen. *omnipotēntis;* nom. sing. m., qualifying *pater. Omnipotens* is compounded of *omnis* and *potens*. —— **spēluncīs,** abl. plur. of *spēlunca, -ae,* f., 1st (Greek σπῆλυγξ); abl. of place where; see note on *antro,* l. 52. —— **abdidit,** 3d pers. sing. perf. ind. act. of *abdō, -ere, abdidī, abditum,* 3 (*ab* + *do;* cf. *condo, con* + *do,* l. 5); the subj. is *pater* above. Most of the compounds of *do* have the reduplicated perfect. —— **ātrīs,** abl. plur. of *āter, ātra, ātrum;* qualifies *speluncis.* Synonyms: *niger* is the generic word, and admits of comparison; *ater* is specific, and = *coal black,* i.e. the greatest degree of black possible. *Ater* often has the derived meaning of *gloomy,* hence *dies atri* are *unlucky* days.

LINE 61. **Hōc,** acc. sing. n. of demonstr. adj. *hĭc, haec, hōc* (see *hoc,* l. 17); gov. by *metuens.* Wagner has shown that *hoc metuens* differs from *id metuens* in this respect — the former being used when it is feared a calamity is about to happen *immediately,* the latter when someone fears an impending disaster, but does not know when exactly to expect it. —— **metuēns,** nom. sing. m. of *metuēns, -tis,* pres. part. act. of *metuō, -ere, metuī, metūtum,* 3 (*metus* = *fear*); agrees with *pater,* of which it is a participial enlargement. See note on *hoc* above, and refer to *id metuens,* l. 23. —— **mōlemque** (*mōlem* + *que*), acc. sing. of *mōlēs, mōlis,* f., 3d; obj. of *imposuit. Moles* here = *mass;* in l. 33 it has the derived meaning of *labor.* The words *molem* and *montes altos,* both direct objects of *imposuit,* are by the figure *hendiadys* (ἓν διὰ δυοῖν) put for *molem altorum montium;* cf. l. 111, *brevia et Syrtes* = lit. *the shoals and the Syrtes,* i.e. *the shoals of the Syrtes,* and consult A. & G. 385; B. 374, 4; G. 698; H. 636, III, 2. This figure is common in Vergil. *que,* enclitic conj., joins *imposuit* to *abdidit* above; cf. *que, l.* 1. By *elision,* the diphthong *ne* is not sounded in scansion; cf. *quoque,* l. 5. —— **et,** cop. conj., connecting *molem* and *montes* together. It should be remembered that *que* joins two members very closely connected internally, as are *abdidit* and *imposuit; et* simply connects two equal ideas, e.g. *molem* and *montes,* though, except for the figure, there is only one substantive before the mind. —— **montēs,** acc. plur. of *mons, montis,* m., 3d (for gender, cf. *montis,* l. 55); direct obj. of *imposuit.* The plural is merely intensive and poetic, for in l. 55 we read of the *loud groaning of the mountain,* not *mountains.* —— **insuper** (*in* = *on,* + *super* = *above*), adv. of place; modifying *imposuit. Insuper,* as an adverb, has two meanings: (1) *overhead,* (2) *besides.* In l. 29, *super* was used adverbially in the second sense. *Insuper* occurs in late Latin as a prep. gov. the acc. and abl. cases. —— **altōs,** acc. plur. m. of *altus, -a, -um;* qualifies *montes.*

62 **móntes** , **ínsuper** , **áltos** **Ímposu,ít,** **re,gémque**
  mountains   *above*   *high*   *placed*   *and a king*
63 **de,dít,** „ **qui** , **fóedere** , **cérto** **Ét**
  gave (them) *who*   *by compact*   *fixed*   *both*
  preme,re **ét** **la,xás** _ „ **sci,rét** **dare** ,
  to draw tight *and* *loosened*   *would know* *to give*

mass of towering
mountains, and es-
tablished over them
a king, who by
predetermined rule
should know at the
command to tighten

LINE 62. **Imposuit**, 3d pers. sing. perf. ind. act. of *impōnō, -ere, imposuī, im-positum*, 3 (*in = on*, + *pono = I place*); the subj. is *pater* in l. 60. —— **rēgemque** (*rēgem* + *que*), acc. sing. of *rēx, rēgis*, m., 3d; direct obj. of *dedit. Que*, cop. conj., joins *dedit* to *imposuit*. The king is, of course, Aeolus. —— **dedit**, 3d pers. sing. perf. ind. act. of *dō, dare, dedī, datum*, 1, irreg.; joined by *que* to *imposuit*.—— **qūi**, nom. sing. m. of the rel. pron. *quī, quae, quod*, gen. *cūius*, dat. *cuī*, abl. *quō, quā, quō*, acc. *quem, quam, quod;* it is masculine and singular in agreement with its antecedent *regem*, and nom. because it is subj. of *sciret* in the next line. *Qui* here = *ut is*, introducing the *final* clause *qui . . . sciret*, etc.; cf. *quae*, l. 20. —— **foedere**, abl. sing. of *foedus, foederis*, n., 3d (*fidus*, and *fido*); probably an abl. of cause. A. & G. 245; B. 165; G. 408; H. 416. It is hard to distinguish the various uses of the abl.; *foedere* might be taken as giving the cause, stating the means, or pointing out the manner, but as Aeolus had to accept a *fixed compact* before becoming ruler of the winds, the idea of *cause* seems to preponderate. Vergil uses *foedus* as = to *lex*. —— **certō**, abl. sing. n. of *certus, -a, -um;* agrees with *foedere*. *Certus*, of things = *fixed*, *established;* of qualities = *firm, constant;* of persons = (1) *sure, positive*, e.g. *certiorem te facio = I inform you;* (2) *reliable.*

LINE 63. **Et**, cop. conj., correlatively with *et* below, = *both . . . and*. Other combinations are: (1) *que . . . et;* this is rare in early Latin, and Cicero and Caesar avoid it, but it is found in later writers; (2) *et . . . que*, very rare; (3) *que . . . que*, very common in poets; it begins with Plautus, and is used in prose by Sallust and his successors, though Cicero has it once only. See references on *et*, l. 3. —— **premere,** pres. inf. act. of *premō, -ĕre, prĕssī, prĕssum*, 3; objective complementary infinitive, regular with verbs meaning to *dare, learn, know how, be able*, etc. A. & G. 271; B. 326; G. 423; H. 533. The question arises as to what is the object of *premere, ventos* or *habenas;* if *ventos, premere = to check, control;* if *habenas* is obj. (which is more probable), *premere* has the forced sense of *tighten;* cf. Aen. XI, 600, *pressis habenis*. Thus *premere habenas* is the natural opposite of *dare laxas habenas*. The final *e* is *elided* before *et*. —— **et**, cop. conj., correl. of *et* above. —— **lāxās**, acc. plur. f. of *lāxus, -a, -um;* agrees with *habenas*, but stands with *dare* to complete the predication of the infinitive. As such, *laxas* is *proleptic*, i.e. antici-pates what is to be done, and represents it as already completed. The stock example in Vergil is Aen. III, 237, *scuta latentia condunt* = lit. *they conceal their hidden shields* (i.e. *their shields in hiding*); cf. *I hurled him* PROSTRATE. A. & G. 385; B. 374, 5; G. no reference, but read 325, at beginning; H. 636, IV, 3. —— **sciret**, 3d pers. sing. imperf. subjunct. act. of *sciō, -īre, -īvī* or *-iī, -ītum*, 4; the subj. is *qui*, and the subjunct. expresses purpose. A. & G. 317; B. 282; G. 545; H. 497. The purpose is the purpose of the *pater omnipotens* in making the *foedus* with Aeolus. Synonyms: *scire = to know* facts or truths as the objects of conviction, e.g. *scio quis sit = I know who he is. Scio*, and its neg. *nescio*, also = *I know how; noscere = to know* things or attributes as the objects of perception, e.g. *novi hominem = I know the man; cognoscere = to know, to recognize, to ascertain; intelligere = to*

and let slack the	iússus	ha,bénas.	Ad quem	, túm	Iu,nó „ 64
reins. To him now	*being ordered*	*reins.*	*To whom*	*then*	*Juno*
Juno in supplica- tion addressed these	sup,pléx	his	, vócibus	, úsa est:	"Aeole, , 65
words: "Aeolus, —	*(as) a suppliant*	*these*	*words*	*used:*	*O Aeolus,*
for to thee the father of the gods	námque	ti,bí „	di,vúm	pater	, átque
and king of men	*for*	*to thee*	*of the gods*	*the father*	*and*

perceive by the senses or the understanding. —— **dare**, pres. inf. act. of *dŏ, dare, dedĭ, datum*, 1; joined by *et* to *premere*. *Dare* is used with participles and adjectives as a *periphrasis* for a simple verb; thus *dare laxas habenas = laxare habenas;* cf. Aen. IX, 323. *haec . . . vasta dabo = haec vastabo.* It illustrates the tendency for analysis to supplant synthesis in languages. —— **iūssus**, nom. sing. m. of the perf. part. pass. of *iubeō, -ēre, iŭssī, iŭssum*, 2; predicate or attribute part. limiting *qui*, taking the place of a temporal clause in English. A. & G. 292; B. 337, 2; G. 437; H. 549, 5. Thus, *iussus = whenever ordered* to do so by Jupiter. Synonyms: *iubeo = I order*, and is followed by the acc. and inf., e.g. *iubeo te hoc facere; impero = I order*, and takes the dat. of the person, and *ut* with the subj., e.g. *impero tibi ut* (neg. *ne*) *hoc facias.* —— **habēnās**, acc. plur. of *habēna, -ae*, f., 1st (*habeo*, hence *the holding thing*); obj. of the combinate predicate *laxas dare.*

LINE 64. **Ad**, prep. with the acc. gov. *quem.* A. & G. 153; B. 182, 3; G. 416, 1; H. 433, I, under *Ad.* —— **quem**, acc. sing. m. of the rel. pron. *quī, quae, quod;* agrees in gender and number with its antecedent *Aeolus*, and in case gov. by *ad.* The relative is here used, as very often in Latin, to connect two independent sentences; it practically = a conjunction and a demonstrative pronoun, and may be so translated, e.g. *ad quem = itaque* or *et ad eum.* The most common forms of this use are with relative adverbs, e.g. *quo cum progressus esset*, and the phrase *quae cum ita sint.* A. & G. 180, *f*; B. 251, 6; G. 610; H. 453. —— **tum**, temporal adv., limiting *usa est;* see *tum*, l. 18. Observe, that there is no *ecthlipsis*, as the initial *i* of *Iuno* is consonantal. —— **Iūnō**, nom. sing., subj. of *usa est.* There has been a descriptive digression since l. 52, but the narrative again proceeds with Juno's request to Aeolus. —— **supplēx**, nom. sing. f., gen. *supplicis*, adj., 3d; agrees with *Iuno*, but haz the force of an adverbial apposite; see note on *rapidi*, l. 59. —— **hīs**, abl. plur. f. of demonstr. adj. *hīc, haec, hōc*, gen. *hūius*, dat. *huīc*, acc. *hunc, hanc, hōc*, abl. *hōc, hāc, hōc;* agrees with *vocibus.* See *hoc*, l. 17. —— **vōcibus**, abl. plur. of *vōx, vōcis*, f., 3d; gov. by *usa est. Vox* (*voc-s*, from *voco*) = (1) *sound*, (2) *voice*, (3) a *word*, (4) *language*, (5) *accent;* here it = *word.* —— **ūsa est**, 3d pers. sing. perf. ind. of the dep. verb *ūtor, ūtī, ūsus sum*, 3; agrees with its subj. *Iuno.* The perf. of dep. and pass. verbs is made up of the pres. tense of *sum* and the past part. of the verb, e.g. *amatus um;* similarly the pluperf. = the past part. + imperf. of *sum*, e.g. *amatus eram.* The participle must agree in gender, number, and case with the subject of the verb; the tense of *sum* agrees in person and number. *Vocibus* is abl., because *utor* regularly governs that case; so do *fungor, fruor, vescor, potior, dignor*, and *supersedeo.* A. & G. 249; B. 218, 1; G. 407; H. 421, I.

LINE 65. **Aeole**, voc. sing. of *Aeolus;* case of the person addressed. —— **namque** (*nam* + *que*); *nam* is an explanatory conj., with the cop. conj. *que* as a suffix. A combination of conjunctions as above (cf. *at enim, itaque*, etc.) lends emphasis and connects a sentence more definitely with what has preceded. A. & G. 208, *e;* B. 345; G. 498; H. 554, V. There is perhaps an ellipse of some such words as, *I address you, for*, etc., but causal conjunctions often introduce a parenthesis, and

66 homi,núm	rex	Ét	mul,cére	de,dít	has bestowed it both
of men	*the king*	*both*	*to calm*	*has granted it*	to assuage and up-
67 fluc,tús	„ et ,	tóllere ,	vénto,	Géns	stir the waves by the power of the
the waves	*and*	*to upraise*	*with the wind,*	*a race*	wind, — a race

so we may regard it here, with the request postponed till *incute vim*, l. 69. —— **tibī**, dat. sing. of the 2d personal pron. *tū*, acc. *tē*, gen. *tuī*, abl. *tē*, nom., voc., acc. plur. *vōs*, gen. *vestrum* or *vestrī*, dat. and abl. *vōbīs; dat. of the indirect object following *dedit*. Notice that the final *i* is here long in quantity. Final *i* is usually long, but *mihi, tibi, sibi, ibi, ubi* are generally exceptions to this rule; the *i*, however, is in this and several other instances long. —— **dīvūm** (sometimes written *dīvōm*), contracted gen. plur. of *dīvus, -ī*, m., 2d; poss. gen. limiting *pater*. For this genitive, see note on *divum*, l. 46. —— **pater**, nom. sing., subj. of *dedit*. —— **atque**, cop. conj., joining *pater* and *rex*. For use of *atque*, see note on *que*, l. 1. The final syllable is *elided;* cf. *quoque*, l. 5. —— **hominum**, gen. plur. of *homŏ, hominis*, m., 3d (derivation uncertain); poss. gen., limiting *rex*. Synonyms: *homo* in the sing. = *man*, as distinguished from gods on the one hand, and beasts on the other; in the plural, *homines = mankind*, often including men and women: *vir = man*, as distinguished from a boy (*puer*) and particularly from a woman (*femina*); *vir* also has sometimes the meaning of *hero*.—— **rēx**, nom. sing., joined by *atque* to *pater*, and referring to the same person, Jupiter. The majesty of Jupiter is brought into view not only by the great titles which Vergil gives him, but also by the rhythm of the line; the final monosyllable *rex* is very emphatic; cf. Aen. V, 481, *procumbit humi bos*, and the famous Horatian example *parturiunt montes, nascetur ridiculus mus*.

LINE 66. **Et**, cop. conj., correlative of *et* below; see note on *et*, l. 63. —— **mulcēre**, pres. inf. act. of *mulceō, -ēre, mulsī, mulsum* or *mulctum*, 2; the inf. is direct obj. of *dedit*. In prose we should expect *ut* with the subjunct. or a gerundive construction after *dedit;* the inf. is poetical, expressing purpose, and is borrowed from the common Greek idiom, e.g. Iliad XXIII, 512, δῶκε δ' ἄγειν ... καὶ φέρειν; cf. l. 319, *dederatque comam diffundere ventis*. A. & G. 331, *g*; B. 326, NOTE; G. 421, NOTE 1, *b*; H. 535, IV. The notion of the winds soothing and arousing the sea is frequent in Vergil. —— **dedit**, 3d pers. sing. perf. ind. act. of *dō, dare, dedī, datum*, 1; the subj. is *pater*. —— **flūctūs**, acc. plur. of *flūctus, -ūs*, m., 4th (*fluo = I flow*); obj. of *mulcere*. —— **et**, conj.; see *et* above. —— **tollere**, pres. inf. act. of *tollō, -ere, sustulī, sublātum*, 3 (perf. and supine are borrowed from *suffero*); joined by *et* to *mulcere*, and similar in syntax. —— **ventō**, abl. sing. of *ventus, -ī*, m., 2d; abl. of means or instrument, limiting both *mulcere* and *tollere*. A. & G. 248, *c*; B. 218; G. 401; H. 420.

LINE 67. **Gēns**, gen. *gēntis*, f., 3d (*gigno*); nom. sing., subj. of *navigat*. The first part of the parenthesis introduced by *namque* above referred to Aeolus; this, the second, part is a brief, pithy reason assigned for the request that follows. —— **inimīca**, nom. sing. f. of *inimīcus, -a, -um (in = not, + amicus = friendly)*; agrees with *gens*. *Inimicus* is used of a personal enemy, whereas *hostis* = a public enemy, i.e. the enemy of a state and the occasion of war. —— **mihī**, dat. sing. f. of *ego* (see *mihi*, l. 8); dat. of indirect object. A. & G. 226; B. 187; G. 359; H. 382. —— **Tyrrhēnum**, acc. sing. n. of *Tyrrhēnus, -a, -um;* agrees with *aequor*. The *Tyrrhenian* is a Greek name for the Tuscan Sea, but it stands here for any part of the Mediterranean off the shores of Italy. The *Tyrrheni* were probably a Pelasgian race which imigrated from Greece or elsewhere to Etruria in north Italy; they are distinct from other Italian races in many respects, notably in language. —— **nāvigat**, 3d

hostile to me sails	ini,míca	mī,hí	„	Tyr,rhénum	,	návigat	,
the Tuscan sea,	*hostile*	*to me*		*Tyrrhenian*		*is sailing*	
bearing Troy to	aéquor,	Ílium	in	,	Ítali,ám	por,táns	„ 68
Italy and the van-							
quished gods of	*the sea*	*Ilium*	*into*		*Italy*	*carrying*	
their home. Lash	vic,tósque		Pe,nátes:		Íncute	,	vím 69
the winds to fury,	*and conquered*		*household gods.*		*Strike*		*force*
and overwhelm the	ven,tís	„	sub,mérsas,que		óbrue	,	púppes,
sunken barks, or	*into the winds*		*and overwhelmed*		*overthrow*		*the ships*

pers. sing. pres. ind. act. of *nāvigō, -āre, -āvī, -ātum*, 1, trans. and intrans.; agrees with its subj. *gens.* In this passage it is possible to regard *navigat* as trans., in which case the acc. *aequor* is quite regular. If it is intrans., *aequor* is a *cognate* acc.; cf. *vecti maria*, l. 524. The acc. is usually either of the same stem or the same signification as the verb, though there are instances in Vergil of variations from this rule. A. & G. 238; B. 176, 4; G. 333, 2; H. 371, II, and esp. NOTE. —— **aequor**, acc. sing. of *aequor, -is*, n., 3d (*aequus = level*); *cognate* acc. after *navigat.* For synonyms, see note on *aequore*, l. 29.

LINE 68. **Ilium**, acc. sing. of *Ilium, -ī*, n., 2d (Greek Ἴλιον); obj. of *portans.* *Ilium* is a common poetic name for Troy, derived from Ilus, one of the Trojan kings. The adjectives *Ilius* and *Iliacus* are similarly derived. Aeneas is described as carrying Troy metaphorically to Italy; the household gods mentioned below are a sign of authority, and these Aeneas had with him, and so more than a mere figurative transplantation is in the poet's mind. It would be possible to take *Ilium* . . . *Penates* as a case of *hendiadys* (= *Penates Iliacos*), but this is not necessary. By *ecthlipsis*, the final syllable is suppressed; cf. *multum*, l. 3. —— **in**, prep. with the acc. and abl.; gov. *Italiam.* *In* + the acc. = motion to; *in* + the abl. = rest at. A. & G. 153; B. 143; G. 418, 1; H. 435, 1. —— **Italiam**, acc. sing. of *Italia, -ae*, f., 1st; gov. by *in.* —— **portāns**, nom. sing. of the pres. part. act. of *portō, -āre, -āvī, -ātum*, 1; agrees with *gens* above. —— **victōsque** (*victōs + que*), acc. plur. m. of *victus, -a, -um*, perf. part. pass. of *vincō, -ere, vīcī, victum*, 3; qualifies *Penates.* The household gods are described as *vanquished*, because they were unable to save Troy from the Greeks. —— **Penātēs**, gen. *Penātium;* acc. plur. of *Penātēs*, m., 3d, no sing.; gov. by *portans.* The *Penates* included the greater or lesser divinities or some of them, and particular heroes, deified ancestors, etc., in fact, all the powers which exercised a tutelary influence over the home and native city.

LINE 69. **Incute**, 2d pers. sing. imperat. mood act. of *incutiō, incutere, incussī, incussum*, 3 (*in = against*, + *quatio = I shake*); the subj. is *tu* unexpressed, i.e. *Aeolus.* When used with two objects, *incutio* takes the acc. of the direct, and the dat. of the remoter object; it is seldom found in this way, except when the direct object is an emotion, e.g. *iram* and *timorem* follow it in various authors. —— **vim**, acc. sing. of *vīs*, abl. *vī*, f., 3d (gen. *vīs*, and dat. *vī* very rare); direct obj. of *incute.* *Vis* in the sing. = *violence;* the plural *vires = strength.* —— **ventīs**, dat. plur. of *ventus, -i*, m., 2d; dat. of the remoter object after the trans. verb *incute.* —— **submersāsque**, acc. plur. f. of *submersus, -a, -um*, perf. part. pass. of *submergō, -ere, submersī, submersum*, 3; *proleptic* part., qualifying *puppes.* *Submersas obrue =* *submerge et obrue*, or else *obrue ut submergantur.* For *prolepsis*, see the note on *laxas*, l. 63. The final syllable is *elided.* —— **que**, cop. conj., connecting *incute* and *obrue.* —— **obrue**, 2d pers. sing. imperat. mood act. of *obruō, -ere, obruī, obrutum*, 3 (*ob +*

70 **Aút** age   ,   díver,sós „   et ,   dísiice , | drive   them   scat-
or   *drive*   (*the men*) *in different ways*   *and*   *scatter* | tered   far   and
71 córpora   ,   pónto.   Súnt   mĭhi ,   bís | strew   their   bodies
their bodies   *in the sea.*   (*There*) *are*   *to me*   *twice* | over   sea.   Twice
sep,tém   „   prae,stánti ,   córpore ,   Nýmphae, | seven Nymphs are
seven   *exceptional*   *form*   *nymphs* | mine of overpass-
                                                       ing beauty; of these

---

ruo); joined by *que* to *incute*. —— **puppēs**, acc. plur. of *puppis*, f., 3d, gen. *puppis*, acc. *puppim* or *puppem*, dat. and abl. *puppī;* direct obj. of *obrue*. *Puppis* = lit. *the stem* of a ship, but in poetry becomes a synonym for *navis*. The use of the name of a part for the whole is called *synecdoche.* A. & G. 386; B. no reference; G. 695; H. 637, IV.

LINE 70. **Aut,** co-ordinate disjunctive conj., connecting *age* with *obrue* above. For distinctions between *aut, vet, sive,* etc., see the notes on *aut,* l. 49, and *ve,* l. 9. —— **age,** 2d pers. sing. imperat. mood act. of *agō, -ere, ēgī, actum,* 3; joined to *obrue* by *aut. Ago* here = *to drive;* it has numerous other meanings and applications, which should be studied in a dictionary. —— **dīversōs,** acc. plur. m. of *dīversus, -a, -um (dis + verto);* agreeing with *viros* or *Troas* understood. *Diversos,* like *submersas* in the line above, is *proleptic. Diversas,* qualifying *puppes,* is expected by the reader, but by the construction called *synesis* or *constructio ad sensum* the crews of the ships are mentioned, as being prominent in Vergil's mind. A. &. G. 385; B. 235, B, 2, *c,* and 254, 4, for partial statement; G. 211, REM. 1; H. 636, IV, 4. —— **et,** cop. conj., joining *age* and *disiice.* —— **dīsiice,** 2d pers. sing. imperat. mood act. of *dīsiiciō, -ere, dīsiēcī, dīsiectum,* 3 (*dis + iacio*); joined by *et* to *age.* —— **corpora,** acc. plur. of *corpus, corporis,* n., 3d; direct obj. of *disiice.* —— **pontō,** abl. sing. of *pontus, -ī,* m., 2d; locative abl., indicating place over which. See *aequore,* l. 29.

LINE 71. **Sunt,** 3d pers. plur. pres. ind. of *sum, esse, fuī;* agreeing with *Nymphae. Sunt mihi = habeo.* —— **mihi,** dat. sing. of *ego,* the 1st personal pron.; dat. of the possessor. A. & G. 231; B, 190; G. 349; H. 387. Compare l. 11, *tantaene animis . . . irae,* for a similar dative, but in that instance *sunt* was omitted and understood. —— **bis,** numeral adv. (in composition written *bi,* e.g. *bi-remis = a vessel with two banks of oars);* limiting *septem. Bis = duis,* from the cardinal number *duo.* In prose we should not find a numeral adverb thus qualifying a cardinal, but it is common in poetry for two reasons, firstly because the periphrasis is poetic and therefore employed also by English poets, secondly because large numbers are too unwieldy to be introduced in verse so artificial as Latin. —— **septem,** cardinal numeral adj., indeclinable; qualifying *Nymphae.* —— **praestantī,** abl. sing. n. of the adj. *praestans, -antis,* properly the pres. part. act. of *praestō, praestāre, praestiti, praestitum* or *praestātum,* 1 (*prae = before,* + *sto = I stand*); agrees with *corpore.* As an adjective, *praestans* admits of comparison; comparative *praestantior,* superlative *praestantissimus.* —— **corpore,** abl. sing. of *corpus, corporis,* n., 3d; abl. of quality, also called the descriptive ablative. This abl. is the case of a noun used to describe another noun in the place of an adjective; the gen. of description is similarly used. A. & G. 251; B. 224; G. 400; H. 419, II. *Corpus =* (1) *a dead body,* (2) *beauty,* of features but especially figure. *Praestanti corpore = pulcherrimae.* Synonyms: *corpus = beauty,* as above; *forma = beauty,* in the sense of graceful shape, but is often general; *pulchritudo = beauty,* of regular features, complexion, symmetry, etc. —— **Nymphae,** nom. plur. of *Nympha, -ae,* f., 1st (Greek νύμφη); subj. of *sunt. Nympha* bears the first of the two following meanings: (1) *a nymph,* i.e. a demi-goddess, living in the seas, woods (*hamadryads*), trees, rivers, or mountains; (2) *a bride.*

her that is of	Quárum	, quae	for,má	„	pul,chérrima	, 72
the fairest grace, Deiopeia, will I	of whom	(her) who (is)	in beauty		most fair	
join to thee in lasting wedlock and	Déio,péia,	Cónnu,bió	iun,gám		stabi,lí	„ 73
consecrate her thine	Deiopeia	in marriage	I will join		sure	

LINE 72. **Quārum**, gen. plur. of rel. pron. *quī, quae, quod;* agrees with *nymphae* in gender and number, and is a partitive gen. after *Deiopeia.* A. & G. 216; B. 201; G. 367, ff.; H. 397. This genitive states the whole, of which a part is taken. —— **quae**, nom. sing. f. of *quī, quae, quod;* agrees with *Deiopeia*, and is subj. of *est* understood. See note on *Deiopeia* below. —— **fōrmā**, abl. sing. of *fōrma, -ae*, f., 1st; abl. of specification, showing wherein or in respect of what *Deiopeia* was *pulcherrima.* A. & G. 253; B. 226; G. 397; H. 424. The scansion here shows that *forma* must be the abl. case, for the final *a* is long; *pulcherrima* on the contrary is nom., for the last three syllables form a dactyl and the final *a* is consequently short. See note on *corpore* above for synonyms. *Est* is understood here, but the copula is often left out, esp. when it would be in the indicative or infinitive moods. A. & G. 206, *c*, 2; B. 166, 3; G. 209; H. 368, 3. —— **pulcherrima**, nom. sing. f. of *pulcherrimus, -a, -um*, the superl. of *pulcher, pulchra, pulchrum (polio = I polish);* agrees with *quae*, and stands in the predicate with *est* understood. Positive = *pulcher;* comparative = *pulchrior.* Adjectives in *er* form their superlative by adding *rimus* to the nom. m. sing. of the positive. A. & G. 89, *a*; B. 71, 3; G. 87, 1; H. 163, 1. —— **Dēiopēia**, nom. sing. f., 1st (Δηϊόπεια); attracted to the case of the rel. *quae*, and inserted within the rel. clause. What we should expect is *iungam Deiopeiam quae forma pulcherrima est.* Attraction of the antecedent to the case of the rel. is less common than attraction of the rel.; the rel. attracted to the case of the antecedent is found in prose and poetry, but attraction of the antecedent is rare in prose, and not at all common in poetry. A noted Vergilian example is *urbem, quam statuo, vestra est.* The idiom probably arose from the antecedent often being repeated in the rel. clause, e.g. *eo die, quo die = on that day, on which;* it is then easy to drop one of the nouns. A. & G. 200, *b*; B. 251, 4; G. 617, NOTE 2; H. 445, 9. *Deiopeia* belonged to the sea-nymphs, called *Nereides, Naiades, or Oceanides;* mountain-nymphs are called *Oreades.*

LINE 73. **Cōnnūbīō** (sometimes written *cōnūbīō*), abl. sing. of *cōnnūbium, -ī*, n., 2d (*cum + nubo = I marry*, of a woman marrying; *duco = I marry*, of a man); abl. of manner, with the prep. *cum* omitted. A. & G. 248, at the end; B. 220; G. 399, NOTE 2; H. 419, III. There are difficulties about the scansion of this word; cf. *nūbo* and yet *pronŭba.* The quantity of the *u* seems to have been uncertain even among the Romans, but when the accent falls it, the *u* must be regarded as long. Thus *connubio* may be scanned: (1) as a word with four syllables, the first three forming a dactyl, e.g. connŭbĭō; (2) as a trisyllable, e.g. cōnnūbīō, with the *i* =⟨to *y*, by *synizesis.* A. & G. 347, *c*, and REM. on *d;* B. 367, 4; G. 727; H. 608, III, NOTE 2. *Connubium = marriage*, as an institution observed and upheld by the state; *coniugium = marriage*, as a personal affair. —— **iungam**, 1st pers. sing. fut. ind. act. of *iungō, -ere, iunxī, iunctum*, 3; subj. is *ego*, i.e. *Iuno.* —— **stabilī**, abl. sing. n. of *stabilis, -e*, adj., 3d (*sto = I stand*, hence *firm);* qualifies *connubio.* —— **propriam**, acc. sing. f. of *proprius, -a, -um;* agrees with *Deiopeiam* understood, though *Deiopeiam* was attracted to *quae* and inserted in the rel. clause. *Proprius* conveys the notion of absolute possession and control for ever; cf. Horace, *Archilochum proprio rabies armavit iambo = rage armed Archilochus with his own peculiar* (satiric weapon, viz.) *iambus.* —— **que**, enclitic conj., joining *iungam* and *dicabo.* ——

74 propri,ámque	di,cábo,	Ómnes	, út	te,cúm „	for ever, that in
and for thy own	*I will set apart*	*all*	*that*	*with thee*	return for thy

75 meri,tís pro , tálibus , ánnos Éxigat ,
favors for such her years she may spend

ét pul,chrá „ faci,át te , próle pa,réntem.”
and beautiful make thee of offspring the parent.

good service she
may pass with
thee all her years
and make thee
the father of good-
ly children.” Thus

---

dicābō, 1st pers. sing. fut. ind. act. of *dicō, -āre, -āvī, -ātum,* 1; joined by *que* to *iungam.* *Dicabo,* a word with religious sense of *dedicate,* is fitly applied to Juno, one of whose titles was *Pronuba,* the goddess presiding over marriage, another of her titles being *Lucina,* presiding over births. There is a strong contrast implied between *propriam dicabo* and the pure sensuality of the marriage arranged by Venus between Paris and Helen.

LINE 74. **Omnēs,** acc. plur. m. of *omnis, -e,* adj., 3d (see *omnibus,* l. 15); agrees with *annos.* —— **ut** (original form *uti*), conj., here final, expressing purpose; gov. *exigat.* *Ut* is sometimes an adverb, and = (1) *how;* (2) *as,* esp. as correl. of *ita,* e.g. *ut . . . ita;* (3) *since the time that;* (4) *as, when, while,* of time. The conj. *ut* is used in two ways: (1) *ut* final, as above, followed by the subjunct., = *in order that;* the negative is *ne;* (2) *ut* consecutive, expressing result, taking the subjunct., = *so that;* the negative is *ut non.* The uses will be treated as they occur; see *exigat* below. —— **tēcum** (*tē* + *cum*); *tē* is abl. sing. of *tu* (see *tibi,* l. 65); gov. by *cum,* in accompaniment. *Cum* is the prep. with the abl., used as an enclitic, for which read the note on *secum,* l. 37. —— **meritīs,** abl. plur. of *meritum, -ī,* n., 2d (*mereo* = *I deserve*); gov. by *pro.* —— **prō,** prep. with the abl.; gov. *meritis. Pro* here = *for,* i.e. *because of.* It has other shades of meaning, for which see the note and references on *pro,* l. 24. —— **tālibus,** abl. plur. n. of *tālis, -e;* qualifies *meritis.* —— **annōs,** acc. plur. of *annus, -ī,* m., 2d; direct obj. of *exigat* in next line.

LINE 75. **Exigat,** 3d pers. sing. pres. subjunct. act. of *exigō, -ere, exēgī, exactum,* 3 (*ex* + *ago*); gov. by *ut* in purpose-clause; see note on *ut* above. For final clauses, consult A. & G. 317; B. 282; G. 545; H. 497. *Exigat* is pres. tense in accordance with the rule for sequence of tenses, viz. when the tense of the main verb is *primary* (pres., fut., perf., and fut. perfect), the verb in the subordinate clause is *primary;* when the main verb is *historic* (imperf., aorist, or pluperfect), the subordinate verb is also *historic.* A. & G. 286; B. 267, 268; G. 509; H. 491. —— **et,** cop. conj., joining *exigat* and *faciat.* —— **pulchrā,** abl. sing. f. of *pulcher, pulchra, pulchrum;* agrees with *prole.* See note on *pulcherrima,* l. 72. —— **faciat,** 3d. pers. sing. pres. subjunct. act. of *faciō, -ere, fēcī, factum,* 3 (passive is *fio*); joined by *et* to *exigat,* and gov. by *ut.* —— **tē,** acc. sing. of 2d personal pron. *tū* (see *tibi,* l. 65); obj. of *faciat.* —— **prōle,** abl. sing. of *prōlēs, -is,* f., 3d (for *pro-ol-es; pro* = *forth,* *ol* is root in *olesco* = *I grow*); abl. of means or instrument, for which see references on *fatis,* l. 32. — NOTE. This ablative has troubled some scholars. It is treated: (1) as descriptive abl., for which consult the references on *corpore,* l. 71; *pulchra prole parens* thus becomes a closely-knit phrase, but it is very doubtful Latin; (2) Thiel calls *prole pulchra* a loose kind of abl. absolute, and reconstructs *quae te faciat parentem, ut pulchra proles sit;* this seems entirely inadmissible; (3) the best Vergilian scholars call the abl. instrumental; thus the sentence = *make thee a father* (or we might say *happy*) *by means of* (the birth of) *beautiful offspring.* —— **parentem,** acc. sing. of *parens, -entis,* m. and f., 3d; predicate acc., referring to *te.* Verbs of *calling, making, appointing,* etc., may take a noun or an adj. in the acc., referring to the direct object, but not in apposition nor as a mere attribute. A. & G. 239, 1, *a;* B. 177; G. 340; H. 373. Some few commentators reject ll. 74 and 75 as superfluous.

Aeolus replied: "Thine, O queen, the task to search out what thou desirest; my duty it is to fulfil thy commands. Thou winnest me all this my kingdom, thou my sceptre

A̓eolus	,	haec	con,trá:	„	"Tuus,	,	Ó 76
Aeolus		*(spake) these words*	*in reply:*		*"Thy,*		*O*
re,gína,	quid	,	óptes,	Éxplo,ráre	la,bór;	„ 77	
queen,	*what*		*thou desirest*	*to examine*	*(it is) task*		
mihi	,	iússa	ca,péssere	,	fás	est.	
for me		*thy commands*	*to execute*		*right*	*it is.*	
Tú	mihi	,	quódcum,que	hóc	reg,ní,	„ 78	
Thou	*for me*		*whatsoever*	*this (is)*	*of kingdom*		

Line 76. **Aeolus**, nom. sing., subj. of *dixit* understood. —— **haec**, acc. plur. n. of *hīc, haec, hōc* (see *hoc*, l. 17); direct obj. of *dixit* understood. The verb of *speaking* introducing speeches in the Aeneid is often omitted. —— **contrā**, adv.; here = *in reply;* commonly = *on the other hand.* For *contra* as a preposition, cf. *Italiam contra*, l. 13. —— **Tuus**, nom. sing. m. of *tuus, -a, -um*, poss. pronominal adj. of the 2d person; agrees with *labor*. It is emphatic by position, being in contrast with *mihi* below.——**O**, exclamation, accompanying the voc. *regina*. The exclamation expresses joy, sorrow, surprise, and desire, and is used with other cases, besides the vocative; it sometimes accompanies adverbs and particles, especially in unfulfilled wishes for the past or future; e.g. *o si*. —— **rēgīna**, voc. sing.; case of person addressed, referring to *Iuno*. —— **quid**, acc. sing. n. of the interrogative pron. *quis, quae, quid* (other cases like the rel. *qui*)*;* direct obj. of *optes*. —— **optēs**, 2d pers. sing. pres. subjunct. act. of *optō, -āre, -āvī, -ātum*, 1 ; its subj. is *tu* understood, i.e. Juno. The subjunct. mood is due to the indirect question introduced by *explorare;* for explanation of this construction, read the note on *impulerit*, l. 11, and consult the references. It is possible, but unnecessary, to call *optes* a *deliberative* subjunctive, translating: *it is thy task to search out what you are to wish for.*

Line 77. **Explōrāre**, pres. inf. act. of *explōrō, -āre, -āvī, -ātum*, 1 (*ex* = *out, + ploro* = *I call out*)*;* the inf. is here a noun, being subj. of the pred. *labor (est)*, but it retains its verbal right of governing an object, viz. the phrase *quid optes*. As a noun, the infinitive can be either subject or object in a sentence. A. & G. 270; B. 326-328; G. 280; H. 532, 538. *Exploro* = (1) *I cry out;* (2) *I search out*, originally by calling; (3) *I reconnoitre*, in military phraseology; cf. *explorator = scout;* (4) *I examine, test.* —— **labor**, gen. *labōris*, m., 3d; it is *complement* of *est* understood in the predicate; see note on *forma*, l. 72, for omission of the copula. Aeolus declares his entire submission to the will of Juno, but for all that *explorare quid optes* has a note of supplication in it, and the responsibility for the future is laid upon Juno. —— **mihi**, dat. sing. of *ego;* dat. of the indirect obj. after *fas*. *Mihi*, like *tuus* in the line above, is very emphatic, and the two words are in strong contrast. The contrast is increased by the absence of any connecting conjunction (*asyndeton; cf. adire*, l. 10). —— **iussa**, acc. plur. n. of *iussum, -ī*, n., 2d (properly past part. pass. of *iubeō, -ēre, iussī, iussum*, 2)*;* gov. by *capessere*. The word *command* makes Juno responsible for the future disasters. —— **capessere**, pres. inf. act. of *capessō, -ere, capessīvī* or *capessiī, capessītum*, 3 (*capio*)*;* subj. of *est*, in the pred. *fas est;* cf. *explorare* above. —— **fās**, nom. sing. n., indecl.; *complement* of *est;* see *labor* above. *Fas* = divine *law*, and *fas est* = *est officium meum; ius* = *law*, human, divine, or legal. The negative of *fas* is *nefas* = *unlawful*. —— **est**, 3d pers. sing. pres. ind. act. of the copula *sum, esse, fuī;* its subj. is *capessere*.

Line 78. **Tū**, nom. sing., subj. of *concilias*. The personal pronouns, when subjects, are omitted as a rule, but sometimes given for emphasis or contrast; *tu* is

79 tu ，　scéptra　　Io,vémque　　Cóncili,ás,　　tu ，
thou　*my sceptres*　*and Jupiter*　　*winnest,*　*thou*

dás　　　　epu,lís　　„　ac,cúmbere　　，　dívum,
dost give　*at the feasts*　　*(the right) to lie*　　*of the gods*

80 Nímbo,rúmque　　　fa,cís　„　tem,pésta,túmque
and of the storms　　*thou makest*　　*and of the tempests*

and Jove's favor;
thou dost grant me
to recline at the
banquets of the
gods, and makest
me lord over storm-
clouds and tem-

emphatic, and more so because it is first word in the sentence. —— **mihi**, dat. of *ego ;*
dat. of the indirect obj. after *concilias*, a verb compounded with *con*. A. & G. 228;
B. 187, III; G. 347; H. 386. The juxtaposition of *tu* and *mihi* is for the sake of
contrast. —— **quodcumque**, nom. sing. n. of *quīcumque, quaecumque, quodcumque*,
indefinite or universal rel. pron. (declined like *qui*, with the suffix *cumque*); agrees
with *hoc, hoc* being an attracted antecedent. The adverbial suffix *cumque* may
be used with any relative, making it indefinite; e.g. *quocumque = whither soever.*
A. & G. 105, *a*; B. 91, 8; G. 111, 2; H. 187, 3, FOOTNOTE 3. Some call *quodcumque*
depreciatory, e.g. this kingdom, *such as it is*, a modest reference to the rule of
Aeolus; others say it is universal, and = this kingdom, *all there is of it.* The final
syllable is *elided* before *hoc*. The sentence put simply would be *tu mihi concilias
hoc regnum, quodcumque regni est.* —— **hōc**, nom. sing. of *hīc, haec, hōc ;* subj. of *est*
understood, in the pred. *quodcumque est. Hoc* agrees in gender with *regni*, and has
marked deictic force. For attraction, see note on *Deiopeia*, l. 72. —— **rēgnī**, gen.
sing. of *regnum, -ī,* n., 2d; a partitive gen., often used with neuter adjectives and
pronouns. A. & G. 216, 3; B. 201, 2; G. 369; H. 397, 3. Compare *nihil novi =
nothing new. Regni* may be said to limit either *hoc* or *quodcumque.* —— **tū**, nom.
sing.; see *tu* above. The repetition of a word is called *anaphora ;* cf. *hic . . . hic,*
l. 17, and the references there given. —— **scēptra**, acc. plur. of *scēptrum, -ī,* n., 2d;
direct obj. of *concilias.* —— **Iovemque ;** *que,* the cop. conj., joins *sceptra* and
Iovem. Iovem is the acc. of *Iupiter,* gen. *Iovis,* dat. *Iovī,* abl. *Iove,* m., 3d, irreg.;
direct obj. of *concilias.* By *Jupiter* is meant the *good-will of Jupiter.*

LINE 79. **Conciliās**, 2d pers. sing. pres. ind. act. of *conciliō, -āre, -āvī, -ātum,* 1 ;
its subj. is *tu. Concilio* = (1) *I make friendly*, the regular meaning; (2) *I procure ;*
in this passage it is applied loosely to a person and to things, to *sceptra* and *regnum*
in the second sense, to *Iovem* in the first. This connection between Juno and
Aeolus is more clear from the myth that Juno is the lower air personified. The
present tense, instead of the perfect, denotes the continuation of those favors. ——
tū, nom. sing., subj. of *das. Tu* is repeated by *anaphora ;* see *tu* above. —— **dās**,
2d pers. sing. pres. ind. act. of *dō, dare, dedī, datum,* 1, irreg.; agrees with subj. *tu.*
—— **epulīs**, dat. plur. of *epulum, -ī,* n., 2d (plural is heterogeneous, *epulae, -ārum,* f.,
1st); dat. of the indirect obj. after *accumbere* (compound of *ad*). Consult the note
and references under *mīhi*, l. 78. —— **accumbere**, pres. inf. act. of *accumbō, -ere,
accubuī, accubitum,* 3 (*ad + cumbo = I lie down*); direct obj. of *das*, instead of *ut
accumbam.* Refer to the note on *mulcere*, l. 66. It was the Roman costum to recline
on couches at meals. —— **dīvūm** (contracted for *dīvōrum*), gen. plur. of *dīvus, -ī,* m.,
2d; poss. gen. limiting *epulis.*

LINE 80. **Nimbōrum**, gen. plur. of *nimbus, -ī,* m., 2d; gov. by *potentem.* Adjectives,
of the class called *relative* or *transitive* adjectives, denoting *fulness, knowledge, power,
memory*, etc., and their opposites take the genitive. A. & G. 218, *a*; B. 204, 1 ; G. 374;
H. 399, I, 2. —— **que**, cop. conj., joining *das* and *facis.* —— **facis**, 2d. pers. sing.
pres. ind. act. of *faciō, -ere, fēcī, factum,* 3, irreg.; subj. is *tu.* See note on *concilias,*
l. 79, for the tense of *facis,* and of *das.* —— **tempestātumque**, gen. plur. of *tempestās,*

pests." These words spoken, with spear turned he smote the hollow mountain on the side, and the winds, as if in banded column, rush forth wherever an out-

po,téntem." Haéc ubi , dícta, „ ca,vúm 81
(me) ruler." These things when were said, hollow

con,vérsa , cúspide , móntem Ímpulit , ín 82
inverted with spear the mountain he struck on

latus: , ác ven,tí „ velut , ágmine , fácto,
the side: and the winds as though a line having been made

-atis, f., 3d; joined by the conj. *que* to *nimborum*. —— **potentem**, acc. sing. m. of *potens*, *-entis* (originally pres. part. of *possum = I am able*); predicate acc., gov. *nimborum* and *tempestatum*. For the predicate acc., refer back to *parentem*, l. 75.

LINE 81. **Haec**, nom. plur. n. of demonstr. pron. *hic, haec, hoc;* subj. of *dicta* (*essent*) in the temporal clause *haec ubi dicta*. From a comparison of *haec*, l. 76, with *haec* here, it is seen that the demonstrative can refer both to what is to follow and what has preceded. —— **ubi**, temporal conj., gov. *dicta essent*. *Ubi* has many uses: (1) interrog. of place = *where?* also of time = *when;* (2) rel. local adv. = *where, in which place;* (3) of persons and things = *with* or *by which, whom;* (4) temporal conj. = *when*. Its use as a particle is like that of *postquam, simul atque*, etc.; with the perf. and *historic* present it takes the indicative; less commonly they take the imperf. and pluperf. indicative (rarely the subjunct.). The mood of the verb depends on whether the particle itself marks the time of the main clause, or whether it describes by details the time which the main clause itself marks; in the first case the mood is indicative, in the second it is subjunctive. A. & G. 323–324; B. 287; G. 561, ff.; H. 518. —— **dicta**, nom. plur. n. of *dictus, -a, -um*, perf. part. pass. of *dico, -ere, dixi, dictum*, 3; agrees with *haec*, and *essent* is understood, forming the pluperf. tense of *dico* as predicate of subj. *haec;* see note on *usa est*, l. 64. The main *caesura* seems to follow here, though there is an ordinary one after *cavum*. —— **cavum**, acc. sing. m. of *cavus, -a, -um;* qualifies *montem*. Observe the *alliteration* in *cavum conversa cuspide*, and cf. *indignantes*, l. 55. —— **conversā**, abl. sing. of *conversus, -a, -um*, perf. part. pass. of *converto, -ere, converti, conversum*, 3 (con + *verto*); agrees with *cuspide*. *Conversa = turned*, i.e. in the direction of the mountain, and is used simply as an adjective. —— **cuspide**, abl. sing. of *cuspis, -īdis*, f., 3d; abl. of means or instrument. Some call *cuspide conversa* an abl. absolute, for which see note on *laeso*, l. 8. *Cuspis* properly = *a point* of a spear, and is used for *spear*, the whole, by *synecdoche;* cf. *puppes*, l. 69 and note. —— **montem**, acc. sing. of *mons, montis*, m., 3d; direct obj. of *impulit*. See *latus* below.

LINE 82. **Impulit**, 3d pers. sing. perf. ind. act of *impello, -ere, impuli, impulsum*, 3 (*in* + *pello*); subj. is Aeolus. *Impello = to drive on*, but here has a rarer meaning, *to strike*. The rhythm of the line suggests blows dealt with vigor. —— **in**, prep. with the acc.; gov. *latus;* cf. *in*, l. 34. *In* marks the direction of the blow. — **latus**, acc. sing. of *latus, -eris*, n., 3d; obj. of *in*. — NOTE. *Montem impulit in latus.* Those who refine upon l. 56, *celsa arce*, etc., have much to say on these words; some say that if the throne was outside of the cave and on the mountain-top, it would be impossible to strike *in latus = against the side*. Some take *montem* to = (*a part* of) *the mountain*, giving *impulit* its literal meaning; viz. *forced a part of the mountain into the side*. On the whole the true sense seems to be: *struck the mountain on the side;* cf. l. 115, *unam* (sc. *navem*) *in puppim ferit = smites against the stern of one ship*. The construction is really that of the *whole* and *part*. —— **āc**, cop. conj., connecting the cause in *impulit* with the result in *ruunt*. *Ac* is short for *atque;* see note on *que*, l. 1. *Ac* here = *ac statim*. —— **ventī**, nom. plur. of *ventus, -i*, m., 2d;

⁸³Quā　data　, pórta,　ru,únt „ et , térras ,
where　*was given*　*a gateway*　*rush*　*and*　*the lands*

⁸⁴túrbine　, pérflant.　Íncubu,ére　ma,rí, „
in whirlwind　*blow through.*　*They lay*　*upon the sea,*

let offered and sweep the earth with whirling hurricane. Down on the sea they swoop, and East wind

subj. of *ruunt*. —— **velut** (*vel* = *even*, + *ut* = *as*), sometimes written *veluti*; a comparative adv., frequently introducing comparisons and metaphors. —— **āgmine**, abl. sing. of *agmen, agminis*, n., 3d (*ago* = *I lead*, hence *that which is led*); abl. abs. with *facto*. *Agmen* = (1) *a multitude*; (2) *the march* of an army; (3) most often, as here, *a column* of an army in motion. Synonyms: *agmen* = *line of march*; *acies* = *line of battle*; *exercitus* = *army*, the general term. —— **factō**, abl. sing. n. of *factus, -a, -um*, perf. part. of *fio, fieri, factus sum* (used as passive of *facio*); agrees with *agmine* in the abl. abs. construction. Any clause independent of the main sentence may have its subject put in the abl. with a participle, adjective, or other noun in agreement. A. & G. 255; B. 227; G. 409, 410; H. 431.

LINE 83. **Quā**, adv. of place; originally abl. of the rel. *qui*. Other uses are: (1) manner = *in whatever way*; (2) limitation = *so far as*; (3) correlatively, e.g. *qua : . . qua* = *both . . . and.* —— **data**, nom. sing. f. of *datus, -a, -um*, perf. part. pass. of *do, dare, dedi, datum*, 1; *est* is understood, making the 3d pers. sing. perf. ind. pass. of *do*, agreeing with the subj. *porta*. —— **porta**, nom. sing., gen. *portae*, f., 1st; subj. of *data* (*est*). This line is *alliterative*, *t* and *r* prevailing; it represents the hurry and scurry of the winds escaping. —— **ruunt**, 3d pers. plur. pres. ind. act. of *ruo, -ere, rui, rutum*, 3, intrans., but rarely trans.; the subj. is *venti*, l. 82. *Ruunt* is here intransitive. —— **et**, cop. conj., joining *ruunt* and *perflant*. —— **terrās**, acc. plur. of *terra, -ae*, f., 1st; direct obj. of *perflant*. —— **turbine**, abl. sing. of *turbo, turbinis*, m., 3d (*turben, -inis*, n., 3d); abl. of the instrument. —— **perflant**, 3d pers. plur. pres. ind. act. of *perflo, -are, -avi, -atum*, 1 (*per* = *through*, + *flo* = *I blow*); gov. *terras*, and joined to *ruunt* by *et*.

LINE 84. **Incubuēre**, 3d pers. plur. perf. ind. act. of *incumbo, -ere, incubui, incubitum*, 3 (*in* = *on*, + *cumbo* = *I lie*); the subj. is *venti* understood. See note on *tenuere*, l. 12, for the termination *ere*. The perf. is *aoristic*, i.e. *historic*, and here conveys the idea of instantaneous action. The prep. *in* makes *incubuere* = *swooped down upon*. —— **marī**, dat. sing. of *mare, -is*, n., 3d; dat. of the indirect obj. after the compound verb *incubuere*; cf. *accumbere*, l. 79. —— **tōtumque** (*totum* + *que*), acc. sing. of *totus, -a, -um*; agreeing with *mare* understood from *mari* above. For the signification of *totum*, cf. *aequore toto*, l. 29. *que*, cop. conj., joining *incubuere* and *ruunt*. The diphthong is subject to *elision* before the following vowel; cf. *quoque*, l. 5. —— **ā**, prep. with the abl., showing 'place from which.' *A* or *ab* is used before consonants, *ab* before words beginning with a vowel or *h*. Other uses of *a* or *ab* are: (1) with abl. of the agent; (2) *cause*; (3) *origin*; (4) *separation in time*. A. & G. 152, *b*, and 153; B. 142, 1; G. 417, 1; H. 434. —— **sēdibus**, abl. plur. of *sedes, sedis*, f., 3d (*sedeo* = *I sit*, hence *seat, throne, abode, foundations*); gov. by *a*. —— **īmīs**, abl. plur. f. of *imus, -a, -um*; agrees with *sedibus*. *Imis* is partitive, and = *from the bottom of the foundations*; this idiom is most common with *summus*, *imus*, and similar superlatives. A. & G. 193; B. 241; G. 291, REM. 2; H. 440, 2, NOTE 1. *Imus* is a contracted form of *infimus*, a superl. formed from the prep. *infra* (cf. prep. *prope*, no positive, comparative *propior*, superl. *proximus*); the positive *inferus* is very rare, but is found in *mare inferum* = *the lower* (Tuscan) *sea*, and in the plural *Inferi* = *the gods of the nether world*; the comparative is *inferior*.

and South and | to,túmq*ue* a , sédibus , ímis Úna Eu,rúsque 85
Southwest heavy | *and the whole from the seats lowest together both Eurus*
with storms to- |
gether they up- | No,túsque ru,únt „ cre,bérque pro,céllis Áfricus,, 86
turn it utterly | *and Notus tear up and abounding with storms Africus,*
from its lowest |
depths, and roll | ét vas,tós „ vol,vúnt ad , lítora , flúctus.
vast billows shore- | *and vast roll to the shores waves.*
wards. Thereon fol- |
lows a shouting | Ínsequi,túr cla,mórque vi,rúm „ stri,dórque 87
of men and a | *Follows both the shouting of men and the creaking*

LINE 85. **Ūnā**, adverbial abl. sing. of the cardinal *unus, -a, -um;* gen. *unius,* dat. *uni;* limits *ruunt.* The final syllable is *elided* before *Eurus.* —— **Eurus,** gen. *Euri,* m., 2d (Greek Εὑρος); nom. sing., one of the subjects of *ruunt. Eurus* is the East wind. —— **que,** cop. conj., used with *que . . . que* below in *polysyndeton,* i.e. multiplication of copulative conjunctions. A. & G. 385; B. 341, 4, *b*; G. 476, NOTE 2; H. 636, III, 1. The effect of the *polysyndeton* here is to make a number of *onomatopœic dactyls.* —— **Notusque** (*Notus + que*), gen. *Noti,* m., 2d ; joined by the cop. conj. *que* to *Eurus. Notus* is the South wind. The names of the winds are masculine. This line is a very close imitation of a line in Homer. —— **ruunt,** 3d pers. plur. pres. ind. act. of *ruo, -ere, rui, rutum,* 3 ; agrees with its subjects *Eurus, Notus,* and *Africus* in combination. *Ruunt* is transitive in this passage, and = *eruunt,* i.e. *upturn;* cf. *verteret* for *everteret,* l. 20; in l. 83, *ruunt* was, as usually, intransitive. —— **crēberque,** nom. sing. m. of *creber, crebra, crebrum* (related to *cresco*); agrees with and describes *Africus. que,* cop. conj., joining *Africus* and *Notus.* —— **procellīs,** abl. plur. of *procella, -ae,* f., 1st; abl. of specification. A. & G. 253; B. 226; G. 397; H. 424.

LINE 86. **Africus,** gen. *Afrĭci,* m., 2d; joined by *que* to *Notus. Africus* is the Southwest wind, and is entirely Latin, whereas Eurus and Notus are names drawn from the Greek; it is so called, because it blows across the Mediterranean from Africa, and now Italians know it by the name of Affrico or Gherbino. The names have no signification here beyond a poetical one; poets are fond of describing storms as the boisterous play of the winds let loose. —— **et,** cop. conj., joining *ruunt* and *volvunt.* —— **vāstōs,** acc. plur. m. of *vastus, -a, -um;* qualifies *fluctus.* —— **volvunt** (sometimes written *volvont*), 3d pers. plur. pers. ind. act. of *volvo, -ere, volvi, volutum,* 3; joined by *et* to *ruunt.* For other meanings, cf. *volvere,* l. 9. It should be noticed that *volvunt* (also *perflant,* l. 83, *ruunt,* l. 85, etc.) is a vivid *historic present.* A. & G. 276, *d*; B. 259, 3; G. 229; H. 467, III. —— **ad,** prep. with the acc.; gov. *litora;* cf. *ad,* l. 24, for note and references. —— **lītora,** acc. plur. of *litus, litoris,* n., 3d; obj. of *ad.* The plural is poetic. —— **fluctūs,** acc. plur. of *fluctus, -ūs,* m., 4th (*fluo = I flow*); direct obj. of *volvunt.* Synonym: *unda = wave; unda* is more regular in prose, but Cicero uses *fluctus,* often metaphorically.

LINE 87. **Insequitur,** 3d pers. sing. pres. ind. of the dep. verb *insequor, -i, insecutus sum,* 3 (*in = in* or *onto,* + *sequor*). —— **clāmor,** gen. *clamoris,* m., 3d (*clamo = I shout*); nom. sing., subj. of·*insequitur.* —— **que,** cop. conj., correlative of *que* below. Refer to the note on *et,* l. 63, for the combination *que . . . que.* —— **virūm** (contracted for *virorum*), gen. plur. of *vir, -i,* m., 2d; poss. gen. limiting *clamor.* For the contraction of the gen. plural of certain nouns of the 2d declension, consult A. & G. 40, *e;* B. 25, 6; G. 33, REM. 4; H. 52, 3. *Virum = Troum, the Trojans.* With picturesque vividness Vergil paints the storm and its effect upon the Trojans and upon their ships. —— **strīdor,** gen. *stridoris,* m., 3d (*strideo*); nom.

88 ru,déntum.	Éripi,únt	subi,tó	nu,bés	„	shrieking of cord-
of ropes.	*Seize away*	*suddenly*	*the clouds*		age. On a sud-den clouds snatch
89 coe,lúmque	di,émque	Téucro,*rum*	éx	ocu,lís; „	both sky and day-light from the Tro-
both sky	*and daylight*	*of the Trojans*	*from*	*the eyes;*	jans' eyes; night

sing., joined by *que* to *clamor*. Observe that there are two separate subjects, but the verb remains singular; in such cases it is said to agree with one, and be understood with the rest. A. & G. 205, *d*; B. 255, 3; G. 285, EXCEPTION 1; H. 463, I. *Stridor* is an *onomatopœic* word, representing the sound of *hissing, creaking, whistling, shrieking*, etc.; it must be translated freely to suit the context. —— **que**, cop. conj., correlative of *que* above. —— **rudentum**, gen. plur. of *rudens, -entis*, m., 3d; poss. gen. limiting *stridor*. *Rudens* is an exception to the rule that 3d-declension words ending in *s* preceded by a consonant are feminine; cf. *mons, dens*, etc., and see references on *montis*, l. 55.

LINE 88. **Eripiunt**, 3d pers. plur. pres. ind. act. of *eripio, -ere, eripui, ereptum*, 3 (*e* + *rapio*); agrees with subj. *nubes*. By the metaphor of the 'clouds *snatching* the sky' from the Trojans eyes, Vergil is refining upon Odyssey V. 293, σὺν δὲ νεφέεσσι κάλυψε Γαῖαν ὁμοῦ καὶ πόντον· ὀρώρει δ' οὐρανόθεν νύξ; ll. 88 and 89 are a fairly close copy of the above. —— **subitō**, temporal adv.; limiting *eripiunt*. *Subito* is the adverbial abl. neuter of *subitus;* the neuter and sometimes the feminine abl. sing. of adjectives, pronouns, and nouns, may be used as adverbs, e.g. *cito = quickly, forte = by chance.* A. & G. 148, *c*; B. 77, 2; G. 91, *c, d*; H. 304, II. —— **nūbēs**, nom. plur. of *nubes, -is*, f., 3d; subj. of *eripiunt*. —— **coelum**, acc. sing. of *coelum, -i*, n., 2d; direct obj. of *eripiunt*. —— **que**, enclitic cop. conj., correlative of *que* below; *que . . . que = both . . . and*. —— **diemque**; *diem* is acc. sing. of *dies, diei* (old gen. *dii*, cf. l. 636), m., but sometimes f. in the sing., always m. in the plural, 5th; obj. of *eripiunt;* joined to *coelum* by *que*. *Dies* and *res* are the only nouns of the 5th declension completely declined in singular and in plural. *Dies* = (1) *day*, a period of time; (2) *day*, as opposed to *nox*; (3) *daylight*, with which sense *Jupiter* (*Diespiter*) is connected; (4) *day*, in legal and civil reference, e.g. *dies fasti = days* on which law matters could be attended to, and also = *holy days*, devoted to religious purposes; *dies nefasti = days* on which legal business was forbidden. *que*, cop. conj.; see *que* above.

LINE 89. **Teucrōrum**, gen. plur. of *Teucri*, m., 2d, plural noun (see *Teucrorum*, l. 38); poss. gen. limiting *oculis*. *Teucrorum = Troum, the Trojans*. Observe the suppression (*ecthlipsis*) of *um* before *ex;* see *multum*, l. 3. —— **ex**, prep. with the abl.; gov. *oculis*. *E* or *ex* before consonants, *ex* before vowels and *h*. A. & G., 152, *b*; B. 142, 2; G. 417; H. 434. —— **oculís**, abl. plur. of *oculus, -i*, m., 2d; gov. by *ex*. The expression *ex oculis* is poetic; *e conspectu*, l. 34, is admissible in prose or poetry. —— **pontō**, dat. sing. of *pontus, -i*, m., 2d (Greek πόντος); dat. of the indirect obj. after *incubat*, a compound of *in*. See note on *mihi*, l. 78, for this dative. The omission of a conjunction before *ponto* (*asyndeton;* see note on *adire*, l. 10) makes the description of desolation more impressive. —— **nox**, gen. *noctis* (cf. Greek νύξ, gen. νύκτος), f., 3d; nom. sing., subj. of *incubat*. —— **incubat**, 3d pers. sing. pres. ind. act. of *incubo, -are, incubui* (rarely *incubavi*), *incubitum* (rarely *incubatum*), 1 (closely akin to *incumbo*, cf. *incubuere*, l. 84); agrees with subj. *nox*. *Incubat* = (1) *to lie in;* (2) *to overhang;* translate *hovers over* or *swoops upon*, in metaphor drawn from the floating of a bird in the air with outspread wings. Being a verb compounded with the prep. *in, incubat* takes the dat. case. —— **ātra**, nom. sing. f. of *ater, atra, atrum;* agrees with *nox*. For the difference between *ater* and *niger*, see note on *atris*, l. 60.

broods black up- on the main. The poles thunder and	pon,tó	nox ,	íncubat ,	átra.	Íntonu,ére po,lí 90
	on the sea	*night*	*lies down*	*black.*	*Thundered the poles*
the air quivers with quick-follow- ing flashes, and	ét	cre,brís „	micat ,	ígnibus ,	aéther,
	and	*frequent*	*gleams*	*with fires*	*the air,*
all things threaten the crews with in- stant death. Forth-	Praésen,témque	vi,rís „	in,téntant ,	ómnia , 91
	and instant	*to the man*	*hold out*	*all things*
with Aeneas' limbs are loosed in icy	mórtem.	Éxtem,plo	Aéne,ae „	sol,vúntur , 92
	death.	*At once*	*of Aeneas*	*are loosed*

LINE 90. **Intonuēre**, 3d pers. plur. perf. ind. act. of *intono, -are, intonui*, no supine, 1, intrans. (*in + tono = I thunder*); agrees with subj. *poli.* As all the principal verbs in this description are in the *historic* present tense, *intonuere* is clearly the *aoristic* perfect of sudden and instantaneous action; cf. *incubuere*, l. 84. —— **polī**, nom. plur. of *polus, -i*, m., 2d (Greek πόλος); subj. of *intonuere. Polus = the end of an axis*, hence the (*north*) *pole.* The poetic plural *poli* is often trans- lated *the heavens* (= *coelum*), but the apparent reverberation of thunder above and under the ground-surface probably gives rise to the plural here. The final *i* is elided. —— **et**, cop. conj., joining *intonuere* and *micat.* —— **crēbrīs**, abl. plur. m. of *creber, crebra, crebrum;* qualifying *ignibus.* In l. 85, *creber = abounding with;* here it has the more common meaning = *frequent.* —— **micat**, 3d pers. sing. pres. ind. act. of *mico, -are, micui*, no supine, 1; agrees with subj. *aether. Mico* originally indicates tremulous motion, and, applied to light, swift flashing; so it may be rendered either *quivers*, or *gleams.* —— **ignibus**, abl. plur. of *ignis, -is*, m., 3d (cf. *ignem*, l. 42); abl. of the instrument. Here used in its sense of *lightning-flashes.* —— **aethēr**, gen. *aetheris*, m., 3d (Greek word, derived from αἴθω = *I burn;* Greek αἰθήρ); nom. sing., subj. of *micat.* Synonyms: *aer = the lower air*, which we breathe; *aether = the upper air*, a fiery element and so lighter and higher than *aer.*

LINE 91. **Praesentem**, acc. sing. f. of *praesens, -entis*, adj., 3d (properly pres. part. of *praesum*); agrees with *mortem.* The abl. sing., of things, is *praesenti;* of persons, *praesente. Praesens* = (1) lit., *that which is before*, hence *at hand;* (2) *instant, prompt*, as here; (3) *efficacious;* (4) of character, *resolute;* (5) sometimes in Vergil of persons, *propitious.* —— **que**, enclitic cop. conj., joining *aether micat* and *omnia intentant.* —— **virīs**, dat. plur. of *vir, -i*, m., 2d; dat. of indirect obj. after *intentant.* —— **intentant**, 3d pers. plur. pres. ind. act. of *intento, -are, -avi, -atum*, 1 (*in + tento*, akin to *intendo*); agrees with subj. *omnia.* —— **omnia**, nom. plur. n., used as noun, of *omnis, -e;* subj. of *intentant.* See *omnibus*, l. 15. —— **mortem**, acc. sing. of *mors, mortis*, f., 3d (*mor-ior = I die*); direct obj. of *intentant.*

LINE 92. **Extemplō**, adv. of time, qualifying *solvuntur. Extemplo* = lit. *immediately after the time*, being a compound of *ex* (separation of time) and *tempulo*, abl. of *tempulum* (diminutive of *tempus*). The last syllable undergoes *elision.* —— **Aenēae**, gen. sing of *Aeneas* (voc. *Aeneā*, acc. *Aeneam* or *Aenean*, dat. *Aeneae*, abl. *Aeneā*) m., 1st-decl. Greek noun; poss. gen., limiting *membra.* For the declension of *Aeneas* and other 1st-decl. Greek nouns, consult A. & G. 37; B. 22; G. 65; H. 50. Aeneas, the hero of the Aeneid, was son of *Anchises* and Venus; he married a distant relative, *Creusa*, a daughter of Priam, but was unable to save her when he rescued his father from burning Troy. He finally marries Lavinia, daughter of king Latinus and the promised bride of Turnus (hence the war in Italy,

93 **frígore** , **mémbra**; **Íngemit,** , **ét** **dupli,cés** „ chill; he groans,
with cold *the limbs;* *he groans,* *and* *the two* and stretching his
94 **ten,déns** ad , **sídera** , **pálmas** **Tália** , **vóce** two hands towards
stretching *to* *the stars* *palms* *such (words)* *with his voice* the stars · uplifts
re,fért: „ **"O** , **térque** **qua,térque** **be,áti,** his voice to cry
he utters: **"O** *both thrice* *and four times* *blessed,* aloud: "O thrice
and four times
blessed they whose

Aen. VII–XII), and becomes (in Vergil's hands) the ancestor of Romulus. ——
solvuntur, 3d pers. plur. pres. ind. pass. of *solve, -ere, solvi, solutum,* 3 (*se = apart,*
+ *luo = I loosen*); vivid present, agreeing with subj. *membra.* The idea of a sort
of nervous paralysis seizing the limbs in times of danger or in act of dying is
borrowed from Homer, who is more exact in applying the *loosing* to the knees
(γούνατα). Mr. Page well observes that Vergil purposely imitates Homer; the
ancients liked to have familiar passages brought on in a new dress. For all that,
Vergil has a genius of his own, and of him it may well be said that "he touched
nothing which he did not adorn." —— **frígore,** abl. sing. of *frigus, frigoris,* n., 3d
(*frigeo = I shiver* with cold; cf. Greek verb φρίσσω); abl. of cause. A. & G. 245;
B. 219; G. 408; H. 416. —— **membra,** nom. plur. of *membrum, -i,* n., 2d; subj. of
solvuntur.

LINE 93. **Ingemit,** 3d pers. sing. pres. ind. act. of *ingemo, -ere, -ui,* no supine, 3
(*in + gemo = I groan*); agrees with *Aeneas* as subj., understood from *Aeneae* in the
previous line. The ancient Greeks thought it wholesome and no shame to give rein
to the emotions; Homer depicts the brave hero Odysseus as weeping and moaning
on occasions when according to modern standards it would be unmanly. The stoic
philosophers later taught self-restraint. —— **et,** cop. conj., joins *ingemit* and *refert.*
—— **duplicēs,** acc. plur. f. of *duplex, -icis,* adj., 3d; qualifies *palmas. Duplex* (*duo,*
and *plico = I fold*) lit. = *twofold;* cf. *triplex.* Here it = *ambas, both;* cf. Aen.VII. 140,
duplices . . . parentes: others with less probability understand by it *folded.* ——
tendēns, gen. *tendentis;* nom. sing. m. of the pres. part. act. of *tendo, -ere, tetendi,*
tensum or *tendum,* 3; agrees with *Aeneas* (supplied), subj. of *refert.* The ancients
stood when praying, and raised the hands above the head, keeping the palms of the
hands up. —— **ad,** prep. with the acc.; gov. *sidera.* —— **sīdera,** acc. plur. of
sidus, sideris, n., 3d; obj. of *ad.* Synonyms: *sidus = a cluster of stars,* a con-
stellation; stella = a star, as a single heavenly body. —— **palmās,** acc. plur. of
palma, -ae, f., 1st (Greek παλάμη); direct obj. of the part. *tendens. Palma*
= (1) *palm* of the hand; (2) *palm-tree;* (3) *blade* of an oar; (4) *palm-wreath,*
hence *prize.*

LINE 94. **Tālia,** acc. plur. n. of *talis, -e,* adj., 3d; obj. of *refert.* —— **vōce,** abl.
sing. of *vox, vocis,* f., 3d; abl. of the instrument. *Voce* is not strictly necessary, but
Homer and Vergil use a more or less peculiar and stereotyped phraseology in intro-
ducing speeches. —— **refert,** 3d pers. sing. pres. ind. act. of *refero, referre, retuli,*
relatum, irreg. (*re + fero*); subj. is *Aeneas;* cf. *ingemit. Refert = utters,* not
answers; other meanings of *refero* are (1) *carry back,* (2) *answer,* (3) *relate.* ——
O, interjection; cf. *O,* l. 76. —— **terque** (*ter + que*); *ter* is a numeral adverb.
que, conj., correlative of *que* below. —— **quater,** numeral adv., joined by *que* to
ter. Ter and *quater* are poetical, and = a prose adv., e.g. *praecipue.* —— **que,**
conj., joining *ter* and *quater;* correlative of *que* above. —— **beātī,** voc. plur.
m. of *beatus, -a, -um;* case of the person addressed. The above words are
in imitation of Odyssey V. 706, τρισμάκαρες Δαναοὶ καὶ τέτρακις, οἳ τότ'
ὅλοντο, etc.

fate it was to	Quéis	an,te	óra	pa,trúm	„	Tro,iaé	sub	, 95
die under Troy's	to whom	before	the faces	of their fathers		of Troy	under	
lofty walls be-								
fore their fathers'	moenibus	,	áltis	Cóntigit	,	óppete,re!	„	Ó 96
gaze! O Tydeus'	the walls		high	it befell		to perish!		O
son, bravest of								
the Grecian race,	Dana,úm	for,tíssime	, géntis			Týdi,dé,	me,ne	97
could I not have	of the Greeks	bravest	of the race			son of Tydeus	(was) I	

LINE 95. **Queïs** (sometimes written *quis = quibus*), old form of dat. (also abl.) plur. of rel. pron. *qui, quae, quod*; indirect obj. of the intransitive verb *contigit*. This dat. is used with trans. and intrans. verbs compounded with *in, con, prae*, etc. A. & G. ?28; B. 187, III; G. 347; H. 386. *Queïs* is a monosyllable. —— **ante,** prep. with the acc.; gov. *ora*. *Ante = before*, in respect of place, time, and degree. A. & G. 153; B. 141; G. 416, 3; H. 433, I. Observe the *elision* of *e*. —— **ōra,** acc. plur. of *os, oris*, n., 3d; obj. of *ante*. *Os* = (1) *face*, (2) *mouth;* distinguish it from *os, ossis*, n., 3d, = *a bone*. —— **patrum,** gen. plur. of *pater, patris*, m., 3d; poss. gen., limiting *ora*. —— **Trōiae,** gen. sing. of *Troia*, f., 1st; poss. gen., limiting *moenibus*. —— **sub,** prep. with acc. and abl.; gov. the abl. *moenibus*. See the note and references under *sub*, l. 36. —— **moenibus,** abl. plur. of *moenia, -ium*, n., 3d (no sing.); obj. of *sub*. See note on *moenia*, l. 7, for synonyms. —— **altis,** abl. plur. n. of *altus, -a, -um;* qualifies *moenibus*.

LINE 96. **Contigit,** 3d pers. sing. perf. ind. act. of *contingo, -ere, contigi, contactum*, 3, trans. and intrans. (*con* + *tango*); its subj. is *oppetere*, the inf. as a verbal noun. When used impersonally, *contingit* (like *efficitur, accidit, evenit, fit, licet*, etc.) takes *ut* with the subjunctive (neg. *ut non*). A. & G. 332, *a*, 2; B. 297, 2; G. 553, 4; H. 501, I, 1. Apart from the reason given under *queis* above, *contingo* as an intrans. verb of advantage or disadvantage is entitled to govern the dative of the indirect object. A. & G. 226, NOTE 1; B. 187, II; G. 346, particularly; H. 384, I. Synonyms: *contingit = it happens*, usually in a happy sense; *accidit = it happens*, usually in an unfortunate sense; *evenit = it happens*, lit. *comes out*, indicating the cause and often including it, e.g. *ex quo evenit*. —— **oppetere,** pres. inf. act. of *oppeto, -ere, oppetivi* or *-ii, oppetitum*, 3 (*ob = towards*, + *peto = proceed towards, seek*) ; subj. of *contigit*. For the inf. as a verbal noun, capable of standing as subject or object of a sentence, cf. *condere*, l. 33, and note. *Oppeto* takes the acc. of the direct object, sc. *mortem;* poets frequently use *oppetere* and *obire* simply, with *ellipse* of *mortem*. Synonyms: *oppeto = I die*, in the field courageously (points a contrast with such a shameful death as drowning); *obire* and *occumbere* (l. 97) = *to die*, in same sense as *oppetere; interire = to be destroyed*, irrevocably; *perire = to perish* (often = in battle); *mori = to die*, the ordinary word. Observe the *elision* of the final *e*. —— **Ō,** exclamation; cf. l. 76. —— **Danaûm,** gen. plur. of *Danai, -orum*, plur. noun, m., 2d (see *Danaum*, l. 30); a subjective gen., describing *gentis*. In Gildersleeve this gen. is called *epexegetical*, a kind of adnominal gen. of specification instead of a noun in apposition. A. & G. 214, *f*; B. 202; G. 361, especially; H. 395. —— **fortissime,** voc. sing. m. of *fortissimus, -a, -um*, superlative of *fortis, -e*, adj., 3d (comparative, *fortior*) ; agrees with *Tydide*. —— **gentis,** gen. sing. of *gens*, f., 3d; partitive gen., limiting *fortissime*. This genitive is regular with comparatives and superlatives of adjectives, e.g. *maior fratrum, the elder of the brothers*. A. & G. 216, 2; B. 201, 1; G. 372; H. 397, 3.

LINE 97. **Tydidē,** voc. sing. of *Tydides;* case of person addressed. For the declension of Greek patronymic nouns in *des* and *ides*, consult A. & G. 37, *Aeneades*, and 63; B. 22, under *Cometes*; G. 65, under *Anchises*; H. 50, under *Pyrites*.

98 Ília,cís „ oc,cúmbere , cámpis **Nón** potu,ísse | fallen on the plains
Iliam   *to fall*   *on the plains*   *not*   *able* | of Ilium and poured

tu,áqυe   ani,mam „ hánc ef,fúndere , déxtra, | forth this life be-
and thy   *life*   *this*   *pour out*   *by hand,* | neath thy right hand? where fierce

99 Saévus u,bi   Áeaci,dae „ te,ló iacet Héctor, | Hector lies be-
fierce   *where of the son of Aeacus by the dart lies*   *Hector,* | low the spear of Aeacides, where

---

Tydides (Greek Τυδείδης) = *son of Tydeus,* i.e. *Diomedes,* from whom Venus rescued Aeneas near Troy; cf. Iliad V. 239 ff. —— **mēne** (*me + ne*); *me* is acc. sing. of *ego;* subj. of *potuisse,* in exclamation of despair. For the explanation of this idiom, refer to note on *mene,* l. 37. *ne,* enclitic and interrog. particle; see note on *mene,* l. 37. The final syllable is *elided.* —— **Īliacīs,** abl. plur. m. of *Iliacus, -a, -um* (*Ilium = Troy*); agrees with *campis.* —— **occumbere,** pres. inf. act. of *occumbo, -ere, occubui, occubitum,* 3 (*ob + cumbo*); *prolative* inf., completing *potuisse.* A. & G. 271; B. 326; G 423; H. 533. There is an *ellipse* of the object, *morti;* cf. the *ellipse* of *mortem* after *oppetere,* l. 96. When *ob* is compounded with verbs of motion, they take the accusative; when with other verbs, usually the dative; *ob* marks *hindrance* in composition. For synonyms, see note on *oppetere,* l. 96. —— **campīs,** abl. plur. of *campus, -i,* m., 2d; abl. of 'place where.' A. & G. 258, 4, under *f;* B. 228; G. 385; H. 425, II, 1.

LINE 98. **Nōn** (originally *ne + unum*), negative adv., limiting *potuisse. Non* is the common negative adverb; *haud* (= *not*) is very rarely used with verbs, except *scio* (*haud scio an*), but is common with adjectives and adverbs. —— **potuisse,** perf. inf. of *possum, posse, potui,* irreg.; agrees with subj. *me* in the exclamatory acc. and inf. construction. For this, see note on *posse,* l. 38. —— **tuā,** abl. sing. f. of *tuus, -a, -um,* poss. adj. of the 2d personal pron. *tu;* agrees with *dextra.* —— **que,** enclitic conj., joining *potuisse* and *effundere.* Observe the *elision* of *que.* —— **animam,** acc. sing. of *anima, -ae,* f., 1st (Sanskrit root AN = *to breathe*); direct obj. of *effundere. Anima* = (1) *air,* (2) *breath,* (3) *soul, life.* By *ecthlipsis* the final *am* is not scanned. Final *m,* together with the vowel preceding it, is suppressed before words beginning with *h* (as *hauc* here) or a vowel (as *Teucrorum,* l. 38). A. & G. 359, *d;* B. 366, 7; G. 719, 2; H. 608, I. —— **hanc,** acc. sing. f. of demonstr. adj. *hic, haec, hoc* (for decl., see *hoc,* l. 17); agrees with *animam,* and is strongly deictic = *this of mine.* —— **effundere,** pres. inf. act. of *effundo, -ere, effudi, effusum,* 3 (*ex + fundo*); *prolative* inf., completing *potuisse,* and co-ordinate with *occumbere.* —— **dextrā** (sometimes *dextera*), abl. sing. of *dextra, -ae,* f., 1st (properly f. of adj. *dexter, dextra, dextrum,* agreeing with *manus = hand* understood; cf. *sinistra = left hand;* abl. of instrument.

LINE 99. **Saevus,** nom. sing. m. of adj. 1st and 2d; qualifies *Hector. Saevus* here does not mean *cruel,* for the character of Hector in the Iliad is wholly against it; it = *fiercely brave,* a proper attribute of the Trojan hero who always led the fighting. —— **ubī,** adverbial conj. of place; introducing *Hector iacet,* etc., in adverbial extension of *effundere animam.* For the meanings and uses of *ubi,* cf. *ubi,* l. 81. The final *i* undergoes *elision.* —— **Aeacidae,** gen. sing. of *Aeacides,* m., 1st-decl. Greek patronymic noun (for decl., see *Tydide,* l. 97); poss. gen., limiting *telo.* The termination *des* or *ides = son of,* or descendent of. Achilles is meant, the grandson of *Aeacus.* Achilles was the son of Peleus and Thetis, leader of the Myrmidons in the Trojan War, slayer of Hector, and finally the victim of Paris who shot him in the heel. —— **tēlō,** abl. sing. of *telum, -i,* n., 2d; abl. of the instrument. *Telum* = (1) *weapon,* (2) *javelin.* —— **iacet,** 3d pers. sing. pres. ind.

mighty Sarpedon lies too, where Simois has caught	u,bɩ	íngens	Sárpe,dón,	ubi	,	tót	Simo,ís	„ 100
	where	*huge*	*Sarpedon,*	*where*		*so many*	*Simois*	
and whirls beneath his wave so many shields	cor,répta		sub	,	úndis	Scúta	vi,rúm 101
	snatched away		*beneath*		*the waves*	*shields*	*of men*
and helmets and brave bodies of men." As he let	gale,ásq*ue*	„	et	,	fórtia	,	córpora	,	vólvit?"
	and the helmets		*and*		*brave*		*the bodies*		*rolls?"*

act. of *iaceō, -ēre, iacuī, iacitum*, 2, intrans.; agrees with subj. *Hector.* The present is the vivid *historic*, for which cf. *volvit*, l. 101, and consult note on *tendit*, l. 18. Notice that *iacet* = a passive verb, e.g. *interficitur* (for *interfectus est*); hence it takes the abl. of instrument *telo* above. Some translate *iacet* as *lies buried*, but this is incorrect, for it is predicate also of *Sarpedon*, l. 100, and Homer says that Sarpedon's body was removed to Lycia; *it = lies slain.* —— **Hector,** gen. *Hectoris,* m., 3d; nom. sing., subj. of *iacet.* Hector was a son of Priam, and the lion-hearted leader of the Trojan warriors; he was slain by Achilles, and his body was dragged round the walls of Troy, but finally, in answer to Priam's prayers, given back on receipt of a ransom. —— **ubi,** adverbial conj. of place; see *ubi* above; it is repeated by *anaphora* for the sake of impression. For *anaphora*, see note on *hic*, l. 17. The final *i* is elided. Observe the omission of a conj. with *ubi* (*asyndeton*). —— **ingēns,** gen. *ingēntis,* adj., 3d; qualifies *Sarpedon.*

LINE 100. **Sarpēdōn,** gen. *Sarpēdonis,* m., 3d; subj. of *iacet* understood. It is clear from *iacet* above what to supply with *Sarpedon.* Sarpedon was the son of Jupiter and Europa (or Laodamia), and king of Lycia; he assisted the Trojans, and was slain by Patroclus. —— **ubi,** local adv.; see *ubi* above. This clause is not united to the preceding one by a conjunction (*asyndeton*); cf. Caesar's brief message to Rome *veni, vidi, vici*, and the praetor's formula in the court *do, dico, addico.* —— **tot,** indeclinable adj., qualifies *scuta*, and understood with *galeas* and *corpora.* Its correlative is *quot;* cf. *talis . . . qualis.* —— **Simoīs,** gen. *Simoentis,* m., 3d; nom. sing., subj. of *volvit* below. The river Simois (now the Mendes), one of the rivers in the Troad, flows from Mount Ida and is a tributary of the Scamander; it played a not unimportant part in the events of the siege of Troy. —— **correpta,** acc. plur. n. of *correptus, -a, -um,* perf. part. pass. of *corripiō, -ere, corripuī, correptum,* 3 (*con + rapio*); predicate part., agreeing with *scuta.* *Correpta scuta volvit = scuta corripuit et volvit,* i.e. in English two co-ordinate sentences. A. & G. 292, REM.; B. 337, 2; G. 437; H. 549, 5. —— **sub,** prep. with the abl.; gov. *undis.* —— **undīs,** abl. plur. of *unda, -ae,* f., 1st; obj. of *sub.*

LINE 101. **Scúta,** acc. plur. of *scutum, -ī,* n., 2d (akin to Greek σκῦτ-os, and Sanskrit root SKU = *to cover*, hence *the covering thing*); direct obj. of *volvit.* Synonyms: *scutum* = *shield;* the generic term, but also = a special kind of shield, made of wood, oblong in form, and concave on the inside to give better protection; it was the regular shield of the Roman foot-soldier; *parma* = *shield,* round in shape, usually made of leather (so Suidas states), and (according to Polybius) 3 feet in diameter; *clipeus* = *shield,* round like the *parma,* but frequently of bronze or brass; *ancile* was a small shield of peculiar shape, and made of bronze. —— **virūm** (contracted for *virōrum*), gen. plur. of *vir, -ī,* m., 2d; poss. gen., limiting *scuta, galeas,* and *corpora.* —— **galeās,** acc. plur. of *galea, -ae,* f., 1st (akin to κάλυπτω = *I conceal,* hence *helmet,* protecting by hiding the head); obj. of *volvit,* joined by *que* to *scuta.* Synonyms: *galea* is a helmet made either of leather or bronze, and

102 Tália   , iáctan,tí „ stri,déns   Aqui,lóne | these words burst
Such words (*to him*) *casting forth* *shrieking* *with the N. wind* | forth, a storm-blast
| hissing before the
103 pro,célla **Vé**lum ad,vérsa fe,rít, „ fluc,túsque | North wind smites
the storm   *the sail* *adverse* *strikes,*   *and the waves* | the sail in front,
| and raises the
104 ad , sídera , tóllit. Frángun,túr re,mí; „ tum , | waves to the
towards *the stars* *raises.*   *Are broken* *the oars;* *then* | stars. The oars
| are shattered; then

surmounted by a plume; *cassis* is a metal helmet. With *galeas* is understood
correptas (supplied from *correpta* above), for Simois seized all, shields, helmets, and
bodies. —— **que,** cop. conj., *elided* before *et.* —— **et,** cop. conj., joining *galeas* and
corpora. —— **fortia,** acc. plur. n. of *fortis, -e,* adj., 3d; qualifies *corpora.* ——
corpora, acc. plur. of *corpus, corporis,* n., 3d; obj. of *volvit,* joined to *galeas* by *et.*
—— **volvit,** 3d pers. sing. pres. ind. act. of *volvō, -ere, volvī, volūtum,* 3; *historic*
present, agreeing with subj. *Simois* above.

LINE 102. **Tālia,** acc. plur. n. of *tālis, -e,* adj., 3d; obj. of *iactanti,* applied to
the preceding speech. —— **iactantī,** dat. sing. m. of *iactans, -antis,* pres. part. act. of
iactō, -āre, -āvī, -ātum, I (intensive of *iacio*); *ethic* dative, agreeing with *Aeneae*
understood. The *ethic* dative or dative of reference is used of persons who are
principally affected by the action of the main sentence, or from whose point of view
such action is described; cf. the familiar example from Horace, *quid* MIHI *Celsus*
agit? = *what is my Celsus doing?* or *tell me what is Celsus doing.* A. & G. 235, *b,*
and 236; B. 188; G. 351-353; H. 389. —— **strīdēns,** nom. sing. f. of the pres. part.
act. of *strīdeō, -ēre, strīdī,* no supine, 2 (or of *strīdō, -ĕre, strīdī,* no supine, 3); agrees
with *procella.* *Strideo* and *strido* both have the same meaning, being *onomatopœic*
verbs imitating the sound of *creaking, whistling,* etc. —— **Aquilōne,** abl. sing. of
Aquilō, -ōnis, m., 3d (akin to Greek ὠκύς = *swift*); abl. of the instrument
(= *roused by* the north wind). The Latin *Aquilo* = the Greek βορέας, i.e. *the North*
wind. —— **procella,** nom. sing.; subj. of *ferit.*

LINE 103. **Vēlum,** acc. sing. of *vēlum, -ī,* n., 2d· direct obj. of *ferit.* The fina
syllable suffers *ecthlipsis.* —— **adversa,** nom. sing. f. of *adversus, -a, -um* (*ad* + *versus,*
from *verto;* cf. *a-versus*); agrees with adverbial force with *procella;* cf. *laeti,* l. 35,
and note. We should naturally expect *adversum,* i.e. the sail struck *in front,* but as
the sail and the wind are face to face, as it were, the adjective may be used with
either subject or object. —— **ferit,** 3d pers. sing. pres. ind. act. of *feriō, -īre,* no
perf. or supine, 4; agrees with the subj. *procella.* —— **fluctūs,** acc. plur of *fluctus, -ūs,*
m., 4th; direct obj. of *tollit.* —— **que,** conj., joining *ferit* and *tollit;* undergoes
elision. —— **ad,** prep. with the acc.; gov. *sidera.* —— **sīdera,** acc. plur. of *sīdus,*
sīderis, n., 3d; obj. of *ad.* See *sidera,* l. 93, for meaning. *Ad sidera* may = *towards*
the stars; or *to the stars,* by *hyperbole,* i.e. intentional exaggeration for rhetorical
effect. A. & G. 386; B. no reference; G. no reference; H. 637, VII. —— **tollit,** 3d
pers. sing. pres. ind. act. of *tollō, -ere, sustulī, sublātum,* 3 (perf. a..d supine borrowed
from *suffero*); agrees with subj. *procella.*

LINE 104. **Franguntur,** 3d pers. plur. pres. ind. pass. of *frangō, -ere, frēgī.*
fractum, 3; agrees with subj. *remi,* and again the *historic* present. —— **rēmī,** nom,
plur. of *rēmus, -ī,* m., 2d (probably for *ret-mus,* akin to Greek ἔρετμον = *an oai,*
from the verb ἐρέσσω); subj. of *franguntur.* —— **tum,** adv. of time; limits *averti..*
Tum properly = *at that time,* not *next* (*deinde*). It marks the veering of the ship
as due to and almost instantaneous with the breaking of the oars. See *tum,* l. 13.

the prow swings round, and gives her side to the waves; a towering mountain of water in a heap o'ertakes her. These hang on the crest of the wave; to	prṓra a,vértit et , úndis **Dát** latus; , 105
	the prow *turns away and* *to the waves* *surrenders* *the side;*
	ínseqᵤi,túr cumu,ló „ prae,rúptus a,quaé mons.
	follows *in a heap* *steep* *of water* *a mountain.*
	Hí sum,mo ín fluc,tú pen,dént, „ his , 10:
	These (men) *highest* *on* *the wave* *hang,* *to these*

—— **prōra**, gen. *prōrae*, f., 1st (πρώρα); nom. sing., subj. of *avertit*. *Prora* = *the prow* of a ship, as opposed to *puppis* = *the stern;* rising with a high curve from the prow was the *rostrum* = *beak,* or figure-head. Final *a* is *elided.* —— **āvertit**, 3d pers. sing. pres. ind. act. of *āvertō, -ere, āvertī, āversum,* 3 (*a* + *verto*); agrees with its subj. *prora. Averto* is here used intransitively, and = *avertit se* or *avertitur,* cf. l. 402, *et avertens rosea cervice refulsit;* Vergil uses *verto, volvo, fero,* etc., frequently as intrans. verbs. Several MSS. read *proram avertit,* in which case *procella,* l. 102 above, is subj. of *avertit,* and *proram* is the direct object. This is a very awkward reading, for the subject has been changed by the interposition of *franguntur remi;* and apart from that *dat* does not suit *procella* as a predicate. —— **et**, cop. conj., joining *avertit* and *dat.* —— **undīs**, dat. plur. of *unda, -ae,* f., 1st; dat. of the indirect object after *dat.*

LINE 105. **Dat**, 3d pers. sing. pres. ind. act. of *do, dare, dedi, datum,* 1; agrees with its subj. *prora.* —— **latus**, gen. *lateris,* n., 3d; acc. sing., direct obj. of *dat.* —— **insequitur**, 3d pers. sing. pres. ind. of the deponent verb. *insequor, -ī, insecūtus sum,* 3 (*in* + *sequor*); agrees with the subj. *mons.* The *asyndeton* attaches emphasis to the succession of disasters that overtake the Trojans. —— **cumulō**, abl. sing. of *cumulus, -ī,* m., 2d; abl. of manner, limiting *insequitur* adverbially. A. & G. 248, at the end; B. 220; G. 399, III. —— **praeruptus**, nom. sing. m. of the perf. part. pass. of *praerumpō, -ere, praerūpī, praeruptum,* 3 (*prae* = *in front,* + *rumpo* = *I burst*); agrees with *mons. Praeruptus,* lit. *broken in front,* acquires the meaning of *steep, sheer;* but some prefer to take it in its original sense = *broken,* and so the *praeruptus mons* = *a high breaker.* —— **aquae**, gen. sing. of *aqua,* f., 1st; a descriptive gen., stating the material or substance, limiting *mons.* This gen. illustrates one of the simplest uses of the gen. case. A. & G. 214, *e*; B. 197; G. 361; H. 395. —— **mōns**, gen. *mōntis,* m., 3d; subj. of *insequitur. Mons aquae* is of course a metaphor; in prose metaphors are qualified by being introduced by such words as *sicut, quasi,* etc. The force and vigor of this line should be studied; every word is carefully chosen so that the rhythm represents the swift approach of the wave, culminating in its crashing descent (*mons*) upon the vessels. The monosyllable at the end is a favorite device for emphasis; cf. *procumbit humi bos* = *the ox falls* (with a thud) *upon the ground.* A commentator points out that the Greeks thought every third wave to be the largest and most dangerous, while the Romans had the same idea of every tenth wave.

LINE 106. **Hī**, nom. plur. m. of the demonstr. adj. *hīc, haec, hōc;* agrees with *homines* understood, subj. of *pendent. Hi* is contrasted with *his* below, the contrast being between the crews of different ships, and not (as Heyne thinks) between the right and left oarsmen of a single ship. —— **summō**, abl. sing. m. of *summus, -a, -um,* superlative formed from *supra* = *above* (the post *superus* is rare, but *Superi* = *the gods above;* comparative *superior*); agrees with *fluctu* as a partitive adjective. The partitive adjective defines a particular part of the noun, which it thus describes and

107 únda   de,híscens Térr*am* in,tér fluc,tús ape,rít, „
   a wave   *yawning*   *the earth* *among* *the billows* *lays open,*

108 furit ,   a'estus   a,rénis.   Trés   Notus ,
   rages   *the tide*   *with the sand.* *Three (ships)* *Notus*

   ábrep,tás „ in , sáxa   la,téntia , tórquet;
   seized   *onto*   *rocks*   *hidden*   *hurls;*

these the yawn-
ing main disclos-
es land amid the bil-
lows, the churning
waters boil with
sand. Three ships
the South wind
seizes and dashes
on hidden rocks,

---

limits; the most common are *summus, imus,* and *medius,* but other adjectives are sometimes used partitively. A. & G. 193; B. 241; G. 291, REM. 2; H. 440, 2, NOTE I. The final *o* is *elided.* —— **in,** prep. with the acc. and abl.; gov. the abl. *fluctu.* For its position with noun and adjective, consult A. & G. 345, *a*; B. 350, 7, *b*; G. 413, REM. 1; H. 569, II, 1. —— **fluctū,** abl. sing. of *fluctus, -ūs,* m., 4th; obj. of prep. *in.* —— **pendent,** 3d pers. plur. pres. ind. act. of *pendeō, -ēre, pependī,* no supine, 2, intrans. (*not* of *pendo, -ere, pependi, pensum,* 3 = *I hang* [trans.], or *weigh*); agrees with subj. *hi.* —— **hīs,** dat. plur. m. of *hīc, haec, hōc*; dat. of the indirect object, agreeing with *hominibus* understood. The contrast is heightened by the *asyndeton.* —— **unda,** nom. sing. of *unda, -ae,* f., 1st; subj. of *aperit.* The meaning is that those on one ship are carried high on the crest of a wave, while others sink in the trough of the sea between the waves, and owing to the shallowness of the water can see the sand of the bottom thick in the water. —— **dehīscēns,** nom. sing. f. of *dehīscēns, -ēntis,* pres. part. act. of *dehīscō, -ere, dehīvī,* no supine, 3, intrans. (*de,* intensive = here *deep down,* + *hisco* = *I yawn*); agrees with subj. *unda.*

LINE 107. **Terram,** acc. sing. of *terra, -ae,* f., 1st; direct obj. of *aperit.* The final *am* undergoes *ecthlipsis.* —— **inter,** prep. with the acc.; gov. *fluctus. Inter* = *between,* or *among;* here it = *between,* referring to the hollow between two waves. *Inter* has other idiomatic uses, e.g. with the gerund, *inter bibendum* = *while* or *in the midst of drinking; inter nos* = *among ourselves,* colloquially; *inter viam* = *on the way.* A. & G. 153, under *Inter;* B. 141; G. 416, 13; H. 433, under *Inter.* —— **fluctūs** (see *fluctu,* above); acc. plur., gov. by prep. *inter.* —— **aperit,** 3d pers. sing. pres. ind. act. of *aperiō, -īre, aperuī, apertum,* 4; agrees with its subj. *unda. Aperio* = lit. *I open,* hence *I reveal.* —— **furit,** 3d pers. sing. pres. ind. act. of *furō, -ere, furuī,* no supine, 3; agrees with *aestus,* the subject. Note the absence of a conjunction (*asyndeton*). —— **aestus,** gen. *aestūs,* m., 4th (probably akin to Greek αἴθω = *I burn,* and so = *burning,* denoting agitated motion); nom. sing., subj of *furit.* It has several meanings: (1) *heat;* hence (2) *excitement, rage;* (3) *swell* ot the sea, hence *tide;* (4) *embarrassment,* in Cicero. —— **arēnīs,** abl. plur. of *arēna, -ae,* f., 1st (from *areo* = *I am dry,* hence *that which is dry*); abl. of the instrument with *furit.* The expression is vague and poetical, but the abl. should not be taken for an abl. of 'place where,' as those take it who translate *on the sands.* The *arena* of a circus or amphitheatre derives its name from the fact that it was sprinkled with *sand* to lend a firm hold to the feet, especially necessary when the blood of beasts and gladiators was flowing.

LINE 108. **Trēs,** acc. plur. f. of the cardinal numeral *trēs,* m. and f., *tria,* n., gen. *trium,* dat. and abl. *tribus;* agrees with *naves* understood, as direct obj. of *torquet.* —— **Notus,** gen. *Notī,* m., 2d; nom. sing., subj. of *torquet.* —— **abreptās,** acc. plur. f. of *abreptus, -a, -um,* perf. part. pass. of *abripiō, -ĕre, abripuī, abreptum,* 3 (*ab* + *rapio*); predicate part., agreeing with *tres* (*naves*). *Tres abreptas torquet* = *tres abripit et torquet;* in Latin, compression plays a very important part.

rocks in mid sea-way which Italians call the Altars, a huge reef on the sea's surface. Three the East wind impels from the deep into shal-	Sáxa (those) rocks	vo,cánt call	Ita,lí the Italians	„	medi,ís middle (of)	quae which	in 109 in
	flúctibus the billows	, áras, the Altars,	Dórsum a ridge		im,máne immense	ma,rí 110 in the sea
	sum,mó, highest (part of);	„	tres , three	Eúrus Eurus	ab , from	álto the deep	Ín 111 Into

A. & G. 292, REM.; B. 337, 2; G. 437; H. 549, 5. ── in, prep. with the acc. and abl.; gov. the acc. *saxa*. ── saxa, acc. plur. of *saxum, -ī*, n., 2d; gov. by the prep. *in*. ── latentia, acc. plur. n. of *latens, -entis*, pres. part. act. of *lateō, -ēre, latuī*, no supine, 2 (akin to root λαθ, in λανθάνω = *I escape notice*); qualifies *saxa*. *Lateo* is usually intransitive, but cf. *latuere*, l. 130, for its transitive use. ── torquet, 3d pers. sing. pres. ind. act. of *torqueō, -ēre, torsī, tortum*, 2; agrees with subj. *Notus*.

LINE 109. Saxa, acc. plur., in apposition to *saxa* above; *saxa . . . aras* is in parenthesis. For apposition, see note on *loca*, l. 51. ── vocant, 3d pers. plur. pres. ind. act. of *vocō, -āre, -āvī, -ātum*, 1; in agreement with subj. *Itali* in the rel. clause *vocant quae . . . Aras*. ── Italī, nom. plur. m. of *Italus, -a, -um*, adj. used as noun in the masculine (*Italia*); subj. of *vocant*. ── mediīs, abl. plur. m. of *medius, -a, -um*; agreeing partitively with *fluctibus*. For note on partitive adjectives, cf. *summo*, l. 106. ── quae, acc. plur. n. of the rel. pron. *qui, quae, quod*; agrees in gender and number with *saxa*, and is the direct obj. of *vocant*. If the sentence were prose, *quae* would follow *saxa* immediately, but in poetry considerable license is allowed and usurped in the arrangement of words. Observe the *elision* of the diphthong before the word *in*, and see *quoque*, l. 5. ── in, prep. with the abl. or acc.; gov. the abl. *fluctibus*. ── fluctibus, abl. plur. of *fluctus, -ūs*, m., 4th; gov. by the prep. *in*. ── Ārās, acc. plur. of *Arae, -ārum*, f., 1st (personified plural of *ara*); predicate acc., in the same case as *quae* to which it refers, after the *factitive* verb *vocant*; see note on *parentem*, l. 75. The *Arae* rocks are usually identified with the Aeigimori islands, some miles north of Carthage, where, Servius says, the Romans and Carthaginians made peace at the end of the First Punic War. Others say Arae = a reef between Sicily and Sardinia, mentioned by Varro. It seems most probable that no specific spot is intended, but that *Arae* was a name given to any such hidden reefs; in which case *saxa* = not THE *rocks*, but simply *rocks* (i.e. rocks of that kind).

LINE 110. Dorsum, acc. sing. of *dorsum, -ī*, n., 2d (contracted from *devorsum* = *turned downwards*, from *de* and *versus*· [*verto*]); acc. in apposition to *saxa*. Observe the *ecthlipsis*, to which in future (as also to *elision*) no reference will occur in the notes. ── immāne, acc. sing. n. of adj. *immānis, -e*, 3d; qualifies *dorsum*. *Immanis* = (1) *huge*, of seize; (2) *terrible*, of appearance, or character. ── marī, abl. sing. of *mare, -is*, n., 3d; abl. of 'place where,' for which cf. *mente*, l. 26. ── summō, abl. sing. n. of *summus, -a, -um;* agrees as a partitive attribute with *mari*. ── trēs, acc. plur. of *trēs, tria* (see *tres*, l. 108, above); agrees with *naves* understood as obj. of *urguet*. ── Eurus, gen. *Eurī*, m., 2d; nom. sing., subj. of *urguet*. ── ab, prep. with the abl. (cf. *ab*, l. 1); gov. *alto*, here expressing separation. ── altō, abl. sing. of *altum, -ī*, n., 2d; gov. by *ab*.

LINE 111. In, prep. with acc. and abl.; gov. the acc. *brevia*. ── brevia, acc. plur. n. of adj. *brevis, -e*, used as a plural noun; obj. of prep. *in*. *Brevis* as an adj. is the opposite of *longus;* in reference to time, longitudinal (not of width) measure-

brevia ,	ét	syr,tés	ur,guét,	„ mise,rábile	, vísu,
shallows	*and*	*quicksands*	*forces*	*miserable*	*to be seen*

lows and quick-
sands, piteous to
see, and dashes
them on shoals and

112 Ílli,dítque va,dís „ at,que ággere , cíngit

and dashes ˙*on shoals* *and* *with a mound* *surrounds*

girds them about
with a bank of sand.

113 a,rénae. Únam, . quáe Lyci,ós „ fi,dúmque

of sand. *One* *which* *the Lycians* *and faithful*

One, wherein were
sailing the Lycians

ment, depth and height = *short.* —— **et,** cop. conj., joining *brevia* and *syrtes.* ——
syrtēs, acc. plur. of *syrtis, -is,* f., 3d; joined by *et* to *brevia* as obj. of *in.* Some
write *Syrtes,* i.e. the particular sandbanks in the sea off the north coast of Africa
(*Syrtēs, -ium,* f., 3d); the *Syrtes* were divided into *Syrtis maior* (now off Sidra) and
Syrtis minor (now off Cabes). It is little likely that these are meant, but if
they are, *brevia et Syrtes = brevia Syrtium,* an instance of *hendiadys;* cf. *ob noxas et
furias,* l. 41, and note. If the reference is not particular, it is unnecessary to regard
brevia et syrtes as a case of *hendiadys.* —— **urguet,** 3d pers. sing. pres. ind. act. of
urgueō, -ēre, ursī, no supine, 2 (commonly *urgeo*); agrees with its subj. *Eurus.* ——
miserābile, acc. sing. n. of adj. *miserābilis, -e,* 3d (*miseror = I pity*); acc. in appo-
sition to the preceding clause.   The construction is borrowed from the Greek;
cf. Sophocles' Electra, l. 130, ἥκετ᾽, ἐμῶν καμάτων παραμύθιον = *ye have come,* (your
coming being) *a solace to my pain.* A. & G. 240, *g*; B. no reference, but perhaps 185, 1;
G., 324; H. 363, 5. —— **vīsū,** supine in *u* of *video, -ēre, vīdī, vīsum,* 2; defining
miserabile. The supine is a verbal abstract of the 4th declension; that in *um*
expresses purpose and follows verbs of motion, e.g. *abiit pugnatum = he went away
to fight;* that in *u* is an abl. of specification. There are only a few supines in *u* in
use, e.g. *dictu, visu, auditu,* etc., and they go closely with an adj. (or the nouns *fas,
nefas,* and *opus*) to explain its reference.   A. & G. 303; B. 340, 2; G. 436; H. 547.

LINE 112. **Illīdit,** 3d pers. sing. pres. ind. act. of *illīdō, -ere, illīsī, illīsum,* 3
(sometimes written *inlido;* from *in + laedo = I strike*); agrees with subj. *Eurus.*
—— **que,** enclitic cop. conj., joining *illidit* to *urguet.* —— **vadīs,** dat. plur. of
vadum, -ī, n., 2d; dat. of the indirect object after a compound of the prep. *in,* viz.
illidit; cf. *scopuloque infixit,* l. 45, and note. —— **atque,** cop. conj., here joining
cingit, the third member of the series of predicates, to *urguet* and *illidit* abo·e.
See *atque, que, et,* etc., compared under *que,* l. 1. —— **aggere,** abl. sing. of *agger, -is,*
m., 3d (*ad = to,* + *gero = I bring,* hence materials brought somewhere); abl. of the
instrument. *Agger* has the following meanings: (1) *materials;* (2) *a heap,* of any-
thing; (3) *a mound,* for mounting siege-engines; (4) *a mound,* used as a platform
for speeches to soldiery; (5) *an embankment,* of a road; the famous *via Appia* was
so embanked. —— **cingit,** 3d pers. sing. pres. ind. act. of *cingō, -ere, cinxī, cinctum,* 3,
agrees with subj. *Eurus,* and joined to *illidit* by *atque.* —— **arēnae,** gen. sing. of
arēna, f., 1st; gen. of substance or material, limiting *aggere;* cf. *aquae mons,* l. 105;
and see references.

LINE 113. **Ūnam,** acc. sing. f. of *ūnus, -a, -um,* gen. *ūnīus,* dat. *ūnī;* agrees
with *navem* understood as obj. of *ferit* below. —— **quae,** nom. sing. f. of rel. pron.
quī, quae, quod; agrees with *unam,* and is subj. of *vehebat.* —— **Lyciōs,** acc. plur. of
Lyciī, -ōrum, m., 2d (m. plur. of adj. *Lycius,* i.e. belonging to *Lycia,* as substantive);
direct obj. of *vehebat.*   Lycia was a country of Asia Minor, settled from Crete, and
called after its king *Lycus,* the son of Pandion. —— **fīdum,** acc. sing. m. of *fīdus, -a,
-um* (cf. *fidelis,* from *fido = I trust*); qualifies *Oronten.*   As *pius* is a stock attribute

| and trusty Orontes, before his very eyes a mighty sea smites from above upon the stern. The helmsman is hurled off and rolls headlong for- | ve,hébat
was carrying

in,géns
huge

ferit:
strikes: | O,rónten,
Orontes

a , vértice ,
from the top

, éxcuti,túr
is shaken out | Ípsius ,
of himself

póntus
a sea

„ pro,nús-que
and prone | ánte
before

Ín
On

má,gister
the master | ocu,lós „ 114
the eyes

pup,pím 115
the stern |

of Aeneas, so is *fidus* of his followers; cf. the familiar *fidus Achates.* Vergil herein follows the lead of Homer, whose hero Odysseus is always δῖος = *divine*, πολύμητις = *wily*, or πολύτλας = *much enduring*, and whose less reputable characters, e.g. Aegisthus, are described by the stock epithet *blameless.* —— **que**, enclitic conj., joining *Lycios* and *Oronten.* —— **vehēbat**, 3d pers. sing. imperf. ind. act. of *vehō*, *-ere*, *vēxī*, *vectum*, 3; agrees with its subj. *quae.* This tense serves to remind the reader that all the present tenses in this narrative are *historic*, i.e. take for the sake of vividness the place of perfects. —— **Oronten**, acc. sing. of *Orontēs*, m., 3d; direct obj. of *vehebat.* Other cases are: gen. *Oron-tis, -tae*, or *-tī*, dat. *Orontī*, abl. *Oronte.* Orontes was the chief of the Lycians, and a follower of Aeneas.

LINE 114. **Ipsĭus**, gen. sing. m. of the intensive adj. *ipse, -a, -um* (cf. *ipsos*, l. 40); intensifying *eius* or *illius* understood from Oronten, and a poss. gen. limiting *oculos.* Note that, whereas the *penultimate i* is usually long, it is here short, forming a *dactyl*; cf. *unĭus*, l. 41. —— **ante**, prep. with the acc.; gov. *oculos.* —— **oculōs**, acc. plur. of *oculus, -ī*, m., 2d; gov. by the prep. *ante.* A diminutive form of *oculus* is *ocellus*, as a term of endearment. —— **ingēns**, nom. sing. m. of *ingēns, -entis*, adj., 3; qualifies *pontus.* —— **ā**, prep. with the abl.; gov. *vertice.* —— **vertice**, abl. sing. of *vertex, verticis*, m., 3d (*verto = I turn*); governed by the prep. *a.* *Vertex =* (1) *whirlpool*, (2) *the top* of anything. *A vertice* is a phrase *= perpendicularly*, lit. *from the height*; cf. Odyssey V. 313, κατ' ἄκρης . . . ἐπεσσύμενον. —— **pontus**, gen. *pontī*, m., 2d; nom. sing., subj. of *ferit.* *Pontus =* (1) *sea*, cf. l. 40; (2) *wave*, as here.

LINE 115. **In**, prep. with the acc. and abl.; gov. the acc. *puppim.* —— **puppim** (rarely *puppem*), acc. sing. of *puppis, -is*, f., 3d (abl. *puppī*); governed by the prep. *in.* With *in puppim*, cf. *in latus*, l. 82. —— **ferit**, 3d pers. sing. pres. ind. act. of *feriō, -īre*, no perf. or supine, 4; agrees with the subj. *pontus.* Observe the long pause after *ferit*; it is *the* pause in the line, although the *caesura* falls after *excutitur.* The skilfully arranged *diaeresis* (i.e. simultaneous ending of a word and a foot) is mainly accountable for this checking effect. A. & G. 358, *c*; B. 366, 8; G. 753; H. 602, 2. —— **excutitur**, 3d pers. sing. pres. ind. pass. of *excutiō, -ere, excussī, excussum*, 3 (*ex + quatio = I shake*); agrees with the subj. *magister.* Vergil's mastery over the *hexameter* is very apparent in this line. He wishes to poin' strongly the cause and its effect, and does so by these three means: (1) the pause after *ferit* (see above); (2) the absence of a conjunction (*asyndeton*); (3) *chiasmus* (so called from the Greek letter X, as ₄¹X²₁), i.e. the placing of antithetical words in a pair of ideas in the opposite order; e.g. *pontus . . . ferit, excutitur . . . magister.* A. & G. 344, *f*; B. 350, 11, *c*; G. 682, and REM.; H. 562. —— **prōnus**, nom. sing. m. of adj. *prōnus, -a, -um*; agrees with *magister*, but qualifies the action like an adverb; cf. *laeti*, l. 35 and note. *Pronus =* here *headlong*; when applied to a state of rest it *= prostrate* with face down, as opposed to *supinus = lying on the back*, with face up. —— **que**, conj., joining *excutitur* and *volvitur.* —— **magister**, gen. *magistrī*, m., 2d; nom. sing., subj. of *excutitur* and *volvitur.* *Magister* often *= gubernator*, i.e. *helmsman* or pilot in Vergil; cf. Aen. V. 867, *amisso . . . magistro.* From Aen. VI. 334, we learn that the name of Orontes' pilot was Leucaspis.

116 Vólvitur	, ín	caput;	,	ást	il,lám	„	ter	,
is rolled	*onto*	*his head;*		*but*	*it*		*thrice*	

117 flúctus	i,bídem	Tórquet	a,géns		cir,cum,	„
the wave	*in the same place*	*whirls*	*driving* (*it*)		*round*	

ét	rapi,dús	vorat	,	aéquore	,	vértex.
and	*rapid*	*swallows*		*in the sea*		*a whirlpool.*

118 Áppa,rént		ra,rí ·	„	nan,tés	in	,	gúrgite	,
Appear		(*men*) *scattered*		*swimming*	*in*		*the gulf*	

ward; for the ship,
— thrice in the
same spot the bil-
low drives around
and spins her,
and the swift eddy
engulphs her in
its swirl. Here
and there show
men swimming in
the vast whirlpool,

LINE 116. **Volvitur**, 3d pers. sing. pres. ind. pass. of *volvō, -ere, volvī, volūtum,* 3; agrees with subj. *magister. Volvitur* must not be rendered *is rolled,* for the passive is intransitive in meaning, = *rolls;* cf. *verto = I turn,* trans.; *vertor = I turn,* intransitive. —— **in**, prep.; gov. the acc. *caput.* This use of *in* is not regular, but idiomatic; for the regular meanings, see *in,* l. 51. —— **caput.** acc. sing. of *caput, capitis,* n., 3d; governed by the prep. *in.* This is a case of *diaeresis* similar to that in the line above. —— **ast** (an old or poetic form of *at*), adversative conj., here (as often) introducing a new point. For distinctions between *sed, at, autem, verum,* etc., refer to the note and references under *sed,* l. 19. —— **illam,** acc. sing. f. of the demonstr. pron. *ille, illa, illud* (see *illum,* l. 44); *illam = navem,* and is direct obj. of *torquet.* It is in emphatic position, and = *as for the ship, thrice,* etc. —— **ter,** numeral adverb, limiting *torquet.* One commentator says *ter* should not be translated literally, but as *several times;* there is no adequate reason for it. —— **fluctus, -ūs,** m., 4th; nom. sing., subj. of *torquet.* —— **ibīdem** (*ibi* + the suffix *dem;* cf. *idem = is + dem*), adv. of place, limiting *torquet.*

LINE 117. **Torquet,** 3d pers. sing. pres. ind. act. of *torqueō, -ēre, torsī, tortum,* 2; agrees with the subj. *fluctus.* Note how expressive this line is in rhythm, and observe further the alliteration in the last four words. —— **agēns,** gen. *agēntis;* nom. sing. m. of the pres. part. act. of *agō, -ĕre, ēgī, actum,* 3; predicate part., enlarging the subj. *fluctus.* —— **circum,** adv. of place, limiting *agens. Circum* originally is an adverbial acc. of *circus,* and = *in a ring;* it is also used as a prep. with the accusative. As the pause in the line follows *circum,* it seems preferable to place the *caesura* mark after it, instead of after *et,* even in spite of the *ecthlipsis* of *um.* —— **et,** cop. conj., joining *fluctus* and *vertex.* —— **rapidus,** nom. sing. m. of the adj. *rapidus, -a, -um;* qualifies *vertex.* It is possible to consider it an adverbial attribute = *swiftly.* —— **vorat,** 3d pers. sing. pres. ind. act. of *vorō, -āre, -āvī, -ātum,* 1; agrees with the subj. *vertex.* —— **aequore,** abl. sing. of *aequor, -is,* n., 3d; abl. of the instrument. For synonyms, see *aequore,* l. 29. —— **vertex,** nom. sing. f., 3d; subj. of *vorat.*

LINE 118. **Appārent** (*adparent*), 3d pers. plur. pres. ind. act. of *appāreō, -ēre, -uī, -itum,* 2 (*ad = at,* + *pāreo = I appear*); agrees with the subj. *viri* understood. Synonyms: *appareo = I appear,* i.e. in visual presence; *videor = I appear, seem,* as a matter of belief. —— **rārī,** nom. plur. m. of *rārus, -a, -um;* agrees with *viri,* understood subj. of *apparent.* It has the force of an adverb, = *here and there. Rarus =* (1) *thin,* as opposed to *densus;* (2) in plural, *scattered = disiecti;* (3) *rare.* —— **nantēs,** nom. plur. m. of *nans, -antis,* pres. part. act. of *nō, -āre, -āvī,* no supine, 1 (akin to Greek νέω); agrees with an understood subj. *viri.* —— **in,** prep.; gov. the abl. *gurgite.* —— **gurgite,** abl. sing. of *gurges, -itis,* m., 3d; obj. of the prep. *in.* —— **vāstō,** abl. sing. m. of *vāstus, -a, -um;* qualifies *gurgite. Vastus* conveys the idea of great extent in space and of desolation. This line, being *spondaic,* well expresses intense exertion.

arms of men, and planks, and treasure of Troy in the waves. Now the storm has o'ercome the stout bark of Ilioneus, now that of brave	vásto, vast	Árma the arms	vi,rúm of men	tabu,láeque and boards	„ et , and	Tróïa , 119 Trojan
	gáza treasure	per through	, úndas. the waves.	Iám vali,dam Already strong		Ílio,neí 120 of Ilioneus
	na,vém, the ship,	„ iam already	, fórtis A,chátae, Ét (that) brave of Achates and			qua , 121 (that) in which

LINE 119. **Arma**, nom. plur. (see *arma*, l. 1); a subj. of *apparent*. Note the absence of a cop. conj. with *arma*, and its presence with *tabulae* and *gaza*, the other subjects. —— **virūm**, contracted gen. plur. (*virōrum*) of *vir, -ī,* m., 2d; poss. gen., limiting *arma*. The only *arms* that could be floating would be such things as helmets of leather, shields, etc. —— **tabulae**, nom. plur. of *tabula, -ae,* f., 1st; a subj. of *apparent*, joined by *que* to *arma*. —— **que**, cop. conjunction. —— **et**, cop. conj., joining *gaza* to *tabulae*. —— **Trōïa**, nom. sing. f. of *Trōïus, -a, -um* (*of Troia*); qualifying *gaza*. Synonyms: *Troicus,* and *Troianus,* both formed from the noun *Troia.* —— **gāza**, gen. *gāzae,* f., 1st (Greek γάζα, a word of Persian origin); a subj. of *apparent*, joined by *et* to *tabulae*. —— **per**, prep. with the acc.; gov. *undas*. For its uses in reference to *time, place*, etc., consult A. &. G. 153, *Per;* B. 181, 2; G. 416, 18; H. 433, *Per*. —— **undās**, acc. plur. of *unda, -ae,* f., 1st; gov. by *per*.

LINE 120. **Iam**, adv. of time, = *now, already*. It is repeated below (by *anaphora*) both to mark quick succession and also to point the antithesis. A. & G. 344,*f*; B. 350, 11, *b*; G. 682, and 636, NOTE 4; H. 636, III, 3. *Iam* is often used, in conjunction with *diu* (sometimes as one word *iamdiu*), with the present tense to signify that an action begun in the past is continued into the present; e.g. *iam diu paro* = *I have been preparing for a long time*. —— **validam**, acc. sing. f. of *validus, -a, -um* (from *valeo* = *I am strong*); qualifies *navem*. Vergil sometimes uses *valida* as a complimentary or stock epithet of a ship, just as Homer calls them over and over again θοή, etc. —— **Ílioneī**, gen. sing. of *Ílioneus,* Greek m. noun of mixed declension; poss. gen., limiting *navem*. The final *ei* is a long diphthong, contracted from *Ilionëi;* the contraction is sometimes a single long *i;* cf. *Oili,* l. 40. For the declension, read the note on *Achilli,* l. 30, and consult the references there given. On l. 611, the acc. is *Iliona*. Ilioneus was one of the followers of Aeneas; his name ('Ιλιονεύς) = *a man from Ilium,* and so he is perhaps a creation of Vergil's imagination. Homer has a character of the same name, but refers to his death —— **nāvem**, acc. sing. o *nāvis, -is,* f., 3d; direct obj. of *vicit*. —— **iam**, adverb (see *iam* above). There is no cop. conjunction, a case of *asyndeton*. —— **fortis**, gen. sing. m. of *fortis, -e,* adj., 3d qualifies *Achatae*. —— **Achātae**, gen. sing. of *Achātēs,* Greek m. noun of mixed 1st and 3d declension; poss. gen., limiting *navem* understood from the clause above. This form of the gen. is 1st declension; others read *Achātū* (= Greek ov). A. & G. 37, *Perses;* B. 22, *Cometes;* G. 65, *Anchises;* H. 50, *Pyrites*. For the 3d-declension forms, see note on *Achilli,* l. 30. Greek nouns are declined very loosely in Latin verse. Achates was the most trusty companion of Aeneas, called *fidus Achates*.

LINE 121. **Et**, cop. conj., connecting *navem* understood as antecedent of *qua* with the *navem* understood above and limited by *Achatae*. —— **quā**, abl. sing. f. of the rel. pron. *qui, quae, quod;* agrees with *navem* understood as antecedent, and an abl. of the instrument. The repetition of *qua* below is *anaphora;* see *iam,* l. 120 above. —— **vectus**, nom. sing. m. of the perf. part. pass. of *veho, -ere, vēxī, vectum,* 3, forming with *est* understood the perf. ind. pass. of *veho;* agrees with the subj. *Abas*. *Est* and *sunt* are frequently omitted from the perf. pass., just as they are when

véctus A,bás, „ et , quá gran,daevus A,létes,
was borne Abas, and (that) in which old Aletes
122 **Vícit** hi,émps; „ la,xís late,rúm
has conquered the storm; having been loosened of the sides
123 com,págibus , ómnes Áccipi,únt ini,mícum
the joints all receive hostile

Achates, that too wherein sailed Abas, and that wherein the aged Aletes; through the loosened joints of their sides all let in the fatal flood, and

simply acting as *copula*. See note on *forma*, l. 72. —— **Abās**, *-antis*, m., 3d; nom. sing., subj. of *vectus* (*est*). Nothing is known of Abas, except that he was a follower of Aeneas; he cannot be the same (for an obvious reason) as the Abas whose death Homer mentions. —— **et**, cop. conj., joining *navem* or *eam* understood before *qua*, with *navem* or *eam* understood before *qua* above. —— **quā**, abl. sing. f. of *qui, quae, quod;* abl. of the instrument. —— **grandaevus** (*grandis, -e*, = *great*, + *aevum* = *age*), adj., nom. sing. m.; qualifies *Aletes*. —— **Alētēs**, gen. *Alētis* or *Alētī;* nom. sing. m., 3d; subj. of *vectus est*, understood from the preceding clause. Nothing is known of him outside the Aeneid. We may re-arrange and fill up ll. 120 and 121 as follows: *Iam hiemps validam Ilionei navem, iam* (*eam*) *fortis Achatae, et* (*eam*) *qua Abas vectus* (*est*), *et* (*eam*) *qua grandaevus Aletes* (*vectus est*), *vicit.*

LINE 122. **Vīcit**, 3d pers. sing. perf. ind. act. of *vincō, -ere, vīcī, victum*, 3; agrees with its subj.-nom. *hiemps*. The perfect, a variation from the constant succession of *historic* presents, is (like *incubuere*, l. 84) the perfect of instantaneous action. —— **hiemps** (sometimes written *hiems*), gen. *hiemis*, f., 3d (akin to Greek χειμών = *winter*, and χεῖμα = *wintry weather*); nom. sing., subj. of *vicit. Hiemps* = (1) *winter*, (2) as here, *stormy weather* or *a storm*, i.e. such as occur in winter. The *caesural* pause has been marked after *hiemps*, owing to the sudden check in rhythm and in the narrative description, emphasized as the pause is by the *asyndeton* between this clause and the next (see *laxis* below). The ordinary *caesura* in the 4th foot occurs after *laterum*, but it is not the principal one. Hitherto, when more than one *caesura* occured, only those in the 3d and 4th feet were marked in the text, with the intention of familiarizing the reader with the swing and simplest rules of the *hexameter*. A. & G. 362, *b*, and REM.; B. 368, 3, *b*; G. 784, NOTE 2; H. 611, 1. —— **laxīs**, abl. plur. f. of *laxus, -a, -um;* agrees with *compagibus* in the abl. abs. construction. Usually the noun or pronoun is modified by a participle, but it may be modified by another noun or pronoun, or by an adjective. The adj. *laxis* thus modifies *compagibus*, without a participle of *esse*, for the pres. part. of *esse* is not found in Latin, though a participle of the verb *to be* is found in Sanskrit and in Greek. A. & G. 255; B. 227; G. 409, 410; H. 431. —— **laterum**, gen. plur. of *latus, -eris*, n., 3d; poss. gen., limiting *compagibus*. —— **compāgibus**, abl. plur. of *compāgēs, -is*, f., 3d (*cum + pango* = *I fasten*); abl. abs. with *laxis*. Some call *compagibus* an abl. of the instrument. —— **omnēs**, nom. plur. of *omnis, -e;* agrees with *naves*, understood subj. of *accipiunt*.

LINE 123. **Accipiunt**, 3d pers. plur. pres. ind. act. of *accipiō, -ere, accēpī, acceptum*, 3; agrees with subj. *omnes* (*naves*). —— **inimīcum**, acc. sing. m. of *inimīcus, -a, -um* (*in* = *not*, + *amicus*); qualifies *imbrem;* cf. *inimīca*, l. 67. —— **imbrem**, acc. sing. of *imber, imbris*, m., 3d; direct obj. of *accipiunt. Imber* properly = *rain*, but is used by Lucretius (as by Vergil here) to = *water*, salt or fresh; it = *sea-water* in Ennius. —— **rīmīs**, abl. plur. of *rīma,-ae*,f., 1st; abl. of manner. A.& G. 248, at end; B. 220; G. 399, NOTE 2; H. 419, III. —— **que**, enclitic conj. —— **fatīscunt**, 3d pers. plur. pres. ind. act. of *fatiscō,-ere*, no perfect nor supine, 3 (akin to Greek χαίνω = *I yawn*); agrees with *omnes* (*naves*), subj. of *accipiunt*, to which it is joined by *que.*

gape with opened	im,brém	„	ri,mísque	fa,tíscunt.	Íntere,á 124
seams. Meanwhile	*the water (lit. rain)*		*and with cracks*	*gape.*	*Meanwhile*
Neptune, deeply angered, perceived	mag,nó	„	mis,céri ,	múrmure ,	póntum,
the mighty-roaring	*great*		*to be disturbed*	*with rumbling*	*the sea*
turmoil of the	Émis,sámq*ue*		hie,mém „	sen,sít	Nep,túnus 125
sea, the storm let	*and to have been sent forth*		*the storm*	*felt*	*Neptune*

LINE 124. **Intereā**, adv. of time. This word, compounded of the prep. *inter* and *ea*, is (like *postea, videlicet = videre licet*, etc.) a survival from the time when different words began to be used together in a special connection, and in process of time united in a single word. The termination *ea* is: (1) either an ablative, with which *inter* and the like were once admissible, or (2) the neut. acc. plural; in each case of the demonstr. pron. *is, ea, id*. Some, however, say *ea = eam*, acc. feminine of *is*, comparing the synonym of *interea*, viz. *interim*, compounded of *inter* and *eum*, acc. masculine of *is*. —— **māgnō**, abl. sing. n. of *magnus, -a, -um;* qualifying *murmure*. —— **miscērī**, pres. inf. pass. of *misceō, -ēre, miscuī, mixtum* or *mistum*, 2; agrees with *pontum* in the subject-acc. and inf. construction after *sensit* (a verb of the class *sentiendi vel declarandi*, i.e. *saying, knowing, feeling, thinking*, etc.). The inf.-clause *pontum misceri* is the direct obj. of the verb *sensit*, answering the possible question *quid sensit? = what did he perceive?* Sometimes the inf.-clause is subject of the verb, especially after words like *fama*, or impersonal verbs like *constat;* e.g. *Hannibalem clarum ducem fuisse constat = (it) is well known that Hannibal was a famous general.* A. & G. 272, and REM.; B. 330, 331; G. 527; H. 534, and 535. See the note on *duci*, l. 19. The example in this instance is of the simple acc. and inf.; it is capable of great extension, becoming *Oratio obliqua* in the narrow sense of the construction of lengthy reported speech. The verbs of subordinate clauses pass into the subjunct. mood; cf. l. 20, *verteret*, and study the note and references. —— **murmure**, abl. sing. of *murmur, -is*, n., 3d; abl. of manner, with *cum* omitted, owing to the presence of an adjective modifying the noun; cf. *magno cum murmure*, l. 55. Note the *alliteration* in *Magno Misceri Murmure*. —— **pontum**, acc. sing. of *pontus, -ī*, m., 2d; subject-acc. of the inf. *misceri*.

LINE 125. **Ēmissam**, acc. sing. f. of *ēmissus, -a, -um*, perf. part. pass. of *ēmittō, -ere, ēmīsī, ēmissum*, 3 (*ē + mittō); agrees with its subject-acc. *hiemem*, not as a participle, but as the perf. inf. passive with *esse* understood. For the omission of *esse*, which is common both when *copula* and as part of the complex perf. inf. pass., consult A. & G. 206, *c*, 2; B. 166, 3; G. 209; H. 368, 3. Instead of *emissam* a few read *immissam* (from *immitto*), but Neptune had no interest in the storm as *sent* UPON the Trojans, but as *sent* FORTH by Aeolus. —— **que**, enclitic conj., joining the two subject-accusatives, *pontum* and *hiemem*. —— **hiemem**, acc. sing. of *hiemps* (see *hiemps*, l. 122); subject-acc. of *emissam (esse)*, after *sensit*, a *verbum sentiendi*. See note on *misceri* above. —— **sēnsit**, 3d pers. sing. perf. ind. act. of *sentiō, -īre, sēnsī, sēnsum*, 4; agrees with its subj. *Neptunus*. The description is interrupted here by a new incident and the introduction of a new character; hence the return to the perfect tense, usual in describing past events. —— **Neptūnus**, gen. *Neptūnī*, m., 2d; subj. of *sensit*. Neptune (in Greek myth, Poseidon) was a son of Saturn, and brother of Jupiter and Juno; cf. *fratrem*, l. 130. He was absolute ruler over the sea, and therefore resented the presumption of Aeolus in rousing it with the winds. —— **et**, conj., joining *stagna* and *hiemem*. —— **īmīs**, abl. plur. of *īmus, -a, -um* (see note on *imis*, l. 84); agrees with partitive force with *vadis*.

126 et	, ímis	Stágna		re,fúsa	loose, and the still
and	lowest	the standing-waters	to have been thrown back		waters upheaved
va,dís,	„	gravi,tér	com,mótus; et	, álto	from the lowest depths, and gaz-
from the shoals		deeply	moved; and	on the deep	ing o'er the deep
127 Próspici,éns	sum,má „	placi,dúm	caput,	éxtulit,	has raised his
looking forth	highest	calm	his head	he raised	head serene above
128 únda.		Dísiec,tam	A'ene,áe „	to,tó videt,	the water's rim. He sees Aeneas'
on the wave.		Scattered	of Aeneas	whole he sees	fleet scattered all

LINE 126. **Stāgna**, acc. plur. of *stăgnum, -ī,* n., 2d (from *sto,* hence *that which does not move*); subject-acc. of *refusa* (*esse*), the inf.-clause obj. of *sensit. Stagna =* *the still waters* at the depth of the ocean, which scarcely moved as a rule, but were set in motion from the bottom (*vadis*) towards the surface. —— **refūsa**, acc. plur. n. of *refūsus, -a, -um,* perf. part. pass. of *refundō, -ere, refūdī, refūsum,* 3 (*re = back,* + *fundo = I pour*); forms with *esse* understood (cf. *emissam* above) the perf. inf. pass. of *refundo,* the participial part agreeing with *stagna.* For the force of *re* or *red* in composition, refer to the note on *repostum,* l. 26. *Refusa = forced back,* i.e. *forced up,* away from the *vada;* some translate *shifted,* not necessarily of movement upwards, but of mere change of position. —— **vadīs,** abl. plur. of *vadum, -ī,* n., 2d; abl. of separation after *refusa.* A. & G. 243; B. 214; G. 390, 1 and 2, NOTE 3; H. 414, I. —— **graviter** (from *gravis, -e,* adj., 3d), adv. of manner, limiting *commotus.* For the for- mation of adverbs in *ter* and *iter* from 3d-declension adjectives, consult A. & G. 148, *b;* B. 76; G. 92; H. 304. —— **commōtus,** nom. sing. m. of the perf. part. pass. of *commoveō, -ēre, commōvī, commōtum,* 2 (*cum,* in composition *con,* + *moveo*); modifying *Neptunus.* The participle takes the place of a clause or a coordinate sentence; e.g. *and was greatly moved,* or *whereat he was greatly moved.* —— **et,** conj., joining *sensit* and *extulit.* —— **altō,** abl. sing. of *altum, -ī,* n., 2d; abl. of 'place where' or 'place over which' in regard to vision; cf. l. 181, *prospectum late pelago petit,* where *pelago =* *in pelagus,* just as *alto = in altum.* A. & G. 258, 4, under *f,* 2 and 3; B. 228; G. 385; H. 425, II, 1 and 2. Beware of taking *alto* as an abl. of separation, as some do who render *looking forth from the sea;* the best scholars reject this rendering.

LINE 127. **Prōspiciēns,** nom. sing. m. of the pres. part. act. of *prospiciō, -ĕre, prospēxī, prospectum,* 3; agreeing with a pronoun, referring to *Neptunus* above, subj. of *extulit.* The pres. participle is somewhat *proleptic,* for Neptune could not *look forth* until his head was *above* the sea; in prose we should expect *ut prospiceret,* a purpose- clause. —— **summā,** abl. sing. f. of *summus, -a, -um,* adj. used partitively; agrees with *unda.* See note on *summo,* l. 106. —— **placidum,** acc. sing. n. of *placidus, -a, -um;* qualifies *caput.* This epithet is intended to denote the majesty of Neptune, and = *serene.* Others, with less probability, give it an active verbal sense = *tranquilising, causing peacefulness.* —— **caput,** acc. sing. of *caput, capitis,* n., 3d; direct obj. of *extulit.* —— **extulit,** 3d pers. sing. perf. ind. act. of *efferō, efferre, extulī, ēlātum,* irreg. (compound of *ē* or *ex,* and *fero*); joined by *et* to *sensit* above, agreeing with the same subj. *Neptunus.* For the conjugation of *fero,* and list of its compounds, consult A. & G. 139, and 170, *a;* B. 129; G. 171; H. 292. —— **undā,** abl. sing. of *unda, -ae,* f., 1st; abl. of separation after *extulit.* For references, see note on *animo,* l. 26.

LINE 128. **Dīsiectam,** acc. sing. f. of *disiectus, -a, -um,* perf. part. pass. of *disiiciō, -ĕre, disiēcī, disiectum,* 3 (*dis,* marking separation, + *iacio*); agrees with *classem.*

ocean over, the Trojans overwhelmed by the billows and the deluge from the sky. And far from hidden from	a'equore , clássem, Flúctibus , óppres,sós Tro,ás „ 129	
	on the sea the fleet by the waves overwhelmed the Trojans	
	coe,líque ru,ína. Néc latu,ére do,lí „ 130	
	and of the sky by the downfall. Nor did lie hid from the tricks	

The participle is perhaps used in a predicate way, as is common in Greek after verbs of perceiving, e.g. αἰσθάνομαι, γιγνώσκω, etc. The ordinary prose rule is that Latin verbs of perceiving are followed by an acc. and inf. object clause; it is quite easy to understand *esse* with *disiectam*, and with *oppressos* in the next line. —— **Aenēae**, gen. sing. of *Aenēās* (for declension, see note on *Aeneae*, l. 92); poss. gen., limiting *classem*. —— **tōtō**, abl. sing. n. of *tōtus, -a, -um;* agrees with *aequore;* cf. *toto*, l. 29. —— **videt**, 3d pers. sing. pres. ind. act. of *videō, -ēre, vīdī, vīsum*, 2; agrees with a pronoun as subj. referring to *Neptunus*, l. 125. Once more the *historic* present tense. A. & G. 276, *d*; B. 259, 3; G. 229; H. 467, III. —— **aequore**, abl. sing. of *aequor, -is*, n., 3d; abl. of 'place where' or 'place over which.' See note on *aequore*, l. 29, and on *alto*, l. 126. —— **classem**, acc. sing. of *classis, -is*, f., 3d; direct obj. of *videt*. For the meanings of *classis*, see note on *classem*, l. 39.

LINE 129. **Fluctibus**, abl. plur. of *fluctus, -ūs*, m., 4th; abl. of the instrument. —— **oppressōs**, acc. plur. m. of *oppressus, -a, -um*, perf. part. pass. of *opprimō, -ēre, oppressī, oppressum*, 3 (*ob* + *premo*); agrees with the object-acc. *Troas*. See note on *disiectam* above. —— **Trōās**, Greek acc. plur. of *Trōes, -um*, dat. and abl. *Trōibus*, m.; direct obj. of *videt*. A conjunction is omitted (*asyndeton*) so as to oppose the fate of the ships (*classem*) on the one hand to the condition of the crews (*Troas*) on the other. For declension of *Troas*, etc., see note on *Troas*, l. 30. —— **coelī**, gen. sing. of *coelum*, n., 2d; subjective poss. gen., limiting *ruina*. —— **que**, enclitic conj., joining *ruina* to *fluctibus*. —— **ruinā**, abl. sing. of *ruīna, -ae*, f., 1st (from *ruo = I rush*); abl. of the instrument after *oppressos*. *The downfall of heaven* is a vigorous poetic phrase, including the thunder and rain-storm. The verb *ruo* is similarly used by Vergil; cf. Aen. V. 695, *ruit aethere toto Turbidus imber aqua.*

LINE 130. **Nec** (short form of *neque*, in lit. sense *ne* + *que*, = *and . . . not*), coordinate disjunctive conj., joining *videt* and *latuere*. Used correlatively, *nec . . . nec* = *neither . . . nor;* cf. *neque . . . neque*. —— **latuēre**, 3d pers. plur. perf. ind. act. of *lateō, -ēre, latuī*, no supine, 2, usually intrans.; agrees with the subject-nom. *doli*, and transitively governs *fratrem*. Like its philological Greek relative λανθάνω, *lateo* is in rare cases transitive; for the ordinary use, cf. *latet anguis in herba = a snake lurks in the grass; latet* is sometimes impersonal, = *it escapes notice, is unknown*, esp. with an indirect question; e.g. Aen. V. 4 and 5, *Quae tantum accenderit ignem Causa,* — *latet*, where the indirect interrog. clause is the logical subject. The change of the subject from *Neptunus* to *doli* is abrupt, but intentional; *nec . . . latuere* practically = *he knew very well*, and is a case of *litotes*, also called *meiosis* (or *understatement*), i.e. making an affirmation through the medium of two words (very commonly both negative; e.g. *haud ignoro = I am not ignorant of*, i.e. *I know well*), one of which negatives the other, cf. *non simili*, l. 136. The effect of *litotes* is to convey very much more meaning than at first sight appears. It is very common in Greek; cf. Plato's Apology, 17, B, ὁμολογοίην ἂν ἔγωγε οὐ κατὰ τούτους εἶναι ῥήτωρ, = I would confess that *I am not an orator of their stamp*, i.e. am much better. A. & G. 386, and 209, *c*; B. 375, 1; G. 700; H. 637, VIII. —— **dolī**, nom. plur. of *dolus, -ī*, m., 2d (Greek δόλος); subj. of *latuere*. *Dolus* = (1) *a trick;* (2) *guile*, sometimes *treachery*.

131 fra,trém Iu,nónis et , írae. Eúrum ad , sé

her brother of Juno and the passions. Eurus to himself

Zephy,rúmque vo,cát, „ dehinc , tália , fátur:

and Zephyrus he calls, then such things he speaks:

132 "Tántane , vós gene,rís „ tenu,ít fi,dúcia,véstri?

(Has) so great you in race possessed trust your?

her brother were Juno's guile and anger. Eurus to him he summons, and Zephyrus, and thereafter thus speaks: "Is the trust that has possessed you indeed so sure, your trust in your birth?

—— frātrem, acc. sing. of *frāter, frātris,* m., 3d; direct obj. of *latuere.* Saturn was the father of Jupiter, Juno, and Neptune. —— Iūnōnis, gen. sing. of *Iūnō,* f., 3d; poss. gen., limiting *doli* and also by implication *fratrem.* —— et, conj., joining *doli* and *irae.* —— īrae, nom. plur. of *īra, -ae,* f., 1st; a subj. of *latuere.*

LINE 131. Eurum, acc. sing. of *Eurus, -ī,* m., 2d; direct obj. of *vocat.* The choice of Eurus and Zephyrus as scape-goats is an example of the *seeming* reality of facts in poetry, and by no means implies that they were more active in destruction than the other winds; they are merely representative. —— ad, prep. with the acc.; gov. *se.* —— sē, acc. sing. of the reflexive pron. *sē (sēsē),* gen. *suī,* dat. *sibi,* abl. *sē (sēsē),* reflexive of the 3d person, sing. or plural; obj. of *ad,* and = Neptune. —— Zephyrum, acc. sing. of *Zephyrus, -ī,* m., 2d; direct object of *vocat.* —— que, enclitic conj., joining *Eurum* and *Zephyrum.* —— vocat, 3d pers. sing. pres. ind. act. of *vocō, -āre, -āvī, -ātum,* 1; agrees with the subject-nom. *Neptunus* or a pronoun understood. —— dehinc *(de = from,* + *hinc = hence),* adv., here marking the succession of actions. By *synizesis* (also called *synaeresis,* though some distinguish them), *dehinc* becomes a long monosyllable, the *h* being ignored; cf. *deinde, antēīre,* etc. A. & G. 347, *c*; B. 367, 1; G. 727; H. 608, III. —— tālia, acc. plur. n. of *tālis, -e*; direct obj. of *fatur.* —— fātur, 3d pers. sing. pres. ind. of the defective dep. verb *fāri = to speak, fatus sum = I have spoken;* agrees with the same subject as *vocat.* In the present tense, *fātur* and *fantur* occur; in the fut., *fābor* and *fābitur;* the perf. tenses are regular and complete, e.g. *fātus eram,* the pluperf. For further details and peculiarities, consult A. & G. 144, *c*; B. 136; G. 175, 3; H. 297, II, 3.

LINE 132. Tantane *(tanta + ne); tanta* is nom. sing. f. of *tantus, -a, -um; ne,* enclitic interrog. particle. It is appended to the emphatic word at the beginning, and asks for information; *num,* introducing questions, expects a negative reply; *nonne* expects an affirmative answer. A. & G. 210, *a-d*; B. 162, 2, *c*; G. 454; H. 351, 1 and 2. —— vōs, acc. plur. of the 2d personal pron. *tū* (in plural, nom. *vōs,* gen. *vestrum* or *vestrī,* dat. and abl. *vōbīs);* direct obj. of *tenuit.* —— generis, gen. sing. of *genus,* n., 3d; objective gen., limiting *fiducia.* A. & G. 217; B. 200; G. 363, 2; H. 396, III. This genitive = a preposition such as *erga, in,* etc., and the case it governs of the noun. The allusion is sarcastic, for the winds did not hold a high place among the deities; they were sprung from the Titan Astraeus and the goddess of the dawn, Aurora (Greek *Eos).* —— tenuit, 3d pers. sing. perf. ind. act. of *teneō, -ēre, tenuī, tentum,* 2; agrees with the subj. *fiducia.* This verb, commonly meaning possession, has its exact equivalent in the English *possessed* (= *seized).* Observe that Neptune refers through the perfect *tenuit* to the time when the storm was raised: the winds rebuked by him doubtless appeared anything but self-confident. —— fidūcia, gen. *fidūciae,* f., 1st *(fido = I trust);* nom. sing., subj. of *tenuit.* —— vestrī, gen. sing. n. of the poss. pronominal adj. of the 2d pers. plur. *(vos) vester, vestra, vestrum;* agrees with *generis.*

Dare you now, O winds, without my will tò mix in turmoil sky and earth, and up-raise such mighty mountains(of ocean)? You whom I—! but 'tis best to assuage	Iám coe,lúm ter,rámque „ me,ó sine , númine, , 133 Already sky and earth my without consent, vénti, Mísce,re, ét tan,tás „ au,détis , tóllere , 134 O winds to mingle and so great do you dare to raise móles? Quós ego , — séd mo,tós „ prae,stát 135 masses? Whom I — but set in motion it is better

LINE 133. **Iam,** adv. of time; standing as it does first it is emphatic; we might render it "have you *actually at last* come to dare, etc." See note on *iam*, l. 120. —— **coelum,** acc. sing. of *coelum, -ī,* n., 2d; direct obj. of *miscere.* —— **terram,** acc. sing. of *terra, -ae,* f., 1st; direct obj. of *miscere.* —— **que,** enclitic conj., joining *coelum* and *terram.* The *caesura* is the *feminine* in the 3d foot. See references under *cano,* l. 1. —— **meō,** abl. sing. n. of *meus, -a, -um,* the poss. pronominal adj. of the 1st personal pron. sing. *ego;* agrees with *numine.* *Meo* is emphatic, both by position and rhythm. —— **sine,** prep. with the abl.; gov. *numine.* *Sine* is opposed to *cum,* in reference to accompaniment and manner. A. & G. 152, *b*; B. 142; G. 417, 13; H. 434. —— **nūmine,** abl. sing. of *nūmen, nūminis,* n., 3d (from *nuo,* = *I nod*); obj. of the prep. *sine.* *Numine* here = *will, command;* for other meanings, refer to the note on *numine,* l. 8. —— **ventī,** voc. plur. of *ventus, -ī,* m., 2d; the case of the object addressed by the speaker. The ancients regarded the winds as deities baleful to mankind, who would reduce the earth once more to chaos if they escaped altogether the control of Aeolus. We have already met Eurus, Notus, and Africus: of the rest *Auster,* the south wind, is the bringer of rain; *Boreas,* the north, is rough and boisterous; *Zephyrus,* the west wind, is the gentlest wind; *Corus,* the north-west, brings snow.

LINE 134. **Miscēre,** pres. inf. act. of *misceō, -ēre, miscuī, mixtum,* or *mistum,* 2; *prolative* or *epexegetical* inf. dependent on *audetis.* A. & G. 271; B. 326; G. 423; H. 533. *Misceo* is often used by Vergil figuratively, especially in reference to tumult in the sea; cf. Georgics, I, 359, *aut resonantia longe Litora misceri.* —— **et,** conj., joining *miscere* and *tollere.* —— **tantās,** acc. plur. f. of *tantus, -a, -um;* agrees with *moles.* —— **audētis,** 2d pers. plur. pres. of the semi-deponent verb *audeō, -ēre, ausus sum,* 2; in agreement with the unexpressed subject-pronoun *vos.* Semi-deponent verbs are those which form their present-stem tenses regularly in the active; but, having no perfect stem, they form the past tenses in passive form with active meaning, like deponents. A. & G. 136; B. 114, 1; G. 167, 1; H. 268, 3, and 465, 2, NOTE 2. —— **tollere,** pres. inf. act. of *tollō, -ere, sustulī, sublātum,* 3; joined by *et* to *audetis,* and in the same grammatical construction. —— **mōlēs,** acc. plur. of *mōlēs, -is,* f., 3d; direct obj. of *tollere.* The *masses* referred to are of course masses of water; in l. 61, *molem = mass,* of a mountain; in l. 33, *molis = labor.* — NOTE. In the above interrogative sentence the natural order of words yields to metrical exigencies; reconstructed the sentence runs: *venti, iam coelum terramque miscere et tollere tantas moles sine meo numine audetis?* Observe that the sentence has no introductory particle such as *ne* in the preceding question. In such cases, the only sign that the sentence is interrogative is the question mark. There is, besides, a possibility that the supposed question is an ironical statement. A. & G. 210, *b*; B. 162, 2, *d*; G. 453; H. 351, 3.

LINE 135. **Quōs,** acc. plur. m. of the rel. *quī, quae, quod;* direct obj. of a verb not expressed, owing to the sudden break. The clause, if concluded, would be a threat, '*whom I'll—.*' Such an interruption is called *aposiopesis* (ἀποσιώπησις) or *reticentia, i.e.* a break off into silence; cf. Aen. V, 195, *Quamquam O—sed superent,* etc. A. & G. 386; B. no reference; G. 691; H. 637, XI, 3. —— **ego,** nom. sing. of the 1st personal pron. sing. *ego,* acc. *mē,* gen. *meī,* dat. *mihi,* abl. *mē;* subj. of a verb not expressed (by *aposiopesis*). ——

186 com,pónere, flúctus: **Póst** mihi, nón simi,lí ,,
 to calm *the waves: afterwards to me* *not* *like (this)*

187 poe,ná　　　com,míssa　　lu,etis.　**Mátu,ráte**
 with punishment *your faults* *you will atone for.* *Hasten*

fu,gám, ,, re,gíque　　haec , dícite , véstro:
 your flight *and to king* *these words* *say (ye)* *your*

the troubled billows: Hereafter with punishment far unlike to this you will atone your misdeeds. Speed your flight, and tell this to your king ;

---

sed, adversative conj.; cf. *sed*, l. 19, for discriminations between *sed, verum, at,* and *autem.*
—— **mōtōs**, acc. plur. m. of *mōtus, -a, -um,* perf. part. pass. of *moveo, -ēre, mōvī, mōtum,* 2; predicate part., modifying *fluctus. Motos* = a clause *qui moti sunt.* —— **praestat**, 3d pers. sing. pres. ind. act. of *praestō, -āre, praestitī, praestitum,* or *praestātum,* 1; here impersonal, = *it is better* (lit. *stands before*), with the clause *motos componere fluctus* as the logical subject. —— **compōnere**, pres. inf. act. of *compōnō, -ere, composuī, compositum* (sometimes, by *syncope, compostum*), 3 (*cum + pono*); logical subj. of *praestat.* —— **fluctūs**, acc. plur. of *fluctus, -ūs,* m., 4th; direct obj. of the inf. *componere.*

LINE 136. **Post,** adv. of time, limiting *luetis. Post* is also used as a prep. with the acc., = *after,* in relations of time and place. We may compare *circum,* which in l. 32, *maria omnia circum,* is a prep., but in l. 117, *agens circum,* an adverb. The explanation of this is that originally there was no distinction between adverbs and prepositions either in form or in meaning; the distinction arose as they became specialized in use. *Post* and *ante* being prepositions or adverbs implying comparison may be united with *quam,* e.g. *postquam,* or followed by it, e.g. *post . . . quam,* forming a temporal conjunction. —— **mīhi,** dat. sing. of *ego* (see previous line); dat. of reference, or, as it is often called, *dativis commodi aut inccmmodi,* i.e. dat. of advantage or disadvantage. A. & G. 235; B. 188, 1; G. 350; H. 384, II, 1, 2). —— **nōn,** negative adverb, limiting *simili.* For distinction between *non* and *haud,* refer to the note on *non,* l. 98. —— **simili,** abl. sing. of the adj. *similis, -e,* 3d; agrees with *poena. Similis* is here used absolutely; it may also be used relatively, followed by the gen. of personal pronouns, but as a rule the dative of other parts of speech. *Non simili* is a very good example of litotes, of that kind in which only one of the two words is negative; it = *not by a similar punishment,* i.e. by a much more severe one. Notice, however, that no present punishment is stated. —— **poenā,** abl. sing. of *poena, -ae,* f., 1st (Greek ποινή); abl. of manner. *Poenam luere* as a phrase = *to pay the penalty,* to another, like the Greek δίκην δίδοναι. Synonyms: *poena* = *any* kind of *punishment,* the generic word; *supplicium = severe punishment,* esp. capital. —— **commīssa,** acc. plur. of *commīssum, -ī,* n., 2d (originally sing. n. perf. part. pass. of *committo*); direct obj. of *luetis.* —— **luētis,** 2d pers. plur. fut. ind. act. of *luō, -ere, luī, luitum,* or *lūtum,* 3; in agreement with the unexpressed pronoun-subj. *vos,* referring to *venti.* The ordinary phrase for 'to give satisfaction,' 'to make atonement,' is *dare poenas,* e.g. *mihi poenas dedit,* = *he made atonement to me ; sumere poenas,* = *to exact atonement.*

LINE 137. **Mātūrāte,** 2d pers. plur. imperative mood act. of *mātūrō, -āre, -āvī, -ātum,* 1 (*maturus,* = *ripe*); the inflection indicates the subj. (*vos*). *Maturo* is transitive in such uses as *maturare uvas,* = *to ripen grapes,* and also in Vergil. It is usually intransitive in prose, = *to hasten,* either absolutely or followed by a *prolative* infinitive. If it were necessary to regard it as transitive here, the acc. *fugam* would be a *cognate* acc., like *vitam vivere,* and *navigat aequor,* l. 67. —— **fugam,** acc. sing. of *fuga, -ae,* f., 1st; direct obj. of *maturate.* —— **rēgī,** dat. sing. of *rēx, rēgis,* m., 3d; dat. of the indirect obj. after *dicite.* —— **que,** enclitic conj., joining *maturate* and *dicite.* —— **haec,** acc. plur. n. of the demonstr. adj. *hīc, haec, hōc ;* neut. used as substantive, direct obj. of *dicite. Haec* refers to what follows. —— **dīcite,** 2d pers. plur. imperative mood act. of

| not his, but mine by the lot's award, are the empire of the sea and the stern trident. His sway is over the fearful rocks, the | Nón   il,lí ímperi,úm pela,gí „ sae,vúmque 138 *(that) not to him (is) the rule of the sea, and dread* tri,déntem, Séd mihi , sórte da,túm. „ Tenet , ílle 139 *the trident, but to me by lot given. Holds he* |

---

dīcō, -ere, dīxī, dictum, 3 ; joined by *que* to *maturate,* and in the same construction. The 2d pers. sing. imperative act. is *dic (dice* only in early Latin); so also *fac* from *facio, duc* from *duco,* and *fer* from *fero ;* compounds of *facio* form the 2d pers. regularly, e.g. *perfice.* A. & G. 128, *c;* B. 116, 3; G. 130, 5; H. 238. —— **vestrō,** dat. sing. m. of *vester, vestra, vestrum,* (see *vestri,* l. 132); agrees with *regi.*

LINE 138. **Nōn,** negative adv., limiting *datum (esse);* but see note on *illi* below. —— **īllī,** dat. sing. m. of *ille, illa, illud,* the demonstr. pron. of the 3d person (for declension, see *illum,* l. 44); dat. of the indirect obj. after *datum.* It would be possible to regard *illi* (and *mihi* below) as dat. of the possessor after the copula *esse* understood with each, viz., *non illi (esse), sed mihi (esse) = non illum habere, sed me habere; datum* would then be simply a participle. But alter *imperium* and *tridentem* we should naturally expect *data,* the acc. n. plural usual after two or more nouns of different genders; the sing. might then be explained on the ground that it agrees with *tridentem,* the nearer noun. —— **imperium,** acc. sing. of *imperium, -i,* n , 2d; subj. in the acc. and inf. construction of *datum (esse),* or of *esse* alone (as in the note above). The whole acc. and inf. object clause *non illi . . . datum* is logically in apposition to *haec,* the direct obj. of *dicite,* l. 137. For acc. and inf., see *miscere,* l. 124. —— **pelagī,** gen. sing. of *pelagus, -i,* n., 2d (Greek πέλαγos); objective gen., dependent on *imperium.* A. & G. 217; B. 200; G. 363, 2; H. 396, III. *Pelagus* has only the nom. and acc. plural cases, *pelagē.* For gender, etc., consult A. & G. 39, *b;* B. 26, 2; G. 34, EXCEPTIONS; H. 51, 7. —— **saevum,** acc. sing. m. of *saevus, -a, -um ;* qualifies *tridentem.* In poetry attributes of persons are not uncommonly applied to things; Aeolus, the king of the winds, is *saevus,* a *stern* or *grim* ruler, and so his sign of office, *the trident,* is *saevum.* —— **que,** conj., joining *imperium* and *tridentem.* —— **tridentem,** acc. sing. of *tridens, -entis,* m., 3d (originally an adj. = *with three teeth,* from *tres, tria,* + *dens*): joined by *que* to *imperium,* and in the same construction. With *tridens* we may compare *bidens,* adj. and noun: as an adj. it = *with two teeth ;* as a noun it = (1) *a sheep,* for sacrifice, (2) *a mattock,* or *hoe.*

LINE 139. **Sed,** adversative conj.; see *sed,* l. 19. —— **mihi,** dat. sing. of *ego ;* dat. of the indirect obj. after *datum (esse).* But see note on *illi* above. —— **sorte,** abl. sing. of *sors, -tis,* f., 3d; abl. of manner. *Sors =* (1) *a lot ;* cf. the pieces of turf thrown into a helmet by the Greek heroes to decide a question; (2) *lot, destiny.* The abl. ends sometimes in *i.* On the death of their father Saturn (Kronos), his three sons drew lots for his spheres of rule; Jupiter (Zeus) drew the heavens, Pluto (Hades) drew the lower world, and Neptune (Poseidon) drew the sea. —— **datum,** acc. sing. m. of *datus, -a, -um,* perf. part. pass. of *do, dare, dedī, datum,* 1; agrees with the nearest of the nouns to which it refers, viz. with *tridentem ; datum* is the perf. inf. pass. with *esse* (supplied). —— **Tenet,** 3d pers. sing. pres. ind. act. of *teneō, -ēre, tenuī, tentum,* 2; agrees with the subject-nom. *ille.* Neptune in his excitement deserts the indirect form in which he began his warning, and passes to the more pointed direct form. —— **ille,** nom. sing. m. of the demonstr. pron. of the 3d person; subj. of *tenet.* —— **immānia,** acc. plur. n. of *immānis, -e,* adj., 3d; agrees with *saxa.* —— **sāxa,** acc. plur. of *sāxum, -i,* n., 2d; direct obj of *tenet.* By *saxa* is meant the *antrum,* or *cave ;* cf. *antro,* l. 52.

140 im,mánia , sáxa, **V**estras, , Eúre, do,mós; „ il,lá
　　huge　　　*the rocks*　*your*　*O Eurus,*　*homes;*　　　*that*

141 se , iáctet in , aúla **A**éolus , ét clau,só „
　　himself let boast in　*court*　*Aeolus*　*and*　　*closed*

142 ven,tórum , cárcere , régnet." **S**íc ait, ,
　　of the winds　*in the prison*　*let him rule."*　　*So he speaks,*

home of thee, O Eurus, and thy fellows; in his court yonder let Aeolus vaunt himself and rule it in the barred prison of the winds." So he speaks and

LINE 140. **Vestrās,** acc. plur. f. of *vester, vestra, vestrum;* agrees with *domos.* The plur. poss. adj. (instead of *tuas*) is given because *Eurus,* though alone mentioned by name, represents the rest of the winds; cf. Aen. IX, 525, *Vos, O Calliope, precor.* —— **Eure,** voc. sing. of *Eurus. -ī,* m., 2d; addressed by Neptune. —— **domōs,** acc. plur. of *domus, -ūs,* f., 4th (also forms of 2d); 2d decl. acc. plur., in apposition to *saxa.* *Domus* is declined completely in the 4th declension, though the abl. *domu* is scarce: it has the following 2d decl. cases; gen. sing., *domi* (rare); dat. and abl., *domo;* acc. plur., *domos;* gen. plur., *domorum.* From *domus* we find a survival of the old locative case, viz. *domi, = at home;* cf. *ruri, = in the country.* The acc. *domum* may express limit of motion, e.g. *domum ibo, = I shall go home;* the abl. *domo* is used for ' place whence,' *= from home.* —— **illā,** abl. sing. f. of *ille, illa, illud;* agrees with *aula.* It is emphatically deictic, e.g., ' in THAT fine court of his,' etc., and we might imagine Neptune pointing his finger in the direction of the cavern of the winds. —— **sē,** acc. sing. of the reflexive pronoun (see *secum,* l. 37); direct obj. of *iactet,* and referring to *Aeolus,* the subject. Compare with *iactet se* (= *let him boast* or *vaunt himself*), the familiar words, " Why boastest thou thyself, O tyrant, that thou canst do mischief ?" —— **iactet,** 3d pers. sing. pres. subjunct. act. of *iactō, -āre, -āvī, -ātum,* 1 (intensive of *iacio*); *hortatory* subjunct., agreeing with the subj. *Aeolus.* The *hortatory* subjunct. here expresses a command, but it can also express a concession or a simple exhortation. A negative command or exhortation requires *ne* with this subjunctive. The present or perfect tense is used for the 3d pers. sing. or plural; the present tense for the 1st person; the present for affirmative exhortations, etc., in the 2d person; and the perfect (less commonly the present) for negative commands in the 2d person. A. & G. 266; B. 274–276; G. 263; H. 484. —— **in,** prep.; gov. the abl. *aula.* —— **aulā,** abl. sing. of *aula, -ae,* f., 1st; governed by *in.* *Aula* = (1) *a court* or *yard;* (2) *a palace,* the home of a ruler; (3) *the power,* of a prince (in Cicero); (4) *the court,* i.e. courtiers (in Tacitus).

LINE 141. **Aeolus,** nom. sing.; subj. of *iactet.* —— **et,** cop. conjunction. —— **clausō,** abl. sing. m. of *clausus, -a, -um,* perf. part. pass. of *claudō, -ere, clausī, clausum,* 3; predicate participle, agreeing with *carcere.* *Clauso* is very emphatic and ironical, = ' let him rule in his prison, provided it be barred up.' The participle often contains the principal notion contained in a phrase or clause; cf. *ante urbem conditam, = before the* FOUNDING *of the city.* A. & G. 292, *a;* B. 337, 5; G. 437, NOTE 2; H. 549, 5, NOTE 2. —— **ventōrum,** gen. plur. of *ventus, -ī,* m., 2d; poss. gen., limiting *carcere.* —— **carcere,** abl. sing. of *carcer, -is,* m., 3d; abl. of ' place where'; see note on *mente,* l. 26, for references. —— **rēgnet,** 3d pers. sing. pres. subjunct. act. of *regnō, -āre, -āvī, -ātum,* 1; *hortatory* subjunct., joined by *et* to *iactet,* and agreeing with the same subj. *Aeolus* or a pron. referring to him.

LINE 142. **Sīc,** adv. of manner. —— **ait,** 3d pers. sing. pres. ind. act. of the defective verb *āiō,* 3; *historic* present, agreeing with *is* understood (i.e. *Neptunus*). In the pres. ind. the sing. persons and the 3d pers. plural are found; the imperf. ind. is complete. For other deficiencies, consult A. & G. 144, *a;* B. 135; G. 175, 1; H. 297, II, 1. *Aio* may be used absolutely, but often introduces indirect discourse, like the common

quicker than his word	ét	dic, tó	citi, ús ,, tumi, da áequora, plácat,
he calms the swollen main, routs flying the	and	than the speech quicker	swollen the sea he soothes,
gathered clouds, and brings back the sun.	Cóllec, tásque fu, gát nu, bés ,, so, lémque re, dúcit. 143		
	and collected puts to flight the clouds and the sun brings back.		
Cymothoë and Triton together lean and push the vessels off	Cýmotho, é simul , ét Tri, tón ,, an, níxus 144		
	Cymothoë at the same time and Triton having pushed		

word *dico;* occasionally it stands parenthetically in a direct speech (e.g. *ait,* = *says he*), but parts of another defective verb, *inquam* = *I say,* are nearly always employed. —— **et,** cop. conjunction. —— **dictō,** abl. sing. of *dictum, -ī,* n., 2d (properly n. sing. of the perf. part. pass. of *dīcō*); abl. of the compared, after the comparative adv. *citius.* In this case, *citius dicto* may = a clause, *quicker than he had spoken;* but see *citius* below. *Dicto* is an idiomatic abl. like *opinione, spe, solito,* etc., for which consult A. & G. 247, *b*; B. 217, 4, where *opinione* alone is given; G. 398, NOTE 1; H. 417, NOTE 5. For the ordinary abl. of comparison, and comparisons with *quam,* refer to the note on *terris,* l. 15. —— **citius,** comparative degree of the adv. *cito;* the adverbial phrase *dicto citius* limits *placat.* The superlative is *citissime.* The comparative scheme of adverbs closely follows that of the adj. from which the adv. is formed : the comparative is the same as the acc. n. sing. of the comparative of the adj.; the superl. is the adv. in *e* regularly formed from the superl. adj. in *us.* Thus, positive adj. *bonus* and adv. *bene,* comparative adj. *melior* and adv. *melius,* superl. adj. *optimus* and adv. *optime.* A. & G. 92; B. 76, 2, and 77, 1; G. 93; H. 306. Here *dicto citius* refers not to Neptune's rebuke of the winds, but to the authoritative words with which he calms (*placat*) the sea. —— **tumida,** acc. plur. n. of adj. *tumidus, -a, -um (tumeo,* = *I swell*); qualifies *aequora.* —— **aequora,** acc. plur. of *aequor, -is,* n., 3d; direct obj. of *placat. Aequor* by derivation from *aequus, -a, -um* (= *level surface*) does not admit a plural, but as a poetical synonym of *mare* it is often plural in Vergil. —— **plācat,** 3d pers. sing. pres. ind. act. of *plācō, -āre, -āvī, -ātum,* 1; *historic* present, joined by *et* to *ait,* and agreeing with the same subject.

LINE 143. **Collectās,** acc. plur. f. of *collectus, -a, -um,* perf. part. pass. of *colligō, -ere, collēgī, collectum,* 3 (*con* + *lego*); predicate part., agreeing with *nubes.* —— **que,** conj. —— **fugat,** 3d pers. sing. pres. ind. act. of *fugō, -āre, -āvī, -ātum,* 1 trans. ; joined by *que* to *placat,* and agrees with the same subject. —— **nūbēs,** acc. plur. of *nūbēs, -is,* f., 3d ; direct obj. of *fugat.* —— **sōlem,** acc. sing. of *sol, sōlis,* m., 3d (akin to Greek ἥλιος); direct obj. of *reducit.* As a deity, Sol is identical with Apollo ; in the personified nature-worship of the Ancients, Sol = the Baal of the Chaldeans, Mithras of the Persians, and Osiris of the Egyptians. —— **que,** conj. —— **redūcit,** 3d pers. sing. pres. ind. act. of *redūcō, -ere, redūxī, reductum,* 3 (*re,* = *back,* + *duco*); joined by *que* to *fugat,* and agrees with the same subj., i.e. *Neptunus,* the understood subj. of *ait,* l. 142 above.

LINE 144. **Cȳmothoē,** nom. sing. of the first decl. Greek noun, f.; one of the subjects of *detrudunt* (*Triton* is the other subject). The other cases are : voc. and abl., *Cymothoē;* acc., *Cymothoen;* gen., *Cymothoes;* dat , *Cymothoae.* A. & G. 37 ; B. 22 ; each like Epitome ; G. 65, Penelope ; H. 50, like Epitome. *Cymothoë* is a word of four syllables, final *e* being distinct from the *o,* as the *trema* or dotted sign indicates. She was a Nereid or Sea-nymph, and daughter of Nereus and Doris. —— **simul,** adv., limiting *adnixus. Simul,* with *ac* added, becomes a temporal conjunction. —— **et,** cop. conj. —— **Tritōn,** gen. *Trītōnis* (or *Trītōnos,* a Greek gen.), m., 3d ; nom. sing. joined by *et* to *Cymothoë,* both together forming the subj. of *detrudunt.* Triton was the son of Neptune and Amphitrite (others say his mother was the nymph Salacia), always depicted as half man, half fish, and blowing with distended cheeks on a conch. —— **adnīxus,** nom. sing. m. of the perf. part. pass. of the dep. verb *adnitor, adnītī, adnīxus* or *adnīsus sum,*

145 a, cúto **Détru**, dúnt	na, vés	scopu, ló;	,, levat ,	the sharp rock; him-
sharp	*thrust*	*the ships*	*from the rocks; lifts* (them)	self he floats them
146 ípse	tri, dénti,	**Ét**	vas, tás	ape, rít	with his trident, makes
he himself	*with his trident,*	*and*	*vast*	*opens*	a passage through
					the vast quicksands
147 syr, tés	,, et ,	témperat ,	áequor,	**Átque**	and calms the sea,
the shoals	*and*	*calms*	*the sea*	*and*	and then in his light
ro, tís	sum, más ,, levi, bús per, lábitur ,	úndas.	car skims over the
with wheels	*highest*	*light*	*glides over*	*the waves.*	crest of the waves.

---

3 (*ad,* + *nitor,* = *I lean*); agrees with the nearest noun *Triton,* but really enlarges *Cymothoë* as well. A. & G. 187 ; B. 235, B, 2, *b* ; G. 286, 1 ; H. 439, 2. It is seen that when an adj. qualifies two living objects of different genders, the masculine gender preponderates ; when two inanimate objects are qualified by a predicate adj., the adj. is usually neuter plural. By this rule, we should expect *adnixi,* the m. plural, but the sing. is due to metrical necessity.——**acūtō,** abl. sing. m. of *acūtus, -a, -um ;* qualifies *scopulo.*

LINE 145. **Dētrūdunt,** 3d pers. plur. pres. ind. act. of *dētrūdō, -ere, dētrūsī, dētrūsum,* 3 ; agrees with the double subj. *Cymothoe et Triton.*——**nāvēs,** acc. plur. of *nāvis, -is,* f., 3d ; direct obj. of *detrudunt.*——**scopulō,** abl. sing. of *scopulus, -ī,* m., 2d ; abl. governed by *de* in *detrudunt.* It will be remembered that verbs compounded with *a, ab, de, e,* or *ex* may take the abl. when used figuratively, but when denoting actual separation or motion always require the prep. with which the verb is compounded to be repeated before the noun ; e.g. *ex Italia excessit.* See references on *animo,* l. 26.—— **levat,** 3d pers. sing. pres. ind. act. of *levō, -āre, -āvī, -ātum,* 1 ; agrees with the subj. *ipse.*——**ipse,** nom. sing., agreeing with *Neptunus* as supplied from the context. A. & G. 102, *e* ; B. 88 ; G. 103, 3 ; H. 186, and 452.——**tridentī,** abl. sing. of *tridens* (see *tridentem* and note, l. 138) ; abl. of the instrument.

LINE 146. **Et,** conj.——**vāstās,** acc. plur. f. of *vāstus, -a, -um ;* qualifying *syrtes.* *Vastas,* here implying desolation, is an epithet of the *syrtes,* because they were very dangerous to navigation.——**aperit,** 3d pers. sing. pres. ind. act. of *aperiō, -īre, aperuī apertum,* 4 ; is joined by *et* to *levat,* and agrees with the same subject. *Aperit* = *makes a passage through* the sandbanks, so as to free the ships which had been imprisoned by them ; cf. *aggere cingit arenae,* l. 112 above.——**syrtēs,** acc. plur. of *syrtis, -is,* f., 3d ; direct obj. of *aperit.* The reference is to the shifting of the sand caused by the storm. ——**et,** conj.——**temperat,** 3d pers. sing. pres. ind. act. of *temperō, -āre, -āvī, -ātum,* 1 ; joined by *et* to *aperit,* and in agreement with the same subject.——**aequor,** acc. sing. of *aequor, -is,* n., 3d ; direct obj. of *temperat.*

LINE 147. **Atque,** cop. conj. adding *rotis . . . undis,* something quite new ; see note on *que,* l. 1.——**rotīs,** abl. plur. of *rota, -ae,* f., 1st ; abl. of the instrument. *Rotae,* though only parts of a chariot, by *synecdoche* stands for the whole. A. & G. 386 ; B. no definite reference ; G. 695 ; H. 637, IV. Observe what a light, smooth sound this line has, admirably suiting the subject ; there are no harsh syllables, and liquids and sibilants abound.——**summās,** acc. plur. f. of *summus, -a, -um ;* used partitively, quali- fying *undas.*——**levibus,** abl. plur. f. of adj. *levis, -e,* 3d ; qualifies *rotis.* The adj. is appropriate, because the car does not sink. Distinguish *lēvis* = *light,* from *lĕvis* = *smooth.* ——**perlābitur,** 3d pers. sing. pres. ind. of the dep. verb *perlābor, perlābī, perlapsus sum,* 3 (*per,* = *through,* + *labor,* = *I glide*) ; joined by *atque* to *temperat,* and agreeing with the same subject, i.e. the noun (*Neptunus*) or pronoun intensified by *ipse,* l. 145. ——**undās,** acc. plur. of *unda, -ae,* f., 1st ; direct obj. of *perlabitur.*

Like as when amid	Ắc velu,tí mag,no ín popu,ló „ cum , sáepe	148
a thronging popu-	And as great in a people when often	
lace strife, as is wont,		
has arisen, and the	co,órta est Séditi,ó, sae,vítque an,imís „	149
base mob rage angrily	has arisen civil strife, and rages in their minds	
at heart, and now	ig,nóbile , vúlgus, Iámque fa,cés et , sáxa	150
the brands and stones	low born the mob and already torches and stones	

LINE 148. **Ắc**, conj.; often used before comparisons, to mark their connection with
what has preceded. —— **velutí**, comparative adv., an older form of *velut* (*vel,=or,+ut,
=as*); introducing the simile which runs on to the end of l. 153. *Velut* is often con-
joined to *si, velut si* or *velutsi;* cf. *acsi* (*ac+si*)*; ceu,=as if,* also introduces similes.
When used as a comparative conj., *velut* (like *tamquam, quasi, acsi, velut,* etc.) takes
the pres. or perf. subjunct., unless the imperf. or pluperf. are needed by the rule govern-
ing the sequence of tenses. A. & G. 312; B. 307; G. 602; H. 311, 2. As the following
comparison is a simile and not a conditional comparative clause, the tenses of the indica-
tive are employed. —— **magnō**, abl. sing. m. of *magnus, -a, -um;* agrees,with *populo.*
A large, *frequens,* or dense throng, such as the streets of Rome presented in later-republi-
can and empire days, is before Vergil's eyes. —— **in**, prep., governing the abl. *populo.*
For position, see note on *cum,* l. 47.—— **populō**, abl. sing. of *populus, -ī,* m., 2d obj.
of the prep. *in.* —— **cum**, temporal conj., followed by the perf. ind. *coorta est.* For full
note and references on the use of *cum,* see note on *cum,* l. 36. —— **saepe**, adv. of time,
=an adverbial phrase *id quod saepe accidit, as frequently occurs,* and is an extension of
coorta est. The comparative of *saepe* is *saepius,* the superl. *saepissime.* —— **coōrta est,**
3d pers. sing. perf. ind. of the dep. verb *coörior, coorīrī, coōrtus, sum,* 3, irreg.; the
coorta agrees with *sedito* as a participle, and *coorta est* with the same for its subject; cf.
usa est, l. 64.

LINE 149. **Sēditiō**, gen. *sēditiōnis,* f., 3d; nom. sing., subj. of *coorta est.* This com-
parison of divine actions with human is a clever way of flattering the *one man* (*gravis
pietate,* l. 151), i.e. Augustus, the emperor. *Seditio* is the usual word for civil strife;
scenes of riot were only too common in Rome from the time of the Gracchi to the
empire under Augustus; with such men as Marius, Sulla, Catiline, Clodius, Milo, etc.,
before his memory, Vergil might have tinged the whole simile with the red hue of blood.
—— **saevit**, 3d pers. sing. pres. ind. act. of *saeviō, -īre, saeviī, saevītum,* 4 (*saevus*)*;*
agrees with the subj. *vulgus.*—— **que**, enclitic conj., joining the sentence *saevit . . .
vulgus* to the preceding one.—— **animīs**, abl. plur. of *animus, -ī,* m., 2d; idiomatic
abl. of 'place where.' A. & G. 254, *a*; B. 228; G. 389; H. 425, II, 1, 2). It is a sort
of plural locative (sing. *animo) ; animis* is plural because *vulgus* is *collective.* The real
loc. sing. is *animī,* cf. *domi.* —— **ignōbile**, nom. sing. n., of the adj. *ignōbilis, -e,* 3d
(*in,=not,+* (*g*)*nobilis,=known) ;* agrees with *vulgus.* —— **vulgus** (some prefer *volgus*),
gen. *vulgī,* n. (m. rarely), 2d; nom. sing., subj. of *saevit.* Educated Greeks and Romans
despised the mob as 'the dregs of the people'; cf. Horace, Odes III, I, 1, *Odi pro-
fanum vulgus et arceo.* For *vulgus* as an exception in gender, cf. *pelagi,* l. 138, and
note.

LINE 150. **Iam**, adv. of time; cf. *iam,* l. 120. —— **que**, enclitic conj., joining this
sentence to the one immediately before it. —— **facēs**, nom. plur. of *fax, facis,* f., 3d (akin
to the Greek φαίνω, = *I shine);* subj. of *volant.* —— **et**, cop. conj. —— **sāxa**, nom.
plur. of *sāxum, -ī,* n., 2d; joined by *et* to *faces.* —— **volant**, 3d pers. plur. pres. ind. act.
of *volō, -āre, -āvī, -ātum,* 1; agrees with the subject *faces.* The pres. of vivid descrip-
tion with an idea (introduced by *saepe*) of universal application. —— **furor**, gen. *furōris,*

151 vo , lánt,	„	furor	,	árma	min , ístrat:	Túm	are flying (frenzy sup-
fly,		*fury*		*weapons*	*supplies :*	*then*	plies the arms) : then
pie , táte				gra , vem	ác	meri , tís „	if perchance they
by his noble character				*eminent*	*and*	*by his merits*	sight any man hon-
si	,	fórte			vi , rúm	quem	ored for his virtue
if		*by chance*			*man*	*any*	and good deeds,

m., 3d; nom. sing., subj. of *ministrat. Furor arma ministrat* is a parenthesis, explain-
ing the use of *faces* and *saxa.* —— **arma,** acc. plur. of *arma,* n., 2d (see *arma,* l. 1);
direct obj. of *ministrat.* By *arma* are meant *weapons,* such as sticks, torches for firing
houses, stones, etc. The word is used freely in poetry, and indeed this much-quoted
sentence would not pass in prose, for a concrete subj. would be required in place of the
abstract *furor.* —— **ministrat,** 3d pers. sing. pres. ind. act. of *ministrō, -āre, -āvī, -ātum,*
1 (from *minister, = an attendant*) ; agrees with the subject *furor.* Parentheses in Vergil
are sometimes introduced by a cop. conj., e.g. *nec* in *necdum,* l. 25, or a causal conj., e.g.
nam, or *enim ;* occasionally there is no conjunction (*asyndeton*), as in this instance.
    LINE 151. **Tum,** adv., usually of time, = *then,* but here marking succession of events,
= *then, next.* —— **pietāte,** abl. sing. of *pietās, -ātis,* f., 3d (*pius*); abl. of cause, if we
give *gravis* a passive sense, = *revered.* This abl. seems preferable and best suits *meritis*
(*because of his good deeds*). A. & G. 245; B. 219; G. 408; H. 416. Others call the abl.
an abl. of respect or specification; the phrase then = *a man of weight in respect of virtue
and noble deeds.* A. & G. 253; B. 226; G. 397; H. 424. Beware of rendering *pius* and
pietas as 'pious' and 'piety'; see the note on *pietate,* l. 10, for the proper signification.
Pietate and *meritis* are distinguished, and would in Greek be followed respectively by
μὲν and δέ, not in contrast but = *not only . . . but; pietate* is used of the character of the
man, and *meritis* of its manifestation in deeds. —— **gravem,** acc. sing. m. of *gravis, -e,*
adj., 3d; qualifies *virum. Gravis* is the opposite of *lĕvis:* of things, it = *heavy;* of
character, it = *weighty,* or *dignified,* in respect of thought, demeanor, etc. The most
eminent Romans exhibited this characteristic, and the famous 'Roman law' which has
survived the degenerate empire and the ability to keep the empire for centuries after the
enervating influence of luxury and vice set in, testify strongly to *gravitas* as an essen-
tially Roman virtue. Some see an allusion to Cicero, who suppressed Catiline's conspiracy;
but he also defended Milo, as violent a rioter as Clodius himself. —— **āc,** cop. conj. ——
meritīs, abl. sing. of *meritum, -ī,* n., 2d (see *meritis,* l. 74); abl. of cause; cf. *pietate*
above, with which *meritis* is coördinately connected by *ac.* —— **sī,** conditional conj.,
governing *conspexere.* The *apodosis* or main sentence (*silent, ff.*) is put in the form of a
pure fact and is therefore in the ind. mood; consequently the *hypothetical* clause (*si . . .
conspexere*) has its verb also in the indicative. For conditional sentences, refer to the
note on *si,* l. 18, and consult the references given there. It should, however, be observed
that *si* adds a notion of *time* to the condition in this instance, and practically = *if (by
chance) and as soon as,* etc. —— **forte,** abl. sing. of *fors,* f., 3d, a noun with only these
two cases (*diptotes*); abl. of manner, used as an adverb, modifying *conspexere.* A. & G.
77, 3; B. 57, 2, *a*; G. 70, B (though not included); H. 134. As a personified noun,
Fors (Chance) is declined completely in the singular. *Forte* differs in use, though not in
extraction, from *forsan* and *fortasse; forte = by chance;* e.g. *forte accidit ut,* etc.; *forsan*
and *fortasse = perhaps,* e.g. Vergil, *forsan et haec olim meminisse iuvabit;* but *fors* or
fors sit with *ut* and the subjunct. approach the meaning of *forsan,* as also does the com-
bination *nisi forte, = unless perchance.* —— **virum,** acc. sing. of *vir, -ī,* m., 2d; direct
obj. of *conspexere.* —— **quem,** acc. sing. m. of the indef. pron., m. and f. *quis,* n. *quid;*
used adjectively to qualify *virum.* The indef. *quis* is rarely used except in combination

they are silent and stand fast with inclined ear; he with his words directs their minds and soothes their hearts: in such fashion is hushed the crash of the waters, so soon as	Cónspex,ére, si,lént „ ar,réctis,que aúribus , 152 *they have seen they are silent and up-pricked with ears* ádstant ; Ílle re,gít dic,tís ani,mós, „ et , 153 *stand by; he guides with words their minds, and* péctora , múlcet´: Síc cun,ctús pela,gí „ 154 *their breasts soothes : So all of the sea* ceci,dít fragor,, áequora, póstquam Próspici,éns 155 *fell (quiet) the din, the sea after looking forth*

with *si* or *ne*, e.g. *si* and *ne*, or in the compounds *aliquis, quisquam*. A. & G. 105, *d*;
B. 91, 5; G. 107, 1, REM.; H. 190.

LINE 152. **Conspēxēre**, 3d pers. plur. perf. ind. act. of *conspiciō, -ĕre, conspēxī, conspectum*, 3; agrees with a plural pron. *ii* or *illi*, understood from the collective noun *vulgus*, l. 149. The perfect tense is here because logically the *seeing* of the dignified man is prior to the *silence* of the mob; at the same time, the perfect expresses instantaneous action. —— **silent**, 3d pers. plur. pres. ind. act. of *sileō, -ĕre, siluī*, no supine, 2; vivid present, agreeing with an understood pronoun, *ii*. The juxtaposition of *conspexere* and *silent* is for effect. The *apodosis* begins with *silent*. —— **arrēctīs**, abl. plur. f. of *arrectus,-a, -um*, perf. part. pass. of *arrigo, -ere, arrēxī, arrēctum*, 3 (*ad* + *rego*); agrees adjectively with *auribus*. Some call *arrectis auribus* an abl. absolute. *Erectus* is more common in this phrase, but the prep. *ad* (in the composition) gives an idea of direction, viz. that the mob waits listening upon the *vir gravis;* cf. *adstant* below. —— **que**, enclitic conj. —— **auribus**, abl. plur. of *auris, -is*, f., 3d; abl. of manner. —— **adstant**, 3d pers. plur. pres. ind. act. of *adsto (asto), -are, adstiti, adstitum*, 1 (*ad* + *sto*); joined by *que* to *silent*, and in agreement with the same subject. All compounds of *sto* which have a perfect act. make it in *-stiti*, e.g. *ob-stiti*, except *antesto*, perf. *antesteti*, and *circumsto*, perf. *circumsteti*.

LINE 153. **Ille**, nom. sing. m. of the demonstr. pron. *ille, illa, illud;* refers to *virum* above, and is subj. of *regit*. *Ille* is emphatic. —— **regit**, 3d pers. sing. pres. ind. act. of *regō, -ere, rēxī, rēctum*, 3; agrees with subj. *ille*. —— **dictīs**, abl. plur. of *dictum, -ī*, n., 2d; abl. of the instrument. —— **animōs**, acc. plur. of *animus, -ī*, m., 2d; direct obj. of *regit*. For the distinction between *animus* and *meus*, see *animis*, l. 11. —— **et**, cop. conj. —— **pectora**, acc. plur. of *pectus, pectoris*, n., 3d; direct obj. of *mulcet*. *Pectus* is a poetical synonym of *animus*. —— **mulcet**, 3d pers. sing. pres. ind. act. of *mulceō, -ēre, mulsī, mulsum* or *mulctum*, 2; joined by *et* to *regit*, and in agreement with the subj. *ille*.

LINE 154. **Sīc**, adv. of manner. —— **cūnctus**, nom. sing. m. of *cūnctus, -a, -um;* agrees with *fragor*. The plural *cuncti, -ae, -a*, is more common. Synonyms: *cuncti,* = *all*, i.e. together and in one mass (*coacervatim*, as Apuleius says); *omnes,* = *all*, whether in different places or not; *universi,* = *all*, in respect of the same time or unanimity. —— **pelagī**, gen. sing. of *pelagus*, n., 2d (see *pelagi*, l. 138); subjunctive gen., limiting *fragor*. A. & G. 213, 1; B. 199; G. 363, 1; H. 396, II. —— **cecidit**, 3d pers. sing. perf. ind. act. of *cadō, -ĕre, cĕcĭdi, cāsum*, 3, intrans. (mostly used in compounds, e.g. *occido*); agrees with the subj. *fragor*. Distinguish this verb from *caedo, -ĕre, cecīdi, caesum*, 3, = *I kill*. —— **fragor**, gen. *fragōris*, m., 3d (from root FRAG in *frango*, = *I break*, hence a *crash* of breaking); nom. sing., subj. of *cecidit*. —— **aequora**, acc. plur. of *aequor, -is*, n., 3d; gov. by *prospiciens*. —— **postquam**, temporal adv. and conj.; followed by *flectit*. It is often separated, as *post . . . quam*. It takes the ind. as a rule, but see note on *ubi*, l. 81, and references.

LINE 155. **Prōspiciēns**, gen. *prōspiciĕntis;* nom. sing. m. of the pres. part. act. of *prōspiciō, -ere, prōspēxī, prōspectum*, 3; enlarging the subj. *genitor*. —— **genitor**, gen.

geni‚tór	„	coe‚lóque	in‚véctus	the Sire looks o'er
little father		*and through the sky*	*riding*	the deep and turns
156 a‚pérto	**Fléctit**	e‚quós	cur‚rúque	his steeds, riding
open	*turns*	*his horses*	*and to his chariot*	under a cloudless
				sky, and gives rein
vo‚láns	„	dat	‚ lóra	se‚cúndo.	as he hastes to
while flying	„	*gives*	*the reins*	*speedy.*	his speeding car.

---

genitōris, m., 3d (from *geno*, old form of *gigno*, = *I beget;* the same root γεν in Greek,
cf. ἐγέν-ομην, 2d aor. of γίγνομαι); nom. sing., subj. of *flectit.* An honorable title of
Neptune. —— **coelō**, abl. sing. of *coelum, -ī*, n., 2d; abl. abs. with *aperto*, i.e. *the sky
being cloudless;* it may be rendered freely *under a cloudless sky.* Some call *coelo* an abl.
of 'place where' or 'in which,' for which see references under *mente*, l. 26; but as Nep-
tune is riding on the waves under or through the sky, such an abl. would be even too
loose for poetry, and besides the locative abl. is used of states of rest not of motion. The
participle of *esse* (wanting) is understood as the *copula* or link between the noun *coelo*
and the predicate adj. *aperto.* For a complete explanation of this construction and
grammatical references, refer to the note on *laxis.* l. 122. —— **que**, enclitic conj. ——
invēctus, nom. sing. m. of the perf. part. pass. of *invehō, -ere, invēxī, invēctum*, 3 (*in*
+ *veho*); joined by *que* to *prospiciens*, and agrees with *genitor.* The passive of *veho*
and compounds (and several other trans. verbs) is used as if it were an intrans. depo-
nent; e.g. *veho*, = *I carry; vehor*, = *I ride.* —— **apertō**, abl. sing. n. of *apertus, -a,
-um*, perf. part. pass. of *aperiō, -īre, aperuī, apertum*, 4; part. used attributively, i.e. as
an adj., in agreement with *coelo* in the abl. abs. construction. Participles may be :
(1) attributive, i.e. purely adjectival, e.g. *apertus*, = *open ;* (2) verbal, e.g. *apertus*, =
opened, having been opened.
     LINE 156.   **Flectit**, 3d pers. sing. pres. ind. act. of *flectō, -ere, flēxī, flēxum*, 3;
agrees with the subj. *genitor* in the subordinate temporal clause introduced by *postquam.*
The pluperf. tense is naturally expected, especially as this clause is prior in time to the
principal sentence, and the verb in the principal sentence is itself past (viz. *cecidit*, the
aorist or perfect indefinite).   It is explained as a vivid present, used somewhat freely
here but common in picturesque description; see the note on *tendit*, l. 18, and cf. most
of the verbs between this and l. 83. —— **equōs**, acc. plur. of *equus, -ī*, m., 2d; direct
obj. of *flectit.* *Equus* has a corresponding feminine, *equa, -ae*, f., 1st, = *a mare*, with
dat. and abl. *equabus* to distinguish them from *equis*, usually dat. and abl. of *equus ;* cf.
deus, deis, and *dea, deabus.* —— **currū**, for *currui ;* an old dat. of *currus, -ūs*, m., 4th;
dat. of the indirect obj., dependent on *dat.* This old dat. of m. nouns in *u* is common
in Vergil. —— **que**, conj. —— **volāns**, gen. *volāntis ;* nom. sing. m. of the pres. part.
act. of *volō, -āre, -ārī, -ātum*, 1; agrees with and enlarges the subj., viz. a pronoun
referring to *genitor.* —— **dat**, 3d pers. sing. pres. ind. act. of *dō, dare, dedī, datum*, 1;
joined by *que* to *flectit*, and agreeing with the same subj. or a pron. recalling it. *Dare
lora*, = *to give rein to ;* cf. l. 63, *laxas sciret dare habenas.* The phrase is figurative, for
equis rather than *curru* should be the object. *To slacken the reins* is *lora remittere.*
—— **lōra**, acc. plur. of *lōrum, -ī*, n., 2d; direct obj. of dat. The sing. *lorum*, = (1) *a
thong*, (2) *a leash*, for dogs; the plur., = *reins.* There are one or two other rare mean-
ings. —— **secundō**, dat. sing. m. of the adj. *secundus, -a, -um* (from *sequor*, = *I follow*) ;
agrees with *curru.* *Secundus* = (1) lit. *following;* (2) *second;* (3) *favorable*, or *pros-
perous*, of fortune or the elements, e.g. *ventus secundus*, = a *following*, and so a *favor-
able* wind; and *res secundae*, = *prosperity*, lit. *prosperous things*, as opposed to *res adver-
sae*, = adversity. *Secundus* is really a *participial* form of *sequor* (root *sec*); a similar

The weary followers	Défes, sī	Aénea, dǽ	„	quae	, próxima , 15i
of Aeneas hasten	*Worn out*	*the Aeneadae*		*which*	*(are) nearest*
hurriedly to win	lítora	, cúrsu	Cónten, dúnt	pete, re,	ét 158
the nearest shores,	*the shores*	*in their course*	*hasten*	*to gain,*	*and*
and turn to the	Li, byǽ	„	ver, túntur	ad	, óras.
coasts of Libya.	*of Libya*		*are turned*	*to*	*the shores.*

termination is -*bundus*, e.g. *vitabundus*, from *vito*, 1. Such adjectives are usually active in meaning, and sometimes keep enough of their verbal character to govern an obj.; e.g. *vitabundus castra*, = *avoiding the camp*. A. & G. 164, *p*, and 237, *f*; B. 150, 1; G. 330, NOTE 4; H. 330, 1.

LINE 157. **Dēfessī**, nom. plur. m. of *dēfessus, -a, -um*, perf. part. pass. of *dēfetiscor, -ī, defessus sum*, dep. 3; attributive part., qualifying *Aeneadae*. —— **Aeneadǽ**, nom. plur. of the 1st decl. Greek patronymic noun *Aeneadēs*, = *son of Aeneas*, m.; subj. of *contendunt*. For decl. of *Aeneades*, consult A. & G. 37; B. 21, 2, *d*, and like 22, Cometes; G. 65, FIRST DECLENSION; H. 50, like Pyrites. Like *Aeneadae* are declined *Dardanidae, Hyperidae*, etc. Aeneas, as the leader of the remnant of the Trojans, is like a tribal father (cf. children of Israel, Abraham, etc.); as regards actual relationship, the Trojans were not his descendants. —— **quae**, nom. plur. n. of the rel. *quī, quae, quod;* agreeing with *litora* which is attracted as subj. into the rel. clause. The full phrase would be *contendunt petere litora, quae litora proxima (sunt)*. For the attraction of the antecedent object into the rel. clause, refer to the note on *Deiopeia*, l. 72. Some editors, however, transfer the comma after *litora*, and place it after *proxima*. In this case, *litora* is the acc. obj. of *petere*, and the regular antecedent of *quae* (in poetical disregard of the natural order, *litora, quae proxima*); *quae* then agrees with *litora* and is subj. of *sunt* understood. —— **prōxima** (others *prōxuma*, a variant spelling), nom. plur. n. of *prōximus, -a, -um;* agrees with *litora*, and is complement of *sunt* understood in the predicate. *Proximus* is the superl. formed from the prep. *prope*, = *near;* no positive; comparative, *propior;* cf. *summus* from *supra*, and *imus* from *infra* (though these have a rare positive), and see the note on *imis*, l. 84. For the omission of the *copula sunt*, which often happens when it would be ind. or inf., consult A. & G. 206, *c*, 2; B. 166, 3; G. 209; H. 368, 3. —— **litora**, nom. plur. of *lītus, lĭtoris*, n., 3d; the phrase *quae litora* is subj. of *sunt* understood. See *quae* above for (1) attraction, (2) variant punctuation and consequent variant construction. —— **cursū**, abl. sing. of *cursūs, -ūs*, m., 4th (from *curro*, = *I run*); abl. of manner, used adverbially. *Cursu* = lit. *with running*, hence *speedily*.

LINE 158. **Contendumt**, 3d pers. plur. pres. ind. act. of *contendō, -ere, contendī, contentum* (*con*,+*tendo*, = *I stretch*, hence of effort, *I strive*); agrees with the subj. *Aeneadae*. From the notion of *striving* are derived two other meanings: (1) *I demand persistently;* (2) *I hasten*, as here. —— **petere**, pres. inf. act. of *petō, -ĕre, petīvī*, or *petiī, petītum*, 3 (root PET, as in Greek πέτομαι, = *I fly*, hence *I fly towards, seek*); prolative inf. after *contendunt;* see note on *occumbere*, l. 97. The obj. of *petere* (with the punctuation in the text) is *litora* understood, *litora* being included by attraction in the rel. clause; see *quae* above. —— **et**, cop. conj. —— **Libyae**, gen. sing. of *Libya*, f., 1st; poss. gen., limiting *oras;* see *Libyae*, l. 22. —— **vertuntur**, 3d pers. plur. pres. ind. pass. of *vertō, -ere, vertī, versum*, 3; joined by *que* to *contendunt*. *Vertor* = the intrans. act. '*I turn*,' and is used reflexively; it is a survival of a middle voice, which is regular with Greek verbs, e.g. τύπτω, = *I strike*, act.; τύπτομαι, = *I strike myself* (*myself* obj.), or *I get* (*some one*) *to strike*, middle; τύπτομαι, = *I am struck*, pass. Verbs like *vertor* may be

159 **Ést** in , séces,sú „ lon,gó locus: , ínsula ,
(*There*) *is* *in* *recess* *long* *a place:* *an island*

160 pórtum **Éfficit** , óbiec,tú late,rúm, „ quibus,
a harbour *makes* *by the jutting* *of its sides,* *by which*

161 ómnis ab , álto **Frángitur** , ínque si,nús „
every *from* *the deep* *is broken* *and into* *curves*

In far retreat there is a spot: an island forms a harbor by its jutting sides, whereon every wave from the deep breaks and divides

---

included in the same class as regular deponents. A. & G. 111, *b*; B. no definite reference; G. 218; H. 465.——**ad**, prep. with the acc.; gov. *oras.*——**ōrās**, acc. plur. of *ōra, -ae*, f., 1st; obj. of *ad.*

LINE 159. **Est**, 3d pers. sing. pres. ind. act. of *sum, esse, fuī;* agrees with the subj. *locus.* The following picture is probably imaginary, with details perhaps suggested by actual places in southern Spain or north Africa. Homer has a description of a harbor not unlike this in Vergil. Some editors pick out definite places, e.g. one says that the harbor of Carthagena in Spain is Vergil's model.——**in**, prep., governing *secessu.*—— **sēcessū**, abl. sing. of *sēcessus, -ūs*, m., 4th (from *secedo (se + cedo) = I retire*); obj. of *in.*——**longō**, abl. sing. of *longus, -a, -um;* qualifies *secessu. Longus* here *= longinquus*, i.e. *distant.*——**locus**, gen. *locī*, m., 2d ; nom. sing., subj. of *est. Locus*, m. in the sing. has two plural forms, (1) *loci*, m., 2d, *= topics*, (2) *loca*, n., 2d, *= places ;* cf. *loca*, l. 51.——**īnsula**, *-ae*, f., 1st ; nom. sing., subj. of *efficit.* The change of subject is a little abrupt, but *est . . . locus* is really introductory, the sense being 'in a spot far remote an island makes a harbor,' etc. —— **portum**, acc. sing. of *portus, -ūs*, m., 4th ; direct obj. of *efficit. Portus* may have either the old dat. and abl. plur. *portubus*, or the ordinary later *portibus ;* cf. for *portubus, artus, tribus, veru, partus,* and dissyllables in *-cus*, e.g. *arcus = a bow.* A. & G. 70, *d* ; B. 49, 3 ; G. 61, REM. 1; H. 117, 1.

LINE 160. **Efficit**, 3d pers. sing. pres. ind. act. of *efficiō, -ěre, effēcī, effectum*, 3 (*ex, out*, marks completion, *+ facio*); agrees with the subj. *insula.*——**ōbiectū**, abl. sing. of *ōbiectus, -ūs*, m., 4th (*obicio, = I throw in the way of*) ; abl. of the means or instrument.——**laterum**, gen. plur. of *latus, -eris*, n., 3d ; poss. gen., limiting *obiectu.* The meaning is that an island lying across the mouth of a bay acted as a barrier against the violence of the sea, forming a harbor entered by passages between the island and the mainland on either side the bay.——**quibus**, abl. plur. n. of the rel. *quī;* abl. of the instrument ; agrees with *laterum* in gender and number.——**omnis**, nom. sing. f. of *omnis, -e ;* agrees with *unda.* This adj. is rather more distant from the noun it qualifies than is usual even in poetry. The order is: *Quibus omnis unda ab alto frangitur scinditque sese in reductos sinus.*——**ab**, prep. with the abl.; gov. *alto*, marking 'place whence.' See note on *ab*, l. 1.——**altō**, abl. sing. of *altum, -ī*, n., 2d ; abl. governed by *ab.*

LINE 161. **Frangitur**, 3d pers. sing. pres. ind. pass. of *frangō, -ere, frēgī, fractum*, 3 ; agrees with the subj. *unda* in the rel. clause.——**in**, prep. with the acc. and abl.; gov. the acc. *sinus.* A. & G. 153; B. 143 ; G. 418, 1; H. 435, 1.——**que**, enclitic conj.——**sinūs**, acc. plur. of *sinus, -ūs*, m., 4th; obj. of *in. Sinus =* lit. *a fold*, or *curve*, as in the toga of the Romans. Derived meanings: (1) *bosom*, hence (2) *protection ;* (3) *a bay* or *inlet.* Commentators differ as to the meaning here: (1) some translate "(the wave) divides 'itself into retiring curves," i.e. the sinuous curves of the wave as it breaks on the island and recedes in ripples ; *reductos* is then lit. *= ' brought back,'* i.e. *retiring;* (2) others render "*into retired inlets* or *creeks ;*" *reductos* then has the figurative but common meaning *withdrawn*, i.e. *remote ;* (3) Mr. Page renders "and divides itself into the shore's retreating curves." As each of these three methods has much in its

towards hidden creeks. On this side and on that vast cliffs and twin crags tower threatening to heaven, beneath whose height the sheltered waters far and wide spread silent ; and

scin,dít se,se únda re,dúctos.   **Hínc**   at,que 162
parts   itself   wave   receding.   On this side   and

hínc   vas,tǽ ru,pés „ gemi,níque mi,nántur
on that side   vast   rocks   and twin   rise threatening

Ín coe,lúm scopu,lí, „ quo,rúm sub , vértice , 163
to   the sky   cliffs   of which   under   the summit

láte   **Aéquora** , túta si,lént: „ tum , 164
far and wide   the sea-waters   safe   are silent: then

favor, the reader is left to make his choice. —— **scindit**, 3d pers. sing. pres. ind. act. of *scindō, -ere, scĭdī, scissum*, 3 (akin to the Greek σχίζω = *I cleave*) ; joined by *que* to *frangitur*, and agrees with subj. *unda*. —— **sēsē**, acc. sing. of the reflexive pron. *sē* or *sēsē* (see *secum*, l. 37) ; direct obj. of *scindit*. —— **unda**, gen. *undae*, f., 1st ; nom. sing. subj. of *scindit*. —— **reductōs**, acc. plur. m. of *reductus, -a, -um*, perf. part. pass. of *re-dūcō, -ere, redūxī, reductum*, 3 (*re*, = back, + *duco*, = *I lead*) ; agrees with *sinus*. For the meaning, see note on *sinus* above.

LINE 162. **Hīnc**, adv. of place, correlative of *hīnc* below, = *on this side . . . on that*. *Hinc* generally denotes separation in time and place, = *after this*, and *hence* ; also of origin, *hence*. —— **atque**, conj.; joins *hinc* and *hinc*. —— **hīnc**, adv.; see above. —— **vāstae**, nom. plur. f. of *vāstus, -a, -um* ; qualifies *rupes*. —— **rūpēs**, nom. plur. of *rūpēs, -is*, f., 3d ; subj. of *minantur*. By *rupes* are meant the cliffs lining the sides of the bay. —— **geminī**, nom. plur. m. of *geminus, -a, -um* ; agrees with *scopuli*. *Gemini* = *twins*, or as an adj. *double* ; but here, as elsewhere, Vergil uses it as a synonym of *duo*, = *two* ; cf. Aen. II, 203, *gemini . . . angues*, = *two snakes*. —— **que**, conj. —— **minantur**, 3d pers. plur. pres. ind. of the dep. verb *minor, -ārī, minātus sum*, 1 (akin to *mineo*, = *I project*) ; agrees with the subjects *rupes* and *scopuli*. *Minor* in prose = *I threaten;* so we may translate *project threateningly*.

LINE 163. **In**, prep.; gov. *coelum*. —— **coelum**, acc. sing. of *coelum, -ī*, n., 2d; obj. of *in*. *In coelum* is an adverbial phrase, = *heavenwards*. —— **scopulī**, nom. plur. of *scopulus, -ī*, m., 2d ; joined by *que* to *rupes*. By *scopuli* are meant high buttresses of rock at the extremity of each line of *rupes* or cliffs. *Scopulus* = the Greek σκόπελος, i.e. *a watch-tower*, or a place from which one may take observations (σκοπεῖν, = *to see*). —— **quōrum**, gen. plur. m. of *quī, quae, quod*, the rel. pron.; agrees with its antecedent *scopuli*, and is a poss. gen. limiting *vertice*. —— **sub**, prep. with the acc. or abl.; gov. the abl. *vertice*, as marking a state of rest. A. & G. 153, 260; B. 143; G. 418; H. 435. —— **vertice**, abl. sing. of *vertex, verticis*, m., 3d ; obj. of *sub*. —— **lātē**, adv. (formed from *lātus, -a, -um*). For the formation of adverbs in *e* from 2d decl. adjectives, consult A. & G. 148, *a, b, c, d*; B. 76 ; G. 91–93 ; H. 304. In the above references, the formation of adverbs is completely treated, and should be thoroughly mastered.

LINE 164. **Aequora**, nom. plur. of *aequor, -is*, n , 3d ; subj. of *silent*. —— **tūta**, nom. plur. n. of *tūtus, -a, -um*, adj. (properly the perf. part. pass. of *tueor, tuērī, tuitus* or *tūtus sum*, dep. 3, = *I watch*, hence *protect*) ; qualifies *aequora*. Lucretius uses *tueor* in a passive sense, = *I am seen* or *appear*, and *tutus* is passive here = *guarded*, i.e. *screened*. *Tutus* usually = *safe ;* also very rarely = *cautious*. —— **silent**, 3d pers. plur. pres. ind. act of *sileō, -ēre, siluī*, no supine, 2 ; agrees with the subj. *aequora*. The *silence* or calmness of the water in the bay is due to the island which acts as a break-water. —— **tum**, adv. of time, here introducing a further point in the description of the natural surroundings ; *tum* has scarcely more force than a conj. —— **silvīs**, abl. plur. of

165 sílvis	scǽna	co,rúscis	Désuper	o'erhead hangs a
with woods	*a scene*	*waving*	*above*	background of

hórren,tíque	,, a,trúm	nemus	ímminet	shimmering forest
and awful	*black*	*a grove*	*overhangs*	and a grove black with its grim shade ;

166 úmbra ;	Frónte	sub	ádver,sá ,,	beneath the cliff's
with shade;	*the brow*	*under*	*opposite*	brow fronting them

silva, -ae, f., 1st ; a descriptive abl. enlarging *scaena.* A. & G. 251 ; B. 224 ; G. 400 ; II. 419, II. —— **scaena,** gen. *scaenae,* f., 1st (Greek σκηνή, = lit. *a booth,* i.e. a hut formed of osiers or the branches of trees ; originally it meant little more than a *shady spot,* from σκιά, = *shade*) ; nom. sing. subj. of *imminet. Scaena* is also used of the *stage* of a theatre ; but more commonly it = the painted *scene* or *background* of the stage (so σκηνή) ; we may render *background* here. The origin of this sense is that choral songs, with a little dialogue added, of a tragic or comic character (the forerunner of tragedy and comedy) were sung by travelling actors either in a shady place under the trees or in wagons in which the actor was protected from the sun by a canopy of branches. —— **coruscis,** abl. plur. of *coruscus, -a, -um* (from *corusco,* = lit. *I quiver, vibrate,* hence of the effect of tremulous motion, *I gleam ;* cf. *mico); qualifies silvis.*

LINE 165. **Dēsuper,** (*dē,* = *from,* + *super,* = *above*) adv., limiting *imminet. Desuper* = *above,* from the point of view of one who is above. —— **horrenti,** abl. sing. of *horens, -entis,* pres. part. act. of *horreō, -ēre,* no perf. or supine, 2 (for other tenses a collateral form *horresco, -ĕre, -horrui,* no supine, 3, is used) ; qualifies *umbra. Horrere* = lit. *to bristle,* hence some render *horrenti umbra,* as *bristling shade* (*bristling* referring to the density of the branches), i.e. the adj. *bristling,* properly an attribute of the *grove* (*nemus*), is poetically transferred to the *shade* in the grove. *Horridus,* the adj., commonly = *bristling.* If this be correct, *nemus horrenti umbra* is an instance of *hypallage,* i.e. the transference of the adj. from one noun to another closely connected with it ; cf. Aen. VIII, 526, for the stock Vergilian example, *Tyrrhenusque tubae clangor,* = *clangor Tyrrhenae tubae* (*the blast of the Tyrrhene trumpet*). A. & G. 385 ; B. no reference ; G. 693, HYPALLAGE ; H. 636, IV, 2. Others give to *horrenti* the derived sense (which *horridus* also may have) of '*terrible,*' '*awe-inspiring.*' —— **que,** enclitic conj. —— **ātrum,** nom. sing. n. of *āter, ātra, ātrum* (see *atris,* l. 60) ; qualifies *nemus.* The grove is *atrum,* because the sunlight could penetrate through. —— **nemus,** (Greek νέμος) nom. sing. of *nemus, nemoris,* n., 3d ; joined by *que* to *scaena.* Synonyms : *nemus,* = *a grove,* with clearings suitable for pasture (Greek verb νέμειν) ; *lucus,* = *a wooded glade,* esp. one sacred to a god, but Vergil often uses it as = to *silva ; silva,* = *a wood,* or *forest,* the generic word. —— **imminet,** 3d pers. sing. pres. ind. act. of *immineō -ēre,* no perf., no supine, 2 (*in,* = *upon,* i.e. *over,* + *mineo,* = *I project*) ; agrees with the subj. *nemus.* It happens sometimes, as here, that a verb may agree with one of several separate subjects, and be understood with each of the rest. A. & G. 205, *d* ; B. 255, 3 ; G. 285, EXCEPTION 1 ; H. 463, I. There is besides the explanation that the verb is singular because the two subjects represent one general notion, viz. woody highland. —— **umbrā,** abl. sing. of *umbra, -ae,* f., 1st ; abl. of manner, not an abl. of quality, like *silvis,* above ; i.e. *umbra* does not mean that ' a shady grove overhangs,' but ' a grove overhangs with its shade,' in such a way as to enshroud the front view in its black shade. It seems possible to consider *umbra* as an abl. of cause, after *atrum.*

LINE 166. **Fronte,** abl. sing. of *frons, -tis,* f., 3d ; governed by *sub. Fronte* = *the brow,* i.e. of the cliff, probably at the head of the recess. Distinguish *frons, frontis,* from *frons, frondis,* f., 3d, = *foliage. A fronte,* = *in the van,* opposed to *a tergo,* = *in the rear.* —— **sub,** prep.; gov. *fronte.* —— **adversā,** abl. sing. f. of *adversus, -a, -um ;*

is a cave of hanging | scopu‚lís pen‚déntibus ,   ántrum,   Íntus a‚quæ 167
rocks, within sweet | *with rocks   hanging   (there is) a cave within   waters*
waters and seats of | dul‚cés „ vi‚vóque se‚dília ,   sáxo,   Nýmpha‚rúm 168
living stone, a home | *sweet   and living   seats (made) by stone   of Nymphs*
of nymphs. Here no
cables confine the | domus. , Híc „ fes‚sás non , víncula , náves Ulla 169
weary ships, no | *the home.   Here   weary   not   bonds   the ships   any*
anchor moors them | te‚nént, un‚có „ non , álligat , áncora , mórsu.
with crooked bite. | *do hold   curved   not   fastens   an anchor   bite.*

agrees with *fronte*.   *Adversa*, = *opposite to* or *facing*, i.e. those who entered from the
sea into the bay. —— **scopulīs**, abl. plur. of *scopulus, -ī*, m., 2d (see *scopuli*, l. 163);
abl. of quality, often called the descriptive abl., here describing *antrum*.   For this abl.,
see note on *silvis*, l. 164. —— **pendentibus**, abl. plur. of *pendens, -entis*, pres. part. act.
of *pendeo, -ēre, pependi, pensum*, 2; qualifying *scopulis*. —— **antrum**, gen. *antrī*, n., 2d
(Greek ἄντρον); nom. sing., subj. of *est* understood.   A. & G. 206, *c*, 2; B. 166, 3; G.
209; H. 368, 3.
    LINE 167. **Intus** (akin to Greek ἐντός), adv. of place, limiting *sunt* understood.
—— **aquae**, nom. plur. of *aqua, -ae*, f., 1st; subj. of *sunt* understood. 'The waters'
are undoubtedly springs. —— **dulcēs**, nom. plur. f. of *dulcis, -e*, adj., 3d; qualifies *aquae*.
Dulcis (which some say is akin to γλυκύς) = lit. *sweet to the taste*, hence figuratively
dear.   Of water, it = *fresh;* cf. Georgic II, 243, *dulcesque a fontibus undae*. —— **vīvō**,
abl. sing. of *vīvus, -a, -um;* agrees with *saxo*.   *Vivus*, as an attribute of really inanimate
objects, = *living* in the sense of *natural*, i.e. not artificial. —— **que**, enclitic conj. ——
sedīlia, nom. plur. of *sedīle, -is*, n., 3d (from *sedeo*, = *I sit*, hence *a seat*); joined by *que*
to *aquae*. —— **sāxō**, abl. sing. of *saxum, -ī*, n., 2d; abl. of quality, describing *sedilia*.
    LINE 168. **Nymphārum**, gen. plur. of *nympha, -ae*, f., 1st (see note on *Nymphae*,
l. 71); poss. gen., limiting *domus*. —— **domus**, gen. *domūs*, .f., 4th (for peculiarities in
decl., see note on *domos*, l. 140); nom. sing., in apposition to *sedilia*, but in sense refer-
ring to the cave (*antrum*), for nymphs are very commonly associated with caves and
welling springs. —— **hīc**, adv. of place. —— **fessās**, acc. plur. f. of *fessus, -a, -um*, adj.
(connected with *fatiscor*, = *I grow weary*); qualifies *naves*. —— **nōn**, negative adv.,
limiting *ulla*.   *Non . . . ulla* is a negative combination, = *nulla* (cf. *non unquam*,
= *nunquam*), mostly poetic, but sometimes used in prose for emphasis, and often when
a co-ordinative conj. connects the sentence with a previous one, e.g. *neque unquam*
(for *et nunquam*); cf. Cicero, *Verres nihil unquam fecit* (=*quidquam nunquam*).
—— **vincula**, nom. plur. of *vinculum, -ī*, n., 2d (sometimes contracted to *vinclum;*
from *vincio*, = *I bind*); subj. of *tenent*.   *Vincula* = lit. *the binding things*, i.e. *cables* in
respect of ships; it usually = *fetters*. —— **nāvēs**, acc. plur. of *navis, -is*, f., 3d; direct
obj. of *tenent*.
    LINE 169. **Ulla**, nom. plur. n. of *ullus, -a, -um*, gen. *ullīus*, dat. *ullī*, otherwise reg-
ular; agrees with *vincula*.   *Ullus*, like *quisquam*, is mainly employed in negative sen-
tences, or in sentences of negative implication which may in form be either interrogative
or conditional; *ullus* = *any one at all*, very sweeping and emphatic; its negative is
nullus.   A. & G. 105, *h*; B. 66; G. 317; H. 457. —— **tenent**, 3d pers. plur. pres. ind.
act. of *teneō, -ēre, tenuī, tentum*, 2; agrees with the subj. *vincula*. —— **uncō**, abl. sing.
of *uncus, -a, -um*, adj. (from *uncus, -ī*, m., 2d, = *a hook;* Greek ὄγκος); qualifies *morsu*.
Uncus = *crooked*, or *curved*, sometimes of a bird's talons.   The two sentences, *hic . . .*
tenent, and *unco . . . morsu*, are not joined by any conj.   A. & G. 208, *b*; B. 346; G.
473, REM.; H. 636, I, 1. —— **nōn**, negative adv., restricting *alligat*.   *Ulla*, however,

170 Húc sep,*tem* Aéne,ás ,, col,léctis , návibus ,
  Hither   *seven*   *Aeneas* *having been gathered*   *ships*

171 ómni **Éx** nume,ró subit; ,, ác mag,nó tel,lúris
  all   *from the number* *enters;*   *and* *great* *of the land*

Hither Aeneas, mus-
tering seven ships of
all his fleet, runs for
shelter, and with
mighty yearning for

---

seems to be understood with *ancora*, and *non* perhaps might be taken with the verbs
tenent and *alligat*, though it is usual for the negative word to precede in such combina-
tions; but the sense is clear enough, though the grammatical construction is a little
involved. We may therefore render: *no cables hold* . . ., *no anchor fastens*, etc. ——
alligat, 3d pers. sing. pres. ind. act. of *alligō, -āre, -āvī, -ātum*, 1 (*ad, = to*, + *ligo, = I
bind*); agrees with the subj. *ancora*. —— **ancora**, gen. *ancorae*, f., 1st (Greek ἄγκυρα);
subj. of *alligat*. Homer never speaks of anchors being used, but of ἐυναί, large stones
for mooring vessels. Consequently Vergil's application of the anchor of his own age to
Homeric times is an instance of *anachronism*. Although Vergil is true to his subject as
regards life, custom, and the principal facts, yet he occasionally substitutes later Roman
ideas in describing matters of less importance; we shall have occasion to notice this
later on. —— **morsū**, abl. sing. of *morsus, -ūs*, m., 4th (from *mordeo, = I bite*); abl. of
the instrument. *Morsus*, = lit. *a bite*; it = *the fluke*, or biting part of an anchor, here.
    LINE 170. **Hūc**, adv. of direction, = lit. *to this place* (from *hic, haec, hoc*, demonstr.
pron.); limiting *subit*. As *hic* is locative, = *here, at this place*, and *huc* marks direction,
so *illic* and *istic* (from *ille* and *iste*) are locative, and *illuc* (*to that place*) and *istuc* (*to
that place of yours* or *which you mention*) point the limit of motion. —— **septem**,
numeral indecl. adj., qualifying *navibus*. The entire fleet was eventually saved, except
the ship of Orontes, which was sucked down by a whirlpool; cf. l. 117. Apart from the
vessel of Aeneas, the reader will remember that the other six owed their escape from
destruction to Cymothoë and Triton, l. 144, and to Neptune himself, l. 145; the former
saved three which ran on the rocks, l. 108, and the latter three which grounded on
sandbanks, ll. 111, 112; the rest were scattered, *disiectam . . . toto . . . aequare clas-
sem*, l. 128. —— **Aenēās**, nom. sing. (for decl., see *Aeneae*, l. 92); subj. of *subit*. ——
collectīs, abl. plur. f. of *collectus, -a, -um*, perf. part. pass. of *colligo, -ere, collēgī, col-
lectum*, 3 (*cum*, + *lego*); agrees with *navibus* in the abl. abs. construction. —— **navi-
bus**, abl. plur. of *navis, -is*, f., 3d; with *collectis*, as abl. abs. See note on *laeso*, l. 8.
—— **omnī**, abl. sing. m. of *omnis, -e*, adj., 3d; agrees with *numero*.
    LINE 171. **Ex**, prep. with the abl., *ex* before vowels or 'h,' *e* or *ex* before consonants;
gov. *numero*. Observe that *ex = from*, or *out of* the centre of a place; *a* or *ab = from*
the outside borders of some object or region; *de = from* a definite spot, often *down from*.
A. & G. 152, *b*; B. 142, 2; G. 417; H. 434. —— **numerō**, abl. sing. of *numerus, -ī*, m.,
2d (akin to Greek νέμειν, = *to apportion*, hence *that which is apportioned*); governed by
ex. —— **subit**, 3d pers. sing. ind. act. of *subeō, subīre, subiī, subitum*, irreg. (*sub = towards*,
+ *eo, = I go*); agrees with subj. *Aeneas*. In this compound, *sub* keeps its meaning as a
prep. with the acc., = *up to*, e.g. Horace, *quos aquae subeunt; subeo* may be used with
the acc. of the object. As a prep. with the abl., its meaning of *under* (of states of rest)
survives in composition, e.g. *substruo, = I build beneath*. —— **āc**, conj., introducing a
new and important feature; see note on *que*, l. 1. —— **magnō**, abl. sing. m. of *magnus,
-a, -um;* agrees with *amore*. —— **tellūris**, gen. sing. of *tellūs*, f., 3d (akin to *terra*);
objective gen., limiting *amore*. See note on *generis*, l. 132. — Synonyms: *tellus = the
earth*, mostly poetical, but found in Cicero; personified *Tellus* = the Greek goddess Γαῖα,
also known as Cybele, Ceres, etc.; *terra, = the earth*, as opposed to sky, and sea; *orbis
terrarum, = the world;* i.e. all the separate *terrae*, or regions of earth; *humus = the
surface earth, the ground*, e.g. *humi, = on the ground; mundus, = the universe.* ——

the land the Trojans	a, móre	Égres, si	ópta, tá	,,	poti, úntur	, 172
disembark and gain	love	having disembarked	longed for		possess	
the longed-for sand, and lay their brine-drenched limbs upon	Tróes	a, réna,	Ét	sale ,	táben, tés ar, tús	,, 173
	the Trojans	the sand,	and	with brine	soaking	their limbs
the beach. And	in ,	lítore ,	pónunt.	Ác	pri, múm	sili, cí ,, 174
forthwith Achates	on	the shore	lay.	And	first	from a flint

---

amōre, abl. sing. of *amor, amōris*, m., 3d (*amo*); abl. of manner, with *cum* omitted because of the presence of the adj. *magno* as an attribute. A. & G. 248; B. 220; G. 399; H. 419, III.—Synonyms: *amor*, = *love*, as a passion, no matter whether good or bad; it is the generic term; *caritas*, = *love*, *affection*, of that virtuous kind which one feels towards some one superior in admirable qualities. When personified, *Amor* = *Cupido*, the son of Venus, and the god of love.

LINE 172. **Egressī**, nom. plur. m. of *ēgressus, -a, -um*, perf. part. of the dep. verb *ēgredior, -ī, ēgressus sum*, 3 (*e + gradior*); agrees with *Troes*. The participle saves the necessity of two co-ordinate verbs, e.g. *egrediuntur et potiuntur*. See note and references on *Iactatos*, l. 29. —— **optātā**, abl. sing. of *optātus, -a, -um*, perf. part. pass. of *optō, -āre, -āvī, -ātum*, 1; agrees with *arena*, in place of a rel. clause, *quam optaverant*. —— **potiuntur**, 3d pers. plur. pres. ind. of the dep. verb *potior, potīri, potītus sum*, 4 (from *potis*, = *powerful*, hence *to become powerful over*); agrees with the subj. *Troes*. —— **Trões**, gen. *Trōum*, m. plur. nom. 3d (see *Trōas*, l. 30); subj. of *potiuntur*. The final syllable is short, because the word is a Greek one. —— **arēnā**, abl. sing. of *arēna, -ae*, f., 1st; direct obj. of *potiuntur*. A few verbs have their objects in the abl. case, viz. *potior, fungor, fruor, utor, dignor, supersedeo*, and *vescor*. A. & G. 249; B. 218, 1; G. 407; H. 421, I.

LINE 173. **Et**, conj. —— **sale**, abl. sing of *sāl, salis*, m., 3d (Greek ἅλς, gen. ἅλ-ος); abl. of the means. A. & G. 248, *c*; B. 218; G. 401; H. 420. —— **tābentēs**, acc. plur. m. of *tābens, -entis*, pres. part. act. of *tābeō, -ēre*, no perf., no supine, 2; qualifies *artus*. *Tcbentes* implies a more serious condition of discomfort than *madidos*, = *drenched*, for the noun *tabes* = *decay*. —— **artūs**, acc. plur. of *artus, -ūs*, m., 4th; direct obj. of *ponunt*. —— **in**, prep. governing the abl. *litore*. —— **lītore**, abl. sing. of *lītus, lītoris*, n., 3d; governed by *in*. —— **pōnunt**, 3d pers. plur. pres. ind. act. of *pōnō, -ere, posuī, positum*, 3; joined by *et* to *potiuntur* and in agreement with the same subj. *Troes*. *Pono* has several meanings: (1) *I place;* (2) commercially, *I put out at interest;* (3) *I lay aside*, like *depono;* (4) absolutely, of the winds, *to abate;* (5) *I put* or *suppose*, as an assumption; (6) *I appoint*, e.g. *pono leges*.

LINE 174. **Ac**, cop. conj., joining the sentence in which it stands (*ac Achates excudit*, etc.) to the preceding one (*Troes potiuntur*, etc.). —— **prīmum**, adv. of time; denoting the order of events (followed by *tum*, l. 177), and restricting *excudit*. *Primum* is the adverbial acc. sing. n. of the adj. *primus, -a, -um;* cf. *multum* = *much*, adv., from *multus*. Distinguish *primum* from *primo*, the adverbial abl. sing. n. of *primus; primum* usually = *in the first place* or *for the first time*, but may be used like *primo* of succession, = *firstly*, as here, with such words as *tum, tunc, deinde*, following. Discriminate carefully between *primum* and *primus* in such uses as: *primum fecit*, = *he did it for the first time*, or *at first; primus fecit*, = *he was the first to do it*. *Primum* is really a superlative abv. formed from the prep. *prae* — no positive; comparative, adj *prior*, adv. *prius;* superlative, adj. *primus*, adv. *primum*. —— **silicī**, dat. sing. of *silex, silicis*, m. (rarely f.), 3d; dat. instead of the abl. of separation, which (esp. of persons) may follow compounds *ab, ex, de*, and in some cases *ad*. *Silici* is governed then by *excudit*, = *struck* FROM *a*

¹⁷⁵ scin,tíll*am* ex,cúdit A,chátes Súsce,pítq*ue* ig,ném | struck a spark from a
   a spark   *struck*   *Achates*   *and caught* *the fire* | flint, and caught the
¹⁷⁶ foli,ís ,, at,q*ue* árida , círcum **N**útri,ménta de,dít ,, | fire with leaves, and
  with leaves and   *dry*   *around*   *fuel*   *supplied* | strewed   dry   fuel
                                    | around, and fanned
¹⁷⁷ rapu,ítq*ue* in , fómite , flámmam. T úm Cere,rém | the flame in the
  and hurried *in* *the tinder* *the flame.*   *Then*   *the corn* | tinder.   Then weary

---

flint. Some wrongly call *silici* an abl. of the instrument. For this dat., consult A. & G. 229, and *c*; B. 188, 2, *d*; G. 345, REM. 1; H. 385, 4, 2). —— **scintillam**, acc. sing. of *scintilla, -ae*, f., 1st; direct obj. of *excudit.* —— **excūdit**, 3d pers. sing. perf. ind. act. of *excŭdō, -ere, excŭdī, excūsum*, 3 (*ex = out*, + *cŭdō* (rare) = *I strike*)*;* agrees with the subj. *Achates.* —— **Achātēs**, gen. *Achătae* or *Achātī* (see *Achătae*, l. 120); nom. sing., subj. of *excudit.*

LINE 175. **Sus-cēpit**, 3d pers. sing. perf. ind. act. of *sus-cipiō, -ĕre, suscēpī, suscep-tum*, 3 (*sub* + *capiŏ*)*;* joined by the enclitic *que* to *excudit.* Most MSS. and several commentators read *succēpit*, an archaic form of *suscēpit*, but as there seems to be no adequate reason for an archaism here and the choice of readings is hard to determine, the ordinary prose form of the word is inserted in the text. The process of kindling a fire seems to be as follows : a flint is struck on some light dry bark or twigs, and the little flare is at once caught on other dry leaves, etc., and by the process of fanning more substantial pieces of wood (*nutrimenta, fomes*) are in time set ablaze. —— **que**, enclitic conj., joining *excudit* and *suscepit.* —— **īgnem**, acc. sing. of *īgnis, -is*, m., 3d; direct obj. of *suscepit.* —— **foliīs**, abl. plur. of *folium, -ī*, n., 2d (akin to Greek φύλλον); abl. of the means. —— **at-que**, cop. conj., joining to *suscepit* the new feature in the process, *dedit*, etc. —— **ārida**, acc. plur. n. of *āridus, -a, -um* (from *ārēre*, = *to be dry*)*;* qualifies *nutrimenta.* —— **circum**, adv., limiting *dedit.* As the best commentators are silent, it is unnecessary to regard *circum ... dedit* as = to *circumdedit* by *tmesis*, as the separation of two parts of a compound word is called. *Tmesis* is very common in Homer, occurs in Greek tragedy and comedy, but (though found in Horace) is rare in Latin ; Ennius supplies the stock example, *saxo cere - comminuit - brum*, = *cerebrum comminuit.* A. & G. 385; B. 367, 7; G. 726; H. 636, V, 3. In the weaker forms *prius ... quam, qui ... cumque, post ... quam*, however, it is quite common in Latin.

LINE 176. **Nūtrīmenta**, acc. plur. of *nūtrīmentum, -ī*, n., 2d (from *nutrio*, = *I nour-ish*)*;* direct obj. of *dedit.* —— **dedit**, 3d pers. sing. perf. ind. act. of *dŏ, dare, dedī, datum*, 1 ; joined by *atque* to *suscepit*, and in agreement with the same subject. —— **rapuit**, 3d pers. sing. perf. ind. act. of *rapiō, -ĕre, rapuī, raptum*, 3; joined by *que* to *dedit. Rapuit* here is by most translated *fanned*, i.e. = *raptim suscitavit;* Mr. Page considers this too far-fetched a meaning, and renders *quickly caught*, from the original meaning of *rapiō*, = *I seize* or *snatch.* —— **que**, enclitic conj. —— **in**, prep., governing the abl. *fomite.* —— **fōmite**, abl. sing. of *fōmes, fomitis*, m., 3d (probably for *fov-mes*, from *foveo*, = *I foster*)*;* governed by *in. Fomes* = lit. *the fostering thing*, in reference to fire, and may be applied to any inflammable material, especially *touchwood* or *dry twigs.* —— **flammam**, acc. sing. of *flamma, -ae*, f., 1st; direct obj. of *rapuit.*

LINE 177. **Tum**, adv., of succession ; see *primum*, l. 174 above. —— **Cererem**, acc. sing. of *Cerēs, Cereris*, f., 3d ; direct obj. of *expediunt. Cererem* = *frumentum* (*grain*), the name of the goddess standing by the figure *metonymy*, for that over which she exercised special care; similarly *Bacchus* is often used for *vinum, Mars* for *bello*, e.g. *aequo Marte*, etc. This figure embraces not only such instances as the above, but also **any** cases in which a word is used for another, e.g. *aurum* for *aureum vasum, laurea* for

of their lot they bring	cor, rúpt*am*	un, dís	„	Cere, ália, q*ue*		árma	
forth corn spoiled by	*spoilt*	*by the waves*		*and wheaten*		*the implements*	
the waves and imple-ments of Ceres, and	Éxpedi, únt,	fes, sí		re, rúm ;	„	fru, gésque	178
make ready to roast	*they get out*	*weary*		*of things ;*		*and the grain*	
the grain that was	re, céptas	Ét	tor, rére	pa, ránt	flam, mís	„ et ,	179
saved and to crush	*rescued*	*both*	*to roast*	*they prepare*	*with flames*	*and*	

victoriā, etc. A. & G. 386; neither B. nor G. refer to it; H. 637, III. Vergil elsewhere calls bread *Cereale solum.* As a goddess, Ceres was the daughter of Saturn and Ops, and the mother of Proserpine. She is '*the ripener*' of the fruits of the earth. —— **cor-ruptam**, acc. sing. f. of *corruptus, -a, -um*, perf. part. pass. of *corrumpō, -ere, corrūpī, corruptum*, 3 ; attributive part., qualifying *Cererem.* The corn had of course been *injured* by the salt water. —— **undīs**, abl. plur. of *unda, -ae*, f., 1st; abl. of the instrument, enlarging *corruptam.* —— **Cereālia**, acc. plur. n. of *Cereālis, -e*, adj., 3d (=*pertaining to Cerēs*); qualifies *arma.* This word survives in the English ' cereals.' —— **que**, enclitic conj. —— **arma**, acc. plur. of *arma, -ōrum*, n., 2d (no sing.) ; joined by *que* to *Cererem*, and an obj. of *expediunt. Arma* here has the special sense of *implements*, viz. : such things as the hand-mill, etc. Martial uses *arma* as = to a barber's scissors and razor, and Vergil employs it of a ship, = *the tackling* or *fittings.* For the usual sense, refer to l. 1.

LINE 178. **Expediunt**, 3d pers. plur. pres. ind. act. of *expediō, -īre, -īvī* or *-iī, -ītum*, 4 (*ex* = *out*, + *pēs*, = *the foot*, hence *to extricate*) ; agrees with a plural pron. as subj., referring to *Troes*, l. 172. *Expedio* = (1) *I disentangle ;* (2) *I fetch out*, or *I prepare*, as here ; (3) *I disclose*, of a speech; (4) with reflexive pron. and the abl. of the thing, e.g. *me cura expediam,* = *I will free myself from care ;* (5) with reflexive pron., = *I make ready*, e.g. *me expedio.* —— **fessī**, nom. plur. of *fessus, -a, -um ;* agrees with the understood subj. of *expediunt*, viz.: *iī* or *Troes.* —— **rērum**, gen. plur. of *rēs, reī*, f., 5th; objective gen. after *fessi. Fessi rerum* is an imitation of a Greek construction, the gen. becoming a complement as it were to adj. with which it is connected, on the analogy of the objective gen. following adjectives denoting fulness, power, knowledge, desire, etc. and their opposites; cf. Horace, *integer vitae scelerisque purus.* This gen. is often called the gen. of reference, and is frequently employed by Horace and other poets of the Augustan age. A. & G. 218, *c*; B. 204, 4; G. 374, esp. NOTE 6; H. 399, III, 1. In this phrase *rerum* has a bad sense, = *troubles ;* usually it is indefinite, = *things*, either as *res secundae*, = *prosperity*, or *res adversae*, = *adversity. Res* has so many meanings and applications that the reader should study it in a dictionary. —— **frūgēs**, acc. plur. of *frūgēs, frūgum*, f., 3d; direct obj. of *torrere. Fruges*, complete in the plural, is defective in the singular : it has no nom. or voc. sing., but it has acc. *frugem*, gen. *frugis*, dat. *frugi*, abl. *fruge ;* the nom. wanting would be *frux.* A. & G. 77, 5, *a*; B. 57, 6; G. 70, D ; H. 133, 3. —— **que**, enclitic conj., joining *parant* to *expediunt.* —— **receptās**, acc. plur. f. of *receptus, -a, -um*, perf. part. pass. of *recipiō, -ere, recēpī, receptum*, 3 (*re* = *back*, + *capio*) ; qualifies *fruges*, and = *recovered*, i.e. from the sea.

LINE 179. **Et**, conj., correlative of *et* below, = *both . . . and.* For *et . . . et*, see note on *et*, l. 3, and for other combinations, *que . . . et, et . . . que*, and *que . . . que*, refer to the note on *et*, l. 63. —— **torrēre**, pres. inf. act. of *torreō, -ēre, torruī, tostum*, 2; *epexegetical* or *prolative* inf., after *parant.* A. & G. 271; B. 326 ; G. 423; H. 533. The corn would require *roasting* before being ground (*frangere saxo*) after the soaking in the sea. —— **parant**, 3d pers. plur. pres. ind. act. of *parō, -āre, -āvī, -ātum*, 1; joined by *que* to *expediunt*, and in agreement with the same subject. *Paro* may be used with a direct obj., or with an explanatory inf., as above. —— **flammīs**, abl. plur. of *flamma, -ae*,

180 **frángere** , **sáxo.**   **Aéne, ás** scopu ,lum   „ | it with the stone.
to pound   *with a stone.*   *Aeneas*   *a rock* | Meantime   Aeneas
181 **íntere, á con, scéndit, et , ómnem Próspec, túm** | climbs the crag and
meanwhile   *climbs   and   entire*   *a view* | seeks a full wide view
la, té „ pela, gó petit, , Ánthea , sí quem | o'er the sea, if he may
far   *over the sea he seeks,   Antheus   if   any* | haply see Antheus

---

f., 1st; abl. of the means or instrument. —— et, cop. conj.; see *et* above. —— **frangere**, pres. inf. act. of *frangō, -ere, frēgī, fractum,* 3; *prolative* inf., like *torrere,* to which it is joined by *et.* The wealthy used hand-mills, but the poor farmers used the crushing-stone ; cf. Georgics, I, 267, *Nunc torrete igni fruges, nunc frangite saxo,* which proves that *roasting* was not an exception to the rule before the crushing. —— **sāxō,** abl. sing. of *sāxum, -ī,* n., 2d ; abl. of the instrument.

LINE 180. **Aenēās,** nom. sing., subj. of *conscendit.* —— **scopulum,** acc. sing. of *scopulus, -ī,* m., 2d (like Greek σκόπελος, = *a look-out spot*); direct obj. of *conscendit.* The *scopulus* referred to is one of the two *scopuli* (see l. 163) at the two extremities of the harbor. —— **intereā,** adv. of time. For derivation, etc., see the note on *intereā,* l. 124. —— **conscendit,** 3d pers. sing. pres. ind. act. of *conscendō, -ere, conscensī, conscensum,* 3 (*cum,* + *scando,* = *I climb*); agrees with the subj. *Aeneas.* The present is the vivid *historic.* —— et, cop. conj. —— **omnem,** acc. sing. m. of *omnis, -e* ; agrees with *prospectum.* For the distinction between *omnis* and *totus,* refer to the note on *toto,* l. 29. *Omnem prospectum* = *a complete view,* such as might be had from a high point only.

LINE 181. **Prōspectum,** acc. sing. of *prōspectus, -ūs,* m., 4th (derived from *prospicio*); direct obj. of *petit.* — NOTE. *Prospectum,* being a verbal noun, is qualified as a noun by *omnem,* and restricted in its verbal character by the adv. *late;* moreover its verbal origin permits it to govern an obj., *pelago.* *Omnem prospectum pelago* is not a case of *hypallage* (*a view over all the sea*), but rather = *a perfect view;* as *late* is an adv. describing the limits of the view over the sea, *omnem* would be redundant if it were a transference of case from *omni* (qualifying *pelago*). But understood as above (under *omnem*), it adds something new and to the point to the sentence. For *hypallage,* refer to the note on *horrenti,* l. 165. —— **lātē,** adv., modifying *prospectum.* See *late* and note, l. 21. —— **pelagō,** abl. of *pelagus, -ī,* n., 2d; abl. of 'place over which,' for which cf. *alta,* l. 126. For decl. and gender of *pelagus,* consult A. & G. 39, *b*; B. 26, 2; G. 34, EXCEPTIONS; H. 51, 7. Observe the *alliteration* in *prospectum pelago petit.* Synonyms : *pelagus* and *altum* = *the open sea ; mare,* = *sea,* as distinguished from *terra* = *land,* and *coelum* = *sky ; oceanus,* = *the sea,* or *the vast sea,* often particularly of the river encircling the earth; *aequor,* = *the sea,* as presenting a *level* (*aequus*) surface; *marmor* (often = *marble*) = *the sea,* as showing a *glistening* surface. —— **petit,** 3d pers. sing. pres. ind. act. of *petō, -ere, petivī* or *-iī, petitum,* 3; joined by *et* above to *conscendit,* and agreeing with *Aeneas.* —— **Anthea,** acc. sing. of *Antheus, -eī,* etc., m., Greek mixed decl. noun; direct obj. of *videat.* For the declension of *Antheus,* read carefully the note on *Achilli,* l. 30, and comparing *Orpheus* or *Achilleus* in the references given; also cf. *Oīli,* l. 41. Nothing is known of this Antheus. —— **sī,** conj., introducing conditions (= Greek εἰ); has the subjunct. *videat* (which see) dependent upon it. For the general laws on conditional sentences, see the note on *si,* l. 18; also refer to the note on *qua,* l. 18. —— **quem,** acc. sing. m. of the indef. pron. m. and f. *quis,* n. *quid;* used adjectively, in agreement with *Anthea.* Others, however, assert that *quem* is a pronoun, with the nouns *Anthea, Capyn,* etc., in apposition to it. Most

wind tossed and the	Iácta,túm	ven, tó	vide, át,	„	Phrygi, ásque	182
Phrygian barks, or	tossed	by the wind	he may see		and Phrygian	
haply Capys, or the						
arms of Caicus upon	bi,rémes, Aút Capyn, , aút cel,sís „ in , púppibus,					183
the ship's high stern.	the biremes, or	Capys,	or	high	on	the poops

commentators say *quem* is adverbial, i.e., = *if he can* ANYWHERE *see Antheus.* This is, perhaps, a little pedantic, for *quem* can quite easily be a colloquial use = *any (to see) if he can see some* (or *any*) *Antheus or Capys*, etc. This colloquial use has parallels in other languages.

LINE 182. **Iactātum**, acc. sing. m. of *iactātus, -a, -um*, perf. part. pass. of *iactō, -āre, -āvī, -ātum*, I (frequentative of *iaciō*) ; predicate part., agreeing with *Anthea.* —— **ventō**, abl. sing. of *ventus, -ī*, m., 2d; abl. of the instrument, describing *iactatum.* —— **videat**, 3d pers. sing. pres. subjunct. act. of *videō, -ēre, vīdī, vīsum*, 2; agrees with the subj. (a pron. referring to *Aeneas*) in the *si* clause. The subjunct. *si videat* virtually expresses a purpose, and like the Greek εἰ and the English *if* is used in a kind of indirect question introduced by some words understood, e.g. Aeneas scans the horizon (*to find out*) *if* or *whether he can see.* The subjunct. mood, necessary in indirect questions (see note on *impulerit*, l. 11), is thus clearly accounted for. In point of origin, Allen and Greenough say the *si* clause in cases like this is really a *protasis.* A. & G. 334, *f*; B. 300, 3, esp. *a*; G. 460, *b*; H. 529, 1, NOTE 1. This use of *si* is only after verbs of *wondering*, e.g. *miror*, and verbs of *trying*, e.g. *conor*, expressed or understood before *si ;* the usual particles introducing indirect questions being *utrum* and *num.* —— **Phrygiās**, acc. plur. f. of *Phrygius, -a, -um* (lit. pertaining to the *Phryges, -um*, m. plur., 3d; Greek Φρύγες) ; qualifying *biremes.* *Phrygias* = *Troicas* or *Troianas*, for Troy and the Troad were a part of Phrygia, which was a district of Asia Minor. —— **que**, enclitic conj.; the cop. conj. (not *aut*) is used because Antheus was in command of the *Phrygias biremes*, whereas Capys and Caicus were not. —— **birēmēs**, acc. plur. of *birēmis, -is*, f., 3d (*bis* or *bi*, adv. of *duo*, + *remus*, = *an oar*) ; joined (as an obj. of *videat*) to *Anthea* by the conj. *que.* *Biremis* is strictly an adj. = *having two oars*, and Livy applies it as such to *lembus*, = *a cutter.* But its chief meaning is *a vessel with two banks of oars ;* cf. *triremis* (*tres, tria*, + *remus*), = *a trireme*, i.e. *a vessel with three banks of oars.* *Navis*, at first expressed and modified by *biremis* or *triremis*, in time dropped out; hence the substantival origin. Biremes were unknown in the time of Homer, so this is another instance of *anachronism ;* cf. *ancora*, and note, l. 168.

LINE 183. **Aut**, disjunctive conj., at once connecting and opposing *Capyn* and *Anthea.* *Aut* is used when each alternative excludes the other (as *Capys* and *Antheus* do); *sive* offers a choice between two names of the same thing; *vel* and *ve* (probably old imperative of *volo*) give a choice between two alternatives. The principal correlatives are : *aut . . . aut, vel . . . vel, sive (seu) . . . sive (seu).* A. & G. 156, *c*; B. 342; G. 494; H. 554, II, 2. —— **Capyn**, acc. sing. of *Capys*, gen. *Capyos*, m , Greek 3d decl. noun; obj. of *videat*, connected with *Anthea* by *aut.* For declension, consult A. & G. 63, *g*; B. no reference; G. 66, NOTE 5; H. 68, 2. He was a follower of Aeneas, and founded Capua; he was one who wanted to destroy the wooden horse that proved Troy's ruin. —— **aut**, disjunctive conj., connecting *Capyn* and *arma.* —— **celsis**, abl. plur. f. of *celsus, -a, -um ;* qualifies *puppibus.* —— **in**, prep., governing the abl. *puppibus.* —— **puppibus**, abl. plur. of *puppis, -is*, f., 3d; obj. of the prep. *in.* *Puppibus* here = lit. *the stern*, i.e. is not, as commonly, = to *navis.* —— **arma**, acc. plur. of *arma, -ōrum*, n., 2d; direct obj. of *videat*, and joined by *aut* to *Capyn.* The phrase *celsis . . . Caici* is little more than a periphrasis for *Caicum*, coördinate with *Anthea* and *Capyn ;* but even so it lends brightness and picturesqueness to the scene. The

184 árma Ca, íci.   **Návem** in , cónspec,tú nul, lám, „
the arms of Caïcus.   *Ship*   *in*   *sight*   *no*

185 tres   , lítore , cérvos **Próspicit** , érran,tés ; „
three   *on the shore*   *stags*   *he sees*   *wandering;*

186 hos , tóta ar,ménta se,quúntur **Á** ter,go, ét
these   *whole*   *herds*   *follow*   *from behind and*

No ship in sight he sees, only three stags straying on the beach; these whole herds follow behind, and the trailing line

---

arma = shields, and perhaps some other weapons displayed at the stern, a fashion followed by the sea-faring Norsemen. —— **Caïcī**, gen. sing. of *Caïcus*, m., 2d; poss. gen., limiting *arma*. *Caicus* was a prominent follower of Aeneas, and apparently in command of a ship; he is mentioned again in Aen. IX, 35, in connection with the warfare between Aeneas and Turnus.

LINE 184. **Nāvem**, acc. sing. of *nāvis, -is,* f., 3d; direct obj. of *prospicit.* —— **in,** prep., governing the abl. *conspectu.* —— **conspectū**, abl. sing. of *conspectus, -ūs,* m., 4th (derived from *conspicio,* = *I view*) ; obj. of *in.* —— **nullam,** acc. sing. f. of *nullus, -a, -um* (*ne* + *ullus*), gen. *nullīus,* dat. *nullī,* otherwise regular; limits *navem. Nullius* and *nullo, -a, -o* serve as gen. and abl. of the defective neg. pron. *nemo,* = *no one.* —— **trēs,** acc. plur. m. of the numeral adj. *trēs, tria,* gen. *trium,* dat. and abl. *tribus;* agrees with *cervos.* Observe the *asyndeton,* i.e. the absence of a conjunction connecting *navem* and *cervos.* In order to better contrast what Aeneas did see with what he did not, Vergil resorts to *chiasmus,* a cross-fashioned arrangement of words, viz. *navem nullam, tres cervos,* where the natural order *nullam navem, tres cervos,* is changed so as to put *nullam* and *tres* in emphatic opposition. A. & G. 344, *f*; B. 350, 11, *c*; G. 682, and REM.; H. 562. —— **lītore,** abl. sing. of *lītis, lītoris,* n., 3d; locative abl. or abl. of 'place where.' In prose a prep. *in* would be required; see note on *aequore,* l. 29. —— **cervōs,** acc. plur. of *cervus, -ī,* m., 2d; direct obj. of *prospicit.*

LINE 185. **Prōspicit**, 3d pers. sing. pres. ind. act. of *prōspiciō, -ĕre, prōspēxī, prōspectum,* 3; agrees with an understood subj., *Aeneas,* or a pronoun referring to him. —— **errantēs,** acc. plur. m. of *errans, -antis,* pres. part. act. of *errō, -āre, -āvī, -ātum,* 1 ; agrees with *cervos.* The pres. part. is not so common after a verb *sentiendi* as the inf., but it is more vivid: in strict prose we should have had *errare.* Only the pres. participle is used in this way in Latin, though it is usual in Greek. A. & G. 292, *e*; B. 336, 2; G. 536; H. 535, I, 4. —— **hōs,** acc. plur. m. of the demonstr. pron. *hīc, haec, hōc;* refers to *cervos* above, and is the direct object of *sequuntur.* —— **tōta,** nom. plur. n. of *tōtus, -a, -um,* gen. *tōtīus,* dat. *tōtī,* other cases regular; agrees with *armenta. Tota armenta* = *whole herds,* collectively, i.e. as complete totals; *omnia armenta* would = *all the herds, every herd,* a meaning very different from the previous one. —— **armenta,** nom. plur. of *armentum, -ī,* n., 2d (for *ar-a-mentum,* from *aro,* = *I plough,* hence *a beast used in ploughing) ;* subj. of *sequuntur. Armentum* usually = *a herd of cattle,* as oxen were used for ploughing; but Vergil uses it of herds or droves of horses, deer, and even seals. —— **sequuntur,** 3d pers. plur. pres. ind. of the dep. verb *sequor, sequī, secūtus sum,* 3; agrees with the subj. *armenta.*

LINE 186. **Ā**, prep. with the abl.; gov. *tergo. A* or *ab* before consonants, *ab* before vowels or *h.* With the abl. *a* or *ab* may indicate: (1) the agent; (2) separation of time or place; (3) cause; (4) origin. See references on *ab,* l. 1. *A tergo* is an idiomatic phrase, = lit. *from the rear,* i.e. *behind, in the rear;* it is opposed to *a fronte,* = *in the front* or *van.* —— **tergō,** abl. sing. of *tergum, -ī,* n., 2d; governed by *a.* —— **et,** cop. conj., joining the sentence whose subj. is *armenta* with the next whose subj. is *agmen.*

grazes along the val- | lon,gúm ,, per , válles , páscitur , ágmen.
leys. Here he stops, | long   through the valleys   feeds   the column.
and with his hand | Cónstitit , híc, ,, ar,cúmque ma,nú cele,rés-que 187
snatches a bow and | He halted   here   and his bow in his hand   and swift
swift arrows, weapons |
which trusty Achates | sa,gíttas Córripu,ít, ,, fi,dús quae , téla 188
was carrying, and | his arrows   he snatched,   faithful which   weapons
first the leaders only | ge,rébat   A,chátes ;   Dúcto,rés-que   ip,sós 189
he lays low as they | was carrying   Achates ;   and the leaders   themselves

――longum, nom. sing. n. of *longus, -a, -um;* qualifies *agmen.* ――per, prep. with the acc.; gov. *valles.* ―― vallēs, acc. plur. of *vallēs,* or *vallis, -is,* f., 3d; obj. of *per.* ―― pascitur, 3d pers. sing. pres. ind. pass. of *pascō, -ere, pāvī, pastum,* 3; agrees with the subj. *agmen.* *Pasco,* = *I feed,* trans.; the passive is used reflexively (of animals) and = *to graze; pascitur* here = *grazes,* or *feeds itself,* like the Greek *middle* voice. See the NOTE and REFERENCES on *vertuntur,* l. 158. ―― āgmen, gen. *āgminis,* n., 3d (from *ago,* = *I drive,* hence of a large body of men or animals in motion); nom. sing., subj. of *pascitur.* *Agmen* is connected with *armenta* by *et,* and refers to the herds as a kind of marching column; cf. *agmine,* l. 82.

LINE 187. **Constitit,** 3d pers. sing. pres. ind. act. of *constō, -āre, constitī, constitum,* 1 irreg. and intrans.; agrees with the subj. *Aeneas* understood. The impersonal form *constat* = *it is well known.* ―― hīc, adv. of place where, extending *constitit.* For *huc,* see l. 170. ―― arcum, acc. sing. of *arcus, -ūs,* m., 4th; direct obj. of *corripuit.* *Arcus,* being a 4th decl. dissyllable in *-cus,* retains the old dat. and abl. plur. in *-ŭbus (arcubus).* A. & G. 70, *d* ; B. 49, 3 ; G. 61, REM. 1 ; H. 117, 1. ―― manū, abl. sing. of *manus, -ūs,* f., 4th; abl. of the instrument. Nouns of the 4th decl. are masculine, but *manus* belongs to a small list of feminine exceptions, of which the chief are *domus, Idus, porticus, acus, anus, tribus,* and the names of trees, e.g. *quercus,* = *an oak.* A. & G. 69 ; B. 50 ; G. 62, EXCEPTIONS ; H. 118. ―― celerēs, acc. plur. f. of *celer, celeris, celere,* 3d decl. adj. of 3 terminations ; agrees with *sagittas.* The comparative of *celer* is *celerior,* superl. *celerrimus.* ―― que, enclitic conj. ―― sagittās, acc. plur. of *sagitta, -ae,* f., 1st; direct obj. of *corripuit,* like *arcum,* to which it is joined by *que.*

LINE 188. **Corripuit,** 3d pers. sing: perf. ind. act. of *corripiō, -ĕre, corripuī, correptum,* 3 *(cum + rapio) ;* agrees with the same subj. as *contitit,* to which it is joined by *que* appended to *arcum.* ―― fidus, nom. sing. m. of *fīdus, -a, -um ;* qualifies *Achates.* *Fidus* is a constant attribute of Achates. ―― quae, acc. plur. n. of the rel. pron. *quī, quae, quod ;* agrees with the attracted antecedent *tēla.* ―― tēla, acc. plur. of *tēlum, -ī,* n., 2d; direct obj. of *gerebat.* *Tela* is attracted into the rel. clause *quae . . . gerebat Achates ;* logically it is the antecedent of *quae,* an acc. in apposition with *arcum* and *sagittas.* A. & G. 201, *d* ; B. 251, 4, *b* ; G. 616, 2 ; H. 445, 9. ―― gerēbat, 3d pers. sing. imperf. ind. act. of *gerō, -ere, gessī, gestum,* 3 ; agrees with its subj. *Achates* in the rel. clause. *Gero* = (1) *I carry,* (2) *I perform,* e.g. *res gestae ; gerere bellum* = *to wage* or *carry on war.* ―― Achātēs (for decl. see *Achātae,* l. 120) ; nom. sing., subj. of *gerebat.*

LINE 189. **Ductōrēs,** acc. plur. of *ductor, ductōris,* m., 3d (from *duco,* = *I lead) ;* direct obj. of *sternit.* Cicero and Vergil use *ductor* in the sense of *a chief.* ―― que, enclitic conj., joining the clause whose pred. is *sternit* with the preceding clause. ―― ipsōs, acc. plur. m. of the intensive adj. *ipse, ipsa, ipsum ;* agrees with *ductores.* For the use of *ipse,* consult A. & G. 102, *e* ; B. 88 ; G. 103, 3 ; H. 186, and 452. ―― prīmum, adv. of time, limiting *sternit ductores ; primum* is used here to mark the order of events,

| pri, múm, | „ | capi, ta | álta | fe, réntes | bear their heads aloft |
| *first* | | *heads* | *high* | *carrying* | with branching ant- |

190 Córnibus , árbore, ís, ster, nít, „ tum , vúlgus ;　with branching ant-／lers; then the com-／mon herd in general
with horns　branching　he lays low,　then　the mass;

191 et , ómnem **Míscet** a, géns te, lís „　throng, plying them／with his shafts, he
and　all　he confounds　driving (them)　with darts

192 nemo, ra ínter , fróndea , túrbam. **Néc** prius ,　routs amid the leafy／groves; nor does he
the groves　among　leafy　the crowd.　Nor　before　stay his hand ere he

---

cf. *tum, = next,* l. 190.　Refer to the note on *primum,* l. 174. —— **capita,** acc. plur. of
caput, capitis, n., 3d; direct obj. of *ferentes.*　The order of the words may be simplified :
*primumque sternit ductores ipsos, ferentes capita alta arboreis cornibus, tum (sternit)
vulgus, et, agens telis, miscet omnem turbam inter frondea nemora.* —— **alta,** acc. plur.
n. of *altus, -a, -um ;* agrees with *capita.*　Some say *capita alta cornibus = capita altis
cornibus,* by *hypallage ;* see note on *horrenti,* l. 165.　This is possible, but the order of
the words (*alta* and *ferentes* next to one another) suggests that Vergil intended the
phrase to be taken literally, *carrying their heads high with branching horns.　Alta* thus
extends the predicate, and the whole idea is made more striking and poetic. —— **feren-
tēs,** acc. plur. m. of *ferēns, -ēntis,* pres. part. act. of *ferō, ferre, tulī, lātum,* irreg. (see
note on *extulit,* l. 127); agrees with and enlarges *ductores.*
　Line 190.　**Cornibus,** abl. plur. of *cornu, -ūs,* n., 4th; abl. of description, with *cap-
ita.*　A. & G. 251 ; B. 224 ; G. 400 ; H. 419, II. —— **arboreīs,** abl. plur. n. of *arboreus,
-a, -um* (from *arbor, -is,* f., 3d, = *a tree*) ; qualifies *cornibus.　Arboreis = branching,*
like the spreading branches of a tree. —— **sternit,** 3d pers. sing. pres. ind. act. of *sternō,
-ere, strāvī, strātum,* 3; agrees with the subj. *Aeneas* or a pron. understood. —— **tum,**
adv. of time, here of order of events, cf. *primum,* l. 189 above.　As *primum* limits *ster-
nit,* so *tum* limits *sternit* understood in repetition and governing the obj. *vulgus.* ——
vulgus, acc. sing. of *vulgus, -ī,* n. (rarely m.), 2d (see *vulgus,* l. 149) : direct obj. of a
second *sternit* understood.　*Vulgus = the mass,* or *lower order* of the herd, in opposition
to *ductores* above; applied to deer, *vulgus* and *ductores* (divisions of a political com-
munity) are figurative. —— **et,** conj., joining the sentence *miscet,* etc., to the preceding
one. —— **omnem,** acc. sing. f. of *omnis, -e ;* agrees with *turbam.*
　Line 191.　**Miscet,** 3d pers. sing. pres. ind. act. of *misceō, -ēre, miscuī, mixtum,* or
mistum, 2; agrees with a pron. as subj., referring to *Aeneas.*　In l. 124 *misceri =* the
confusion of the sea; here *miscet = he drives in confusion,* or *routs.* —— **agēns,** nom.
sing. m. of the pres. part. act. of *agō, -ere, ēgī, actum,* 3; agrees with and enlarges the
subj. of *miscet.* —— **tēlīs,** abl. plur. of *tēlum, -ī,* n., 2d; abl. of the instrument, after
agens. —— **nemora,** acc. plur. of *nemus, nemoris,* n., 3d (see *nemus,* l. 165) ; governed
by *inter.* —— **inter,** prep. with the acc.; gov. *nemora.*　As a rule, only monosyllabic
prepositions are put between a noun and its adjective, and then the adjective usually
stands first ; see note on *cum,* l. 47.　For the prep. *inter,* see l. 107. —— **frondea,** acc.
plur. n. of *frondeus, -a, -um* (from *frons, -dis,* f., 3d); qualifies *nemora.*　Vergil used
another adj. similarly derived, *frondosus, -a, -um.* —— **turbam,** acc. sing. of *turba, -ae,*
f., 1st (Greek τύρβη); direct obj. of *miscet.*　Cicero uses *turba* as = to : (1) *the disorder*
or *uproar* of a mob; (2) *a crowd* or *throng* (as here), of persons, animals, or things.
Vulgus et turbam really expresses only one idea, = *thronging herd (hendiadys).*
　Line 192.　**Nec** (short for *neque, ne + que, = and . . . not*) coördinate disjunctive
conj., connecting what follows it with what has gone immediately before. —— **prius,**

may in victory bring	ábsis,tít,	„	quam	,	séptem	in,géntia	,	víctor
to earth seven mighty	*does he stop,*		*ere*		*seven*	*immense*		*as victor*

Córpora , fúndat   hu,mo, „ ét numc,rúm cum , 198,

| bodies and make | | | | | | | |
| their number equal | *bodies* | *he strew on the ground and* | *the number* | *with* |

---

comparative adv., logically and often actually united to *quam* (*priusquam*) as a temporal conjunction. By *tmesis*, *prius* is placed in main sentence, and *quam* introduces the subordinate clause; read the note and consult the references under *circum*, l. 175. *Prius*, the adverbial neuter acc. sing. of *prior*, has no positive, but has two superl. forms, *primum* and *primo*, the acc. n. sing. and abl. n. sing. respectively of *primus*. *Prior*, *prius*, and *primus* (+ adverbial cases) are formed from the prep. *prae;* cf. *pro-prior* (*proprius*) and *proximus* (*proxime*) from *prope*. —— **absistit**, 3d pers. sing. pres. ind. act. of *absistō, -ere, abstiti, abstitum*, 3 (*ab* = *away from*, + *sisto* [1st conjugation *sto*], = *I stand*)*;* agrees with an unexpressed pron.-subj. referring to Aeneas. —— **quam**, adv., connected with *prius* above = the conj. *before*. A. & G. 262, and 327; B. 291, 292; G. 574–577; H. 520. When the action is regarded as an actual fact, the ind. mood is used in all tenses, except the imperf. and pluperf. (which must be subjunct. always); when the action is regarded as conceived in thought or anticipated, the subjunct. mood is necessary in all tenses. Observe that *non prius . . . quam, = non* (*abstitit*) . . . *dum*, etc. (*dum, = until*)*;* if there is any suggestion of *purpose*, the subjunct. must be employed. Other uses of *quam* are: (1) in exclamations, e.g., *quam mirabile! = how;* (2) interrog., e.g. *quam diu, = how long?;* (3) correl. of *tam, = so . . . as;* (4) in extension of (3) with superl. adjectives and adverbs, e.g. *quam celer- rime, = (tam) celerrime quam (potuit);* (5) after comparative adjectives and adverbs, = *than*, e.g. *haec arbor altior est quam illa;* (6) with adjectives and adverbs, in indirect questions; (7) many other special uses, which may be studied in a dictionary, or in the grammars (see the references at the end of the grammars). —— **septem**, numeral indecl. adj., qualifying *corpora*. —— **ingentia**, acc. plur. n. of *ingens, -entis*, adj., 3d; agrees with *corpora*. —— **victor**, gen. *victōris*, m., 3d (from *vincō*)*;* predicate noun, qualifying the subj. of *fundat* like an adj. See note and references under *regina*, l. 46.

LINE 193. **Corpora**, acc. plur. of *corpus, -oris*, n., 3d; direct obj. of *fundat*. —— **fundat**, 3d pers. sing. pres. subj. act. of *fundō, -ere, fūdī, fūsum*, 3; agrees with the subj. *Aeneas* or a pron. understood. The subjunct. mood is due to the intention or purpose which *nec prius absistit quam* implies; see *quam* above. Had Vergil said, "nor *did* he stop," etc., the case would have been one of fact pure and simple, but "nor *does* he stop" shows the underlying idea in Aeneas' mind to slay as many deer as he had ships. There are various readings *fundit* and *aequat*, but they have very little authority. The tense in *fundat* and *aequet* is present, because in the sequence of tenses primary follows primary (as *fundat* follows *absistit*), and historic follows historic. A. & G. 286; B. 267, 268; G. 509; H. 491. *Fundere =* lit. *to pour out*, of liquids primarily, then of words; extended to other objects, it = *to scatter*, and *to bring down to earth*. —— **humō**, abl. sing. of *humus, -ī*, f., 2d (= *the ground* underfoot); abl. of 'place where'; cf. *mente*, l. 26. *Humō* is the reading of all the best MSS., and is, therefore, preferable to *humī*, the old locative case (like *domi, = at home*) = *on the ground*, in spite of the difficulty that *humō* elsewhere always = *from the ground*. —— **et**, cop. conj., joining *fundat* and *aequet*. ——- **numerum**, acc. sing. of *numerus, -ī*, m., 2d; direct obj. of *aequet*. —— **cum**, prep. with the abl.; gov. *navibus*. *Cum = with*, in reference to time and place; in other cases it is used idiomatically, e.g. here, of coincidence of circumstances, and frequently to express manner. A. & G. 153; B. 142; G. 417, 4; H. 434. It may be said that *cum* is used in Latin in almost all cases where 'with' is used in English. ——

194 návibus , ǽquet. Hínc por,túm   petit, ,   ét | to his ships. Thence
 the ships   *makes equal.* *Hence   the harbor   he makes for, and* | he seeks the harbor,
195 soci,ós ,, par,títur in , ómnes. Vína bo,nús | and shares among all
 comrades   shares   among   all   The wines   good | his company. Next
quae , déinde ca,dís ,, one,rárat A,céstes | wine that good Aces-
which   next   in casks   had loaded   Acestes | tes had filled in casks

---

návibus, abl. plur. of *návis, -is,* f., 3d; obj. of *cum.* —— **aequet,** 3d pers. sing. pres.
subj. act. of *aequō, -āre, -āvī, -ātum,* 1; joined by *et* to *fundat,* and in exactly similar
grammatical construction.
    LINE 194. **Hīnc,** adv. of separation in place (or in time, often); limits *petit,* and
refers to *scopulum,* l. 180. —— **portum,** acc. sing. of *portus, -ūs,* m., 4th (cf. l. 159);
direct obj. of *petit.* —— **petit,** 3d pers. sing. pres. ind. act. of *petō, -ere, petīvī,* or *-ii,*
petītum, 3; agrees with the subj. *Aeneas* understood. —— **et,** conj., joining *petit* and
partitur. —— **sociōs,** acc. plur. of *socius, -ī,* m., 2d (cf. adj. *socius, -a, -um,* and f., 1st
decl. noun *socia, -ae*); governed by the prep. *in.* —— **partitur,** 3d pers. sing. pres. ind.
of the dep. verb *partior, -īrī, -ītus sum,* 4 (from *pars, -tis,* f., 3d, = *a part,* hence *par-*
tiri = *to divide;* cf. active form *partio);* has the same subj. as *petit.* Understand the
obj. *corpora* from l. 193. —— **in,** prep., governing the acc. *socios. In* with the acc.
= *into the midst of,* hence *among;* see *in,* l. 51 and references. —— **omnēs,** acc. plur.
m. of *omnis, -e;* agrees with *socios.*
    LINE 195. **Vina,** acc. plur. of *vīnum, -ī,* n., 2d (Greek οἶνος, with original initial ϝ
or *digamma* ellipsed); direct obj. of *dividit.* —— **bonus,** nom. sing. m., agreeing with
Acestes. The comparative is *melior,* superl. *optimus.* —— **quae,** acc. plur. n. of *quī,*
quae, quod; agrees with the antecedent *vina,* and is the obj. of *onerarat.* —— **dēinde,**
adv. of order, misplaced but really modifying *dividit. Deinde* in prose is usually three
syllables, but in the poets frequently only two (by *synizesis*). A. & G. 347, *c*; B. 367,
1; G. 727; H. 608, III. The poets are very lax in the arrangement of sentences and
their component parts; cf. Aen. V, 14, *sic deinde locutus, Colligere arma iubet,* when
the order should be *deinde, sic locutus,* etc.   So here the proper order is: *deinde vina,*
quae . . . heros, dividit. —— **cadīs,** dat. plur. of *cadus, -ī,* m., 2d; dat. of the indirect
obj. after *onerarat. Quae cadis onerarat = quibus cados onerarat.* Vergil not seldom
varies a sentence thus; cf. Aen. VIII, 180, *onerantque canistris Dona,* for *onerantque*
canistra donis. Hypallage presents like, but not exactly similar, variations, e.g. Aen.
III, 61, *dare classibus Austros* (for *classes Austris);* see references under *horrenti,*
l. 165. Vergil clearly uses *onero* and some other verbs like *dono, exuo, circumdo,* etc.,
which may take the acc. of the person and the abl. of the thing, or the dat. of the
person (or indirect obj.) and the acc. of the thing. A. & G. 225, *d*; B. 187, I, *a*; G.
348; H. 384, 2, and FOOTNOTE 1. Synonyms: *cadus,* = a large *cask,* or *jar,* for holding
liquids, esp. *wine; amphora,* = *a jar,* usually earthenware, shaped like a wasp's body,
with an ear-like handle on either side at the top; it was fixed with the point in the
earth, or hung by the handles in the smoke of the fireplace to mellow. —— **onerārat**
(*syncopated* for *oneraverat*), 3d pers. sing. pluperf. ind. act. of *onero, -āre, -āvī, -ātum,*
1 (from *onus, -eris,* n., 3d, = *a burden);* agrees in the rel. clause with the subj. *Acestes.*
A. & G. 128, I, 2; B. 367, 8, and 7, 2; G. 131, 1; H. 235. —— **Acestēs,** gen. *Acestae,*
acc. *Acestam* or *Acesten* (see references under *Aeneae,* l. 92); subj. of *onerarat.* Aces-
tes was the son of Crimisus, the Sicilian river-god, and Segesta, a Trojan maiden. He
ruled in Sicily, near Drepanum, and, after helping Priam in the Trojan War, received
Aeneas well and helped him to bury Anchises on Mount Eryx. For this Aeneas built
the Sicilian town of Acesta.

upon the Sicilian shore, and had given them, true hero, on their departure, he apportions out and with his utterance soothes their sorrowing hearts, "Comrades, for not ere this are we unversed in ill

Lítore   ,   Trínacri,ó   „   dede,rátque 196
on the shore   *Trinacrian*   *and had given*

abe,úntibus   ,   héros,   Dívidit, ,   ét   dic,tís ,, 197
to them departing   *the hero,*   *he divides,*   *and   with words*

mae,réntia   péctora   ,   múlcet: " Ó soci,í, 198
sorrowing   *their breast*   *he soothes :*   *"O companions,*

neque en,*im* ígna,rí „ sumus , ánte   ma lórum,
neither   for   ignorant   we are   previously   of ills,

LINE 196. **Lītore,** abl. sing. of *lītus, -oris,* n., 3d; abl. of 'place where.' —— **Trīnacriō,** abl. sing. of *Trīnacrius, -a, -um* (from the Greek τρεῖς ἄκραι, = *three corners* or *promontories;* so *Trinacria, -ae,* f., 1st, = *Sicily,* lit. *the three-cornered land*); qualifies *litore.* The three promontories of Sicily are *Pachynus, Pelorus,* and *Lilybaeum.* Note that the first *i* is long (because it = the Greek diphthong *ei* in τρεῖς); also that the *a* before *cr* is short, although the general rule is that a vowel before two consonants is long. When a mute consonant, preceded by a naturally short vowel, is followed by *l* or *r* (as here), the syllable is called common, i.e. may be either long or short; cf. *pātris* and *pătris.* A. & G. 347, *d*; B. 5, B, 3; G. 13; H. 578. —— **dederat,** 3d pers. sing. pluperf. ind. act. of *dō, dare, dedī, datum,* 1; joined by *que* to *onerarat,* and in the same construction. —— **que,** enclitic conj. —— **abeuntibus,** dat. plur. of *abiens* (gen. *abeuntis,* acc. *abeuntem,* dat. *abeunti,* abl. *abeunte*). pres. part. act. of *abeō, -īre, abii, abitum,* irreg. (*ab = from,* + *eo,* = *I go*); dat. of the indirect obj. after *dederat.* The participles are often used absolutely, but in reality they agree with some noun or pronoun understood, e.g. (*iis*) *abeuntibus.* —— **hērōs,** gen. *herōis,* m., 3d (Greek ἥρως); nom. sing., in apposition with *Acestes.* For decl., consult A. & G. 64; B. 41, like SUS, except that acc. sing. and plur. may be *herōa* and *herōas,* and dat. and abl. plur. *heroibus;* G. 65, Heros; H. 68. *Heros* is emphatic in position at the end of the line and sentence, and = *in true heroic fashion,* i.e. generous as the noblest heroes are generous.

LINE 197. **Dividit,** 3d pers. sing. pres. ind. act. of *dīvidō, -ere, dīvīsī, dīvīsum,* 3; connected, in order of actions, by *deinde* with *partitur* above, and in agreement with the same subject, viz. *Aeneas.* —— **et,** conj. —— **dictīs,** abl. plur. of *dictum, -ī,* n., 2d (*dico,* = *I say,* hence *word*); abl. of the means or instrument. —— **maerentia,** acc. plur. n. of *maerens, -entis,* pres. part. act. of *maereō, -ēre,* no perf., no supine, 2 (akin to *miser,* = *wretched*); qualifies *pectora. Maerentia* is intrans. here, = '*sorrowing*'; sometimes *maereo* is used transitively, taking the acc. case. —— **pectora,** acc. plur. of *pectus, -oris,* n., 3d; direct obj. of *mulcet. Pectora* is a poetical synonym of *animos.* —— **mulcet,** 3d pers. sing. pres. ind. act. of *mulceō, ēre, mulsī, mulsum* or *mulctum,* 2; joined by *et* to *dividit.*

LINE 198. **Ō,** exclamation, accompanying the voc. *socii;* see *O,* l. 76. —— **sociī,** voc. plur. of *socius, -ī,* m., 2d; the case of the object addressed. —— **neque** (*ne + que,* = *and . . . not*), conj. *Neque enim* = lit. *and . . . for . . . not,* with an *ellipse* of some idea, thought but not expressed in words, between *and* and *for,* e.g. *O my friends and* (comrades in peril), *for,* etc.; *neque enim* = Greek καὶ γάρ οὐ, and passed in time into a strongly asserverative conj. A similarly *elliptical* adversative combinate-conj. is *sed enim,* = *but . . . for* (Greek ἀλλὰ γάρ). *Neque . . . malorum* is in parenthesis as far as the complete grammatical sentence is concerned, though Mr. Page thinks the speech gains in rhetorical intensity if *neque — malorum* is not treated as a parenthesis. —— **enim,** causal conj., combined with *neque* above; see *enim,* l. 19. —— **ignārī,** nom. plur. m. of *ignārus, -a, -um* (*in = not,* + (*g*)*nārus,* = *knowing*); agrees with *nos* understood as subj. of *sumus,*

199 O   pas, si   gravi, óra,   „   da, bít
    O   ye who have endured   more serious things,   will give

200 deus , hís quoque , fínem.   Vós et , Scýllae , ám
    god   to these also   an end.   You both   Scyllaean

201 rabi, ém   „   peni, túsque   so, nántes   Ácces, tís
    the frenzy   and deep within   sounding   have gone to

happenings. O ye
that have endured
even heavier woes, to
these also will God
grant an end. You
have come nigh to
the rage of Scylla,
and to her crags
sounding deep with-

and is also complement to *sumus* in the predicate.   *Ignarus* = (1) *ignorant of;* (2) *unknown*, not a prose use. —— **sumus**, 1st pers. plur. pres. ind. of *sum, esse, fuī;* agrees with the understood subj. *nos* (= *et ego et vos*). —— **ante** (= *antea*), adv., limiting *ignari sumus*, = *we are not previously ignorant of ill*, i.e. *we have not previously lacked experience in misfortune.* This use of *ante* with the pres. tense is in imitation of a Homeric line, quoted by all commentators who thus regard *ante*, viz. Odyssey, XII, 208, Ὦ φίλοι, οὐ γάρ πώ τι κακῶν ἀδαήμονές εἰμεν. A few editors make *ante* qualify *malorum*, = *malorum praeteritorum*, like the Greek τῶν πρὶν κακῶν, the adv. and the noun or adj. with which it goes being welded almost into a single word. This construction, called *hyphen*, though common in Greek, is entirely discordant with Latin idiom. —— **malōrum**, gen. plur. of *malum, -ī,* n., 2d (properly n. sing. used substantively of the adj. *malus, -a, -um*); objective gen., after *ignari*. This gen. follows adjectives expressing fulness, memory, knowledge, power, etc., and their opposites.   A. & G. 218, *a;* B. 204, 1; G. 374; H. 399, I, 2.

LINE 199. **Ō**, exclamation ; see *O* in the line above. —— **passī**, voc. plur. m. of *passus, -a, -um,* the perf. part. of the dep. verb *patior, -ī, passus sum,* 3 ; agreeing with and enlarging the understood obj. of address, *socii* or *vos.* *O passi graviora* = *O vos qui passi estis graviora.* —— **graviōra**, acc. plur. n. *gravior, -ius,* comparative degree of *gravis, -e;* direct obj. of *passi,* = *worse (things).* The superl. is *gravissimus, -a, -um.* —— **dabit,** 3d pers. sing. fut. ind. act. of *dō, dare, dedī, datum,* 1 ; agrees with the subj. *deus.* —— **deus,** gen. *deī,* m., 2d (plur. nom. *deī, diī,* or *dī;* gen. *deōrum* or *deūm ;* dat. and abl. *deīs, diīs, dīs*) ; nom. sing., subj. of *dabit.* —— **hīs,** dat. plur. n. of *hīc, haec, hōc;* dat. of the indirect obj. after *dabit.* *His* is either used substantively, = *to these things* (as *haec* often), or we may understand *malis* from *malorum* above. —— **quoque,** adv., not quite so strong in force as *etiam;* intensifies *his.* *Quoque* usually is the second or third word in its sentence, but never the first.   A. & G. 151, *a,* and 345, *b ;* B. 347, 1 ; G. 479 ; H. 554, I, 4. —— **fīnem,** acc. sing. of *finis, -is,* m. or f., 3d (abl. *fine,* rarely *fīnī*); direct obj. of *dabit. Finem =* here *an end.* Other meanings of *finis* are: (1) *a boundary;* (2) *the mark,* or *finishing post,* in races, cf. Aen. V, 327, *sub ipsam finem. Finis* is m. in prose, and sometimes f. in poetry.

LINE 200. **Vōs,** gen. *vestrum* or *vestrī,* acc. *vōs,* dat. and abl. *vōbīs ;* nom. plur. of the 2d pers. pron. (sing. *tū,* etc.), subj. of *accestis. Vōs* is emphatic ; see *vōs* below. —— **et,** cop. conj., correlative of *et* in next line. —— **Scyllaeam,** acc. sing. f. of *Scyllaeus, -a, -um* (from *Scylla, -ae,* f., 1st) ; agrees with *rabiem. Scylla* in the myth was the barking monster guarding the rocks in the Strait of Messina. —— **rabiem,** acc. sing. of *rabiēs,* f., 5th (abl. *rabie ; rabiēs* is gen. in Lucretius ; other cases wanting) ; direct obj. of *accestis.* —— **penitus,** adv., modifying *sonantes.* —— **que,** enclitic conj., joining *rabiem* and *scopulos.* —— **sonantēs,** acc. plur. of *sonans, -antis,* pres. part. act. of *sonō, -āre, sonuī, sonitum,* 1 ; qualifies *scopulos.*

LINE 201. **Accestis** (syncopated for *accessistis*), 2d pres. plur. perf. ind. act. of *accēdō, -ere, accessī, accessum,* 3 (*ad + cēdō*); agrees with the subj. *vos.* Contractions of

in ; of the rocks of Cyclops, too, you have had knowledge.	scopu,lós ; the rocks ;	,,	vos you	,	ét also	Cy,clópea Cyclopean	,	sáxa the stones	
Summon your courage back, and drive gloomy fear away :	Éxper,tí. have had experience of.				Revo,cáte Summon back		ani,mós, your spirits,	,, •	202
haply the memory of this too will one day	maes,túmque and gloomy		ti,mórem fear		Mittite. send away.	,	Fórsan Perhaps	et , even	203

this kind only occur in tenses of perfect stems in *s*; cf. Aen. IV, 606, *extinxem = extinxissem;* so Vergil uses *traxe = traxisse*, etc. A. & G. 128, 2, *b*; B. 116; G. 131 ; H. 235, 3. —— **scopulōs**, acc. plur. of *scopulus, -ī*, m., 2d; direct obj. of *accestis*. Some compounds of *ad, ante, ob, circum, trans*, etc., govern a direct obj. transitively. A. & G. 228, *a* ; B. 175, 2, *a* ; G. 331 ; H. 372. —— **vōs**, nom. plur. (see *vos*, l. 200); subj. of *experti (estis).* *Vos* is repeated for rhetorical effect ; this repetition is called *anaphora.* A. & G. 344, *f*; B. 350, II, *b* ; G. 682, and 636, NOTE 4 ; H. 636, III, 3. —— **et**, conj., correlative of *et* above. It is possible in each case to regard *et* as = to *etiam*, i.e. *even*. —— **Cyclōpea**, acc. plur. n. of *Cyclōpeus, -a, -um* (adj. from the noun *Cyclōps, Cyclōpis*, m., 3d = *Cyclops*, or generally *a Cyclops;* Greek Κύκλωψ, = a man with a round eye) ; agrees with *saxa.* Homer describes the adventures of Odysseus in Sicily, where Cyclops and his fellow giants lived — how he blinded the one-eyed monster and made his escape, and how Cyclops hurled tremendous rocks at the hero's departing vessels. So *Cyclopea saxa* contains two notions: (1) that the rocks were near Sicily, where the *Cyclopes* dwelt ; (2) that the rocks were huge and very dangerous, just as the giant was himself. Near these rocks was the whirlpool of Charybdis, which, with the mythical Scylla (above), made navigation very perilous. Although Homer does not assign them any definite location, tradition represents them as in or near the Strait of Messina, between Sicily and Italy. —— **sāxā**, acc. plur. of *sāxum, -ī*, n., 2d ; direct obj. of *experti (estis)*.

LINE 202. **Expertī**, nom. plur. m. of *expertus, -a, -um*, perf. part. of the dep. verb *experior, -īrī, expertus sum*, 4 ; agrees with the subj. *vos*, in the predicate *experti (estis* understood). —— **revocāte**, 2d pers. plur. imperative mood act. of *revocō, -āre, -āvī, -ātum*, 1 (*re = back*, + *voco = I call*)*;* the subj. *vos* is understood. The whole of this address is highly rhetorical in form ; from *O socii* to *experti*, was introduction, but the direct exhortation begins with *revocate.* —— **animōs**, acc. plur. of *animus, -ī*, m., 2d ; direct obj. of *revocate.* —— **maestum**, acc. sing. of *maestus, -a, -um* (from *maereō*)*;* agrees with *timorem.* The noun *maeror = grief*, displayed in the countenance, and so *maestus* is properly used of persons, but here is poetically assigned to the abstract *timorem.* —— **que**, enclitic conj. —— **timōrem**, acc. sing. of *timor, -ōris*, m., 3d (from *timeō*)*;* direct obj. of *mittite.*

LINE 203. **Mittite**, 2d pers. plur. imperative mood act. of *mittō, -ere, mīsī, missum*, 3; joined by *que* to *revocate*. *Mitto* = lit. *I send*, but here and in poetry elsewhere is used like *dimitto* (cf. *verteret*, l. 20, = *everteret);* cf. Horace, Odes, III, 8, 17, *Mitte civiles super urbe curas.* *Mitto = I cease* sometimes, and takes an inf. object, e.g. Horace, Odes, I, 38, 3, *Mitte sectari.* For the other numerous meanings of *mitto*, consult a good dictionary. —— **forsan** (short form of *forsitan*, = *fors sit an*), adv. = *perhaps. Forsan* is here followed by the ind. *iuvabit,* but like *forsitan, fortasse, fors sit*, etc., it very commonly takes the subjunctive mood. The subjunct. is then potential, e.g. *forsitan quispiam dixerit*, = *perhaps some one will say.* A. & G. 334, *g* ; B. no reference ; G. 457, 2, NOTE; H. page 267, FOOTNOTE I. —— **et**, conj., here = *etiam, even*. —— **haec**, acc. plur. n. of *hīc, haec, hōc;* direct obj. of *meminisse.* A. & G. 219; B. 206; G. 376; H. 406, II, and 407. Verbs *of remembering* and *forgetting* take the gen.

hǽc	„	o, lím	memi, nísse		iu, vábit.	afford pleasure.
these things		*once*	*to remember*		*will please (you).*	Through changing

<table>
<tr><td colspan="7">fortunes, through</td></tr>
</table>

204	Pér	vari, ós	ca, sús,	„	per	,	tót	dis, crímina,	many perilous hazards
	Through various happenings,				*through so many*			*crises*	we press on towards

205	rérum	Téndimus ,	ín	Lati, úm,	„	se, dés	ubi,	Latium, where the
	of matters we are proceeding to			*Latium,*		*abodes*	*where*	fates hold out to us

206	fáta	qui, étas	Osten, dúnt :		il, líc	„	fas	,	peaceful homes.
	the fates	*quiet*	*point out :*		*there*		*it is right*		There 'tis granted

of the object when it is a person, the gen. or acc. of the object when it is a thing. ——
ōlim, adv., by position limiting *meminisse*, but may be taken with *iuvabit*. *Olim* =
(1) *formerly, once upon a time*, of the past ; (2) *some day*, of the future. —— **memi-
nisse**, perf. inf. act. of the defective verb *memini*, = *I remember ;* governs *haec*, the inf.
clause *meminisse haec* being the subj. of *iuvabit.* A. & G. 270; B. 326–328; G. 280;
H. 532 and 538. An inf. clause may be either the subj. or obj. of the main verb. *Me-
mini* (root *men*) is a perfect form, but has the meaning of the present (cf. *odi*, = *I hate*).
It has the regular perfect-stem tenses, e.g. *meminero, memineram,* etc.; also the imper-
ative, *memento, mementote.* A. & G. 143, *c*; B. 133; G. 175, 5, *b*; H. 297, I. —— **iu-
vābit**, 3d pers. sing. fut. ind. act. of *iuvō, -āre, iūvī, iūtum,* 1; agrees with subject-inf.
clause *meminisse haec.* *Iuvo* = (1) *I please ;* (2) *I aid ;* (3) impersonally, *iuvat*, = *it
delights.*

LINE 204. **Per**, prep.; gov. *casus.* —— **variōs**, acc. plur. m. of *varius, -a, -um ;*
agrees with *casus.* —— **cāsūs**, acc. plur. of *cāsus, -ūs,* m., 4th; obj. of *per.* —— **per**,
prep.; gov. *discrimina.* Observe the *asyndeton.* —— **tot**, indecl. adj., qualifying *dis-
crimina.* —— **discrīmina**, acc. plur. of *discrīmen, -inis,* n., 3d (from *discerno*, = *I dis-
tinguish,* hence (1) *distinction,* (2) *danger*) ; obj. of *per.* *Discrimina rerum* = lit.
perils of things, i.e. *crises of fortune.* Synonyms : *periculum,* = lit. *a trial,* then *danger ;
discrimen,* = *a crisis,* hence *danger, id quod dividit inter bonum malumque eventum*
(quoted). —— **rērum**, gen. plur. of *rēs, reī,* f., 5th; poss. gen., limiting *discrimina.*

LINE 205. **Tendimus**, 1st pers. plur. pres. ind. act. of *tendō, -ere, tetendī, tensum*
or *tentum,* 3; trans. and intrans. ; the subj. is *nos* understood. *Tendo* = (1) trans., *I
stretch ;* (2) intrans., *I go,* also *I strive ;* (3) trans., with *cursum* or *iter,* = *I direct,* cf.
656, *iter tendebat.* —— **in**, prep.; gov. the acc. *Latium.* —— **Latium**, acc. sing. of
Latium, -ī, n., 2d; obj. of *in.* See *Latio,* l. 6. —— **sēdēs**, acc. plur. of *sedes, -is,* f., 3d;
direct obj. of *ostendunt.* —— **ubi**, adv. of place, with *ostendunt.* For other uses of *ubi*,
see l. 81. —— **fāta**, nom. plur. of *fātum, -ī,* n., 2d; subj. of *ostendunt.* *Fata* may be
rendered either *our destinies,* or personified (= *Parcae*) *the Fates.* —— **quiētās**, acc.
plur. f. of *quiētus, -a, -um,* adj. (by origin, perf. part. pass. of *quiescō, -ere, -ēvī, -ētum,*
3); qualifies *sedes.* Synonyms : *Quietus,* = *quiet, calm,* i.e. not subject to changes of
state bodily, or free from restlessness mentally; *tranquillus,* = *quiet, undisturbed,* with
a passive notion that the subject is not acted upon in any way. *Tranquillus* is applied
to things, but *quietus* is used of persons as well, but both may be employed in reference
to the mind (*animus*).

LINE 206. **Ostendunt**, 3d pers. plur. pres. ind. act. of *ostendō, -ere, ostendī, ostensum*
or *ostentum,* 3 (*obs = ob,* + *tendo,* = *I stretch out before* some one) ; agrees with the subj.
fata. Synonyms : *ostendo = I show,* for the purpose that the object may be observed,
without any implied discrimination; *monstro = I point out,* i.e. any object near, implying
distinction from other objects. *Ostendo* (*aliquid*) *ut videatur ; monstro, ut dignoscatur.*
—— **illīc**, adv. of place, referring to *Latium.* *Illic* is emphatic in position. *Illic* is
from *ille*, as *hic* from *hic, haec, hoc,* and as *istic* from *iste,* —— **fās**, indeclinable noun,

that the realm of Troy	régna	re,súrgere	, Tróiae.	Dúra,te,	ét 207
may spring to new life. Steel your	*(that) the rule*	*rise again*	*of Troy.*	*Endure,*	*and*

hearts and keep	vos,mét „ re,bús ser,váte se,cúndis." Tália , 208
yourselves against the day of prosperity."	*yourselves for affairs keep prosperous." Such things*

So speaks he, and sick with heavy care	vóce re,fért; „ cu,rísque in,géntibus ,
	with his voice he utters; and with cares mighty

he feigns hope in his face, hiding his sor-	æger Spém vul,tú simu,lát, „ premit , 209
	sick hope in his countenance he feigns, checks

complement in the predicate *fas (est)* of the *copula est* understood. A. & G. 176; B. 167, 168; G. 205, 206; H. 360–362. —— rēgna, acc. plur. of *rēgnum, -ī,* n., 2d; acc.-subj. of *resurgere.* The plur. *regna* for *regnum* is poetic. —— resurgere, pres. inf. act. of *resurgō, -ere, resurrēxī, resurrectum,* 3 *(re = again, + surgō, = I rise)*; the clause *regna resurgere* is subj. of *est* understood in the predicate. The simple acc. and inf. may be either the subj. or the obj. in a sentence, e.g. *hostes adesse nuntiant* (obj.) or *hostes adesse nuntiatur* (subj.). A. & G. 272, REM.; B. 330, 331; G. 527 ; H. 534, 535. With this idea of a *new Troy,* cf. that of a *new Salamis,* in Horace, Odes, I, 8, 29, *Certus enim promisit Apollo ambiguam tellure nova Salimina futuram.* —— Trōiae, gen. sing. of *Trōia,* f., 1st; poss. gen., limiting *regna.*

LINE 207. Dūrāte, 2d pers. plur. imperative mood act. of *dūrō, ˋ-āre, -āvī, -ātum,* 1 (from *durus,* = *hard,* hence trans. and intrans. *I harden,* and intrans. as here *I endure);* the subj. *vos* is unexpressed. —— et, conj. —— vōsmet *(vōs + met),* *vōs* is acc. plur. used reflexively after *servate,* of which it is the object; *met* is an enclitic suffix which may be appended for emphasis to any personal or reflexive pron. except the nom. case of *tu.* A. & G. 99, *f*; B. 84, 2; G. 102, NOTE 2, and 103, NOTE 5 ; H. 184, 3, and 185, NOTE 2. *Met* may not be joined to gen. plurals; it may in some cases be joined to poss. adjectives, e.g. *suomet.* —— rēbus, dat. plur. of *rēs, reī,* f., 5th; dat. of the indirect obj. after the trans. verb *servate.* A. & G. 225; B. 187, I; G. 345; H. 384, II. *Res* and *dies* alone in the 5th decl. are declined fully in the plural. —— servāte, 2d pers. plur. imperative mood act. of *servō, -āre, -āvī, -ātum,* 1; joined by *et* to *durate,* and in the same grammatical construction. —— secundīs, dat. plur. f. of *secundus, -a, -um* (study the note on *secundo,* l. 156); agrees with *rebus.* The combination *res secundae = prosperity ;* so the combination *res publica = common wealth, commonwealth* or *state.*

LINE 208. Tālia, acc. plur. n. of *tālis, -e ;* direct obj. of *refert.* —— vōce, abl. sing. of *vōx, vōcis,* f., 3d; abl. of the instrument. —— refert, 3d pers. sing. pres. ind. act. of *referō, referre, retulī (rettulī), relātum,* irreg.; agrees with the subj. *Aeneas* understood. *Talia voce refert* is a set phrase in the Aeneid; cf. l. 94. —— cūris, abl. plur. of *cūra, -ae,* f., 1st; abl. of cause, enlarging *aeger.* A. & G. 245; B. 219; G. 408, and NOTE 2; H. 416, I, NOTE 1. —— Que, enclitic conj. —— ingentibus, abl. plur. f. of *ingens,* 3d decl. adj. of one termination; qualifies *curis.* —— aeger, nom. sing. m. of *aeger, aegra, aegrum ;* qualifies the understood subj. of *simulat, viz. Aeneas* or a pron. referring to Aeneas. *Aeger = sick,* in mind or body: *aegrotus, = sick,* in body. *Aeger* here stands for a concessive clause, and = *though ill,* or *ill as he was.*

LINE 209. Spem, acc. sing. of *spēs, speī,* f., 5th (gen. plur. *sperum* found sometimes); direct obj. of *simulat.* —— vultū, abl. sing. of *vultus, -ūs,* m., 4th; abl. of the instrument. —— simulat, 3d pers. sing. pres. ind. act. of *simulō, -āre, -āvī, -ātum,* 1 *(similis, = like);* coördinate with *refert,* to which it is joined by *que. Simulo = I feign* either with an acc. obj. as *spem,* or more commonly an acc. and inf. object-clause. *Simulo*

210 áltum , córde do,lórem. Ílli , sé prae ,dae
    deep   in his heart   the grief.   They themselves for booty

211 áccin,gúnt dapi,bús-que fu ,túris : Térgora ,
    gird   and for feasts   future: the skins

212 déripi,únt cos,tís, „ et , víscera , núdant ; Párs
    they rip off from ribs, and the entrails expose;   part

row deep within his heart. His company make ready for their spoil and their feasting that shall be : they tear the hide from the ribs, and show the flesh bare ; some cut it into

---

= *I pretend*, that something is, which really is not; *dissimulo = I pretend*, that something is not, which really is. This difference has been well expressed in the following *hexameter : Quae non sunt simulo, quae sunt ea dissimulantur.* —— **premit**, 3d pers. sing. pres. ind. act. of *premō, -ere, pressī, pressum*, 3; has the same subj. as *simulat*, although for contrast's sake they are not connected by any conjunction (*asyndeton*). A. & G. 208, *b*; B. 346; G. 473, REM.; H. 636, I, I. This line presents an excellent example of the figure called *chiasmus*, i.e. wherein the order of words is inverted for the sake of bringing a pair of ideas into strong contrast. Thus *spem*, the first word, answers *dolorem*, the last; the less important words *vultu* and *corde* lie between the verb and the object in each pair; the verbs *simulat* and *premit*, as it were, meet only to diverge. A. & G. 344, *f*; B. 350, II, *c*; G. 682, and REM.; H. 562. —— **altum**, acc. sing. m. of *altus, -a, -um*; agrees with *dolorem*. *Premit altum corde dolorem* = not *conceals his deep grief in his heart*, but *conceals his sorrow deep in his heart*, i.e. the adjective is used with adverbial force. A. & G. 191; B. 239; G. 325, REM. 6; H. 443. There is also a suggestion of *prolepsis*, i.e. *conceals so as to be deep ;* see note on *laxas*, l. 63. —— **corde**, abl. sing. of *cor, cordis*, n., 3d; abl. of 'place where.' —— **dolōrem**, acc. sing. of *dolor, dolōris*, m., 3d (*doleo, = I grieve*); direct obj. of *premit*.

LINE 210. **Illī**, nom. plur. m. of *ille, illa, illud ;* subj. of *accingunt*. —— **sē**, acc. plur. of the reflexive pron.; refers to the same persons as *illi* (viz. the *socii* of Aeneas), and is direct obj. of *accingunt*. —— **praedae**, dat. sing. of *praeda, -ae*, f., 1st; dat. of the indirect obj. after *accingunt*. See note on *rebus*, l. 207. —— **accingunt**, 3d pers. plur. pres. ind. act. of *accingō, -ere, accinxī, accinctum*, 3 (*ad + cingō*); agrees with the subj. *illi*. *Se accingunt* here = *gird themselves*, i.e. *prepare*. In connection with two objects, *accingo* has the same variable construction as *dono*, etc., for which see the note and references under *cadis*, l. 195. —— **dapibus**, dat. plur. of *dāps, dapis*, f., 3d (gen. plur. very rare); dat. of the indirect obj., like *praedae*, to which it is joined by *que*. **que**, enclitic conj. —— **futūrīs**, dat. plur. of *futūrus, -a, -um*, fut. part. of *sum, esse, fuī ;* agrees attributively with *dapibus*.

LINE 211. **Tergora**, acc. plur. of *tergus, -oris*, n., 3d (a collateral form of *tergum, -i*, n., 2d); direct obj. of *deripiunt*. —— **dēripiunt**, 3d pers. plur. pres. ind. act. of *dēripiō, -ere, -uī, dereptum*, 3 (*dē + rapiō) ;* the subj. *illi* is understood from the context. —— **costīs**, abl. plur. of *costa, -ae*, f., 1st; abl. of separation, governed by *de* in composition in *deripiunt*. Such compounds, except when used figuratively, properly require the preposition repeated with the noun. —— **et**, conj. —— **viscera**, acc. plur. of *viscus, -eris*, n., 3d (rare in the sing.); direct obj. of *nudant*. The *viscera* are not necessarily the entrails of an animal, but the *flesh* or *carcase* as it is when the skin has been removed. —— **nūdant**, 3d pers. plur. pres. ind. act. of *nūdō, -āre, -āvī, -ātum ;* coördinate with *deripiunt*, to which *et* joins it.

LINE 212. **Pars**, gen. *partis*, f., 3d; nom. sing., in partitive apposition with *illi*, l. 210, and subj. of *secant*. *Pars . . . pars* is often correlatively used, = *some . . . others;* here *alii* takes the place of a second *pars*. *Pars* and *alii* are both in apposition with the whole *illi ;* sometimes the whole may be in apposition with the parts. A. & G. 184, *a ;* B. 169, 5; G. 322, 323; H. 364. *Pars = part*, i.e. *some*, being a collective noun, by the

pieces, and impale them yet quivering upon the spits;	in , frústa sc,cánt,	„ veri,bús-que tre,méntia ,	212
	into pieces cut (the flesh),	*and on spits*	*quivering*
others set caldrons on the shore, and supply the fires for them. Then they	fígunt ; Lítore a,ḗna lo,cánt	ali,í, „	213
	they fix (them) ; on the shore brazen (vessels) set	*others,*	
recall their strength with food, and	flam,más-que mi,nístrant. Túm	vic,tú	214
	and flames *furnish.* *Them*	*with food*	
stretched upon the grass take their fill	revo,cánt vi,rés, „ fu,síque per ,	hérbam	
	they call back *strength,* *and spread* *over*	*the grass*	

figure *synesis* (κατὰ σύνεσιν), also called *constructio ad sensum,* is subject of plural verbs, *secant* and *figunt:* note also that *pars* is feminine, and the gender implied by the verbs is masculine; cf. Aen. V, 108, *pars et certare parati,* for different numbers and genders. A. & G. 187, *d,* and 182, *a;* B. 235, B, 2, *c;* G. 211, REM. 1, and EXCEPTIONS *a, b;* H. 438, 6. The word *synesis* means agreement according to sense, not grammatical form. —— **in,** prep.; gov. the acc. *frusta.* —— *frusta,* acc. plur. of *frustum, -ī,* n., 2d; obj. of *in.* —— **secant,** 3d pers. plur. pres. ind. act. of *secō, -āre, secuī, sectum,* 1; agrees *ad sensum* with the subj. *pars.* —— **veribus,** abl. plur. of *veru, -ūs,* n., 4th; abl. of the instrument, after *figunt.* This abl. is more probable than a locative abl., as some regard it; in any case we may render *fix upon spits. Veru* has dat. and abl. plural *verubus.* A. & G. 70, *d;* B. 49, 3; G. 61, REM. 1; H. 117, 1. —— **que,** conj. —— **trementia,** acc. plur. n. of *tremens, -entis,* pres. part. act. of *tremō, -ere, tremuī,* no supine, 3; agrees with *ea* understood, referring to *frusta. Trementia* implies that the beasts were recently killed, and moreover that the Trojans spared no haste in their hunger. —— **figunt,** 3d pers. plur. pres. ind. act. of *figō, -ere, fīxī, fīxum,* 3; joined by *que* to *secant,* and in exactly similar grammatical construction.

LINE 213. **Lītore,** abl. sing. of *lītus, -oris,* n., 3d; locative abl. —— **aēna,** acc. plur. of *aēnum, -ī,* n., 2d (properly the n. of the adj. *aēnus, -a, -um,* from *aes, aeris,* n., 3d = *bronze;* with *aenum* supply *vos* understood); direct obj. of *locant.* It is scarcely likely that Mr. Conington was right in asserting that in Homeric times meat was never boiled for eating; those who support him maintain that the *aena* in this case were used for boiling water for washing purposes. —— **locant,** 3d pers. plur. pres. ind. act. of *locō, -āre, -āvī, -ātum,* 1 (*locus, -ī,* m., 2d); agrees with the subj. *alii.* For the mercantile meanings of this verb, see any dictionary. —— **alii,** nom. plur. m. of *alius, -a, -ud* (gen. *alīus,* dat. *alī* (contracted for *aliī*), otherwise regular); subj. of *locant,* and partitive appositive of *illi,* l. 210 (see *pars,* l. 212). *Alius ... alius = one ... another,* of more than two persons or things. *Alius,* with some part of *alius* or with adverbs like *alibi, alia,* etc., formed from *alius,* denotes a plurality of subjects, e.g. *alius aliud dicit, = one says one thing, another (says) another; alius* is thus often incorporated in a sentence with a plural subject, as a partitive appositive of that subject, e.g. *oratores alius alio modo locuti sunt.* —— **flammās,** acc. plur. of *flamma, -ae,* f., 1st; direct obj. of *ministrant.* —— **que,** conj. —— **ministrant,** 3d pers. plur. pres. ind. act. of *ministrō, -āre, -āvī, -ātum,* 1; joined by *que* to *locant.*

LINE 214. **Tum,** adv. of time; here = *next,* of succession of events. —— **victū,** abl. sing. of *victus, -ūs,* m., 4th (from *vivo*); abl. of the means. *Victus =* (1) *manner of living;* (2) *food,* as here. —— **revocant,** 3d pers. plur. pres. ind. act. of *revocō, -āre, -āvī, ātum,* 1; the subj. *illi* is understood. —— **vīrēs,** acc. plur. of *vis,* acc. *vim,* abl. *vī,* f., 3d (defective in sing.; plural, nom., voc., acc., *vires,* gen. *virium,* dat. an l abl. *viribus*); direct obj. of *revocant.* The sing., *vis, = force, violence,* e.g. *vi = by force;* the plural = strength. —— **fūsī,** nom. plur. m. of *fūsus, -a, -um,* perf, part. pass. of *fundō, -ere, fūdī, fūsum,* 3;

215 **Ímplen,túr** vete,rís Bac,chí „ pin,guís-que | of old wine and fat
they fill themselves *old* *with wine* *and fat* | venison.

216 **fe,rínae.** **Póstqu**a*m* ex,émpta fa,més | After hunger has
with venison. *After* *had been driven away* *hunger* | been banished from
| the board, and the
| tables removed, in
217 **epu,lís,** „ men,sǽque re,mótae, **Á**mis,sós | long-continued talk
by the feast, *and the tables* *had been removed,* . *lost* | they mourn their

---

agrees with a pron. understood as subj. of *implentur*. It = *stretched out*, i.e. in luxurious
ease after their former exhaustion. —— **que,** enclitic conj., joining the sentence to the
preceding one. —— **per,** prep., governing *herbam.* —— **herbam,** acc. sing. of *herba, -ae,*
f., 1st; obj. of *per.*
　　LINE 215.　**Implentur,** 3d pers. plur. pres. ind. pass. of *impleō, -ēre, -ēvī, -ētum* (*in*
+ *pleo,* cf. *com-pleo*); subj. *illi* understood, as with *revocant* above. The passive here
almost = a dep. verb; at any rate, it is reflexive, = *fill themselves,* corresponding to the
Greek middle voice. *Revocant* + *implentur* = *revocant implendo se.* —— **veteris,** gen.
sing. m. of *vetus, veteris,* adj., 3d of one termination; qualifies *Bacchi.* —— **Bacchi,** gen.
sing. of *Bacchus, -ī,* m., 2d; gen. governed by *implentur.* Verbs of *abundance* or *want*
may govern the gen. case, though most of them more frequently govern the abl. case.
A. & G. 223 ; B. 212, 1; G. 383, 1, NOTES 1, 2; H. 410, V, 1. Observe that *Bacchi*
= *vini,* the patron god being named, by *metonymy,* instead of that of which he was
patron; cf. *Cererem,* l. 177, note and references. *Bacchus,* the god of wine, was the son
of Jupiter and Semele, and was known by various names, e.g. *Liber, Lyaeus,* etc. ——
pinguis, gen. sing. of *pinguis, -e ;* qualifies *ferinae.* —— **que,** conj. —— **ferinae,** gen.
sing. of *ferīna,* f., 1st (properly f. sing. of the adj. *ferīnus, -a, -um,* from *fera, a wild
beast;* supply *caro,* = *flesh,* understood); governed by *implentur,* and joined by *que* to
Bacchi. Ferina commonly = *venison,* deer being the only wild animals usually eaten as
food; cf. *agnina (caro),* = *lamb.*
　　LINE 216.　**Postquam,** temporal conj., with *exempta (est).* A. & G. 323, 324; B.
287; G. 561*ff.*; H. 518. —— **exempta,** nom. sing. f. of *exemptus, -a, -um,* perf. part.
pass. of *eximō, -ere, exēmī, exemptum,* 3 (*ex* + *emō,* cf. *adimo*) ; agrees with *fames,* of
which it is the predicate with *est* understood. —— **famēs,** gen. *famis,* f., 3d ; nom. sing.,
subj. of *exempta (est).* —— **epulis,** abl. plur. of *epulae, -ārum,* f., 1st; abl. of the means
or instrument. —— **mensae,** nom. plur. of *mensa, -ae,* f., 1st; subj. of *remotae* (sunt).
Mensa = (1) *a table ;* hence, as the Romans used very small tables at the *triclinia* (or
lounges for dining, placed at right angles to one another, in the form of a square with one
side wanting), and the tables were often removed together with the food left upon them,
mensa comes to mean *a course ;* so *secunda mensa* = *the second course.* Here *mensae*
may = *course ;* or perhaps = *tables,* in the sense of large bread-cakes used for that pur-
pose; cf. the fulfilled prophecy that the Trojans would find a home when they had eaten
their tables, i.e. the cakes used as such. —— **que,** conj., joining this sentence to the pre-
ceding one. —— **remōtae,** nom. plur. f. of *remōtus, -a, -um,* perf. part. pass. of *removeō,
-ēre, remōvī, remōtum,* 2 (*re* = *back* + *moveō* = *I move*) ; agrees with *mensae,* and pred-
icate of it with *sunt* understood. The *copula* is frequently omitted in Latin, especially
in the ind. and inf. moods, and in combinate tenses.
　　LINE 217.　**Amissōs,** acc. plur. m. of *āmissus, -a, -um,* perf. part. pass. of *āmittō,
-ere, āmīsī, āmissum,* 3 (*ā* + *mittō*) ; predicate part., agreeing with *socios.* In *amissos
socios,* the main idea is contained in the participle, as often in Latin; e.g. *ante urbem
conditam.* A. & G. 292, *a*; B. 337, 5; G. 437, NOTE 2; H. 549, 5, NOTE 2. —— **longō,**

comrades lost to them, halting between hope and fear whether to believe they lived or even now were suffering the last doom and no

lon,gó	,,	soci,ós	ser,móne	re,quírunt,
long		*comrades*	*in speech*	*they seek again,*

Spémque me,túmq*ue* in,tér　　dubi,í, ,, seu, 218

both hope　　*and fear*　　*between*　　*doubtful,*　　*whether*

vívere　　,　　crédant,　　Síve　　ex,tréma 219

(that they) live　　*they may believe,*　　*or (that they)*　　*the worst*

abl. sing. m. of *longus, -a, -um;* qualifies *sermone.* —— **sociōs,** acc. plur. of *socius, -ī,* m., 2d; direct obj. of *requirunt.* —— **sermōne,** abl. sing. of *sermō, -ōnis,* m., 3d; abl. of manner, with *cum* omitted, because the adj. *longo* qualifies the noun. —— **requírunt,** 3d pers. plur. pres. ind. act. of *requīrō, -ere, requīsīvī, requīsītum,* 3 (*re* = *back* or *again* + *quaerō = I seek*) ; understand *illi* as subj. *Requiro,* which usually = *I search for, I need,* here is equivalent to *desidero, = I miss;* translated lit. *they search for,* it is very pathetic, and is an instance of Vergil's skill in choosing words which give a vivid reality to the scenes he describes.

LINE 218. **Spem,** acc. sing. of *spēs, speī,* f., 5th; governed by *inter.* —— **que,** conj., repeated below, = *both . . . and.* —— **metum,** acc. sing. of *metus, -ūs,* m., 4th (*metuo, = I fear*) ; governed by *inter,* and joined by *que* to *spem.* —— **que,** conj.; see *que* above. —— **inter,** prep.; gov. *spem* and *metum. Inter* (*circum, ante,* etc.) may sometimes follow the word (as here) which it governs; in Cicero this is most common with the rel. or other pronouns, but in poetry it is quite common with nouns. A. & G. 263, NOTE ; B. 144, 3; G. 413, REM. I; H. 569, II, I. —— **dubii,** nom. plur. m. of *dubius, -a, -um;* agrees with and enlarges the subj. of *requirunt.* The adj. *dubius* may introduce indirect questions, as the verb *dubito,* to which it is akin, regularly does; the most common method is *dubium est* or *erat, = it is* or *was doubtful,* impersonally. —— **seu,** disjunctive conj., repeated in the form *sive* below, properly = *if either . . . or if,* and is particularly used in distinguishing two names of the same thing. Strictly *sive* (*seu*) . . . *sive* (*seu*) may only be used in *oratio recta,* but sometimes in poetry it may take the place of the correct *utrum . . . an,* as in the indirect question here *dubii seu credant.* For *sive* (*seu*), distinguished from *ve, aut,* etc., consult the notes on *ve,* l. 9, and *aut,* l. 183. —— **vívere,** pres. inf. act. of *vīvō, -ere, vīxī, victum,* 3; inf. gov. by the subj.-acc. *eos* (understood from *socios*) in the indirect discourse introduced by *credant.* The omission of the subj.-acc. is very rare, and is only permissible in poetry. The pres. inf. represents continued action in the present time. For this simple form of the acc. and inf. construction, unaccompanied by subordinate clauses, refer to the note and references on *miscere,* l. 124. —— **crédant,** 3d pers. plur. pres. subjunct. act. of *crēdō, -ere, crēdidī, crēditum,* 3 ; deliberative subjunct., which remains unchanged as a rule even when incorporated in an indirect question offering alternative suggestions and introduced by *utrum . . . an* (or poetically *sive . . . sive*). A. & G. 334, *b;* B. 300, 2 and 4; G. 460, 2, and 265; H. 529, 3. *Credant* is pres. tense in sequence with *requirunt.*

LINE 219. **Síve,** disjunctive conj., introducing an alternative proposition, viz. *extrema pati.* See *seu* above. —— **extrēma,** acc. plur. n. of *extrēmus, -a, -um,* superl. adj., = *the extreme* (things), i.e. *the worst;* direct obj. of *pati.* The n. sing. *extremum* is sometimes a noun, = *the boundary. Extremus* has a rare positive, *exterus* (found in n. plur. *extera*); the comparative is *exterior;* superl. may also be *extimus:* like *imus* from *infra,* and *summus* from *supra, extremus* is formed from the adv. or prep. *extra.* —— **patī,** pres. inf. of the dep. verb *patior, patī, passus sum,* 3; governed by the subj.-acc. *eos* understood (see *vivere*), in indirect discourse after *credant.* The pres. inf. has reference to thȩ lasting character of the state of death; if the mere occasion of the death

pa,tí „ nec , i*am*　　éxau,díre　　　vo,cátos.
suffer　*and not*　*now*　*(that they) hear*　*being called.*

220 Præcipu,é pius , Aéne,ás „ nunc , ácris O,rónti
Particularly　*loyal*　*Aeneas*　*now*　*eager of Arontes*

221 Núnc　Amy,cí　ca,súm „ gemit , ét cru,délia ,
now　*of Amycus*　*the fate*　*moans*　*and*　　　*cruel*

222 sécum　　　Fáta　Ly,cí, for,témque Gy,án, „
with himself　*the destinies of Lycus,*　*and brave*　　*Gyas*

223 for,témque　Clo,ánthum.　Ét　iam　,　fínis
and brave　　*Cloanthus.*　*And　already*　*the end*

longer heard when called. Chiefly does knightly Aeneas in his heart lament the fate now of impetuous Orontes, now of Amycus, the cruel doom of Lycus, and brave Gyas and brave Cloanthus. And now the end was, when

---

had been meant, *passos esse* would have been used.——**nec**, neg. adv., = *and . . . not; et non* would not be Latin. —— **iam**, adv. of time. —— **exaudīre**, pres. inf. act. of *ēxaudiō, -īre, -īvī,* or *-iī, -itum,* 4; joined by *nec*, to *pati*, and in exactly the same grammatical construction. —— **vocātōs**, acc. plur. m. of *vocātus, -a, -um*, perf. part. pass. of *vocō, -āre, -āvī, -ātum,* 1; agrees with the understood subj.-acc. of the infinitives, viz. *eos. Vocatos* = a temporal or conditional clause, *when they are*, or *if they are called upon.* There is perhaps an allusion to the custom of calling thrice upon the dead.

LINE 220. **Praecipuē**, adv., from *praecipuus, -a, -um* (*prae,* = *before, in preference,* + *capiō,* = *I take*); it = an adverbial phrase, e.g. *more than others.*——**pius**, nom. sing. m. of *pius, -a, -um;* qualifies *Aeneas.* For the meaning of *pius*, cf. *pietate,* l. 151. —— **Aenēās**, nom. sing., subj. of *gemit.*——**nunc**, adv., with *nunc* below, = *now . . . now.*——**ācris**, gen. sing. m. of *ācer, ācris, ācre,* adj. of three terminations; qualifies *Oronti. Acer* = (1) of things, *sharp;* (2) of intellect, *quick;* (3) of character, *eager;* (4) of sight or hearing, *acute;* (5) of speed, *swift.*——**Orontī**, gen. sing. of *Orontēs,* m.; poss. gen., limiting *casum;* cf. *Oronten,* l. 113.

LINE 221. **Nunc**, adv. of time; see *nunc* above. —— **Amycī**, gen. sing. of *Amycus,* m., 2d; poss. gen., limiting *casum.*——**cāsum**, acc. sing. of *cāsus, -ūs,* m., 4th; direct obj. of *gemit.*—— **gemit**, 3d pers. sing. pres. ind. act. of *gemō, -ere, -uī, -itum,* 3; agrees with the subj. *Aeneas. Gemo* is here trans., governing *casum ;* it is almost always intransitive.——**et**, conj., joining *fata* and *casum.*——**crūdēlia**, acc. plur. n. of *crūdēlis, -e,* adj. 3d; agrees with *fata.*—— **sēcum** (*sē + cum*), *sē* is abl. sing. of the reflexive pron., referring to *Aeneas,* and governed by *cum. cum* is the prep., appended as an enclitic to *se ;* consult the note and references under *secum,* l. 37. *Secum = with,* i.e. *to himself, in privacy,* so as not to trouble his companions.

LINE 222. **Fātā**, acc. plur. of *fātum, -ī,* n., 2d; direct obj. of *gemit.*—— **Lycī**, gen. sing. of *Lycus,* m., 2d; poss. gen., limiting *fata.* He was a follower of Aeneas. —— **fortem**, acc. sing. m. of *fortis, -e,* adj. 3d; qualifies *Gyan.* Observe the repetition *fortemque . : . fortemque;* it is at once dignified and pathetic, for *fortis* is a term of honour with Vergil. *Acer*—— **que**, enclitic conj., joining *fata* and *Gyan.*—— **Gyan**, acc. sing. of *Gyas, -ae,* m., 1st decl. Greek noun (see *Aeneae,* l. 92 for decl.); a direct obj. of *gemit.* —— **fortem**, acc. sing. m.; qualifies *Cloanthum.*—— **que**, conj. —— **Cloanthum**, acc. sing. of *Cloanthus, -ī,* m., 2d; joined by *que* to *Gyan.* Gyas and Cloanthus survived (see l. 612), and the former distinguished himself in the funeral games in Sicily (Aen. V), the latter founded the distinguished family of the Cluentii.

LINE 223. **Et**, cop. conj., connecting a new sentence with the one gone before. ——**iam**, adv. of time.——**fīnis**, gen. *fīnis,* m., 3d (see *fincm,* l. 199); nom. sing.,

Jupiter looking down	e,rát: „ cum , Iúpiter , ǽthere , súmmo
from the height above	*was when Jupiter from the ether highest*
upon the sail-winged	Déspici,éns mare , vélivo,lúm „ ter,rás-que 224
sea, the low-lying	*looking down on the sea sail-winged and the lands*
lands, the shores, and	ia,céntes, Lítora,que ét la,tós 225
wide-spread peoples,	*lying low, and the shores and widely spread*
stood still therewith	popu,lós, „ sic , vértice , cœli Cónstitit, , 226
on heaven's crest and	*peoples, so on the height of heaven halted,*
fixed his downward	ét Li,byǽ „ de,fíxit , lúmina , régnis.
gaze on the realm of	*and of Libya fixed his eyes on the kingdoms.*

subj. of *erat*. —— **erat**, 3d pers. sing. imperf. ind. act. of *sum ;* agrees with the subj. *finis.* —— **cum,** temporal conj., introducing the clause *Jupiter . . . constitit.* For a full list of the uses of *cum,* see the note on *cum,* l. 36. —— **Iūpiter,** gen.⁓*Iovis,* m., 3d irreg.; nom. sing., subj. of *constitit,* l. 226. —— **aethere,** abl. sing. of *aether, -is,* m., 3d; abl. of separation, governed by *de* in *despiciens.* *Aether = the upper air ; aer, = the lower air.* —— **summō,** abl. sing. m. of *summus, -a, -um,* superl. adj.; agrees with *aethere,* and qualifies it partitively; see note, etc. on *summo,* l. 106.

LINE 224.   **Dēspiciēns,** gen. *dēspiciēntis ;* nom. sing. m. of the pres. part. act. of *dē-spiciō, -ere, dēspēxī, dēspectum,* 3 (*dē = down from,* + *spiciō, = I took,* rare) ; agrees with and enlarges *Iupiter.* —— **mare,** acc. sing. of *mare, maris,* n., 3d ; direct obj. of *despi-ciens.* —— **vēlivolum,** acc. sing. n. of *vēlivolus, -a, -um,* adj. (from *vēlum, = a sail,* + *volō, = I fly) ;* qualifies *mare.* Vergil has borrowed this epithet of the sea from Lucre-tius. —— **terrās,** acc. plur. of *terra, -ae,* f., 1st; direct obj. of *despiciens.* —— **que,** en-clitic conj., joining the two objects, *mare* and *terras.* —— **iacentēs,** acc. plur. f. of *iacens, -entis,* pres. part. act. of *iaceō, -ēre, iacuī, iacitum,* 2 ; qualifying *terras.* The lands were *lying, spread out,* as seen from above by Jupiter.

LINE 225. **Litora,** acc. plur. of *lītus, lītoris,* n , 3d ; direct obj. of *despiciens,* and joined by *que* to *terras.* —— **que,** conj. —— **et,** conj., joining *litora* and *populos.* —— **lātōs,** acc. plur. m. of *lātus, -a, -um ;* agrees with *populos.* *Latos,* though properly be-longing to measurement, = *wide,* and so applicable to the countries inhabited by the *po-puli,* is made to qualify the peoples themselves, = *wide-spread.* —— **populōs,** acc. plur. of *populus, -ī,* m., 2d ; direct obj. of *despiciens.* —— **sīc,** adv. of manner. *Sīc =* the Greek οὕτως ; in Greek it is frequently employed in a long period, after extended parti-cipial and other clauses, to pick up the thread of the sentence and renew the main con-struction. —— **vertice,** abl. sing. of *vertex, -icis,* m , 3d (see l. 114) ; abl. of 'place where.' —— **coelī,** gen. sing. of *coelum,* n., 2d ; poss. gen., limiting *vertice.*

LINE 226.   **Constitit,** 3d pers. sing. perf. ind. act. of *constō, -āre, constiti, constitum.* 1 irreg.; agrees with its subj. *Iupiter,* l. 223. —— **et,** conj. —— **Libyae,** gen. sing. of *Libya,* f., 1st; poss. gen , limiting *regnis.* —— **dēfīxit,** 3d pers. sing. perf. ind. act. of *dē-fīgō, -ere, dēfīxī, dēfīxum,* 3 (*dē = down,* + *fīgō, = I fix) ;* joined by *et* to *constitit,* and in the same construction. —— **lūmina,** acc. plur. of *lūmen, -inis,* n., 3d (= *luc-men,* from root in *luceo, = I shine) ;* direct obj. of *defixit.* *Lumen =* (1) *light,* of the sun, a lamp, etc., opposed to *lux, = daylight ;* (2) *daylight,* sometimes in Vergil ; (3) *the eye ;* (4) *the light,* or *excellence,* of things. —— **rēgnīs,** dat. plur. of *rēgnum, -ī,* n., 2d ; dat. of the recipient, loosely used by Vergil instead of *in regna,* which prose requires. Some editors prefer to consider *regnis* a locative abl., but the phrase *defixit lumina* suggests *direction* rather than *position.* It is not quite clear what branch of the dative *regnis* is,

227 **Átque** il,lúm ta,lés „ iac,tántem , péctore ,
And   him   such   turning over   in his breast

228 cúras **Trístior** , ét lacri,mís „ ocu,lós suf,fúsa
cares somewhat sad and with tears   as to her eyes   suffused

229 ni,téntes **Álloqui**,túr Venus: , “ Ó „ qui ,
shining   addresses   Venus :   “ O (thou)   who

Libya.   Him as he
ponders this tale of
cares within his
breast Venus sad be-
yond wont, her shin-
ing eyes bedewed
with tears, addresses:
“ O thou that rulest

---

but as the dat. in all uses is the case of the indirect obj., it suffices to call it a poetic da-
tive. It is possible, however, to suggest two explanations: (1) that *defixit* is used like
other compounds (though *de* is not included). A. & G. 228; B. 187, III; G. 347; H.
386; (2) that *regnis* is a variation of the poetic dat. of the end of motion; e.g. *it clamor
coelo* (= *to the sky*). A. & G. 258, 2, NOTE 1; B. 193; G. 358; H. 380, II, 4.

LINE 227. **Atque**, cop. conj., joining the sentence in which it stands to the preced-
ing one, and suggesting that a new incident follows. —— **illum**, acc. sing. m. of *ille, illa,
illud*, demonstr. pron. of the 3d person; direct obj. of *alloquitur; illum* refers to Jupi-
ter. —— **tālēs**, acc. plur. f. of *tălis, -e;* agrees with *curas*. By *tales* is meant such anxiety
as the state of things among the Trojans, just arrived in Libya, would give rise to. ——
iactantem, acc. sing. m. of *iactans, -antis*, pres. part. act. of *iactō, -āre, -āvī, -ātum*, 1;
agrees with and enlarges *illum*. —— **pectore**, abl. sing. of *pectus, pectoris*, n., 3d; loca-
tive abl., with *iactantem*. —— **cūrās**, acc. plur. of *cūra, -ae*, f., 1st; direct obj. of
iactantem.

LINE 228. **Tristior**, nom. sing. f. of *tristior, -ius*, gen. *tristioris*, the comparative
of *tristis, -e;* agrees with *Venus*. *Tristior* = *rather sad*, i.e. sadder than was usual.
The comparative, apart from its ordinary expression of a higher degree in a quality, has
two uses: (1) expressing a considerable degree, e g. *tristior*, as above; (2) expressing
an excessive degree, = *too*, e.g. *audacius* = *too boldly*. A. & G. 93, *a*; B. 240, 1; G.
297, 2, and 298; H. 444, 1. —— **et**, cop. conj., joining *tristior* and *suffusa*. —— **lacri-
mis**, abl. plur. of *lacrima, -ae*, f., 1st (*lachryma*); abl. of the instrument. —— **oculōs**,
acc. plur. of *oculus, -ī*, m., 2d; the acc. of respect, denoting the part affected. This acc.
(very common in Greek) is also called the acc. of specification, *synecdochical*, or Greek
acc.; it is akin to the cognate acc., and also to the acc. of the direct obj. after verbs
used reflexively in the passive (like the Greek middle voice, e.g. Aen. II, 510, *inutile
ferrum Cingitur*). It is especially common after intransitive verbs, e.g. *tremit artus*, =
he trembles (as to or *in) his limbs*, and after past participles, e.g. *os impressa toro*, =
buried as to her face (= *with her face buried*) *in the couch;* cf. ll. 320, 481, etc. This
acc. may also (like the Greek) be used after adjectives, e.g. *nuda genu*, = *bare as to the
knee*. A. & G. 240, *c*; B. 180; G. 338; H. 378. —— **suffūsa**, nom. sing. f. of *suffūsus,
-a, -um*, perf. part. pass. of *suffundō, -ere, suffūdī, suffūsum*, 3 (*sub + fundo);* agrees
with *Venus*. —— **nitentēs**, acc. plur. m. of *nitens, -entis*, pres. part. act. of *niteō, -ere,
nituī*, no supine, 2 (*nitescō* is more common); qualifies *oculos*.

LINE 229. **Alloquitur**, 3d pers. sing. pres. ind. of the dep. verb *alloquor, -ī, allo-
cūtus sum*, 3 (*ad*, become *al* by assimilation, + *loquor*); agrees with the subj. *Venus*.
Observe that some intransitive verbs when compounded with *ad, trans*, and a few other
prepositions, may govern an acc. of the direct object; see note on *scopulos*, l. 201. ——
Venus, gen. *Veneris*, f., 3d; subj. of *alloquitur*. Venus (= Aphrodite, of Greek mythol-
ogy) was the goddess of love, beauty, pleasure, and laughter. She was married to Vul-
can (in Greek, Hephaestus), but also had a mortal husband, Anchises, to whom she bore
a son, Aeneas. —— **O**, exclamation. —— **qui**, nom. sing. m. of the rel. pron.; agrees

with thy eternal commands the affairs of men and gods, and with thy lightning terrifiest, what sin so great against thee can my Aeneas, can the Trojans have wrought? against whom, after bearing

rés   homi,númque de,úmque Aéter,nís regis, 230
the affairs   of men   and of the gods   eternal   rulest

imperi,ís, „   et ,   fúlmine ,   térres,
by thy commands, and with the thunderbolt terrifiest (them),

Quíd meus , Aéne,ás „ in , té com,míttere , 231
what my   Aeneas   against thee   to commit

tántum, Quíd Tro,és potu,ére, „ qui,bús, 232
so great, what the Trojans were able to whom,

with *tu* understood (the voc. sing. of the 2d pers. pron.), and is subj. of *regis.* —— **rēs,** acc. plur. of *rēs, reī,* f., 5th; direct obj. of *regis.* —— **hominum,** gen. plur. of *homō, -inis,* m., 3d; poss. gen., limiting *res.* —— **que,** enclitic conj.; repeated below, = *both . . . and.* —— **deūm** (for *deōrum*), gen. plur. of *deus, -ī,* m., 2d (see *deūm,* l. 9); joined by *que* below to *hominum.* —— **que,** enclitic conj.; see *que* above.

LINE 230. **Aeternīs,** abl. plur. of *aeternus, -a, -um;* agrees with *imperiis.* —— **regis,** 2d pers. sing. pres. ind. act. of *regō, -ere, rēxī, rectum,* 3; agrees with the subj. *qui.* —— **imperiīs,** abl. plur. of *imperium, -ī,* n., 2d; abl. of the means. —— **et,** conj. —— **fulmine,** abl. sing. of *fulmen, -inis,* n., 3d (from the root in *fulgeō, = I shine);* abl. of the means or instrument, with *terres.* —— **terrēs,** 2d pers. sing. pres. ind. act. of *terreō, -ēre, terruī, territum,* 2; joined by *et* to *regis,* and in agreement with the same subj. *qui.*

LINE 231. **Quid,** acc. sing. n. of the interrog. pron. *quis, quae, quid* (in other cases like the rel.); direct obj. of *committere.* —— **meus,** nom. sing. m. of *meus, mea, meum,* poss. pronominal adj. of the 1st pers. sing. (the voc. m. sing. is *mi*) ; agrees with *Aeneas.* Venus might well claim possession and protection of her own son, but *meus* here is at once endearing and plaintive. —— **Aenēās,** nom. sing.; subj. of *potuit* understood from *potuere* in the next line. —— **in,** prep., governing the acc. *te.* *In = against* in this passage. For the ordinary and idiomatic uses, consult A. & G. 153; B. 143; G. 418, 1; H. 435, 1. —— **tē,** acc. sing. of *tū,* sing. of the 2d pers. pron. ; governed by *in.* Observe the artfulness of this appeal: (a) Venus, the 'smile-lover,' assumes an aspect of gloom (*tristior*); (b) she flatters the lord of heaven and earth (l. 230); (c) she becomes pathetic (*quid meus Aeneas,* fi.); (d) she pretends that Jupiter, not Juno, is harassing the Trojans (*in te);* (e) she reminds Jupiter of his promise (l. 237) ; (f) she contrasts the successful escape of Antenor to Italy with the misadventures of Aeneas. —— **committere,** pres. inf. act. of *committō, -ere, commīsī, commissum,* 3 (*cum + mittō) ;* prolative or explanatory inf. dependent on *potuit* understood (see note on *Aeneas* above). A. & G. 271; B. 326; G. 423; H. 533. *Committere = to bring into contact,* hence idiomatically with acc. *pugnam* or *proelium, = to engage in battle.* *Admittere* is more common than *committere,* of committing crimes. —— **tantum,** acc. sing. n. of *tantus, -a, -um;* agrees with *quid.*

LINE 232. **Quid,** acc. sing. n. (see *quid* above); direct obj. of *committere* understood from the preceding line. —— **Trōēs,** gen. *Trōum,* m., 3d (Greek Τρῶες, acc. Τρῶας, hence Latin acc. *Troas) ;* nom. plur., subj. of *potuere.* —— **potuēre,** 3d pers. plur. perf. ind. of *possum, posse, potuī,* irreg.; agrees with the subj. *Troes.* For the termination *-ere* (for *-erunt*), see note on *tenuere,* l. 12. —— **quibus,** dat. plur. m. of *qui, quae, quod;* dat. of reference (*dativus incommodi*), after *clauditur.* A. & G. 235; B. 188, 1; G. 350; H. 384, II, 1, 2. Observe that after *quid tantum* (= *what so great*) a result clause is naturally expected, and the verb should then be in the subjunct. mood ; thus

233 tot , fúnera , pássis, Cúnctus ob
so many   deaths   having suffered,   all   on account

234 Ítali,ám ,, ter,rárum , claúditur , órbis?   Cérte
of Italy   of lands   is closed   the circle?   Surely

hinc , Róma,nós o,lím, ,, vol,véntibus , ánnis,
from them   the Romans some day,   revolving   the years,

235 Hínc   fore , dúcto,rés, ,, revo,cáto a ,
from them   to be about to be   chiefs,   ·   restored   from

through so many deaths, the whole world is closed for the sake of Italy.
With surety (foreshowing) that one day from them, as the years rolled by, would spring the Romans, would spring leaders of Teucer's

---

quibus claudatur (= *ut iis claudatur*). But the indic. represents the result not so much as a result as an actual state of things at the time. —— **tot**, indecl. adj.; qualifies *funera*. —— **fūnera**, acc. plur. of *fūnus, funeris*, n., 3d; direct obj. of *passis*. —— **passīs**, dat. plur. m. of *passus, -a, -um*, perf. part. of the dep. verb *patior, pati, passus sum*, 3; agrees with and enlarges *quibus*.

LINE 233. **Cūnctus**, nom. sing. m. of *cūnctus, -a, -um ;* agrees with *orbis. Cunctus* is emphatic, and hints at the previous wanderings of Aeneas in the vain attempt to find a home. —— **ob**, prep. with the acc.; gov. *Italiam. On account of Italy* = on account of Juno's desire to keep the Trojans from Italy. —— **Ītaliam**, acc. sing. of *Italia, -ae*, f., 1st; obj. of *ob*. —— **terrārum**, gen. plur. of *terra, -ae*, f., 1st; subjective poss. gen., limiting *orbis*. —— **clauditur**, 3d pers. sing. pres. ind. pass. of *claudō, -ere, clausī, clausum*, 3; agrees with the subj. *orbis*. The ind. mood *clauditur* represents the *closing of the world* as an accomplished fact, and is therefore more vivid than the subjunct. usual in such sentences (see note on *quibus*, l. 232). —— **orbis**, gen. *orbis*, m., 3d; nom. sing., subj. of *clauditur. Orbis terrarum* is also the prose phrase = *the world;* it is distinct from *terra*, a division of the world or land as opposed to sea and sky, and also from *mundus*, = *the universe*, including the world.

LINE 234. **Certē**, adv. (from adj. *certus, -a, -um*), extending *pollicitus (es)*. —— **hīnc**, adv. (from demonstr. pron. *hīc*), limiting *fore; hīnc* = *from this*, so *hence*, and here *from these men*. —— **Rōmānōs**, acc. plur. of *Rōmānus, -ī*, m., 2d (properly the m. sing. of the adj. *Rōmānus, -a, -um*, from *Rōma, -ae*, f., 1st); acc.-subj. of *fore* understood from *fore*, l. 235. —— **ōlim**, adv., extending *fore*. —— **volventibus**, abl. plur. m. of *volvens, -entis*, pres. part. act. of *volvō, -ere, volvī, volūtum*, 3; agrees with *annis* in the abl. abs. construction. Observe that the trans. verb *volvo* is here intrans., = *se vol ventibus; volvo, verto*, and a few other verbs are trans. or intrans. in Vergil, though never in prose. —— **annīs**, abl. plur. of *annus, -ī*, m., 2d; in the abl. abs. construction with *volventibus*, = *as the years keep rolling on*, hence the pres. participle.

LINE 235. **Hīnc**, adv.; see *hinc* above. This repetition of a word is *anaphora;* cf. *hic . . . hic*, l. 17. —— **fore**, fut. inf. of *sum, esse, fuī;* inf. mood in the object clause *fore ductores*. The verb *sum* has two future infinitive forms, *fore* and the more common *futurus, -a, -um, esse*. —— **ductōrēs**, acc. plur. of *ductor, ductōris*, m., 3d (from *dūcō);* acc. subj. of *fore*, an acc. and inf. clause directly governed by the *verbum declarandi, pollicitus*. —— **revocātō**, abl. sing. m. of *revocātus, -a, -um*, perf. part. pass. of *revocō, -āre, -āvī, -ātum*, 1; agrees attributively with *sanguine. Revocato* = lit. *recalled*, i.e. into vigorous existence after the destruction of Troy by the Greeks. —— **ā**, prep. with the abl.; gov. *sanguine. A (ab)* in this case expresses *origin.* A. & G. 152, *b*, and 153; B. 142, 1; G. 417, 1; H. 434. —— **sanguine**, abl. sing. of *sanguis, sanguinis*, m., 3d; governed by *a*.

blood renewed, who	sánguine , Teúcri, Qúi mare, , quí ter,rás ,, 236
should with full power	*the blood* *of Teucer, who the sea, who the lands*
bear sway o'er sea	
and land, thou didst	om,ní diti,óne te,nérent, Póllici,tús: ,, quae , 237
make promise: what	*all with power should hold, thou hast promised: what*

—— **Teucrī**, gen. sing. of *Teucer* (another form *Teucrus*), m., 2d; poss. gen., limiting *sanguine*. This Teucer was a son of the Cretan river-god Scamander by Ida, and the region which he ruled was called *Teucria* after him, and his subjects *Teucri*. He was succeeded in power by his son-in-law Dardanus (hence *Dardanidae, = Trojans*). Carefully distinguish Teucer the king from Teucer, son of Telamon and brother of Ajax, who made a new home in Cyprus, where he founded a city, Salamis.

LINE 236. **Quī**, nom. plur. m. of the rel. pron.; subj. of *tenerent*, understood from the next clause, agreeing with the antecedent *ductores*. —— **mare**, acc. sing. of *mare,-is*, n., 3d; direct obj. of *tenerent*, understood from the next clause. —— **quī**, nom. plur. m.; subj. of *tenerent*. With *qui . . . qui*, cf. *hinc . . . hinc* above (*anaphora*); observe the omission of a conjunction to connect the two clauses, called *asyndeton*. A. & G. 208, *b*; B. 346; G. 473, REM.; H. 636, I, I. —— **terrās**, acc. plur. of *terra, -ae*, f., 1st; direct obj. of *tenerent*. *Mare* and *terras = the world;* the known world was subject to the Roman empire in the time of Vergil, or nearly all subject, for the Parthians were destined to give further trouble. —— **omnī**, abl. sing. of *omnis, -e;* agrees with *ditione*. *Omni ditione =* with *full* power. —— **ditiōne** (*dicione*), abl. sing. of *ditiō* (*diciō*), *-ōnis*, f., 3d (from root in *dō, = I give*, hence a *giving up of oneself* to some one); abl. of manner, showing how the Romans would rule, rather than an abl. of the means. A. & G. 248, at the end; B. 220; G. 399, NOTE 2; H. 419, III. This noun only occurs in the gen., dat., acc., and abl. sing.; it is used by Vergil, Livy, Cicero, etc. = *dominion, sway, power*. —— **tenērent**, 3d pers. plur. imperf. subjunct. act. of *teneō, -ēre, tenuī, tentum*, 2; agrees with the subj. *qui;* the subjunct. mood expresses *purpose*, after *qui final, = ut ei*. A. & G. 317; B. 282; G. 545; H. 497, I. The imperf. tense is in sequence after the *historic* perf. *pollicitus* (*es*). A. & G. 286; B. 267, 268; G. 509; H. 491.

LINE 237. **Pollicitus**, nom. sing. m. of the perf. part. of the dep. verb *polliceor, pol-licēri, pollicitus sum*, 2; agrees with its subj. *tu* understood (referring to Jupiter), and forming, with *es* or *eras* supplied from *sum*, the perf. or pluperf. (respectively) ind. of *polliceor*. The omission of the 2d pers. in compound tenses is rare, though very common in the 3d person; but cf. Aen. V, 687, *si nondum exosus* (*es*) *ad unum Troianos*. Various emendations have been attempted : (1) Ribbeck reads *pollicitu's* (also *exosu's*), instance of apocope found in Plautus but never occurring in Vergil; (2) some change *pollicitus* to *pollicitum*, the acc. sing. m. of the participle, placing a comma after it; in that case *pollicitum* agrees with and enlarges the obj. *te*, in the main sentence *quae te sententia vertit?* = " what thought changes you, after you have promised (*having prom-ised*) that hence, etc."; (3) others place a *comma* after *pollicitus*, and regard the sentence as an example of *anacoluthon* (a Greek word = *want of sequence*), whereby the scheme of the sentence has been changed grammatically, leaving the sense fairly clear. If *pollicitus* is a part. only, something like *cur verteris*, or *qua sententia* (abl.) *verteris* would grammatically be expected. A. & G. 385; B. 374, 6; G. 697; H. 636, IV, 6. However, *pollicitus* (sc. *es*) is the simplest way out of the difficulty. Synonyms: *polliceor*, of promises made freely and spontaneously; *promitto*, of promises generally, but often in answer to requests. —— **quae**, nom. sing. f., of the interrog. adj. *quī, quae, quod;* agrees with *sententia*. This adj. is declined like the rel. pron. *qui* —— **tē**, acc. sing. of *tū;* direct obj. of *vertit*. —— **genitor**, gen. *genitōris* (from *genō, = I beget*), m., 3d; voc. sing.,

238 té,	geni,tór,	sen,téntia ,	vértit ?	Hóc	counsel, Sire, changes
thee,	*O sire,*	*opinion*	*changes?*	*With this*	thee ? Therein in-
equi,*dem*	ócca,súm	Tro,iǽ	„ tris,tésque		deed I found solace for
indeed	*the fall*	*of Troy*	*and sad*		Troy's downfall and
239 ru,ínas	Sóla,bár,		fa,tís „		her sad ruins, with
its ruins	*I comforted myself for,*		*against (good) fates*		other destiny com-
240 con,tráría ,	fáta re,péndens		Núnc ea,dém		pensating destiny;
adverse	*fates weighing.*		*Now same*		now the same fortune

= *O Sire,* referring to Jupiter, whom Venus is addressing. —— **sententia,** gen. *senten-
tiae,* f., 1st (from *sentio,* = *I think,* hence *thought*); nom. sing., subj. of *vertit. Sententia,*
= (1) *sentiment, opinion;* (2) *decision, verdict,* given officially : *sententia* is the word
used for giving one's views in the senate. The following phrases are common : *ex or.
de mea (tua,* etc.) *sententia, praeter sententiam,* etc.; a word worth consultation in a
dictionary. —— **vertit,** 3d pers. sing. pres. ind. act. of *vertō, -ere, vertī, versum,* 3, agrees
with the interrog. subj. *quae sententia.* The inversion "what thought changes you?"
for "why do you change your opinion?" is one of a kind common in Vergil, and is quite
common in English.

LINE 238. **Hōc,** abl. sing. n. of *hīc, haec, hōc ;* abl. of the means referring to the body
of the promise narrated above. —— **equidem,** corroborative adv., = *indeed, for my (your,*
etc.) *part.* It is probably compounded of *ec* = *ce,* a demonstrative suffix, and *quidem,*
though some say of *et* and *quidem.* Others think (with less probability) that it is com-
pounded of *ego* and *quidem,* cf. ἔγωγε, = *I at least,* as one word; its frequent use with
the 1st pers. sing. of verbs accounts for this, but there are many examples of its use with
other persons, e.g. Cicero has, *equidem id erat primum.* —— **occāsum,** acc. sing. of
occāsus -ūs, m., 4th (from *occīdo*) ; direct obj. of *solabar.* Its chief meanings are :
(1) *opportunity ;* (2) lit., *a falling,* hence *occasus solis,* = *the setting of sun ;* (3) of the
quarter in which the sun sets, *the west ;* (4) *destruction, death,* as the verb may = *to die.*
—— **Trōiae,** gen. sing. of *Trōia,* f., 1st; subjective gen., limiting *occasum.* —— **tristēs,**
acc. plur. f. of *tristis, -e ;* qualifies *ruinas.* —— **ruīnās,** acc. plur.
of *ruīna, -ae,* f., 1st (from *ruō*) ; direct obj. (joined by *que* to *occasum*) of *solatar.*

LINE 239. **Sōlābar,** 1st pers. sing. imperf. ind. of the dep. verb *sōlor, -ārī, -ātus,
sum,* 1; agrees with the unexpressed subj. *ego* (i.e. Venus). *Solor,* properly with per-
sons = *I comfort* or with things = *I soothe ;* here it = *I find solace for,* being extended
in its object-governing capacity over the actual cause of the grief that troubles the mind.
Mr. Conington compares Cicero, *pro Milone,* 35, *solari brevitatem vitae.* —— **fātīs,**
dat. plur. of *fātum, -ī,* n., 3d; dat. of the remoter obj. governed by the whole phrase
contraria fata rependens. Some call *fatis* an abl. of the instrument = *compensating
opposite fate with (better) fate,* but the order of the words tends to show that by *fatis* is
meant not the better, but the adverse fate : others again call the abl. one of price, but
this is hardly possible. The dat. is more natural; render *balancing opposite* (i.e. better)
fate against (evil) *fate.* We may compare the use of intransitive compounds of *re,* e.g.
resisto, repugno, which govern the dat. of the indirect obj., the dat. being in addition one
of advantage or the reverse (disadvantage in the case of *fatis*). A. & G. the examples to
227, *f* ; B. 187; G. 346, also 345; H. 385, I. —— **contrāria,** acc. plur. n. of *contrārius, -a,
-um* (from *contrā,* = *against*); agrees with *fata.* —— **fāta,** acc. plur. of *fātum, -ī,* n., 2d;
direct obj. of *rependens.* —— **rependēns,** nom. sing. f. of the pres. part. act. of *rependō,
-ere, rependī, repensum,* 3 (*re* + *pendō*) ; agrees with *ego* understood as subj. of *solabar.*

LINE 240. **Nunc,** adv. of time, but here with adversative force, = *as it is.* ——
eadem, nom sing. f. of *īdem* (= *is-dem*), *eadem, īdem* (= *id-dem*), determinative

follows the heroes,	for, túna	vi, rós	„	tot	,	cásibus	,	áctos
driven by all these	*the fortune*	*the heroes*		*so many*		*by disasters*		*driven*
many disasters. What	Ínsequi, túr.	Quem	,	dás	fi, ném,	„	rex	, 241
term, great King,	*follows.*	*What*		*givest thou*	*end,*		*king*	
settest thou for their	mágne,	la, bórum ?		Ánte, nór		potu, ít,	„	242
sorrows ? Antenor	*great,*	*of their toils?*		*Antenor*		*was able,*		
escaping from the	medi, ís		e, lápsus			A, chívis,		
Achaeans' m i d s t	*midmost*		*having escaped*			*from the Achivi,*		

pron.; agrees with *fortuna.* *Idem* is declined like the pron. *is, ea, id,* except that
m changes to *n* before *d*, e.g. *eundem (eum + dem).* A. & G. 101, and *c*; B. 87;
G. 103, 2; H. 186, VI, and footnote 6 on page 73.——**fortūna,** gen. *fortūnae,* f., 1st;
nom. sing., subj. of *insequitur. Fortuna = luck,* or *fortune,* without necessarily imply-
ing whether good or bad; the adjectives *secunda* and *adversa* mark such distinction.
——**virōs,** acc. plur. of *vir, -ī,* m., 2d; direct obj. of *insequitur.* It will be remembered
that intransitive verbs, compounded with *in* (gov. the acc.), *ad,* etc., become transitive,
and take a direct object.——**tot,** indecl. adj., agreeing with *casibus. Tot* is often used
with a corresponding correlative *quot, tot . . . quot, = so many . . . as.*——**cāsibus,**
abl. plur. of *cāsus, -ūs,* m., 4th; abl. of the instrument, after *actos. Casus* (from *cado, =
I fall) = a falling,* i.e. *chance,* with no original implication as to good or bad, but in
process of use gradually acquiring a bad signification.——**actōs,** acc. plur. m. of *actus,
-a, -um,* perf. part. pass. of *agō, -ere, ēgī, actum,* 3; agrees with and enlarges *viros.*

LINE 241.   **Insequitur,** 3d pers. sing. pres. ind. of the dep. verb *insequor, -ī, insecū-
tus sum,* 3 (*in = against* or *towards,* + *sequor = I follow*)*;* agrees with the subj. *fortuna.*
——**quem,** acc. sing. m. of the interrog. adj. *quī, quae, quod;* agrees with *finem.*——
das, 2d pers. sing. pres. ind. act. of *dō, dare, dedī, datum,* 1; its subj. *tu* is unexpressed,
as usually, except when emphasis or contrast are desired.——**fīnem,** acc. sing. of *fīnis,
-is,* m., 3d; direct obj. of *das.* Vergil often uses *finis* as feminine; e.g. Aen. III, 145,
quam fessis finem rebus ferat.——**rēx** (*reg* + *s*), gen. *rēgis,* m., 3d; voc. sing., as Jupi-
ter, the king of gods and men, is the object of address.——**magne,** voc. sing. of *mag-
nus, -a, -um;* agrees with *rex.*——**labōrum,** gen. plur. of *labor, -ōris,* m., 3d; subjec-
tive gen., defining *finem.*

LINE 242.   **Antēnor,** gen. *Antēnoris,* m., 3d; nom. sing., subj. of *potuit.* Antenor
was a Trojan prince who during the war had advised the restoration of Helen, and who
assisted the Greeks in the means which led to the capture of Troy.   On his escape he
led a band of Paphlagonians of Asia Minor called *Eneti* or *Heneti* to Italy, settling in
the north, and also founding the city of Patavium or Padua.   The similarity between the
names *Heneti* and *Veneti* gave rise to the story that, when Antenor's colony was settled,
his followers called themselves *Veneti.* For Antenor's name in a controversial point, see
note on *primus,* l. 1.——**potuit,** 3d pers. sing. perf. ind. act. of *possum; posse, potuī,* no
supine, irreg.; agrees with the subj. *Antenor.* For its conjugation, consult A. & G. 137,
b ; B. 126 ; G. 119 ; H. 290.——**mediīs,** abl. plur. of *medius, -a, -um;* adj., used par-
titively to mark a particular part of the noun, agreeing with *Achivis. Summus* and *imus*
are the most common partitive adjectives, but *medius* occurs very frequently.   A. & G.
193 ; B. 241 ; G. 291, REM. 2 ; H. 440, 2, NOTE 1.   *Mediis elapsus Achivis* thus = not
escaped from the middle Greeks, but *from the midst of the Greeks;* so *summus mons*
usually = *the top of the mountain,* not *the highest mountain.*——**ēlapsus,** nom. sing. m.
of the perf. part. of the dep. verb *ēlabor, -ī, ēlapsus sum,* 3 (*ē = out of, from,* + *labor =
I slip*)*;* agrees with and enlarges *Antenor,* the participial clause taking the place of a
temporal clause, e.g. *cum elapsus esset.*——**Achīvīs,** abl. plur. of *Achīvī, -ōrum,* m., 2d *;*

243 Íllyri, cós	pene, tráre	si, nús	,,	at, que	availed to win safely
Illyrian	*to penetrate*	*the bays*		*and*	through to the Illy-rian bays and to the
244 íntima	tútus	Régna	Li, búrno, *rum*, ,,		inmost realm of the
inmost	*safe*	*the kingdoms*	*of the Liburni*,		Liburnians, and to
ét	fon, tém	supe, ráre	Ti, mávi,		o'erpass the source
and	*the source*	*to pass over*	*of Timavus*,		of Timavus, whence

abl. of separation after *elapsus*. This use of the abl., where the separation and motion are definite and not figurative, is poetical: in prose *e* or *ex* would have to be repeated with the ablative. A. & G. 243 ; B. 214 ; G. 390, 1, and 2, NOTE 3 ; H. 414, I. The Greeks have various names in Vergil, *Achivi, Grai, Argivi, Danai*, etc. ; so the Trojans are *Troiani, Troes, Dardanidae*, etc.

LINE 243. **Illyricōs**, acc. plur. m. of *Illyricus, -a, -um* (= pertaining to *Illyria, -ae*, f., 1st) ; agrees with *sinus*. The coast on the east of the Adriatic sea was called *Illyricum*. —— **penetrāre**, pres. inf. act. of *penetrō, -āre, -āvī, -ātum*, 1 (the root PEN = *within*) ; prolative inf., dependent on *potuit*. This word, like *elapsus*, hints at the diffi-culties which Antenor had to face ere he could reach Italy ; yet he succeeded, and Venus endeavors to persuade Jupiter to grant Aeneas like good fortune. —— **sinūs**, acc. plur. of *sinus, -ūs*, m., 4th ; direct obj. of *penetrare*. *Sinus* here = *bays* or *gulfs*, with which the coasts of the Adriatic sea abound. —— **atque**, cop. conj., joining *sinus* and *regna*. *Atque* (*ac* before consonants, except *c, g*, and *qu*) emphasizes the second of the words or sentences it connects, and sometimes is used to introduce a third member into a series. Thus *penetrare regna intima* is something more important for Antenor to do than to sail up the Adriatic. Of *et* and *que, et* simply connects two words or sentences of equal value (as *et* in l. 244) ; *que*, the enclitic, joins two members of a pair or series which are closely connected with one another internally. A. & G. 156, *a* ; B. 341 ; G. 475-477, and 481, NOTE ; H. 554, I. —— **intima**, acc. plur. n. of *intimus, -a, -um*, superl. adj. ; a partitive attribute of *regna* (see note on *mediis*, l. 242). The superl. *intimus* is formed from the prep. or adv. *intrā* ; the positive *interus* is very rare ; the comparative is *inte-rior*, often used partitively. *Intima* may be taken as merely descriptive, not partitive ; it then = *remote*; but *inmost* (i.e. the inmost parts of) is preferable. —— **tūtus**, nom. sing. m. ; agrees with *Antenor*, but has adverbial force, = *in safety*. A. & G. 191 ; B. 239; G. 325, REM. 6 ; H. 443.

LINE 244. **Rēgna**, acc. plur. of *rēgnum, -ī*, n., 2d ; direct obj. of *penetrare*, joined by *atque* to *sinus*. —— **Liburnōrum**, gen. plur. of *Liburnī*, m. plur., 2d; poss. gen., lim-iting *regna*. The *Liburni* inhabited Liburnia (now Croatia), between Istria and Dal-matia, from which place settlers left to found a colony in Italy. The *Liburnian* ships were strongly though lightly built. —— **et**, cop. conj., connecting the *penetrare* and *supe-rare*. —— **fontem**, acc. sing. of *fons, fontis*, m., 3d ; direct obj. of *superare*. *Fons* (like *mons, dens, pons*, etc.) belongs to a list of 3d decl. nouns in *-ns* which are masculine. A. & G. 67, *d*; B. 43, 2, and 45, 5, *a* ; G. 55 ; H. 110. —— **superāre**, pres. inf. act. of *superō, -āre, -āvī, -ātum*, 1 ; prolative inf., joined by *et* to *penetrare*, and dependent on *potuit*. *Superare* conveys an idea of exertion ; transitively it● (1) *to pass over*, as here; (2) *to outstrip*, in any quality ; (3) *to conquer*; intransitively, it = *to excel*. —— **Ti-māvī**, gen. sing. of *Timāvus*, m., 2d ; poss. gen., limiting *fontem*. The Timavus (Timao) is a stream, rising between Aquileia and Trieste, and not very much more than a mile in length. Vergil describes it as having nine mouths, but commentators differ as to his exact meaning in other points. NOTE.— From the reference to *mare* and *pelago*, l. 246, some have supposed that the river is just a brook, and that for its last mile it flows under-

through nine mouths	Únde	per	, óra	no, vém	„	vas, tó	cum	, 245
with vast mountain-	*whence*	*through*	*mouths*	*nine*		*vast*	*with*	
roaring it spreads a	múrmure	, móntis	Ít	mare	, prórup, *tum*	„ 246
bursting sea and with	*a noise*	*of the mountain*	*it goes*	*a sea*	*burst forth*	
its sounding flood	ét	pela, gó	premit	, árva	so, nánti.
covers the fields.	*and with its waters*	*overwhelms*	*the fields*	*resounding.*

ground, and that the sea is sometimes driven up underground through nine channels, inundating the plains with salt water. This explanation is in all probability wrong. The correct solution seems to be that the Timavus flows underground for some distance, gaining force and volume, and roaring under the earth (*vasto cum murmure*, l. 245), then *bursts forth* (*proruptum*) at the apparent *fons*, viz.: the *nine mouths*, and floods the land like a sea (*mare* and *pelago* being metaphors). This is Mr. Page's explanation, and the best; Mr. Page says that Servius quotes Varro to prove that the Timavus was known among the natives as *mare*.

LINE 245. **Unde**, adv. of place, denoting separation. *Unde* refers to *fontem*, the underground source of the Timavus. Note that the *mare* rushes *from*, not *to*, the *fontem*. —— **per**, prep. with the acc.; gov. *ora.* —— **óra**, acc. plur. of *ōs, ōris*, n., 3d ; obj. of *per*. *Os* = (1) *face*, (2) *mouth;* distinguish it from *os, ossis*, n., 3d, = *a bone*. —— **novem**, indecl. numeral adj.; an attribute of *ora.* —— **vāstō**, abl. sing. of *vāstus, -a, -um ;* qualifies *murmure*. —— **cum**, prep. with the abl.; gov. *murmure*, denoting manner. For its position between the noun and its adjective, refer to the note on *cum*, l. 47. —— **murmure**, abl. sing. of *murmur, -is*, n., 3d (from *mur*, an *onomatopoeic* sound); governed by *cum*. —— **montis**, gen. sing. of *mons*, m., 3d (see note on *fontem*, l. 244); subjective poss. gen., limiting *murmure*. This phenomenon of the rumbling in the mountains is best explained by the theory given in the note under *Timavi*, l. 244.

LINE 246. **It**, 3d pers. sing. pres. ind. act. of *eō, īre, īvī* or *iī, itum*, irreg. intrans. ; agrees with a pron. (referring to *Timavus*) as subj. The passive of *eo* is used impersonally, e.g. *itur ad astra* (*it is gone*) ; the supine in *um* expressing purpose after verbs of motion is very common after *eo*, and the future inf. pass. of all verbs is a periphrastic form, made up of the supine in *um* + the pres. inf. pass. of *eo, iri*, e.g. *amatum iri, = to be about to be loved* (lit. *to be a going to love*). For the conjugation of *eo*, consult A. & G. 141; B. 132; G. 169; H. 295. Compounds of *eo* nearly always form the perf. tense in -*ii* instead of -*ivi*. —— **mare**, gen. *maris*, n., 3d; nom. sing., in apposition with the subj. of *it*. *Mare* is metaphorical, = *it goes forth a sea*. As said in the note on l. 244, some take *mare* literally, = *the sea*, in which case *mare* is subj. of *it*. —— **proruptum**, nom. sing. n. of *prōruptus, -a, -um*, perf. part. pass. of *prōrumpō, -ere, prōrūpī, prōruptum*, 3 (*prō* = forth + *rumpō* = trans. *I break*, and intrans. *I burst out*) ; agrees with *mare*. *Proruptum* has a mid lle voice meaning, = *se prorumpens, bursting forth*. This word can only literally refer to the bursting out of the river after running underground; referring to the sea, the force of *pro* is quite lost. The natural pause is after this word; and so, in spite of the *ecthlipsis* of *um*, the caesura is better marked after it than after *et ;* there is another *caesura* after *pelago*, but clearly not the important one. —— **et**, cop. conj. —— **pelagō**, abl. sing. of *pelagus, -ī*, n., 2d; abl. of the instrument, after *premit*. *Pelago* is metaphorical, like *mare* above; render *with its flood*. —— **premit**, 3d pers. sing. pres. ind. act. of *premō, -ere, pressī, pressum*, 3; coördinate with *it* above, to which it is joined by *et*. *Premit = covers, deluges*, with an implied idea of hostility, as a foe *presses* a foe. —— **arva**, acc. plur. of *arvum, -ī*, n., 2d (properly n. sing. of *arvus, -a, -um = ploughed*, from *aro ;* supply *solum*) ; direct obj. of *premit*. Synonyms: *ager, = a field*, whether cultivated or not; *arvum, = arable land.* —— **sonantī**,

247 Híc	tamen	,	ílle	ur,bém	Pata,ví „	Yet here he estab-
Here	*nevertheless*		*he*	*the city*	*of Patavium*	lished the city of Pa-
248 se,désque		lo,cávit		Teúcro,rum,	ét	tavium and the homes
and the homes		*he founded*		*of the Trojans,*	*and*	of his Trojans, gave
gen,tí	„	no,mén	dedit,	, ármaque	, fíxit	his name to the peo-
to the race		*a name*	*gave,*	*and arms*	*fixed*	ple, and hung up the

---

abl. sing. n. of *sonans, -antis*, pres. part. act. of *sonō, -āre, sonuī, sonitum*, 1 ; agrees with *pelago*. When the pres. part. of verbs is used attributively, like an adj., the abl. sing. ends in *i*; but when used as a verb, e.g. in the abl. abs. construction, the abl. ends in *e*.

LINE 247. **Hīc**, adv. of place, limiting *locavit*. —— **tamen** (probably a longer form of *tam*), adv. or conj. of adversative force, = *nevertheless*. It is often the correlative of such concessive particles as *etsi* or *quam vis*, e.g. *etsi, although . . . tamen, notwithstanding*. *Tamen* is generally post-positive, i.e. follows one or more words in its clause. It is often used to strengthen other conjunctions (especially adversative ones), e.g. *attamen, sed tamen.* A. & G. 156, *i, k*; B. 343, 1, *f*); G. 485, NOTE 3, and 490; H. 310, 3, and 554, III. —— **ille**, nom. sing. m. of the 3d demonstr. pron.; refers to Antenor, and is subj. of *locavit*. *Ille* is emphatic, suggesting the contrast between Antenor and Aeneas. —— **urbem**, acc. sing. of *urbs, urbis*, f., 3d; direct obj. of *locavit*. —— **Patavī**, gen. sing. of Patavium, n., 2d; descriptive or adnominal gen., describing *urbem*. A. & G. 214, *f*; B. 202; G. 361; H. 395. The gen. would not occur in prose, but *Patavium* in apposition with *urbem;* in English we speak of *the city of Rome*, but in Latin it is *urbs Roma;* cf. Aen. V, 52, *urbe Mycenae*. Vergil always writes the contracted gen. in *-i* (instead of *-ii*) of 2d decl. nouns in *-ium*. The testimony of examples from the best period of Latin literature lends greater support to this contracted gen. than to the other full form; e.g. *filius*, gen. *fīli* (not *fīlii*). Thus Vergil and Cicero almost invariably have *-i*, but Ovid constantly *-ii*. A. & G. 40, *b*; B. 25, 1 and 2; G. 33, REM. 1; H. 51, 5. *Patavium*, now Padua, is famous as the birthplace of Livy, the historian. —— **sēdēs**, acc. plur. of *sēdēs, -is*, f., 3d (from *sēdeo*, = *I sit*, hence *abode*)*;* direct obj. of *locavit*, joined by *que* enclitic to *urbem*. —— **que**, conj. —— **locāvit**, 3d pers. sing. perf. ind. act. of *locō, -āre, -āvī, -ātum*, 1 (from *locus*)*;* agrees with the subj. *ille*.

LINE 248. **Teucrōrum**, gen. plur. of *Teucrī*, m. plur. 2d; poss. gen., limiting *sedes*. —— **et**, cop. conj., joining *dedit* to *locavit*. —— **gentī**, dat. sing. of *gens, gentis*, f., 3d; dat. of the indirect obj. after *dedit*. —— **nōmen**, acc. sing. of *nōmen, nōminis*, n., 3d (= lit. that by which something is known, from *nosco*)*;* direct obj. of *dedit*. The Romans had each 3 names, one for himself, one for his *gens*, and one for his family; thus in Publius Cornelius Scipio: *Publius*, the *praenomen*, serves as a Christian name in English; the *nomen Cornelius* shows that Publius was of the house or *gens* of the Cornelii (founded by a Cornelius); *Scipio*, the family name or *cognomen* is, as often, a nickname, = *a staff*. Any extra title is called an *agnomen* (*ad* + (*g*)*nomen*, = *name in addition*), e.g. of Scipio, *Africanus*, because of his military renown won in Africa. Women used to have no Christian names, only the *nomen* of their house; e.g. *Cornelia, Tullia*, etc. What the name was that Antenor gave his people is not known; tradition has it that his settlement was called *Troia*, and Mr. Conington supposes that Antenor called his subjects *Veneti*. —— **dedit**, 3d pers. sing. perf. ind. act. of *dō, dare, dedī, datum*, 1; agrees with the same subj. as *locavit*, to which it is joined by *et*. —— **arma**, acc. plur. of *arma, -ōrum*, n., plur. 2d; direct obj. of *fixit*. It was the custom to hang up weapons, shield, etc., in a temple on the conclusion of a war. —— **que**, enclitic conj. —— **fīxit**, 3d pers. sing. perf. ind. act. of *fīgō, -ere, fīxī, fīxum*, 3; joined by *que* to *dedit*, and agrees with the same subj., viz. *ille*. *Fixit = fastened* or *hung up*, i.e. on temple walls, in token of peace.

arms of Troy; now	Tróïa ; , núnc placi,dá „ com,póstus , páce 249
settled in peaceful	*Trojan;* *now* *quiet* *settled* , *in peace*
calm he rests. We,	qui,éscit: Nós, tua , prógeni,és, „ coe,lí quibus, 250
thy offspring, who by	*he rests:* *We,* *thy* *offspring,* *of heaven to whom*
thy nod are heirs of	ánnuis , árcem, Návibus , ínfan,dum! 251
heaven's citadel,	*thou dost promise* *the citadel,* *the ships* *alas!*
our ships alas! lost,	ámis,sís, „ u,níus ob , íram
for the sake of one	*having been lost,* *of one* *on account of* *the anger*

LINE 249. **Trōïa,** acc. plur. of *Trōïus, -a, -um;* agrees with *arma.* —— **nunc,** adv. of time. —— **placidā,** abl. sing. f. of *placidus, -a, -um;* an attribute of *pace.* —— **compostus** (*syncopated* for *compositus*), nom. sing. m. of the perf. part. pass. of *compōnō, -ere, composuī, compositum,* 3 (*cum,* in composition *con + pōnō*)*;* agrees with and enlarges *ille* understood as subj. of *quiescit. Compono* may = (1) *I arrange, settle;* (2) *I lay out,* for burial, hence *bury;* it is doubtful whether Venus is speaking of the peacefulness of Antenor in a state of life or death, probably the former. For the *syncope,* consult A. & G. 128, I, 2; B. 367, 8; G. 131, 1; H. 235. —— **pāce,** abl. sing. of *pāx, pācis,* f., 3d; abl. of manner, without *cum,* as *pace* is qualified by the adj. *placida* (by the regular rule). —— **quiescit,** 3d pers. sing. pres. ind. act. of *quiescō, -ere, quiēvī, quiētum,* 3 (*quies, = rest*)*;* agrees with subj. *ille* understood. Verbs in *-sco* are *inceptive* or *inchoative* verbs, which = *to begin to do* something; e.g. *quiesco, irascor,* etc. A. & G. 167, *a;* B. 155, 1; G. 133, V; H. 337.

LINE 250. **Nōs,** nom. plur. of *nōs,* gen. *nostrum* or *nostrī,* acc. *nōs,* dat. and abl. *nōbīs,* 2d personal pron. (plur.; in sing. *tu*)*;* subj. of *prodimur,* l. 252. The contrast has been working since *Antenor,* l. 242; now it is being painted, and skilfully, for Venus classes herself as one of the Trojans (*we,* very emphatic). —— **tua,** nom. sing. f. of *tuus, -a, -um,* poss. pronominal adj. of 2d sing. personal pron.; agrees with *progenies.* —— **prōgeniēs,** gen. *prōgeniēī,* f., 5th; nom. sing. in apposition with *nos.* —— **coelī,** gen. sing. of *coelum,* n., 2d; subj. gen., limiting *arcem.* —— **quibus,** dat. plur. m. of the rel. *quī, quae, quod;* agrees with the antecedent *nos* (wherein the masculine gender predominates), and is dat. of the indirect obj. after the notion of promising in *adnuis.* It was to Aeneas that the promise of translation to heaven was made : like Romulus, Aeneas was supposed not to have died, but to have become one of the *Dei Indigetes.* Venus, like a lawyer, identifies herself with her client. —— **annuis** (*adnuis*), 2d pers. sing. pres. ind. act. of *annuō* (*adnuō*), *-ere, -uī, -ūtum,* 3 (*ad = to + nuo = I nod*)*;* the subj. is *tu* unexpressed, in the rel. clause *coeli . . . arcem. Adnuo,* from the affirmative signification of a nod, esp. the nod of Jupiter, = *I assent to,* hence *promise.* —— **arcem,** acc. sing. of *arx, arcis,* f., 3d; direct obj. of *annuis.*

LINE 251. **Nāvibus,** abl. plur. of *nāvis, -is,* f., 3d; abl. abs. with *amissis.* —— **infandum,** acc. sing. n. of *infandus, -a, -um* (*in = not, + fandus* (gerundive of *fāri*), *that must be spoken,* i.e. *unutterable*)*;* exclamatory acc., = to an interjection, e.g. *eheu, alas.* This acc. may be used with or without *O* or *pro,* etc., e.g. *O fallacem spem ! = O treacherous hope ! me miserum, = unhappy me !* A. & G. 240, *d* ; B. 183; G. 343, 1; H. 381. —— **āmissīs,** abl. plur. f. of *āmissus, -a, -um,* perf. part. pass. of *āmittō, -ere, āmīsī, āmissum,* 3; agrees with *navibus* in the abl. abs. construction. —— **ūnīus,** gen. sing. of *ūnus, -a, -um ;* poss. gen., limiting *iram. Unīus = Iunonis.* Observe that the vowel *i* is long; less commonly it is short. —— **ob,** prep. with the acc.; gov. *iram.* —— **īram,** acc. sing. of *īra, -ae,* f., 1st; governed by *ob.*

252 Pródimur, , átque Ita,lís ,, lon,gé dis,iúngimur	foe's anger are aban-
are betrayed, and Italian far we are severed	doned and severed
	far from the shores
253 óris. Híc pie,tátis ho,nós? ,, sic , nós in ,	of Italy. Is this the re-
from shores. (Is) this of virtue the reward? thus us to	ward of virtue ? thus
	dost thou restore us
254 scéptra re,pónis?" Ólli , súbri,déns ,,	to empire?" Smiling
our sceptres dost thou restore?" At her smiling	upon her with that

LINE 252. **Prōdimur**, 1st pers. plur. pres. ind. pass. of *prōdō, -ere, prōdidi, prōditum*, 3 (*prō = forth*, + *dō = I give*); agrees with the subj. *nos*. *Prodimur* has a bad sense here, = *we are betrayed* or *abandoned.* —— **atque**, cop. conj. —— **Italīs**, abl. plur. f. of *Italus, -a, -um* (pertaining to *Italia, -ae*, f., 1st); agrees with *oris*. —— **longē**, adv., extending *disiungimur*. —— **dīsiungimur**, 1st pers. plur. pres. ind. pass. of *dīsiungō, -ere, dīsiunxī, dīsiunctum*, 3 (*dīs*, marks separation, + *iungo*, hence *unjoin*, i.e. *sever*) ; joined by *atque* to *prodimur*. —— **ōrīs**, abl. plur. of *ōra, -ae*, f., 1st; abl. of separation, properly used without a prep. after *disiungimur*, as the verb implies both deprivation and removal. The abl. alone follows verbs meaning to *deprive, remove, want*, and *set free.* A. & G. 243, *a*; B. 214, esp. 2; G. 390, 2, and NOTE 2; H. 413.

LINE 253. **Hīc**, nom. sing. m. of the demonstr. pron. *hīc, haec, hōc ;* agrees with *honos* in gender and number, and subj. of *est* understood. *Hic* refers to the state of things described just before, but is attracted, as it frequently is, into agreement with the predicate noun or an appositive. A. & G. 195, *d*; B. 246, 5; G. 211, 5; H. 445, 4. —— **pietātis**, gen. sing. of *pietās*, f., 3d; objective gen. after *honos*, which is here a noun of *agency*, = *reward.* A. & G. 217; B. 200; G. 363, 2; H. 396, III. For the meaning of *pietas*, see the note on *pietate*, l. 10. —— **honōs** (*honor*), gen. *honōris*, m., 3d; complement of *est* understood in the predicate. For *honos* = *reward, recompense*, cf. *honores*, l. 28, and note. Observe that the above question is not introduced by an interrogative particle, *ne*, or *num ;* such questions are usually emotional and rhetorical, and in many cases are little more than exclamations (the nom. case being occasionally used instead of the regular acc. for exclamations). A. & G. 210, *b*; B. 162, 2, *d*; G. 453; H. 351, 3. —— **sīc**, adv. of manner, limiting with much emphasis the predicate *reponis ; = is it thus that you*, etc.? Observe that, as just above, the interrogative particle is omitted; as an exclamation, the sentence = *thus you restore us*, etc.! spoken with intense surprise and indignant sorrow. —— **nōs**, acc. plur. of *nōs*, 1st personal plur. pron. (sing. *ego*); direct obj. of *reponis*. —— **in**, prep., governing the acc. *sceptra*. —— **scēptra**, acc. plur. of *scēptrum, -ī*, n., 2d (Greek σκῆπτρον, = a *staff*, used for walking by noble Greeks; also the sign of royal power); governed by *in. In sceptra = in imperium, to empire.* —— **repōnis**, 2d pers. sing. pres. ind. act. of *repōnō, -ere, reposuī, repositum*, 3 (*re = back*, + *pōnō = I place*); the subj. is *tu* (i.e. Jupiter) unexpressed.

LINE 254. **Ollī** (archaic form of *illī*), dat. sing. of the 3d demonstr. pron. *ille, illa, illud* (gen. *illīus*, dat. *illī*, otherwise regular); dat. of the indirect obj., after the compound of *sub, subridens*. A. & G. 228; B. 187, III; G. 347; H. 386. There were other old and rare forms of *ille*, viz. *illus*, with a sing. gen. *illi, -ae, -i*, and dat. *illo, -ae, -o ;* also *ollus* or *olle*. *Ollus, olla* (nom. m. and f.), *olle* (nom. m.), *olli* and *olla* (nom. m. and n. plur.), and *ollis* (dat. and abl. plur.) are nearly the only survivals of the old pronoun, and they for the most part are single instances. The adv. *olim* (= *ollim*) is a classical survival. —— **subrīdēns**, nom. sing. m. of the pres. part. act. of *subrīdeō, -ēre, subrīsī*, no supine, 2 (*sub*, with diminutive force, = *slightly*, + *rīdeō*, = *I laugh*) ; agrees with and enlarges the subj. *sator*. —— **hominum**, gen. plur. of *homō, -inis*, m., 3d; objective gen., after *sator*, = lit. *sower*, but regarding *sator* as = to *father*, the gen. may

look wherewith he	homi,núm sator , átque de,órum **V**últu, 255
clears the sky and	*of men* ▪ *the father and* *of gods _with the countenance*
storms, the father of	
men and gods lightly	quó co,elúm „ tem,**pé**sta,tés-que se,rénat, **Ó**scula, 256
touched his daugh-	*with which the sky* *and the storms* *he calms,* *the lips*
ter's lips, then speaks	líba,vít na,tǽ; „ dehinc , tália , fátur :
as follows: "Spare	*sipped* *of his daughter;* *then* *such words* *he speaks:*

be possessive. —— **sator,** gen. *satōrīs*, m., 3d (from *serō, -ere, sēvī, satum*, 3, = *I sow*); subj. of *libavit. Sator hominum*, etc., = *Iupiter.* Apart from other considerations, Jupiter as the supreme god might be called 'father of men and gods'; but when Jupiter, angered by the impiety of mankind, sent a flood over the earth, he allowed Deucalion and Pyrrha to live, and to create men and women from the stones they threw behind them. —— **atque,** cop. conj., joining *hominum* and *deorum.* —— **deōrum,** gen. plur. of *deus, -ī,* m., 2d; limits *sator,* and is the same sort of gen. as *hominum.* Jupiter was actually the father of many of the deities.

LINE 255. **Vultū,** abl. sing. of *vultus, -ūs,* m., 4th; abl. of the instrument, or rather of manner. —— **quō,** abl. sing. m. of the rel. *quī, quae, quod;* abl. of the instrument in the rel. clause *quo . . . serenat.* —— **coelum,** acc. sing. of *coelum, -ī,* n., 2d; direct o' j. of *serenat.* —— **tempestātēs,** acc. plur. of *tempestās, -ātis,* f., 3d (akin to *tempus, -oris,* n., 3d); direct obj. of *serenat,* joined by enclitic *que* to *coelum.* —— **que,** conj.—— **serēnat,** 3d pers. sing. pres. ind. act. of *serēnō, -āre, -āvī, -ātum,* 1 (*serēnus, -a, -um,* = *clear, bright*); agrees with a pron. as subj. referring to *sator* above (Jupiter). The verb *serenat* properly applies only to *coelum,* but from the general idea which it conveys it is easy to supply a cognate signification with *tempestates.* The figure whereby one verb governs two substantives, to only one of which it is strictly applicable, is called *zeugma* (Greek ζεῦγμα, from ζεύγνυμι = *I join*) or *syllepsis;* cf. Tacitus, Annals, II, 29, 2; *Manus ac supplices voces tendens,* = *stretching hands and (raising) suppliant cries;* cf. also Dickens' description of a lady going home "in a bath chair and a flood of tears," though not exactly similar. A. & G. 385; B. 374, 2, *a;* G. 690; H. 636, II, 1.

LINE 256. **Oscula,** acc. plur. of *osculum, -ī,* n., 2d (diminutive of *ōs, ōris,* n., 3d, = *mouth*); direct obj. of *libavit.* Diminutive forms generally express endearment, e.g. *filiolus,* diminutive of *filius.* The regular sense of *oscula* is *kisses,* but it sometimes = *lips,* as here. —— **lībāvit,** 3d pers. sing. perf. ind. act. of *lībō, -āre, -āvī, -ātum,* 1; agrees with the subj. *sator. Libo* has many meanings: *I cull, take, taste, sip, sprinkle, pour out* wine or milk in honor of the gods (i.e. *make a libation*); render freely *lightly touched the lips of his daughter.* —— **nātae,** gen. sing. of *nāta,* f., 1st (originally f. of the perf. part. of *nascor, -ī, nātus sum,* 3, = *I am born*); poss. gen., limiting *oscula.* Some editors who regard *olli* as an *ethic* dative (and *subridens* as used absolutely), take *natae* as dat. sing., referring to *olli* and making it more clear. *Natae* seems redundant after *olli* above, but Vergil sometimes adds a noun to refer to and explain another; cf. l. 691, *At Venus . . . irrigat, et fotum* DEA *tollit,* etc., where *Venus* and *dea* are one person. —— **dehinc** (*dē + hinc,* = lit. *from hence*), adv., here of succession in time, = *then, next. Dehinc,* usually dissyllabic in prose, by *synizesis* or *synaeresis* becomes a monosyllable in poetry; so *deinde* (3 or 2 syllables). A. & G. 347, *c;* B. 367, 1; G. 727; H. 608, III —— **tālia,** acc. plur. n. of *tālis, -e;* direct obj. of *fatur,* referring to what follows. —— **fātur,** 3d pers. sing. pres. ind. of the defective dep. verb *fāri,* = *to speak,* 1 ; connected by *dehinc* (= *deinde*) with *libavit,* and agrees with the same subj. On *fari,* consult A. & G. 144, *c;* B. 136; G. 175, 3; H. 297, II, 3.

257 "**Párce** me,tú, Cythe,réa; ,, ma,nént im,móta | fear, Cytherea; the
    "*Spare*   *fear,*   *Cytherea,*   *remain*   *unchanged* | destinies of thy people thou shalt find to

258 tu,órum   **Fáta**   ti,bí;   ,, cer,nés   ur,bem | abide   unchanged.
   of thy people   the fates   for thee;   thou shalt see   the city | Thou shalt see Lavi-nium's city and her

---

LINE 257. **Parce**, 2d pers. sing. imperative mood act. of *parcō, -ere, pepercī* (*parsī* in Plautus, but not in best Latin), *parsum*, 3; the unexpressed subj. is *tu*, i.e. *Venus Cytherea*. *Parco* = lit. *I spare*, and applied to indulgence of emotions, = *I refrain from:* the English *spare* is used similarly. —— metū (archaic form of *metui*), contracted dat. sing. of *metus, -ūs*, m., 4th; governed by *parce*. Vergil regularly uses this form of the 4th decl. dative, cf. *curru*, l. 156. *Parcere* is one of a large list of verbs (over 60) that regularly take the dat. in classical Latin: some of the others most common are: *I obey, persuade, believe, pardon, resist, help, please, envy*. A. & G. 227; B. 187, II; G. 346, and REM. 2; H. 385, I, II. These verbs are intransitive in Latin, though apparently transitive in English, and are, therefore, only used impersonally in the passive, e.g. *parcitur mihi*, = lit. *it is spared to me*, i.e. *I am spared*. —— **Cytherēa**, voc. sing. of *Cytherēa, -ae*, f., 1st (properly f. sing. of the adj. *Cytherēus, -a, -um*, = *the Cytherean one*); case of the goddess addressed. *Cytherea* is a name by which Venus was known, because the island from which the adj. is formed, *Cythera* (*-orum*, n., 2d, now called *Cerigo*), was sacred to her. Near this island (on the south of the Peloponnesus) she rose from the sea, and she had a splendid temple there dedicated to her worship. The *penultimate* syllable *e* is long; some write *Cytheraea*. —— manent, 3d pers. plur. pres. ind. act. of *maneō, -ere, mansī, mansum*, 2 irreg.; agrees with its subj. *fata*. —— immōta, nom. plur. n. of *immōtus, -a, -um* (adj. formed from *in*, = *not*, + *mōtus*, = *moved*, perf. part. pass. of *moveō*); agrees with *fata*, but modifies *manent* adverbially, = *abide immovably;* see note and references under *laeti*, l. 35. Some prefer to take *immota* as complement of *manent* (as if merely = to *sunt*); this is unnecessary, for *manent* is a complete predicate; but see the references given under *regina*, l. 46. —— tuōrum, gen. plur. m. of the poss. adj. (of the 2d sing. personal pron. *tu*) *tuus, -a, -um;* poss. gen., limiting *fata*. The m. plur. of the poss. adjectives is used substantively, e.g. *mei*, = *my (friends);* so the n. plur., e.g. *mea (bona)*, = *my (property);* cf. *necessarii, consanguinei*, etc.

LINE 258. **Fāta**, nom. plur. of *fātum, -ī*, n., 2d; subj. of *manent*. —— tibī, dat. of *tū;* dat. of reference (*dativus commodi vel incommodi*, of advantage or disadvantage ↑ here of advantage), dependent on the whole sentence. A. & G. 235; B. 188, 1; G. 350; H. 384, II, 1, 2). There is not much internal difference between this dative and the *ethic* dative; see note, etc., on *iactanti*, l. 102. The sentence *parce . . . tibi* is a direct reply to *quae te sententia vertit?* l. 237. —— cernēs, 2d pers. sing. fut. ind. act. of *cernō, -ere, crēvī, cretum*, 3; the subj. *tu* is unexpressed, the personal ending making it unnecessary, except for emphasis or contrast. Synonyms: *cernere*, = *to see clearly*, usually implying discrimination; *videre*, = *to see*, the general word for the function of the visual sense; *as picere*, = *to behold, look at; spectare* and *intueri*, = *to gaze at*, long and intently; *animadvertere*, = *to observe*, or *notice* anything, as an object of mental interest. —— urbem, acc. sing. of *urbs, urbis*, f., 3d; direct obj. of *cernes*. Observe the *hendiadys* in *urbem et . . . moenia (Lavini)*; the two coördinate nouns only really convey one idea, and the phrase = *moenia urbis Lavini (walls of the city of Lavinium)*. A. & G. 385; B. 374, 4; G. 698; H. 636, III, 2. Observe that there are several *caesurae*, viz.: after *tibi, cernes*, or *urbem;* the rhythm is against the one after *cernes*, and of the rest it is preferable to consider that after *tibi* the chief, because of the change in the

promised walls, and shalt bear aloft to the stars of heaven brave Aeneas; nor does any counsel change me. He to thy joy — for I will speak since this care eats thy heart, and will further unroll and dis-

ét pro,míssa La,víni **Mœ**nia, , súbli,mémque ,, 259
and   promised   of Lavinium   the walls,   and high

fe,rés   ad , sídera , cœli   **M**ágnani,m*um* 260
thou shalt carry to   the stars of heaven   . great-souled

Aéne án; ,, neque , mé sen,téntia , vértit.   **H**íc 261
Aeneas;   nor   me   opinion   changes.   He

— tibi , fábor   e,ním, ,, quan,d*o* hǽc te ,
— to thee   I will tell (it)   for,   since   this   thee

grammatical construction, and the consequent pause. —— et, conj. —— **prōmissa**, acc. plur. n. of *prōmissus, -a, -um*, perf. part. pass. of *prōmittō, -ere, prōmīsī, prōmissum*, 3 ; agrees with *moenia*. *Promissus* sometimes has the literal derived sense (*sent forth*) *long*, e.g. *promissae comae*. —— **Lavīnī**, contracted gen. of *Lavīnium*, n., 2d ; poss. gen., limiting *moenia*. For *Lavīnī* instead of *Lavīnii*, cf. *Patavī*, l. 247, and note. *Lavinium*, mentioned *proleptically* in prophecy by Jupiter, was afterwards founded in Latium by Aeneas, who called it after *Lavinia*, his Italian wife ; it was the capital of Latium under Aeneas. Observe the quantity *Lăvini* here, but *Lāvinia*, l. 2 ; so *Sȳchaeus*, l. 343, but *Sȳchaeum*, l. 348, and other instances. The poets allow themselves much license as regards the quantity of vowels in proper names.

LINE 259. **Moenia**, acc. plur. of *moenia, -iŭm*, n., 3d (no sing.) ; joined by *et* to *urbem* and direct obj. of *cernes*. See note on *moenia*, l. 7. —— **sublīmem**, acc. sing. m. of *sublīmis, -e*, adj. 3d ; agrees with *Aenean*. *Sublimem* is *proleptic*, as also the English *aloft* in *thou shalt carry Aeneas aloft*, i.e. so as to be aloft ; so *scuta latentia condunt,* = *they conceal their* (lit. *hidden shields*, i.e.) *shields in hiding* (so as to be hidden). A. & G. 385; B. 374, 5; G. 325, PREDICATIVE ATTRIBUTION; H. 636, IV, 3. —— **que**, enclitic conj. —— **ferēs**, 2d pers. sing. fut. ind. act. of *ferō, ferre, tulī, lātum*, irreg.; joined by *que* to *cernes*. For the conjugation of *fero*, consult A. & G. 139 ; B. 129 ; G. 171 ; H. 292. The allusion is to the apotheosis of Aeneas, who (according to Livy) disappeared from earth to be worshipped as one of the 'native gods,' *Iupiter Indiges*. —— **ad**, prep.; gov. the acc. *sidera*. —— **sīdera**, acc. plur. of *sīdus, sīderis*, n., 3d ; obj. of *ad*. —— **coelī**, gen. sing. of *coelum*, n., 2d; subjective gen., qualifying *sidera* instead of an adj. (*coelestia*).

LINE 260. **Magnanimum**, acc. sing. m. of *magnanimus, -a, -um* (compounded of the adj. *magnus* and the noun *animus*) ; an attribute of *Aenean*. *Magnanimity* (Greek μεγαλοψυχία) is that spirit of generosity, tempered by the perfect self-pride and self-confidence of the man who knows he is perfect, of which Aristotle speaks so highly. *Magnanimus* here probably = *lion-hearted, brave*. —— **Aenēan**, acc. sing. of *Aenēās* (for decl., see *Aenēae*, l. 92); direct obj. of *feres*. —— **neque** (*ne* + *que*, = *and not*), conj., connecting its own and the preceding sentences. The change of subject, and the use of the same phrase (*sententia vertit*) by Jupiter as that which Venus had employed (l. 237), show that Jupiter thinks he has answered Venus' charge as to his change of mind ; *neque* introductory here conveys a gentle reproof. —— **mē**, acc. of *ego;* direct obj. of *vertit*. —— **sententia**, gen. *sententiae*, f., 1st ; nom. sing., subj. of *vertit*. —— **vertit**, 3d pers. sing. pres. ind. act. of *vertō, -ere, vertī, versum*, 3 ; agrees with the subj. *sententia*. Refer to l. 237.

LINE 261. **Hīc**, nom. sing. m. of the demonstr. pron. of the 1st pers.; subj. of *geret*, l. 263. *Hic* is emphatic as first word, referring to Aeneas in opposition to *Ascanius*, l. 267. —— **tibi**, dat. of *tū ; ethic* dat., a dat. superfluous so far as the sense is concerned, but indicating that the person to whom the pron. refers (i.e. Venus) takes a lively interest

262 cúra	re,mórdet,	Lóngius	,	ét	vol,véns	,,	cover the hidden
care	*gnaws,*	*further*		*and*	*unrolling*		screeds of fate—shall
263 fa,tórum	ar,cána	mo,vébo —		Béllum	in,géns		wage a mighty war in
of the fates	*the secrets*	*I will display —*		*a war*	*mighty*		Italy and shall crush
							proud nations and

in, and is mentally or emotionally affected by the action of the sentence; cf. the familiar *quid mihi Celsus agit?* = (*tell me*) *what is Celsus doing?* A. & G. 236; B. 188, 2, *b*); G. 351; H. 389. The *ethic* dative is most common with personal pronouns; it is sometimes called the *dative of feeling* (ἠθικός).——**fābor,** 1st pers. sing. fut. ind. of the defective dep. verb *fāri;* the personal ending shows that *ego* is the subj. For references on *fāri,* see *fatur,* l. 256.——**enim,** causal conj., standing post-positive, introducing the parenthesis from *fabor* . . . *movebo.*——**quandō,** causal conj., = *because, since, as* (in poetry, but not in the prose of the *golden age* of Latin literature). *Quando* is followed by the ind. mood *remordet,* and as a rule may only take the subjunctive when stating something as an idea in the speaker's mind, or the mind of the person about whom he is speaking (*virtual oratio obliqua*). A. & G. 321, NOTE 3; B. 286, 3; G. 540; H. 516. *Quando* is also used: (1) as an interrog. adv. in direct questions, = *when?* (2) adv. relatively, = *when;* (3) as an indefinite adv., = *at any time;* (4) in composition, e.g. *quandoque, quandoquidem.*——**haec,** nom. sing. f. of the demonstr. adj. ; agrees with *cura. Haec* refers to the anxiety of Venus about Aeneas.——**tē,** acc. of *tū;* direct obj. of *remordet.*——**cūra,** gen. *cūrae,* f., 1st; nom. sing., subj. of *remordet. Cura* = *care, trouble, guardianship,* all kindred meanings; it most commonly = *anxiety, solicitude,* here of the *anxiety* caused by affection for one in danger (so *securus* = *free from care,* not *secure* in the sense of *safe*).——**remordet,** 3d pers. sing. pres. ind. act. of *remordeō, -ēre,* no perf., *remorsum,* 2 (*re + mordeo*)*;* agrees with its subj. *cura,* and = lit. *bites,* hence *vexes.* For the force of *re* in composition generally, refer to the note on *repostum,* l. 26. Commentators differ as to its force in *remordet:* (1) some say it is entirely without force; (2) very many follow Professor Conington in supposing that *re* marks iteration or constant repetition, so that *remordet* = *mordet iterum atque iterum, keeps biting;* (3) Mr. Page with much reason thinks the above unlikely; he gives *re* its common signification of *back,* as in *repono,* and very aptly compares remorse and care to worms which eat *back* from the surface of a thing to the core, so that *eats back* = *eats deep.*

LINE 262. **Longius,** comparative of the adv. *longē,* extending *volvens.* Superl. *longissime.* For the comparison of adverbs, consult A. & G. 92; B. 76, 2, and 77, 1; G. 93; H. 306.——**et,** conj., joining *fabor* and *movebo.* In prose *et* stands before the words it introduces, but here, as elsewhere in poetry, we find it after; sometimes it is even in the middle of a sentence.——**volvēns,** nom. sing. m. of the pres. part. act. of *volvō, -ere, volvī, volūtum,* 3 ; agrees with and enlarges the unexpressed subj. *ego. Volvens* = *evolvens* (*unrolling*) is a metaphor taken from a book, which, in ancient times consisted of sheets of parchment rolled around a stick or cylinder (*volumen*).—— **fātōrum,** gen. plur. of *fātum, -ī,* n., 2d; poss. gen., limiting *arcana. Fatorum* probably = *destinies,* not personified = *the Fates.* Jupiter was acquainted with the decrees of the *Parcae,* and though he might defer their accomplishment, could not annul or reverse them; in all other respects he was absolute lord of heaven and earth.—— **arcāna,** acc. plur. of *arcānum, -ī,* n., 2d (properly n. of adj. *arcānus, -a, -um,* = *secret,* from *arca,* = *a chest*)*;* direct object of *movebo.*——**movēbō,** 1st pers. sing. fut. ind. act. of *moveō, -ēre, mōvī, mōtum,* 2; the subj. is ego, i.e. Jupiter. *Movere* = *disclose,* in this and some other instances.

LINE 263. **Bellum,** acc. sing. of *bellum, -ī,* n., 2d; direct obj. of *geret.*——**ingēns,** acc. sing. n. of *ingēns, -ēntis,* adj. 3d, of one nom. termination; qualifies *bellum.*——

assign his people laws	geret	,	Itali,á,	„	popu,lósque	fe,róces
and city walls, till the	*will wage*		*in Italy,*		*and nations*	*fierce*
third summer has	Cóntun,dét;	„	mo,résque	vi,rís et	,	mœnia, 264
	he will crush;		*and customs*	*for men and*		*city-walls*
seen him ruling in	pónet,		Tértia	, dúm Lati,ó	„	reg,nántem, 265
Latium and three	*he will establish,*	*third*		*until in Latium*		*ruling*

---

geret, 3d. pers. sing. fut. ind. act. of *gerō, -ere, gessī, gestum,* 3; agrees with its subj. *hic,* from which it is separated by the parenthesis in ll. 261, 262. Observe the artistic skill with which Vergil, by the mouth of Jupiter, prepares his readers for the warfare of the last six books of the *Aeneid.* —— **Italiā,** abl. sing. *Italia, -ae,* f., 1st; abl. of 'place where,' poetical for *in Italia.* The locative abl. is not uncommon in prose when the noun is qualified by an adj., e.g. *totus, medius,* etc.; it is very common in poetry, e.g. *litare, aequare,* etc. Here we find it used of countries; cf. *Epiro, = in Epirus.* A. & G. 258, 4, *f,* 3; B. 228; G. 385; H. 425, 3. —— **populōs,** acc. plur. of *populus, -ī,* m., 2d; direct obj. of *contundet.* The allusion is to the Rutulians and Etruscans. —— **que,** enclitic conj. —— **ferōcēs,** acc. plur. m. of *ferōx, ferōcis,* adj. 3d; qualifies *populos.* *Ferox* = (1) *fierce,* (2) *high-spirited, proud,* as here.

LINE 264. **Contundet,** 3d pers. sing. fut. ind. act. of *contundō, -ere, contūdī, contūsum,* 3 (*con* [*cum*] + *tundō*); joined by *que* above to *geret.* —— **mōrēs,** acc. plur. of *mōs, mōris,* m., 3d; direct obj. of *ponet. Mores* (= customs) is poetical for *leges.* In the sing. *mos = custom, manner,* e.g. *more, ad morem,* etc.; in the plur. it properly = *habits,* hence *character,* as a state of mind built up from individual actions of one kind (ἠθική, ἕξις, Aristotle; so Greek ἔθος, sing. = *custom,* plur. ἔθη = *character*). —— **que,** enclitic conj., joining the sentence with *ponet* to the previous one with *contundet.* —— **virīs,** dat. plur. of *vir, -ī,* m., 2d; dat. of the indirect obj. after *ponet* (as though *dabit*). —— **et,** cop. conj., joining the two equally important words *mores* and *moenia.* —— **moenia,** acc. plur. of the plur. noun *moenia, -ium,* n., 3d; direct obj. of *ponet. Moenia = the walls* of a city; *murus = wall,* any wall; *paries = a house-wall.* —— **pōnet,** 3d pers. sing. fut. ind. act. of *pōnō, -ere, posuī, positum,* 3; joined by *que* (appended to *mores*) to *contundet. Ponet* by the figure *zeugma* governs two objects, *mores* and *moenia,* having a slightly different sense with each; thus *ponet mores = will establish* or *make laws,* while *ponet moenia = will set up,* or *build walls.* For note and references on *zeugma,* refer to *serenat,* l. 255. But it is well to remember that laws were often literally *set up* in a public place, being engraved on wood or metal, as the laws of the Athenian legislator, Solon, which were set up in the market-place.

LINE 265. **Tertia,** nom. sing. f. of the ordinal numeral adj. *tertius, -a, -um;* agrees with *aestas.* —— **dum,** temporal conj., followed by the ind. *viderit. Dum* here = *until,* and takes the ind. to mark a point of time, but the subj. when purpose or aim is suggested. *Dum* often = *while,* taking the pres. (rarely the imperf.) ind. of past or present action, retaining the ind. even when in a subordinate clause in *oratio obliqua.* The fut. *ponet* indicates that the process of civilization is continued *until* three years shall have elapsed (fut. perf. *viderit*). A. & G. 328; B. 293, III; G. 571; H. 519, II. —— **Latiō,** abl. sing. of *Latium, -ī,* n., 2d; locative abl., with *regnantem.* See note on *Italia,* l. 263 above. —— **rēgnantem,** acc. sing. m. of *rēgnans, -antis,* pres. part. act. of *rēgnō, -āre, -āvī, -ātum,* 1; direct obj. of *viderit,* properly agreeing with *eum* or *Aenean* understood. The plur. of participles may sometimes be used substantively, e.g. *mortui, the dead,* or *regentes, rulers* (lit. *men ruling*); but *regnantem* is scarcely = to the noun *regem,* as it conveys *continuation of rule* with true participial force. The part. is used, in imitation of the

266 víderit	,	ǽstas,	Térnaque	,	tránsie, rínt ,,	winter watches have
shall have seen		*the summer,*	*and three*		*shall have passed*	passed o'er the
267 Rutu, lís		hi, bérna	sub, áctis.		Át puer ,	crushed Rutulians.
to the Rutulians		*winters*	*having been subdued.*		*But the boy*	But the boy Ascanius,

Greek construction, as being more vivid than the inf. *regnare* (which strict prose would require). A. & G. 292, *e*; B. 336, 2; G. 536; H. 535, I, 4. —— **vīderit**, 3d pers. sing. fut. perf. ind. act. of *video, -ēre, vīdī, vīsum*, 2; agrees with the subj. *aestas*. For tense and mood, see note on *dum*. The phrase *till three summers have seen him ruling* is poetical, and could not be used in prose composition, though much of Cicero's phraseology is poetical (cf. the poetical prose-writer of the Greeks, Plato). —— **aestās**, gen. *aestātis*, f., 3d; nom. sing., subj. of *viderit. Aestas* here = *annus*, a meaning derived from the fact that the summer was = to a whole year as far as the prosecution of a military campaign was concerned, as fighting was usually postponed in the winter (*hiems*); as a rough division, summer lasted from April to September (inclusive), and winter the other months. In English we should invert the above phrase, *till, ruling, he has seen three summers;* for *summer = year* in English, cf. such expressions as 'a maiden of eighteen summers.'

LINE 266.   **Terna**, nom. plur. n. of *ternus, -a, -um*, distributive numeral adj.(= *three each*, but here = *trēs, tria, three*); agrees with *hiberna*. When a noun plur. in form (e.g. *castra*) but sing. in meaning is used in a really plural sense (being qualified in English by a cardinal number), it takes a distributive instead of a cardinal number; so *castra bina, terna,*= *two*, or *three camps.* A. & G. 95; B. 81, 4; G. 97, and REMARKS; H. 174, 2. —— **que**, enclitic conj., connecting the sentence in which it stands with the preceding one. —— **trānsierint**, 3d pers. plur. fut. perf. ind. act. of *trānseo, -īre, -iī* (less common *-īvī*), *-itum*, irreg. (*trāns* + *eō*) agrees with its subj. *hiberna*, and in tense and mood similar to *viderit* above. *Transeo* may be used as trans. or intrans.: (1) trans. *I cross;* (2) *I pass by*, hence of time, *to elapse.* —— **Rutulis**, dat. plur. of *Rutulī, -ōrum*, m., 2d plur.; *ethic* dat. of the persons affected; cf. a very similar dat. *iactanti*, l. 102, and consult the references there given. This dative is common in Greek. A few prefer to consider *Rutulis* as abl. plur., in the abl. abs. construction with *subactis*. The Rutulians were an ancient people of Latium, who were ruled by Turnus (to whom Lavinia was promised as bride) when Aeneas reached Italy, and fought for Turnus against Aeneas when the latter won the hand of Lavinia. The capital of the country of the *Rutuli* was *Ardea.* —— **hīberna**, gen. *hibernōrum*, n., 3d; nom. plur. (no sing.), subj. of *transierint. Hīberna* (properly n. plur. of the adj. *hibernus, -a, -um, = of winter, wintry;* akin to *hiems*) = *winter-quarters* in prose, i.e. with *castra* understood; here it seems to suggest the military character of Aeneas' rule, and all his wars with Turnus. We may, however, render *terna hiberna* as *three winters*, supplying *tempora. Three summers* and *three winters = three years;* see *aestas* above. —— **subactis**, dat. plur. m. of *subactus, -a, -um*, perf. part. pass. of *subigō, -ere, subēgī, subactum*, 3 (*sub* + *agō*, = lit. *I bring under*, hence *subdue*); agrees with *Rutulis*. Some take it as abl. plur. in abl. abs. construction with *Rutulis*. The poet makes Jupiter allow Aeneas a reign of 3 years (ll. 265, 266), Ascanius or Iulus a reign of 30 years (l. 269), the king's ruling at the new capital of Alba Longa a rule of 300 years (l. 272), but to the power and empire of Rome no season or limit is fixed (ll. 278, 279).

LINE 267.   **At** (sometimes *ast*), adversative conj., introducing Ascanius in opposition to Aeneas, mentioned before. For the distinctions between *at, autem, verum*, and *sed*, refer to the note and references under *sed*, l. 19. —— **puer**, gen. *puerī*, m., 2d; nom. sing., in apposition with *Ascanius. Pueri = children; a puero = from boyhood; Cyrus puer socios rexit, = Cyrus in his boyhood ruled his companions.* The period of boyhood

to whom is now added | Áscani, ús, „ cui , núnc cog,nómen I,úlo
the surname Iulus | Ascanius,   to whom   now   the name   Iulus
(Ilus he was, while |
Ilium's state stood | Additur, , —Ílus e,rát, „dum , rés stetit , Ília , 268
firm in sovereignty), | is added,   — Ilus he was,   while the state stood   Ilian

---

(*pueritia*) lasted till the 16th to the 18th year, when the *toga praetexta* (with purple edge) was discarded and the *toga virilis* assumed. Gradations of age are expressed by: *infantulus, infans, puerulus, puer, adolescentulus, adolescens, iunior, iuvenis, senior, senex* (quoted). Of these the chief divisions are *puer, adolescens, iuvenis,* and *senex*. Some try to fix the years definitely, but they probably overlap one another: a child is *puer* till about 17; becomes *adolescens* (and with it *vir*), onwards till perhaps 30; *iuvenis* from 25 or 30 to 40 or 50; then *senex*.——**Ascanius,** gen. *Ascani,* m., 2d; nom. sing. subj. of *explebit,* l. 270. Ascanius, the son of Aeneas by Creusa, accompanied his father from Troy to Italy; he succeeded Aeneas, and transferred his regal seat from Lavinium to Alba Longa, which he built. Vergil, and later poets in like manner, give him the name of *Iulus* (invented, as also *Ilus,* next line) in compliment to Augustus, who belonged to the *gens Iulia.* Observe that all the best Roman qualities are attributed to Aeneas (as law-maker, soldier, etc.), and that Vergil implies that they have descended through the *Julian house* to the emperor Augustus.——**cui,** dat. sing. m. of *qui;* agrees with the antecedent *Ascanio,* and is dat. of the recipient or indirect obj. after *additur.*——**nunc,** adv. of time, = *now,* in opposition to the time when the name was *Ilus* (next line).——**cognōmen,** gen. *cognōminis,* n., 3d; nom. sing., subj. of *additur.* Strictly the *cognōmen* is the 3d name, distinguishing the *familia;* e.g. Marcus Tullius *Cicero;* it was often a nickname. Here Vergil uses it for the *nomen* or name of the *gens,* as Augustus and earlier Julius Caesar belonged to the *gens Iulia.*——**Iūlō,** dat. sing of *Iūlus, -i,* m., 2d (from the Greek ιουλος = *down* on the face, considered a mark of youthful beauty in ancient times); attracted into agreement in opposition with the rel. *cui.* This construction is found chiefly in poetry, or in early and post-Ciceronian Latin. The most common and best construction is for the proper name (e.g. *Iulus*) to be put in apposition with the word *nomen* (*cognomen,* etc.); the adnominal gen., e.g. *nomen Marci = the name of Marcus* is comparatively rare (see note on *Danaum,* l. 96). A. & G. 231, *b;* B. 190; G. 349, REM. 5; H. 387, NOTES 1 and 2.

LINE 268. **Additur,** 3d pers. sing. pres. ind. pass. of *addo, -ere, addidi, additum,* 3 (*ad + do*); agrees with the subj. *cognomen.*——**Ilus,** gen. *Ili,* m., 2d; nom. sing., complement of *erat* in the predicate. A. & G. 176; B. 167, 168; G. 205, 206; H. 360–362. *Ilus . . . regno* is a parenthesis. *Ilus* was the name of a mythical king of Troy, viz.: Ilus son of Tros.——**erat,** 3d pers. sing. imperf. ind. of *sum, esse, fui;* agrees with a pron. (e.g. *id*) as subj., referring to *cognomen.*——**dum,** temporal conj., here = *while.* For its use generally, see *dum* and note, l. 265; for its use with the perf. tense here, see *stetit* below.——**res,** gen. *rei,* f., 5th; nom. sing., subj. of *stetit. Res = power, sway,* or *empire* here. Consult a good dictionary for its many and various uses.——**stetit,** 3d pers. sing. perf. ind. act. of *sto, stare, steti, statum,* 1 (perf. and supine *-stiti,* and *-stitum,* usually in compounds, e.g. *consto*); agrees with its subj. *res. Sto* means originally *I stand,* as opposed to sitting or moving about; hence *I remain, endure, stand firm,* and the like. *Dum* may be used with the perf. ind., as it is with *stetit,* when it is wished to make the point of time emphatic by contrast, or when (as here) the emphasis is laid, not on the time or its duration, but on the *fact* embodied in the verb; thus *dum . . . stetit = while the power of Ilium actually endured.* A. & G. 276, *e,* NOTE, and *ff.;* B. 293, I, II; G. 569, 570; H. 467, 4, and 519.——**Ilia,** nom. sing. f. of *Ilius, -a, -um* (adj. formed from the noun *Ilus*); agrees with *res. Ilius* is one of the many synonyms of

269 régno, *in kingship,—*	—Trígin,tá *thirty*	mag,nós *great*	„	vol,véndis , *rolling on*	will in empire fulfil thirty great circles of
270 ménsibus , *the months*	órbes *circles*	Ímperi,o *with empire*	éxple,bít, *will fulfil*	„	rolling months, and
reg,númque *and the kingdom*	ab , *from*	séde *the seat*	La,víni *of Lavinium*		transfer his kingdom from its seat in La-
271 Tránsferet, , *will transfer,*	ét *and*	lon,gám *long*	„	mul,tá vi , *much with strength*	vinium and valiantly guard about Alba
272 múniet , *will fortify*	Álbam. *Alba!*	Híc *Here*	iam , *now*		Longa. Here for full

Troianus.——**rēgnō,** abl. sing. of *rēgnum, -ī,* n., 2d ; probably abl. of respect, after *stetit;* cf. Aen, II, 88, *dum stabat regno incolumis.* Others take *regno* as: (1) abl. of manner ; (2) dat. of recipient, after *stetit;* however, (2) appears impossible.

LINE 269. **Trīgintā,** indecl. cardinal number, qualifying *orbes.*——**magnōs,** acc. plur. m. of *magnus, -a, -um;* agrees with *orbes.*——**volvendīs,** abl. plur. m. of *volvendus, -a, -um,* gerundive of *volvō, -ere, volvī, volūtum,* 3 ; agrees with *mensibus. Volvendis = rolling,* the gerundive being used in Latin where in Greek the pres. part. middle or passive would be employed ; thus *volvendis mensibus = mensibus se volventibus,* or even *volventibus mensibus* (like *volventibus annis,* l. 234). This is the old and participial use of the gerundive, cf. *secundus=following,* etc.; the passive use of the gerundive probably arose later. With *volvendis mensibus,* cf. *volvenda dies* in Vergil ; *volvenda aetas,* etc., in Lucretius.——**mensibus,** abl. plur. of *mensis, -is,* m., 3d ; probably a descriptive abl., describing *orbes.* A. & G. 251; B. 224; G. 400; H. 419, II. Some take *volvendis mensibus* as abl. abs., *volvendis* being used just as though it were a pres. part. passive.——**orbēs,** acc. plur. of *orbis, -is,* m., 3d ; direct obj. of *explebit. Orbes* (lit. *circles*) clearly = *annos.*

LINE 270. **Imperiō,** abl. sing. of *imperium, -ī,* n., 2d ; abl. of manner, with *explebit.*——**explēbit,** 3d pers. sing. fut. ind. act. of *expleō, -ēre, -ēvī, -ētum,* 2 (*ex + pleō*); agrees with the subj. *Ascanius,* l. 267. Vergil does not make it clear whether (1) Ascanius was to reign 30 years at Lavinium, and *after that* found Alba Longa, or (2) whether he was to reign altogether 30 years, founding Alba at some time *within* those 30 years : Forbiger, guided by other passages in Vergil, is in favor of (1).——**rēgnum,** acc. sing. of *rēgnum, -ī,* n., 2d ; direct obj. of *transferet.*——**que,** enclitic conj.——**ab,** prep.; gov. *sede,* marking separation.——**sēde,** abl. sing. of *sēdes, -is,* f., 3d ; governed by *ab.*——**Lavīnī,** gen. sing. of *Lavīnium,* n., 2d (not *Lavīnum,* for the adj. is *Lavīniensis,* not *Lavīnensis*); gen. of specification. A. & G. 214, *f*; B. 202 ; G. 361 ; H. 395.

LINE 271. **Trānsferet,** 3d pers. sing. fut. ind. act. of *trānsferō, transferre, trānstulī, trānslātum,* irreg. (*trāns + ferō*); joined by *que (regnumque)* to *explebit.*——**et,** conj.——**longam,** acc. sing. f. of *longus, -a, -um;* qualifies *albam.*——**multā,** abl. sing. f. of *multus, -a, -um;* agrees with *vi.*——**vī,** abl. sing of *vīs,* acc. *vim,* f., 3d (other cases in sing. wanting; plur. *vīres, -ium,* f. = *strength*); abl. of manner, after *muniet.*——**mūniet,** 3d pers. sing. fut. ind. act. of *mūniō, -īre, -īvī* or *iī, -ītum,* 4 (old form *moen-io,* from *moen-ia, = walls*); joined by *et* above to *transferet. Munio = lit. I build defences,* hence *I build and fortify. Alba Longa* was little more than a hill camp, surrounded by walls.——**Albam,** acc. sing. of *Alba, -ae,* f., 1st; direct obj. of *muniet. Alba* or *Alba Longa* (so called because built by Ascanius on a mountain ridge) gave Rome much trouble in later days, but was finally destroyed (and its inhabitants carried off to Rome) by Tullus Hostilius.

LINE 272. **Hīc,** adv. of place, referring to *Alba Longa.*——**iam,** adv. of time. Jupi-

thrice a hundred years shall the kingdom endure under Hector's line till the royal priestess Ilia shall bear to Mars as sire twin offspring.	tér cen,túm *thrice a hundred* Génte sub *The race under* sa,cérdos *priestess* par,tú *at birth*	„ to,tós *complete* , Héctore,á, *Hectorean,* Márte *by Mars* dabit *shall give*	reg,nábitur *it will be ruled* „ do,néc *until* gra,vís *pregnant* , Ília *Ilia*	, ánnos *for years* re,gína 273 *the queen* gemi,nám „ 274 *twin* , prólem. *offspring.*

ter, foreseeing the future, uses this adv. because to his mind the occasion appears present *now*. Or we may consider *iam* as marking a fresh stage in the progress of events, = *then* or *thenceforth*. —— **ter**, numeral adv., modifying *centum*. In poetry large numbers are often treated in this manner, partly because it is more poetic in character, and partly because it better suits the scansional requirements of the *hexameter*. —— **centum**, indecl. numeral, qualifying *annos*. *Ter centum* is approximate, not exact. —— **tōtōs**, acc. plur. m. of *tōtus, -a, -um;* agreeing with *annos.* —— **rēgnābitur**, 3d pers. sing. fut. ind. pass. of *rēgnō, -āre, -āvī, -ātum,* 1; impersonally, = *it will be ruled,* i.e. *the kingdom will continue.* The impersonal passive use of intrans. verbs is very common; e.g. *pugnatur, pugnatum est.* —— **annōs**, acc. plur. m. of *annus, -ī,* m., 2d; acc. of duration of time, answering the question *how long?* A. & G. 256; B. 181; G. 336; H. 379.

LINE 273. **Gente**, abl. sing. of *gens, gentis,* f., 3d; governed by *sub.* —— **sub**, prep.; gov. the abl. *gente.* —— **Hectoreā**, abl. sing. f. of *Hectoreus, -a, -um* (from *Hector, -is,* m., 3d); qualifies *gente. The race of Hector = the Trojans:* Hector is picked out as the principal Trojan hero, though he was only distantly related by blood to Aeneas; both, however, were of royal descent. —— **dōnec**, temporal conj., taking the ind. *dabit = until. Dōnec* (= *until*) takes the ind., when the verb expresses an actual fact; the subjunct. follows it when there is any suggestion of intention, desire, or purpose. *Dōnec* is also used of contemporaneous action, = *while = as long as,* with the indicative. A. & G. 328; B. 293, III; G. 571; H. 519, II. —— **rēgīna**, gen. *rēgīnae,* f., 1st; nom. sing., in apposition with *sacerdos. Rēgīna = rēgia,* for Ilia was the daughter of Numitor, whom his younger brother, Amulius, dispossessed of the throne. —— **sacerdōs**, gen. *sacerdōtis,* m. or f., 3d (from *sacer, = sacred*); nom. sing., in apposition with *Ilia.* Ilia was a priestess of Vesta, the goddess of hearth and home, whose sacred fire was never allowed to die out. The Vestal Virgins were chosen very young, and served Vesta for 30 years, after which period they were given the liberty of marriage and freedom. Amulius made Ilia a Vestal, because he wished his own children to succeed, not his brother's, though Numitor was the rightful king; in spite of precautions, Ilia became the mother of Romulus and Remus.

LINE 274. **Marte**, abl. sing. of *Mars, Martis,* m., 3d; abl. of the means. Mars, the god of war, was the son of Jupiter and Juno; in Greek mythology his name was Ares. At Rome he was much worshipped, and the Salii were his own especial priests. In the Trojan war, he assisted the Trojans, because of his affection for Venus (Aphrodite), but he retired when he was wounded by Diomedes. Vergil represents him as the ancestor of Augustus. —— **gravis**, nom. sing. f. of the adj. *gravis, -e;* agrees with *Ilia.* —— **geminam**, acc. sing. f. of *geminus, -a, -um;* qualifies *prolem.* —— **partū**, abl. sing. of *partus, -ūs,* m., 4th (from *pario,= I bring forth*); abl. of manner, with *dabit; partu dabit = pariet.* —— **dabit**, 3d pers. sing. fut. ind. act. of *dō, dare, dedī, datum,* 1; agrees with its subj.-nom. *Ilia.* —— **Ilia**, gen. *Iliae,* f., 1st; nom. sing., subj. of *dabit.* Ilia, a poetic name signifying Trojan origin, is another name for Rhaea Sylvia, the daughter of Numitor; she bore Romulus and Remus to Mars, and was buried alive, by order of Amulius,

275 Índe lu, pǽ ful, vó „ nu , trícis , tégmine ,
    Them   she-wolf   tawny   of his nurse   in the hide
276 lǽtus   Rómulus ,   éxcipi, ét   gen, tem, „
    exulting   Romulus   will receive (and rule)   the race,
277 ét   Ma, vórtia ,   cóndet   Mœ́nia,   ,
    and   of Mars   will found   the walls,
    Róma, nósque „ su , ó de , nómine ,
    and Romans   his own   from   name

Thereafter shall Romulus, exulting in the tawny hide of the wolf his nurse, take up his people's rule, found the walls of Mars, and call them from his own name, Romans. To their

for violating her Vestal vow of chastity. —— **prŏlēs**, acc. sing. of *prŏlēs, -is*, f., 3d; direct obj. of *dabit*.

LINE 275. **Inde**, adv. with connective force = *from it* (the *gens Hectorea*), or *after that, next. Inde* is derived from the demonstr. *is*, with the suffix *de* = *from* (corresponds to the Greek suffix θε or θεν, denoting separation): it may refer to time = *next*, place = *thence*, and persons = *from him* (*her, them*, etc.); cf. its correlative *unde*, l. 6. —— **lupae**, gen. sing. of *lupa, -ae*, f., 1st (with a corresponding m. noun, *lupus, -ī*; Greek λύκος); poss. gen., limiting *tegmine*. Romulus and Remus, when exposed to die in the Tiber, are said to have been saved and suckled by a she-wolf. Their foster-mother is stated by others to have been Acca Laurentia, the wife of the shepherd of the king's flocks, who was nicknamed Lupa. Most historians reject as myth the whole story of the life of Romulus, which was invented to account for the name and foundation of Rome (ll. 276, 277). —— **fulvō**, abl. sing. n. of *fulvus, -a, -um;* qualifies *tegmine*. —— **nū-trīcis** (from *nūtriō*), gen. sing. of *nūtrīx*, f., 3d; in apposition with *lupae*. —— **tĕg-mine**, abl. sing. of *tĕgmen, -inis*, n., 3d (other forms *tegimen, tegumen*, from *tegō, = I cover*)*;* abl. of cause, dependent on *laetus*. A. & G. 245; B. 219; G. 408; H. 416. A wolf-skin seems to have been the traditional costume of Romulus; *tegmine* suggests some sort of robe, rather than the *galea lupina* (*helmet*) with which Propertius adorns Romulus. —— **laetus**, nom. sing. m. of *laetus, -a, -um;* agrees with *Romulus. Laetus* = *ex-ulting in*, out of gratitude to the wolf that tended him; Heyne and others very unneces-sarily make it = to *utens*, apparently to account for the abl. *tegmine*.

LINE 276. **Rŏmulus**, nom. sing.; subj. of *excipiet*. Romulus was founder and first king of Rome. He and his brother eventually slew the usurper Amulius, and Romulus afterwards killed Remus in a quarrel which arose when Rome was building. Upon his death or disappearance, he was worshipped under the name Quirinus. —— **excipiet**, 3d pers. sing. fut. ind. act. of *excipiō, -ere, excēpī, exceptum*, 3 (*ēx + capiō*)*;* agrees with the subj. *Romulus. Excipere* = lit. *to take from* another, here *from the race of Hector*. —— **gentem**, acc. sing. of *gens, gentis*, f., 3d; direct obj. of *excipiet*. —— **et**, cop. conj. —— **Māvortia**, acc. plur. n. of *Māvortius, -a, -um* (*Māvors, -tis*, m., 3d, another name for *Mars*)*;* agrees with *moenia. Mavortius* = *Romanus*, as Romulus was son of Mars. —— **condet**, 3d pers. sing. fut. ind. act. of *condō, -ere, condidī, conditum*, 3; joined by *et* to *excipiet*.

LINE 277. **Moenia**, acc. plur. of *moenia, -ium*, n., 3d; direct obj. of *condet*. —— **Rōmānōs**, acc. plur. of *Rōmānī, -ōrum*, m., 2d (plur. m. of adj. *Rōmānus, -a, -um*)*;* direct obj. of *dicet*. —— **que**, = enclitic conj. The *caesura* after *que* is called *feminine*, because it occurs after the 2d syllable in the foot. —— **suō**, abl. sing. n. of *suus, -a, -um*, poss. adj. of the reflexive pron. of the 3d person; agrees with *nomine*. Like *se, sui*, the adj. *suus* may only be used when the noun which it qualifies belongs or appertains to the subject. Thus, *his friends* = *amici ejus*, but *he loves his friends* = *amicos suos amat*. A. & G. 196; B. 86, 1, and 244; G. 309; H. 449.—— **dē**, prep. with the abl.; gov.

power I set nor goal	dícet.	**Hís** ego , néc me, tás	re, rúm	„ 278
nor season; empire	*will call.*	*To them I neither goals*	*for their fortunes*	
without end have I	nec , témpora , póno ; Ímperiúm	sine ,	fíne 279	
given. Nay more,	*nor seasons I fix;*	*rule*	*without end*	
harsh Juno, who now	de, dí. „ Quin , áspera , Iúno,	Quæ	mare 280	
with her alarms keeps	*I have given. Nay but harsh Juno*	*who*	*sea*	

nomine. De = down from, and then *from,* of time, place, or source, especially after compound verbs, e.g. *araneas de pariete deiiciam;* it is also used of the whole from which a part is taken, *unus de compluribus.* In other relations, *de = concerning (de rerum natura),* according to *(de more),* of *(de marmore signum),* etc. A. & G. 153; B. 142; G. 417, 5; H. 434, I. —— **nōmine,** abl. sing. of *nōmen, -inis,* n., 3d; governed by *de.* —— **dīcet,** 3d pers. sing. fut. ind. act. of *dīcō, -ere, dīxī, dictum,* 3; joined by *que* to *condet.*

LINE 278. **Hīs,** dat. plur. m. of *hīc, haec, hōc;* dat. of the indirect obj. after *pono; his = Romanis.* It is emphatic, contrasting the unlimited empire of the Romans with the restricted power of their predecessors. —— **ego,** nom. sing.; subj. of *pono.* —— **nec** *(neque),* conj., repeated below, *= neither . . . nor.* —— **mētās,** acc. plur. of *mĕta, -ae,* f., 1st (from *mētior,* hence *the measuring thing);* direct obj. of *pono. Meta =* (1) *a pillar,* set up for marking a measured distance, (2) *the turning point,* or *goal,* in a race course, cf. Horace, Odes, I, 1, 5, *metaque fervidis evitata rotis. Nec . . . nec* connect *metas* and *tempora* in opposition to one another, *metas* being limits of area in space, *tempora* limits of duration in time. —— **rērum,** gen. plur. of *rēs, reī,* f., 5th; objective gen. dependent on the notion of *agency* in *metas. Rerum = affairs,* hence *fortunes, empire.* —— **nec,** conj.; see above. —— **tempora,** acc. plur. of *tempus, -oris,* n., 3d (lit. = *a division made by cutting;* akin to Greek τέμνω *= I cut);* direct obj. of *pono.* See *metas* above. —— **pōnō,** 1st pers. sing. pres. ind. act. of *pŏnō, -ere, posuī, positum,* 3; agrees with its subj. *ego.*

LINE 279. **Imperium,** acc. sing. of *imperium, -ī,* n., 2d; direct obj. of *deaī.* —— **sine,** prep. with the abl.; gov. *fine.* —— **fīne,** abl. sing. of *fīnis, -is,* m. (less commonly f.), 3d; governed by *sine.* This majestic prophecy has been far more fully realized than the poet himself was likely to imagine. The German emperors of the Hapsburg line were the real successors of the Roman emperors, after the dissolution took place, and each heir claimed the title of King of the Romans: thus we may regard the empire of Rome as still surviving in the Germany of to-day. —— **dedī,** 1st pers. sing. perf. ind. act. of *dŏ, dare, dedī, datum,* 1; its unexpressed subj. *ego =* Jupiter. —— **quin** (for *quī + ne, quī* being an old locative abl. of the rel.; *= by which not),* corroborative conj., *= nay but, verily* (like the Greek μέν οὖν). Other uses of *quin* are: (1) in interrogatives, *= why not?* with the ind. mood; (2) as a final conj. with the subjunct., after verbs of *hindering, refusing,* and the like; e.g. *neque recusare quin armis contendant, = and (that they) do not refuse to contend in arms;* (3) as a consecutive conj., after verbs of *doubting;* or in negative or implied negative sentences = *ut non.* The student would do well to look up the references in the grammars. —— **aspera,** nom. sing. f. of *asper, -a, -um;* qualifies *Iuno.* —— **Iūnō,** nom. sing.; subj. of *referet.* Juno and Jupiter afterwards had splendid temples in Rome, of which they were the most important guardians; Minerva was also another guardian deity.

LINE 280. **Quae,** nom. sing. f. of the rel. pron.; agrees with *Iuno,* and is subj. of *fatigat* in the rel. clause. —— **mare,** acc. sing. of *mare, -is,* n., 3d; direct obj. of *fatigat.*

				sea and land and sky
núnc	ter, rás-que	me, tú ,,	coe, lúmque fa, tígat,	astir, will lead to
now	*and lands*	*with fear*	*and sky stirs,*	better ways her coun-
281 Cónsili, a	ín	meli, ús refe, rét,	,, me, cúmque	sels, and with me will
her plans	*to*	*the better will change,*	*and with me*	cherish the Romans,
282 fo, vébit		Róma, nós,	re, rúm	lords of earth, the
will cherish		*the Romans,*	*of things (the world)*	nation of the gown.
domi, nós,	,,	gen, témque	to, gátam.	
rulers,		*and the race*	*clad in the toga.*	

—— **nunc**, adv., modifying in respect to time the action of *fatigat*. —— **terrās**, acc. plur. of *terra, -ae*, f., 1st; joined by *que* to *mare*. —— **que**, enclitic conj. —— **metū**, abl. sing. of *metus, -ūs*, m., 4th (*metuo*, = *I fear*); probably instrumental abl. after *fatigat*, = *torments by her fears*. Some make it abl. of cause, = *in her fear*, comparing *id metuens* in l. 23. —— **coelum**, acc. sing. of *coelum, -ī*, n., 2d; joined by *que* to *terras*. Observe that all the firmaments (earth, sea, and sky) are mentioned, = the world. —— **que**, enclitic conj. —— **fatigat**, 3d pers. sing. prcs. ind. act. of *fatīgō, -āre, -āvī, -ātum*, 1; agrees with its subj. *quae*. *Fatigare*, = lit. *to weary*, hence *harass;* it commonly expresses the relation between a hunter and his quarry, = *pursues hard*.

Line 281. **Consilia**, acc. plur. of *consilium, -ī*, n., 2d (from *consulo*, = *I consult*); direct obj. of *referet*. *Consilium* = (1) *consultation;* (2) *plan*, as here; (3) *prudence;* (4) *advice;* (5) *a senate, a council*, e.g. of war. Distinguish the above from *concilium* (*con* + *culo* = Greek καλῶ, *I call together*), = *council, deliberative assembly*. —— **in**, prep. with the acc. or abl.; gov. *melius* in the idiomatic phrase *in melius*. See *in*, l. 51. —— **melius**, acc. sing. n. of *melior, melius*, comparative adj.; obj. of *in*. Comparison: positive, *bonus;* comparative, *melior;* superl., *optimus*. The n. adj. *melius* is here, as in many instances in Vergil, used substantively; cf. *extrema*, l. 219, *in altum*, l. 34, etc. *In melius referet* = *emendabit, will amend*. —— **referet**, 3d pers. sing. fut. ind. act. of *referō, referre, retulī, relātum*, irreg. (compound of *re* = *back*, and *fero*); agrees with the subj. *Iuno*. —— **mēcum** (*mē* + *cum*), *me*, is abl. case of *ego;* governed by the prep. *cum: cum*, prep. with the abl., appended to and governing *me.* *Cum* is thus used with the abl. of the personal, reflexive, and relative pronouns. A. & G. 99, *e*, and 104, *e*; B. 142, 4; G. 413, rem. 1; H. 184, 6, and 187, 2. —— **que**, enclitic conj. —— **fovēbit**, 3d pers. sing. fut. ind. act. of *foveō, -ēre, fōvī, fōtum*, 2; joined by *que* to *referet*.

Line 282. **Rōmānōs**, acc. plur. of *Rōmānī, -ōrum*, m., 2d; direct obj. of *fovebit*. —— **rērum**, gen. plur. of *rēs, reī*, f., 3d; objective gen., dependent on the noun of agency *dominos*. A. & G. 217; B. 200; G. 363, 2; H. 396, III. —— **dominōs**, acc. plur. of *dominus, -i*, m., 2d; in apposition with *Romanos;* cf. Horace, Odes, I, 1, 6, *palmaque nobilis* TERRARUM DOMINOS *evehit ad deos*. Some derive *dominus* from *domus*, = *a house*, the connotation of *dominus* being absolute mastery of a house and its usual company of household slaves and retainers; others derive it from *domo*, = *I tame*. Synonyms: *dominus*, = *master*, i.e. owner of property; *herus*, = *master*, i.e. in relation to his *famuli* and *servi; magister*, = *master, overseer*, often in respect of skill in some art or science, hence *teacher* (in which sense it = *praeceptor*). —— **gentem**, acc. sing. of *gens, gentis*, f., 3d; joined by *que* to *Romanos*. As the *toga-clad race* is the Roman race, *Romanos + gentem togatam* is an instance of *hendiadys;* however, the latter phrase adds a little piece of picturesque description. —— **que**, enclitic conj. —— **togātam**, acc. sing. f. of *togātus, -a, -um* (from the noun *toga, -ae*, f., 1st); qualifies *gentem*. The *toga*, or civil dress of the Roman citizen, was a long and full garment of white wool, reaching to the feet, and fastened at the shoulder by a *fibula* or pin, frequently so as to leave the right arm free. As

Thus is it decreed.	Sïc	placi, túm.	,,	Veni, ét	lus, trís	283
With the lapsing of the sacred season will	*Thus*	*it has been decided.*		*Will come*	*the lustra*	
come an age when	la, béntibus	,	ǽtas,	Cúm	domus	, 284
the house of Assaracus shall subdue to	*gliding on*		*an age,*	*when*	*the house*	
serfdom Phthia and	Ássara, cí	,, Phthi, ám	cla, rás-que	My, cénas		
famed Mycenae, and	*of Assaracus*	*Phthia*	*and famous*	*Mycenae*		

a general costume, it began to go out of fashion in Vergil's time, but was worn on occasions of state and ceremony. There is perhaps a contrast between *rerum dominos* and *gentem togatam*, the former describing the Romans in their character of *soldiers*, the latter as citizens in times of *peace*.

LINE 283. **Sïc,** adv. of manner, summing up the matter of this prophetic utterance. —— **placitum,** nom. sing. n. of *placitus, -a, -um,* perf. part. of *placeo, -ēre, placui, placitum,* 2; *placitum* is used impersonally with *est* understood, = *it has been decided.* The impersonal paradigm is *placet, placere, placuit* or *placitum est.* *Placet* may be followed by a subject-clause introduced by *ut* with the subjunctive, e.g. Cicero, *placitum est mihi . . . ut ducerem,* etc. For the double perf. form, cf. *licuit* or *licitum est, miseruit* or *miseritum est.* *Placet* was often used expressing the decision of official bodies in civil matters, = *it pleases* (e.g. *senatui*), with the dat. of the object; e.g. *mihi placet = I decide.* A. & G. 146, *c,* and 330, A; B. 138, III, and 327, 1; G. 553, 4; H. 301. An acc. and inf. clause may also be subj. of *placet;* e.g. *placuit Caesari mittere legatos.* —— **Veniet,** 3d pers. sing. fut. ind. act. of *venio, -īre, vēni, ventum,* 4; agrees with the subj. *aetas.* —— **lūstrīs,** abl. plur. of *lūstrum, -ī,* n., 2d (from *luo,* = *I wash,* hence *expiate*) ; abl. abs. with *labentibus.* *Lustrum* = (1) *expiatory offering, purification;* (2) hence, as the Censors at Rome enjoined a solemn purification every five years, *lustrum* = the religious period of *five years.* We may render *lustris* freely, *as the sacred years glide on.* —— **lābentibus,** abl. plur. n. of *lābens, -entis,* pres. part. of the dep. verb *lābor, -ī, lapsus sum,* 3; agrees with *lustris* in the abl. abs. construction. A. & G. 255; B. 227; G. 409, 410; H. 431. Deponent verbs are the only verbs in Latin which have participles of present and past time with active meaning. A. & G. 135; B. 112; G. 113, 220; H. 231. —— **aetās,** gen. *aetātis,* f., 3d (akin to *aevum*) ; nom. sing., subj. of *veniet.*

LINE 284. **Cum** (sometimes *quum, quom,* and rarely *qum*) temporal conj., followed by the ind. *premet. Cum* temporal takes the subjunct. in the imperf. and pluperf. tenses, and the ind. in the rest. *Cum* may also introduce: (1) *causal* clauses, = *since;* (2) *concessive* clauses, = *although;* in both cases the mood of the verb is subjunct. in all tenses. For *cum* temporal, consult A. & G. 325; B. 288, 289; G. 580–585; H. 521. —— **domus,** gen. *domūs,* f., 4th (for decl., refer to *domos,* l. 140); nom. sing., subj. of *premet.* —— **Assaracī,** gen. sing. of *Assaracus,* m., 2d; poss. gen., qualifying *domus.* Assaracus was a son of the Trojan king Tros, and the great-grandfather of Aeneas. Ilus, the brother of Assaracus, was the grandfather of king Priam, so Aeneas was only remotely connected with the royal house of Troy. *Domus Assaraci* is a poetical variation for *Troiani.* —— **Phthīam,** acc. sing. of *Phthīa, -ae,* f., 1st; direct obj. of *premet.* Phthia was a town of Thessaly, famous as the birthplace of the great Greek hero, Achilles. —— **clārās,** acc. plur. f. of *clārus, -a, -um ;* qualifies *Mycenas.* *Clarus* is a favorite epithet, but it very likely is made a literal attribute of Mycenae, which the testimony of Homer and archaeologists prove to have been a splendid city in Homeric times and considerably advanced in the uses and adornments of civilization. —— **que,** enclitic conj. —— **Mycēnās,** acc. of the plur. noun *Mycēnae, -ārum,* f., 1st (less commonly in the sing. forms *Mycena, Mycene* (Greek 1st decl. nom.)); joined by *que* to

285 Sérviti, ó　　premet,, ác　vic, tís ,, domi, nábitur,
with servitude　will press,　and　conquered　　　will rule

286 Árgis.　　Násce, túr pul, chrá ,, Tro, iánus o, rígine,
over Argos.　Will be born　fair　　Trojan　　by descent

287 Cǽsar,　Ímperi, *um*　ócea, nó,　,, fa, mám　qui,
Caesar,　his empire　by the ocean,　his fame　who

shall rule o'er con-
quered Argos. A
Trojan shall be born
of noble lineage, a
Caesar destined to
bound his empire with
Ocean, his glory with

Phthiam. In Homer, Mycenae is stated to have been the home of Agamemnon, who led the Greek host against Troy.

LINE 285. **Servitiō**, abl. sing. of *servitium, -ī,* n., 2d (from *servio,* = *I am a slave*); abl. of the means, or equally well abl. of manner, after *premet.* The allusion is to the final subjugation of Greece by Aemilius Paullus (in the north), and particularly Mummius, who destroyed Corinth in 146 B.C. (the same year that Scipio destroyed Carthage). The enumeration of Greek cities is intended to convey the idea that the descendants of the old Trojans (i.e. the Romans) enjoyed a full revenge upon the descendants of the ancient Greeks who sacked Troy. Under the Roman empire, Greece was allowed considerable freedom and self-government. —— **premet,** 3d pers. sing. fut. ind. act. of *premō, -ere, pressī, pressum,* 3; agrees with its subj. *domus.* —— **āc,** conj., adding another important feature. —— **victīs,** abl. plur. m. of *victus, -a, -um,* perf. part. pass. of *vincō, -ere, vīcī, victum,* 3; agrees with *Argis* (which see). —— **dominābitur,** 3d pers. sing. fut. ind. of the dep. verb *dominor, -ārī, -ātus sum,* I (*dominus*) ; joined by *ac* to *premet.* —— **Argīs,** abl. of the plur. noun *Argī, -ōrum,* m., 2d (see *Argīs,* l. 24); locative abl. Some take *victis Argis* as abl. absolute. Argos was near Mycenae, and was the chief city of Argolis in the Peloponnese and the home of the hero Diomedes (who wounded the god Mars).

LINE 286. **Nascētur,** 3d pers. sing. fut. ind. of the dep. verb *nascor, -ī, nātus sum,* 3; agrees with the subj. *Caesar.* —— **pulchrā,** abl. sing. f. of *pulcher, pulchra, pulchrum;* agrees with *origine.* *Pulchra* here = *noble,* not *beautiful.* —— **Trōiānus,** nom. sing. m. of the adj.; qualifies *Caesar.* Augustus was *Trōiānus* through the *gens Iulia.* —— **orīgine,** abl. sing. of *orīgo, -inis,* f., 3d; abl. of description, with *Troianus.* —— **Caesar,** gen. *Caesaris,* m., 3d (from the regal implication in this name are derived the titles *Kaiser, Czar,* etc.); nom. sing., subj. of *nascetur.* The reference is to the Emperor Augustus, not to his uncle C. Julius Caesar. The emperor's own name before his adoption by Julius Caesar was C. Octavius but, according to custom, on adoption he took the adopter's name, with Octavianus as an *agnomen.* He is called *Iulius* in l. 288 to point his descent from Aeneas. The title *Augustus* was not adopted by him till 27 B.C. With Caesar's adopted name, cf. P. Cornelius Scipio *Aemilianus* (because originally an *Aemilius,* and adopted by the elder Scipio).

LINE 287. **Imperium,** acc. sing. of *imperium, -ī,* n., 2d; direct obj. of *terminet.* *Imperium,* which in golden Latin = *the authority or command* of a Roman consul, praetor (or proconsul, propraetor) outside the walls of Rome, here has the poetical and late-prose meaning of *empire.* Augustus was made perpetual *Imperator* in B.C. 29. He set out upon a career of conquest, but later devoted himself to consolidating his empire. The Rhine was the northern boundary of his western dominions, the buffer-state Armenia the boundary of his eastern. —— **ōceanō,** abl. sing. of *ōceanus, -ī,* m., 2d; abl. of the means or instrument. *Oceanus* ('Ωκεανός) is the river that flows round the earth, so Augustus is implied to be the destined conqueror of the whole world. —— **fāmam,** acc. sing. of *fāma, -ae,* f., 1st; direct obj. of *terminet.* Observe the *asyndeton,* intended to give greater rhetorical effect to the line. —— **quī,** nom. sing. m. of the rel. pron.; agrees

the stars, Julius, a	términet	,	ástris,	Iúlius,	, á	mag,nó	, , 288
name passed down	*is to bound*		*by the stars,*	*Julius,*	*from*	*great*	
from great Iulus.	de,míssum	,	nómen	I,úlo.	Húnc	tu	o,lím 289
Him laden with the	*passed down*		*a name*	*Iulus.*	*Him*	*thou some day*	
spoils of the East thou	coe,ló,	,,	spoli,ís	Ori,éntis	o,nústum,		
shalt one day, thy	*in the sky,*		*with the spoils*	*of the East*	*laden,*		
cares departed, wel-	Áccipi,és		se,cúra ;	,,	vo,cábitur	,	híc 290
come to heaven: he	*thou shalt receive*		*fearless;*		*will be called upon*		*he*

with *Caesar,* and is subj. of *terminet.* *Qui* is here final, = *ut is;* refer to the NOTE on *tenerent,* l. 236. —— **terminet,** 3d pers. sing. pres. subjunct. act. of *terminō, -āre, -āvī, -ātum,* 1 (*terminus,* = *a boundary*); agrees with its subj. *qui,* in the *purpose* clause *qui terminet,* etc., = *destined to bound,* etc. —— **astrīs,** abl. plur. of *astrum, -ī,* n., 2d; abl. of the means or instrument.

LINE 288. **Iūlius,** nom. sing. m., 2d (properly m. of adj. *Iūlius, -a, -um;* so *Iūlia*); in apposition with *Caesar;* or it may be taken as the adj., agreeing with *Caesar,* and marking the *gens.* —— **ā,** prep.; gov. *Iulo.* —— **magnō,** abl. sing. m. of *magnus, -a, -um;* agrees with *Iulo.* —— **dēmissum,** nom. sing. n., of the perf. part. pass. of *dēmittō, -ere, dēmīsī, dēmissum,* 3 (*de* + *mitto*); agrees with *nomen.* —— **nōmen,** nom. sing. n., 3d (gen. *nōminis*); in apposition with *Iulius.* —— **Iūlō,** abl. sing. of *Iūlus, -ī,* m., 2d; governed by the prep. *a.* The derivation of the name *Iulius* from *Iulus* (Ascanius) is entirely fanciful.

LINE 289. **Hunc,** acc. sing. m. of the demonstr. pron. *hīc, haec, hōc;* direct obj. of *accipies; hunc* refers to Caesar Augustus. —— **tū,** nom. sing.; subj. of *accipies.* By *tu,* of course, Venus is meant, to whom Jupiter is disclosing the mysteries of fate respecting the Trojans. —— **ōlim,** adv. of time; here of the future, = *in time to come.* —— **coelō,** abl. sing. of *coelum, -ī,* n., 2d; abl. of 'place where.' —— **spoliīs,** abl. plur. of *spolium, -ī,* n., 2d; instrumental abl., with *onustum.* —— **Orientis,** gen. sing. of *Oriens,* m., 3d (by origin, the pres. part. of *orior,* = *I rise,* agreeing with *sol* understood); poss. gen., limiting *spoliis.* With *Oriens* compare *Occidens* (*sol*), and *occasus* used absolutely without *solis.* The allusion in the text is to the progress of victory through the East made by Augustus after his victory over Antony and Cleopatra at Actium in 31 B.C.; it is not to the expedition to Armenia made in 21 B.C., for the Aeneid was not then complete, and besides, Augustus did not win victories over the Parthians, but rather made a diplomatic treaty with them, receiving back the standards lost by Crassus. The words *spoliis Orientis onustum* clearly prove that *Iulius Caesar* above = Augustus, for Julius Caesar, the Dictator, won his laurels, not in the East, but in Gaul and Britain. —— **onustum,** acc. plur. m. of *onustus, -a, -um* (from *onus,* = *a burden*); qualifies *hunc.*

LINE 290. **Accipiēs,** 2d pers. sing. fut. ind. act. of *accipiō, -ere, accēpī, acceptum,* 3 (*ad* + *capiō*); agrees with the subj. *tu.* —— **sēcūra,** nom. sing. f. of *sēcūrus, -a, -um* (*sē,* = *without,* + *cūra,* = *anxiety*), agrees with *tu.* —— **vocābitur,** 3d pers. sing. fut. ind. pass. of *vocō, -āre, -āvī, -ātum,* 1; agrees with the subj. *hic; vocabitur = invocabitur.* —— **quoque,** conjunctive adv. *Hic quoque* (*he* ALSO) signifies that Augustus will be deified as a *deus indiges* or patron god of his country *as well as* Aeneas. *Quoque* never stands first in a sentence, but usually second, or even third if the second word is emphatic. A. & G. 151, *a,* and 345, *b;* B. 347, 1; G. 479; H. 554, I, 4. —— **vōtīs,** abl. plur. of *vōtum, -ī,* n., 2d (from *vōveō,* = *I vow*); instrumental ablative. After his return from the East in 29 B.C. Augustus consecrated a temple to the worship of Julius Caesar, and also began to permit and even encourage his

291 quoque　,　vótis.　　Áspera　,　túm　posi,tís　„
   I also　　*with prayers.*　　*Rough*　　*them being laid aside*

292 mi,téscent　,　sǽcula　,　béllis ;　Cána Fi,dés et ,
   will soften　　*the ages*　　*wars ;*　*hoary　Faith　and*

Vésta,　„　Re,mó　cum　,　frátre　Qui,rínus
Vesta,　　*Remus　with*　　*his brother　Quirinus*

too shall be invoked in prayer. Then warfare shall cease and the rough ages grow gentle. Hoary Faith and Vesta, Quirinus and his brother Re-

own worship. Henceforth the Roman emperors allowed themselves to be called divine in their lifetime, for this religious innovation was readily taken up in Spain and in other provinces, and proved a very useful part in the political machinery of Rome. The regular title of a deceased emperor was *divus*. In course of time a royal college of priests came into being (*sodales*), and the deification of the emperor grew to be such a matter of course as to prompt and win servile recognition of the extravagant claims of weakminded men such as Nero, and his predecessors Gaius and Claudius.

LINE 291. **Aspera**, nom. plur. n. of *asper, -a, -um;* qualifies *saecula.*——**tum**, adv. of time, alluding to that happy period when the worship of Augustus should have become general. ——**positis**, abl. plur. n. of *positus, -a, -um,* perf. part. pass. of *pōnō, -ere, posuī, positum,* 3; agrees with *bellis* in the abl. abs. construction; this verb here = *being laid aside.* ——**mītescent,** 3d pers. plur. fut. ind. act. of *mītescō, -ere,* no perf., no supine, 3 (from *mītis,* = *gentle,* adj., 3d); agrees with its subj. *saecula.* The termination in *-sco* expresses the beginning of an action, e.g. *vesperascit,* = *it grows toward evening.* Verbs in *-sco* are called *inceptive* or *inchoative.* A. & G. 167, *a*; B. 155, 1; G. 133, V; H. 337. With the sentiment expressed here compare Aen. VI, 793, where Vergil, in speaking of Augustus (*divi genus*), says that he *will institute a golden age* (*aurea condet saecula*) wherein the earth will untended give her bounties, as it did in the golden age under the rule of Saturn. A future golden age of peace was a vision that appealed very strongly to the poets of Rome. —— **saecula**, gen. *saeculōrum,* n., 2d; nom. plur., subj. of *mitescent.* ——**bellis**, abl. plur. of *bellum, -ī,* n., 2d; in the abl. abs. construction with *positis.* From 29 B.C. to the death of Augustus, Rome was free from the terrible internal strife which began about the time of the Gracchi, and continued on with scarcely any intermission till the empire.

LINE 292. **Cāna**, nom. sing. f. of *cănus, -a, -um;* qualifying *Fides.* The deity Faith is called *gray* or *hoary-headed* (and therefore to be specially revered) because she was much worshipped in the early days of Rome, when the nobles in the *simplicity* of their character handled the plough in peace and the sword in war. The worship of Faith was enjoined by king Numa, but was neglected in the later republic. Commentators quote Horace, *Carmen Saeculare,* l. 57: *Iam Fides et Pax et Honos Pudorque priscus et neglecta redire virtus audet,* all this as a result of the peace under Augustus and his revival of primitive forms of religion.——**Fidēs**, gen. *Fideī,* f., 3d; nom. sing., one of the subjects of *dabunt.* *Faith* personified was the goddess of oaths and honesty, one of the deities worshipped before the multiplication of gods in Rome and/the introduction of foreign divinities, e.g. Isis, from Egypt. —— **et**, cop. conj. —— **Vesta**, gen. *Vestae,* f., 1st (Greek ἑστία, *the hearth*) ; nom. sing., joined by *et* to *Fides.* Vesta, the daughter of Rhea and Saturn, was goddess of the hearth and home. The Vestal virgins kept her fire constantly burning. and it was the Greek custom to take some fire from her temple, keep it burning, and keep it alive in every colony that was to be founded. —— **Rĕmō,** abl. sing. of *Rĕmus, -ī,* m., 2d; governed by *cum.* Remus was the brother of Romulus, and their mention together signifies that a new era of civil harmony under Augustus will succeed the intestine warfare of the republic. —— **cum**, prep., governing *Remo.* —— **frātre**, abl. sing. of *frāter, -tris,* m., 3d; in apposition with *Remo.* —— **Quirīnus**, nom.

mus shall establish laws; the gates of war dread with close-fitting bolts of iron shall be shut; within	Iúra da, búnt; „ di, ræ fer, ro ét com, págibus , 293
	laws will give; dread with iron and with bars
	ártis Claúden, túr bel, lí por, tæ ; „ Furor , 294
	tight will be closed of war the gates; Fury

---

sing. m., 2d; one of the subjects of *dabunt;* observe the omission of a cop. conjunction to join *Quirinus* and *Vesta.* Quirinus is the name under which Romulus was worshipped after his translation to heaven.   Horace speaks of the ' *bones of Quirinus,*' and Varro (quoted by Porphyrion) speaks of " a burial place of Romulus behind the Rostra"; but poets, among other prerogatives, often seem to claim a right to be inconsistent.   The *Quirinalia* (or festival of Quirinus) was observed annually on February the 17th.   There is some doubt as to the derivation of the word; some refer it to *quiris* or *curis,* a Sabine word = *a spear,* hence *the warrior;* others refer it to κῦρος = *might, power;* similarly derived is *Quirites,* a name given to Roman citizens in their full civil capacity, *capite non deminuti.*

LINE 293. **Iūra**, acc. plur. of *iūs, iūris,* n., 3d (gen. plur. *iūrum*)*;* direct obj. of *dabunt Iura dare* = *to give,* i.e. *impose laws* for others to obey, and the phrase here means that domestic purity shall be sovereign in Rome. —— **dabunt**, 3d pers. plur. fut. ind. act. of *dō, dare, dedī, datum,* 1; agrees with *Fides, Vesta,* and *Quirinus* as a composite subject. —— **dīrae**, nom. plur. f. of *dīrus, -a, -um ;* agrees with *portae.*——**ferrō**, abl. sing. of *ferrum, -ī,* n., 2d; probably an abl. of description, with *dirae* = *grim with iron,* etc.; some take it as an instrumental abl. dependent on *claudentur.   Ferro et compagibus artis* = lit. *with iron and close-fitting fastenings,* i.e. *with tightly-closed fastenings of iron,* an instance of *hendiadys;* cf. l. 648, (*pallam*) *signis auroque rigentem,* = *signis aureis rigentem.*   A. & G. 385; B. 374, 4; G. 698; H. 636, III, 2. —— **et**, cop. conj. —— **compāgibus**, abl. plur. of *compāgēs, -is,* f., 3d (*com* [*cum*] *together* + root PAG in *pangō, I fasten,* and in Greek πήγνυμι); joined by *et* to *ferro,* and similar to *ferro* in construction.   The gen. plur. of *compages* is *compagum;* there is a 3d decl. f. collateral form *compago, -inis.* —— **artīs** (*arctīs*), abl. plur. f. of *artus, -a, -um* (akin to *arceō ;* cf. the form *arctus*).

LINE 294. **Claudentur**, 3d pers. plur. fut. ind. pass. of *claudō, -ere, clausī, clausum,* 3; agrees with the subj. *portae.* —— **bellī** (some write *Bellī*), gen. sing. of *bellum,* n., 2d; poss. gen., qualifying *portae.*   By the *gates of war* are meant the gates of the temple of Janus (also called *Ianus Quirini*)*;* the gates were kept open in time of war (as Niebuhr says, to allow the Latin and Sabine divisions of ancient Rome to go through and assist one another against enemies attacking), and tradition adds that before the time of Augustus they were only shut twice, viz. (1) in the reign of Numa, (2) by Titus Manlius, at the end of the First Punic War, B.C. 235.   The gates were closed three times under Augustus, viz. in B.C. 29, in B.C. 24, and one other unspecified occasion. ——‐portae, nom. plur. of *porta, -ae,* f., 1st; subj. of *claudentur‐.* Synonyms: *porta,* = the *gate,* esp. of a city, a camp, or any fortified place; *ianua,* = the *gate,* esp. of doors between rooms ("*parietis ac domorum*"). —— **Furor**, gen. *furōris,* m., 3d; nom. sing., subj. of *fremet. Furor impius* is a personification of *civil war,* and = the *Furor civilis* of Horace, Odes IV, xv, 17 ("while Caesar Augustus guards our fortunes, neither civil rage nor violence will banish peace "; the subject and treatment of this ode are very similar to Vergil's in this passage). —— **impius**, nom. sing. m. (*in,* = *not,* + *pius,* = *dutiful*)*;* qualifies *Furor.* Civil war, parricide, want of respect for parents or the aged, and disbelief in the gods are all forms of the notion expressed by *impietas.*   The commentators suggest that Vergil derived the idea of Rage imprisoned in the temple of Janus from a picture by the Greek Apelles representing War fastened as a prisoner by the hands to the car of Alexander

295 ímpius	,	íntus,	Sǽva	se, déns	super	,	árma, ,,
accursed		within	cruel	sitting	upon		arms
296 et	, céntum	,	vínctus	a, ḗnis	Póst	ter, gúm
and	a hundred		bound	brazen	behind	his back
no, dís, ,,	fremet	,	hórridus	,	óre	cru, énto.''
with knots,	will rave		fearful		with mouth	gory.''
297 Hǽc		ait: ,	ét	Mai, á	geni, túm ,,
These things		he says:	and	from Maia	(the son) born

accursed Rage, seated on savage weapons and bound behind the back with a hundred brazen bonds, shall gnash fearfully with blood-dyed lips." So speaks he, and sends from the height Maia's son

---

the Great; Augustus presented this picture to the Forum at Rome. —— **intus,** adv. of place, modifying *sedens*.

LINE 295. **Saeva,** acc. plur. n. of *saevus, -a, -um;* agrees with *arma*. —— **sedēns,** nom. sing. m. of the pres. part. act. of *sedeō, -ēre, sēdī, sessum,* 2; agrees with and enlarges the subj. *Furor.* —— **super,** prep. with the acc. and abl.; gov. the acc. *arma.* A. & G. 153, and 260; B. 143; G. 418, 4; H. 435. Observe the *alliteration* here, and in *impius intus.* —— **arma,** acc. of the plur. noun, n., 2d; governed by *super.* —— **et,** cop. conj. —— **centum,** indecl. cardinal numeral; qualifies *nodis. Centum* is not exact here, but indicates a large number; so often *mille,* etc. —— **vinctus,** nom. sing. m. of the perf. part. pass. of *vinciō, -īre, vinxī, vinctum,* 4; joined by *et* to *sedens.* —— **aēnis,** abl. plur. of *aĕnus, -a, -um* (from *aes, aeris,* n., 3d); qualifies *nodis.*

LINE 296. **Post,** prep. with the acc.; gov. *tergum. Post =* (1) *behind,* of place; (2) *after,* of time (the most common use); (3) *after, under,* of rank (rare). A. & G. 152, *a;* B. 141; G. 416, 20; H. 433. —— **tergum,** acc. sing. of *tergum, -ī,* n., 2d; governed by *post.* —— **nōdīs,** abl. plur. of *nōdus, -ī,* m., 2d; abl. of the instrument, with *vinctus.* —— **fremet,** 3d pers. sing. fut. ind. act. of *fremō, -ere, fremuī, fremitum,* 3; agrees with the subj. *Furor. Fremere = to rage,* implying an accompaniment of furious, muttering sound, and so is very expressive. —— **horridus,** nom. sing. m. of *horridus, -a, -um* (from *horreō, = I bristle,* hence, *I shiver*); qualifies *Furor. Horridus* usually has the literal meaning *bristling,* e.g. Aen. V, 37, *horridus . . . pelle Libystidis ursae,* but occasionally the derivative sense of *dreadful.* —— **ōre,** abl. sing. of *ōs, ōris,* n., 3d; instrumental abl., with *fremet.* It may be considered an abl. of respect, defining *horridus;* probably both ideas are intended, the picture of *Furor* being a terrible one. —— **cruentō,** abl. sing. n. of *cruentus, -a, -um* (from *cruor, = gore;* cf. *crudus*); qualifies *ore.*

LINE 297. **Haec,** acc. plur. n. of *hīc, haec, hōc;* direct obj. of *ait.* —— **ait,** 3d pers. sing. pres. ind. act. of the defective verb *aio;* the subj. implied by the personal ending is *Iupiter.* A. & G. 144, *a;* B. 135; G. 175, 1; H. 297, II, 1. For the use of *aio,* etc., refer to the NOTE on *ait,* l. 142. —— **et,** cop. conj. —— **Māiā,** abl. sing. of *Māia, -ae,* f., 1st (Μαῖα); abl. of source or origin, with *genitum.* The abl. of source without a preposition (*ex* or *ab*) is common in poetry, esp. following participles; cf. Horace, Odes, I, i, 1, *Maecenas, atavis edite regibus.* A. & G. 244, *a;* B. 215; G. 395, and NOTE 1; H. 415, II. Maia was the daughter of Atlas and Pleione, and the mother of Mercury by Jupiter. Maia was the brightest of the stars in the constellation of the Pleiades. —— **genitum,** acc. sing. m. of *genitus, -a, -um,* perf. part. pass. of *gignō, -ere, genuī, genitum,* 3; direct obj. of *demittit;* the part. is used as a noun. A. & G. 113, *f;* B. cf. 236; G. 437; H. 441. The noun to be supplied with *genitum* is *fīlium.* Mercury, son of Maia, was born on Mount Cyllene, in Arcadia; in Greek myth his name is Hermes. He was the messenger of the gods, and esp. of Jupiter, the patron god of thieves, the inventor of the lyre, and

below that the land	de,míttit	ab	,	álto,	Út	ter,rae, 298
and citadels of new-	*sends down*	*from*		*the high (heaven), in*	*order that*	*the lands*
springing　Carthage	útque	no,vé	„	pate,ánt	Car,tháginis	,
may be open to wel-	*and that*	*new*		*may lie open*	*of Carthage*	
come the Trojans, lest	árces	Hóspiti,ó		Teu,crís,	„ ne	, fáti , 299
Dido, ignorant of fate,	*the citadels*	*for a refuge*		*for the Trojans,*	*lest*	*of destiny*

the conductor of the dead to Hades. —— **dēmittit,** 3d pers. sing. pres. ind. act. of *dē-mittō, -ere, dēmīsī, dēmissum,* 3 (*dē,* = *down from,* + *mittō*)*;* joined by *et* to *ait.* — NOTE. *Demittit,* like *ait,* is an *historic* present used to represent more vividly an act in the past. A. & G. 276, *d*; B. 259, 3; G. 229; H. 467, III.　As such, the sequence of subordinate tenses may either be *primary* or *historic.*　Observe that in l. 298 it is followed by the pres. subjunct. *pateant,* and again in l. 300 by the imperf. subj. *arceret:* at first glance one would expect *demittit . . . pateant . . . arceat,* or *demittit . . . paterent . . . arceret,* i.e. the two subordinate verbs corresponding in tense.　But there is a reason for the difference, viz. that *pateant* merely denotes the order given to Mercury, while *arceret* denotes the *motive* behind the order, a difference which is preserved in the tenses in the text. —— **ab,** prep. with the abl.; gov. *alto.*　It is written *a* or *ab* before consonants, *ab* before vowels and *h.* —— **altō,** abl. sing. of *altum, -i,* n., 2d; governed by *ab.*　*Altum* = *the height,* from the point of view of one below.

LINE 298.　**Ut,** *final* conj. taking the subjunct. *pateant* understood from the following; its neg. is *ne.*　*Purpose* may be expressed by *ut* or *ne* with the subjunctive, = *in order that* (. . . *not*).　Distinguish *ut final* from *ut consecutive,* i.e. *ut* with clauses of result, neg. *ut . . . non.*　For final clauses, consult A. & G. 317; B. 282; G. 545; H. 497. —— **terrae,** nom. plur. of *terra, -ae,* f., 1st; subj. of *pateant.* —— **ut,** final conj.; see above. —— **que,** enclitic conj., joining the clauses *ut terrae* (*pateant*) and *ut . . . pateant . . . arces.* —— **novae,** gen. sing. f. of *novus, -a, -um ;* qualifies *Carthaginis,* cf. *novae Carthaginis,* l. 366.　Some, however, prefer to make *novae* nom. plur. f. qualifying *arces.* Carthage is called *new,* because it was just then being founded : do not confound it with the town in Spain built much later and called *Nova Carthago* to distinguish it from *Carthago* in Africa.　*Novissimus,* the superl., has the derived meaning of *last;* in military phraseology *novissimi* = *the rear-guard, the soldiers in the rear.* —— **Carthāginis,** gen. sing. of *Carthāgō,* f., 3d; poss. gen., limiting *arces.*　Carthage (derived from two Phoenician words) = *new town.*　It was a colony in Northern Africa, founded by Phoenicians of Tyre.　Carthage in time far surpassed the mother-city in wealth and power, acquiring an immense merchant navy and planting numerous colonies in Spain, Sicily, and elsewhere in the Mediterranean.　As an imperial city she was nearing maturity when she came into conflict with the growing power of Rome, and the result was that three great wars were fought with varying success on the whole, in the second of which Hannibal nearly overpowered the Romans, but in the third of which the Carthaginians were utterly defeated by Scipio Aemilianus, and Carthage was destroyed (146 B.C.).　Reference will be made later on to Vergil's account of the foundation of Carthage. —— **arcēs,** nom. plur. of *arx, arcis,* f., 3d, subj. of *pateant.*

LINE 299.　**Hospitiō,** dat. sing. of *hospitium, -ī,* n., 2d (from *hospes*)*;* dat. of the predicate, followed by the dat. of the indirect obj. (advantage or disadvantage) *Teucris.* This construction is sometimes called the *double dative,* and the dat. of the predicate sometimes is named the *dative of purpose* or *service.*　A. & G. 233, *a*; B. 191; G. 356; H. 390.　*Hospitio* is by some incorrectly taken to be an ablative of manner. —— **Teucrīs,** dat. plur. of *Teucrī, -ōrum,* m., 2d; dat. of the indirect obj.; see *hospitio.* —— **nē,** negative conj., here = *lest.*　It takes the subjunct. mood: (1) after verbs of fearing,

800	néscia	,	Dído	Fínibus	,	árce, rét.	,,	might debar them
	ignorant		*· Dido*	*From her territory*		*should keep (them).*		from her borders. He

801	Volat	,	ílle	per	,	áëra	,	mágnum	Rémigi, o	flies through the wide
	Flies		*he*	*through*		*the air*		*wide*	*with the oarage*	air with the oarage of

ála, rum,	,,	ác	Li, byǽ	citus	,	ádstitit	,	his wings and speedily
of his wings		*and*	*of Libya*	*quick*		*has taken stand*		alights on the shores

of Libya. And now he

= *lest;* we may understand *because Jupiter feared lest,* etc.; (2), as the neg. of *ut* final, = *in order that . . . not, lest;* (3) in neg. commands, e.g. *ne hoc feceris;* (4) other idiomatic constructions, for which *vide* references in the grammars. Distinguish *nē,* the conj., from *nĕ,* the enclitic particle. As the logical train of thought leads one to supply a participle or clause = *fearing* or *as he feared* before *ne arceret, ne* here is a *final* object clause. A. & G. 331, *f*; B. 296, 2; G. 550; H. 498, III. —— **fātī,** gen. sing. of *fātum, -ī,* n., 2d; objective gen., dependent on *nescia,* and regularly with adjectives expressing fulness, power, knowledge, memory, and their opposites. A. & G. 218, *a*; B. 204, 1; G. 374; H. 399, I, 2. Jupiter feared that Dido, *ignorant of fate,* and of the promise that the Trojans would find a home in Italy and not in Africa, might drive them away. As Vergil is a poet, it is useless to argue whether Dido could have interfered against fate if she wished to do so: probably if she had known fate (that Aeneas would cause her death), she would have expelled the Trojans. —— **nescia,** nom. sing. f., of *nescius, -a, -um* (*nĕ,* = *not,* + *sciō*) *;* agrees with *Dido.* —— **Dīdō,** gen. *Dīdūs* and *Dīdōnis,* f., 3d; nom. sing., subj. of *arceret.* For declension, consult A. & G. 63, *h*; B. 47, 8; G. 65; H. 68. Dido, also called Elissa, was a daughter of Belus, king of Tyre, and the wife of Sychaeus. To escape Pygmalion, who murdered her husband for his wealth's sake, Dido sailed to Africa and founded Byrsa (Carthage). Dido stabbed herself on a funeral pyre, out of grief (as Vergil says) caused by the departure of Aeneas, whom she loved, or (as others say) because her subjects were forcing her to a marriage with a Mauritanian prince, who threatened war as an alternative of marriage.

Line 300. **Fīnibus,** abl. plur of *fīnis, -ium,* m., 3d, = *territory* (sing. *finis* = *end*) *;* abl. of separation, after *arceret.* A. & G. 243, *a*; B. 214, esp. 2; G. 390, 2, and note 2; H. 413. —— **arcēret,** 3d pers. sing. imperf. subjunct. act. of *arceō, -ēre, -uī,* no supine, 2; agrees with its subj. *Dido,* in the clause *ne . . . arceret.* For the tense, refer to the note under *demittit,* l. 297. —— **Volat,** 3d pers. sing. pres. ind. act. of *volō, -āre, -āvī, -ātum,* 1; agrees with the subj. *ille.* —— **ille,** nom. sing. m. of the demons. pron. of the 3d person : subj. of *volat; ille* refers to Mercury, *Maia genitum.* —— **per,** prep.; gov. the acc. *aëra.* —— **āëra,** acc. sing. of *āër, āëris,* m., 3d (acc. *āëra,* sometimes *āërem*) *;* governed by *per.* *Aër* = *the air,* the lower atmosphere of the earth, as opposed to *aether, the upper air.* —— **magnum,** acc. sing. m. of *magnus, -a, -um ;* qualifies *aëra.*

Line 301. **Rēmigiō,** abl. sing. of *rēmigium, -ī,* n., 2d (from *remigo,* = *I row*) *;* abl. of the means. The metaphor 'oarage of wings' is imitated from Aeschylus, *Agamemnon,* l. 52, πτερύγων ἐρέτμοισιν ἐρεσσόμενοι. —— **ālārum,** gen. plur. of *āla, -ae,* f., 1st; descriptive gen., stating the substance or material, and limiting *remigio.* A. & G. 214, *e*; B. 197; G. 361; H. 395. —— **āc,** cop. conj., connecting the following with the preceding sentence. —— **Libyae,** gen. sing. of *Libya ;* f., 1st; poss. gen., limiting *oris.* See *Libyae,* l. 22. —— **citus,** nom. sing. m.; agrees with the understood subj. of *adstitit* (*ille*), but modifies the action of the verb adverbially. A. & G. 191; B. 239; G. 325, rem. 6; H. 443. —— **adstitit,** 3d pers. sing. perf. ind. act. of *adstō, -āre, adstitī, adstitum,* 1; joined by *ac* to *volat,* agreeing with the same subj. *ille;* the perf. tense expresses instantaneous accom-

does his commands, and the men from Phoenicia put off their pride of temper at the will of the god; among the first the queen assumes a gentle spirit and kindly purpose towards the					
óris.	Ét iam ,iússa	fa,cít;	„	po,núntque 302	
on the shores.	*And now his commands he does;*			*and lay aside*	
fe,rócia	, Póéni	Córda,	vo,lénte	de,o ; „ 303	
fierce	*the Carthaginians*	*their hearts,*	*willing*	*the god;*	
in	pri,mís	re,gína	qui,étum	Áccipit 304	
among	*the first*	*the queen*	*calm*	*receives*	
in	Teu,crós	„	ani,múm	men,témque	
towards	*the Trojans*		*a disposition*	*and a purpose*	

plishment. —— ōrīs, dat. plur. of *ōra, -ae,,* f., 1st; dat. of the indirect obj. after the compound of *ad, adstitit.* A. & G. 228; B. 187, III; G. 347; H. 386.

LINE 302. **Et,** cop. conj., joining what follows to what has immediately preceded. —— **iam,** adv. of time. —— **iussa,** acc. plur. n. of *iussum, -ī,* n., 2d (properly n. of the perf. part. pass. of *iubeō, -ēre, iussī, iussum,* 2; direct obj. of *facit.* —— **facit,** 3d pers. sing. pres. ind. act. of *faciō, -ere, fēcī, factum,* 3 (*fīō, fierī, factus sum* is used as the passive); the subj. understood is a pron. referring to Mercury. —— **pōnunt,** 3d pers. plur. pres. ind. act. of *pōnō, -ere, posuī, positum,* 3; agrees with the subj. *Poeni. Ponunt,* here = *deponunt,* i.e. *lay* ASIDE. The two present tenses *facit* and *ponunt,* standing close to one another, express the immediate result of Mercury's mission. —— **que,** enclitic conj., joining the two closely connected sentences whose predicates are *facit* and *ponunt;* see note on *que,* l. 1. —— **ferōcia,** acc. plur. n. of *ferōx, -ōcis,* 3d decl. adj. one nom. termination; agrees with *corda.* —— **Poeni,** gen. *Poenārum,* m., 2d (noun formed from the adj. *Poenus, -a, -um);* nom. plur., subj. of *ponunt.* The adj. *Poenus* is the Latin correspondent of the Greek Φοῖνιξ = *Phoenician,* and *Phoenices, Punicus, -a, -um,* Φοινίκιος are all akin. *Poeni* is the name by which the Romans spoke of the Carthaginians, who were colonists from Phoenicia.

LINE 303. **Corda,** acc. plur. of *cor, cordis,* n., 3d; direct obj. of *ponunt; corda =* *animos,* a feeling to be laid aside like a garment. —— **volente,** abl. sing. *volō, velle, voluī,* irreg.; agrees with *deo* in the abl. abs. construction. The abl. sing. of participles ends in *e* when they are used in a verbal way, in *i* when used adjectively. For the conjugation of *volo,* consult A. & G. 138; B. 130; G. 174; H. 293. The negative of *volo* is *nolo; volo* compounded with *magis* (*magis volo,* hence) *malo = I wish rather, I prefer.* Synonyms: *cupere,* = *to desire eagerly; velle,* = *to wish,* implying a less keen desire; cf. Horace, *Cupio omnia quae vis,* where the distinction expresses a compliment. —— **deō,** abl. sing. of *deus, -i,* m., 2d; in the abl. abs. construction with *volente; deo volente =* a causal clause, *as the god wished it.* —— **in,** prep. with the acc. or abl.; gov. the abl. *primis. In* here has the same force as *inter.* A. & G. 153; B. 143; G. 418, 1; H. 435, 1. —— **prīmīs,** abl. plur. m. of *prīmus, -a, -um;* governed by *in.* The plural *prīmi* (*prima*) is often used substantively, as it is here. *In primis* is sometimes written *inprimis,* or *imprimis,* i.e. the adverbial phrase becomes an actual adverb. —— **rēgīna,** gen. *rēgīnae,* f., 1st; nom. sing., subj. of *accipit.* The queen referred to is Dido. — **quiētum,** acc. sing. m. of *quiētus, -a, -um;* agrees with *animum.* See the note on *quietas,* l. 205.

LINE 304. **Accipit,** 3d pers. sing. pres. ind. acc. of *accipiō, -ere, accēpī, acceptum,* 3 (*ad* + *capiō);* agrees with the subj. *regina.* —— **in,** prep.; gov. the acc. *Teucros. In,* with the acc., marks direction of feeling or motion; see the references on *in,* l. 303 above. —— **Teucrōs,** acc. plur. of *Teucrī, -ōrum,* m., 2d; governed by *in.* —— **animum,** acc. sing. m. of *animus, -ī,* m., 2d; direct obj. of *accipit.* —— **mentem,** acc. sing. of

305	be,nígnam.	Át	pius	,Aéne,ás	„	per	,	Teucrians.	But
	kindly.	*But*	*loyal*	*Aeneas*		*through*		knightly	Aeneas,
306	nóctem	,	plúrima	,	vólvens,		Út	pondering full many things throughout the
	the night		*many things*		*rolling (in his mind),*		*When*	night, as soon as
	pri,múm	lux	,	álma	da,ta ést,	„	ex,íre	kindly light was
	first	*the light*		*gentle*	*was given,*		*to go out*	given, resolves to

mens, mentis, f., 3d; direct obj. of *accipit,* joined by *que* to *animum.* There is usually a distinction between *animus* and *mens,* the former being the seat of the emotions, the latter the seat of the intellect; but here they are almost exact synonyms.——*que,* enclitic conj. —— **benīgnam,** acc. sing. f. of *benīgnus, -a, -um;* agrees with the nearest object *mentem,* though it qualifies *animum* as well. A. & G. 187; B. 235, B, 2, *b*; G. 286, 1; H. 439, 2.

LINE 305. **At,** adversative conj., introducing a change of subject.——**pius,** nom, sing. m.; qualifies *Aeneas.*——**Aenēās,** nom. sing. m.; subj. of *constituit,* l. 309.—— **per,** prep. with the acc.; gov. *noctem,* to express duration of time. A. & G. 153; B. 181, 2; G. 416, 18; H. 433.——**noctem,** acc. sing. of *nox, noctis,* f., 3d (Greek *νύξ,* gen. *νυκτός*); governed by *per.*——**plūrima,** acc. plur. n. (used substantively) of *plūrimus, -a, -um;* direct object of *volvens. Plurimus* is the superl. of the adj. *multus;* the comparative is *plus.*——**volvēns,** nom. sing. m. of the pres. part. act. of *volvō, -ere, volvī, volūtum,* 3; agrees with and enlarges the subj. *Aeneas. Volvens,* as the next line shows, refers to past time, and = a relative clause expressing continued action in the past, *who had been pondering.*

LINE 306. **Ut,** temporal conj., followed by the ind. *data est. Ut* and *ut primum* in temporal clauses take the indicative, generally (1) in the *historic present* or the *perfect,* and (2) less commonly in the imperfect and pluperfect tenses: in the case of (1) the time is defined by the description of circumstances (as in the text, *when day dawned*); in the case of (2) the imperfect describes an existing condition of affairs at the time of the action of the principal verb, and the pluperfect is used of action already completed in the past. A. & G. 324; B. 287; G. 561, *ff.*; H. 518. *Ut* is used in a variety of ways: (1) causal, = *as;* (2) as correl. of *ita, sic,* etc., e.g. *ut . . . ita, as . . . so;* (3) in wishes, (= *utinam*); (4) in exclamations, = *how . . . !* (5) in direct and indirect questions, = *how;* (6) as *final* conjunction, = *in order that* (negative *ne*); (7) as *consecutive* conjunction, = *so that* (negative *ut non*); (8) as conjunction, expressing apprehension that something will *not* happen, after verbs of *fearing,* e.g. *timeo ut veniat = I fear he will not come.* For the syntax of *ut* and its other idiomatic uses, consult the references appended to the grammars.——**primum,** adv. of time, here used with *ut, ut primum = as soon as;* cf. *cum primum.* For a full treatment of *primum,* refer to the note on l. 174.——**lūx,** gen. *lūcis,* f., 3d; nom. sing., subj. of *data est. Lux* specially = *daylight,* e.g. *prima luce* = lit. *at first light, at daybreak; lumen = light,* of any object, e.g. *solis, lucernae,* etc.——**ālma,** nom. sing. f. of *ālmus, -a, -um* (from *alō, = I cherish*); an attribute of *lux.* This adj. is applied to the *sun,* as the nourisher of the earth, to the *earth, Ceres, light,* etc., as the cherishers of life.—— **data est,** 3d pers. sing. perf. ind. pass. of *dō, dare, dedī, datum,* 1; a composite tense, of which *data* agrees in gender and number, and *est* in person with the subj. *lux;* cf. *usa est,* l. 64.—— **ēxīre,** pres. inf. act. of *ēxeō, -īre, -iī, -itum,* irreg. (*ēx + eō*); *prolative* inf., dependent on *constituit,* l. 309. The order may be simplified: *At pius Aeneas . . . constituit exire locosque explorare novos,* | *quaerere quas oras vento accesserit, qui teneant* (*nam inculta videt*) *hominesne feraene,* | *sociisque exacta referre.* Observe that all the infinitives are *epexegetical* or

sally forth and explore the new country — to what coasts the wind has brought him, who inhabit them, men or wild beasts (for he sees a wilderness) — to	loc, ósque *and the places*	Éxplo, ráre *to explore*	nov, ós, *new,*	,,	quas , 807 *(to see) what*
	vénto *by the wind*	ac, césserit *he has arrived at*	óras, *shores,*	Quí *who*	tene, ánt, 808 *hold (them),*
	nam *for*	in, cúlta *uncultivated (regions)*	vi, dét, *he sees, —*	,,	homi, nésne *whether men*

prolative, after the main verb *constituit.* —— **locōs**, acc. plur. of *locus, -ī*, m., 2d; direct obj. of *explorare. Locus* (cf. *iocus*) is one of a class of heterogeneous nouns which have plural forms in both masculine and neuter of the 2d declension: thus (1) *loci = topics*, or *passages* in a book or discourse, but in this instance =(2) *loca*, which is generally used properly in the sense of *places.* A. & G. 78, 2, *b*; B. 60, 2; G. 67, 2: H. 141. —— **que**, enclitic conj., joining the infinitives *exire* and *explorare.*

LINE 307. **Explōrāre**, pres. inf. act. of *explōrō, -āre, -āvī, -ātum*, I; *prolative* inf., dependent on *constituit*, and joined by *que* to *exire.* —— **novōs**, acc. plur. m. of *novus, -a, -um;* agrees with *locos.* —— **quās**, acc. plur. f. of the interrog. adj. *qui, quae, quod* (declined like the rel. *qui*) ; agrees with *oras* in the indirect question *quas vento accesserit oras.* —— **ventō**, abl. sing. of *ventus, -ī*, m., 2d; abl. of the instrument, with *accesserit, quas oras vento accesserit* practically = *quas ad oras vento actus sit.* —— **accēsserit**, 3d pers. sing. perf. subj. act. of *accēdō, -ere, accēssī, accēssum*, 3 (*ad + cēdō = I go*) ; agrees with an understood pron. as subj. referring to Aeneas. *Accedere*, being a compound of the prep. *ad* and the intrans. verb *cedere*, is permitted a direct obj., viz. *quas oras.* A. & G. 228, *a* ; B. 175, 2, *a*; G. 331; H. 372. Observe that *quas . . . accesserit* is an indirect question, and an object-clause of *explorare;* that *explorare* also has a direct object *locos;* that the indirect question is explanatory of *locos.* The student should remember that an indirect question is introduced by an interrog. adj., pron., or adverb, and is contained within a principal sentence ; the verb of the contained interrog. sentence must be in the subjunctive. A. & G. 334 ; B. 300 ; G. 467; H. 528, 2, and 529, I. The perfect *accesserit* is in proper sequence after the present *explorare*, marking a time anterior to it. A. & G. 286 ; B. 267, 268; G. 509; H. 491. —— **ōrās**, acc. plur. of *ōra, -ae*, f., 1st; direct obj. of *accesserit.*

LINE 308. **quī**, nom. plur. m. of the interrog. pron. *quis, quae, quid;* subj. of *teneant* in indirect question after *explorare.* The direct question would be *qui tenent? = who hold (the land)?* Some think it preferable to make *explorare* govern *locos* only, and assign the two indirect questions *quas . . . oras* and *qui teneant* as object-clauses, of *quaerere*, l. 309. While this is quite possible and perhaps simpler, it is nevertheless common for a verb to govern an acc.-object and an object-clause as well, as *explorare* governs *locos* and the following indirect questions. Note that the two objects of Aeneas' search, viz. the study of the country and the search for the inhabitants, are so closely connected that Vergil omits a connecting conjunction (*asyndeton*). —— **teneānt**, 3d pers. plur. pres. subj. act. of *teneō, -ēre, tenuī, tentum*, 2; agrees with its subj. *qui; qui teneant* is an indirect question, the present subjunctive being due to the fact that the time of the action of the introductory inf. *explorare* (or *quaerere*) and of the subordinate verb *teneant* is the same. —— **nam**, causal conj., introducing the explanatory parenthesis *nam inculta videt.* —— **inculta**, acc. plur. n. of *incultus, -a, -um* (compounded of *in, = not*, and *cultus*, the perf. part. pass. of *colō, -ere, coluī, cultum*, 3), used substantively (understand *loca*) as direct obj. of *videt.* —— **videt**, 3d pers. sing. pres. ind. act. of *videō, -ēre, vīdī, vīsum*, 2 ; a pron.-subject referring to Aeneas is understood. Note that the two chief *caesurae* fall after *teneant* and *videt*, and that the final syllable of *videt*

809 fe,ráe̅ne, Quǽrere , cónstitu,ít, ,, soci,ísque
or wild beasts, to search *he resolves,* *and to his comrades*

810 ex,ácta re,férre. Clássem in ,
the things ascertained *to relate.* *The fleet* *in*

cónvex,ó ,, nemo,rúm sub , rúpe ca,váta
a recess *of groves* *beneath a cliff* *hollowed*

search this out, and report to his comrades what he has done. The fleet he hides in a wood-bound recess beneath a hollowed cliff,

is long, in spite of the fact that a word beginning with *h* follows, viz. *homines :* this lengthening is called *diastole,* and owes itself to the *ictus* on the last syllable accompanied by the pause of the *caesura* after it. Vergil frequently resorts to this artifice, cf. l. 651, *Pergama cum* PETERĒT *inconcessosque hymenaeos ;* so Horace affords the well-known example, PERRUPĪT *Acheronta Herculeus labor.* A. & G. 359, *f ;* B. 367, 2; G. 721; H. 608, V. Vergil lengthens *que* by *diastole* on no less than sixteen occasions. —— **homine̅s,** nom. plur. of *homo̅, hominis,* m., 3d ; subj. of *teneant* understood from *qui teneant. Homines* is used, not *vi̅ri,* because *homo = a man,* as distinguished from gods on the one hand and from animals (*ferae*) on the other. —— **ne,** enclitic interrog. particle, used in repetition *ne . . . ne,* the first *ne* introducing the indirect question and the second introducing the alternative. *Ne . . . ne* is poetical, the usual prose particles being *utrum . . . an,* or if the second member be a simple negation, *utrum . . . necne* (*or not*). *Utrum . . . an,* and *utrum . . . annon* are used in direct alternative questions. A. & G. 211, *d,* and 334, *b ;* B. 300, 2 and 4 ; G. 460, 2, and 265 ; H. 529, 3. —— **fera̅e,** nom. plur. of *fera, -ae,* f., 1st (properly the f. of the adj. *ferus, -a, -um*) ; alternative subj. of *teneant* understood ; see *homines.* —— **ne,** enclitic interrog. particle, appearing with the second member of the alternatives.

LINE 309. **Quaerere,** pres. inf. act. of *quae̅ro̅, -ere, quae̅si̅vi̅, quae̅si̅tum,* 3; prolative inf. dependent on *constituit. Quaerere* may be regarded as introducing the indirect questions from *quas,* l. 307, to *feraene,* l. 308; but very likely it is only a rather superfluous repetition intended to make this involved sentence more clear. —— **constituit,** 3d pers. sing. pres. ind. act. of *constituo̅, -ere, -ui̅, -u̅tum,* 3 (*con*[*cum*] + *statuo̅*); historic present, agreeing with the subj. *Aeneas,* l. 305. —— **sociis,** dat. plur. of *socius, -i̅,* m., 2d; dat. of the indirect obj. after *referre.* —— **que,** enclitic conj., connecting *referre* with *quaerere,* and so with the preceding infinitives. —— **exacta,** acc. plur. n. of *exactus, -a, -um,* perf. part. pass. of *exigo̅, -ere, exe̅gi̅, exactum,* 3 (*ex* + *ago̅*) ; used substantively as the direct obj. of *referre. Exacta = the things accomplished,* i.e. *what he had discovered ;* it does not mean *accurate tidings,* as some translate it from the occasional meaning of *I weigh mentally,* or *I ponder,* which *exigo* may have. The best commentators render *the end,* i.e. the fruit of Aeneas' observations. —— **referre,** pres. inf. act. of *refero̅, referre, retuli̅* (*rettuli̅*), *rela̅tum,* irreg. (*re* + *fero̅*) ; prolative inf., dependent on *constituit.* For the compounds and conjugation of *fero,* consult A. & G. 139, and 170, *a ;* B. 129; G. 171; H. 292. *Refero =* lit. *I carry back,* from which are derived the meanings of (1) *I carry back news,* i.e. *I report,* as here; (2) *I answer, speak in reply,* e.g. the frequent expression *talia voce refert.*

LINE 310. **Classem,** acc. sing. of *classis, -is,* f., 3d; direct obj. of *occulit.* —— **in,** prep. with the acc. or abl.; gov. the abl. *convexo.* —— **convēxo̅,** abl. sing. n. of *convēxus, -a, -um,* used substantively; governed by *in.* Vergil frequently forms neuter nouns from adjectives, or uses the neuter of adjectives substantively on occasions; cf. *in melius referet,* l. 281; *inculta,* l. 308; *extrema,* l. 219, etc.; very commonly he uses the neuters with a preposition, e.g. *ab alto.* A. & G. 188, 189; B. 236-238; G. 204, NOTES 1-4; H. 441. —— **nemorum,** gen. plur. of *nemus, nemoris,* n., 3d; partitive gen. after *convexo.*

enclosed around by	Árbori͵bús	clau͵sám	cir͵cum	„	átque 311
trees of bristling	*by trees*	*shut in*	*around*		*and*
shade. Himself, com-	hor͵réntibus	úmbris	Ócculit:	ípse	u͵nó „ 312
panioned by Achates	*dreadful*	*by shadows*	*he hides:*	*he himself*	*alone*

The partitive gen. is common after neuter adjectives or pronouns used as nouns; e.g. *id temporis, plana urbis*, etc.; it may even follow adverbs, e.g. *ubi terrarum*, = *where in the world.* A. & G. 216, 3; B. 201, 2; G. 369; H. 397, 3. Compare Aen. IV, 451, *coeli convexa.* —— **sub**, prep. with the acc. or abl.; gov. the abl. *rupe*, denoting a state of rest. —— **rūpe**, abl. sing. of *rūpēs, -is*, f., 3d; governed by *sub.* —— **cavātā**, abl. sing. f. of *cavātus, -a, -um*, perf. part. pass. of *cavō, -āre -āvī, -ātum*, 1 (from *cavus*, = *hollow*, hence, *I hollow out*)*;* qualifies *rupe* attributively.

LINE 311. **Arboribus**, abl. plur. of *arbor, -is*, f., 3d; instrumental abl.͵ with *clausam.* —— **clausam**, acc. sing. f. of *clausus, -a, -um*, perf. part. pass. of *claudō, -ere, clausī, clausum*, 3; predicate part., agreeing with *classem.* *Classem clausam occulit* = *classem claudit et occulit, he hides and conceals the fleet:* A. & G. 292, REM.; B. 337, 2; G. 437; H. 549, 5. But perhaps there is a notion of purpose in *clausam*, = *ut claudetur;* in this case *clausam* is *proleptic,* and the expression here is very similar to the stock instance in Vergil, *scuta latentia condunt.* A. & G. 385; B. 374, 5; G. 325, PREDICATIVE ATTRIBU-TION; H. 636, IV, 3. —— **circum**, adv., extending *clausam.* Many Latin words are used without change of form as adverbs or prepositions, between which there was no original difference, though such arose gradually in use. *Circum* is the adverbial acc. n. of *circus,* and = *in a ring,*͵hence, *around.* —— **atque**, cop. conj. —— **hōrrentibus**, abl. plur. of *hōrrens, -entis*, pres. part. act. of *hōrreō, -ēre*, no͵ perf., no supine, 2; qualifies *umbris.* For the meaning of *horrentibus*, refer to the note on *horrenti . . . umbra*, l. 165. —— **ūmbrīs**, abl. plur. of *ūmbra, -ae*, f., 1st; abl. of the instrument, joined by *atque* to *arboribus. Arboribus atque umbris* is a case of *hendiadys*, = *arborum umbris.* A. & G. 385; B. 374, 4; G. 698; H. 636, III, 2.

LINE 312. **Occulit**, 3d pers. sing. pres. ind. act. of *occulō, -ere, occuluī, occultum*, 3 (a compound of *ob* and a root found in *celo, I hide*)*;* the subj. implied by the termina-tion is *Aeneas.* —— **ípse**, nom. sing. m. of the intensive pron. *īpse, īpsa, īpsum;* intensi-fies and agrees with a pron.-subj. of *graditur* referring to Aeneas. A. & G. 102, *e*; B. 88; G. 103, 3; H. 186, and 452. —— **ūnō**, abl. sing. m. of *ūnus, -a, -um* (gen. *ūnīus,* dat. *ūnī*)*;* agrees with *Achate.* —— **graditur**, 3d pers. sing. pres. ind. of the dep. verb of *gradior, gradī, gressus sum* (chiefly used in compounds, e.g. *egredior, progredior, aggredior*, etc.); agrees with *ipse.* —— **comitātus**, nom. sing. m. of the perf. part. of the dep. verb *comitor, -ārī, -ātus sum*, 1 (from *comes*)*;* predicate part., agreeing with and enlarging the subj. of *graditur.* There is an active verb *comitō, -āre, -āvī, -ātum*, 1, and some refer *comitatus* in this passage to it, because *comitatus* is passive in meaning = *accompanied.* Probably, however, *comitatus* is the part. of the deponent *comitor*, for Vergil uses *comitor* rather than *comito*, and the perf. participles not seldom have ͏a pas-sive͏ signification. A. & G. 135, *b* and *f*; B. 112, *b*; G. 167, NOTE 2; H. 231, 2. Fur-ther observe that the perf. part. of deponents, when used passively, is sometimes = to a pres. part. pass. (wanting in Latin, but general in Greek verbs); so *comitatus* = not *having been accompanied*, but *being accompanied.* —— **Achāte**, abl. sing. of *Achātēs,* gen. *Achāt -ae* or *-ī*, m. (see *Achātae*, l. 120); apparently a poetical abl. of the agent with the prep. *a* or *ab* omitted. It is impossible to regard the abl. as an instrumental one, though some do: perhaps it may be described as a forced use of the abl. of accom-paniment. There are many instances in poets of this abl. after the verb *comitor;* cf. Aen. IX,͵ 48, *Viginti lectis equitum comitatus.* Commentators explain in various ways:

818 gradi,túr comi,tátus A,cháte, Bína   ma,nú
   advances   *accompanied*   *by Achates, two (each) in his hand*

814 la,tó ,, cris,páns has,tília ,   férro.   Cuí
   broad   *brandishing*   *spears*   *with iron (tip).* *To whom*

   ma,tér medi,á ,, se,sé tulit , óbvia ,   sílva,
   his mother *middle*   *herself betook in the way in the wood,*

815 Vírginis   ,   ós habi,túmque ge,réns ,, et ,
   of a Virgin   *the face*   *and the dress*   *bearing*   *and*

alone, he proceeds on, grasping in his hand two spears broadly tipped with steel. And in mid-forest his mother appeared before him, wearing a maiden's face and dress, and

---

certain examples from Horace are capable of being considered ablative absolute con-structions, but here that is impossible; in another instance, a similar abl. *viris* is explained as = *turba virorum*, hence instrumental. As the dative of the agent is com-mon after perf. participles passive (or any passive form in poetry), so the abl. seems in some cases to be used without a prep. in poetry. For the ablative of the agent, consult A. & G. 246; B. 216, and 222, 1; G. 401, and REM. 1; H. 415, I, 1.

LINE 313. **Bīna**, acc. plur. n. of the distributive numeral *bīni, -ae, -a* (sing. *bīnus* very rare); agrees with *hastilia*. *Bina* is poetical for *duo;* cf. l. 381, *bis* DENIS (= *decem*) *navibus*. Distributives are used properly in two ways: (1) as = to *2, 3, 4* (and so on) *each;* e.g. *equitibus binos equos dedit* (= *two horses each*)*;* (2) qualifying nouns of plural form and single meaning, when a plural meaning is intended; e.g. *bina castra* = *two camps* (not *duo castra*, which is not Latin, except in the sense of *forts* and as the plural of *castrum* = *a fort*). —— **manū**, abl. sing. of *manus, -ūs*, f., 4th; abl. of the instrument. —— **lātō**, abl. sing. n. of *lātus, -a, -um;* qualifies *ferro.* —— **crispāns**, nom. sing. m. of the pres. part. act. of *crispō, -āre, -āvī, -ātum*, 1; agrees with *ipse*. —— **hastīlia**, acc. plur. of *hastīle, hastīlis*, n., 3d (cf. *hasta*); direct obj. of *crispans*. —— **ferro**, abl. sing. of *ferrum, -i*, n., 2d; abl. of quality, describing *hastilia*. A. & G. 251; B. 224; G. 400; H. 419, II. The head of the spears was made of iron.

LINE 314. **Cui**, dat. sing. m. of the rel. pron. *qui, quae, quod;* agrees with the ante-cedent *ipse*, i.e. Aeneas, and is governed by *obvia*. The relative *cui* here = *et ei*, connect-ing a new sentence with the one preceding. A. & G. 180, *f;* B. 251, 6; G. 610; H. 453. —— **māter**, gen. *mātris*, f., 3d; nom. sing., subj. of *tulit*. *Mater* = Venus; this meeting between Aeneas and the goddess disguised recalls passages of the same kind in the Odyssey. —— **mediā**, abl. sing. f. of *medius, -a, -um;* agrees with *silva*, and has a partitive force; see note on *alta*, l. 26. —— **sēsē**, acc. sing. of the reflexive pron. *sē* or *sēsē;* referring as the direct obj. of *tulit* to the subj. *mater*. —— **tulit**, 3d pers. sing. perf. ind. act. of *ferō, ferre, tulī, lātum*, irreg.; agrees with the subj. *mater*. *Se ferre, se agere*, etc., = *ire*, and so with other like phrases; e.g. *se recipere, = regredi*. —— **obvia**, nom. sing. f. of *obvius, -a, -um;* agrees with the subj. *mater*. We should have expected *sese obviam tulit*, but Vergil is fond of variations; cf. Aen. II, 388, *quaque (fortuna) ostendit se* DEXTRA, *sequamur*. The dative follows the adjective *obvius*, and also its adverb *obviam;* it may also follow many compounds of *ob*, e.g. *obesse, obstare*, etc. A. & G. 228, *b;* B. 187, III; G. 347, and REM. 2; H. 386. —— **silvā**, abl. sing. of *silva, -ae*, f., 1st; abl. of 'place where.'

LINE 315. **Virginis**, gen. sing. of *virgō*, f., 3d; poss. gen., limiting *os*. —— **ōs**, acc. sing. of *os, ōris*, n., 3d; direct obj. of *gerens*. —— **habitum**, acc. sing. m. of *habitus, -ūs*, m., 4th (from *habeo*, hence of the way in which one holds oneself, *condition, appearance, attire*, etc.); joined by *que* to *os*. —— **que**, enclitic conj. —— **gerēns**, nom. sing. f. of the pres. part. act. of *gerō, -ere, gessī, gestum*, 3; agrees with and enlarges the subj.

the arms of a Spartan	vírginis, árma Spárta,næ, vel, quális e,quós ,, 316
maiden or one such	*of a virgin the arms Spartan, or (such) as horses*
as Harpalyce of	
Thrace who wearies	Thre,íssa fa,tígat Hárpaly,cé, volu,crémque 317
her steeds and out-	*Thrasian tires Harpalyce, and swift*

mater. The verb *gero* may be used not only of attire, as *habitum*, but also of features, as *os; se gerere = se praestare, to show oneself.* —— **et,** cop. conj. —— **virginis,** gen. sing. (see above); poss. gen., limiting *arma.* Some say that *virginis* here is an unnecessary repetition, but others affirm that it is necessary in order to restrict the application of *arma* to the Spartan maiden. —— **arma,** *-ōrum,* n., 2d; direct obj. of *gerens,* joined by *et* to *habitum.* The type of beauty that satisfied the old Greek standard in male or female was essentially that which could only be attained by athletics, viz. a lithe and graceful symmetry: Spartan women went through the same kind of physical drill and exercises as the men, and so Venus condescended to pose as a Spartan maid.

LINE 316. **Spartānae,** gen. sing. f. of *Spartānus, -a, -um* (*Sparta, -ae,* f., 1st); agrees with *virginis.* Sparta, though an unwalled town, was the capital of Laconia in the Peloponnesus; the Spartans called themselves not *Spartani,* but *Lacedaemonii,* and their town *Lacedaemon.* —— **vel** (probably the imperative of *volŏ,* with a weaker form *ve*), disjunctive conj., offering a choice of comparison between a Spartan and a Thracian maiden. For distinctions between *vel, aut,* and *sive,* consult the note and references under *ve,* l. 9. —— **quālis,** relative adj., corresponding to an understood demonstrative *tālis* (gen. sing. f., agreeing with *virginis*). *Qualis* is nom. sing. f. of *qualis, -e,* agreeing with the subj. in the relative clause, *Harpalyce.* We should expect something like *vel* (*talis virginis*) *qualis* (*est*) *Harpalyce* (*quae*) *fatigat,* etc., but comparisons introduced by *qualis* are often abbreviated as in the text. —— **equōs,** acc. plur. of *equus, -ī,* m., 2d; direct obj. of *fatigat.* —— **Threïssa** (sometimes *Thrēssa*), a nom sing. f. borrowed from the Greek adj. Θρῇιξ which has the f. Θρηίσσα (the Attic Greek being Θρᾷξ, Θρᾷσσα); agrees with *Harpalyce.* *Threïssa* is attracted into the rel. clause, = *vel Threissae qualis,* etc.; see note on *tela,* l. 188. As *Threïssa* is a f. adj., so is *Thrax* a m. adj.: the commonest adjectives are *Thracius, -a, -um,* and *Threïcius, -a, -um,* = *Thracian,* appertaining to the country (1) *Thracia, -ae,* f., 1st, (2) *Thrace, -ēs,* f., 1st (Θράκη), (3) *Thraca, -ae,* f., 1st, (4) *Threce, -ēs,* f., 1st (Θρήκη). Thrace was the name of a large country in Europe, lying between Macedonia on the west, the Aegean sea on the south, and on the east the Hellespont and Black sea. —— **fatīgat,** 3d pers. sing. pres. ind. act. of *fatīgō, -āre, -āvī, -ātum,* 1; agrees with the subj. *Harpalyce.*

LINE 317. **Harpalycē,** gen. *Harpalycēs,* f., 1st decl. Greek noun; nom. sing., subj. of *fatigat* in the relative clause. For declension, consult A. & G. 37; B. 22; each like Epitome; G. 65, like Penelope; H. 50, like Epitome. Harpalyce was the daughter of a Thracian king named Harpalycus, who repelled an invasion led by Neoptolemus, the son of Achilles, and was a famous huntress. —— **volucrem,** acc. sing. m. of *volucer, volucris, volucre* (the f. *volucris* is sometimes used as a f. noun, = *a bird,* with *avis* supplied); an attribute of *Hebrum.* Most ancient authors describe the *Hebrus* as *lenis* = *sluggish;* but Thrace was to Vergil a wild and unknown country, and in the poetic spirit he invests its river with a quality corresponding to the country. —— **que,** enclitic conj., joining the clauses *fatigat equos* and *praevertitur Hebrum.* —— **fugā,** abl. sing. of *fuga, -ae,* f., 1st; abl. of manner, with *cum* omitted (as often in poetry). A. & G. 248, near the end; B. 220; G. 399, NOTE 2; H. 419, III. —— **praevertitur,** 3d pers. sing. pres. ind. of the dep. verb *praevertor, -ī, praeversus sum,* 3 (with an active collateral form *praeverto, -ere, praeverti, praeversum,* 3); joined by *que* to *fatigat.* *Praevertor* is properly an intransitive,

818 fu,gá „ prae,vértitur , Hébrum.   Námque | strips   the   swift
   in flight   *surpasses*   *Hebrus.*   *for* | Hebrus in her flight.

hume,rís   de ,   móre   habi,lém „ | For in manner due
   from her shoulders   *according*   *to custom*   *light* | she had slung from
   | her   shoulder   the

819 sus,pénderat , árcum   Véna,tríx,   dede,rátque | handy bow, huntress-
   she had suspended   *a bow*   *huntress-fashion,*   *and had given* | fashion,   and   had
   | loosed her hair to the

820 co,mám „ dif,fúndere   véntis,   Núda   ge,nú, „ | winds to scatter, with
   her hair   *to scatter*   *to the winds,*   *bare as to the knee,* | knee bare and her

no,dóque   si,nús   col,lécta | raiment's   flowing
   and in a knot   *as to the folds (of her dress)*   *gathered* | folds gathered in a

---

but in poetry some such verbs (especially those denoting *avoiding* or *escape*, e.g. Aen. V,
438, *tela* . . . *exit*, = *he avoids blows*) acquire a transitive force; cf. l. 580, *erumpere
nubem.*——**Hēbrum,** acc. sing. of *Hēbrus*, -*ī*, m., 2d; direct obj. of *praevertitur.* The
Hebrus, now the Marissa, is a river of Thrace, rising in Mount Haemus and flowing into
the Aegean. There is a different reading *Eurum*, which some few adopt because *volucrem*
seems a more suitable attribute of it than of *Hebrum.* But the MSS. are all against
Eurum, and commentators quote Silius, *cursuque fatigant Hebrum innupta manus.*
   LINE 318.   **Namque** (*nam* + *que*), emphatic causal conj. (see l. 65).——**humerīs,**
dat. plur. of *humerus*, -*ī*, m., 2d; dat. of the indirect obj. after *suspenderat*, a compound
of *sub.*   A. & G. 228; B. 187, III; G. 347; H. 386.   But possibly it is a free locative
ablative.——**dē,** prep. with the abl.; gov. *more* (see note on *de*, l. 277).——**mōre,** abl.
sing. of *mōs, mōris*, m., 3d (the plur. *mores* = *character*); governed by *de.*——**habilem,**
acc. sing. m. of *habilis*, -*e*, adj., 3d (from *habeo*, hence *easily held, handy*) ; qualifies
arcum.——**suspenderat,** 3d pers. sing. pluperf. ind. act. of *suspendō, -ere, suspendī,
suspensum*, 3 (*sub* + *pendō*) ; agrees with *Venus* understood as the subject——**arcum,**
acc. sing. of *arcus*, -*ūs*, m., 4th; direct obj. of *suspenderat.*   See note on *arcum*, l. 187.
   LINE 319.   **Vēnātrīx,** gen. *vēnātrīcis*, f., 3d (from *vēnāri*, = *to hunt*) ; nom. sing.,
in apposition with the unexpressed subj. of *suspenderat.*——**dederat,** 3d pers. sing. plu-
perf. ind. act. of *dō, dare, dedī, datum*, 1; joined by *que* to *suspenderat.*——**que,**
enclitic conj.——**comam,** acc. sing. of *coma*, -*ae*, f., 1st (κόμη); direct obj. of *dederat.*
——**diffundere,** pres. inf. act. of *diffundō, -ere, diffūdī, diffūsum*, 3 (*dis* + *fundō*) ; a
poetic inf., of the *epexegetic* or *prolative* kind; dependent on and explaining *dederat.*
This infinitive expresses *purpose*, and is borrowed from the Greek; it = in prose *dederat
comam ventis diffundendam* (gerundive) or *ut diffunderetur.*   It is common in Vergil
after *do, dono*, etc., and is clearly imitated from the Homeric δῶκε δ' ἄγειν: in Horace
there are numerous examples, following various verbs, e.g. Odes, I, 26, 1, *tristitiam* . . .
tradam protervis in mare Creticum portare ventis (= *portandam, quam portarent*, or
ut portarent).   A. & G. 331, *g*; B. 326, NOTE; G. 421, NOTE 1, *b*; H. 535, IV.——
ventīs, dat. plur. of *ventus*, -*ī*, m., 2d; dat. of the recipient (indirect object), after
dederat.
   LINE 320.   **Nūda,** nom. sing. f. of *nūdus*, -*a*, -*um ;* agrees with the subj. (*Venus* or
a pron.) of *dederat.*——**genū,** acc. sing. of *genu*, -*ūs*, n., 4th (γόνυ); acc. of respect or
specification, called also *synecdochical* or Greek acc., explaining *nuda.*   See note on
sinus below.——**nōdō,** abl. sing. of *nōdus*, -*ī*, m., 2d; abl. of manner, with *collecta.*
——**que,** enclitic conj.——**sinūs,** acc. plur. of *sinus*, -*ūs*, m., 4th (here used of the
folds of her flowing costume); in the grammars this acc. is treated in the same way as

knot. And speaking	flu͵éntes.	Ác	prior,	,	" Heús,"	in͵quít, 321
first " Ho, men ! "	*flowing.*	*And*	*first*		*"Ho!"*	*says she,*
says she, "show me,	" iuve͵nés,	,,	mon͵stráte me͵árum	Vídis͵tís	si , 322	
if haply ye have seen	*" young men,*		*point (her) out*	*my*	*you have seen*	*if*

nuda genu. A. & G. 240, *c*; B. 180; G. 338; H. 378. The best scholars make distinc-
tions with regard to this so-called accusative of respect. It now appears certain that
many participles retain some of an old *middle* use (like the middle voice of Greek verbs),
and the accusative used with these is really the accusative of the direct object. So *collecta
sinus* is to be taken here = *having gathered for herself the folds ;* similarly middle is *tun-
sae pectora,* l. 481. In some cases, however, it is obviously impossible to call the parti-
ciple a middle one, or anything but passive, e.g. *manus post terga revinctum,* for no one
could *fasten his own hands* behind his back (one sense of the middle), and no one
would *get his hands bound* for him (the other meaning of the middle voice). —— col-
lēcta, nom. sing. f. of *collectus, -a, -um,* perf. part. pass. (here with middle governing
power) of *colligō, -ere, collēgī, collectum,* 3 (*con* [*cum*] + *legō*) ; joined by *que* to *nuda.*
—— fluentēs, acc. plur. m. of *fluens, -entis,* pres. part. act. of *fluo, -ere, fluxī, fluctum,*
3; agrees with *sinus.*

    LINE 321. Ác, cop. conj., joining its own sentence to the one before. —— prior,
nom. sing. f. of *prior, prius,* comparative adj.; agrees with *Venus* or a pron. subj. of
inquit; prior is an adverbial attribute modifying *inquit,* = *is the first to speak,* cf. l. 1,
primus . . . venit. Prior is used here, not *prima,* because the persons meeting form
two parties, Venus on the one hand, the Trojans on the other, and Venus anticipates
them in speaking. *Prior* has no positive, but is formed from a preposition, *pro* or *prae ;
primus* is the superlative. —— Heus, interjection, to attract attention before addressing
any one. —— inquit, 3d pers. sing. pres. ind. act. of the irreg. and defective verb
inquam ; agrees with the subj. *Venus* or a pron. unexpressed. *Inquam* has a complete
present ind., *inqu-am, -is, -it, -imus, -itis* (rare), *-iunt ;* in the imperf. the only survival
is *inquiebat;* fut. *inquies, inquiet;* perf. *inquisti, inquit;* imperative, *inque, inquito.*
In prose, and usually in poetry, this verb stands within direct quotations, like the Eng-
lish *quoth he.* A. & G. 144, *b*; B. 134; G. 175, 2; H. 297, II, 2. —— iuvenēs, voc.
plur. of *iuvenis, -is,* adj. commonly substantival; the case of address. *Iuvenis* is ter.n
applied to any man capable of military service; see note on *puer,* l. 267. Comparison :
iuvenis ; iunior ; natu minimus, or occasionally *minimus* alone with *natu* understood.
—— monstrāte, 2d pers. plur. imperative mood act. of *monstrō, -āre, -āvī, -ātum,* 1;
the implied subj. is *vos* (i.e. *iuvenes*) ; supply a demonstr. pron. *eam* (corresponding to
quam sororum) as direct obj. of *monstrate.* For synonyms, refer to *ostendunt,* l. 206.
—— meārum, gen. plur. f. of *meus, -a, -um,* poss. adj. of the 1st personal pron.; agrees
with *sororum.* Observe the involved order : take the words thus : *monstrate, si quam
mearum sororum hic errantem forte vidistis,* etc.

    LINE 322. Vīdistis, 2d pers. plur. perf. ind. act. of *video, -ere, vīdī, vīsum,* 2; the
implied subj. is *vos,* referring to the Trojans. *Monstrate si vidistis* is not an indirect
question, of course, for the subjunct. *videritis* would be necessary; it is a simple condi-
tion of fact, = *if you have seen, point out* (where she is or has gone). If the verb in the
apodosis is a pure indicative or imperative, the verb in the *protasis* (or *if* clause) is indic-
ative. A. & G. 306, *a*; B. 302, 4 ; G. 595; H. 508, 4. In such *logical* conditions, the
elements in question are simply stated, and nothing is implied as to reality : the *apodosis*
may be (1) indicative, e.g. *si hoc credis, erras ;* (2) imperative, *si hoc credis, recte fac ;*
(3) some form of the *independent* subjunctive (*hortatory, deliberative,* etc.), e.g. *si hoc
credis, faciamus.* —— sī, conditional conj., followed by the ind. *vidistis.* For *si* intro-

qu*am*	híc	„	er, rántem	,	fórte	so, rórum,	any of my sisters wan-

quam   híc „ er, rántem , fórte   so, rórum, | any of my sisters wan-
any   *here*   *wandering*   *by chance*   *of my sisters,* | dering here girt with
328 Súccinc, tám   phare, tra „ ét   macu, lósae , | a quiver, and a hide of
girdled   *with a quiver*   *and*   *spotted* | spotted lynx, or press-
324 tégmine , lýncis,   Aút   spu, mántis | ing with a shout on
with the hide   *of a lynx,*   *or*   *foaming* | the track of a foaming

---

ducing imaginary future conditions, or unfilled past conditions, consult A. & G. 304–309; B. 301–304; G. 589, *ff;* H. 507–512. —— **quam,** acc. sing. f. of the indefinite pron. *quis, quis (quae), quid;* direct obj. of *vidistis.* *Quis,* the indefinite, is rarely used except with *si* or *ne* (= *if* or *lest any one*). —— **hīc,** adv. of place, with *errantem.* —— **errantem,** acc. sing. f. of *errans, -antis,* pres. part. act. of *errō, -āre, -āvī, -ātum,* 1; agrees with *quam.* For the participle instead of the infinitive, see the note on *prementem,* l. 324. —— **forte,** adverbial abl. sing. of *fors,* f., 3d; in combination with *si,* and often likewise with *ne,* and *nisi;* see *forte,* l. 151. —— **sorōrum,** gen. plur. of *soror, sororis,* f., 3d; partitive gen., standing for the whole of which a part (*quam*) is taken. A. & G. 216; B. 201; G. 371; H. 397, 3.

LINE 323. **Succīnctam,** acc. sing. f. of *succinctus, -a, -um,* perf. part. pass. of *succingō, -ere, succinxī, succinctum,* 3; agrees with *quam (sororum). Succinctus = girt up,* i.e. with the long robe taken up in folds and fastened by a girdle so as to allow free movement; the *toga* used to be girt up in like fashion when a Roman desired to exert himself out of the ordinary way. Strictly, *succinctam* only applies to *tegmine,* but by a stretch of meaning it covers *pharetra,* as knives, quivers, etc., were often carried in or suspended from the girdle. The figure whereby a verb is used with two nouns, and has a slightly different sense with each, is called *zeugma;* see *serenat,* l. 255. —— **pharetrā,** abl. sing. of *pharetra, -ae,* f., 1st (φαρέτρα); abl. of the instrument. Mr. Page compares *cultro succinctus* (in Livy) = *having a knife fastened in his girdle,* lit. *girt with a knife.* Notice that the *penultimate* syllable *re* is short; it is very often long, e.g. Aen. V, 501, *depromunt tela pharetris.* The rule is that when a naturally short vowel precedes a mute consonant followed by *l* or *r* the vowel is called *common,* i.e. may be either long or short. A. & G. 347, *d;* B. 5, B, 3; G. 13; H. 578. —— **et,** cop. conj., joining *pharetra* and *tegmine;* if we adopted Madvig's reading *maculoso* (for *maculosae*), *et* would be connecting *succinctam* and *prementem;* see *maculosae* below. —— **maculōsae,** gen. sing. of *maculōsus, -a, -um* (from *macula, = a spot);* agrees with *lyncis. Maculosae* is the reading of the MSS., but Madvig, ignoring the canon of classical criticism forbidding unnecessary and especially unauthorized emendation, reads *maculoso. Maculoso* then agrees with *tegmine,* and *maculoso tegmine* is an abl. of description, = *a lynx of spotted hide;* and *lyncis* becomes an objective gen., dependent, like *apri,* on *cursum;* the sentence would thus read *succinctam pharetra et prementem clamore cursum* (direct obj.) *lyncis aut apri.* This reading, admittedly ingenious, is open to the serious objection made above, and also to another, viz. that *tegmine* properly = *the hide* of a dead animal, not of a living one. —— **tēgmine,** abl. sing. of *tēgmen, -inis,* n., 3d (*tegō,* = *I cover);* abl. of the instrument, joined by *et* to *pharetra.* Madvig seems to have read *maculoso* owing to the slight difficulty of taking *succinctam* with both *pharetra* and *tegmine;* but it has been shown that *succinctus* may be used with either, and critical rules lay down that a difficult but well-supported reading is preferable to a simple but unauthoritative change. —— **lyncis,** gen. sing. of *lȳnx,* f., 3d (λύγξ); poss. gen., limiting *tegmine.*

LINE 324. **Aut,** disjunctive conj. There is no very obvious antithesis, however, between *succinctam* and *prementem,* whereas in Madvig's text there is a very natural

boar." Thus Venus;	a, prí	cur, súm	„	cla, móre	pre, méntem."	
and in answer Venus'	*of a boar*	*the course*		*with a shout*	*pressing on.*"	
son thus began: —	Síc Venus;	, ét	Vene, rís	con, trá	„ síc	, 325
	Thus Venus;	*and*	*of Venus*	*in return*	*thus*	
"No sister of thine	fílius	, órsus:	"Núlla	tu, árum	au, díta	326
have I seen or heard,	*the son*	*began:*	"*None*	*thy*	*has been heard*	

---

one, between *lyncis* and *apri*. But *aut* is used like the English *or*, which frequently means little more than *and*. See *aut*, l. 183. —— **spūmantis**, gen. sing. m. of *spūmans*, *-antis*, pres. part. act. of *spūmō, -āre, -āvī, -ātum;* 1; agrees with *apri*. —— **aprī**, gen. sing. of *aper*, m., 2d; poss. gen., after *cursum*. —— **cursum**, acc. sing. of *cursus, -ūs*, m., 4th (from *curro*) *;* direct obj. of *prementem*. —— **clāmōre**, abl. sing. of *clāmor*, *-ōris*, m., 3d; abl. of manner. —— **prementem**, acc. sing. f. of *premens, -entis*, pres. part. act. of *premo, -ere, pressī, pressum*, 3; agrees with *quam sororum = sororem*, and is joined by *aut* to *succinctam*. The participle (*prementem*) is more vivid than the usual inf. (*premere*) after verbs of perception; it is regularly employed in Greek. A. & G. 292, *e*; B. 336, 2; G. 536; H. 535, I, 4.

LINE 325. **Sīc**, adv. of manner, modifying *loquitur* or *ait* understood. *Sic* is used sometimes as correlative of *ut, ut . . . ita* or *sic, = as . . . so*. —— **Venus**, gen. *Veneris*, f., 3d; nom. sing., subj. of *ait* or *loquitur* understood. —— **et**, cop. conj., joining the sentence to *sic Venus (ait)* preceding. —— **Veneris**, gen. sing.; poss. gen., limiting *filius*. *Veneris filius = Aeneas*, the close repetition of the name of the goddess adding dramatic effect to the episode described. —— **contrā**, adv., = *in reply*, with *orsus (est)*. —— **sīc**, adv. of manner. —— **fīlius**, gen. *fīlī* (voc. sing. *fīlī*), m., 2d; nom. sing., subj. of *orsus (est)*. —— **ōrsus**, nom. sing. m. of the perf. part. of the dep. verb *ōrdior, ōrdīrī, ōrsus sum*, 4; agrees with *fīlius*, and is the 3d pers. sing. perf. ind. with *est* understood. *Ordiri* by derivation has reference to *weaving;* cf. its compound *redordiri*, which = *fila dissolvere*, hence in the sense *to begin* it implies a process of some length; furthermore it is distinguished from other synonyms as implying *beginning* from the earliest point, whereas *coepisse* may be used of commencement from any point. Synonyms: *coepisse = to begin*, as opposed to ceasing; *inchoare = to begin*, as opposed to fully completing something.

LINE 326. **Nūlla**, nom. sing. f. of *nūllus, -a, -um* (gen. *nūllīus*, dat. *nūllī*) *;* subj. of *audita (est)*, agreeing with *soror* understood. —— **tuārum**, gen. plur. f. of *tuus, -a, -um*, poss. adj. of the 2d personal pron. sing.; agreeing with *sororum*. —— **audīta**, nom. sing. f. of *audītus, -a, -um*, perf. part. pass. of *audiō, -īre, -īvī* or *-iī, -ītum*, 4; agreeing with *nulla*, and forming with *est* understood the 3d pers. sing. perf. ind. pass. *Audita* = lit. *heard*, answering the reference to shouting in *clamore*. —— **mihī**, dat. sing. of *ego ;* dat. of the agent. This use of the dative is poetical, and is especially common after the perfect passive tense and perfect participles passive. The dat. is explained as originally being a dat. of the indirect object after *sum* (used to form the perfect passive); e.g. *nulla audita (est) mihi* = lit. *no one is to me heard;* its use with participles alone and with other tenses is accordingly an extension. As it is most common in Augustan poets who favored Greek models, many say it is an imitation of the Greek dat. of the agent after the perf. ind. or participle passive, e.g. τὰ μοι πεπραγμένα; cf. l. 440, *neque cernitur ulli*. A. & G. 232; B. 189; G. 354; H. 388, I. —— **neque**, conj. —— **visa** (*est* supplied), 3d pers. sing. perf. ind. pass. of *video, -ēre, vīdī, vīsum*, 2; the participle agrees with *nulla*, and *visa* is joined by *neque* to *audita*. —— **sorōrum**, gen. plur. of *soror, -ōris*, f., 3d; partitive gen., after *nulla*.

327 mi,hí ,, neque , vísa so,rórum, O — quam , té O — how must I call
   by me   *nor*   *seen*   *of sisters,*   *O — whom thee*   thee, maiden ? for

memo,rém, vir,gó? ,, nam,que haúd tibi , not mortal is thy
  am I to call,   *maiden?*   *for*   *not*   *to thee* aspect, nor sounds

328 vúltus   Mórta,lís, ,, nec , vóx   homi,ném thy voice of human
  (is) the countenance mortal,   *nor thy voice human* (lit. *a man*) kind ; O, goddess

329 sonat. , Ó dea , cérte : **An** Phoe,bí ,, soror ? , truly, whether sister
  sounds.   *O goddess surely : whether of Phoebus*   *the sister?* of Phoebus, or one

---

LINE 327. **Ŏ,** exclamation; no vocative follows it immediately, because Aeneas is not acquainted with the maiden's name, but imagining her to be a goddess, he resumes in l. 328, with the address *O dea.* —— **quam,** acc. sing. f. of the interrog. pron. *quis;* predicate acc. after the verb of *calling, memorem.* A. & G. 239, 1, *a*; B. 177; G. 340; H. 373. —— **tē,** acc. sing. of *tū;* direct obj. of *memorem.* —— **memorem,** 1st pers. sing. pres. subjunct. act. of *memoro, -āre, -āvī, -atum,* 1; *ego* is the unexpressed subject. The subjunctive is the *deliberative* or *dubitative,* employed in questions (usually requiring no answer) implying *doubt* or *indignation,* and in exclamations of a rhetorical kind; *memorem* expresses the doubt in Aeneas' mind. A. & G. 268 ; B. 277; G. 259; H. 484, V. —— **virgō,** voc. sing. of *virgō, virginis,* f., 3d; case of the person addressed. —— **namque** (*nam* + *que*), *nam,* causal conj. strengthened by *que;* see *namque,* l. 65. —— **haud,** negative adv.; negatives the adj. *mortalis. Haud* is never used with verbs by Vergil, and rarely by any Latin writer except with *scio,* e.g. *haud scio an :* it is common with adjectives and adverbs. Caesar uses *haud* only once, viz. in *haud scio an :* so Cicero uses it, and he also has *haud dubito, haud ignoro,* and a few other like expressions. *Haud* with verbs is fairly common in early writers, and reappears in Livy and Tacitus. —— **tibi,** dat. sing. of *tū;* dat. of the possessor, with *est* understood. A. & G. 231; B. 190; G. 349; H. 387. —— **vultus,** gen. *vultūs,* m., 4th; nom. sing., subj. of *est* understood.

LINE 328. **Mortālis,** nom. sing. m. of *mortālis, -e,* adj., 3d (from *mors*)*;* agrees with *vultus* and is the *complement* of *est* understood in the predicate *mortalis (est). Mortalis = mortal,* i.e. subject to death; but *a mortal wound* is not *vulnus mortale* but *vulnus funestum.* —— **nec,** conj., = *et non.* —— **vōx,** gen. *vōcis,* f, 3d; nom. sing., subj. of *sonat.* —— **hominem,** acc. sing. of *homo, hominis,* m., 3d; a poetical extension of the *cognate* acc. The ordinary *cognate* acc. would be *sonitum sonat,* and with the adj. qualifying *sonitum* added, *sonitum humanum sonat;* so far the acc. is familiar, but the noun and adj. are poetically condensed in *hominem* (*man-fashion*). Horace has *Cyclopa saltare* = lit. *to dance a Cyclops* (i.e. *like a Cyclops,* or *to dance a Cyclopean dance*). A. & G. 238, *a*; B. 176, 5; G. 333, 2, NOTE 3; H. 371, II, NOTE. —— **sonat,** 3d pers. sing. pres. ind. act. of *sono, -āre, sonuī, sonitum,* 1; agrees with the subj. *vox.* —— **Ŏ,** exclamation, with the voc. *dea.* —— **dea,** voc. sing. of *dea, -ae,* f., 1st (dat. and abl. plur. *deabus* or *deis*)*;* case of the object addressed. —— **certē,** adv. (from *certus*)*;* emphasizing *dea,* as if *dea = divina.*

LINE 329. **An,** interrog. particle, introducing the direct question *Phoebi soror (es)* ? *An . . . an* do not introduce double questions here, but two distinct questions. Double questions are introduced by *utrum . . . an,* and if other alternatives are stated, *an* is repeated before them. When *an* introduces a single question, there is usually a previous question either spoken or conceived in the mind. A. & G. 211; B. 162, 4, and *a*; G. 457, esp. 1, NOTE 3; H. 353, NOTE 4. —— **Phoebī,** gen. sing. of *Phoebus,* m., 2d (Φοῖβος

of the nymphs' blood?	án nym,phárum , sánguinis , úna? Sís 330
Be gracious, and	or of nymphs of the race one? May'st thou be
whosoe'er thou art	fe,líx, nos,trúmque le,vés, ,, quae,cúmque,
lighten our toil, and	propitious, and our may'st thou lighten; whoever (thou art),
instruct us beneath	la,bórem, Ét quo , súb coe,ló tan,dém, ,, quibus , 331
what sky indeed, on	labor, and what under sky at length, what
what shores of the	órbis in , óris Iácte,múr, doce,ás. ,, 332
world we are cast; we	of the world in shores we are tossed, may thou instruct (us).

= *the radiant one;* akin to φάος = *light*) ; poss. gen., limiting *soror.* Phoebus is one of the names of Apollo, the sun-god. —— **soror,** gen. *sorōris,* f., 3d; nom. sing., *complement* in the predicate *soror (es).* The allusion is to Diana (Artemis), daughter of Latona (or Leto) and Jupiter, and twin-sister of Apollo; she and her brother were born in the island of Delos, hence Horace speaks of *Delius . . . Apollo.* Diana was a warrior-goddess, who sided with the Greeks at Troy; she was the goddess of hunting. Sometimes the poets identify her with Luna (the moon). —— **an,** interrog. particle ; see *an* above. —— **Nymphārum,** gen. plur. of *Nympha, -ae,* f., 1st; poss. gen., limiting *sanguinis;* see *Nympharum,* l. 168. —— **sanguinis,** gen. sing. of *sanguis,* m., 3d ; *sanguinis = gentis,* partitive gen. after the numeral *una.* See references under *sororum,* l. 322. —— **ūna,** nom. sing. f. of *ūnus, -a, -um;* agrees with *tū* understood as subj., and is complement in the predicate *(es) una.*

LINE 330. **Sīs,** 2d pers. sing. pres. subj. of *sum, esse, fuī;* agrees with the implied subj. *tu;* the subjunct. expresses a wish. The *optative* subjunctive may be used either independently or with *ut, o si,* and *utinam;* it sometimes follows *velim* and *vellem.* The present tense denotes a wish that something may happen in the future; the imperfect of wishes unfulfilled *now* in the present time ; the pluperfect of wishes unfulfilled in the past. A. & G. 267; B. 279; G. 260-262; H. 483, 484. The negative in wishes is *ne,* rarely *non.* —— **fēlīx,** gen. *fēlīcis,* adj., 3d ; nom. sing. f., agreeing with *tu* (i.e. *dea*), and in the predicate with *sis.* *Felix* = (1) *propitious,* as here ; an active sense ; (2) *happy;* a passive sense. —— **nostrum,** acc. sing. m. of *noster, nostra, nostrum,* poss. adj. of the plur. 2d personal pron. *nōs;* agrees with *laborem.* —— **que,** enclitic conj. —— **levēs,** 2d pers. sing. pres. subjunct. act. of *levō, -āre, -āvī, -ātum,* 1 ; joined by *que* to *sis,* and in the same grammatical construction. —— **quaecumque,** nom. sing. f. of the universal rel. pron. *quīcumque, quaecumque, quodcumque* (rel. *quī* + the suffix *cumque*) ; subj. of *es* understood. For the force of *cumque* in making the relative universal, consult A. & G. 105, *a;* B. 91, 8; G. 111, 2; H. 187, 3, FOOTNOTE 3. —— **labō-rem,** acc. sing. of *labor, -ōris,* m., 3d; direct obj. of *levēs.*

LINE 331. **Et,** cop. conj., joining the equally important request *doceas* to *leves* preceding. —— **quō,** abl. sing. n. of the interrog. adj. *quī, quae, quod;* agrees with *coelo,* and introduces one part of the double indirect question, *quo sub coelo iactemur,* as *quibus* below the second, *quibus in oris iactemur.* —— **sub,** prep. with the acc. or abl.; gov. the abl. *coelo.* —— **coelō,** abl. sing. of *coelum, -ī,* n., 2d ; governed by *sub.* —— **tandem,** adv. (usually of time, = *at length*), emphasizing the question asked. *Tandem* is so used by Cicero, and other orators and poets ; it corresponds to the Greek particle δή, e.g. τίς δή = *who exactly.* —— **quibus,** abl. plur. f. of the interrog. adj. *quī;* agrees with *oris.* —— **orbis,** gen. sing. of *orbis,* m., 3d; poss. gen., limiting *oris. Orbis,* usually with *terrarum* added, = *the world.* —— **in,** prep. with the acc. or abl.; gov. the abl. *oris.* —— **ōrīs,** abl. plur. of *ōra, -ae,* f., 1st; governed by *in.*

LINE 332. **Iactēmur,** 1st pers. plur. pres. subjunct. pass. of *iactō, -āre, -āvī, -ātum,* 1; the implied subj. is *nōs* (the Trojans); the subjunctive is due to the indirect question;

333 Ig,nári homi,númque lo,córum*que* Érra,mús,
Ignorant   both of the men   and of the regions   we wander,
334 ven,to „ húc et, vástis, flúctibus, ácti. Múlta
by the wind hither and vast by waves driven. Many
ti,bī ánte a,rás „ nos,trá cadet , hóstia ,
to thee before the altars   our   shall fall   a victim

are wandering know-
ing nought of the peo-
ple or the land, driven
hither by the wind
and the grim billows.
Many a victim shall
fall by our hand be-
fore the altar in thine

see *quo* above. For indirect questions, refer to the note on *accesserit*, l. 307. —— **doceās,**
2d pers. sing. pres. subjunct. act. of *doceō, -ēre, docuī, doctum*, 2; *optative* subjunct., joined
by *et* to *leves* above; *doceās* is the principal verb so far as the indirect question *quo* . . .
iactemur is concerned. —— **ignārī,** nom. plur. m. of *ignārus, -a, -um* (*in, = not, + gnā-*
rus, = knowing) ; agrees with *nos*, the implied subj. of *erramus*. —— **hominum,** gen.
plur. of *homō, hominis*, m., 3d; objective gen., dependent on the adj. of *knowledge,*
ignārī. A. & G. 218, *a*; B. 204, 1; G. 374; H. 399, I, 2. —— **que,** enclitic conj.;
repeated below, = *both* . . . *and*. The combination *que* . . . *que* is common in poetry;
Sallust and his successors use it in prose, but Cicero presents only one instance of it; *que*
. . . *et* is shunned by Caesar and Cicero, but appears in later authors; *et* . . . *que* is very
rare; *et* . . . *et* is by far the most common. See the note and references to *et*, l. 3. ——
locōrum, gen. plur. of *locus, -ī*, m., 2d (plur. *loci*, m., or *loca*, n.) ; joined by *que* below to
hominum; an objective genitive. —— **que,** enclitic conj. This line is *hypermetrical;*
such license is only permitted when the extra syllable (as *que* here) is one that it is
capable of *elision*, and when the next line begins with a vowel or *h*, so that the extra syl-
lable may be and actually is *elided* before it (as *que* is *elided* before *Erramus*). The
continuation of the scansion caused by the joining of the last syllable of one line with the
first of the next is called *synapheia.* There is another example in l. 448, *nexaequ*e *Aere*
trabes. A. & G. 359, *c*, REM.; B. 367, 6; G. 728; H. 608, I, NOTE 5.
      LINE 333. **Errāmus,** 1st pers. plur. pres. ind. act. of *errō, -āre, -āvī, -ātum*, 1; the
implied subj. is *nos*. —— **ventō,** abl. sing. of *ventus, -ī*, m., 2d; abl. of the means or
instrument. A. & G. 248, *c*; B. 218; G. 401; H 420. —— **hūc,** adv. of place whither,
extending *acti ;* see *hūc*, l. 170. —— **et,** cop. conj. —— **vāstīs,** abl. plur. m. of *vāstus,*
-a, -um ; qualifying *fluctibus*. —— **fluctibus,** abl. plur. of *fluctus, -ūs*, m., 4th; abl. of
the instrument, joined by *et* to *vento*. —— **āctī,** nom. plur. m. of *āctus, -a, -um*, perf.
part. pass. of *agō, -ere, ēgī, āctum*, 3; agrees with and extends *nos* understood as subj. of
erramus.
      LINE 334. **Multa,** nom. sing. f. of *multus, -a, -um ;* agrees with *hostia*. *Multus,*
denoting amount or degree, is regular in the sing., e.g. *multum frumentum, = much*
corn ; multa auctoritas, = much influence : the plural *multi, -ae, -a* is an indefinite
numeral, = *many*. *Multa hostia* here = *multae hostiae*, an uncommon and poetical use
of the singular. —— **tibi,** dat. sing. of *tū ;* dat. of advantage, = *in thy honor* A. & G.
235; B. 188, 1; G. 350; H. 384, 4. —— **ante,** prep. with the acc.; gov. *aras*. A. & G.
153; B. 141; G. 416, 3; H. 433, I. —— **ārās,** acc. plur. of *āra, -ae*, f., 1st; governed
by *ante*. —— **nostrā,** abl. sing. f. of *noster, nostra, nostrum ;* agrees with *dextra*. ——
cadet, 3d pers. sing. fut. ind. act. of *cadō, -ere, cecĭdī, cāsum*, 3; agrees with the subj.
hostia. —— **hostia,** gen. *hostiae*, f., 1st (from an obsolete verb *hostio, = I strike*) ; nom.
sing., subj. of *cadet*. —— **dextrā,** abl. sing. of *dextra, -ae*, f., 1st (properly f. of the adj.
dexter, dextra, dextrum, with *manus* supplied; cf. *sinistra* (*manus*), = *the left hand*) ;
abl. of the instrument, with *cadet* (which has a passive signification = to *necabitur*).
The meaning of this line is that Aeneas will sacrifice victims to the maiden, i.e. provided
she will grant his requests.

honor." Then	déxtra." Túm Venus: , "Haúd equi, dém „ 335
Venus: "Nay, not	*by right hand."* *Then* *Venus:* *"Not* *indeed*
worthy of such offering do I deem me ;	ta, lí me , dígnor ho, nóre ; Vírgini, bús Tyri, ís „ 336
it is the wont of	*such myself I am worthy of honor;* *for maidens* *Tyrian*
Tyrian maidens to	mos , ést ges, táre pha, rétram, Púrpure, óque 337
bear the quiver, and	*the custom* *is* *to carry* *a quiver,* *and purple*

LINE 335. **Tum**, adv. of time, = *then*, or order, = *next*. —— **Venus**, nom. sing. subj. of *loquitur*, or some such verb understood. —— **Haud**, negative adv.; negatives *tali;* see note on *haud*, l. 327. —— **equidem**, demonstr. corroborative particle; see note on *equidem*, l. 238. —— **tālī**, abl. sing. m. of *tālis, -e;* agrees with *honore; tali* is emphatic, and *haud tali = not such reverential offerings*. *Talis*, the demonstrative, may be used absolutely, or with its corresponding relative *qualis;* so *quantus . . . tantus*, etc. —— **mē**, acc. sing. of *ego;* direct reflexive obj. of *dignor*. —— **dīgnor**, 1st pers. sing. pres. ind. of the dep. verb *dignor, dīgnārī, dīgnātus sum*, 1 (from *dīgnus, worthy*); supply *ego* as subject. *Me dignor = me dignum (esse) aestimo*. *Dignor* takes the accusative of the person and the ablative of the thing, *aliquem aliqua re*. Like *dignor*, the adjectives *dignus* and *indignus* are followed by the abl. of the cause without a preposition. A. & G. 245, *a;* B. 226, 2, where the abl. is described as one of *specification;* G. 397, NOTE 2; H. 421, III, NOTE 2. *Dignor* is very often used as a passive verb, = *I am deemed worthy*, governing the ablative of the cause. —— **honōre**, abl. sing. of *honōs, honōris*, m., 3d; abl. of cause or respect, dependent on *dignor; honore = offering, sacrifice*, cf. *honores*, l. 28, and note.

LINE 336. **Virginibus**, dat. plur. of *virgō, virginis*, f., 3d; dat. of the possessor, after *est;* see note on *tibi*, l. 327. —— **Tyriis**, dat. plur. f. of *Tyrius, -a, -um* (pertaining to *Tyros* or *Tyrus, -ī*, f., 2d, = *Tyre*, the chief city of Phoenicia); agrees with *virginibus*. *Virginibus Tyriis*, by its emphatic position, disclaims at once any claim to that divinity with which Aeneas had in suggestion invested the disguised goddess. *Tyrius =* Carthaginian; so *Phoenicius* and *Sidonius* in Vergil; all three have reference to the Phoenician origin of Carthage. —— **mōs**, gen. *mōris*, m., 3d; nom. sing., in the predicate with the *copula est*. —— **est**, 3d pers. sing. pres. ind. of the *copula sum*, *esse, fuī;* agrees with its subj.-inf. *gestare*. The verb *to be* (except when it = *to exist*) does not form a complete predicate; it requires a noun or adj. (called the *complement*) referring to the subject to make the predication perfect. —— **gestāre**, pres. inf. act. of *gestō, -āre, -āvī, -ātum*, 1; subj. of *mos est*. The infinitive exercises both verbal and substantival functions; it admits of different tenses, can be modified by adverbs, and may govern an object like a verb, and like a noun may be the subject or object of a sentence. A. & G. 270; B. 326-328; G. 280; H. 532 and 538. —— **pharētram**, acc. sing. of *pharētra, -ae*, f., 1st; direct obj. of *gestare*. For scansion, see note on *pharetra*, l. 323.

LINE 337. **Purpureō**, abl. sing. m. of *purpureus, -a, -um* (from *purpura, = purple;* cf. Greek πορφύρα); qualifies *cothurno*. In statues Diana was represented as wearing the *cothurnus* or high boot, and this led Aeneas to say *an Phoebi soror ;* moreover, purple was to the Romans a color restricted to nobles, adorning the *togae* of senators, priests, etc. Venus explains the purple boot as an ordinary Tyrian part of the attire, Tyre being noted for its purple dyes (*puniceus* and *Phoenician = purple*). Vergil and the poets use *purpureus* of many kinds of objects; Vergil has *purpureos flores, purpureum ver*, and the adjective is made to qualify *eyes, love, the sea, light, swans*, etc. —— **que**, enclitic conj. —— **alte**, adv. of manner (from *altus, = high*); modifies *vincire*. —— **sūrās**, acc.

838 al,té ,, su,rás vin,círe co,thúrno.　　Púnica , régna
　　high　　the calves　to bind　　with boot.　　Phoenician　realms

839 vi,dés, ,, Tyri,ós et A,génoris , úrbem; Séd
　　thou seest,　the Tyrians and　of Agenor　　the city ;　　but

fi,nés　　　　Liby,cí, ,, genus , íntrac,tábile ,
　　the territory (is)　Libyan,　　a race　　　unmanageable

840 béllo.　　Imperi,úm　Di,dó ,, Tyri,á regit ,
　　in war.　　The empire　　Dido　,,　Tyrian　　rules

to bind high the leg with purple buskin. The realm thou seest is Punic, Tyrian the folk, and Agenor's the city ; but the land is Libyan, a race unfitamable in war. The rule is swayed by Dido, who left the Tyrian

---

plur. of *sūra, -ae,* f., 1st; direct obj. of *vincire.* —— **vincīre**, pres. inf. act. of *vinciō, -īre, vinxī, vinctum,* 4; subject-inf., joined by *que* above to *gestare.* —— **cothurnō**, abl. sing. of *cothurnus, -ī,* m., 2d (Greek κόθορνος); abl. of the instrument. The *cothurnus* was a Greek hunting-boot, which came half-way (*alte*) up the calf, and was laced in front; its main service was to support the leg in heavy exertion, and to protect it against thorny bushes and the like. The *cothurnus* or buskin of Greek tragedy was different, being a very high and artificially raised boot, intended to give dignity; the *soccus* of comedy was a low shoe.

LINE 338. **Pūnica**, acc. plur. n. of *Pūnicus, -a, -um* (a corruption of Φοῖνιξ; cf. *Poeni*); agrees with *regna;* the adj. is predicate, = *the kingdom which you see is Punic* (Phoenician or Carthaginian). —— **rēgna**, acc. plur. of *rēgnum, -ī,* n., 2d; direct obj. of *vides. Regna* is in answer to *quibus in oris,* l. 331. —— **vidēs**, 2d pers. sing. pres. ind. act. of *videō, -ēre, vīdī, vīsum,* 2; the implied subj. is *tu.* —— **Tyriōs**, acc. plur. m. of *Tyrii, -ōrum,* m., 2d (or perhaps predicate adj. agreeing with *homines* understood); direct obj. of *vides.* It is best to regard *Tyrios et urbem* as appositives of *regna,* being the constituent *parts* of the *whole, regna. Tyrios* answers *hominum,* l. 332. —— **et**, cop. conj. —— **Agēnoris**, gen. sing. of *Agēnor,* m , 3d; poss. gen., limiting *urbem.* Agenor was the brother of Belus, king of Egypt; the father of Cadmus, Phoenix, Europa, etc.; and the ancestor of Dido. Because of the last fact, Carthage is by a kind of poetic *metonymy* called *urbs Agenoris.* —— **ūrbem**, acc. sing. of *urbs, urbis,* f., 3d; direct obj. of *vides.*

LINE 339. **Sed**, adversative conj.; see *sed,* l. 19, note and references. —— **fīnēs**, nom. plur.· of *fīnis, -is,* m., 3d (in sing., = *end;* in plur., = *territory*); subj. of *sunt* understood in the predicate; *finis* is opposed to *regna,* and answers *quo sub coelo,* l. 331. The land is Libyan, but the colony is Phoenician. —— **Libycī**, nom. plur. m. of *Libycus, -a, -um* (pertaining to *Libya, -ae,* f., 1st); *complement* of *sunt* understood. —— **genus**, gen. *generis,* n., 3d; nom. sing., in loose apposition with *fines,* for *fines (sunt) Libyci* practically = *finitimi sunt Libyci, genus,* etc.; the apposition is clear enough in sense; cf. Aen. IV, 40, *Gaetulae urbes, genus insuperabile bello.* —— **intrāctābile**, nom. sing. n. of *intrāctābilis, -e,* adj., 3d (*in,* = *not,* + *trāctābilis,* = *manageable,* from *tractō, I manage*); qualifies *genus.* Some incorrectly regard *genus* as not an appositive, but as subj. of (*est*) *intractabile;* in that case we must note that there is *asyndeton,* and that *intractabile* becomes a part of the predicate. —— **bellō**, abl. sing. of *bellum, -ī,* n., 2d; abl. of specification. A. & G. 253; B. 226; G. 397; H. 424.

LINE 340. **Imperium**, acc. sing. of *imperium, -ī,* n., 2d; probably direct obj. of *regit;* then *imperium* = *empire,* referring to the area of government, a sense which the word began to acquire in the time of Vergil. Those who prefer to do so may take it as a *cognate* acc.; cf. *servitutem servire.* A. & G. 238; B. 176, 4; G. 333, 2; H. 371, II. —— **Dīdō**, gen. *Dīdōnis* or *Dīdūs;* nom. sing. f., subj. of *regit.* For declension and biographical notice of Dido, refer to the note on *Dido,* l. 299. —— **Tyriā**, abl. sing. f. of

city fleeing her	úrbe	pro,fécta,	Gérma,núm	fugi,éns. „341
brother. Long is the	*from the city*	*having set out,*	*her brother*	*fleeing from.*
story of wrong, long	Lon,*ga*	ést	in,iúria,	, lóngae
its mazes ; but the	*Lengthy*	*is*	*the (story of) wrong,*	*lengthy*
chief heads of the	Ámba,gés;	sed ,	súmma se,quár „	fas,tígia , 342
matter I will trace.	*the details;*	*but*	*chief I will follow*	*the heads*

Tyrius, -a, -um ; agrees with *urbe.* —— regit, 3d pers. sing. pres. ind. act. of *regō, -ere,* *rēxī, rectum,* 3; agrees with the subj. *Dido.* —— **urbe,** abl. sing. of *urbs, urbis,* f., 3d; abl. of ' place from which.' The ablative with a preposition (*ab, de* or *ex*) denotes *place from which;* the names of towns or small islands (not countries), provided *urbs, oppidum,* etc., be not expressed, may be put in the ablative without a preposition. The omission of the preposition here is poetical. A. & G. 258, 1, and *a,* NOTE 3; B. 229, 1, and esp. *c;* G. 390, esp. 2, NOTE 2; H. 412. —— **profēcta,** nom. sing. f. of the perf. part. of the dep. verb *proficiscor, -ī, profectus sum,* 3; agrees with *Dido,* and takes the place of a relative or temporal clause.

LINE 341. **Germānum,** acc. sing. of *germānus, -ī,* m., 2d (properly m. of adj. *germānus, -a, -um ;* cf. *germāna, -ae,* f., 1st, = *a full sister*) *;* direct obj. of *fugiens; germanum* = Pygmalion. —— **fugiēns,** nom. sing. f. of the pres. part. act. of *fugiō, -ere, fūgī, fūgitum,* 3 (akin to the Greek root φυγ, whence φυγή, φεύγω); agrees with the subj. *Dido. Fugiens* has a meaning common in the Greek noun and verb just mentioned, viz. *being in a state of exile from, avoiding by expatriation* (φεύγειν often has the passive sense *to be banished*). This is clear, for *fugiens* cannot =*fleeing from*, as she had settled in a new home. —— **Longa,** nom. sing. f. of *longus, -a, -um ;* agrees with *iniuria. Longa = longa dictu,* a poetical and somewhat forced meaning; but cf. *longae ambages, = a long story.* —— **est,** 3d pers. sing. pres. ind. of *sum ;* agrees in the predicate *longa est* with the subj. *iniuria.* —— **īniūria,** gen. *īniūriae,* f., 1st; nom. sing., subj. of *est.* —— **longāē,** nom. plur. f. of *longus, -a, -um ;* predicate adj., agreeing with *ambages.*

LINE 342. **Ambāgēs,** nom. plur. of *ambāgēs, -is,* f., 3d, rare in the sing., complete in plur. with gen. *ambagum* (*ambi,* = *around* (ἀμφί), + *ago,* = *I go,* hence *a going roundabout*) *;* subj. of *sunt* understood. Notice the intentionally effective *asyndeton. Ambages* = (1) lit. *the twistings and turnings* of a labyrinth; e.g. Aen. VI, 29, (*Daedalus*) *dolos tecti ambagesque resolvit;* hence (2) *an intricate story,* as here; or sometimes *evasions,* e.g. Horace, *missis ambagibus,* = *omitting circumlocution ;* cf. the adj. *ambiguus.* —— **sed,** adversative conj. —— **summa,** acc. pl. n. of *summus, -a, -um,* superl. adj.; agrees with *fastigia.* Comparison : from prep. *supra* = *above ;* positive, *superus* rare, but plur. *superi* = *the gods above ;* comparative, *supuerior ;* superl. *supremus* or *summus.* —— **sequar,** 1st pers. sing. fut. ind. of the dep. verb *sequor, sequī, secūtus sum,* 3; understand *ego* as subj. —— **fastīgia,** acc. plur. of *fastīgium, -ī,* n., 2d (from *fastigō,* = *I make pointed,* hence *that which is pointed*) *;* direct obj. of *sequar ; fastigia* = *capita, heads* in a story, but this is a rare sense. *Fastigium* is properly used : (1) of a *gable* of a building, or the *summit* of anything; hence (2) of *rank, dignity.* Synonyms : *cacumen, the top* of anything, but never used like *fastigium* of the *lowest part ; vertex* = *the crown* of the head, hence *summit ; apex* = *the top,* esp. of a cap; *culmen* = *the top* of a house, i.e. *the roof,* originally covered with straw (*culmus*). —— **rērum,** gen. plur. of *rēs, reī,* f., 5th; poss. gen., limiting *fastigia.*

343 rérum.   Huíc   con,iúnx   Sy,chǽus   e,rát,   „   Her   husband   was
of the affairs.   *To her*   *husband*   *Sychaeus*   *was,*   Sychaeus, richest of
344 di,tíssimus ,   ágri   Phœni,cum,   ét   mag,nó ,,   the Phoenicians in
richest   *in land of the Phoenicians, and*   *great*   land and beloved
345 mise,rǽ   di,léctus   a,móre,   Cuí   of his hapless wife
of the miserable (woman)   *beloved*   *with the affection, to whom*   with a mighty
                                                                         passion; to whom

LINE 343. **Huic**, dat. sing. of the demonstr. pron. *hīc, haec, hōc;* dat. of the possessor; *huic coniunx Sychaeus. erat = haec coniugem Sychaeum habebat.* See note on *tibi,* l. 327. —— **coniūnx**, gen. *coniugis,* m. or f., 3d *(cum + iungo);* predicate noun with *erat,* agreeing with the subj. *Sychaeus; conjunx* is more often f. = *wife,* cf. l. 47, *et soror et coniunx.* Synonyms : *coniunx* = husband, as equal partner with the wife in marriage; *maritus* = husband, with emphasis on the difference in sex; *vir,* one of its special senses. —— **Sȳchaeus**, gen. *Sȳchaeī,* m., 2d; nom. sing., subj. of *erat.* Observe that the first syllable is long; in l. 348 it is short, and elsewhere it is commonly so. Proper names are treated with considerable freedom by the poets; cf. *Lāvinia,* l. 2, and *Lăvini,* l. 258; *Sidōnia,* l. 446, and *Sidŏniam,* l. 678. Sychaeus (also called Acerbas) was a priest of the temple of Hercules in Phoenicia, and married Elissa (Dido), the sister of King Pygmalion. Pygmalion murdered him to gain his immense riches, and persuaded Dido to believe her husband had gone away upon some affair, until his shade appeared to her, informed her of the truth and where to find much wealth, and advised her to flee from Tyre. —— **erat**, 3d pers. sing. imperf. ind. of *sum;* agrees with the subj. *Sychaeus.* —— **dītīssimus**, nom. sing. m., superl. of *dīves;* agrees with *Sychaeus.* Comparison: *dīves; dīvītior (dītior); dīvitissimus (dītissimus).* —— **āgrī**, gen. sing. of *ăger,* m., 2d; gen. of respect or specification. A. & G. 218, *c* ; B. 204, 4; G. 374, NOTE 1; H. 399, III, 1. An ingenious emendation, *auri (rich in gold),* has been adopted by some, on the ground that Phoenician wealth consisted in money and not estates, as the Phoenicians were great merchants; but wealth at Rome was measured by the estates, slaves, houses, etc., that a citizen possessed, and it is natural that Vergil should translate to Roman ideas when referring to something foreign.

LINE 344. **Phoenīcum**, gen. plur. of *Phoenīces,* m. plur. (see *Poenī,* l. 302); partitive gen. limiting the superl. adj. *ditissimus.* For this gen. after comparative and superlative adjectives, consult A. & G. 216, 2; B. 201, 1; G. 372; H. 397, 3. —— **et**, cop. conj. —— **māgnō**, abl. sing. m. of *mǎgnus, -a, -um ;* qualifies *amore.* —— **miserae**, gen. sing. f. of *miser, misera, miserum ;* subjective gen. after *amore; miseriae* agrees with *uxoris* understood. Some prefer to consider *miserae* the dat. sing. f., dat. of the agent after the participle *dilectus,* like *mihi,* l. 326; consult the note and references on *mīhi.* *Misera* = hapless, and Dido is called *misera* on account of the murder of her husband, to whom she was very strongly attached; perhaps there is a secret allusion to her future infatuation for and desertion by Aeneas. —— **dīlectus**, nom. sing. m. of the perf. part. pass. of *dīligō, -ere, dīlēxī, dilectum,* 3 *(di = dis,* apart, + *lego,* = *I* choose, hence *I value particularly) ;* joined by *et* to *ditissimus,* and agreeing with *Sychaeus.* The student should keep distinct in his memory the verbs *diligo, delego, deligo* (2 verbs, 1st and 3d conjugation). —— **amōre**, abl. sing. of *amor, -ōris,* m., 3d; abl. of manner, with *dilectus;* the phrase = *loved with the passion of a hapless (woman).* The prep. *cum* may be used or omitted at will, whenever the noun is qualified by an adjective. A. & G. 248; B. 220; G. 399; H. 419, III.

LINE 345. **Cui**, dat. sing. m. of the rel. *quī;* agrees with the antecedent *Sychaeus,* and dat. of the recipient (indirect obj.) following *dederat.* —— **pater**, gen, *pătris,* m., 3d ;

her father had	pater , íntac,tám dede,rát, „ pri,mísque
given her as a virgin,	*her father* *untouched* *had given (her),* *and first*
uniting her with	
the rites of first	iu,gárat Ómini,bús. Sed , régna Ty,rí „ 34t
wedlock. But her	*had united (her)* *with omens.* *But* *the realm* *of Tyre*
brother held the	ger,mánus ha,bébat Pýgmali,ón, „ scele,re 347
realm of Tyre, Pyg-	*her brother* *held* *Pygmalion,* *in crime*
malion—monstrous	
in crime beyond all	ánte ali,ós im,mánior, ómnes. Quós in,tér 348
others. Between	*beyond other men more monstrous* *all.* *Whom* *between*

nom. sing., subj. of *dederat; pater* = *pater miserae*, i.e. Belus, king of Tyre. —— **intāctam,** acc. sing. f. of *intāctus, -a, -um*, (*in,* = *not,* + *tāctus,* = *touched,* perf. part. pass. of *tangō, -ere, tetigī, tāctum,* 3); agrees with *eam* (understood from *miserae*, l. 344), the direct obj. of *dederat.* *Intactam* and *primis ominibus* indicate that Dido was a maiden, not a widow, before she married Sychaeus. —— **dederat,** 3d pers. sing. pluperf. ind. act. of *dō, dare, dedī, datum,* 1; agrees with the subj. *pater.* —— **prīmis,** abl. plur. n. of *prīmus, -a, -um ;* qualifies *ominibus; primis* is literal, = *first,* i.e. auspices taken *for the first time ;* see *intactam* —— **que,** enclitic conj. —— **iugārat** (= *iugāverat*), 3d pers. sing. pluperf. ind. act. of *iugō, -āre, -āvī, -ātum,* 1 (*iugum, -ī,* n., 2d, = *a yoke*) *;* joined by *que* to *dederat; iugarat* is a contraction of *iugaverat.* For syncopation and contraction, consult A. & G. 128, *a;* B. 116, 1; G. 131, 1; H. 235.

LINE 346. **Ōminibus,** abl. plur. of *ōmen, ōminis,* n., 3d ; abl. of the means ; *omina* here has the derived meaning *marriage,* originating from the regular custom of taking the auspices, and observing certain signs of good or bad luck exhibited in nature, previous to celebrating the ceremony. The best known omen was the flight of birds. —— **Sed,** adversative conj. —— **rēgna,** acc. plur. of *rēgnum, -ī,* n., 2d ; direct obj. of *habebat.* ——**Tyrī,** gen. sing. of *Tyrus,* f., 2d ; *adnominal* gen., describing *regna.* A. & G. 214*f;* B. 202 ; G. 361 ; H. 395. Tyre was an ancient and splendid city of Phoenicia, about 20 miles to the south of Sidon, whence it was founded ; it had two fine harbors. —— **germānus,** nom. sing. m. (see *germānum,* l. 341); subj. of *habebat.* —— **habēbat,** 3d pers. sing. imperf. ind. act. of *habeō, -ēre, habuī, habitum,* 2 ; agrees with the subj. *germanus.*

LINE 347. **Pȳgmaliōn,** gen. *Pȳgmaliōnis,* m., 3d ; nom. sing., in apposition with the subj. *gērmanus.* —— **scelere,** abl. sing. of *scelus, sceleris,* n., 3d ; abl. of specification ; see references under *bello,* l. 339. —— **ante,** prep. with the acc., = *more than, beyond;* gov. *alios.* See references under *ante,* l. 334. —— **aliōs,** acc. plur. m. of *alius, -a, -ud* (gen. *alīus,* dat. *aliī*) *;* governed by *ante.* It seems as though the positive *immanis* would have been quite enough with *ante alios,* = *beyond others,* sc. *frightful;* but Vergil wishes to intensify the enormity of Pygmalion's guilt, hence the comparative. The superlative is sometimes similarly strengthened, e.g. Aen. VII, 55, *ante alios pulcherrimus omnes.* —— **immānior,** nom. sing., m., of the comparative of *immānis, -e,* adj. 3d (*in,* = *not,* + Sanskrit root MÂ, = *to measure,* hence *vast,* and metaphorically *terrible*) *;* agrees with *Pygmalion.* —— **omnēs,** acc. plur., m., of *omnis, -e ;* agrees with *alios.*

LINE 348. **quōs,** acc. plur. m. of the rel. *quī, quae, quod;* refers to *Sychaeus* and *Pygmalion* as antecedents, and is governed by the prep. *inter.* Observe that *quos* is connective, and = a copulative conjunction and a demonstrative pronoun (*et eos*). A. & G. 180,*f;* B. 251, 6 ; G. 610 ; H. 453. —— **inter,** prep. with the acc.;.gov. *quos.* Observe that *inter* here follows the word it governs ; certain dissyllabic prepositions are allowed this, e.g. *contra, circum,* etc. A. & G. 263, NOTE ; B. 144, 3 ; G. 413, REM. I ;

| medi,ús | „ | ve,nít | furor. | , | Ílle | Sy,chǽum | these mad frenzy |
| *midway* | | *came* | *rage.* | | *He* | *Sychaeus* | arose. He, in wicked |

849 **Ímpius** , ánte a,rás „ at,que aúri , cǽcus — sin and blind with
wicked *before the altars* *and of gold* *blind* — lust of gold, with his
sword before the altar
850 a,móre **Clám** fer,ro íncau,túm supe,rát, „ — overcomes Sychaeus
with love secretly with the sword unsuspecting *overcomes* — whom he surprised
851 se,cúrus a,mórum Gérma,nǽ; fac,túmque „ — in secret, heedless of
regardless of the love of his sister; *and the deed* — his sister's love ; and

H. 569, II, 1. —— **medius**, nom. sing. m. of *medius, -a, -um;* agrees with *furor; medius* is not partitive here as it is in l. 109, *mediis . . . in fluctibus,* but is an adverbial attribute modifying the verbal action.   *Quos inter medius venit furor = between whom rage came middlewise,* i.e. *in the middle, betwixt.*   A. & G. 191 ; B. 239 ; G. 325, REM. 6 ; H. 443. —— **venit**, 3d pers. sing. perf. ind. act. of *veniō, -īre, vēni, ventum,* 4 ; agrees with subj. *furor; medius venit = intervenit.* —— **furor**, gen. *furōris,* m., 3d (*furere = to rage*) ; nom. sing., subj. of *venit;* the personification of *furor* as the subj. of the verb is poetical, and would not be permissible in Latin prose. —— **Ille**, nom. sing. m. of the 3d demonstr. pron.; subj. of *superat,* and refers to *Pygmalion.* —— **Sychaeum**, acc. sing. of *Sychaeus, -ī,* m., 2d ; direct obj. of *superat.* Observe that the first syllable is short, as it should be ; but cf. *Sȳchaeus,* l. 343, where it is long.

LINE 349.   **Impius**, nom. sing. m. (*in, = not, + pius, = dutiful*) ; agrees with *ille,* and is an adverbial attribute, cf. *medius* above.   Murder is a crime of *impietas;* the *impietas* is greater if the murder be secret (*clam*) and that of a kinsman (Sychaeus was Pygmalion's brother-in-law); it is absolutely heinous if the murder be committed in a sanctified place (*ante aras*). —— **ante**, prep. with the acc.; gov. *aras.* —— **ārās**, acc. plur. of *āra, -ae,* f., 1st ; governed by *ante.* The reference is to the altars of the household gods, *Penates.* —— **atque**, cop. conj.; the emphatic *atque* is employed to introduce the reason, *caecus amore auri.* —— **auri**, gen. sing. of *aurum,* n., 2d ; objective gen., governed by *amore.*   A. & G. 217 ; B. 200 ; G. 363, 2 ; H. 396, III.   Sychaeus possessed great wealth. —— **caecus**, nom. sing. m. of *caecus, -a, -um;* joined by *atque* to *impius; caecus* has adverbial force, = a clause *quod auri amore caecus factus erat* (or *esset,* if the *blindness* be a suggestion which Vergil wishes to make).   *Caecus* in poetry sometimes has another, viz. a passive meaning, *dark, concealed,* etc. —— **amōre**, abl. sing. of *amor, -ōris,* m., 3d ; abl. of the cause, with *caecus.*   A. & G. 245, and 2, *b*; B. 219 ; G. 408, and NOTE 2 ; H. 416.

LINE 350.   **Clam**, adv. of manner, = *secretly* (akin to *celo, = I hide*).   It is sometimes a preposition, governing the ablative, and meaning *without the knowledge of.* —— **ferrō**, abl. sing. of *ferrum, -ī,* n., 2d; abl. of the means or instrument. —— **incautum**, acc. sing. m. of *incautus, -a, -um* (derived from *in, = not, + caveo, = I am on my guard against,* with obj.-acc.); agrees with *Sychaeum,* l. 348; *incautum* = a temporal clause, *dum incautus est.* —— **superat**, 3d pers. sing. pres. ind. act. of *superō, -āre, -āvī, ātum,* 1; agrees with the subj. *ille.   Superare* expresses mastery on a particular occasion; *vincere* expresses complete and permanent mastery. —— **sēcūrus**, nom. sing. m. (*sē, = without, + cūra, = care, anxiety*); agrees with the subj. *ille; securus amorum germanae = heedless of the love of his sister* (i.e. for her husband). —— **amōrum**, gen. plur. of *amor, -ōris,* m., 3d; poetic gen. of reference.   The poets use this gen. freely with any adj., denoting that in respect to which the quality is indicated.   A. & G. 218, *c*; B. 204, 4; G. 374, NOTE 6; H. 399, III, 1.

LINE 351.   **Germānae**, gen. sing. of *germāna,* f., 1st (properly f. of adj. *germānus, -a, -um*); poss. gen., limiting *amōrum.* —— **factum**, acc. sing. of *factum, -ī,* n., 2d

long he hid the deed, and by many a cunning pretext tricked the love-sick wife with idle hopes. But in her slumber there came the very phantom of her un-

di,ú ce,lávit, et , ǽgram, Múlta ma,lús 852
long   he concealed, and   sick   many things   evil
simu,láns, ,, va,ná spe , lúsit a,mántem. Ípsa 853
pretending,   vain with hope deluded the lover.   Itself
sed , ín som,nís ,, inhu,máti , vénit i,mágo
but   in   dreams   unburied   came   the phantom

(properly n. of the perf. part. *factus,* of *fīō*) ; direct obj. of *celavit.* ——— **que,** enclitic conj., connecting its own and the preceding sentence. ——— **diū,** adv. of time, = *for a long time;* originally = *dium,* adverbial acc. of *dius* (= *dies*), and so an acc. expressing duration of time. ——— **cēlāvit,** 3d pers. sing. perf. ind. act. of *cēlō, -āre, -āvī, ātum,* I (akin to Greek καλύπτω); joined by *que* to *superat,* agreeing with the same subject. *Celare* is often followed by a double accusative, on the direct object, the other of the indirect; e.g. *hoc me celavit,* = *he concealed this from me.* ——— **et,** cop conj. ——— **aegram,** acc. sing. f. of *aeger, aegra, aegrum;* qualifies *amantem; aegram* = *love-sick,* or *sick with anxiety* for the return of Sychaeus.

LINE 352. **Mūlta,** acc. plur. n. of *mūltus, -a, -um* (in the plur. an indefinite numeral, *mūltī* and *mūlta,* m. and n. often substantival) ; direct obj. of *simulans.* ——— **malus,** nom. sing. m. of the adj. *malus, -a, -um ;* agrees with the subj. (*Pygmalion*) of *lusit,* but is adverbial in force. ——— **simulāns,** nom. sing. m. of the pres. part. act. of *simulō, -āre, -āvī, -ātum,* I; agrees with the subj. of *lusit.* *Simulare* = *to pretend* that something is what it is not, *dissimulare* = *to pretend* that something is not what it is; so *simulans* conveys the idea that Pygmalion invented stories representing that Sychaeus was *safe,* to quiet Dido's suspicions that he was *not safe.* ——— **vānā,** abl. sing. f. of *vānus, -a, -um ;* agrees with *spē ;* the original meaning of *empty* is very suitable here (the derived sense is *vain, fruitless, idle*). ——— **spē,** abl. sing. of *spēs, speī,* f., 3d; abl. of the means, with *lusit.* ——— **lūsit,** 3d pers. sing. perf. ind. act. of *lūdō, -ĕre, lūsī, lūsum,* 3; agrees with the understood subj. *Pygmalion* or a pron. referring to him. *Lūdo* may be used : *transitively,* (1) as in the text; (2) = *I imitate;* (3) *I compose* (e.g. *carmina*) *for amusement; intransitively,* (4) *I play, I sport;* (5) with *cognate* acc., e.g. *ludum ludere, to play a game.* ——— **amāntem,** acc. sing. f. of the pres. part. act. (used as a noun) of *amō, -āre, -āvī, -ātum,* I ; direct obj. of *lusit.* A. & G. 113, *f*; B. no reference, but see 236; G. 437; H. 441. Synonyms : *amare* = *to love,* as opposed to hate or indifference; *diligere* = *to love ardently,* esp. of love tempered by respect and esteem.

LINE 353. **Ipsa,** nom. sing. f. of the intensive pron. *ipse, ipsa, ipsum ;* agrees with *imago; ipsa* is emphatic, even displacing *sed* to gain emphasis by position. ——— **sed,** adversative conj., frequently post-positive in poetry. For the use of *sed,* and distinctions between *sed, verum, autem,* and *at,* refer to the note on *sed,* l. 19. ——— **in**₂ prep. with the acc. or abl.; gov. the abl. *somnis.* ——— **somnīs,** abl. plur. of *somnus, -i,* m., 2d; governed by *in.* ——— **inhumātī,** gen. sing. m. of *inhumātus, -a, -um* (derived from *in,* = *not,* and *humus,* = *the ground*) ; qualifies *coniugis.* To a Roman, to die unburied was a terrible calamity, as the spirit of the dead man was compelled to wander restlessly about, unable to cross the Styx to Hades; three handfuls of earth thrown on the body was sufficient burial. ——— **vēnit,** 3d pers. sing. perf. ind. act. of *veniō, -īre, vēnī, ventum,* 4; agrees with the subj. *imago.* ——— **imāgō,** gen. *imāginis,* f., 3d (root IM, denoting *imitation;* cf. μιμ-εῖσθαι) ; nom. sing., subj. of *venit; imago* = *manes, the spirit* of the dead. The Romans called the wax busts of distinguished ancestors *imagines;* they were kept in little cupboards in the *atrium,* and were carried in procession when the funeral of one of the house took place.

854	Cóniugis ;	,	óra	mo,dís	„	at,tóllens ,
	of her husband;		*its face*	*in manner*		*raising*
855	pállida		míris,	Crúde,lés		a,rás „
	pallid		*wondrous*	*cruel*		*the altars*
856	tra,iéctaque	,	péctora	,	férro	Núda,vít,
	and pierced		*the breast*		*by the sword*	*laid bare,*
	cae,cúmque	do,mús	„	scelus ,	ómne	re,téxit.
	and hidden	*of the house*		*the crime*	*all*	*exposed.*

buried husband; raising a face pale in wondrous wise, he exposed the cruel altars and his breast pierced by the steel, and un-folded all the secret guilt of the house.

LINE 354. **Cōniugir**, gen. sing. (here m.) of *cŏniunx*, m. or f., 3d; poss. gen., limiting *imago*. —— **ōra**, acc. plur. of *ōs, ōris*, n., 3d; direct obj. of *attollens;* the plur. *ora* is poetic for the sing. *os*, and the difference in number does not mark any difference in meaning; cf. *pectora*, l. 355, and innumerable other instances. —— **modīs**, abl. plur. of *modus, -ī*, m., 2d; abl. of manner, *miris modis* being an adverbial phrase qualifying *pallida*. Cases of *modus* are used in certain adjectival and adverbial relations; e.g. *ad modum, modo, in modum;* and frequently with demonstr. and rel. pronouns, e.g. *eiusmodi, cuiusmodi, quemadmodum (quem ad modum)*, etc. —— **attōllēns**, nom. sing. f. of the pres. part. act. of *attōllō, -ĕre*, no perf., no supine, 3 (*ad + tōllō; tollō* borrows perf. *sustulī*, and supine *sublātum* from *sufferō*) ; agrees with *imago*. —— **pāllida**, acc. plur. n. of *pāllidus, -a, -um* (from *pālleō, = I am pale*) ; agrees with *ōra*. Horace uses *pallida* with *mors* personified. —— **mirīs**, abl. sing. m. of *mīrus, -a, -um ;* qualifies *modīs*. Vergil has borrowed the archaic phrase *modis miris*, as well as the notion of the phantom being *pallida*, from a passage in Lucretius.

LINE 355. **Crūdēlēs**, acc. plur. f. of *crūdēlis, -e*, adj., 3d; qualifies *aras; crudeles aras = the altar of cruelty*, i.e. where the cruel murder was committed. The application of the adj. suitable to the murderer to the place where the murder was done is a poetic figure; this figure comes under the head of *enallage*. A. & G. 385; B. no reference; G. 693; H. 636, IV. —— **ārās**, acc. plur. of *āra, -ae*, f., 1st; direct obj. of *nudavit*. —— **trāiecta**, acc. plur. n. of *trāiectus, -a, -um*, perf. part. pass. of *trāiciō, -ĕre, trāiēcī, trāiectum*, 3 (*trāns + iaciō*) ; agrees with *pectora*. —— **que**, enclitic conj., joining the two obj.-accusatives *aras* and *pectora*. —— **pectora**, acc. plur. of *pectus, pectoris*, n., 3d; direct obj. of *nudavit*. —— **ferrō**, abl. sing. of *ferrum, -ī*, n., 2d; abl. of the instrument, with *traiecta*.

LINE 356. **Nūdāvit**, 3d pers. sing. perf. ind. act. of *nūdō, -āre, -āvī, -ātum*, 1; agrees with the subj. *imago* or *Sychaeus* understood. Observe that *nudavit pectora* = lit. *laid bare (exposed) his breast*, and that *nudavit aras = laid bare (the crime committed at) the altar ;* so one of Dickens's characters goes home " IN a bath chair and a flood of tears," *in* being literal with its first object and idiomatic with the second. This figure is called *zeugma ;* see the note and references to *serenat*, l. 255. —— **caecum**, acc. sing. n. of *caecus, -a, -um ;* qualifies *scelus; caecum* is passive, = *hidden, secret*, cf. *caecus*, l. 349, and note. —— **que**, enclitic conj. —— **domūs**, gen. sing. of *domus, -ūs*, f., 4th (with 2d decl. forms in some cases; see note on *domos*, l 40`· subjective gen., equivalent to an dj. qualifying *scelus*. The crime was of the ' family-skeleton' type, for Pygmalion murdered his sister's husband for his riches, and violated the sacred shrine of the *Penates* of his family (*domūs*). —— **scelus**, acc. sing. of *sce.`, sceleris*, n., 3d; direct obj. of *retexit*. —— **ōmne**, acc. sing. n. of *ōmnis, -e*, adj., 3d; agrees with *scelus ;* it is out of the usual order for the sake of emphasis. —— **retēxit**, 3d pers. sing. perf. ind. act. of *retegō, -ĕre, retēxī, retectum*, 3 (*re, = back, + tegō, = I cover*, hence *I cover back*, i.e. *uncover*) ; joined by *que* to *nudavit*.

Then he counsels | Túm cele,ráre fu,gám ,, patri,áque   ex,cédere, 857
her to make | *Then   to hasten   flight and from her country   to depart*
speedy flight from
the country, and to | suádet,   Aúxili,úmque   vi,áe ,,   vete,rés 358
aid her journeying | *he advises (her)   and (as) a help for the journey   old*
discloses treasures
long hid in the earth, | tel,lúre   re,clúdit Thésau,rós, ,, ig,nótum 359
an untold weight of | *in the ground he reveals   treasures,   unknown*
silver and of gold. | ar,génti , póndus et , aúri.   His 360
Stirred thereby | *of silver   a weight and   of gold. By these things*

LINE 357. **Tum,** adv., here conjunctive = *deinde*. —— **celerāre,** pres. inf. act. of *celerō, -āre, -āvī, -atum,* 1, trans. and intrans.; *epexegetic* inf., instead of the usual prose construction *ut* + the subjunct.; dependent on *suadet.* For this infinitive after verbs such as *suadeo, oro, hortor,* etc., refer to the note on *volvere,* l. 9. —— **fugam,** acc. sing. of *fuga, -ae,* f., 1st; direct obj. of *celerare.* *Celero* is one of a class of intransitive verbs which, owing to having a meaning similar to that of other verbs regularly governing a direct object, are sometimes used transitively; we may consider the acc. really a kind of *cognate* accusative; thus *celerare fugam = celerare celeritatem fuga (in flight)*; cf. *maturate fugam,* l. 137. —— **patriā,** abl. sing. of *patria, -ae,* f., 1st (properly f. of adj. *patrius,* from *pater*) ; abl. of separation, following *excedere.* —— **que,** enclitic conj. —— **excēdere,** pres. inf. act. of *excēdō, -ere, excessī, excessum,* 3 (*ex* + *cēdō*) ; joined by *que* to *celerare,* and in construction exactly similar. —— **suādet,** 3d pers. sing. pres. ind. act. of *suādeō, -ēre, suāsī, suāsum,* 2; agrees with the subj. *imago Sychaei* understood; *suādet* is a *historic* present. A. & G. 276, *d*; B. 259, 3; G. 229; H. 467, III.

LINE 358. **Auxilium,** acc. sing. of *auxilium, -ī,* n., 2d (from *augeo*) ; in apposition with *thesauros.* A. & G. 184; B. 169; G. 320, *ff*; H. 359, NOTE 2. —— **que,** enclitic conj. —— **viāe,** gen. sing. of *via,* f., 1st; objective gen., with *auxilium*; *viae* here = *itineris.* —— **veterēs,** acc. plur. m. of *vetus,* gen. *veteris,* adj. 3d; agrees with *thesauros.* For distinction between *vetus* and *antiquus,* see *veteris,* l. 23. —— **tellūre,** abl. sing. of *tellūs, tellūris,* f., 3d; abl. of separation after *recludit*; in prose *e tellure* would be necessary. Many translate *tellure* as (*treasures long-hidden*) *in the ground,* making it an abl. of 'place where'; there is little to choose between the two renderings '*from the ground*' and '*in the ground.*' —— **reclūdit,** 3d pers. sing. pres. ind. act. of *reclūdō, -ere, reclūsī, reclūsum,* 3 (*re, = back,* + *claudō, = I close,* hence *discloses*); joined by *que* to *suadet.* Verbs compounded with *re* often take the abl. of separation.

LINE 359. **Thēsaurōs,** acc. plur. of *thēsaurus, -ī,* m., 2d (a Greek word, θησαυρός); direct obj. of *recludit.* —— **ignōtum,** acc. sing. n. of *ignōtus, -a, -um,* adj. (*in, = not,* + *nōtus, = known*); agrees with *pondus.* —— **argentī,** gen. sing. of *argentum,* n., 2d (from root ARG transposed from RAJ, = *to shine* ; cf. Sanskrit *rajatam = silver,* and Greek ἄργ-υρος); gen. of substance or material. A. & G. 214, *e*; B. 197; G. 361; H. 395. —— **pondus,** acc. sing. of *pondus, ponderis,* n., 3d (from *pendo, = I weigh*) ; in apposition with *thesauros.* —— **et,** cop. conj. —— **aurī,** gen. sing. of *aurum,* n., 2d (lit. *the burning* i.e. *shining thing,* from a root found in Greek αὔρον); gen. of substance, joined by *et* to *argenti.*

LINE 360. **Hīs,** abl. plur. n. of demonstr. pron. *hīc, haec, hōc*; abl. of the means or instrument, with *commota* ; *his* refers to the revelations and instructions spoken by the phantom of Sychaeus to Dido. —— **commōta,** nom. sing. f. of *commōtus, -a, -um,* perf. part. pass. of *commoveō, -ēre, commōvī, commōtum,* 2 (*cum* + *moveō*); agrees with and enlarges the subj. *Dido,* and = a *causal clause, cum commōta esset.* —— **fugam,** acc. sing.

com,móta fu,gám „ Di,dó soci,ósque　　pa,rábat. | Dido strove to win
moved　　　*flight*　　*Dido and companions was preparing.* | escape and a fol-
361 Cónveni,únt,　　　quibus　,　aút　odi,úm „ | lowing. Those meet
They come together,　*to whom*　*either*　*hatred* | together who had
362 cru,déle　ty,ránni　Aút　metus　,　ácer | cruel hatred or keen
cruel　*of the tyrant*　*or*　*fear*　*sharp* | fear of the tyrant ;
e,rát; „ na,vés,　quae , fórte　pa,rátae, | they seize ships that
there was ;　*ships,*　*which*　*by chance (were) prepared,* | by chance lay ready,

---

of *fuga, -ae,* f., 1st; direct obj. of *parabat.* —— **Dīdō,** gen. *Dīdōnis* or *Dīdūs,* f.; subj.
of *parabat.* —— **sociōs,** acc. plur. of *socius, -ī,* m., 2d; joined by *que* to *fugam.* Observe
that *parabat = was preparing for* with *fugam,* but = *was collecting* with *socios,* an instance
of *zeugma.* A. & G. 385; B. 374, 2, *a*; G. 690; H. 636, II, 1. —— **que,** enclitic conj.
—— **parābat,** 3d pers. sing. imperf. ind. act. of *parō, -āre, -āvī, -ātum,* 1; agrees with
the subj. *Dido.*
　　LINE 361.　**Conveniunt,** 3d pers. plur. pres. ind. act. of *conveniō, -īre, convēnī, con-
ventum,* 4 irreg. (*con + veniō*); agrees with the subj.-nom. *ii* understood. When a
demonstrative pronoun is the antecedent of a relative, it is frequently omitted. ——
quibus, dat. plur. m. of *quī;* agrees with the unexpressed antecedent *ii,* and dat. of the
indirect obj. after *odium . . . erat.* —— **aut,** disjunctive conj., and repeated below =
either . . . or. See the note on *aut,* l. 183. —— **odium,** gen. *odii,* n., 2d; subj. of *erat*
in the rel. clause. —— **crūdēle,** nom. sing. n. of *crūdēlis, -e,* adj., 3d (akin to *cruor,
crudus,* etc., and = *raw,* hence figuratively of wounds fresh or still unhealed); quali-
fies *odium.* The poets constantly qualify abstract ideas with adjectives expressing a
personal quality, but some editors consider *odium crudele tyranni* an instance of *hypal-
lage* (= *odium crudelis tyranni*). *Hypallage* is an interchange of construction, espe-
cially of cases of nouns and adjectives; cf. Aen. VIII, 526, *Tyrrhenusque tubae clangor*
(= *Tyrrhenae tubae*). A. & G. 385; B. no reference; G. 693, HYPALLAGE; H. 636, IV,
2. —— **tyrannī,** gen. sing. of *tyrannus,* m., 2d (Greek τύραννος); objective gen. gov-
erned by the notion of *agency* in *odium.* The Greek word originally signified an *absolute
ruler,* especially one who rose to supreme power from among the ranks of the people, as
opposed to a hereditary king, βασιλεύς; the idea of *oppression* was acquired by *tyrannus*
through the general misgovernment of the Greek tyrants.
　　LINE 362.　**Aut,** disjunctive conj., introducing the alternative motive *metus.* ——
metus, gen. *metūs,* m., 4th (*metuō = I fear*); nom. sing., joined by *aut* to *odium.*
Synonyms : *timor = fear,* the generic word simply expressing the emotion without added
implication, and defined by Cicero as *metus mali appropinquantis ; metus = fear* of
imminent peril, defined by Cicero as *opinio impendentis* (*et intolerabilis*) *mali ; pavor =
fear* of a stupefying kind, which Cicero calls *metus loco movens mentem ; formido = a
lasting fear* (*metus permanens :* Cicero). —— **ācer,** nom. sing. m. of *ācer, ācris, ācre,*
adj., 3d (from AC, root of *acuō = I sharpen ;* hence *sharp, keen, eager*); qualifies *metus.*
—— **erat,** 3d pers. sing. imperf. ind. act. of *sum, esse, fuī;* agrees with each of the dis-
joined subjects, *odium* and *metus.* —— **nāvēs,** acc. plur. of *nāvis, -is,* f., 3d; direct obj.
of *corripiunt.* —— **quae,** nom. plur. f. of the rel. pron. *qui, quae, quod ;* agrees with the
antecedent *naves,* and is subj.-nom. of *paratae* (*sunt*). —— **forte,** abl. sing. of *fors,
fortis,* f., 3d; abl. of manner, and by reason of its constant use in this one way practi-
cally an adverb. —— **parātae,** nom. plur. f. of *parātus, -a, -um,* perf. part. pass. of *parō,
-āre, -āvī, -ātum,* 1; agrees with subj. *quae,* of which it is the predicate with *sunt* under-
stood (3d pers. plur. perf. ind. pass. of *parō*).

and load them | Córripi,únt, one,rántqu*e* au,ró. , Por,tántur 363*
with the gold; the
wealth of the grasper | *they seize,* and load *with gold.* *Are carried*
Pygmalion is car- | a,vári Pýgmali,ónis o,pés pela,gó; ,, dux , 364
ried over seas; a
woman leads the | *avaricious of Pygmalion the riches on the sea; (is) leader*
emprise. They came | fémina , fácti. Déve,nére lo,cós, ,, ubi , núnc 365
to the place where | *a woman of the deed. They reached places, where now*

LINE 363. **Corripiunt**, 3d pers. plur. pres. ind. act. of *corripiō, -ere, corripuī, correptum,* 3 (*con + rapiō*); agrees with the implied subj. *ii* (i.e. *socii Didonis).*—— **onerant**, 3d pers. plur. pres. ind. act. of *onerō, -āre, -āvī, -ātum,* 1 (from *onus, oneris,* n., 3d, = *a burden*); joined by *que* to *corripiunt;* the object of *onerant* is *naves* understood. The construction after *onero* is either acc. of the thing loaded and the abl. of that with which it is loaded, or the dat. of the thing loaded and the acc. of that with which it is loaded; cf. (*onerarat*) *vina cadis,* l. 195, and references.—— **que,** enclitic conj.—— **aurō,** abl. sing. of *aurum, -ī,* n., 2d; abl. of the instrument.—— **portántur**, 3d pers. plur. pres. ind. pass. of *portō, -āre, -āvī, -ātum,* 1; agrees with its subj. *opes.* Observe how the *asyndeton* intensifies the crispness of the description. —— **avārī,** gen. sing. m. of *avārus, -a, -um;* qualifies *Pygmaliōnis.*

LINE 364. **Pygmaliōnis,** gen. sing. of *Pygmaliōn,* m., 3d; poss. gen., limiting *opes.* —— **opēs,** nom. plur. f., 3d (nom. sing. *Ops* only as name of a goddess; acc. *opem,* gen. *opis,* abl. *ope*); sub. of *portantur.* *Opēs Pygmaliōnis* = the buried riches of Sychaeus which Pygmalion regarded as his own property after committing the murder to gain them; *opes* very often includes much more than money, in fact all the *resources* of power, such as arms, men, etc. —— **pelagō,** abl. sing. of *pelagus, -ī,* n., 2d; abl. of 'place over which,' an extension of the locative ablative.—— **dux,** gen. *dúcis,* m. or f., 3d (*dūcō* = *I lead*); complement of *est* understood in the predicate *dux* (*est*), in the same case as the subj. *femina.* —— **fēmina,** gen. *fēminae,* f., 1st (from *feo,* = *I produce*); nom. sing., subj. of *dux* (*est*); *femina* refers to Dido. —— **factī,** gen. sing. of *factum,* n., 2d; a subjective gen., limiting *dux.*

LINE 365. **Dēvēnēre,** 3d pers. plur. perf. ind. act. of *dēvēniō, -īre, aēvēnī,* no supine, 4 irreg. (*dē,* = *down,* + *veniō,* = *I come;* hence *arrive*); the subj. is a pron. understood, referring to Dido and her followers. From very early times the perfect tense had two endings, in *ērunt* and *ēre;* the former is usual in classical prose, and the latter, which was a popular form, is very common in poetry, as it lends itself readily to the hexameter and other metres. —— **locōs,** acc. plur. of *locus, -ī,* m., 2d (two plural forms, *loci,* m., and *loca,* n.); acc. of 'place to which.' In prose, *ad* or *in* with the accusative would be necessary, but poets very often put the name of the 'place to which' in the accusative without a preposition; in this and some other instances Vergil puts the actual place (apart from its name) in the accusative. This construction is an extension of the ordinary rule respecting the names of towns and small islands; e.g. *Romam* = *to Rome;* so some other words, e.g. *domum* = (*to*) *home, rus* = *to the country.* A. & G. 258, *b,* NOTE 5; B. 182, 4 and 5; G. 337; H. 380, 3. —— **ubi,** adv. of place, relative to *locos* (= *in quibus*). For other uses of *ubi,* refer to the note on l. 81. —— **nūnc,** adv. of time. —— **ingentia,** acc. plur. n. of *ingens, -entis,* adj., 3d; qualifies *moenia.* —— **cernis,** 2d pers. sing. pres. ind. act. of *cernō, -ere, crēvī, crētum,* 3; the implied subj. *tu* refers to Aeneas, whom Venus is addressing. The present tense is more suitable than *cernes,* the future which some MSS. read; *nunc* has more meaning with the present, and "where you see" is a common colloquial use of the present to which the arguments of the impossibility of seeing Carthage through the intervening mountain does not apply; poets are

866 in,géntia , cérnis **Mœnia** , súrgen,témque , no,væ
immense *you see* *walls* *and rising* *new*
867 Car,tháginis , árcem, **Mérca**,tíque so,lúm, „
of Carthage *the citadel,* *and bought* *ground,*
868 fac,tí de , nómine , Býrsam, Taúri,nó
of the deed from *the name* *(called) Byrsa,* *bull's*
quan,túm „ pos,sént cir,cúmdare , térgo.
as much as *they could* *enclose* *with a hide.*

thou now seest the vast walls and rising citadel of new Carthage, and bought ground (called Byrsa from the buying), as much as they might compass about with a bull's hide.

rarely exact or altogether consistent in such prose affairs as geographical description and the like.

LINE 366. **Moenia**, acc. of the plural noun *moenia, -ium*, n., 3d ; direct obj. of *cernis ; moenia* always = *city-walls*, or *walls* of a fortified place. —— **surgentem**, acc. sing. f. of *surgens, -entis*, pres. part. act. of *surgō, -ĕre, surrēxī, surrectum*, 3 ; qualifies *arcem* attributively. —— **que**, enclitic conj. —— **novae**, gen. sing. f. of *novus, -a, -um ;* qualifies *Carthāginis*. —— **Carthāginis**, gen. sing. of *Carthāgō* (f., 3d ; poss. gen. limiting *arcem*. This name is made up of two Phoenician words, and = *new town*. —— **arcem**, acc. sing. of *arx, arcis*, f., 3d ; direct obj. of *cernis*, joined by *que* to *moenia*. It was always the Greek custom to build a new settlement round a hill capable of being fortified.

LINE 367. **Mercātī**, nom. plur. m. of *mercātus, -a, -um*, perf. part. of the dep. verb *mercor, -āri, -ātus sum*, 1 *(mercēs = pay);* with *mercati* understand *sunt* (3d pers. plur. perf. ind.) ; this verb is joined by *que* to *devenere*, l. 365. —— **que**, enclitic conj., joining *devenere* and *mercati (sunt)*. —— **solum**, acc. sing. of *solum, -ī*, n., 2d (probably from a root SOL, signifying that upon which anything rested or was set) ; direct obj. of *mercati (sunt)*. —— **factī**, gen. sing. of *factum*, n., 2d ; poss. gen., limiting *nomine ; facti* refers to what is described in the next line. —— **dē**, prep. with the abl.; gov. *nōmine*. *De* with *nomine* indicates *source : de* is used = *down from*, of place; of the *whole* from which a part is taken, e.g. *partem solido demere de die ;* of the object, = *concerning*, and in other ways. A. & G. 153; B. 142; G. 417, 5; H. 434, I. —— **nōmine**, abl. sing. of *nōmen, nōminis*, n., 3d (from *nosco*, = *I know*) ; governed by *de*. —— **Býrsam**, acc. sing. of *Býrsa, -ae*, f., 1st (Greek Βύρσα = *a hide*) ; in apposition with *solum*. The origin of the name Byrsa, as Vergil derives it, is purely fanciful. The original name was *Bosra*, a Phoenician word which = *citadel ;* this the Greeks, by *metathesis*, or change in the position of letters, altered to Βύρσα, and as the original meaning of the name passed out of memory, Vergil is afforded an opportunity of inventing an origin, and takes the Greek noun which = *a hide* to work upon in the process. Very many names and legends in the history of Greece and Rome are inventions, intended to explain something already existing; thus *Romulus* explains *Roma ;* so the legend of Arion and the dolphin was invented to explain a picture representing Arion riding on a dolphin's back.

LINE 368. **Taurīnō**, abl. sing. n. of *taurīnus, -a, -um* (adj. formed from the noun *taurus, -ī*, m., 2d = *a bull*) ; agrees with *tergo*. —— **quantum**, acc. sing. n. of *quantus, -a, -um ;* agrees with *solum*, and is direct obj. of *circumdare* in the clause *taurino . . . tergo; quantum* is the correlative of a demonstrative *tantum* which may be understood with *solum*, but *tantus* is very often omitted before *quantus* as *talis* before its correlative *qualis*. —— **possent**, 3d pers. plur. imperf. subjunct. of *possum, posse, potui ;* its implied subj. is a pron. *ii* or *illi* referring to the new colonists. The verb is subjunctive because " as much as they could encircle," etc., is quoted from the arrangement made; the sub-

But who, pray, are ye? from what coasts are ye come ? or whither shape ye your course ?" At her question he sighed and drawing utterance from the deep of his breast, with this replied :

Séd vos , quí tan,dém, „ quibus , aút ve,nístis 369
But you (are) who at length,   what   or have you come

ab , óris,   Quóve   te,nétis   i,tér ? " „ 370
from shores,   or whither   do you hold   your journey ?"

Quae,rénti ,   tálibus ,   ílle   Súspi,ráns, 371
To (her) inquiring   with such (words)   he   sighing,

i,móque   tra,héns „ a , péctore , vócem:
and lowest   drawing   from   his breast   his voice

junctive is used when some *explanatory* statement or some thought in the mind of the speaker is introduced by a relative adjective or adverb, and the construction is called *virtual oratio obliqua*, or informal indirect discourse. A. & G. 341, *d*; B. 323; G. 628; H. page 289, footnote 2. For the conjugation of *possum*, consult A. & G. 137, *b*; B. 126; G. 119; H. 290.——circumdare, pres. inf. act. of *circumdō, -āre, circumdedi, circumdatum*, 1 (*circum* + *do*); *prolative* inf., completing the meaning of *possent*. The construction after *circumdare* may be either acc. and abl. *aliquid aliqua re* (as here) or acc. and dat. *aliquid alicui rei.*——tergō, abl. sing. of *tergum, -ī*, n., 2d; abl. of the instrument. *Tergo* = *hide*, the usual meaning of *tergus, -oris*, n., whereas *tergum* commonly = *back.* The tale alluded to in this passage is that the natives sold to the Phoenician settlers as much land as they could enclose with the skin of an ox, and the Phoenicians cunningly cut the hide into narrow strips and were thus enabled to enclose sufficient land to build a settlement and citadel.

LINE 369. **Sed**, adversative conj., introducing a new subject of discussion.——**vōs,** gen. *vestrum* or *vestri ;* nom. of the 2d personal pron. plur., subj. in the question *qui vos* (*estis*)? The pronoun is expressed for the sake of emphasis.——**quī,** nom. plur. m. of the interrog. pron. *quis, quae, quid;* agrees with *vos.*——**tandem,** adv., included in the sentence to emphasize it; cf. *tandem*, l. 331.——**quibus,** abl. plur. f. of the interrog. adj. *quī, quae, quod ;* agrees with *oris.*——**aut,** disjunctive conj., connecting the question *quibus ab oris venistis* with the one immediately before it.——**vēnistis,** 2d pers. plur. perf. ind. act. of *veniō, -īre, vēnī, ventum,* 4 irreg.; *vōs* is understood as subject. ——**ab,** prep. with the abl.; gov. *oris ;* see *ab,* l. 1.——**ōrīs,** abl. plur. of *ōra, -ae,* f., 1st; governed by *ab.*

LINE 370. **Quōve** (*quō* + *ve*). *Quō* is the adverbial abl. sing. n. of *qui,* and = *whither.* It is used either interrogatively as here; or relatively = *to which* place, often as correlative of the demonstrative *eo* = *thither.* *Ve* is an enclitic disjunctive conj., joining the question introduced by *quō* with the preceding one; *ve* is a weaker form of *vel.* For distinctions between *ve, aut,* and *sive,* refer to note on *ve,* l. 9.——**tenētis,** 2d pers. plur. pres. ind. act. of *teneō, -ēre, tenuī, tentum,* 2; supply *vōs* as subject.——**iter,** gen. *itineris,* n., 3d; acc. sing., direct object of *tenetis.*——**quaerēntī,** dat. sing. f. of *quaerēns, -ēntis,* pres. part. act. of *quaerō, -ere, quaesīvī, quaesītum,* 3; dat. of the indirect obj. after the understood verb of *saying,* of which *ille* is subject; *quaerenti* agrees with *illi* (dat. f. sing.) understood, = *to her questioning,* etc.——**tālibus,** abl. plur. n. of *tālis, -e ;* abl. of the instrument, substantival or agreeing with *verbis* understood.—— **ille,** gen. *illīus,* dat. *illī ;* nom. sing. m. of *ille, illa, illud,* subj. of *dixit* or some verb of *saying* understood.

LINE 371. **Suspīrāns,** gen. *suspīrāntis ;* nom. sing. m. of the pres. part. act. of *suspīrō, -āre, -āvī, -ātum,* 1 (*sub,* = *from under,* + *spīrō,* = *I breathe,* hence *I sigh*) ; agrees with and enlarges the subj. *ille.*——**īmō,** abl. sing. n. of *īmus, -a, -um* (superl.

372 " **Ó** dea , sí pri,má „ repe,téns   ab o,rígine ,
   "O goddess, if   first   seeking back from the origin

373 pérgam,   **Ét**   vacet   ,   ánna,lés „
   I should proceed, and (if) there were time   the records

374 nos,tró*rum* au,díre la,bórum,   **Á**nte   di,ém
   our   to hear   of labors,   before (that) the day

"O goddess, if I should tell all, retracing from the earliest beginnings, and thou hadst leisure to hear the record of our woes, sooner would evening

---

adj. from preposition *infrā;* comparative *inferior*) *;* agrees partitively with *pectore.* ——
que, enclitic conj. —— **trahēns,** nom. sing. m. of the pres. part. act. of *trahō, -ere,*
trāxī, tractum, 3; joined by *que* to *suspīrāns.* —— **ā,** prep. with the abl.; gov. *pectore.*
—— **pectore,** abl. sing. of *pectus, pectoris,* n., 3d; governed by *a,* expressing ' place from
which.' —— **vōcem,** acc. sing. of *vōx, vōcis,* f., 3d; direct obj♦ of *trahēns.*

    Line 372. **O,** exclamation, with the voc. *dea.* —— **dea,** voc. sing. of *dea, -ae,* f., 1st;
the case of address. Aeneas appears to have ignored Venus' repudiation of divinity, l.
336. —— **sī,** conditional conj., introducing the *protasis, pergam et vacet;* the *apodosis* or
main clause begins on l. 374. —— **prīmā,** abl. sing. f. of *primus, -a, -um;* qualifies *orī-*
gine. —— **repetēns,** nom. sing. m. of the pres. part. act. of *repetō, -ere, repet-īvī* or *-iī,*
repetītum, 3 (*re,* = *back,* + *petō,* = *I seek,* hence *I trace back;* sometimes *re* = *again,* and
repeto then = *I resume*) *;* joined by *que* to *suspirans.*   *Repetens ab origine prima*
= *searching back (into the story) from its earliest beginning.* —— **ab,** prep. with the
abl.; gov. *origine.* —— **orīgine,** abl. sing. of *orīgo, -inis,* f., 3d (from *orior,* = *I arise*) *;*
governed by *ab.* —— **pergam,** 1st pers. sing. pres. subjunct. act. of *pergō, -ere, perrexī,*
perrectum, 3 (*per,* intensive, + *regō* = *I direct,* hence, *I continue*) *;* the implied subj.
is *ego* (i.e. Aeneas); *si pergam* = *if I should proceed (to narrate),* and the present sub-
junctive is the ordinary tense and mood of imaginary conditions respecting the future,
followed regularly by the present subjunctive *componat* in the *apodosis.* A. & G. 307, 2
and *b*; B. 303; G. 596, 1; H. 509.

    Line 373. **Et,** cop. conj., connecting the clauses *si pergam* and *si vacet.* —— **vacet,**
3d pers. sing. pres. subjunct. act. of *vacō, -āre, -āvī, -ātum,* 1; *vacet* is impersonal (*if*
there should be leisure), and is a similar subjunctive to *pergam,* with which it is connected
by *et.* —— **annālēs,** acc. of the plural noun *annālēs, -ium,* m., 3d (properly from the
adj. *annālis* (abl. *annāli*), *pertaining to a year*) *;* direct obj. of *audire.* The *Annales*
was the name given to the records of public events kept by the priests, and was extended
to other historical records, e.g. the Annals of the historian Tacitus. —— **nostrōrum,** gen.
plur. m. of *noster, nostra, nostrum,* pronominal poss. adj. of the 1st pers. plur.; agrees
with *laborum.* —— **audīre,** pres. inf. act. of *audiō, -ire, -īvī, -ītum,* 4; *prolative* inf.,
completing the meaning of *vacet.* —— **labōrum,** gen. plur. of *labor, -ōris,* m., 3d;
objective gen. after *annālēs.*

    Line 374. **Ante,** adv. of time; *anteā* is the regular adverb, *ante* being commonly a
preposition with the accusative, but cf. *ante . . . quam;* here there is a relative clause
understood, *before* (*I could finish the story*). —— **diem,** acc. sing. of *diēs, diei,* f., 5th;
m. always in the plur. and usually in the sing.; direct obj. of *componat.* —— **clausō,** abl.
sing. m. of *clausus, -a, -um,* perf. part. pass. of *claudō, -ere, clausī, clausum,* 3; agrees
with *Olympo* in the abl. abs. construction. A. & G. 255; B. 227; G. 409, 410; H. 431.
—— **compōnat,** 3d pers. sing. pres. subjunct. of *compōnō, -ere, composuī, compositum,* 3
(*cum* + *pōnō*) *;* agrees with the subj. *Vesper,* and is the regular pres. subjunct. in the
apodosis of ideal or less vivid future conditions; see note and references on *pergam*
above. Some good MSS. read *componet,* the future indicative, and there are examples
of this in future conditions, but the future is only used when the speaker or writer wishes

lay the day to rest	clau,só	„	com,pónat	,	Vésper	O,lýmpo.
and close the gates	*having been shut*		*would end*		*evening*	*Olympus.*
of heaven. Us, as we						
sailed from ancient	Nós Tro,ia	ánti,quá,	„	si	, véstras	, fórte 875
Troy (if haply the	*Us from Troy*	*ancient,*		*if*	*your*	*by chance*
name of Troy has	per	, aúres	Tróiae	,	nómen	i, ít, „ 876
passed through your	*through*	*your ears*	*of Troy*		*the name*	*has gone,*
ears) over strange						
seas the storm at its	di, vérsa	per	, æquora	,	véctos	Fórte su, á 877
own wild caprice has	*various*	*through*	*seas*		*carried*	*by chance its own*

to represent that something not merely *might* but *will* happen. However, Aeneas does not intend speaking at length, so *componat* is at once more regular and more suitable; it is a well-supported reading, and is adopted by the best editors. —— **Vesper,** gen. *vesperis* or *vesperī,* m., 3d and 2d; nom. sing., subj. of *componat;* Vesper is the evening star (= Greek ἕσπερος, in which the rough breathing is compensation for an original *digamma*). The abl. of *vesper* is *vespere, vesperi* being a locative case = *in the evening.* For declension, consult A. & G. 41, *b;* B. 23, 2; G. 68, 10; H. 51, 4, and 62, NOTE 2. —— **Olympō,** abl. sing. of *Olympus, -ī,* m., 2d; abl. abs. with *clauso;* the idea of eve closing the gates of heaven and dawn opening them is derived from the shutting and opening of city-gates. Olympus was the vague abode of the gods; it is commonly identified in Greek myth with Mount Olympus, on the borders of Thessaly and Macedonia, its top reaching to heaven, and untouched by wind, rain, or clouds.

LINE 375. **Nōs,** acc. of *nōs,* gen. *nostrum* or *nostrī,* plur. of 1st personal pron.; direct obj. of *appulit.* —— **Trōiā,** abl. sing. of *Trōia, -ae,* f., 1st; abl. of separation, dependent on *vectos.* 'Place from which' is expressed by the abl. with a prep. *ab, de,* or *ex,* but the names of towns or small islands are put in the abl. without a preposition; thus *Troia = from Troy,* but if one wished to write *from the city of Troy,* it would be *ex* or *ab urbe Troia,* the addition of *urbe* rendering a preposition necessary. A. & G. 258, *a ;* B. 229, 1, *a ;* G. 391 ; H. 428, II. —— **antīquā,** abl. sing. f. of *antīquus, -a, -um ;* qualifies *Trōiā.* —— **sī,** conditional conj., in the *protasis* with *iit.* —— **vestrās,** acc. plur. f. of *vester, vestra, vestrum ;* agrees with *aurēs ;* the plural poss. adj. *vestrās = your own and those of your people.* —— **forte,** abl. sing. of *fors, fortis.* f., 3d ; adverbial abl. of manner ; very common in combination with *si* and *ne,* modifying the directness of the clauses they introduce. —— **per,** prep. with the acc.; gov. *aures.* —— **aurēs,** acc. plur. of *auris, -is,* f., 3d ; governed by *per.*

LINE 376. **Trōiae,** gen sing. of *Trōia,* f., 1st ; poss. gen., limiting *nōmen.* —— **nōmen,** gen. *nōminis,* n., 3d ; nom. sing., subj. of *iit.* —— **iit,** 3d per. sing. perf. ind. act. of *eō, īre, īvī* or *iī, itum,* irreg. (for conjugation, see *it,* l. 246); agrees with the subj. *nomen ;* the indicative mood signifies that Aeneas had no doubt that the maiden was acquainted with the name of Troy, and indeed the conditional clause is expressive of Aeneas' Trojan modesty. —— **dīversa,** acc. plur. n. of *dīversus, -a, -um ;* agrees with *aequora.* —— **per,** prep. with the acc.; gov. *aequora.* —— **aequora,** acc. plur. of *aequor, -is,* n., 3d ; governed by *per ;* the plural for singular is frequent in poetry. —— **vectōs,** acc. plur. m. of *vectus, -a, -um,* perf. part. pass. of *vehō, -ere, vēxī, vectum,* 3 ; agrees with *nōs,* the obj. of *appulit ; nōs vectōs appulit* exemplifies the use of a predicate participle. —— **vectōs,** instead of two coördinate sentences, e.g. *nōs vexit et appulit.* A. & G. 292, REM.; B. 337, 2 ; G. 437 ; H. 549, 5.

LINE 377. **Forte,** abl. sing. of *fors, fortis,* f., 3d ; abl. of manner, and not the adverb *forte,* as on l. 375, above. —— **suā,** abl. sing. f. of *suus, -a, -um,* poss. adj. of the reflexive

378 Liby‚cís „ tem‚péstas , áppulit ,   óris.   Súm
   Libyan   *the storm*   *has driven to the shores.*   *I am*

pius , Aéne‚ás, „ rap‚tós quí ex ,   hóste
dutiful   *Aeneas,*   „   *seized* *who* *from the enemy*

379 pe‚nátes   Clásse   ve‚hó   mē‚cúm,   „
   the household gods *in the fleet* *am carrying*   *with me,*

380 fa‚má super , æthera , nótus. Ítali‚ám quae‚ro „
   in glory above the upper air known.   *Italy*   *I seek*

driven onto the Li-
byan shores. Aeneas
the good am I, who
bear with me in my
fleet my household
gods rescued from
the enemy, known by
fame in heaven above.
I seek the Italy

---

pron. of the 3d person ; agrees with *forte ; forte suā* is analogous to *sponte suā*, and = *by
its own* (i.e. the storm's) caprice. A. & G. 196 ; B. 86, 1, and 244 ; G. 309 ; H. 449.
—— **Libycīs,** dat. plur. f. of *Libycus, -a, -um* (adj. of the noun *Libya*) ; agrees with
ōrīs. —— **tempestās,** gen. *tempestātis,* f., 3d ; nom. sing., subj. of *appulit.* —— **appulit,**
3d pers. sing. perf. ind. act. of *appellō (adpellō), -ere, appulī, appulsum,* 3 (*ad,* = *towards,*
+ *pellō,* = *I drive*) ; agrees with the subj. *tempestās.* —— **ōrīs,** dat. plur. of *ōra, -ae,* f.,
1st ; dat. of the indirect obj. after *appulit,* as a compound of *ad.*   A. & G. 228 ;
B. 187, III ; G. 347 ; H. 386.   In prose *ad ōrās* would probably have been written, but
it is not strictly necessary to take *oris* as a dat. of ' place to which.'

    LINE 378.   **Sum,** 1st pers. sing. pres. ind. of *sum, esse, fuī ;* the implied subj. is *ego.* ——
pius, nom. sing m. adj.; qualifies *Aeneas ;* the almost titular epithet of the hero. This
revelation of Aeneas' identity by himself is imitated from Homer, with whose heroes it
was an indispensable rule of etiquette to make themselves known to their hosts after
receiving the first honors of hospitality ; Homer's heroes regularly apply to themselves
those qualities for which they were well known, e.g. Odysseus is a *soi-disant* ' man of
guile.' —— **Aeneās,** gen. *Aenēae,* m., 1st ; decl. Greek noun ; nom. sing., *complement* of
the copula *sum* in the predicate. —— **raptōs,** acc. plur. m. of *raptus, -a, -um,* perf. part.
pass. of *rapiō, -ere, rapuī, raptum,* 3 ; agrees with *Penates ; raptos* is a predicate parti-
ciple similar to *vectos* above, and *Penates raptos veho* = *Penates rapui et veho.* —— **quī,**
nom. sing. m. of the rel. pron.; agrees with its antecedent *Aeneās,* and is subj. of *vehō.*
—— **ēx,** prep. with the abl. ; gov. *hoste ; ex hoste* = *from the midst of the enemy.   Ex* =
oui of the interior ; ab = *from the frontier.* —— **hoste,** abl. sing. of *hostis, -is,* m. and f.,
3d ; governed by *ex. Hostis* = *a public enemy,* i.e. the enemy of a country ; *inimicus*
= *a private* or *personal enemy.* —— **Penātēs,** acc. plur. of *Penātēs, -ium,* m., 3d (no sing.);
direct obj. of *vehō.*   This introduction is not intended to be boasting, though it has the
true and single-minded ring of its Greek models.

    LINE 379.   **Classe,** abl. sing. of *classis, -is,* f., 3d; abl. of the means or instrument.
—— **vehō,** 1st pers. sing. pres. ind. act. of *vehō, -ere, vexī, vectum,* 3; agrees with its
subj. *quī.* —— **mēcum** (*mē + cum*), *mē* is abl. of *ego ;* governed by the enclitic prep. *cum.
Cum,* prep. with the abl., regularly appended to personal, reflexive, and relative pro-
nouns. A. & G. 99, *e,* and 104, *e;* B. 142, 4; G. 413, REM. 1; H. 184, 6, and 187, 2. ——
fāmā, abl. sing. of *fāma, -ae,* f., 1st (Greek φήμη, lit. *a saying,* hence *rumor ; renown*
is a derived meaning); abl. of manner extending *notus.* —— **super,** prep. with the acc.
or abl.; gov. the acc. *aethera.* —— **aethera,** acc. sing. of *aether, -is,* m., 3d (Greek
αἰθήρ); governed by *super.* The acc. *aethera* and the gen. *aetheros* are Greek forms.
Aether is the *upper air,* as opposed to *aër, the lower air.* —— **nōtus,** nom. sing. m. of
nōtus, -a, -um, adj. (properly perf. part. pass. of *noscō, -ere, nōvī, nōtum,* 3); agrees with
the subj. of *sum,* viz. *ego* or the complement *Aeneas.*

    LINE 380.   **Ītaliam,** acc. sing. of *Ītalia, -ae,* f., 1st; direct obj. of *quaerō.* ——
quaerō, 1st pers. sing. pres. ind. act. of *quaerō, -ere, quaesīvī, quaesītum,* 3 ; understand

of my sires and my ancestry of the line of Jove supreme.	patri, *am,* ét genus , áb Iove, súmmo.
	(my) ancestral, and the race (sprung) from Jupiter highest.
With twice ten ships I climbed the Phryg-ian main, pursuing destinies revealed, my goddess mother pointing out the way;	Bís de, nís Phrygi, úm ,, con, scéndi , návibus , 381
	Twice ten Phrygian I climbed with ships
	æquor, Mátre de, á mon, stránte vi, ám, ,, 382
	the sea, my mother goddess pointing out the way,

---

ego, referring to Aeneas, as subject. —— **patriam,** acc. sing. f. of *patrius, -a, -um ;* quali-fies *Italiam ; patriam* may be taken as acc. of the noun *patria* and in apposition with *Italiam.* —— **et,** cop. conj., connecting the two objects, *Italiam* and *genus.* Before Wagner inserted *et,* editors used to place a semicolon after *patriam ;* the *genus* was taken as nom , = *descendant,* and an appositive of the subj. of *conscendi,* and *genus* was an awkward allusion to Aeneas' descent from Jove. —— **genus,** acc. sing. of *genus, generis,* n., 3d; direct obj. of *quaero,* joined by *et* to *Italiam. Quaero genus* may = (1) *I seek my descent,* i.e. the country of my ancestors, or better (2) *I seek my lineage,* i.e. *the race* (descended) *from Jupiter.* —— **ab,** prep. with the abl., here expressing origin; gov. *Iove.* —— **Iove,** abl. sing. of *Iūpiter,* gen. *Iovis,* m., 3d; governed by *ab ;* in prose a participle would be required agreeing with *genus,* e.g. *genus (ortum) ab Iove,* but *genus* by its derivation from *geno* (old form of *gigno*) has a quasi-verbal signification of origin. —— **summō,** abl. sing. m. of *summus, -a, -um* (superl. adj. formed from prep. *suprā*)*;* agrees with *Iove ; summo* is not partitive, but = *highest,* as Jupiter's throne was on the pinnacle of heaven, or perhaps = *most mighty.* The allusion in this line is to the legend that Dardanus, the son of Jupiter and Electra, and the ancestor of Aeneas, was born in Italy, at Corythus (later called Cortona), a town of Etruria. Dardanus is said to have migrated across northern Greece and settled in the Troad in Asia Minor. Aeneas traced his origin back to Jupiter through Anchises, Capys, Assaracus, Tros, Ericthonius, and Dardanus.

LINE 381. **Bis** (= *duis,* from *duo*), numeral adv., multiplying *denis.* —— **dēnīs,** abl. plur. f. of *dēnī, -ae, -a,* distributive numeral adj.; agrees with *navibus ; bis denis* = *viginti.* Observe that Vergil uses the distributive *denis* instead of the cardinal *decem.* —— **Phrygium,** acc. sing. n. of *Phrygius, -a, -um* (adj. of noun *Phrygia*)*;* agrees with *aequor.* —— **cōnscendī,** 1st pers. sing. perf. ind. act. of *cōnscendō, -ere, cōnscendī, cōn-scensum,* 3 (*con* + *scandō* = *I climb*)*; ego* is implied as subject. *Conscendere* = *to climb,* and is common in the phrase *navem conscendere* = (lit., *to climb the ship*) *to embark ;* hence some translate here *I embarked* OVER *the Phrygian sea,* regarding *aequor* as an accusative of *extension over ;* but it. is preferable to render *I climbed the sea,* for the ancients always thought of ships leaving harbor as *going up* the sea, and of ships enter-ing harbor as *going down* the sea (Greek ἀνάγομαι, compound of ἀνά = *up,* = *I put out to sea ;* so κατάγειν = *to bring to land,* from κατά = *down*). —— **nāvibus,** abl. plur. of *nāvis, -is,* f., 3d; abl. of the means or instrument with *conscendi.* —— **aequor,** acc. sing. of *aequor, -is,* n., 3d; direct obj. of *conscendi.*

LINE 382. **Mātre,** abl. sing. of *māter, mātris,* f., 3d (Greek μήτηρ); in the abl. abs. construction with *monstrante.* —— **deā,** abl. sing. of *dea, -ae,* f., 1st; in apposition with *matre,* which it modifies, as if = *to divina ;* the allusion is to Venus, the unrecognized interlocutor of Aeneas. —— **monstrānte,** abl. sing. f. of the pres. part. act. of *monstrō, -āre, -āvī, -ātum,* 1; agrees with *mātre* in the abl. abs. construction. The ablative abso-lute, in this case an abl. combined with a participle (often a predicative substantive or adjective acts as substitute for the participle), serves to modify the verbal predicate of

388 data , fáta se,cútus. Víx sep,tém con,vúlsae
granted destinies following.　Scarcely　seven　　shaken
384 un,dís 　　,, 　Eu,róque 　su,pérsunt. 　　Ípse
by the waves　　and by Eurus　　survive.　I myself,
ig,nótus, 　e,géns, 　,, Liby,áe de,sérta per,ágro,
unknown,　　needy,　　of Libya　the deserts　traverse,
385 Éúro,pa 　átque 　Asi,á 　　pul,sús.” 　,, Nec ,
from Europe　and　from Asia having been driven."　　Nor

hardly do seven, shattered by the waves and eastern wind, survive. My- self unknown, neces- sitous, I wander through the Libyan wastes, driven from Europe and from Asia." But suf-

the sentence. For references, etc., consult the note on *laxis*, l. 122. —— **viam**, acc. sing. of *via*, -*ae*, f., 1st; direct obj. of *monstrante*. —— **data**, acc. plur. n. of *datus*, -*a*, -*um*, perf. part. pass. of *do, dare, dedi, datum*, 1; agrees with *fata*, and = a rel. clause *quae data erant*. —— **fāta**, acc. plur. of *fātum*, -*ī*, n., 2d; direct obj. of *secutus; fata*, as the perf. part. with passive meaning of *fari = to speak*, here = *oracula*, i.e. the spoken warning or decree of destiny, especially of that given by the god at Delphi. —— **secūtus**, nom. sing. m. of the perf. part. of the dep. verb *sequor, sequī, secūtus sum*, 3; agrees with the subj. *ego* implied by the personal ending of the verb *conscendi*.

LINE 383. **Vīx**, adv. of manner, limiting *supersunt; vix = with difficulty;* beware of taking *vix* with *septem* as *scarcely seven*, which is nonsense. —— **septem**, cardinal numeral, qualifying *naves* understood as subj. of *supersunt;* all the rest except one ship survived the storm, ll. 509–512. —— **convulsae**, nom. plur. f. of *convulsus*, -*a*, -*um*, perf. part. pass. of *convellō, -ere, convellī, convulsum*, 3 (*con + vellō = I pluck*); agrees with the subj. *naves* understood; the participle *convūlsae* is peculiar in this sentence, taking the place of a temporal clause, *after being shattered*. —— **undīs**, abl. plur. of *unda*, -*ae*, f., 1st; abl. of the instrument with *convulsae*. A. & G. 248, *c*; B. 218; G. 401; H. 420. —— **Eurō**, abl. sing. of *Eurus*, -*ī*, m., 2d (Greek Εὖρος); abl. of the instrument, joined by *que* to *undis;* Eurus is the East-wind, and is singled out for mention not by any means as being the most violent of the winds, but merely as a representative of all. —— **que**, enclitic conj. —— **supersunt**, 3d pers. plur. pres. ind. of *supersum, superesse, super- fuī (super, = over, + sum, = I am*, hence *I survive;* agrees with the subj. *convulsae (naves)*.

LINE 384. **Ipse**, nom. sing. m., of *ipse*, -*a*, -*um* (gen. *ipsīus*, dat. *ipsī*); intensifies *ego*, the implied subj. of *peragro; ipse* is very emphatic, and in conjunction with *ignotus* and *egens* marks the strong emotion under which Aeneas is laboring as he points the contrast between his present destitution and his former power and fame; see ll. 378, 379. —— **ignōtus**, nom. sing. m. of *ignōtus*, -*a*, -*um* (*in*, = *not*, + *nōtus*, = *known*, perf. part. pass. of *nosco*); agrees with *ipse;* some give *ignotus* its rarer *active* meaning of *not know- ing, ignorant* (i.e. of the country), but it is undoubtedly intended to be in opposition to *notus*, l. 379. —— **egēns**, gen. *egēntis;* nom. sing. m. of the pres. part. act. of *egeō, -ēre, -uī*, no supine, 2; agrees with *ipse*. Observe the omission of a conjunction between *ignotus* and *egens;* the *asyndeton* expresses intense feeling and excitement. A. & G. 208, *b*; B. 346; G. 473, REM.; H. 636, I, I. —— **Libyae**, gen. sing. of *Libya*, f., 1st; poss. gen., limiting *deserta*. —— **dēserta**, acc. plur. n. of *dēsertus*, -*a*, -*um*, perf. part. pass. of *dēserō, -ere, -uī, dēsertum*, 3; used as noun, directly governed by *peragro*. —— **perāgrō**, 1st pers. sing. pres. ind. act. of *perāgrō, -āre, -āvī, -ātum*, 1 (*per*, = *through*, + *āger*, gen. *āgri*, a *field*, hence *I traverse);* its subj. *ego* is implied by the termination.

LINE 385. **Eurōpā**, abl. sing. of *Eurōpa*, -*ae*, f. 1st (Greek Εὐρώπη = *she with the broad face);* abl. of 'place from which'; a preposition *ab* or *ex* is, as often in poetry,

fering not his further	plúra	que,réntem Pássa Ve,nús medi,ó ,, sic , 386
plaint,thus Venus mid	*more things*	*lamenting* *suffering* *Venus* *middle* *thus*
his grief broke in:	ínter,fáta	do,lóre est: " Quísquis es, , haúd, 387
" Whosoe'er thou art,	*interrupted*	*in his grief* — : *whoever* *thou art,* *not,*

omitted. A. & G. 258, *a*; B. 229, 1, *a*; G. 391; H. 428, II. This continent is supposed to have been named after Europa, a daughter of the Phoenician king Agenor; she was carried off to Crete by Jupiter, who assumed the shape of a bull for the purpose, and there she bore to Jupiter three children, Minos, Sarpedon, and Rhadamanthus. —— **atque,** cop. conj. —— **Asiā,** abl. sing. of *Asia, -ae,* f., 1st (Greek Ἀσία); abl. of 'place from which,' joined by *atque* to *Europa.* Asia was one of the daughters of Oceanus, and gave her name to one of the three great divisions of the ancient world. The name was first applied to what is now known as Asia Minor, but in later times was extended to the whole eastern continent. —— **pulsus,** nom. sing. m. of the perf. part. pass. of *pellō, -ere, pepulī, pulsum,* 3; agrees with and enlarges the subj. of *peragro.* The allusion in *Europa atque Asia pulsus* is: (1) *Asia;* to Aeneas' exile from Troy (in Asia Minor) after its capture by the Greeks; (2) *Europa;* in the first place, to the futile attempt made some years before to found a colony in Thrace, and in the second place to the failure of the Trojans in trying to reach Italy and settle there. —— **Nec** (short for *neque,* = *and . . . not*), conj., connecting its own with the preceding sentence. —— **plūra,** acc. plur. n. of *plūres, -a,* gen. *plūrium,* dat. and abl. *plūribus* (in the sing. *plus* is neuter, and is only found in the nom. and acc. cases, and in the gen. *pluris*); direct obj. of *querentem.* Comparison: positive *multus, -a, -um;* comparative, *plus;* superl. *plurimus.* —— **querentem,** acc. sing. m. of *querens, -entis,* pres. part. act. of *queror, -ī, questus sum,* deponent 3, trans. and intrans.; agrees with *eum* or *Aenean* understood. Many editors regard the participle as a variation for the infinitive mood, *nec* (*eum*) *plura queri passa,* but more probably *querentem plura* is to be taken as a direct object of *passa,* i.e. Venus could not endure *Aeneas as he was complaining further.*

LINE 386. **Passa,** nom. sing. of *passus, -a, -um,* perf. part. of the dep. verb *patior, patī, passus sum,* 3; agrees with and enlarges the subj. *Venus; passa* is equivalent to a present participle, the perfect participles of deponents being often used without any implication that the action is anterior to that of the principal verb. —— **Venus,** gen. *Veneris,* f., 3d; nom. sing., subj. of *interfata* (*est*). —— **mediō,** abl. sing. m. of *medius, -a, -um ;* partitive attribute of *dolore.* —— **sīc,** adv. of manner, modifying *interfata* and referring to what follows. —— **interfāta,** nom. sing. f. of the perf. part. of the dep. verb *interfor, interfāri, interfātus sum,* 1 (*inter,* = *between,* + *fāri,* = *to speak,* hence *to interrupt*); agrees with the subj. *Venus,* and constitutes with *est* below the 3d pers. sing. perf. ind. —— **dolōre,** abl. sing. of *dolor, -ōris,* m., 3d (*doleō* = *I grieve*) ; idiomatic abl. of ' time when.' In certain expressions like this it is not always easy to distinguish between the ablative of *time when* and the ablative of *place where;* in the case before us the verb *interfata* indicates *when* (*fata*) and *where* (*inter*), but the interruption occurs on the whole rather in time than in place. A. & G. 259, *a*; B. 230; G. 393, and REM. 5; H. 429. Observe that Vergil uses *dolore,* which properly represents the abstract idea of *grief,* for the *display of grief* made by Aeneas. —— **est,** 3d pers. sing. pres. ind. act. of *sum, esse, fuī;* agrees in person with *Venus,* and with *interfata* makes *interfata est,* the 3d pers. sing. of the combinate perf. indicative. Parts of the verb *sum* are borrowed to form the perfect, future perfect, and pluperfect tenses passive of all other verbs that have these tenses.

LINE 387. **Quisquis,** nom. sing. m. of *quisquis,* f. rare, *quidquid* or *quicquid* (*quodquod* is the adjectival neuter), indefinite rel. pron.; agrees predicatively with the implied

388 cre, do, „ ínvi, sús   coe, léstibus , aúras Víta, lés
  I believe   *hatred*   *by the gods above*   *breath*   *of life*

car, pís, „ Tyri, ám qu*i*   ad, véneris , úrbem.
  'thou drawest   *Tyrian who* (=*as*) (*thou*) *hast come to* *the city.*

389 **Pérge** mo, do, átqu*e* hinc , té re, gínae „ ad ,
  Proceed   *only,*   *and* *hence*   *thee of the queen*   *to*

not hated, me-
thinks, of the heav-
enly host dost thou
draw the breath of
life, for that thou hast
reached the Tyrian
city. Only proceed,
and betake thee
hence to the palace-

---

subj. (*tu*) of *es*. —— **es**, 2d pers. sing. pres. ind. of *sum, esse, fuī;* understand *tu* as subj.
of the predicate *quisquis es*. —— **haud**, negative adv., limiting *invisus*, not *carpis*.
Remember that Vergil never uses *haud* with verbs, and that the best authors rarely use
it with them, except with *scio, ignoro,* and a very few more. —— **crēdō**, 1st pers. sing.
pres. ind. act. of *crēdō, -ere, crēdidī, crēditum*, 3; the contained subj. is *ego; crēdō* is
parenthetic, being constructionally independent of the rest of the sentence; in prose it is
usual to have *quod* or *id quod credo, ut credo,* etc. —— **invīsus**, nom. sing. m. of *invīsus,
-a, -um* (from *invideō = I envy,* hence *detested,* or *detestable*); agrees with the subj. of
carpis. *Haud invisus carpis* is really an abbreviation of *non invisus es qui carpis,* the
emphasis lying on *invisus*. —— **coelestibus**, dat. plur. of *coelestēs, -ium,* m. and f., 3d
(plur. of adj. *coelestis, -e,* from *coelum; coelestes = dī superī*); dat. of the indirect obj.
with *invisus*. —— **aurās**, acc. plur. of *aura, -ae,* f., 1st (Greek ἀύρα); direct obj. of
carpis.
    LINE 388. **Vītālēs**, acc. plur. f. of *vītālis, -e,* adj. 3d (from *vīta, life*); qualifies *aurās;
the breath of life* is an expression borrowed from Lucretius. —— **carpis**, 2d pers. sing.
pres. ind. act. of *carpō, -ere, carpsī, carptum,* 3 (= *to pluck,* here *to draw;* for other
meanings, consult a dictionary); *tu* is the unexpressed subject. —— **Tyriam**, acc. sing.
f. of *Tyrius, -a, -um;* qualifies *urbem*. —— **quī**, nom. sing. m. of the rel. pron.; agrees
with *tū* (subj. of *carpis*) as antecedent, and is subj. of *adveneris*. Observe that *qui* intro-
duces a *causal* clause, = *quippe qui,* or *cum is;* for the relative in *purpose* clauses, cf.
quae verteret arces (= *ut ea*), l. 20; *qui* in *concessive* clauses also takes the subjunctive
(= *cum is, although he*); in statements of general characteristics the subjunctive mood
follows the relative pronoun. —— **advēneris**, 2d pers. sing. perf. subjunct. act. of *adveniō,
-īre, advēnī, adventum,* 4 (*ad,* = *to,* + *veniō,* = *I come*); agrees with its subj. *quī;* the
mood is the *causal* subjunctive. A. & G. 320, *e;* B. 283, 3; G. 633; H. 517. —— **urbem**,
acc. sing. of *urbs, urbis,* f., 3d; direct obj. of *adveneris*. *Venio* is intransitive, but in
composition with *ad* governs a direct object; compounds of *ante, ob, trans,* and a few
other prepositions similarly acquire a transitive force. A. & G. 228, *a;* B. 175, 2, *a;*
G. 331; H. 372.
    LINE 389. **Perge**, 2d pers. sing. imperative mood, act. of *pergō, -ere, perrēxī, per-
rectum,* 3; the subj. *tū* is unexpressed, being contained in the personal ending. ——
modo, adv., strengthening the imperative *perge;* so the English *now* in *proceed now,*
without temporal signification. *Modo* is used in a variety of ways, of which the chief are:
(1) in distributive coördination, *modo . . . modo,* = *now . . . now;* (2) *non modo,* not
only . . . sed etiam, but also; (3) *non modo non,* not only not *. . . sed ne quidem, but
not even;* (4) in provisions, *modo* (usually with *dum,* e.g. *dummodo*) = *provided that,*
followed by the subjunctive, the negative being *modo ne* (*dummodo ne*), *provided that
. . . not;* (5) restrictive adv., = *only, merely;* (6) temporal adv., of time present or
just past, = *just now;* of the immediate future, = *directly, in a moment*. —— **atque**,
cop. conj. —— **hinc**, adv. of 'place whence'; cf. *hīc = here, hūc = hither,* from the
demonstrative pronoun *hīc, haec, hōc*. —— **tē**, acc. sing. of the 2d personal pron. *tū;*

portals of the Queen.	límina ,	pérfer.	Námque	ti, bí	redu, cés	390
For I bring thee news	the threshold	betake.	For indeed	to thee	returned	
of thy comrades re-	soci, ós ,,	clas, sémque re, látam	Núntio,	et ,		391
turned and thy fleet						
driven back and borne	your companions and your fleet	brought back I announce,	and			
into safety by the	ín tu, túm ,,	ver, sís	Aqui, lónibus , áctam,			
changed north winds,	into safety	having changed	by the north winds	driven		

---

reflexive direct obj. of *perfer.* —— **rēgīnae,** gen. sing. of *rēgīna,* f., 1st; poss. gen., lim-
iting *limina ; reginae = Didonis.* —— **ad,** prep. with the acc.; gov. *limina.* The fol-
lowing distinctions are perceptible in prepositions expressing *motion to : in = to, into,*
i.e. into the interior; *ad = to, towards,* i.e. to the borders of a place. —— **limina,** acc.
plur. of *līmen, -inis,* n., 3d (for *ligmen,* from *ligō = I fasten ;* hence of the fastening
timbers of a doorway); governed by *ad.* —— **perfer,** 2d pers. sing. imperative mood act.
of *perferō, perferre, pe.·tulī, perlātum,* irreg. (*per, = through,* + *ferō, = I carry ;* with
reflexive pron. as object, *= to betake one's self*) ; joined by *atque* to *perge. Fer* (not
fere) is the imperative of *fero;* so *dic* of *dico,* and *fac* of *facio.*
    LINE 390. **Namque** (*nam + que*), *nam* is a causal conj., strengthened by the suffix
que ; there is an ellipse in the thought, e.g. *and (go joyfully) for,* etc. There are several
combinate conjunctions like *namque,* e.g. *itaque, sed enim, enimvero,* etc. ; they are
more emphatic than the simple conjunctions, and connect a sentence more closely and
logically with what has preceded. A. & G. 208, *e ;* B. 345 ; G. 498 ; H. 554, V.——
tibī, dat. sing. of *tū ;* dat. of the indirect obj. after *nuntio.* The final *i* of *mihi, tibi,* and
sibi may be either long or short ; it is more often short than long, but the *i* is long in
tibi here. —— **reducēs,** acc. plur. m. of *redūx, reducis,* adj. 3d (*= reducs,* from *redūcō =*
I lead back ; hence passively *led back, returning*) ; agrees with *socios,* and is the comple-
ment of *esse* understood ; *socios reduces* (*esse*) and *classem relatam* (*esse*) are acc. and inf.
object-clauses governed by *nuntio,* the verb implying *saying.* A. & G. 272, REM. ;
B. 330, 331 ; G. 527 ; H. 534, 535. —— **sociōs,** acc. plur of *socius, -ī,* m., 2d ; acc.-subj.
of *reduces* (*esse*), after *nuntio.* —— **classem,** acc. sing. of *classis, -is,* f., 3d ; subj.-acc. of
relatam (*esse*), after *nuntio.* This is the first intimation *Aeneas* had of the safety of his
fleet ; he had supposed that the seven vessels with him were the only ones that survived
the storm roused by Aeolus. —— **que,** enclitic conj., joining the two object-clauses, *reduces*
socios and *classem relatam.* —— **relātam,** acc. sing. f. of *relātus, -a, -um,* perf. part. pass.
of *referō, referre, retulī* (*rettulī*), *relātum,* irreg. (*re, = back,* + *ferō, = I bring*) ; agrees
with *classem ;* supply *esse* with *relatam, relatam* (*esse*) being the perf. inf. passive
governed by the subject-acc. *classem.*
    LINE 391. **Nuntiō,** 1st pers. sing. pres. ind. act. of *nuntiō, -āre, -āvī, -ātum,* 1 ; the
contained subj. is *ego.* —— **et,** cop. conj. —— **in,** prep. with the acc. or abl. ; gov.
the acc. *tutum.* —— **tūtum,** acc. sing. n. of adj. *tūtus, -a, -um* (originally perf. part. of
tueor) ; governed by *in ; tutum* is substantival, *= tutum locum.* Vergil often uses the
neuter of adjectives as substantives, cf. *in altum, in melius,* etc., especially after prepo-
sitions. A. & G. 188, 189 ; B. 236–238 ; G. 204, NOTES 1–4 ; H. 441. —— **versis,** abl.
plur. m. of *versus, -a, -um,* perf. part. pass. of *vertō, -ere, vertī, versum,* 3 ; agrees with
aquilonibus. —— **aquilōnibus,** abl. plur. of *aquilō, -ōnis,* m., 3d; abl. of the instrument
with *actam ;* the plural of *aquilo* (the *north* wind) practically *= ventis. Versis aquilo-*
nibus may be taken as abl. abs., in which case *versis = having changed* (the passive *vertor*
being medial or reflexive, and similar to a regular deponent). —— **actam,** acc. sing. f. of
actus, -a, -um, perf. part. pass. of *agō, -ere, ēgī, actum,* 3 ; agrees with *classem ;* supply
esse with *actam, =* the perf. inf. pass. of *ago,* joined by *et* to *relatam* (*esse*) above.

392 **Ní** frus,tra aúguri,úm „ va,ní docu,ére | unless to no end my
  unless to no purpose *augury* *fond* *taught (me)* | parents have falsely
393 pa,réntes. **Áspice** , bís se,nós „ lae,tántes , | taught me augury.
  my parents. *Behold thou* *twice* *six* *rejoicing* | Behold yon twelve
394 ágmine , cýcnos, **Aétheri**,á quos , lápsa | swans in joyous array,
  in a column *swans,* *heavenly* *whom* *gliding* | whom the bird of
pla,gá „ **Iovis** , áles a,pérto | Jove, swooping from
  from the region *of Jupiter* *the bird* *open* | the tract of aether,

LINE 392. **nī** (old form *nēī*, so probably the same as *ne*, though some think it a contraction of *nisi*), negative conditional particle, followed by the ind. mood *docuere*. *Si* introduces affirmative, and *nisi* or *ni* and *si non* negative conditions. *Nisi* and *ni* (usually = *unless*) are most common in conditions whose apodoses or conclusions are negative. When *nisi* or *ni* is used, the *apodosis* is stated as true generally, except for the single exception introduced by *nisi* or *ni ;* when *si non* is used, the *apodosis* is true only for the case under consideration. A. & G. 315, *a* ; B. 306 ; G. 591 ; H. 507 and 3, NOTE 3.——**frustrā**, adv. of manner, limiting *docuere*.——**augurium**, acc. sing. of *augurium, -ī*, n., 2d (from *augur*) ; direct obj. of *docuere*.——**vānī**, nom. plur. m. of *vānus, -a, -um* (= *vacnus*, cf. *vacuus, empty*) ; agrees with the subj. *parentes*, but limits the verb *docuere* like an adverb. A. &. G. 191 ; B. 239 ; G. 325, REM. 6 ; H. 443.——**docuēre**, 3d pers. plur. perf. ind. act. of *doceō, -ēre, docuī, doctum*, 2 ; agrees with the subj. *parentes*.——**parēntēs**, nom. plur. of *parēns, -entis*, m. or f., 3d ; subj. of *docuēre*.

LINE 393. **Aspice**, 2d pers. sing. imperative mood act. of *aspiciō (adspiciō), -ere, aspēxī, aspectum*, 3 (*ad + speciō*) ; the contained subj. is *tu*. Synonyms : *videre* simply = *to see ; intueri* = *to gaze at ; aspicere* = *to look at*, or *to behold*, whether accidentally or intentionally ; *spectare* = *to look steadily at ; cernere* = *to see*, so as to be able to distinguish.——**bis**, numeral adv., qualifying *senos ; bis senos* is a poetical way of expressing *twelve (duodecim)*.——**sēnōs**, acc. plur. m. of the distributive *sēnī, -ae, -a* (the cardinal is *sex*) ; agrees with *cycnos*. In prose, *bis senos* could only mean *twice six each*, but here it = *bis sex ;* Vergil occasionally puts distributives for cardinals.——**laetāntēs**, acc. plur. m. of *laetāns, -āntis*, pres. part. of the dep. verb *laetor, -ārī, -ātus sum*, 1 (*laetus, glad*) ; agrees with *cycnos ;* the participle *laetantes* is more vivid than the ordinary infinitive *laetari*. A. & G. 292, *e* ; B. 336, 2 ; G. 536 ; H. 535, I, 4.——**āgmine**, abl. sing. of *āgmen, āgminis*, n., 3d ; abl. of manner, with *laetantes*.——**cȳcnōs**, acc. plur. of *cȳcnus, -ī*, m., 2d (Greek κύκνος) ; direct obj. of *aspice*. The swan is said to have not been a bird of augury among the Romans, but Venus naturally selects her own sacred bird to give an omen to the Trojans.

LINE 394. **Aetheriā**, abl. sing. f. of *aetherius, -a, -um (aether)* ; agrees with *plaga*.——**quōs**, acc. plur. m. of the rel. pron. *quī, quae, quod ;* agrees with the antecedent *cycnos* in gender and number, and is direct obj. of *turbabat*.——**lapsa**, nom. f. sing. of *lapsus, -a, -um*, perf. part. of the dep. verb *labor, labī, lapsus sum*, 3 ; agrees with and enlarges the subj. *ales*.——**plagā**, abl. sing. of *plaga, -ae*, f., 1st (akin to Greek πλάξ, gen. πλάγος, *a flat surface*) ; abl. of 'place from which.' *Plaga* = *a region*, always of the sky in Vergil, but also of the earth in Livy : distinguish it from *plaga* = *a net* (from a root in Greek πλέκω = *I entwine*), and from *plāga* = *a blow* (Greek πληγή).—— **Iovis**, gen. sing. of *Iūpiter*, m., 3d ; poss. gen., limiting *ales ; Iovis ales* = *aquila, the eagle*. The eagle was sacred to Jupiter, and the emblem of the supreme god's power ; it

was scattering through the open sky; now they are seen alighting in long line upon the ground or gazing down on the places just taken: as they safe-returned	Túrba, bát	coe, ló; „	nunc,	térras,	órdine,	lóngo 395
	was harassing in the sky;		*now*	*the land*	*in line*	*long*
	Aút	cape, re,	aút	cap, tás „	iam,	déspec, táre 396
	either	*to take*	*or*	*taken*	*already*	*to look down on*
	vi, déntur :	Út	redu, cés	il, lí	lu, dúnt „ 397
	they seem :	*As*	*returning*	*they*	*sport*

was frequently employed by Jupiter, e.g. to carry Ganymede to heaven. —— **āles,** gen. *ālitis,* m. or f., 3d (probably for *ālits,* from *āla = a wing,* and the root *i* of the verb *eo,* hence *the wing-goer*) ; nom. sing., subj. of *turbabat.* —— **apertō,** abl. sing. n. of *apertus,* *-a, -um,* adj. (properly pref. part. pass. of *aperiō*) ; qualifies *coelo; apertus = open,* not in the sense of *clear,* but in the sense of *unsheltered.*

LINE 395. **Turbābat,** 3d pers. sing. imperf. ind. act. of *turbo, -āre, -āvī, -ātum,* 1; agrees with its subj. *ales.* —— **coelō,** abl. sing. of *coelum, -ī,* n., 2d; abl. of 'place where' or 'place through which.' See references to *alto,* l. 126. —— **nūnc,** adv. of time. —— **terrās,** acc. plur. of *terra, -ae,* f., 1st; direct obj. of *capere.* —— **ordine,** abl. sing. of *ordō, ordinis,* m., 3d; abl. of manner; as *ordine* is qualified by an adjective *longo,* the abl. of manner is regular with or without the preposition *cum.* —— **longō,** abl. sing. m. of *longus, -a, -um ;* qualifies *ordine.*

LINE 396. **Aut,** disjunctive conj.; *aut . . . aut* (below) = *either . . . or.* For a complete note on *aut,* see l. 183. —— **capere,** pres. inf. act. of *capiō, -ere, cēpī, captum,* 3; *prolative* inf., completing the meaning of *videntur.* A. & G. 271; B. 326; G. 423; H. 533. For the various meanings of *capere* consult a dictionary : there are, however, two meanings, (1) *to reach,* or *to alight upon,* (2) *to choose,* between which a choice must here be made. If *capere = to choose,* then it is used as the equivalent of *capere oculis,* but it is doubtful if it can = *to choose* when *oculis* is omitted as in this passage : so it is preferable to render *capere* as *to settle upon,* for the above reason and for another important one mentioned in the note on *despectare* below. —— **aut,** disjunctive conj. —— **captās,** acc. plur. f. of *captus, -a, -um,* perf. part. pass. of *capiō* (see *capere* above); predicate part. in agreement with *terras ; terras captas = terras quas ceperant.* —— **iam,** adv. of time, limiting *despectare ;* whereas *nunc* is used of time present, *iam* may be used of time present, just past, or coming immediately. —— **dēspectāre,** pres. inf. act. of *dēspectō, -āre,* no perf., no supine, 1 (*dē, = down from,* + *spectō, = I look at*) ; prolative inf., joined by *aut* to *capere* above. In order to understand this line properly it is necessary to anticipate Vergil's comparison of the 12 swans with the 12 ships which had been driven away by the storm. Clearly the birds *alighting* (*capere*) correspond to the ships *in harbor* (*portum tenet,* l. 400); the birds still *looking down* (*despectare*) but not yet alighted correspond to the ships just entering the port (*subit ostia*) ; so *stridentibus alis* corresponds to *pleno velo.* If *capere* above = *to occupy,* then *videntur aut capere aut despectare = they seem* SOME *of them to settle or* OTHERS *to look down ;* if *capere = to mark,* or *to choose,* all the birds must be in the air, and the comparison loses very much of its point. So *captas = captas ab altera parte cycnorum,* which is a little harsh, but preserves the elaborate completeness of the comparison. —— **videntur,** 3d pers. plur. pres. ind. of the dep. verb *videor, -ēri, visus sum,* 2 (= *I seem ; videor* is properly the passive of *video*) ; agrees with *cycni* or *illi* understood (from *cycnos,* l. 393) as subject.

LINE 397. **Ut,** comparative conj., relative of the demonstrative *haud aliter* (= *ita*), l. 399. For the various uses of *ut,* see l. 306. —— **reducēs,** nom. plur. m. of *redūx, reducis,* adj. 3d (see *reducēs,* l. 390); agrees with *illi.* The swans coll ting together after their flight correspond to the ships gathering together after the storm. —— **illī,**

898 stri , déntibus , ál.is,   Ét coe , tú   cin , xére | disport with noisy
    noisy   *with wings, and in a crowd have encircled* | wings, and encircle
                                                             | with their throng the
899 po , lúm, „ can , túsque de , dére, Haúd ali , tér | sky, breaking into
    the sky   *and songs   have given forth, not   otherwise* | song; in like manner
                                                             | thy ships and thy
400 pup , pésque tu , æ̃ „ pu , bésque tu , órum   Aút | young following are
    both ships   *thy   and the youth of thy followers either* | either safe in port
                                                             | or with full sail
    por , túm tenet, , aút ple , nó „ subit , óstia , vélo. | entering its mouth.
    the harbor hold   or   full   enters the mouth with sail. |

---

nom. plur. m. of the demonstr. pron. *ille, illa, illud;* subj. of *ludunt; illi* refers to the
swans. —— **lūdunt,** 3d pers. plur. pres. ind. act. of *lūdō, -ere, lūsī, lūsum,* 3 ; agrees
with the subj. *illi.* —— **strīdentibus,** abl. plur. f. of *strīdens, -entis,* pres. part. act. of
strīdeō, -ēre, strīdī, no supine, 2 (or of *strīdō, -ere, strīdī,* no supine, 3 ; both forms
common) ; qualifies *alis* attributively. —— **ālīs,** abl. plur. of *āla, -ae,* f., 1st ; abl. of the
means or instrument.

LINE 398. **Et,** cop. conj. —— **coetū,** abl. sing. of *coetus, -ūs,* m., 4th (another form
of *coitus, -ūs,* m., 4th, from *coeo [co = con + eo]*) ; abl. of manner. A. & G. 248, at the
end ; B. 220 ; G. 399, NOTE 2 ; H. 419, III. —— **cinxēre,** 3d pers. plur. perf. ind. act.
of *cingō, -ere, cinxī, cinctum,* 3 ; agrees with the subj. *illi,* and joined by *et* to *ludunt.*
Observe the difference in tense in *ludunt* and *cinxere ;* the perfect shows that the swans
circled about the sky before they alighted. —— **polum,** acc. sing. of *polus, -ī,* m., 2d
(Greek πόλος) ; direct obj. of *cinxere ; polum* is a poetical variation for *coelum,* and
avoids an inartistic repetition (after *coelo,* l. 395). —— **cantūs,** acc. plur. of *cantus, -ūs,*
m., 4th (from *canō, -ere, cecinī, cantum,* 3, = I sing) ; direct object of *dedere ;* with
cantus dare compare *amplexus dare, laxas habenas dare,* and other periphrases of a
similar kind. —— **que,** enclitic conj., joining *dedere* and *cinxere ; que* always connects
very closely, for instance the two perfects ; see *que,* l. 1. —— **dedēre,** 3d pers. plur. perf.
ind. act. of *dō, dare, dedī, datum,* 1 ; joined by *que* to *cinxere.*

LINE 399. **Haud,** negative adv. ; negatives *aliter.* —— **aliter,** adv. of manner.
Aliter is used in comparative sentences, especially when negatived by *haud* or *non,* and
is followed by *quam, atque,* or *ac ; haud aliter ac* (or *quam, quam si,* etc.), = *not other-
wise than, just as if.* —— **puppēs,** nom. plur. of *puppis, -is,* f., 3d ; subj. of *tenent* under-
stood from *tenet,* l. 400 ; *puppes = naves* by synecdoche, the figure whereby the *part* is
used for the *whole.* A. & G. 386 ; B. no reference ; G. 695 ; H. 637, IV. —— **que,**
enclitic conj. —— **tuae,** nom. sing. f. of *tuus, -a, -um ;* agrees with *puppes.* —— **pūbēs,**
gen. *pūbis,* f., 3d ; nom. sing., subj. of *tenet,* and joined by *que* to *puppēs* above. ——
que, enclitic conj. —— **tuōrum,** gen. plur. m. of *tuus, -a, um ;* a kind of adnominal gen.
of specification, supplying the place of a noun in apposition. A. & G. 214, *f ;* B. 202 ;
G. 361 ; H. 395. *Tui, mei, sui* are often used substantively = *thy, my, his (her* or *their)
friends* or *followers.*

LINE 400. **Aut,** disjunctive conj. ; see *aut* below, = *either . . . or.* —— **portum,** acc.
sing. of *portus, -ūs,* m., 4th ; direct obj. of *tenet.* —— **tenet,** 3d pers. sing. pres. ind. act.
of *teneō, -ēre, -uī, tentum,* 2 ; agrees only with *pubes,* a part of the subj. *puppes . . .
pubesque.* It sometimes happens that when there are several subjects and only one verb,
the verb agrees with the nearest subject and is understood with the rest ; this is most
common when all the subjects are singular or the last only plural, but in the present
instance the first subject is plural and the last singular. A. & G. 205, *d ;* B. 255, 3 ;
G. 285, EXCEPTION 1 ; H. 463, I. —— **aut,** disjunctive conj. ; see above. —— **plēnō,** abl.

| Only proceed, and where the path guides, direct thy step." She spake, and as she turned away her roseate neck shone forth and from her head her ambrosial tresses exhaled | Pérge mo,do, ét, „ qua , té du,cít viá, , dírige , 401 *Proceed   only,   and   where thee leads   the way,   direct* gréssum." Díxit; et ,áver,téns „rose , á cer ,více 402 *thy step."   She spoke; and turning away   rosy   with neck* re,fúlsit, Ámbrosi,æque co,mæ „ di,vínum , 403 *gleamed,   and ambrosial   her hair   divine* |

sing. n. of *plēnus, -a, -um ;* agrees with *vēlō.* —— **subit,** 3d pers. sing. pres. ind. act. of *subeō, subīre, subīvī* or *-iī, subitum,* irreg. (*sub,* = *under,* + *eō,* = *I go,* hence *I enter*); agrees with one of the subjects, viz. *pūbēs.* —— **ōstia,** acc. plur. of *ōstium, -ī,* n., 2d (cf. *os, oris,* n., 3d = *a mouth*) ; direct obj. of *subit.* —— **vēlō,** abl. sing. of *vēlum, -ī,* n., 2d (probably for *vehlum,* from *vehō = I carry ;* hence *the carrying thing, a sail*) ; abl. of the instrument, with *subit.*

LINE 401. **Perge,** 2d pers. sing. imperative mood act. of *pergō, -ere, perēxī, perrectum,* 3; the subj. *tū* is implied in the personal ending. —— **modo,** adv., strengthening the imperative *perge,* and here possessing no temporal signification; cf. the English adverb *now.* For the various meanings and uses of *modo,* refer to the note on *modo,* l. 389. —— **et,** copulative conjunction, connecting the two imperatives *perge* and *dirige.* —— **quā,** adv. of place, = *in what direction ;* originally *quā* is the ablative sing. feminine of the relative pronoun *quī.* —— **tē,** acc. sing. of the 2d personal pron. sing. *tū ;* direct obj. of *dūcit ; te* refers to Aeneas, to whom Venus is giving instructions as to what he is to do. —— **dūcit,** 3d pers. sing. pres. ind. act. of *dūcō, -ere, dūxī, ductum,* 3 ; agrees with its subj.-nom. *via ;* the notion of a road performing the active function of a *dux* or guide (*ducit*) is poetical. —— **via,** gen. *viae,* f., 1st; nom. sing., subj. of *dūcit.* —— **dirige,** 2d pers. sing. imperative mood act. of *dirigō, -ere, dīrēxī, dīrectum,* 3 (*dī = dis,* with strengthening force, + *regō = I keep straight*) ; the implied subj.-nom. is *tū.* —— **gressum,** acc. sing. of *gressus, -ūs,* m., 4th (for *grad-sus,* from *gradior = I step*) ; direct obj. of *dirige.*

LINE 402. **Dīxit,** 3d pers. sing. perf. ind. act, of *dīcō, -ere, dīxī, dictum,* 3; agrees with an understood subj.-nom. *Venus* or a pronoun referring to *Venus.* —— **et,** copulative conj. —— **āvertēns,** gen. *āvertēntis ;* nom. sing. f. of the pres. part. act. of *āvertō, -ere, āvertī, āversum,* 3 (*a, = away from,* + *verto, = I turn*) ; agrees with the pronoun *illa* understood as subj. of *refulsit. Avertens = āvertens se,* that is, the verb is here given an intransitive force; Vergil has many examples of this, cf. l. 104, *tum prōra āvertit = then the prow swings round.* Observe the beautiful language and description of the following lines, wherein the goddess, 'only on departing (*avertens*), allows her divinity to become apparent : the signs of her godhead are the beautiful shape and coloring of her neck, the ambrosial unguent (possessed only by the gods) with which her hair was anointed, the dress which, before girt up, now fell down to the feet, and especially the majesty and dignity of her bearing (*incessu*). —— **roseā,** abl. sing. f. of *roseus, -a, -um* (from *rosa = a rose*) ; qualifies *cervīce.* —— **cervīce,** abl. sing. of *cervīx, -īcis,* f., 3d; an abl. of the means or instrument; the expression *cervice refulsit* (= *she shone out with roseate neck*) is a poetical variation for *cervix refulsit* (= *her roseate neck shone out*). —— **refulsit,** 3d pers. sing. perf. ind. act. of *refulgeō, -ēre, refulsī,* no supine, 2 (*re = back,* in contrast to a former merely ordinary aspect, + *fulgeō = I shine*) ; understand *illa* or *Venus* as subject; *refulsit* is joined by *et* to *dixit* above.

LINE 403. **Ambrosiae,** nom. plur. f. of *ambrosius, -a, -um,* adj. (cf. the noun *ambrosia, -ae,* f., 1st, which is probably from the same root as *ambergris ;* agrees with *comae.*

404 vértice   o, dórem Spíra, vére : ,, pe, dés ves, tís | immortal fragrance;
   from her head   a perfume   breathed: her feet her robe | down to her feet her
405 de, flúxit ad , ímos ; Ét ve, ra ínces, sú ,, | flowing robe de-
   flowed down   to   lowest;   and   true   in her progress | scended, and by her
                                                                 | movement the true
   patu, ít   dea. , Ílle ubi , mátrem | goddess was revealed.
   was made manifest a goddess.   He   when   his mother | Her son, when he

---

Ambrosius is a Greek word, and some derive it from two words with the meaning "*not mortal*," hence *divine.* There were two kinds of *ambrosia :* (1) the peculiar food of the gods, just as *nectar* was their peculiar drink; (2) a sweet-scented unguent known and used only by the gods, the fragrance of which was enough to disclose the presence of a deity to a mortal. —— **que**, enclitic copulative conjunction, joining its own to the preceding sentence. —— **comae**, nom. plur. of *coma, -ae,* f., 1st; subj. of *spīrāvēre.* —— **dīvīnum**, acc. sing. m. of the adjective *divinus, -a, -um* (formed from the noun *divus, -ī,* m., 2d); qualifies *odōrem.* —— **vertice**, abl. sing. of *vertex, verticis,* m., 3d; abl. of the 'place from which.' —— **odōrem**, acc. sing. of *odor, odōris,* m., 3d (root OD; akin to the Greek verb ὄζω (= ὄδ-σω) = *I smell ;* the root is the same in the Latin verb *oleō = I smell of) ;* direct obj. of *spiravere.*

LINE 404. **Spīrāvēre**, 3d pers. plur. perf. ind. act. of *spīrō, -āre, -āvī, -ātum,* 1 trans. and intrans.; agrees with its subj. *comae.* —— **pedēs**, acc. plur. of *pēs, pedis,* m., 3d; governed by the preposition *ad.* A robe descending to the feet was a divine distinction; in l. 320 the robe was girt up so that the divinity of Venus might not be noticed (*nodo sinus collecta fluentes*). The noun *pes* = (1) *foot,* of a man or an animal, even the *talons* of a bird; (2) metaphorically, the *foot* of a mountain; (3) *the sheet,* the technical name of a rope which was connected with a sail. —— **vestis**, gen. *vestis,* f., 3d; nom. sing., subj. of *dēflūxit.* —— **dēflūxit**, 3d pers. sing. perf. ind. act. of *dēfluō, -ere, dēflūxī, dēfluctum,* 3 intransitive (*dē, = down from, + fluō, = I flow) ;* agrees with its subj. *vestis.* Observe that there is no conjunction connecting the sentence *vestis defluxit* with the preceding sentences; the omission of a conjunction is called *asyndeton.* A. & G. 208, *b ;* B. 346; G. 473, REM.; H. 636, I, 1. The poets are often lax about connecting their sentences, often intentionally, as in such swift descriptions as that of Venus given in this passage; for instance, the next sentence is properly connected. —— **ad**, prep. with the acc.; gov. *pedes. In* with the acc. = *into,* i.e. into the interior of; *ad = to, towards,* i.e. to the borders of. For other uses of *ad,* consult A. & G. 153; B. 182, 3; G. 416, 1; H. 433, I. —— **īmōs**, acc. plur. m. of *īmus, -a, -um,* superlative adj. (formed from the prep. *infrā ;* comparative *inferior ;* positive *inferus* very rare, but cf. *Inferi = the gods below) ;* agrees with *pedes.* Observe that *imos* is *partitive,* that is, indicates the part alluded to. A. & G. 193; B. 241; G. 291, REM. 2; H. 440, 2, NOTE I.

LINE 405. **Et**, copulative conj. —— **vēra**, nom. sing. f. of the adj. *verus, -a, -um ;* agrees with *dea. Verus = true, actual, real ;* so the substantival neuter *verum = a truth,* or *true thing ;* the abstract *veritas* may = (1) *trueness* (*conditio eius quod verum est) ;* (2) *veracity, moral truth.* —— **incessū**, abl. sing. of *incessus, -ūs,* m., 4th (from the verb *incēdō = I walk majestically) ;* ablative of the means, amplifying *patuit.* A. & G. 248, *c ;* B. 218; G. 401; H. 420. —— **patuit**, 3d pers. sing. perf. ind. act. of *pateō, -ēre, patuī,* no supine, 2 (= (1) *to lie open,* (2) *to be manifest ;* akin to the Greek verb πετάννυμι); agrees with the subj. *dea.* —— **dea**, gen. *deae,* f., 1st; nom. sing., subj. of *patuit.* The final syllable *a* is not elided before the next word *ille ;* such omissions of *elision* are known by the name *hiatus.* They are rare always, and in almost all cases occur where there is a marked break in the sense ; secondly, they are almost invariably found

was ware of her his **Ágno,vít,   ta,lí   „   fugi,éntem   est ,   vóce** 406
mother, with this cry *he recognized,   such   her) fleeing   —— with speech*
pursued her flight :
"Why, cruel as the **se,cútus :   "Quíd na,túm toti,és „ cru,délis , tú** 407
rest, mockest thou *he pursued :   "Why   thy son   so often   cruel   thou*
thy son so oft in **quoque , fálsis Lúdis   i,mágini,bús? „ cur ,** 408
false likenesses? why *too   false dost thou mock   with visions?   why*

---

in syllables which are accented.   But the *a* of *dea* is not accented, being a short vowel, and the only justification for the *hiatus* is the long pause which follows the revelation of Venus, artistically preparing for the change of subject as soon as the astonishment of Aeneas permitted action.   This instance is one of the two in Vergil after a short vowel, the other being Eclogue II, l. 53, *prūnă ; hŏnōs*, etc.   For a full explanation of *hiatus* consult A. & G. 359, *e*; B. 366, 7, *a*; G. 720, and 784, NOTE 6; H. 608, II. —— **Ille,** gen. *illīus ;* nom. sing. m. of the demonstr. pron. of the 3d person; refers to Aeneas, and is subj. of *agnovit*. —— **ubi,** temporal conj., followed by the ind. *agnovit*. As a temporal particle, *ubi* is used like *postquam* and *simul ac*, etc.; it is followed by the indicative in the perfect and *historic* present tenses;   less commonly it governs the imperfect and pluperfect indicative (rarely subjunctive).   A. & G. 323-324; B. 287; G. 561, *ff*.; H. 518. Other uses of *ubi* are : (1) interrog. = *where?* or *when?;* (2) rel. local adv. = *where*, *in which place ;* (3) of persons or things = *with* or *by which*. —— **mātrem,** acc. sing. of *māter, mātris*, f., 3d (Greek μήτηρ); direct obj. of *agnōvit*.

LINE 406. **Agnōvit,** 3d pers. sing. perf. ind. act. of *agnoscō, -ere, agnōvī, agnitum*, 3 (for *ad-gnosco*, from *ad + gnosco ;* cf. γιγνώσκω);   agrees with the subj. *ille*. —— **tālī,** abl. sing. f. of *tālis, -e ;* agrees with *vōce*, and refers to the speech which follows. —— **fugientem,** acc. sing. f. of *fugiens, -entis*, pres. part. act. of *fugiō, -ere, fūgī, fūgitum*, 3; agrees with *matrem* or a pronoun (understood from *matrem*, l. 405) as direct obj. of *secutus est*.   It is possible, but unnecessary, to take *fugientem* as a participle used substantively, for which see note and references to *amantem*, l. 352. —— **est,** 3d pers. sing. pres. ind. of *sum, esse, fuī ;* agrees with *Aeneas* the subj. understood; *est* is to be taken with *secutus* as *secutus est*, the 3d pers. sing. perf. ind. of the deponent verb *sequor*. —— **vōce,** abl. sing. of *vōx, vōcis*, f., 3d; abl. of the means or instrument. —— **secūtus,** nom. sing. m. of the perf. part. of the deponent verb *sequor, sequī, secūtus sum*, 3; agrees with the understood subj.-nom. *Aeneas*, and with *est* above forms the 3d pers. sing. of the perf. indicative.

LINE 407. **Quid,** interrog. adv. = *why ;* see *quid*, l. 9. —— **nātum,** acc. sing. of *nātus, -ī*, m., 2d = *a son* (properly m. of the perf. part. of the deponent verb *nascor, -ī, nātus sum*, 3);   direct obj. of *ludis ; natum*, a pathetic word in this case, = *me*, referring to Aeneas. —— **toti̇̄s,** numeral adv. = *so often* (from the indeclinable adj. *tot* = *so many*) ; modi- fies *ludis*. The demonstrative *totiēs* has a correlative *quotiēs*.   Although Aeneas accuses his mother of *so often* appearing to him in disguise, Vergil only tells us of one other appearance, and then she made herself known at once; cf. Aen. II, 590. —— **crūdēlis,** nom. sing. f. of the 3d decl. adj. *crūdelis, -e ;* agrees with *tū*. —— **tū,** nom. sing. of the 2d (sing.) personal pron. ; subj. of *ludis ; tū* is emphatic, signifying that Aeneas had everything against him if Venus also mocked him. —— **quoque,** adv., going closely with *crudelis ; quoque* expresses Aeneas' feeling of being generally unfortunate. —— **falsīs,** abl. plur. f. of *falsus, -a, -um* (from *fallō*) ; agrees with *imaginibus*.

LINE 408. **Lūdis,** 2d pers. sing. pres. ind. act. of *ludō, -ere, lūsī, lūsum*, 3; agrees with the subj. *tū*. —— **imāginibus,** abl. plur. of *imāgo, imāginis*, f., 3d; abl. of the means or instrument. —— **cūr** (old form *quŏr ;* probably contracted from *quā rē*), interrog. adv.,

409 déxtrae	, iúngere	, déxtram	Nón	datur,	,	ác	is it not granted to
to right hand	*to join*	*right hand*	*not is it granted,*	*and*			join hand to hand,

409 déxtrae , iúngere , déxtram **N**ón datur, , ác | is it not granted to
to right hand *to join* *right hand* *not is it granted, and* | join hand to hand,
ve,rás „ au,díre et , réddere , vóces?" | and hear and utter
true *to hear* *and* *to answer* *words?"* | speech without dis-
| guise?" With this he
410 Tálibus , íncu,sát, „ gres,súmque ad , | makes reproach, and
With such (words) *he reproaches (her),* *and his step* *to* | turns his step towards
411 mœnia , téndit. **Á**t Venus , óbscu,ró „ | the city-walls. But
the walls *turns.* *But* *Venus* *dark* | Venus shrouded

introducing the question following. —— **dextrae,** dat. sing. of *dextra, -ae,* f., 1st (prop-
erly the f. of the adj. *dexter, dextra, dextrum,* with *manus* understood; cf. *sinistra,* =
the left (hand)); a dative of the indirect obj., being a poetical variation for the expected
cum dextrā. —— **iungere,** pres. inf. act. of *iungō, -ere, iunxī, iunctum,* 3; it is prefer-
able to regard *iungere* as substantival, the subj. of *non datur; iungere* may, however, be
regarded as a loose *prolative* infinitive after *non datur* (= *non possumus*), and in any
case prose would require *ut iungamus.* —— **dextram,** acc. sing. of *dextra, -ae,* f., 1st (see
above); direct obj. of *iungere.*

LINE 409. **Nōn** (originally *nē + ūnum*), negative adv., limiting *datur. Nōn* is the
usual negative adverb; *haud* is very rarely used with verbs (except *scio,* e.g. *haud scio
an,* and a few others), but is common with adjectives and adverbs. —— **datur,** 3d pers.
sing. pres. ind. pass. of *dō, dare, dedī, datum,* 1; agrees with the subj.-inf. *iungere; datur*
= *permittitur.* —— **āc** (shortened for *atque*), copulative conj., joining *iungere* and
auaīre; āc is more emphatic than *et,* and is generally used instead of the longer form
atque before consonants, except *c, g,* and *qu.* —— **vērās,** acc. plur. f. of *vērus, -a, -um;*
agrees with *vōces;* there is an intentional contrast between *veras* and *falsis,* l. 407. ——
audīre, pres. inf. act. of *audiō, -īre, -īvī* or *-iī, -ītum,* 4; a subj. of *datur,* joined by *ac* to
iungere above. —— **et,** cop. conj., connecting the two closely joined infinitives *audīre*
and *reddere.* —— **reddere,** pres. inf. act. of *reddō, -ere, reddidī, redditum,* 3 (*re* = *back* +
do = *I give);* joined by *et* to *auaīre.* —— **vōcēs,** acc. plur. of *vōx, vōcis,* f., 3d; direct obj.
of both *audīre* and *reddere.*

LINE 410. **Tālibus,** abl. plur. n. of *tālis, -e* (used substantively, = *with such things,*
or with *verbis* understood); abl. of the instrument. —— **incūsat,** 3d pers. sing. pres. ind.
act. of *incūsō, -āre, -āvī, -ātum,* 1; agrees with the subj.-nom. *Aenēas* understood from
the context. *Incūsō* = lit. *I bring a charge against (in,* = *against,* + *causa,* = *a charge),*
hence *I blame, complain of.* —— **gressum,** acc. sing. of *gressus, -ūs,* m., 4th (from *gradior* =
I walk, I step); direct obj. of *tendit.* —— **que,** enclitic cop. conjunction. —— **ad,** prep. with
the acc.; governing *moenia.* —— **moenia,** acc. plur. of *moenia, -ium,* n., 3d; governed by
the preposition *ad.* —— **tendit,** 3d pers. sing. pres. ind. act. of *tendō, -ere, tetendī, tensum*
or *tentum,* 3 trans. and intrans.; joined by *que* to *incusat* and in agreement with the
same subject. *Tendere* has the following meanings: (1) *to stretch;* (2) *to direct,* e.g.
tendit gressum; (3) absolutely, *I go;* (4) *I aim, strive.*

LINE 411. **At,** adversative conj.; for a comparison of *at, verum, autem,* and *sed,*
consult the note and references on *sed,* l. 19. —— **Venus,** gen. *Veneris,* f., 3d; nom.
sing., subj. of *saepsit.* —— **obscūrō,** abl. sing. m. of *obscūrus, -a, -um;* qualifies *āere.*
Obscūrus (derived probably from *ob* = *in the way,* and the Sanskrit root SKU = *tegere,*
to cover) = (1) *covered over* by anything; this is rare; (2) *dark* in color, or *shady;*
(3) *invisible, unseen;* (4) *obscure, intricate, unintelligible;* (5) of rank, *ignoble;* (6) of
character, *secret.* —— **gradientēs,** acc. plur. m. of *gradiens, -entis,* pres. part. of the

their going with a	gradi, éntes , áëre , sǽpsit, Ét mul, tó nebu, lǽ ,, 412
dense mist, and by	*(them) going with mist enclosed, and plentiful of cloud*
her goddess-power	
wrapt them about	cir, cúm dea , fúdit a, míctu, Cérnere , 413
with a thick veil of	*around the goddess enveloped (them) with a garment, to see*
cloud, lest any might	né quis e, ós, ,, neu , quís con, tíngere , pósset.
see or touch them,	*lest anyone them and lest any one to touch (them) might be able*

deponent verb *gradior, gradī, gressus sum*, 3; substantival participle, direct obj. of *saepsit*. For the participle used as a noun, consult A. & G. 113, *f*; B. no reference, but see 236; G. 437; H. 441. The acc. plur. is given, because Aeneas was accompanied by Achates; see l. 312. —— **āëre**, abl. sing. of *āër, āëris*, m., 3d; abl. of the instrument. The idea of covering a hero with a cloud or body of mist is Homeric; the usual word in Vergil for such a mist is *nebula* or *nubes*. However, ἀήρ is the Homeric word, and is properly applicable, as ἀήρ = *the lower air* as opposed to ἀεθήρ = *the upper air*. Cf. Odyssey, VII, 14, where Athene sheds πολλὴν ἠέρα round about Odysseus. —— **saepsit**, 3d pers. sing. perf. ind. act. of *saepiō, -īre, saepsī, saeptum*, 4 (from *saepēs = a hedge)*; agrees with the subj.-nom. *Venus*.

LINE 412. **Et**, cop. conj., joining *saepsit* and *fudit*. —— **multō**, abl. sing. m. of *multus, -a, -um ;* agrees with *amictū*. —— **nebulae**, gen. sing. of *nebula*, f., 1st (akin to *nūbēs)* ; gen. of the substance or material, describing *amictū*. A. & G. 214, *e*; B. 197; G. 361; H. 395. —— **circum**, adv. (originally acc. of *circus*, and = *in a ring*, hence adv. and prep. = *around*). *Circum* is here by *tmesis* separated from *fudit*, as the construction requires *circumfūdit*. The celebrated example from Ennius is *saxo cere comminuit brum = saxo comminuit cerebrum ;* in later poetry *tmesis* is less common, and is not carried to such lengths. A. & G. 385 ; B. 367, 7; G. 726; H. 636, V, 3. —— **dea**, gen. *deae*, f., 1st; nom. sing., subj. of *circumfūdit;* *dea* = *by divine power*, for unless *dea* had this adverbial sense it would be unnecessary in the sentence, as the subject *Venus* has just been mentioned above. —— **fūdit**, 3d pers. sing. perf. ind. act. of *fundō, -ere, fudi, fusum*, 3; joined by *et* to *saepsit*, and in agreement with the same subj. *Venus ;* for the separation of the one word *circumfudit* into two parts, see the references on *circum* above. —— **amictū**, abl. sing. of *amictus, -ūs*, m., 4th (from *amiciō = I throw around*, hence *that which is cast around, a covering* or *garment) ;* abl. of the means or instrument.

LINE 413. **Cernere**, pres. inf. act. of *cernō, -ere, crēvī, crētum*, 3; *prolative* inf., completing the meaning of *posset*. A. & G. 271; B. 326; G. 423; H. 533. —— **nē**, negative final conj., followed by the subj. *posset;* consult the note on *nē*, l. 299. —— **quis**, nom. sing. m. of the indefinite pron. *quis, quae, quid;* subj. of *posset*. *Quis* is common after *nē* and *si*, but otherwise is little used; it occurs in compounds, e.g. *quis-quam*. —— **eōs**, acc. plur. m. of *is, ea, id*, here used as the 3d personal pronoun; direct obj. of *cernere*. The oblique cases of *is*, as a personal pronoun, are rarely found in poetry. —— **nēu** (= *nē + ve*), conj., used to connect a negative sentence with one which has preceded; such negative sentences may be commands, or imply design or tendency, e.g. *nēve (neu) . . . nēve (neu)*, = *that neither . . . nor*. —— **quis**, nom. sing. m. (see *quis* above); subj. of *posset;* repeated by *anaphora*. —— **contingere**, pres. inf. act. of *contingō, -ere, contigī, contactum*, 3 (*con = cum*, augmentative, + *tangō = I touch) ; prolative* inf. after *posset*. *Contingere* = (1) trans. *to lay hands on, to touch ;* (2) intrans. *to happen*. —— **posset**, 3d pers. sing. imperf. subjunct. of *possum, posse, potuī*, irreg.; agrees with the subj. *quis*. The verb is in the subjunctive mood because *nē* introduces a negative purpose clause; and the tense is imperfect (historic) because the tense of the principal verb *circumfūdit* is the aorist or perfect indefinite (also historic), according to

414 Móli, ríve mo, ram, ,, aút veni, éndi , póscere ,
   or to contrive   delay,   or of (their) coming   to ask
415 caúsas.   Ípsa   Pa, phúm sub, límis ab, ít, ,,
   the causes.   She herself   to Paphos   on high   departs,
416 se, désque re, vísit L&eta su, ás,   ubi , témplum
   and the abodes   revisits   glad   her own, where (is) a temple

or construct delay or demand the causes of their coming. Herself she speeds away on high to Paphos, and gladly revisits her own abode, where her temple is,

---

the rule that primary subordinate tenses follow primary principal tenses, and historic follow historic. A. & G. 286; B. 267, 268; G. 509; H. 491. For purpose clauses after *ut, qui,* and *ne,* consult A. & G. 317; B. 282; G. 545; H. 497.

LINE 414. **Mōlīrī,** pres. inf. of the deponent verb *mōlior, -īrī, -ītus sum,* 4 (*mōlēs = a mass*) ; *prolative* inf., joined by *ve* to *contingere* above. *Molior* has a large number of meanings and applications, e.g. *I build, I remove, I whirl* (*fulmen*), *I design, I destroy,* etc.; the verb implies either great exertion or very careful preparation. —— **ve** (a weaker form of *vel*), enclitic disjunctive conj., in this instance not offering an alternative in opposition to what has been mentioned before (*cernere* and *contingere*), but adding something new. —— **moram,** acc. sing. of *mora, -ae,* f., 1st; direct obj. of *mōlīrī ; mōlīrī moram = to build up delays,* i.e. place obstacles in the way of the Trojans. —— **aut,** disjunctive conj., connecting (without opposing) *poscere* and *mōlīri ;* consult the note on *aut,* l. 183. —— **veniendī,** gen. sing. of the gerund (acc. *veniendum ;* dat. and abl. *veniendo ;* no nom.) of *veniō, -īre, vēnī, ventum,* 4; subjective gen., limiting *causas.* The gerund of a verb is practically a verbal noun, for as a verb it may take an object in the proper case, and as a noun is governed itself by other words. A. & G. 295; B. 338; G. 425, *ff ;* H. 541, 542. —— **poscere,** pres. inf. act. of *poscō, -ere, poposcī,* no supine, 3; *prolative* inf., joined by *aut* to *mōlīri.* —— **causās,** acc. plur. of *causa, -ae,* f., 1st; direct obj. of *poscere.*

LINE 415. **Ipsa,** nom. sing. f. of *ipse, ipsa, ipsum* (gen. *ipsīus,* dat. *ipsī*), intensive pronoun; agrees with *Venus* understood as subj. of *abiit.* —— **Paphum,** acc. sing. of *Paphus* or *Paphos,* gen. *Paphī,* f., 2d ; acc. of the limit of motion, the preposition *ad* or *in* always being omitted in the case of the name of a town or small island. A. & G. 258, *b*; B. 182, 1, *a*; G. 337; H. 380, II. —— **sublīmis,** nom. sing. f. of the 3d decl. adj. *sublīmis, -e* (akin to *sublevō = I raise up*) ; agrees with *ipsa,* and is an adverbial attribute, i.e. modifies the action of the verb *abit.* A. & G. 191; B. 239; G. 325, REM. 6; H. 443. —— **abit,** 3d pers. sing. pres. ind. act. of *abeō, -īre, abiī, abitum,* irreg. (*ab = from + eō = I go*) ; agrees with the subj. *ipsa.* —— **sēdēs,** acc. plur. of *sēdēs, -is,* f., 3d (from *sēdeō = I sit,* hence *a seat, an abode*) ; direct obj. of *revīsit.* Paphos, a town in the island of Cyprus, was a chosen seat of the worship of Venus (Aphrodite); cf. her name *Paphia.* —— **que,** enclitic conj., joining *abit* and *revīsit.* —— **revīsit,** 3d pers. sing. pres. ind. act. of *revīsō, -ere, revīsī* (rare), *revīsum* (rare), 3 (*re, = again, + vīsō, = I visit*) ; agrees with the same subj. as *abit,* to which *que* joins it.

LINE 416. **Laeta,** nom. sing. f. of *laetus, -a, -um ;* agrees with the subj. *ipsa.* Different explanations are given of *laeta :* (1) some follow Servius in regarding *laeta* as a stock epithet, equivalent to φιλομμειδὴς Ἀφροδίτη in Odyssey VIII, l. 362 (which passage Vergil is here imitating and expanding); this view is hardly convincing ; (2) Wagner thinks Venus is *laeta,* because she took particular pleasure in *Paphos,* but it seems unlikely that she would be *glad* to leave her son in order to go to Paphos, and the fact of her having a *templum* at *Paphos* accounts for her visit there ; however, the conjunction of *laeta* and the affectionate adjective *suas* support this view ; (3) the best way to explain *laeta* is to consider it expressive of the relief Venus felt at finding

and   a   hundred | il, lí, „ cen, túmque Sa, bǽo Thúre   ca, lént 417
altars   glow   with
Sabaean incense and | *to her,*   *and a hundred*   *Sabaean*   *with incense*   *glow*
breathe the fragrance | a, rǽ   „   ser, tísque   re, céntibus   ,   hálant.
of fresh-culled gar-
lands.   Meanwhile | *altars,*   *and with garlands*   *fresh*   *breathe fragrant.*
they have hasted on | Córripu, ére vi, *am* íntere, á, „ qua , sémita , 418
their way, where the | *They seized upon the road   meanwhile,*   *where*   *the path*
path guides.   And
now they were climb- | mónstrat.   Iámqu*e* as, cénde, bánt col, lém, „ 419
ing the hill which | *shows (the way).*   *And now*   *they were ascending*   *the hill*

Aeneas safe after the storm ; contrast with it *tristior*, l. 228, when Venus was supplicat-
ing *Jupiter* on behalf of the Trojans. —— **suās**, acc. plur. f. of *suus, -a, -um ;* agrees
with *sēdēs*. —— **ubi**, relative adv. of place, = *where, in which place*, referring to *Paphum ;*
see *ubi*, l. 405. —— **templum**, gen: *templī*, n., 2d ; nom. sing., subj. of *est* understood.
Venus had a celebrated temple at Paphos. —— **illī**, dat. sing. f. of *ille, illa, illud (illīus) ;*
refers to Venus, and is dat. of the possessor after *est* understood. A. & G. 231; B. 190;
G. 349 ; H. 387. —— **centum**, indeclinable cardinal numeral ; qualifying *arae*. Homer
only mentions one altar, but Vergil as usual thinks it necessary to improve upon this.
—— **que**, enclitic conj., joining the sentence in which it stands with the one immediately
preceding. —— **Sabaeō**, abl. sing. n. of *Sabaeus, -a, -um* (of *Saba, -ae*, f., 1st = Saba, the
principal town of Arabia Felix, noted for its myrrh and frankincense) ; agrees with *thure*.
    LINE 417. **Thūre** (*tūre*), abl. sing. of *thūs, thūris*, n., 3d (often written *tūs, tūris ;*
but cf. Greek θύος); abl. of the means or instrument. Venus, as the patron goddess of
the peaceful art of love, preferred offerings of incense and flowers to those of victims.
—— **calent**, 3d pers. plur. pres. ind. act. of *caleō, -ēre, -uī*, no supine, 2 ; agrees with its
subj.-nom. *arae*. —— **ārae**, nom. plur. of *ara, -ae*, f., 1st, subj.-nom. of *calent*. —— **sertīs**,
abl. plur. of *sertum, -ī*, n., 2d (from *sero = I entwine*, hence *a garland*) ; abl. of the
instrument. —— **que**, enclitic conj. —— **recéntibus**, abl. plur. n. of *recens, -entis*, adj. 3d,
= *fresh ;* qualifies *sertīs*. ——**hālant**, 3d pers. plur. pres. ind. act. of *hālō, -āre, -āvī,
-ātum*, 1 ; joined by *que* to *calent* and agrees with the same subj.-nom. *arae*.
    LINE 418. **Corripuēre**, 3d pers. plur. perf. ind. act. of *corripiō, -ere, corripuī, cor-
reptum*, 3 (*con = cum + rapiō*) ; understand *illī* as subj.-nom., i.e. Aeneas and Achates.
Corripere viam is a forcible expression, marking the great haste of the two Trojans ;
Gossrau is quoted as suggesting that the phrase is derived from the notion that a travel-
ler who is hurrying to some place brings the beginning and end of a road together by
quickly traversing it (*corripere* = lit. *to seize together*). —— **viam**, acc. sing. of *via, -ae*,
f., 1st ; direct obj. of *corripuēre*. —— **intereā**, adv. of time. *Intereā*, compounded of
the preposition *inter* and *ea*, is (like *postea*, etc.) a survival from the time when different
words were used together in a special connection, in process of use being united so as to
form a single word. The termination *ea* is : (1) either an abl. f. of *is, ea, id*, with
which *inter* and other prepositions were once admissible ; (2) the neuter acc. plur. of
is ; (3) a few consider *ea* as = *eam*, the acc. f. sing., comparing *interim* which is said to
= *inter + eum*. —— **quā**, adv. .of 'place where,' originally the abl. f. sing. of the rel.
pron. *quī*. —— **sēmita**, gen. *sēmitae*, f., 1st (for *sēmeta*, from *sē*, = *aside*, + *meō*, = *I go*,
hence *that which goes aside, a by-way, a path*) ; nom. sing., subj. of *monstrat*. ——
monstrat, 3d pers. sing. pres. ind. act. of *monstrō, -āre, -āvī, -atum*, 1 ; agrees with the
subj. *sēmita*.
    LINE 419. **Iam**, adv. of time; this adverb expresses the haste which Aeneas had
made. —— **que**, enclitic conj., joining this sentence to the preceding one. —— **ascendē-**

420 qui ，　plúrimus　，　úrbi　ímminet，　，
which　　　*very high*　　*over the city*　　*hangs,*

ádver,sásque ，，as,péctat ，désuper ，árces.
and opposite　　　*faces*　　*from above*　　*the citadels.*

421 Míra,túr mo,lem Aéne,ás，，，ma,gália ，quóndam；
Admires　　*the pile*　*Aeneas*　　　*huts*　　　*once;*

looms massive above the city and looks towards the battlements fronting it below. Aeneas marvels at the city's mass, erewhile but huts,

---

bant, 3d pers. plur. imperf. ind. act. of *ascendō, -ere, ascendī, ascensum,* 3 (*ad* + *scandō* = *I climb*); the implied subj. is *illi,* i.e. Aeneas and Achates. —— **collem,** acc. sing. of *collis, -is,* m., 3d (akin to *celsus = high,* and to the Greek noun κολ-ώνη); direct obj. of *ascendebant*). Synonyms: *mons = a hill* or *mountain,* denoting a rise greater and more precipitous than *collis; collis = a little hill,* suggesting a gradual slope; *tumulus = a hillock* (a diminutive *collis*); *iugum,* specially understood, = *the crest* or *summit* of a hill, but is occasionally used for the hill itself. —— **quī,** nom. sing. m. of the rel. pron.; agrees with its antecedent *collem,* and is subj.-nom. of *imminet.* A. & G. 198; B. 250, 1; G. 614; H. 445. —— **plūrimus,** nom. sing. m. of *plūrimus, -a, -um,* the superl. of the adj. *multus, -a, -um* (comparative *plus*); agrees with *quī,* and is an adverbial attribute = *plūrime. Plurimus = altissimus, very high;* this is one of the peculiar uses of *multus* and its degrees of comparison; cf. *multo amictu = magno* or *denso amictu,* l. 412. —— **urbī,** dat. sing. of *urbs, urbis,* f., 3d; dat. of the indirect object after the compound verb *imminet* (a compound of the prep. *in* and *mineō*). A. & G. 228; B. 187, III; G. 347; H. 386.

LINE 420. **Imminet,** 3d pers. sing. pres. ind. act. of *immineō, -ēre,* no perf., no supine, 2 (*in, = on,* + *mineō, = I hang*); agrees with the subj.-nom. *qui* in the relative clause. —— **adversās,** acc. plur. f. of *adversus, -a, -um* (*ad* + *versus,* perf. part. pass. of *vertō = I turn,* hence *turned towards, facing, opposite*); agrees with *arcēs.* The adjective *adversus* may agree with the subject which faces or the object which is faced; cf. l. 103, *procella velum adversa ferit,* where the adjective agrees with the subject *procella.* In the scansion the chief pause is after *imminet,* where the word and foot end simultaneously (*diaeresis*). A. & G. 358, *c;* B. 366, 8; G. 753; H. 602, 2. There is, however, a *caesura* (marked in the text) after the second syllable of the third foot; this kind of *caesura* is called weak or feminine. —— **que,** enclitic copulative conjunction. —— **aspectat** (*adspectat*), 3d pers. sing. pres. ind. act. of *a(d)spectō, -āre, -āvī, -ātum,* 1 (*ad* + *spectō*); agrees with the subj. *quī,* and is joined to *imminet* by *que.* —— **dēsuper,** adv. of place, = *from above* (*dē, = down from,* + *super, = above*); modifying *aspectat. Dēsuper* is not used by Cicero, but is common in poetry, etc. —— **arcēs,** acc. plur. of *arx, arcis,* f., 3d; direct obj. of *àspectat.*

LINE 421. **Mīrātur,** 3d pers. sing. pres. ind. of the deponent verb *miror, -ārī, -ātus sum,* 1; agrees with its subj. *Aenēās.* —— **mōlem,** acc. sing. of *mōlēs, -is,* f., 3d; direct obj. of *miratur; mōlēs =* (1) *a mass,* as here; (2) *trouble, difficulty,* as in l. 33. —— **Aenēās** (voc. *Aenēā,* acc. *Aenē-ān* or *-an,* dat. *Aenēae,* abl. *Aenēā*), nom. sing. m., 1st decl. Greek noun; subj. of *mīrātur.* A. & G. 37; B. 22; G. 65; H. 50. —— **māgālia,** acc. plur. of *māgālia, -ium,* n., 3d; acc. in apposition with *mōlem,* instead of a relative clause. A. & G. 184; B. 169; G. 320 ff.; H. 359, NOTE 2. *Māgālia = huts,* and is said to be of Phoenician origin; some commentators identify it with *mapālia* in the Georgics, III, 340. —— **quondam** (for *quom-dam,* from *quom,* an old form of *quem,* acc. m. sing. of the rel. *quī,* + the suffix *dam*), adv. of time, = *once, erewhile.* As a temporal adverb, *quondam* has other uses: (1) *sometimes, = aliquando;* (2) *one day* (in the future); cf. *olim = formerly* (in the past) or *one day* (in the future).

| marvels at the gates, at the clash and clamor, and at the paved streets. Zealously the Tyrians press on, some to build the following | Míra,túr *he admires* stráta *the pavements* Tyri,í *the Tyrians* | por,tás, *the gates* vi,árum. *of the streets.* " pars *part* | " , | strepi,túmque *and the bustle* Ínstant *Press on* dúcere *to build* | et , 422 *and* , árden,tés 423 *zealous* , múros, *the walls,* |

LINE 422. **Mīrātur,** 3d pers. sing. pres. ind. of the deponent verb *miror, -ārī, -ātus sum,* 1; agrees with *Aeneās* or a pronoun understood referring to Aeneas. Observe the repetition of the verb *miratur,* expressing the wonder and admiration of Aeneas at the view which met his eyes as he reached the summit of the hill; the repetition of a word at the beginning of a new clause is called *anaphora,* and is a favorite rhetorical device. A. & G. 344, *f*; B. 350, 11, *b*; G. 682, and 636, NOTE 4; H. 636, III, 3. —— **portās,** acc. plur. of *porta, -ae,* f., 1st; direct obj. of *mīrātur.* —— **strepitum,** acc. sing. of *strepitus, -ūs,* m., 4th (from *strepō, -ere, -uī, -itum,* 3, = *I make a noise*); direct obj. of *miratur ;* joined by *que* to *portas* above. —— **que,** enclitic copulative conj. —— **et,** copulative conj., joining *strepitum* and *strāta.* —— **strāta,** acc. plur. n. of *strātus, -a, -um,* perf. part. pass. of *sternō, -ere, strāvī, stratum,* 3 = *I spread out, I strew* (akin to the Greek verb στορέννυμι); direct obj. of *miratur.* *Strāta viārum = strātās viās.* Some take *strāta* as acc. plur. of the noun *strātum, -ī,* n., 2d, and render *the pavements of the streets,* but this is incorrect. The expression *strata viarum* is copied from Lucretius, and = lit. *the strewn things of the streets,* hence *the strewn,* i.e. *paved, streets.* The analogy of several other similar poetical and late prose (Tacitus) expressions, e.g. *augusta viarum* (= *narrow paths*), *tacita suspicionum* (= *silent suspicions*), makes it clear that *strata* is the neuter acc. plur. of the adj. *stratus.* —— **viārum,** gen. plur. of *via, -ae,* f., 1st; partitive gen. after *strāta.* A partitive genitive may be used idiomatically as above, and is even found after adverbs, e.g. *ubi terrarum,* = *where in the world.* In constructions of the kind like *strata viarum* the partitive idea often vanishes; e.g. *amara curarum* (lit. *the bitter things of cares*) = *bitter cares.* A. & G. 216, 3; B. 201, 2; G. 372, NOTE 2, specially; H. 397, 3, NOTE 4. Well-made streets would win a Roman's admiration, for the Romans made excellent roads, as we have still opportunities of observing: the Via Appia from Rome to Brundisium was a marvel of skilled workmanship. Consult the heading *via Appia* in a dictionary of Roman antiquities.'

LINE 423. **Instant,** 3d pers. plur. pres. ind. act. of *instō, -āre, institi, instatum,* 1 (*in,* = *on,* + *stō,* = *I stand,* hence *I hurry on*); agrees with the subj. *Tyrii.* Some editors place a comma or a semicolon after *Tyrii,* in which case *instant* is to be taken absolutely = *work busily,* and the infinitives *ducere, moliri, subvolvere, optare,* and *concludere* in this case become *historic* infinitives, i.e. stand in the place of imperfect indicative tenses (see note on *ducere* below); but it seems more natural to regard *instant* as the main general verb, whose meaning is explained by the *prolative* or explanatory infinitives *ducere,* etc., and whose subject *Tyrii* is subdivided into parts (*pars . . . pars*) mentioned appositively; cf. Aen. II, 627, *instant eruere,* where *eruere* is plainly an explanatory infinitive. The present *instant* is *historic,* depicting the scene more vividly than a past tense. —— **ardentēs,** nom. plur. m. of *ardens, -entis,* the pres. part. act. of *ardeō, -ēre, arsī, arsum,* 2 = (1) *to be on fire,* (2) *to be excited,* (3) *to wish eagerly ;* agrees with the subj. *Tyrii.* —— **Tyrii,** nom. plur. m. of *Tyrius, -a, -um* (adj. of *Tyrus, -ī,* f. 2d = *Tyre,* hence *Tyrii, -ōrum* m., 2d = *the Tyrians*); subj. of *instant.* —— **pars,** gen. *partis,* f., 3d; nom. sing., in partitive apposition with *Tyrii; pars . . . pars = alii . . . alii.* A. & G. 184, *a*; B. 169. 5; G. 322, 323; H. 364. —— **dūcere,** pres. inf. act. of

424 **Móli,ríque** ar,cem, „ ét mani,bús sub,vólvere ,
   and to erect the citadel, and with the hands   to roll up

425 **sáxa** ;   **Párs** **op,táre** **lo,cúm** „ **tec,to,**   ét
  stones ;   *Part* *to choose*   *a site*   *for a house, and*

walls, to raise the citadel and roll up stones by hand; some to choose a site for dwellings and en-

---

dūcō, -ere, dūxī, ductum, 3; prolative inf., dependent on the notion of *eagerness* or *haste* in *instant;* this kind of infinitive is variously called *explanatory, epexegetical, prolative,* and *complementary.* See the note and references under *coluisse,* l. 16. Those who place a stop after *Tyrii* regard *dūcere* and the following infinitives as *historic,* i.e. independent of *instant,* each infinitive being a complete predicate in itself. The *historic* infinitive takes the place of an imperfect indicative, and its subject is in the nominative case; it is used not in stating historical facts but in vivid *descriptions;* Livy uses it frequently in describing the incidents of a battle or a rapid sequence of events. A. & G. 275; B. 335; G. 647; H. 536, 1. The phrase *dūcere mūrōs* expresses the gradual character of the process of building a wall — the wall appears to follow or be led along by the builder; it is imitated from the Greek ἐλαύνειν τεῖχος. —— **mūrōs**, acc. plur. of *murus, -ī,* m., 2d; direct obj. of *dūcere; mūrōs* may refer to city-walls or to house-walls, for the word is general in application, whereas *moenia = city-walls* (*mūniō = I fortify*) and *pariēs = a partition-wall* of a house; here *mūrōs* probably refers to the walls of the *arx,* as a city-wall would be built after the city.

LINE 424. **mōlīrī,** pres. inf. of the deponent verb *mōlior, -īrī, -ītus sum,* 4 (from *mōlēs = a mass*) ; *prolative* inf., joined by *que* to *ducere* and in the same grammatical construction ; *moliri = to build laboriously* and expresses the harder and more difficult nature of the work of building the citadel. —— **que,** enclitic copulative conj. —— **arcem,** acc. sing. of *arx, arcis,* f., 3d ; direct obj. of *moliri.* The colonists of every new settlement made it their first object to build a fort or citadel, to ensure the safety of their lives in case of attack ; a town gradually sprang up around this fort. In the scansion the main *caesura* and pause follows *arcem,* and though the final syllable *-em* is suppressed by *ecthlipsis* (see *multum,* l. 3) before *et* and the first syllable of the third foot is *et,* it seems preferable to mark the pause after *arcem;* those who prefer it may mark the *caesura* after *et,* or after *manibus* in the 4th foot. —— **et,** copulative conj. —— **manibus,** abl. plur. of *manus, -ūs,* f., 4th ; instrumental abl., amplifying *subvolvere.* —— **subvolvere,** pres. inf. act. of *subvolvō, -ere, subvolvī, subvolūtum,* 3 (*sub, = under,* + *volvō, = I roll*) ; *prolative* inf., joined by *et* to *moliri* and in the same grammatical construction; the force of *sub* in the composition is to convey the idea of rolling the stones *from underneath* up the hill on which the citadel was being built. —— **sāxa,** acc. plur. n. of *sāxum, -ī,* n., 2d; direct obj. of *subvolvere.*

LINE 425. **Pars,** gen. *partis,* f., 3d (see *pars,* l. 423 above) ; nom. sing., in partitive apposition with *Tyrii,* constituting the second of the two classes into which the *Tyrians* are divided. It appears that one party of the settlers were at work on the public buildings, the other busy in choosing sites and preparing the foundation of the private dwellings. —— **optāre,** pres. inf. act. of *optō, -āre, -āvī, -ātum,* 1 ; *prolative* inf., dependent on *instant;* the construction simplified is *Tyrii instant, pars (alii) ducere muros,* etc., *pars (alii) optare,* etc. —— **locum,** acc. sing. of *locus, -ī,* m., 2d (plur. *locī,* m., or *loca,* n.); direct obj. of *optāre.* —— **tectō,** dat. sing. of *tectum, -ī,* n., 2d (from *tegō = I cover,* hence *a covering, shelter, house*) ; dat. of the indirect obj. after *optāre locum,* this dative being often called *dat. of purpose.* In prose it occurs in some military phrases, but is employed with freedom by poets ; cf. *receptui canere.* A. & G. 233, *b*; B. 191, 1; G. 356; H. 384, 1, 3). —— **et,** copulative conj. —— **conclūdere,** pres. inf. act. of *conclūdō, -ere,*

trench them with a	con, clúdere , súlco; Iúra ma, gístra, túsque 426
furrow ; laws and	to enclose it with a furrow; Laws and officials
magistrates they	
appoint and a vener-	le, gúnt, ,, sanc, túmque se, nátum ; Híc por, tús 427
able senate; here	they choose, and reverend a senate ; Here harbors

conclūsī, conclūsum, 3 (*cum* + *claudō* = *I shut*) ; joined by *et* to *optāre*. —— *sulcō*, abl. sing. of *sulcus, -ī*, m., 2d ; abl. of the instrument. Probably the phrase *concludere sulco* refers to the drawing of a trench round a site for the purpose of laying foundations ; this explanation best suits the division of the work given here. Some, however, think the reference is to the Roman practice of marking out the city-walls with a *furrow* (*sulcus*) made by a plough ; perhaps there is a hint at the marking out of the amount of land which the strips of bull's hide enclosed (see the note on *tergō*, l. 368).

LINE 426. **Iūra**, acc. plur. of *iūs, iūris*, n., 3d ; direct obj. of *legunt*. It should be noticed that *legunt* does not properly apply to *iura*, but is quite natural with *magistratus;* with *iura* we should expect *constituunt* or some similar verb. The construction whereby one verb is used with two nouns, applying strictly to one only, is called *zeugma;* cf. the Vergilian example, *duces pictasque exure carinas* = (*kill*) *the leaders and set fire to the painted ships*. A. & G. 385 ; B. 374, 2, a; G. 690; H. 636, II, 1. —— **magistrātūs**, acc. plur. of *magistrātus, -ūs*, m., 4th (from *magister*) ; direct obj. of *legunt*, joined by *que* to *iūra; magistratus* may = (1) *magisterial office, magistracy;* (2) as here, *a magistrate*, i.e. one holding such office. —— **que**, enclitic copulative conj. —— **legunt**, 3d pers. plur. pres. ind. act. of *legō, -ere, lēgī, lectum*, 3; the implied subj. is *Tyriī*. This verb must be distinguished from *lēgō, -āre, -āvī, -ātum*, 1 = *I appoint by law*. The principal meanings of *lēgō* (Greek λέγω) are: (1) *I gather, collect;* (2) *I choose, select*, as in this passage; (3) *I levy, enlist;* (4) *I pick, cull*, etc., of fruit and the like; (5) *I read;* there are also other uses. Some editors find much fault with this line, considering that *legunt iura* is opposed to regal apportionment of justice by Dido, in l. 507 (*iura dabat*). It is certainly awkward and inartistic in position between two descriptions of building operations, and is one of those few lines which Vergil would have had occasion to strike out or alter if he had had time to revise the work. But it is essentially a Roman characteristic to take notice of institutions and forms of government, and there is no sufficient reason for supposing that the line is not genuine. —— **sanctum**, acc. sing. m. of *sanctus, -a, -um*, adj. (from *sanciō* = *I render sacred*, hence *august, venerable*) ; agrees with *senatum*. In the early republic a Roman senator was a person revered and respected; cf. the *tribuni plebis*, who were *sacro-sancti*, i.e. *inviolable*. —— **que**, enclitic conj. —— **senātum**, acc. sing. of *senātus, -ūs*, m., 4th; direct obj. of *legunt*, joined by *que* to *magistrātūs*. The Roman Senate (originally composed of men who were nobles and *senes*, = *old men*) was the highest council in the state; its numbers were kept up by admission of those who held curule offices at Rome, e.g. *praetorship, consulship;* but the censors were empowered to dismiss senators overburdened with debt or of bad moral character. After the expulsion of the kings the Senate ruled Rome (through the consuls), but from the time of the Gracchi it had to contend against popular leaders, e.g. Marius. There was a council of *elders* at Rome, called by the Greek name *Gerousia* (γερουσία, from being composed of γερόντες = *old men*).

LINE 427. **Hīc**, adv. of place; it is repeated by *anaphora* below. —— **portūs**, acc. plur. of *portus, -ūs*, m., 4th; direct obj. of *effodiunt*. The harbor of Carthage, called Cothon, was not a natural one, but artificially constructed; it is unlikely that newly-arrived settlers would *make* a harbor before they had built a town, but the detail adds variety to the description. —— **alii**, nom. plur. of *alius, -a, -ud* (gen. *alīus*, dat. *aliī*) ; subj. of *effodiunt; alii . . . alii* (see next line) are partitive appositives of *Tyrii* under-

ali,*i*	éffodi,únt;	„	hic	álta	the,átris
some	*dig out;*		*here*	*deep*	*for theatres*

428 **Fúnda,ménta lo,cánt** ali,*i*, „ ímma,nésque
foundations *place* *others,* *and immense*

429 **co,lúmnas Rúpibus** , éxci,dúnt, „ sce,nís
columns *from the cliffs* *cut out,* *for stages*

430 **deco,ra álta fu,túris :** **Quális a,pés aes,táte**
decorations *tall* *future:* *(such) as* *bees* *in the summer*

some are digging out harbors; here others are setting deep the foundations of a theatre, and are hewing mighty columns from the cliffs, the lofty splendor of a stage to be. Even as the bees are kept

---

stood as subj. of *legunt.* —— **effodiunt**, 3d pers. plur. pres. ind. act. of *effodiō, -ere, effōdī, effossum,* 3 (*ex,* = *out,* + *fodiō,* = *I dig*); agrees with the subj. *alii.* —— **hīc**, adv. of place. —— **alta**, acc. plur. n. of *altus, -a, -um ;* agrees with *fundāmenta ; alta* here = *deep,* as viewed from above. —— **theātrīs**, dat. plur. of *theātrum, -ī,* n., 2d (Greek θέατρον); dat. of the indirect object, like *tectō,* l. 425. There is another reading *theātrī,* the gen. sing.; the only objection to *theatris* is that the settlers would not build more than *one* theatre, but this objection is futile, as the plural is simply the common poetical variation from the singular. The building of a theatre is a very late Roman idea, but Vergil seems to have a Greek colony in his mind in this description; the Greeks would not have omitted to build a theatre for public festivals and plays.

LINE 428. **Fundāmenta**, acc. plur. of *fundāmentum, -ī,* n., 2d (from *fundō,* I = *I found,* and *fundus, -ī,* m., 2d = Greek βυθός, i.e. *depth* or *the bottom*); direct obj. of *locant.* ——**locant**, 3d pers. plur. pres. ind. act. of *locō, -āre -āvī, -ātum,* I (*locus = a place);* agrees with the subj. *alii.* —— **aliī**, nom. plur. of *alius, -a, -ud ;* subj. of *locant,* and in partitive apposition with *Tyrii* understood. —— **immānēs**, acc. plur. f. of *immā-nis, -e,* adj. 3d; qualifies *columnās.* —— **que**, enclitic copulative conjunction. —— **colum-nās**, acc. plur. of *columna, -ae,* f., 1st (Greek κολώνη); *columen* and *culmen* are kindred forms of *columna,* and the root is the same as in *celsus* and *collis);* direct obj. of *excidunt.*

LINE 429. **Rūpibus**, abl. plur. of *rūpēs, -is,* f., 3d; abl. of separation, governed by the preposition *ex* in the compound verb *excidunt.* —— **excīdunt**, 3d pers. plur. pres. ind. act. of *excīdō, -ere, excīdī, excīsum,* 3 (*ex,* = *out,* + *caedō,* = *I cut);* agrees with the subj. *alii* and is joined by *que* to *locant.* —— **scēnīs** (*scaenīs*), dat. plur. of *sc(a)ēna, -ae,* f., 1st (see note on *scēna,* l. 164); dat. of the indirect object implying the end aimed at, for references to which consult the note on *tectō,* l. 425. —— **decora**, acc. plur. of *decus, decoris,* n., 3d (akin to *decet = it becomes ;* hence *that which becomes, an ornament);* acc. in apposition with the acc. *columnas.* —— **alta**, acc. plur. n. of *altus, -a, -um ;* qualifies *decora ; alta* here = *high,* i.e. as viewed from below (but see *alta,* l. 427 above). —— **futūrīs**, dat. plur. f. of *futūrus, -a, -um,* the fut. part. of the verb *sum, esse, fuī ;* in agreement with *scēnīs.*

LINE 430. **Quālis**, nom. sing. m. of *quālis, -e* (correlative of the demonstr. adj. *tālis, -e);* agrees with *labor.* *Quālis* is used here (as often elsewhere) to introduce a simile; the construction is compressed, for the full grammatical construction would be *talis labor est qualis* (*labor*) *exercet apes,* etc. = *the work is such as the work is which busily employs the bees,* etc. —— **apēs**, acc. plur. of *apis, -is,* f., 3d (= lit. *the drinker,* i.e. of the juice of flowers, from the Sanskrit root PI = *to drink,* with *a* as prefix, cf. Greek πί-νω = *I drink);* direct obj. of *exercet.* This simile of the bees is mainly reproduced from Georgics, IV, ll. 162 ff. —— **aestāte**, abl. sing. of *aestās, -ātis,* f., 3d; abl. of 'time when.' Time *when* is expressed by the ablative alone, time *within which* by the ablative alone or by the ablative with the preposition *in.* A. & G. 256;

busy by their toil be-
neath the sun amid
the flowery meadows

while the summer is
young, when they
lead out the grown
brood of their race
or when they press
the flowing honey

no, vá „ per , flórea , rúra Éxer, cét sub , 431
early   through   flowery   the fields keeps busy   under

sóle la, bór, „ cum , géntis a, dúltos
the sun toil,   when   of the swarm full-grown

Édu, cúnt fe, tús, „ aut , cúm li, quéntia , mélla 432
they lead out the brood,   or   when   flowing   the honey

B. 230; G. 393; H. 429.——novā, abl. sing. f. of *novus, -a, -um;* agrees with *aestate.*
——per, prep. with the acc.; gov. *rūra.*——flōrea, acc. plur. n. of *flōreus, -a, -um*
(from *flōs, flōris,* m. = *a flower*)*;* qualifies *rūra.*——rūra, acc. plur. of *rūs, rūris,* n.,
3d (only found in the plural in the nom. and acc. cases, = *fields;* the sing. = *the coun-*
try)*;* governed by the preposition *per.* Synonyms: *rus = the country,* as opposed to
urbs = a city, or *oppidum = a town,* and the adj. *rusticus, = countrified (boorish),* is simi-
larly opposed to the adj. *urbānus, = citified (polite);* *rura,* the plural, = *the fields,*
field-country as distinct from *agri = fields* (the plural number of *ager = a field);* *regio*
= *a region,* a large tract of country including fields, cities, etc.; *patria = country,* i.e.
native country.

LINE 431. Éxercet, 3d pers. sing. pres. ind. act. of *ēxerceō, -ēre, -uī, -itum,* 2 (*ēx,* =
out, + *arceō,* = *I shut up*)*;* agrees with the subj. *labor.* *Exercet* here = *keeps in motion,*
keeps busy; a second meaning of *exercēre* is *to practise,* i.e. a pursuit, or *to engage in* an
occupation.——sub, prep. with the acc. and abl.; gov. the abl. *sōle.*——sōle, abl. sing.
of *sōl, sōlis,* m., 3d; governed by *sub;* with *sub sole,* cf., *sub Iove,* the difference being that
sub Iove = in daylight, while *sub sole = in sunlight.* —— labor, gen. *labōris,* m., 3d;
nom. sing., subj. of *exercet.*—— cum (other forms are *quum, quom,* and rarely *qum,* each
a form of the adverbial acc. of the rel. pron. *quī*), temporal conj., governing the ind.
educunt. *Cum* is here practically a correlative of *aestate nova* (= an adv. *tum*), and =
in which, when. *Cum* temporal takes the subjunctive mood in the imperfect and plu-
perfect tenses, and the indicative in the rest; but when it is merely explanatory of a
time just mentioned (e.g. of an adv. *tum* preceding), *cum* may take the indicative in all
tenses. *Cum* may introduce also (1) a *causal* clause (*cum = since, as*), (2) a *concessive*
clause (*cum = although*)*;* in both cases it is followed by the subjunctive mood. A. & G.
325, 326; B. 286, 2, 288, 289, and 309, 3; G. 581-587; H. 515, III, 517, and 521.——
gentis, gen. sing. of *gens,* f., 3d; partitive gen., after *adultos fetus.*——adultōs, acc.
plur. m. of *adultus, -a, -um,* perf. part. pass. of *adolescō, -ere, adolēvī (adoluī* rare),
adultum, 3 (*ad,* = *up,* + root OL, = *to grow);* agrees with *fētūs.* The inceptive *adolesco*
is more commonly used than the form *adoleō, -ēre, adoluī* (rarely *adolēvī*), *adultum,* 2.

LINE 432. Édūcunt, 3d pers. plur. pres. ind. act. of *ēdūcō, -ere, ēdūxī, ēductum,* 3
(*ē,* = *out,* + *dūcō,* = *I lead*)*;* agrees with *illi* understood as subj., referring to *apes.*——
fētūs, acc. plur. of *fētus, -ūs,* m., 4th (akin to *fēmina);* direct. obj. of *ēdūcunt.*——aut,
disjunctive conj., introducing an alternative source of employment. See the note on *aut,*
l. 183. —— cum, temporal conj., followed by the ind. *stipant* and *distendunt;* see *cum*
in the preceding line.—— līquentia, acc. plur. n. of *līquens, -entis,* pres. part. of the
deponent verb *līquor, līquī,* no perf., 3; agrees attributively with *mella.* Observe that
the first syllable of *līquentia* is long; in Aen. V, 238, *vīna līquentia fundam,* the first
syllable is short, the participle in this case being from the verb *līqueō, -ēre, liquī* or *licuī,*
no supine, 2. The active verb *līquō, -āre, -āvī, -ātum,* 1, has the first syllable short. The
quantity of the *i* seems to have been doubtful, but is in most cases short, cf. the noun
līquor, and the adjective is usually *līquidus,* though Lucretius three times has *līquidus.*

433 **Stípant,　,　ét dul,cí　„ dis,téndunt　,　néctare　,**
they press,　and　sweet　　　　stretch　　　　with nectar

434 **céllas; Aút one,ra áccipi,únt „ veni,éntum, aut,**
the cells; or the loads they receive　of those coming,　or

435 **ágmine　,　fácto　Ígna,vúm fu,cós „ pecus　,　á**
a column having been made　lazy　the droves　a herd from

and with sweet nectar swell their cells or receive the burdens of the comers, or marshalling in array drive the drones, an idle herd, away from

---

—— **mella,** acc. plur. of *mel, mellis,* n., 3d (akin to Greek μέλι); direct obj. of *stipant;* the plural is poetic variation for the singular.

LINE 433. **Stípant,** 3d pers. plur. pres. ind. act. of *stīpō, -āre, -āvī, -ātum,* 1 (= *I stamp tight, I pack*) ; understand a pronoun referring to *apes* as the subject; *stipant* is an expressive word, the sound of the heavy *spondee* representing the labor of packing the honey together. —— **et,** copulative conj. —— **dulcī,** abl. sing. of *dulcis, -e,* adj., 3d; qualifies *nectare.* —— **distendunt,** 3d pers. plur. pres. ind. act. of *distendō, -ere, distendī, distensum* or *distentum,* 3 (*dis,* = *apart,* + *tendō,* = *I stretch*) ; joined by *et* to *stipant* and in the same construction. —— **nectare,** abl. sing. of *nectar, -aris,* n., 3d (Greek νέκταρ); abl. of the instrument, with *distendunt.* *Nectar* is the name of the drink of the gods, as *ambrosia* is the name of their food; *nectar* is sometimes, as here, used metaphorically with reference to something, e.g. wine, honey, of extraordinary sweetness. —— **cellās,** acc. plur. of *cella, -ae,* f., 1st (akin to *cēlō* = *I hide,* hence *cella* = *a storehouse*) ; direct obj. of *distendunt.*

LINE 434. **Aut,** disjunctive conj. —— **onera,** acc. plur. of *onus, oneris,* n., 3d; direct obj. of *accipiunt.* —— **accipiunt,** 3d pers. plur. pres. ind. act. of *accipiō, -ere, accēpī, acceptum,* 3 (*ad* + *capiō*) ; joined by *aut* to *distendunt,* and in agreement with the same subject. The admirable military, social, and economic arrangements and institutions of bees form the chief topic of interest in the fourth Georgic; they are there seen to have an admirable system for dividing labor proportionately, to appreciate the value of work in their own community. Thus the simile given in this passage applies very well, as an illustration of the business of the Carthaginians in building a settlement. —— **venientum,** gen. plur. of *veniens, -entis,* pres. part. (substantival) of *veniō, -ire, vēnī, ventum,* 4; poss. gen., limiting *onera ; venientum* is an old form of the usual genitive *venientium.* A. & G. 113, *f;* B. see 236; G. 437; H. 441. —— **aut,** disjunctive conj. —— **agmine,** abl. sing. of *agmen, agminis,* n., 3d (from *agō* = *I lead*) ; in the abl. abs. construction with *factō.* It should be remembered that the ablative absolute (i.e. a noun in the ablative combined with a participle, adjective, or other noun in agreement) serves to modify the verbal predicate of a sentence; the construction is only allowed when the words in the ablative are not the same as the subject, object, or dependent case of the verbal predicate. A. & G. 255; B. 227; G. 409, 410; H. 431. Bees (and ants) are remarkable for the system and organization in everything they do; most animals and insects put their own interests first, but these think first of the good of the community. —— **factō,** abl. sing. n. of *factus, -a, -um,* perf. part. of *fīō, fierī, factus sum* (used as passive of *faciō, facere, fēcī, factum,* 3; agrees with *agmine* in the abl. abs. construction.

LINE 435. **Ignāvum,** acc. sing. n. of *ignāvus, -a, -um* (*in,* = *not,* + (*g*)*navus,* = *busy*) ; qualifies *pecus.* —— **fūcos,** acc. plur. of *fūcus, -ī,* m., 2d; direct obj. of *arcent.* —— **pecus,** acc. sing. of *pecus, pecoris,* n., 3d (akin to *pecu,* n., = *cattle*) ; acc. in apposition with *fucos.* *Pecus, pecoris,* 3d, = *a herd,* in a collective sense, whether of *cattle, bees, seals,* etc., as opposed to *pecus, pecudis,* f., 3d, which = *a single head of cattle.* Observe the peculiar arrangement of the words; we should expect *fucos, ignavum pecus,* or *ignavum pecus, fucos;* cf Horace, Odes, I, viii, 1, *Lydia, dic, per omnes te deos oro.*

the enclosure; the	prae,sépibus	,	árcent:	Férvet	o,pús, 436
work glows hotly,	*the hives*		*they keep off:*	*glows*	*the work,*
and the sweet-scented	redo,léntque	thy,mó	,,	fra,grántia	, mélla.
honey is fragrant with	*and smells*	*of thyme*		*fragrant*	*the honey.*
thyme. "O happy	"Ó for,túna,tí,	,,	quo,rúm	iam	, mœ́nia , 437
ye, whose city-walls	*"O happy men,*		*whose*	*now*	*walls*
are now arising!"					
Aeneas cries, while	súrgunt!"	Aéne,ás	ait, ,	ét, ,,	fas,tígia , 438
he gazes up at the	*are rising!"*	*Aeneas*	*says,*	*and*	*the pinnacles*

—— ā, prep. with the abl.; gov. *praesēpibus*, expressing separation. —— **praesēpibus,** abl. plur. of *praesēpe, -is,* n., 3d, or *praesēpēs, -is,* f., 3d (cf. another form *praesēpia, -ae,* f., 1st; all from *prae,* = *in front,* + *saepiō,* = *I hedge in,* hence *an enclosure,* or *a hive of bees*); governed by the preposition *a.* —— **arcent,** 3d pers. plur. pres. ind. act. of *arceō, -ēre, -uī,* no supine, 2; joined by *aut* to *accipiunt,* and in agreement with the same subject, viz. *illi* or *apes.*

LINE 436. **Fervet,** 3d pers. sing. pres. ind. act. of *ferveō, -ēre, ferbuī,* no supine, 2 (a collateral form is *fervō, -ere, fervī,* no supine, 3; both are intransitive); agrees with the subj. *opus.* *Fervēre* = *to be hot,* or, of liquids, *to boil, to seethe;* metaphorically it refers to excitement or passion, = *to rave, burn* (with love), *to rage,* etc.: *fervet opus,* = *the work glows,* i.e. *is carried on swiftly,* for motion causes heat. —— **opus,** gen. *operis,* n., 3d; nom. sing., subj. of *fervet.* —— **redolent,** 3d pers. plur. pres. ind. act. of *redoleō, -ēre, -uī,* no supine, 2 (*re* or *red,* + *oleō,* = *I smell of*); agrees with the subj. *mella.* —— **que,** enclitic copulative conj., joining its own to the preceding sentence. —— **thymō,** abl. sing of *thymum, -ī,* n., 2d (Greek θύμον); abl. of the means or instrument, with *redolent.* —— **frāgrantia,** nom. plur. n. of *frāgans, -antis,* pres. part. act. of *frāgrō, -āre, -āvī, -ātum,* 1; agrees attributively with *mella.* —— **mella,** nom. plur. of *mel, mellis,* n., 3d; subj. of *redolent.*

LINE 437. **Ō,** exclamation, with the voc. case *fortunatī.* —— **fortūnātī,** voc. plur. of *fortūnātus, -a, -um,* adj. (strictly perf. part. pass. of *fortūnō, -āre, -āvī, -ātum,* 1 = *I make fortunate;* from *fortuna*); the case of address, for *Aēneas* addresses his soliloquy to the Phoenician settlers. —— **quōrum,** gen. plur. m. of the rel. pron. *qui, quae, quod;* agree in gender and number with its antecedent *fortunati,* and is a poss. gen. limiting *moenia.* —— **iam,** adv. of time, modifying the verb *surgunt.* —— **moenia,** gen. *moenium,* n., 3d; nom. plur., subj. of *surgunt.* The reference to *moenia* = *city-walls* may be taken as supporting the argument that *concludere sulco,* l. 425, refers to marking out the walls of the city; but poetry is never really exact, and *moenia* possibly means nothing more than *urbs* or *tecta.* —— **surgunt,** 3d pers. plur. pres. ind. act. of *surgō, -ere, surrēxī, surrectum,* 3 (*sub* + *regō*); agrees with the subj. *moenia.* The dominating note of the whole of the Aeneid is the difficulty of the Trojans in finding a place where they might make a fixed home.

LINE 438. **Aenēās,** nom. sing., sub. of *ait.* —— **ait,** 3d pers. sing. pres. ind. act. of the defective verb *āiō;* agrees with the subj.-nom. *Aenēās.* The present is more nearly complete than the other defective tenses, having 1st pers. *āiō,* 2d *ais,* 3d *ait,* and 3d plur. *āiunt;* the imperf. *āiēbam* is conjugated throughout. A. & G. 144, *a*; B. 135; G. 175, 1; H. 297, II, 1. —— **et,** copulative conj. The only *caesura* in the line (except one after *Aeneas*) follows *et.* —— **fastīgia,** acc. plur. of *fastīgium, -ī,* n., 2d (see the note on *fastigia,* l. 342); direct obj. of *suspicit.* —— **suspicit,** 3d pers. sing. pres. ind. act. of *suspiciō, -ere, suspēxī, suspectum,* 3 (*sub* + *speciō*); joined by *et* to *ait,* and agrees with

439 súspicit , úrbis.　Ínfert , sé　saep,tús nebu,lá, „| roof-tops of the city.
looks up at　of the city.　He bears himself enveloped　by a cloud, | Cloud-girt　he　goes
440 mi,rábile , díctu,　Pér　medi,ós,　mis,cétque | among them — won-
wonderful　to say,　through　their midst,　and mingles | drous　to　tell — in
vi,rís ;　　„　neque　,　cérnitur　,　úlli. | their midst, mingles
with the men;　nor　is he seen　by any one. | with the men, yet
 | is　seen　of　none.

the same subject *Aeneas. Suspicere = to look at from beneath,* and its use here is one of
the many signs of Vergil's mastery of language and literary devices ; it implies that
Aeneas, who had in l. 420 gazed in wonder at the newly-building city from the hill-top,
has now descended the hill and is approaching with the city still in view on another slope
before him. *Suspicere* sometimes = *to look askance at* (hence *suspectus = suspected ;* cf.
suspicio), apparently from the notion of *looking up at* with the eyes under frowning eye-
brows. —— **urbis**, gen. sing. of *urbs*, f., 3d; poss. gen., limiting *fastigia.*

LINE 439. **Infert**, 3d pers. sing. pres. ind. act. of *inferō, inferre, intulī, illātum,*
irreg. (*in,* = *in* or *into,* + *ferō,* = *I carry*) *;* agrees with *Aeneas* understood or a pron.
referring to Aeneas. —— **sē**, acc. sing. of the reflexive pron. *sē (sēsē),* gen. *suī,* dat. *sibi,*
abl. *sē (sēsē) ;* direct obj. of *infert,* and refers back to the subj. of *infert,* i.e. to Aeneas.
Sē is the reflexive pronoun of the 3d person, singular or plural, irrespective of gender.
A. & G. 196 ; B. 85, and 244 ; G. 309 ; H. 449. —— **saeptus**, nom. sing. m. of the perf.
part. pass. of *saepiō, -īre, saepsī, saeptum,* 4 (*saepes = a hedge,* hence *I hedge in, enclose*) *;*
agrees with and extends (in place of a relative clause) the subj. of *infert.* —— **nebulā**,
abl. sing. of *nebula, -ae,* f., 1st ; abl. of the instrument. —— **mīrābile**, acc. sing. n. of
mīrābilis, -e, adj. 3d (from *mīror,* = *I wonder at*) *;* acc. sing. in apposition to the pre-
ceding sentence. This construction is Greek by origin ; cf. Sophocles' Electra, l. 130,
ἥκετ', ἐμῶν καμάτων παραμύθιον = *you have come,* (your coming being) *a solace to my
woes.* A. & G. 240, *g* ; B. no reference ; G. 324 ; H. 363, 5. —— **dictū**, supine in *u* of
dīcō, -ere, dīxī, dictum, 3 ; defines *mirabile.* The supine in *u* is a verbal abstract of the
4th declension, being probably an ablative of specification ; the supine in *um* is an acc.,
denoting *purpose,* and used instead of a final clause after verbs of motion. Only a few
supines in *u* are found, e.g. *dictu, visu, auditu,* and a few others ; they are used with
adjectives (or the nouns *fas, nefas,* and *opus*) to explain the reference. A. &. G. 303 ;
B. 340, 2 ; G. 436 ; H. 547.

LINE 440. **Per,** prep. with the acc.; gov. *mediōs.* —— **mediōs**, acc. plur. m. of
medius, -a, -um ; governed by *per ;* with *mediōs* supply *viros, Tyrios,* or some plural
noun referring to the inhabitants, with which *medios* agrees partitively, i.e. denoting a
particular place. —— **miscet**, 3d pers. sing. pres. ind. act. of *misceō, -ēre, -uī, mixtum* or
mistum, 2; joined by *que* to *infert ;* understand *se* (from *infert se*) as direct obj. of
miscet. —— **que**, enclitic copulative conj. —— **virīs**, dat. plur. of *vir, virī,* m., 2d; a
poetic dat. (instead of *cum* + the abl. *virīs ;* cf. l. 408, *cur dextrae* (for *cum dextrā*)
iungere dextram non datur ? The dative is frequently used by poets who imitate Greek
idioms, where in prose a noun would be governed by a preposition ; this is specially
common after verbs signifying *to contend,* e.g. *contendis Homero,* = *you vie with Homer.*
A. & G. 229, *c*; B. no reference ; G. 346, NOTE 6; H. 385, 4, 3). —— **neque** (*ne + que,*
= *and . . . not*), coördinate disjunctive conj., joining *miscet* and *cernitur.* —— **cer-
nitur,** 3d pers. sing. pres. ind. pass. of *cernō, -ere, crēvī, crētum,* 3; joined by *neque* to
miscet. —— **ūllī**, dat. sing. of *ullus, -a, -um* (gen. *ullīus,* dat. *ullī*) *;* dat. of the agent
after *cernitur.* The dative of the agent is rare in Latin, except in poets; even then it is
seldom found except after perfect passive tenses or perfect participles passive (the dative

A grove there was in	Lúcus in , úrbe	fu, ít	medi, á,	„ lae, tíssimus , 441
the city's centre, with	*A grove in the city*	*there was*	*middle,*	*very rich*
wealth of shade, the	úmbrae, Quó pri, múm		iac, tátī	un, dís „ 442
spot where first the				
Phoenicians, tossed	*in shade, which*	*first*	*having been tossed*	*by waves*
by wave and whirl-	et , túrbine	,	Pœ́ni	Éffo, dére	lo, có 443
wind, dug out the	*and whirlwind*		*the Carthaginians*	*dug out*	*in place*

---

in such cases being a dat. of the indirect object after a part of *sum* present or supplied; see note on *mihi*, l. 326). The dat. of the agent is regular after gerundives, e.g. *hoc mihi faciendum est*, and is also usually employed after *videor;* but its use with other verbs and other tenses than the perfect passive (or participle) is not a Latin idiom, but an imitation of Greek models; cf. Ovid's *non intelligor ulli.* Some try to avoid the difficulty by considering *ulli* as a dative of the person interested or affected, i.e. *is not seen (visible) to* or *for any one.* A. & G. 232; B. 189; G. 354; H. 388, 1, 3, and 4.

LINE 441. **Lūcus**, gen. *lūcī*, m., 2d; nom. sing., subj. of *fuit.* Synonyms : *silva* = a wild, untended forest; *nemus = a grove*, a cluster of trees; *lucus = a woodland glade,* sacred to some deity. —— **in**, prep. with the acc. or abl.; gov. the abl. *urbe.* —— **urbe**, abl. sing. of *urbs, urbis*, f., 3d; governed by the preposition *in.* —— **fuit**, 3d pers. sing. perf. ind. act. of *sum, esse, fuī ;* agrees with the subj. *lucus.* —— **mediā**, abl. sing. f. of *medius, -a, -um ;* agrees, with partitive signification, with *urbe.* —— **laetissimus**, nom. sing. m. of the superlative degree of the adj. *laetus, -a, -um* (comparative, *laetior) ;* agrees with *lūcus.* The meanings of *laetus* are noticeable : (1) *glad;* (2) *ready, willing;* (3) *delighting in,* e.g. l. 275, *tegmine laetus;* (4) *propitious;* (5) *luxuriant,* of crops; (6) *abounding in, full of,* with the ablative or genitive. —— **umbrae**, gen. sing. of *umbra,* f., 1st; gen. of specification, after *laetissimus.* Some consider a gen. of abundance, such as follows *plenus;* but though there is not a great distinction between the two genitives, *laetus* is scarcely equivalent to *plēnus;* on the other hand, there are many phrases very similar to this, in which the genitive is one of specification. A. & G. 218, *c;* B. 204, 4; G. 374, NOTE 1; H. 399, III, 1. Some editors support the reading *umbrā,* which is an abl. of abundance or else an abl. of specification; this variant reading probably arose from an incomplete knowledge of the two last meanings of *laetus* referred to in the note on *laetissimus* above.

LINE 442. **Quō**, abl. sing. m. of the rel. adj. *quī, quae, quod;* agrees with *loco.* —— **prīmum**, adv. of time (see the note on *primum*, l. 174); *primum* clearly refers to the first arrival of the Phoenicians. Some suppose *primum* to be acc. sing. neuter of the adj. *primus, -a, -um,* agreeing with *signum.* —— **iactātī**, nom. plur. m. of *iactātus, -a, -um,* perf. part. pass. of *iactō, -āre, -āvī, -ātum,* 1; agrees with the subj. *Poeni,* which it enlarges like a temporal clause, *cum iactati essent.* —— **undīs**, abl. plur. of *unda, -ae,* f., 1st; abl. of the instrument. —— **et**, copulative conj., joining *undis* and *turbine.* —— **turbine**, abl. sing. of *turbō, turbinis,* m., 3d (another is found, *turben, turbinis,* n., 3d;) abl. of the means or instrument, like *undis.* The root of the noun *turbo* (also of the verb *turbo*) expresses rotatory motion; hence *turbo* = (1) *a whirlwind;* (2) *a spinning-top ;* (3) *a spindle;* (4) *a circle* of duties. —— **Poenī**, gen. *Poenōrum,* m., 2d; nom. plur., subj. of *effōdēre.*

LINE 443. **Effōdēre**, 3d pers. plur. perf. ind. act. of *effōdiō, -ere, effōdī, effossum,* 3 (*ex, = out,* + *fōdiō, = I dig*); agrees with the subj. *Poeni.* The perfect active has two terminations, viz. in *-ērunt,* and in *-ēre ;* the former occurs more often in classical prose, but the latter (*-ēre*), which was a popular form, is very much in favor with the poets, owing to its adaptability to most metres. Observe that there is nothing to distinguish

444 sig‚núm,	„ quod	, régia	Iúno	Mónstra‚rát,	token which royal
the token,	*which*	*royal*	*Juno*	*had indicated,*	Juno had forewarned,

caput , ácris e‚quí; „ sic , nám fore ,
the head   spirited   of a horse;   (saying) thus   for   would be

445 béllo Égregi‚am ét faci‚lém vic‚tú „ per ,
in war   excellent   and   easy   in living   through

the head of a war-horse — that thereby their race should be glorious in war and rich in store through-

the 3d plur. perf. act. from the present infinitive in form; however, the context and the scansion prove infallible guides. —— **locō**, abl. sing. of *locus, -ī,* m., 2d; abl. of 'place where.' —— **signum**, gen. *signī,* n., 2d; acc. sing., direct obj. of *effodēre; signum* does not = *standard* here, but *token* or *sign,* for see the next line where the sign is shown to be the head of a war-horse. —— *Signum* has several meanings : (1) *sign, token;* (2) *military standard,* especially the *aquila* (*eagle*)*;* (3) *signal, watchword;* (4) *an image;* (5) *constellation.* —— **quod**, acc. sing. n. of the rel. pron. *quī, quae, quod;* agrees with its antecedent *signum* in gender and number, and is the direct obj. of *mon-strārat.* —— **rēgia**, nom. sing. f. of *rēgius, -a, -um* (from *rēx, rēgis,* m., 3d; cf. *rēgina*)*;* qualifies *Iuno.* —— **Iūnō**, gen. *Iūnōnis,* f., 3d: nom. sing., subj. of *monstrārat.*

LINE 444.   **Monstrārat**, 3d pers. sing. pluperf. ind. act. of *monstrō, -āre, -āvī, -atum,* 1 ; agrees with the subj. *Iuno* in the rel. clause introduced by *quo . . . loco; monstrārat* is a syncopated or contracted form of *monstrāverat.* A. & G. 128, I, 2; B. 7, 2, and 367, 8; G. 131, 1; H. 235. *Monstrarat* signifies that Juno had indicated to the Carthaginians where they should find the token, not that she actually pointed it out to them. —— **caput**, gen. *capitis,* n., 3d; acc. sing., in apposition with *signum.* —— **ācris**, gen. sing. m. of *ācer, ācris, ācre* (for *ac-cer,* from *acuō = I sharpen*)*;* qualifies *equi.* Many editors find fault with this adjective as applied to a dead horse, but probably *acer equus* was a regular term for a *war-horse,* just as *navis longa* is the regular phrase for a *war-ship. Acer* has many meanings : (1) *sharp, pointed;* (2) *sharp, keen,* of sight or of wit; (3) *eager, spirited;* (4) in a bad sense, *hot, violent.* —— **equī**, gen. sing. of *equus, -ī,* m., 2d; poss. gen., limiting *caput.* —— **sīc**, adv. of manner; = the notion *hoc signo effosso,* i.e. if the head were dug up; Juno made the finding of the token the condition of the prosperity. —— **nam**, explanatory conj., usually prae-positive. A verb of saying, e.g. *dixerat,* must be supplied, though it is implied by *monstrarat,* to introduce the oblique oration following? the sentence may be thus put together — *nam (dixerat) gentem sic* (= *signo effosso*) *fore egregiam,* etc. —— **fore**, fut. inf. of *sum, esse, fui* (there is also a periphrastic fut. inf. *futurus, -a, -um esse*)*;* agrees with its subj.-acc. *gentem* in the acc. and inf. construction, the oblique oration being introduced by the notion of *speaking, saying,* in *monstrarat;* see *nam* above. The infinitive is future because the fame of Carthage is subsequent to the time of the main verb *monstrarat.* A. & G. 272, and REM.; B. 330, 331; G. 527; H. 534, 535. —— **bellō**, abl. sing. of *bellum, -ī,* n., 2d; abl. of specification. A. & G. 253; B. 226; G. 397; H. 424. The token of the war-horse prefigured military renown. Vergil is doubtless thinking of the struggle between Rome and Carthage for the empire of the world; but in fact, the Carthaginians made better merchants than soldiers, for though Hamilcar and Hannibal were great generals, their soldiery was largely mercenary and barbarian.

LINE 445.   **Ēgregiam**, acc. sing. f. of *ēgregius, -a, -um* (from *ē, = out of,* + *grex,* = *the herd,* hence (1) *extraordinary, excellent,* (2) *illustrious*)*;* predicate adj., agreeing with the subj.-acc. *gentem.* —— **et**, copulative conj., joining *egregiam* and *facilem.* —— **facilem**, acc. sing. f. of *facilis, -e,* adj., 3d (from *facio*)*;* predicate attribute of *gentem;* *egregiam* and *facilem* are each complements of the copula *fore. Facilem victu* = lit. *easy*

out the ages. Here to Juno Sidonian Dido was founding a mighty temple richly blessed with offerings and the divine presence of the goddess, whereof the threshold	sæcula , géntem. Híc tem,plúm Iu,nóni 446			
	the ages	*(that) the race.*	*Here*	*a temple*	*to Juno*

in,géns „ Si,dónia , Dído Cónde,bát, do,nís „ 447
huge *Sidonian* *Dido* *was founding,* *with gifts*

opu,léntum et , númine , divae ; Aérea , cuí 448
wealthy *and* *the favor of the goddess; bronze to which*

in living, i.e. abounding in store; *facilem* is a transferred epithet, for it properly refers to *victu*, i.e. *facile victu = with easy living;* this transference of words is called *hypallage*. A. & G. 385; B. no reference; G. 693, HYPALLAGE; H. 636, IV, 2. —— *victū*, supine in *u* of *vīvō, -ere, vīxī, victum,* 3; a verbal abl. of specification, explaining *facilem ; facilem victu = divitem,* and denotes prosperity in commerce and the arts of peace. For the use of the supine in *u*, consult the note on *dictu*, l. 439. —— **per**, prep. with the acc.; gov. *saecula*. —— **gentem**, acc. sing. of *gens, gentis*, f., 3d; subj.-acc. of *fore* in the reported speech.

LINE 446. **Hīc**, adv. of place, i.e. in Carthage or perhaps the very spot where the *signum* was found. —— **templum**, gen. *templī*, n., 2d; acc. sing., direct obj. of *condebat.* —— **Iūnōnī**, dat. sing. of *Iūnō, -ōnis*, f., 3d; dat. of reference (*commodi vel incommodi*). A. & G. 235; B. 188, 1; G. 350; H. 384, 1, 2). Juno's long-standing hatred of the Trojan race and her foresight of the rivalry between Rome (of Trojan origin) and Carthage induced her to interest herself in the latter city from the very beginning of the circumstances which oaused Dido to leave Phoenicia as Sychaeus directed; naturally Juno was regarded as the patron-goddess of Carthage, and her temple was begun at the same time as the building of the city. —— **ingēns**, gen. *ingentis*, adj., 3d; acc. sing., qualifying *templum.* —— **Sīdōnia**, nom. sing. f. of *Sīdōnius, -a, -um* (adj. of noun *Sīdon*, gen. *Sīdōnis* or *Sīdŏnis*, f., 3d, acc. *Sīdōna*)*;* an attribute of *Dido.* Dido came from Tyre, but she and Carthage (*urbs Sidonia*) are called *Sidonia* because Sidon was the mother-city of Tyre. —— **Dīdō**, gen. *Dīdōnis* or *Dīdūs*, f., 3d; nom. sing., subj. of *condebat.*

LINE 447. **Condēbat**, 3d pers. sing. imperf. ind. act. of *condō, -ere, condidī, conditum,* 3; agrees with the subj. *Iūnō.* —— **dōnīs**, abl. plur. of *dōnum, -ī*, n., 2d; abl. of specification, descriptive of *opulentum.* The *dona* were probably the *gifts* of those who came to the shrine to worship; in this case, this early mention of rich gifts somewhat anticipates the future: others think that *divae* limits *donis* as well as *numine*, and that *donis divae = the gifts belonging to the goddess*, i.e. the various vases, censers, etc., used in her worship. —— **opulentum**, acc. sing. n. of *opulentus, -a, -um* (from *opēs, = wealth);* agrees with *templum ; opulentum* goes with *numine* by a kind of *zeugma.* —— **et**, copulative conj., joining *donis* and *numine.* —— **nūmine**, abl. sing. of *nūmen, nūminis*, n., 3d (from *nuō, = I nod);* abl. of specification, after *opulentum ; numine* probably = *presence* of the goddess, though the adjective *opulentum* induces some to suppose *numine = a statue of the goddess.* —— **dīvae**, gen. sing. of *dīva, -ae*, f., 1st (*dīvus, -ī*, m., 2d, is the corresponding masculine noun); poss. gen., limiting *nūmine.*

LINE 448. **Aerea**, nom. plur. n. of *aereus, -a, -um* (adj. of *aes, aeris*, n., 3d = *bronze);* qualifies *limina ; aerea* is predicative, going closely with *surgebant = of which the threshold* (*was*) *of bronze* (*which*) *ran up*, etc. —— **cuī**, dat. sing. n. of the rel. pron. *quī, quae, quod;* agrees in gender and number with the antecedent *templum*, and is a dat. of reference used to qualify the whole idea in the place of the possessive gen. modifying only a single word. A. & G. 235, *a*; B. 188, 1; G. 350, 1; H. 384, 4, NOTE 2. The relative usually stands first in its clause. —— **gradibus**, abl. plur. of *gradus, -ūs*, m., 4th (from

gradi,bús　„　sur,gébant　,　límina,　,　níxaeque
in steps　　　*were rising*　　*thresholds,*　*and supported*

449 **Aére**　tra,bés :　„　fori,bús　car,dó　stri,débat
by bronze　*beams :*　„　*on the doors*　*the hinge*　*was creaking*

450 a ,énis.　**Hóc**　pri,mum　ín　lu,có　„　nova　,　rés
brazen.　　*This*　　*first*　　*in*　*grove*　　*new*　　*a thing*

with its rising steps was bronze, on bronze the upper lintel rested, bronze the doors whereon the grating hinges fitted. In this grove first a strange sight met

---

gradior, = *I step*); abl. of the means, or it may be considered an abl. of manner. —— **surgēbant,** 3d pers. plur. imperf. ind. act. of *surgō, -ere, surrēxī, surrectum,* 3 (*sub +
regō*); agrees with its subj. *limina* in the rel. clause introduced by *cui.* —— **limina,** nom. plur. of *līmen, līminis,* n., 3d (for *lig-men,* from *ligō* = *I bind,* hence *that which fastens, a door,* and more commonly by extension *a threshold*); subj. of *surgebant.* —— **nīxae,** nom. plur. f. of *nīxus, -a, -um,* perf. part. of the deponent verb *nītor, nītī, nīsus sum* or *nīxus sum,* 3, = *to rest upon something;* agrees with *trabes.* There is a better supported reading *nexae,* but it is hard to explain, and so many commentators prefer to read the easily understood *nixae. Nixae aere* = *leaning on* or *supported by* bronze (i.e. bronze columns); it would not be a perfect description of a temple if the pillars, so imposing and important a feature of ancient architecture, were passed over in silence. If we read *nexae,* it is not apparent what *trabes* can refer to; Conington renders "*door-posts,*" but Mr. Page points out that the ancient door-post was part of the door itself; the latter likewise adds that *trabes* has in Horace the special sense of *architrave,* the *upper lintel,* which is just what is required here to complete the description. Those who read *nexae* (nom. plur. f. of *nexus, -a, -um,* perf. part. pass. of *nexō, -ere, nexī,* or *nexuī, nexum,* 3, = *I bind*) say that *nexae aere* = *aeratae* (*bronze-plated*); they add that it is unlikely the pillars would be of bronze. —— **que,** enclitic copulative conj., joining *līmina* and *trabes.* Observe that this line is hypermetrical, the final *que* being over and above the required number of feet, but permissible because it is *elided* before *aere,* the initial word of the next line; the elision of an extra syllable in a line is called *synapheia.* A. & G. 359, *c,* REM.; B. 367, 6; G. 728; H. 608, 1, NOTE 5.

LINE 449. **Aere,** abl. sing. of *aes, aeris,* n., 3d; abl. of 'place where' with *nixae. Aes* = *bronze,* being a compound of copper and tin, and should not be rendered *brass* (a compound of copper and zinc), which was perhaps unknown to the ancients. Observe the repetition of the composition, *aerea . . . aere . . . aēnis;* it is emphatic, and calls attention to the part which bronze plays in the different divisions of the front of the temple. Incidentally this makes it more likely that *trabes* = *the upper lintel;* for if *trabes* = *door-posts,* the description is very inadequate. —— **trabēs,** nom. plur. of *trabs, trabis,* f., 3d; subj. of *surgebant* (understood from *surgebant* in the previous line). *Trabs* often has the meaning of *beam,* and *trabes* in one place in Horace = *architrave,* so probably *trabes* = *beams,* i.e. *architrave,* in this passage rather than *door-posts;* besides, the door-posts were part of the door, running into sockets at top and bottom and not the supports of the architrave, as we understand door-posts. —— **foribus,** dat. plur. of *foris, -is,* f., 3d; dat. of reference, similar to *cui* in the previous line. —— **cardō,** gen. *cardinis,* m., 3d; nom. sing., subj. of *stridebat;* the *cardines* were the pivots of the door-posts (properly so called), revolving in sockets above and below (the sockets being called *cardines* as well). —— **strīdēbat,** 3d pers. sing. imperf. ind. act. of *strīdeō, -ēre, strīdī,* no supine, 2; agrees with the subj. *cardō.* There is a 3d conjug. form *strīdō, -ere, strīdī,* no supine. —— **aēnis,** dat. plur. f. of *aēnus, -a, -um* (*aes, aeris,* n., 3d); qualifies *foribus.*

LINE 450. **Hōc,** abl. sing. m. of the demonstr. adj. *hīc, haec, hōc;* agrees with *luco,* and is emphatic by position in the sentence. —— **prīmum,** adv. of time. —— **in,** prep.

him and allayed his	ob,láta		ti,mórem	Léniit, ,	híc pri,mum 451
fear, here first Aeneas	*having presented itself*		*his fear*	*soothed,*	*here* *first*
took heart to hope for	Aéne,ás	"	spe,ráre	sal,útem	Aúsus et, 452
	Aeneas		*to hope for*	*safety*	*dared and*
safety and better trust	áfflic,tís	"	meli,ús	con,fídere	, rébus.
his stricken fortunes.	*shattered*		*better*	*to trust in*	*his fortunes.*

with the acc. or abl.; gov. the abl. *luco.* —— **nova,** nom. sing. f. of *novus, -a, -um;* agrees with *rēs; nova* = *strange.* —— **rēs,** gen. *reī,* f., 5th (*res* and *dies* are the only 5th decl. nouns complete in singular and plural); nom. sing., subj. of *lēniit.* —— **oblāta,** nom. sing. f. of *oblātus, -a, -um,* perf. part. pass. of *offerō, offerre, obtulī, oblātum,* irreg. (*ob* + *ferō*); predicate participle agreeing with *res; res oblata* = lit. *a thing brought forward before* (*Aeneas*), and is best rendered by an English abstract noun followed by the gen. of the noun qualified by the participle, e.g. *the meeting of a new sight.* In this case, as in many others, e.g. *ante urbem conditam* = *before the founding of the city,* the principal idea is contained in the participle. A. & G. 292, *a* ; B. 337, 5; G. 437, NOTE 2; H. 549, 5, NOTE 2. —— **timōrem,** acc. sing. of *timor, timōris,* m., 3d (from *timeō,* = *I fear*); direct obj. of *lēniit.*

LINE 451. **Lēniit,** 3d pers. sing. perf. ind. act. of *lēniō, -īre, -īvī* or *-iī, -ītum,* 4 (*lēnis* = *soft, gentle*); agrees with the subj. *res.* —— **hīc,** adv. of place, with demonstrative force (from the demonstrative adj. *hīc, haec, hōc*). Vergil here indulges in a little impassioned rhetoric, and to emphasize the first occasion on which Aeneas " ventured to hope" employs the figure *anaphora, hoc in luco* (= *hic*) . . . *hic,* and also *asyndeton,* for no conjunction connects this with the preceding sentence in spite of the fact that the grammatical subjects are different. —— **prīmum,** adv. of time. Observe the repetition of *primum* from the line above (*anaphora*). —— **Aenēās,** nom. sing., subj. of *ausus* (*est*). —— **spērāre,** pres. inf. act. of *spērō, -āre, -āvī, -ātum,* 1; *prolative* or explanatory inf. after *ausus* (*est*). —— **salūtem,** acc. sing. of *salūs, -ūtis,* f., 3d (*salvus* = *sound, safe*); direct obj. of *spērāre; salus* = (1) *soundness* of condition; (2) *safety;* (3) *welfare;* (4) *greeting;* (5) *Salūs* personified, the goddess of Health, worshipped by the Greeks under the name of *Hygeia.*

LINE 452. **Ausus** (*est*), 3d pers. sing. perf. ind. of *audeō, -ēre, ausus sum,* 2, semideponent; agrees with the subj. *Aeneas;* the indicative of *sum* is very often omitted, both as the copula and as a part of compound tenses. A. & G. 206, *c*, 2; B. 166, 3; G. 209; H. 368, 3. On the form of semi-deponent verbs, consult A. & G. 136; B. 114, 1; G. 167, 1; H. 268, 3, and 465, 2, NOTE 2. —— **et,** cop. conj., joining the complementary infinitives *sperare* and *confidere.* —— **afflictīs,** abl. plur. f. of *afflictus, -a, -um,* perf. part. pass. of *affligō* (*adflīgō,* etc.), *-ere, afflīxī, afflictum,* 3 (*ad* + *flīgō*); predicate participle agreeing with *rebus; afflictis* is equivalent to a *concessive* clause introduced by *cum,* = *although they were crushed.* —— **melius,** adv. modifying *confidere; melius* is the comparative of the adv. *bene;* superlative *optime.* Observe that the comparison of adverbs follows the comparison of the adjectives from which the adverbs are formed; adj. *bonus;* comparative *melior;* superlative *optimus.* A. & G. 92; B. 76, 2, and 77, 1; G. 93; H. 306. —— **confidere,** pres. inf. of the semi-deponent verb *confīdo, -ere, confīsus sum,* 3 (*cum* + the semi-deponent *fīdō*); prolative inf., joined by *et* to *spērāre.* —— **rēbus,** abl. plur. of *rēs, reī,* f., 5th; governed by *confidere. Confido* may take either the dative or the ablative case; it usually takes the abl. in reference to things, the dative in reference to persons. But there are numerous cases in which the dative (of things) follows *confido,* and *rebus* may very well be the dat. here. A. & G. 254, *b*; B. 219, 1, *a*; G. 401, NOTE 6; H. 425, 1, 1), NOTE. *Delector, gaudeo, nitor, fretus,* etc., take a similar ablative.

453 **Námque**   sub   ,   íngen,tí   „   lus,trát   dum ,
For indeed   *under*   *huge*   *he views*   *while*

454 **síngula**   ,   témplo **Régi**,n*am* ópperi,éns, „ dum, ,
each thing   *the temple*   *the queen*   *awaiting,*   *while,*

455 quǽ   for,túna   sit   ,   úrbi,   **Á**rtifi,cúmque
what   *the fortune*   *is*   *to the city*   *and of the workmen*

For while at the mighty temple's foot he scans each scene, waiting the Queen's coming, while he wonders at the city's fortune, the rival handiwork of the

---

LINE 453. **Namque** (*nam* + *que*), *nam* is a causal conj. with enclitic *que* as suffix. A combinate conjunction as above is emphatic and connects a sentence more clearly than a simple conjunction with what has preceded; cf. *at enim, itaque*, etc. A. & G. 208, *e*; B. 345; G. 498; H. 554, V. —— **que**, enclitic conj., strengthening *nam*. —— **sub**, prep. with the acc. or abl.; gov. the abl. *templō; sub templo = at the foot of the temple*, i.e. Aeneas was standing looking up at the temple from below. —— **ingenti**, abl. sing. n. of *ingens, -entis*, adj. 3d of one termination; qualifies *templō*. —— **lustrat**, 3d pers. sing. pres. ind. act. of *lustrō, -āre, -āvī, -ātum*, 1; supply *Aeneas* as subject; the mood is indicative after *dum = while*. —— **dum**, temporal conj., = *while*. *Dum*, meaning *while*, takes the *present indicative* (less commonly the perfect or imperfect) even in reference to the past and even in subordinate sentences in *oratio obliqua : dum* may mean *until*, followed by the indicative or, if doubt or purpose be implied, by the subjunctive. A. & G. 328; B. 293, III; G. 572; H. 519, II, NOTE I. *Dum* follows its verb here, but usually precedes it. —— **singula**, acc. plur. n. of *singulī, -ae, -a*, the distributive of the numeral *ūnus, -a, -um ;* direct object of *lustrat*. —— **templō**, abl. sing. of *templum, -ī*, n., 2d; governed by *sub*.

LINE 454. **Rēgīnam**, acc. sing. of *rēgīna, -ae*, f., 1st; direct obj. of *opperiens ; reginam = Didonem*. A question suggests itself—how did Aeneas know that Dido was going to come? Possibly he was so informed by the workmen. —— **opperiēns**, gen. *opperientis ;* nom. sing of the pres. part. of the deponent verb *opperior, -īrī, opperītus* or *oppertus sum*, 4 ; agrees with and enlarges the subj. of *lustrat*. —— **dum**, temporal conj., governing the indicative *miratur*. *Dum* is repeated for effect from the preceding line ; observe that the repetition takes the place of a conjunction connecting the clause *dum miratur* with the previous one *dum lustrat*. —— **quae**, nom. sing. f. of the interrog. adj. *quī, quae, quod ;* agrees with the subj. *fortuna ;* the clause *quae fortuna sit urbi*, an indirect question or rather an indirect exclamation, is one of the objects of *miratur* and = *egregiam fortunam urbis*. —— **fortūna**, gen. *fortunae*, f., 1st; nom. sing., subj. of *sit* in the indirect exclamation *quae sit fortuna*. —— **sit**, 3d pers. sing. pres. subjunct. of *sum, esse, fui ;* agrees with the subj. *fortuna ;* the mood is subjunctive beca use the clause expresses an indirect exclamation. Mr. Sidgwick quotes Aen. X, 20, *Cernis ut insultent Rutuli*, = *thou seest how the Rutulians insult ;* the direct would be *how the Rutulians insult !* So here the direct would probably be *what fortune the city has !* In indirect questions and indirect exclamations the rule is the same, viz. that the verb of the indirect clause must be subjunctive, and must follow the tense (as *primary* or *historic*) of the principal verb; so *sit* (primary) follows *miratur* (primary). A. & G. 334; B. 300; G. 467; H. 528, 2, and 529, I. —— **urbī**, dat. sing. of *urbs, urbis*, f., 3d ; dat. of the possessor, after *sit ;* we may render *I have* as *habeo* or *est mihi*.

LINE 455. **Artificum**, gen. plur. of *artifex, artificis*, 3d, common gender (*ars + faciō*) ; poss. gen., limiting *manūs*. —— **que**, enclitic cop. conj., connecting *manūs* with the object clause *quae fortuna sit urbi*. —— **manūs**, acc. plur. of *manus, -ūs*, f., 4th; direct obj. of *miratur; manūs =* not the *hands* which do the work, but *the work*

craftsmen and the fine labor of building, he sees presented in their order the battles of Ilium and that warfare already noised abroad by	ma, nús „ in, tér se ope, rúmque la, bórem
	the hands *among themselves and of the works* *the toil*
	Míra, túr, videt, Ília, cás „ ex , órdine , 456
	he marvels at, he sees *Trojan* *according to* *order*
	púgnas, Béllaque , iám fa, má „ to, túm vul, gáta 457
	the battles and the wars *already by report* *whole* *spread*

(*handiwork*) produced by the hands ; cf. *artes*, which sometimes = *art-productions*. —— **inter**, prep. with the acc.; governing *sē*. —— **sē**, acc. plur. of the reflexive pron. *sē ;* governed by *inter*. *Inter se* is very difficult to explain, and the difficulty has given rise to several different views and 'emendations : (1) *se* may refer back to *manūs* (*artificum*), and then *inter se* = (*admires*) the work (*of the artificers*) *as compared, the one with the other ;* (2) *inter se* may go loosely with *artificum*, in which case the sentence is to be taken as if *certantium inter se* were read, = *the work of the craftsmen* (lit. *among themselves*, i.e.) *vieing with one another ;* Conington understands it in this way, and renders *the craftsmen's rival skill ;* (3) many read *mīrantur* instead of *mīrātur*, the subjects being Aeneas and Achates, the main objection to this reading being the change of the subject from singular to plural. In this case *inter se* is easily explained, referring back to the subj. of *mirantur* (viz. to *īllī* understood, i.e. Aeneas and Achates), and the sentence = *they admire among themselves ;* this emendation is very plausible ; (4) a few MSS. have *intrā sē* = *within himself,* i.e. in his own mind ; render then *Aeneas admires within his heart the work,* etc. ; (5) the reading *intrans* his won some support = *Aeneas, as he enters, admires the work,* etc. ; (6) *nitidas* = *shining, resplendent,* is a conjecture, but not very plausible ; if accepted, it agrees with *manus.* —— **operum**, gen. plur. of *opus, -eris,* n., 3d ; poss. gen., limiting *laborem.* —— **que,** enclitic cop. conj. —— **labōrem,** acc. sing. of *labor, labōris,* m., 3d ; direct obj. of *miratur,* joined by *que* to *manūs* above. *Operum laborem* probably = *the labor of* (i.e. involved in) *the works ;* it may be taken as = *the fine finish of the work,* a figurative sense of *labor.*
    LINE 456. **Mīrātur,** 3d pers. sing. pres. ind. of the deponent verb *mīror, -ārī, -ātus sum,* 1 ; agrees with *ille* understood as subj. referring to *Aeneās ;* in some editions the reading *mīrantur* is adopted, for which refer to (3) in the note on *se,* l. 455 above. —— **videt,** 3d pers. sing. pres. ind. act. of *video, -ēre, vīdī, vīsum,* 2 ; the implied subj. is *Aeneas ;* in the complex sentence beginning l. 453 and ending l. 458, the principal verb is *videt.* —— **Īliacās,** acc. plur. f. of *Īliacus, -a, -um* (belonging to *Ilium* = *Troy*) *;* agrees with *pugnās ; Iliacas pugnas* = *the battles fought at Troy,* between the Greeks and Trojans. —— **ēx,** prep. with the abl.; gov. *ordine ; ex* here has the idiomatic sense *according to,* cf. *ex consuetudine.* A. & G. 152, *b ;* B. 142, 2; G. 417; H. 434. —— **ordine,** abl. sing. of *ordō, ordinis,* m., 3d; governed by the preposition *ex ; ex ordine* alludes to the representation of each battle in its proper order of sequence. —— **pugnās,** acc. plur. of *pugna, -ae,* f., 1st; direct obj. of *videt.*
    LINE 457. **Bella,** acc. plur. of *bellum, -ī,* n., 2d; direct obj. of *videt,* joined by *que* to *pugnas* above. —— **que,** enclitic cop. conj. —— **iam,** adv. of time, modifying *vulgata ; iam* refers, not to the times in which Vergil lived, but to the time when Aeneas arrived at Carthage. —— **fāmā,** abl. sing. of *fāma, -ae,* f., 1st (Greek φήμη; cf. *fārī* = *to speak*) *;* abl. of the means, with *vulgata ; fama* = (1) *rumor,* (2) *renown,* as here. —— **tōtum,** acc. sing. m. of *tōtus, -a, -um* (gen. *tōtīus,* dat. *tōtī*) *;* agrees with *orbem ;* see the note on *toto,* l. 29. —— **vulgāta** (*volgāta*), nom. plur. n. of *vulgātus, -a, -um,* perf. part. pass. of *vulgō, -āre, -āvī, -ātum,* 1 = lit. *I spread among the people* (*vulgus* or *volgus, -ī,* m. and n., 2d); agrees with and enlarges *bella ; vulgata* = a relative clause, *quae vulgata erant.*

458 per　　, 　órbenf,　Átri,dás,　　Pria,múmque, ,,　rumor t h r o u g h o u t
　　through　　the world,　the Atridae,　　and Priam,　the world, the sons
　et　　,　　sǽvum　　am,bóbus　　A,chíllen.　of Atreus and Priam,
　and　　fierce　　to both　　Achilles.　and Achilles fierce
459 Cónstitit, , ét lacri,máns, ,, "Quis , iám locus,", foe of both.　He
　He stopped,　and　weeping,　"What　now　place," spake, "What place

──── per, prep. with the acc.; gov. orbem. ──── orbem, acc. sing. of orbis, -is, m., 3d;
governed by per; orbis = (1) a circle; (2) the world, in prose with terrārum added.
　　LINE 458. Ātrīdās, acc. plur. of Ātrīdēs, gen. Ātrīdae, m., 1st decl. Greek patro-
nymic noun, = son of Atreus; a direct obj. of videt, not connected by a conjunction
(asyndeton) with pugnas or bella because Vergil now mentions, not general subjects
depicted on the walls, but particular individuals. For 1st decl. Greek nouns, consult
A. & G. 37; B. 21, 2, d, and 22, like Cometes; G. 65; H. 50, like Pyrites. The sons of
Atreus indicated are Agamemnon and Menelaus, the leaders of the Greek host before
Troy. ──── Priamum, acc. sing. of Priamus, -ī, m., 2d; joined by que to Atridas.
Priam, the son of Laomedon, was the last king of Troy; he married Hecuba, by whom
he had 19 children (so Homer; or 17, according to Cicero), the most famous being
Paris, Hector, Cassandra, Troilus, Deiphobus, and Helenus. Priam was finally slain by
Neoptolemus, son of Achilles. ──── qᴜe, enclitic cop. conj., connecting Atridas and
Priamum. ──── et, cop. conj. ──── saevum, acc. sing. m. of saevus, -a, -um; qualifies
Achillēn. ──── ambōbus, dat. plur. m. of ambō, -ae, -ō, = both, numeral adj.; dat. of the
indirect obj. after saevus. A. & G. 226, a; B. 187; G. 350, DATIVE OF PERSONAL INTER-
EST; H. 382. Ambō is thus declined: acc. ambōs or ambo, ambas, ambō; gen. ambōrum,
ambārum, ambōrum; dat. and abl. ambōbus, ambābus, ambōbus, or occasionally ambis,
m., f., and n. A. & G. 94, b; B. 80, 2, a; G. 95, and NOTE 2; H. 175, NOTE 2. Whereas
duo simply = two, ambō = both, i.e. each of two persons or parties considered together;
uterque = either, i.e. two parties considered separately. The distinction between ambo
and uterque is well exemplified by the following sentence (quoted from Cicero, Fin. II,
7, 20): Qui utrumque probat, ambobus debuit uti = he who approves of either one ought
to have made use of both. Ambōbus is used here because the Atridae are one party,
Priam being the other: Achilles was wrathful against the former because Agamemnon
refused to give him Briseis, his spoil of war, which was the origin of the μῆνις = violent
wrath of Achilles and his refusal to fight till after the death of Patroclus; Achilles was
fierce against Priam with the Greeks in general, but Achilles appears particularly saevus
as the slayer of Hector, son of Priam, whose body he dragged along the ground. ────
Achillēn, acc. sing. of Achillēs, m., mixed decl. Greek noun (see note on Achillī, l. 30);
direct obj. of videt, joined by et to Priamum; some read Achiliem, but in the best MSS.
Greek nouns ending in -es have the acc. in -ēn, and those ending in -as have it in -an
(not -am).
　　LINE 459. Constitit, 3d pers. sing. perf. ind. act. of constō, -āre, constitī, constitum,
1 irreg. and intrans. (con = cum, + stō); the implied subj. is Aenēās or a pron. referring
to him. ──── et, cop. conj. ──── lacrimāns, gen. lacrimāntis, nom. sing. m. of the pres.
part. act. of lacrimō, -āre, -āvī, -ātum, 1 (with a rarer collateral deponent form, lacri-
mor, -ārī, -ātus sum, 1; from lacrima, = a tear (sometimes written lacryma, lachryma,
or lacruma)); agrees with and enlarges the subj. of inquit. Aeneas finds much in the
representation of the war to arouse his emotions and call forth tears; we find him weep-
ing copiously (largo) in l. 465, and still shedding tears in l. 470. The ancient Greeks
did not think it the weak and almost shameful thing which the Anglo-Saxons do for a

is there now, Achates,	ínquit,	"A,cháte,	Quǽ regi,*o* ín ᵗer,rís	,, nos,trí 460
what quarter of the	he says,	"Achates,	what　region　in　lands	our
earth that is not full				
of our sorrow? Lo,	non, plḗna la,bóris?		Én Pria,mús!	,, Sunt, 461
Priam! Even here	not　(is) full of trouble?		Lo　Priam!	There are

man to give vent to his emotion in tears; the hero Odysseus indulges in many weepings
in the Odyssey. —— **quis**, nom. sing. m. of *quis, quae, quid*, the interrog. pron. here used
adjectively (instead of the usual interrog. adj. *quī, quae, quod*); agrees with the subj.
locus. —— **iam**, adv. of time, modifies *plenus est* (understood from *plena*, l. 460); *iam* =
iam nunc, at this time. —— **locus**, gen. *locī*, m., 2d; nom. sing., subj. of *est* understood
in the predicate *plenus est* (*plenus* being also understood, from *plena* in the next line).
—— **inquit**, 3d pers. sing. pres. ind. act. of the defective and irreg. verb *inquam*; joined
by *et* to *constitit*, and in agreement with the same subject. *Inquam* has a complete
pres. ind., but no other tenses are fully gone through. *Inquam* (esp. *inquit*) usually
stands within direct quotations, like the English *quoth he*. A. & G. 144, *b*; B. 134;
G. 175, 2; H. 297, II, 2. —— **Achātē**, voc. sing. of *Achātēs, -ae*, m., 1st decl. Greek
noun (see references under *Atridas*, l. 458); case of the person addressed.

LINE 460. **Quae**, nom. sing. f. of the interrog. adj. *quī, quae, quod*; agrees with the
verb *est* understood in the predicate *plena* (*est*). —— **regiō**, *regiōnis*, f., 3d; nom. sing.,
subj. of *plena* (*est*). —— **in**, prep. with the acc. and abl.; gov. the abl. *terrīs*. —— **terrīs**,
abl. plur. of *terra, -ae*, f., 1st; governed by *in*; *in terris* = *in omnibus terris* or *in orbe*
terrarum. —— **nostrī**, gen. sing. m. of *noster, nostra, nostrum*, poss. adj. of *nōs*, the 1st
(plur.) personal pron.; agrees with *laboris*; *nostri* refers not only to Aeneas and
Achates, but to all the Trojans. —— **nōn**, negative adv., limiting the predicate *plena*
(*est*). *Nōn* negatives verbs, adjectives, or adverbs; *haud* rarely negatives verbs, but
frequently adjectives and adverbs. —— **plēna**, nom. sing. f. of *plēnus, -a, -um*; agrees
with the subj. *regiō*, and is the complement of the copula *est* understood, the full predi-
cate being *plena* (*est*). The indicative and infinitive moods of the copula *sum* are very
often omitted, when it is easy to supply the omission from the context. A. & G. 206, *c*,
2; B. 166, 3; G. 209; H. 368, 3. Observe that the predicate (*plenus est*) of the first
subject *locus* has to be understood from the predicate (*plena est*) of the second subject
regiō. This is frequently the case, especially when there are several singular subjects of
different genders, all having the same predicate. A. & G. 205, *d*; B. 255, 2 and 3;
G. 285, EXCEPTION, 1; H. 463, I. —— **labōris**, gen. sing. of *labor*, m., 3d; objective
gen., which follows adjectives expressing *fulness, knowledge, power, memory*, etc., and
their opposites. A. & G. 218, *a*; B. 204, 1; G. 374; H. 399, I, 2.

LINE 461. **Ēn**, interjection, used with the nom. case. *Ēn* is also often used with
the imperative mood to attract notice, e.g. *en age*. Synonyms: *em* = *lo!* and *ecce* = *lo*
here!, both used with the accusative case in early Latin, e.g. *ecce hominem* = *lo! the*
man! or *there is the man!*; *ecce* takes the nominative only in classical Latin; *en* (distin-
guished from *em*) was not used till Cicero, and is followed by the nominative; *O* takes the
vocative; *prō* takes the vocative, rarely accusative; *vae* and *ei* take the dative, e.g. *vae*
victis = *woe to the conquered*. —— **Priamus**, gen. *Priamī*, m., 2d; nom. sing., nom. after
the exclamatory interjection *en*. —— **sunt**, 3d pers. plur. pres. ind. of *sum, esse, fuī*; agrees
with the subj. *praemia*. —— **hīc**, adv. of place. —— **etiam** (*et + iam*), intensive sociative
conj., or adverb (see *etiam*, l. 25). —— **sua**, nom. plur. n. of the reflexive adj. *suus, -a, -um*;
agrees with *praemia*; *suus* is not often used referring to a word which is not subject of
its sentence, but it is quite allowable here for *praemia sunt laudi* = *laus habet praemia*,
and *sua* = *propria*, i.e. its own. —— **praemia**, nom. plur. of *praemium, -ī*, n., 2d; subj.
of *sunt*. —— **laudī**, dat. sing. of *laus, laudis*, f., 3d; dat. of the possessor, very common

462 híc eti,ám sua , prǽmia , laúdi ;   Súnt lacri,mǽ
here   even   its own   rewards   to merit; there are   tears

re , r*um*,   ,,   ét men,tém mor,tália ,   tángunt.
for things,   and   the mind   mortal (woes)   touch.

463 Sólve   me,tús ;   feret , hǽc ali,quám ,, tibi ,
Drive away   your fears ;   will bring   this   some   for thee

464 fáma sa,lútem."   Síc   ait, , átq*ue* ani,múm ,,
fame   safety."   Thus he says,   and   his mind

worth finds its due reward ; here are tears for trouble and mortal woes touch the heart.   Banish thy fears ;   be sure the fame of this will bring some measure of salvation."   So speaking, he feeds his

---

after parts of the verb *sum ;* see the note and references to *illi,* l. 416.   *Laudi* here has the rare meaning of *worth* (not the ordinary sense of *praise*), and = *virtuti.*

LINE 462.   **Sunt,** 3d pers. plur. pres. ind. of *sum, esse, fui ;* agrees with the subj. *lacrimae.* —— **lacrimae,** nom. plur. of *lacrima, -ae,* f., 1st ; subj. of *sunt.* —— **rērum,** gen. plur. of *rēs, rēi,* f., 5th ; a sort of objective gen., of the *cause,* or it may be considered a gen. of specification expressing the circumstance in respect of which a thing is said to be or to be done ; cf. Aen. II, 413, *ereptae virginis ira = anger at the seizure of the maiden.* —— **et,** cop. conj., joining the following to the preceding sentence. —— **mentem,** acc. sing. of *mens, mentis,* f., 3d ; direct obj. of *tangunt ; mentem* practically = *animum* (the usual word for the seat of emotions), but adds something more, and may be rendered *the reflective mind.* —— **mortālia,** nom. plur. n. of *mortālis, -e,* adj., 3d (from *mors, mortis,* f., 3d = *death*) ; used substantively, subj. of *tangunt ; mortālia* expresses impotence and sadness, denoting *mortal woes.* —— **tangunt,** 3d pers. plur. pres. ind. act. of *tangō, -ere, tetigī, tactum,* 3 ; agrees with the subj. *mortalia.   Tangunt* is here metaphorical, = *touch,* i.e. *affect, move.* The beauty and pathos of this famous line should be noticed.

LINE 463.   **Solve,** 2d pers. sing. imperative mood act. of *solvō, -ere, solvī, solūtum,* 3 ; the subj. *tū* is implied by the personal ending. —— **metūs,** acc. plur. of *metus, -ūs,* m., 4th ; direct obj. of *solve.* —— **feret,** 3d pers. sing. fut. ind. act. of *ferō, ferre, tulī, lātum,* irreg. ; agrees with the subj. *fāma.* —— **haec,** nom. sing. f. of the demonstr. adj. *hīc, haec, hōc ;* agrees with *fama ; haec* is deictic, referring to the history of Troy depicted on the walls of the temple. —— **aliquam,** acc. sing. f. of *aliquis, aliqua* (rare), *aliquid* (or adjectival *aliquod*), indefinite pron. or pronominal adj. ; qualifies *salutem ;* there is a resigned pathos in the addition of *aliquam* as an attribute limiting *salutem,* suggesting that Aeneas would readily welcome even a slight change for the better in his fortunes. —— **tibi,** dat. sing. of *tū ;* dat. of the indirect obj. after *feret.*   Some think that *tibi* is an *ethic* dative, = *you will see that the fame of this will bring some measure of safety.*   A. & G. 236 ; B. 188, 2, *b*) ; G. 351 ; H. 389. —— **fāma,** gen. *fāmae,* f., 1st ; nom. sing., subj. of *feret.* —— **salūtem,** acc. sing. of *salūs, -ūtis,* f., 3d ; direct obj. of *feret.*

LINE 464.   **Sīc,** adv. of manner, modifying *ait.* —— **ait,** 3d pers. sing. pres. ind. act. of the defective verb *āiō* (see *ait,* l. 438) ; agrees with the understood subj. *ille,* referring to Aeneas. —— **atque,** cop. conj., joining the important notion *pascit animum,* etc., to what has preceded.   *Atque* becomes *ac* before consonants (*c, g,* and *qu* excepted), and always adds emphasis to the second of the words or sentences it connects ; it is sometimes used specially to unite the third member of a series.   It is distinguished from *que* insomuch as *que* joins two words or ideas very closely connected internally ; *et* joins members of equal importance.   A. & G. 156, *a*; B. 341 ; G. 475-477, and 481, NOTE; H. 554, I. —— **animum,** acc. sing. of *animus, -ī,* m., 2d ; direct obj. of *pascit.* ——

soul on the lifeless	pic,túra	,	páscit	i,náni,	**Múlta**	ge,méns,	,, 465
painting, deep-groan-	*on the picture*		*feeds*	*unreal,*	*many things*	*groaning,*	

ing, and his face	lar,góq*ue*	hu,méctat	,	flúmine	,	vúltum.
streams with the flood of his tears.	*and copious*	*moistens*		*with a flood*		*his face.*

For he saw how, in	**Námque**	vi,débat,	u,tí	,,	bel,lántes	,	Pérgama	, 466
their warring round	*For indeed*	*he saw,*	*how*		*warring*		*Pergamos*	

Pergamos, on this	círcum	**Hác**	fuge,rént	Grai,í,	,,	preme,rét 467
side fled the Greeks,	*round*	*on this side*	*were fleeing*	*the Greeks,*		*was pressing*

pictūrā, abl. sing. of *pictūra, -ae,* f., 1st (from *pingō, -ere, pinxī, pictum,* 3, = *I paint*); abl. of the means or instrument. —— **pascit**, 3d pers. sing. pres. ind. act. of *pascō, -ere, pāvī, pastum,* 3 (akin to Sanskrit root PÂ = *to nourish*) ; joined by *atque* to *ait,* and in agreement with the same subject. —— **ināni**, abl. sing. f. of *inānis, -e,* adj., 3d (= lit. *empty,* hence *vain, unreal, unsubstantial*); qualifies *pictura; inani* is another skilful word, whereby Vergil draws attention to the inability of Aeneas to leave the pictures, though unreal, i.e. not the living reality.

LINE 465. **Multa,** acc. plur. n. of *multus, -a, -um;* used substantively, and a sort of *cognate* acc. with *gemens,* though some consider the acc. a Greek acc. of respect. Verbs which express emotion, though intransitive, are permitted the above kind of object with adjectives in the neuter singular and plural. A. & G. 237, *b;* B. 175, 2, *b;* G. 333, 1, REM. 2; H. 371, III. —— **gemēns,** gen. *gementis;* nom. sing. m. of the pres. part. act. of *gemō, -ere, -uī, -itum,* 3; agrees with and enlarges the subj. of *pascit.* —— **largō,** abl. sing. n. of *largus, -a, -um;* qualifies *flumine.* —— **que,** enclitic cop. conj. —— **hūmectat,** 3d pers. sing. pres. ind. act. of *hūmectō, -āre, -āvī, -ātum,* 1 (akin to *hūmidus* = *moist*); joined by *que* to *pascit,* and in agreement with the same subject (i.e. a pronoun referring to Aeneas). —— **flūmine,** abl. sing. of *flūmen, flūminis,* n., 3d (*fluō = I flow*) ; abl. of the instrument, with *hūmectat.* —— **vultum,** acc. sing. of *vultus, -ūs,* m., 4th; direct obj. of *hūmectat.*

LINE 466. **Namque** (*nam* + suffix *que*), strengthened causal conj., introducing some-thing explanatory of what has been already narrated; *namque* here gives a reason for *humectat vultum;* see note on *namque,* l. 65. —— **vidēbat,** 3d pers. sing. imperf. ind. act. of *videō, -ēre, vīdī, vīsum,* 2; the implied subj. is *Aeneas;* the imperfect tense is pictorial in its signification. The pictures are mentioned in a sort of series: A. (1) the success of the Trojan youths; (2) the victory of Achilles; B. (1) the death of Rhesus; (2) the flight and death of Troilus; C. suppliant scenes, (1) the procession of Trojan women to the temple of Pallas; (2) Priam ransoming the body of Hector from Achilles; D. battle scenes, (1) Memnon and his Eastern warriors; (2) the Amazonian host. —— **uti** (a form of *ut*), adv. and conj., here introducing the indirect exclamation *uti . . .* *Achilles* —— **bellantēs,** nom. plur. m. of *bellāns, -antis,* pres. part. act. of *bellō, -āre, -āvī, -ātum,* 1 (from *bellum;* there is a collateral deponent *bellor, -ārī, bellātus sum* (rare), 1); agrees with *Graii,* but enlarges all the other subjects as well, viz. *iuventus, Phryges,* and *Achilles.* —— **Pergama,** acc. plur. of *Pergama, -ōrum,* n., 2d (Greek Πέρ-γαμα); governed by *circum;* Pergama was the citadel of Troy. There is a singular form, *Pergamum, -ī,* n., 2d; so in Greek the singulars τὸ Πέργαμον and ἡ Πέργαμος. —— **circum,** prep. with the acc.; gov. *Pergama.* Certain dissyllabic prepositions sometimes follow the nouns they govern, e.g. *circum, contra, inter,* etc.; in Cicero this is most common after the relative or personal pronouns. A. & G. 263, NOTE; B. 144, 3; G. 413, REM. 1; H. 569, II, 1.

LINE 467. **Hāc,** abl. sing. f. (used adverbially) of the demonstr. pron. *hīc, haec, hōc;* probably *viā* is to be supplied with *hac; hac . . . hac = hac . . . illac,* contrasting two

468 Tro,iána   iu,véntus;   Hác   Phryges; ,
   Trojan   *the youth;*   *on this side (fled) the Phrygians;*

469 ínsta,rét   cur,rú „ cris,tátus A,chílles.   Néc
   was pursuing in his car   *plumed*   *Achilles.*   *Nor*

procul , hínc   Rhe,sí „ nive,ís ten,tória , vélis
   far   *from here of Rhesus*   *snowy*   *the tents with canvas*

and the youth of Troy pressed them, on that the Phrygians fled, pursued by plumed Achilles in his chariot. Nor far from these he weeps to recognize the tents of Rhesus with snowy canvas,

---

different scenes. —— **fugerent,** 3d pers. plur. imperf. subjunct. act. of *fugiō, -ere, fūgī, fugitum,* 3 (akin to Greek root φυγ, root of φεύγω = *I flee*) ; agrees with its subj. *Graii ;* the mood is subjunctive, because the sentence is an indirect exclamation, introduced by the conj. *uti* in the previous line (see the note on *sit,* l. 454). —— **Graii** (*Grāī*), nom. plur. of *Graii, -ōrum,* m., 2d = *the Greeks* (properly m. of the adj. *Graius, -a, -um* = *Grecian*) ; subj. of *fugerent; Graii* is a dissyllable.   The scene referred to is generally supposed to be the fight in which the Greeks were driven back and Patroclus was slain. —— **premeret,** 3d pers. sing. imperf. subjunct. act. of *premō, -ere, pressī, pressum,* 3; agrees with the subj. *iuventus,* and in the same construction as the subjunct. *fugerent* above.   Observe the devices employed to bring the flight of the Greeks and the pursuit by the Trojans into strong contrast: (1) *asyndeton,* no conjunction connecting the two clauses; (2) placing the pairs in the same order, viz. verb, then subject (*anaphora*) ; contrast is sometimes obtained by opposite order (*chiasmus*).   A. & G. 344, *f,* 1; B. 350, 11, *b;* G. 682; H. no reference for *anaphora.*   This meaning of the word *anaphora* must be distinguished from that signifying the repetition of a word at the beginning of a sentence for emphasis. —— **Trōiāna,** nom. sing. f. of *Trōiānus, -a, -um* (adj. of *Trōia,* f., 1st); agrees with *iuventus.* —— **iuventūs,** gen. *iuventūtis,* f., 3d (akin to *iuvenis*) ; nom. sing., subj. of *premeret; iuventus* is here collective = *iuvenēs,* the abstract singular standing for the concrete plural.

   LINE 468.   **Hāc,** adv. of place; *hac* here = *illac,* referring to a new scene, distinct from that given in the previous line. —— **Phryges,** gen. *Phrygum,* m., 3d (sing. *Phryx, Phrygis,* m., 3d); nom. plur., subj. of *fugerent* understood from the previous sentence. —— **instāret,** 3d pers. sing. imperf. subjunct. of *instō, -āre, institī, instatum,* 1 (*in,* = *upon,* + *sto,* = *I stand,* hence *I press upon*); agrees with the subj. *Achilles ;* the grammatical construction is the same as in *premeret* in the preceding line, and the contrast is marked in the same way, viz. by *asyndeton* and *anaphora.*—— **currū,** abl. sing. of *currus, -ūs,* m., 4th; abl. of the instrument.   The principal heroes fought from chariots, but often fought on foot where there was a press of fighters. —— **cristātus,** nom. sing. m. of the adj. *cristātus, -a, -um* (*crista* = *a crest, plume*) ; agrees with *Achilles.* —— **Achillēs,** nom. sing. (for declension, see note on *Achilli,* l. 30); subj. of *instaret.*

   LINE 469.   **Nec** (short form of *neque, ne + que = and* . . . *not*), coördinate disjunctive conj., joining its sentence to the one preceding. —— **procul,** adv. ; *not far,* i.e. from the pictures just mentioned. *Procul* may be used absolutely or in conjunction with another adverb or adverbial phrase, e.g. *procul hinc, procul ab urbe.* —— **hinc,** adv. of 'place from which.'   Many adverbs are formed from the demonstrative pronouns, cf. from *hic* and *ille :* (1) *hic* and *illic* = *here* and *there ;* (2) *hac* and *illac* = *on this side,* and *on that side ;* (3) *hinc* and *illinc* = *hence* and *thence ;* (4) *huc* and *illuc* = *hither* and *thither.* Adverbs of similar form are formed from *iste,* and there are several adverbial forms of the pronoun *is,* e.g. *ea, eo.* —— **Rhēsī,** gen. sing. of *Rhēsus,* m., 2d (Greek Ῥῆσος); poss. gen., limiting *tentoria.*   Rhesus, the son of the Strymon and Terpsichore (others say of

which, betrayed by their first slumber, Tydeus' blood-stained son with unceasing slaughter was laying	Ágnos, cit lacri, máns, „ pri, mó quae , pródita , 4;0
	he recognizes weeping, first which betrayed
	sómno Týdi, dés mul, tá „ vas, tábat , cǽde 4ꞏ1
	by sleep Tydides much was ravaging with slaughter

Eioneus and Euterpe), was the king of Thrace. He had fought several successful wars in Europe and came to the aid of the Trojans in the tenth year of the siege of Troy. There was an oracle (in later story, which Vergil weaves into the Homeric tale) that if the horses of Rhesus once tasted the waters of the Trojan river Xanthus and ate of the grass on the Trojan plains, Troy would be impregnable. Aware of this, Odysseus (in Latin, Ulysses) and Tydides (i.e. Diomedes, son of Tydeus) set out by night directly after his arrival, killed Rhesus and led his horses away.——**niveīs**, abl. plur. n. of *niveus, -a, -um,* adj. (from *nix, nĭvis,* f., 3d, = *snow*);· qualifies *vēlīs.*——**tentōria**, acc. plur. of *tentōrium, -ī,* n., 2d (from *tendō,* = *I stretch out,* through the obsolete *tentor* = lit. *a stretcher-out*);· direct obj. of *agnoscit.* Vergil's mention of *tentoria* = *tents* of canvas (*velis*) is an *anachronism,* i.e. an ascription of later notions or facts to an earlier time when they did not exist; the so-called *tents* of the Greek heroes were not *tents* at all, but huts made of osiers and tree-branches, or even of earth. This is one of many instances in which the poet applies modern ideas to heroic times, and the practice is doubtless due to Vergil's desire to expand and work upon the simple features of the Homeric story and bring them into conformity with Roman notions. At the same time it must not be forgotten that Vergil preserves all ancient customs and modes of public and private life in their original simplicity and free from the change which in such matters could only be distortion. —— **vēlīs**, abl. plur. of *vēlum, -ī,* n., 2d; abl. of quality, sometimes called the descriptive abl., describing *tentoria.* A. & G. 251; B. 224; G. 400; H. 419, II.

LINE 470. **Agnoscit** (sometimes written *adgnoscit*), 3d pers. sing. pres. ind. act. of *agnoscō, -ere, agnōvī, agnitum,* 3 (*ad* + (*g*)*noscō*);· the subj. implied by the personal ending is *Aenēās.* —— **lacrimāns**, gen. *lacrimāntis;·* nom. sing. m. of the pres. part. act. of *lacrimō, -āre, -āvī, -ātum,* 1; agrees with and enlarges the subj. of *agnoscit.* —— **prīmō**, abl. sing. m. of *primus, -a, -um,* superl. formed from the prep. *prae* or *pro* (comparative *prior*);· qualifies *somno. Primo* may be taken in two ways: (1) as a descriptive attribute of *somno* = lit. *first,* signifying that the night was the first spent near Troy by Rhesus, and so the sleep of that night actually *the first;* (2) as a partitive attribute, = *the first* (i.e. the earliest and soundest) *sleep,* in which Rhesus was most likely to be surprised; most commentators prefer the latter, though in Homer it is late in the night when the Greeks surprise Rhesus. —— **quae**, acc. sing. n. of the rel. pron. *quī, quae, quod;·* agrees with the antecedent *tentoria,* and is direct obj. of *vastabat.* —— **prōdita,** acc. plur. n. of *prōditus, -a, -um,* perf. part. pass. of *prōdō, -ere, prōdidī, prōditum,* 3 (*prō* + *dō*);· predicate part. agreeing with *quae; quae prodita vastabat* = two coördinate sentences *quae prodebat et vastabat.* A. & G. 292, REM.; B. 337, 2; G. 437; H. 549, 5. —— **somnō**, abl. sing. of *somnus, -ī,* m., 2d; *somnō* may be (1) abl. of the instrument, with *prōdita* = *betrayed by their first slumber;* this is a poetical and vigorous notion; (2) abl. of 'time when,' = *betrayed in their first sleep.* Observe that grammatically *somno* refers to *quae,* i.e. the tents; in English we might speak of *sleeping tents,* but this is scarcely possible in Latin; but it is not necessary to press such an objection, for Vergil in the words *tentoria quae prodita somno* clearly means *the tents and the men inside them.*

LINE 471. **Tȳdidēs**, gen. *Tȳdĭdae,* m., 1st decl. Greek patronymic noun (voc. *Tȳdĭde,* l. 97; Greek Τυδείδης = *son of Tydeus*);· nom. sing., subj. of *vastabat. Tydides* = *Diomedes,* the king of Aetolia, and one of the bravest of the Grecian chiefs before Troy. He fought with Hector and with Aeneas, and accompanied Ulysses on another daring

472 cru,éntus, Árden,tésque a,vértit e,quós „ in ,
blood-stained,   and eager   turns off the horses   to
473 cástra, pri,úsquam Pábula , gústas,sént Tro,iǽ „
the camp,   before   the fodder   they had tasted   of Troy

in ruin, and (there-
after) turns the fiery
steeds towards the
camp, ere they might
taste the Trojan fod-

exploit, viz. to steal the Palladium from the temple of Pallas at Troy. On his return
home after the war, he found his wife Aegiale remarried, and in disgust went off to the
south of Italy (called *Magna Graecia*), where he married the daughter of Daunus, a
king in that region, and founded the city of Argyripa. —— **multā**, abl. sing. f. of *multus*,
-*a*, -*um ;* agrees with *caede*. —— **vastābat**, 3d pers. sing. imperf. ind. act. of *vastō*, -*āre*,
-*āvī*, -*ātum*, 1 (= lit. *I make vastus*, i.e. *desolate*); agrees with the subj. *Tydides ;* the
imperf. (like *videbat*, l. 466) is descriptive, expressing what Aeneas saw happening in
the pictures. Observe that Vergil varies the tenses very skilfully, now a descriptive
imperfect, and now a vivid *historic* present (*agnoscit*, l. 470, and *āvertit*, l. 472). ——
caede, abl. sing. of *caedēs, -is*, f., 3d (from *caedō, = I kill*) ; abl. of manner, with *vasta-
bat ;* manner is expressed by the abl. with the prep. *cum*, but if the noun in the abl. is
qualified by an adjective, the prep. *cum* may either be retained or omitted. A. & G. 248;
B. 220; G. 399; H. 419, III. —— **cruentus**, nom. sing. m. of the adj. *cruentus*, -*a*, -*um*
(from *cruor, = blood ;* cf. *crūdus, = raw*) ; qualifies *Tydides ;* it is possible to take *caede*
with *cruentus* as an abl. of cause = *blood-stained through much killing*, i.e. so represented
in the picture, but on the whole this rendering does not appear as suitable to the order
of the words as that with *caede* modifying *vastabat*.

LINE 472. **Ardentēs**, acc. plur. m. of *ardēns, -entis*, pres. part. act. of *ardeō, -ēre*,
arsī, arsum, 2; qualifies *equōs*. —— **que**, enclitic cop. conj. —— **āvertit**, 3d pers. sing.
pres. ind. act. of *āvertō, -ere, āvertī, āversum*, 3 (*ā, = from*, + *vertō, = I turn*) ; joined by
que to *vastabat*. —— **equōs**, acc. plur. of *equus, -ī*, m., 2d; direct obj. of *āvertit*. —— **in**,
prep. with the acc. and abl.; gov. the acc. *castra ; in* + the acc. = *into*, i.e. into the
interior, while *ad* + the acc. = *to*, i.e. to the borders. —— **castra**, gen. *castrōrum*, n.
plur., 2d (sing. *castrum, -ī*, n., 2d, = *a fort*) ; governed by *in ; castra* is of course the
Grecian camp. —— **priusquam** (*prius*, comparative adv., + *quam ;* cf. *antequam* =
ante + quam), temporal conj., introducing *gustassent* and *bibissent*, the subjunctive being
due to the *purpose* expressed by *avertit priusquam*. *Priusquam* and *antequam* are
sometimes written in two separate parts, e.g. *prius . . . quam*, *prius* (*ante*) modifying
the principal verb in the main clause and *quam* introducing the subordinate temporal
clause. The verb of the temporal clause is indicative when actual facts are recorded
(and so especially in historic tenses), but subjunctive when the purpose in the mind of
the subject of the principal sentence is indicated. A. &. G. 262 and 327; B. 291, 292;
G. 574-577; H. 520.

LINE 473. **Pābula**, acc. plur. of *pābulum, -ī*, n., 2d (from *pascō, = I give to feed*,
hence = *that which feeds, fodder*) ; direct obj. of *gustassent*. —— **gustassent** (for *gustā-
vissent*), 3d pers. plur. pluperf. subjunct. act. of *gustō, -āre, -āvī, -ātum*, 1 (*gustus = a
tasting*) ; agrees with the subj. *illi* understood referring to *equos* in the preceding line;
the subjunctive mood expresses the design of Tydides, a kind of virtual *oratio obliqua*
(see the note and references to *priusquam* above). *Gustassent* is a contracted form of
gustavissent. A. & G. 128, *a*, 1; B. 7, 2; G. 131, 1; H. 235. —— **Trōiae**, gen. sing. of
Trōia, f., 1st; poss. gen., limiting *pābula*. —— **Xanthum**, acc. sing. of *Xanthus, -ī*, m.,
2d (Greek Ξανθός = "*gold-colored*" river); direct obj. of *bibissent*. The Xanthus is the
same river as the Scamander, being called (according to Homer) Xanthus by the gods
and Scamander by men; it is one of the two famous rivers of the Troad, the other being

der and drink of Xanthus. In another place Troilus fugitive, with armor cast away,—luckless boy and no match for Achilles in the conflict,—is rushed along by his steeds,

Xan,thúmque bi,bíssent. Párte ali,á fugi,éns ,, 474

and Xanthus　　　　　had drunk.　　　In part another　　　fleeing

a,míssis , Tróilus , ármis, Ínfe,líx puer, , átque 475

having been lost Troilus　his arms,　luckless　boy　　　and

im,pár ,, con,gréssus A,chílli, Fértur　　　e,quís, 476

unequal having encountered Achilles, is carried off by his horses,

called Simois. —— que, enclitic cop. conj. —— bibissent, 3d pers. plur. pluperf. subjunct. act. of *bibō, -ere, bibī,* no supine (*pōtum* is supplied from *pōtō,* 1), 3; joined by *que* to *gustassent,* and in the same grammatical construction.

LINE 474. Parte, abl. sing. of *pars, partis,* f., 3d; abl. of 'place where'; *parte aliā = in another part,* i.e. of the temple. —— aliā, abl. sing. f. of *alius, -a, -ud* (gen. *alīus,* dat. *aliī*) ; in agreement with *parte.* —— fugiēns, gen. *fugientis;* nom. sing. m. of the pres. part. act. of *fugiō, -ere, fūgī, fugitum,* 3; agrees with the subj. *Troilus.* —— amissīs, abl. plur. n. of *āmissus, -a, -um,* perf. part. pass. of *āmittō, -ere, āmīsī, āmissum,* 3 (*ā + mittō*); agrees with *armis* in the abl. abs. construction. —— Trōilus, gen. *Trōilī,* m., 2d (Greek Τρώϊλος = lit. 'one pertaining to Tros'); nom. sing., subj. of *fertur* below. Troilus was a son of Priam and Hecuba, and his name is mentioned in the last book of the Iliad with the notice that he had been killed before the siege of Troy; his slayer was Achilles. —— armīs, abl. plur. of *arma, -ōrum,* n., 2d (see l. 1); in the abl. abs. construction with *āmissīs; armis* seems to refer to shield and helmet, for in l. 478 he is described as holding his spear which trailed along the ground.

LINE 475. Infēlīx, gen. *infēlīcis,* 3d decl. adj. of one termination (*in, = not, + fēlīx, = fortunate*); qualifies *puer.* —— puer, gen. *puerī,* m., 2d; nom. sing., in apposition with *Troilus.* Troilus appears to have been quite a youth; cf. Horace, Odes, II, ix, 15, *nec* IMPUBEM *parentes Trōilon . . . flevere semper.* For the distinctions of age implied by *puer, iuvenis,* etc., see the note on *puer,* l. 267. —— atque, copulative conj., joining *impar congressus* with *infelix;* as usual, *atque* expresses a very emphatic connection and lays greater stress on the second member of the pairs which it unites; *infelix* and *impar congressus* are not ideas of equal importance, but one gives a reason for the other, i.e. Troilus is unlucky for the reason that he is not an equal match for Achilles. —— impar, gen. *imparis,* adj., 3d (*in, = not, + par, = equal*); nom. sing., in agreement with *puer,* but modifies *congressus* adverbially = *matched unequally.* Synonyms : *similis* (*qui alterum refert*) merely expresses resemblance; *aequalis* (*qui tantundem habet*) denotes mutual and absolute equality; *par = aequalis* and *similis,* denoting "mutual congruity, proportionate equality." For the adverbial modification of *congressus* by *impar,* consult A. & G. 191; B. 239; G. 325, REM. 6; H. 443. —— congressus, nom. sing. m. of the perf. part. of the deponent verb *congredior, -ī, congressus sum,* 3 (*cum + gradior*); agrees with *puer; congressus* (or rather the phrase *impar congressus*), not *impar* alone, is joined by *atque* to *infelix.* —— Achillī, dat. sing. of *Achilles,* m. (for decl. see note on *Achilli,* l. 30); governed by *congressus.* The dative may be explained (1) on the ground that *congressus* is a compound verb (*cum + gradior*); A. & G. 228; B. 187, III; G. 347; H. 386; — (2) or, more probably, as a dat. analogous to the dative *Homero* in the sentence *contendis Homero,* i.e. a poetical dative where in prose we should find a preposition with the noun, e.g. *cum Achille congressus;* this dative is specially common after verbs of *contending.* A. & G. 229, *c;* B. no reference; G. 346, NOTE 6; H. 385, 4, 3).

LINE 476. Fertur, 3d pers. sing. pres. ind. pass. of *ferō, ferre, tulī, lātum,* irreg.; agrees with the subj. *Troilus.* —— equīs, abl. plur. of *equus, -ī,* m., 2d; abl. of the

477 cur,rúque hae,rét „ resu,pínus i,náni, Lóra
and to the car *cleaves* *on his back* *empty,* *the reins*

te,néns „ tamen: , huíc cer,víxque co,mǽque
holding *nevertheless:* *to him* *both the head* *and the hair*

478 tra,húntur Pér ter,ram, ét ver,sá „ pul,vís
are dragged *over* *the ground, and inverted* *the dust*

and fallen on his back is caught in the empty car, still holding the reins; his neck and hair trail along the ground, and the dust is scored

instrument, with *fertur;* the meaning is that the horses have run away with Troilus. —— currū (old form of *currui*), dat. sing. of *currus, -ūs,* m., 4th; dat. of the indirect obj. after *haeret.* Some think that *curru* is the locative ablative, because the construction after *haereō* is commonly *in* with the ablative or the ablative alone, or less frequently the dative. For *haereō* with the dative, consult A. & G. 227, *e,* 3; B. no reference; G. 346, NOTE 6; H. 385, 4, 4). The dative would be thoroughly Vergilian. —— que, enclitic cop. conj. —— haeret, 3d pers. sing. pres. ind. act. of *haereō, -ēre, haesī, haesum,* 2; joined by *que* to *fertur,* and in agreement with the same subject. —— resupīnus, nom. sing. m. of *resupīnus, -a, -um (re = back,* intensive + *supīnus = lying on the back,* opposed to *prōnus = lying face downwards); agrees* with the subj. of *haeret.* —— inānī, dat. sing. m. of *inānis, -e,* adj., 3d; qualifies *curru.* If *curru* be considered an ablative, then *inānī* must be abl. case masculine, in agreement with it. *Inani* denotes that the chariot was *empty,* i.e. deprived of the *aurīga (charioteer);* one has only to read the Iliad to notice how often the charioteers were slain and only the principal hero of the moment left alive in the car.

LINE 477. Lōra, acc. plur. of *lōrum, -ī,* n., 2d; direct obj. of *tenens.* —— tenēns, gen. *tenēntis;* nom. sing. m. of the pres. part. act. of *teneō, -ēre, -uī, tentum,* 2; agrees with and enlarges the subj. of *haeret.* —— tamen (perhaps a longer form of *tam,* and so = *in so far,* with adversative force), adv., limiting *tenens.* —— hūic, dat. sing. m. of the demonstr. pron. *hīc, haec, hōc;* dat. of reference, in the place of a gen. of the possessor, by means of which several events may be narrated with particular reference to the noun in the dative. A. & G. 235; B. 188, 1; G. 350; H. 384, 1, 2). —— cervīx, gen. *cervīcis,* f., 3d; nom. sing. m., one of the subjects of *trahuntur.* —— que, enclitic conj.; repeated after *comae, que ... que = both ... and,* a combination which is very common in the poets and began with Plautus; in prose *que ... que* is used by Sallust and his successors, but it only occurs once in Cicero. Other combinations of correlative conjunctions are: (1) *et ... et,* by far the most frequent; (2) *que ... et,* rare in early Latin, and avoided by Caesar and Cicero, but found in later writers; (3) *et ... que,* very rare. A. & G. 156, *h;* B. 341, 3; G. 476, NOTE 5; H. 554, I, NOTE 5. —— comae, nom. plur. of *coma, -ae,* f., 1st (Greek κόμη); joined by *que* below to *cervix,* one of the subjects of *trahuntur.* —— que, enclitic cop. conj. (see *que* above). —— trahuntur, 3d pers. plur. pres. ind. pass. of *trahō, -ere, trāxī, tractum,* 3; *historic present,* agreeing with the subjects *cervix* and *comae.* A. & G. 276, *d;* B. 259, 3; G. 229; H. 467, III.

LINE 478. Per, prep. with the acc.; gov. *terram; per* here = *over.* A. & G. 153; B. 181, 2; G. 416, 18; H. 433, PER. —— terram, acc. sing. of *terra, -ae,* f., 1st; governed by *per.* —— et, copulative conjunction, joining the following with the preceding sentence. —— versā, abl. sing. f. of *versus, -a, -um,* perf. part. pass. of *vertō, -ere, vertī, versum,* 3; predicate participle, agreeing with *hasta,* and standing instead of a relative clause *(quae versa est); versa = turned down,* i.e. *trailing* behind, instead of being held out in front of him by Troilus against the enemy. —— pulvīs, gen. *pulveris,* m., 3d; nom. sing., subj. of *inscribitur.* Observe that the second syllable is long in quantity, contrary to the usual rule: we find *pulvīs* in Ennius also, and there seems some reason

by his inverted spear.	in,scríbitur	, hásta.	Íntere,*a*	ád	tem,plúm „ 479
Meanwhile the Trojan women with hair flung loose were on their way to the temple of angry Pallas, carrying her sacred robe, in suppliant guise, mourning and beating breasts	*is scored*	*by his spear.*	*Meanwhile*	*to*	*the temple*

non , æquae , Pálladis , íbant   Crínibus ,   Ília , dés 480
not   friendly   of Pallas   were going   their hair   Trojan women

pas , sís,　　　　　„　　　　pep , lúmque　　　　　fe , rébant
having been loosened,　　and the peplum　　　　were carrying

Súpplici , tér   tris , tés „   et ,   túnsae ,   péctora , 481
suppliant-wise　　　sad　　　and　　　beating　　　their breasts

---

to suppose that the syllable was long by origin (Mr. Page writes *pulvis = pulvis-s*, on the analogy of *sanguis = sanguin-s*). If the syllable be not long by nature, we must regard it as lengthened by *arsis* (*diastole*, the lengthening being due to the *ictus*). A. & G. 359, *f*; B. 367, 2; G. 721; H. 608, V. Vergil lengthens *que* by *diastole* sixteen different times. **inscrībitur**, 3d pers. sing. pres. ind. pass. of *inscrībō, -ere, inscripsī, inscriptum,* 3 (*in + scrībō*); agrees with the subj. *pulvis.* —— **hastā**, abl. sing. of *hasta, -ae,* f., 1st; abl. of the instrument, with *inscrībĭtur,* and not in the abl. abs. with *versa.*

LINE 479. **Intereā** (see the note on *intereā,* l. 124), adv. of time, frequently acting as a connective. —— **ad**, prep. with the acc.; gov. *templum.* —— **templum**, gen. *templī,* n., 2d ; acc. sing., governed by *ad.* —— **nōn**, negative adv., limiting the adjective *aequae.* —— **aequae**, gen. sing. f. of *aequus, -a, -um,* adj.; qualifies *Palladis; non aequae = iniquae, unfriendly, angry.* This scene is imitated from Iliad, VI, 297 ff. The uses of *aequus* are worthy of notice : (1) *smooth, level;* (2) of persons, *favorable, friendly,* with negative *iniquus;* (3) *advantageous,* of place or time; (4) *equitable, honorable;* (5) *tranquil, calm;* (6) *equal, like, similar. Non aequae* is an instance of *litotes;* see *latuere,* l. 130. —— **Palladis**, gen. sing. of *Pallas,* f., 3d; poss. gen., limiting *templum.* Pallas is a surname of the goddess Athene (Minerva), daughter of Jupiter, and the name is probably derived from the fact that she is represented in statues as brandishing (πάλλειν) a spear. She was one of the three goddesses who contended for the prize of beauty with Paris as judge. —— **ībant**, 3d pers. plur. imperf. ind. act. of *eō, īre, īvī* or *iī, itum,* irreg.; agrees with the subj. *Iliades.*

LINE 480. **Crīnibus**, abl. plur. of *crīnis, -is,* m., 3d (for *crēnis,* from CRE, root of *cresco = I grow;* Greek θρίξ, gen. τριχός); abl. abs. with *passis.* —— **Īliadēs**, nom. plur. of *Ilias, Iliadis,* f., 3d (Greek Ἰλιάς); subj. of *ibant.* —— **passīs**, abl. plur. m. of *passus, -a, -um,* perf. part. pass. of *pandō, -ere, pandī, pansum,* and *passum,* 3; agrees with *crinibus* in the abl. abs. construction. —— **peplum**, acc. sing. of *peplus, -ī,* m., 2d, or *peplum, -ī,* n., 2d (Greek πέπλος and πέπλον); direct obj. of *ferebant.* The peplum was the long and richly embroidered robe specially connected with Pallas; it was the Athenian custom to carry it in procession at the Panathenaic festival, and finally to invest with it the statue of the goddess. —— **que**, enclitic cop. conj. —— **ferēbant**, 3d pers. plur. imperf. ind. act. of *ferō, ferre, tulī, lātum,* irreg.; joined by *que* to *ibant,* and in agreement with the same subject *Iliades.* For the conjugation of *ferō,* consult A. & G. 139; B. 129; G. 171; H. 292.

LINE 481. **Suppliciter,** adv. of manner, referring to what follows (*tristes,* etc.). *Suppliciter* is formed from the adj. *supplex,* gen. *supplicis.* For the formation of adverbs from adjectives of the third declension, consult A. & G. 148, *b*; B. 76; G. 92; H. 304. —— **tristēs**, nom. plur. f. of *tristis, -e,* adj., 3d; agrees with the subj. *Iliades,* but exerts an adverbial modifying force over the preceding predicates. —— **et**, copulative conj., joining the adverbial attribute *tristes* and the adverbial phrase *tunsae pectora.* —— **tunsae**, nom. plur. f. of *tunsus, -a, -um,* perf. part. pass. of *tundō, -ere, tutudī, tunsum* or

482 pálmis ;   Díva   so,ló   fi,xós ocu,lós ,
with their palms; the goddess; on the ground fixed   her eyes

483 a,vérsa   te,nébat.   Tér cir,cum Ília,cós „
turned away   was keeping.   Thrice   around   of Troy

484 rap,táverat , Héctora , múros, Éxani,múmque
had dragged   Hector   the walls,   and lifeless

with palms; the goddess, turning from them, ever kept her eyes fixed on the ground. Thrice around the walls of Troy had Achilles dragged Hector, and was selling his lifeless

---

tūsum, 3; agrees with *Iliades*. *Tunsae* here has an *active* sense, = *beating their breasts*, and is equivalent to a Greek *middle voice* participle. Moreover, *tunsae* (though a perfect participle) refers to present, not past, time; this use of the participle is common in Vergil, especially in the case of deponent verbs; e.g. Georgics, I, 293, *cantu solata laborem.* —— **pectora**, acc. plur. of *pectus, pectoris*, n., 3d; a kind of direct obj. after the middle *tunsae*, and probably not an acc. of respect as these accusatives after passive participles used to be described; refer to the note on *oculos*, l. 228. —— **palmis**, abl. plur. of *palma, -ae*, f., 1st; abl. of the instrument, with *tunsae.*

LINE 482. **Dīva**, gen. *dīvae*, f., 1st (cf. *dīvus, -ī*, m., 2d); nom. sing., subj. of *tenebat; diva = Pallas*, i.e. in the picture. —— **solō**, abl. sing. of *solum, -ī*, n., 2d; locative ablative, to be taken with *fixos.* —— **fīxōs**, acc. plur. m. of *fīxus, -a, -um*, perf. part. pass. of *fīgō, -ere, fīxī, fīxum*, 3; predicate participle, agreeing with *oculos.* —— **oculōs**, acc. plur. of *oculus, -ī*, m., 2d; direct obj. of *tenebat.* —— **āversa**, nom. sing. f. of *āversus, -a, -um*, perf. part. passive of *āvertō, -ere, āvertī, āversum*, 3 (*ā, = from*, + *vertō, = I turn*); predicate participle, agreeing with *diva ; aversa* is middle or reflexive, and = *se avertens, turning away.* The passive of verbs like *verto* is often used as if the verb were a deponent. A. & G. 111, *b*; B. no reference; G. 218; H. 465. —— **tenēbat**, 3d pers. sing. imperf. ind. act. of *teneō, -ēre, -uī, tentum*, 2; agrees with the subj. *diva.*

LINE 483. **Ter**, numeral adv., modifying *raptaverat.* The dragging of Hector's body thrice round the walls of Troy must be a later addition of the cyclic poets, for Homer does not refer to it. In the last book of the Iliad Homer describes Hector as chased thrice round the walls of the city, and his body afterwards dragged not round the city but round the tomb of Patroclus. —— **circum**, prep. with the acc.; gov. *muros.* —— **Iliacōs**, acc. plur. m. of *Iliacus, -a, -um* (*Ilium, -ī*, n., 2d, = *Troy*)*;* qualifies *mūrōs*, —— **raptāverat**, 3d pers. sing. pluperf. ind. act. of *raptō, -āre, -āvī, -ātum*, 1 (intensive of *rapiō*)*;* agrees with the subj. *Achilles.* Observe the different tenses *raptaverat* and *vendebat;* the pluperfect represents the action it describes as preceding the action described by the imperfect. Of course, Aeneas could not actually see Achilles dragging Hector round the walls, but doubtless the body of Hector was torn and mangled in the picture which Aeneas was studying, and the poet in this line both suggests this and explains it with that wonderful skill that makes the Aeneid a true and original work of literary 'art. —— **Hectora**, acc. sing. of *Hector, -is*, m., 3d (Greek Ἕκτωρ, acc. Ἕκτορα, gen. Ἕκτορος); direct obj. of *raptaverat; Hectora* is an acc. with the Greek accusative termination. —— **mūrōs**, acc. plur. of *mūrus, -ī*, m., 2d; governed by *circum.*

LINE 484. **Exanimum**, acc. sing. n. of *exanimus, -a, -um* (*ex = out of*, hence *without*, + *anima = life*)*;* qualifies *corpus. Exanimum* is more expressive than *mortuum*, for it suggests that the dragging robbed Hector of the last trace of life. —— **que**, enclitic cop. conj. —— **aurō**, abl. sing. of *aurum, -ī*, n., 2d (Greek αὖρον); abl. of price. A. & G. 252; B. 225; G. 404; H. 422. Verbs of buying, selling, hiring, rating, costing, etc., are construed with the ablative when the value is definite, but with the genitive when it

| body for ransom of gold. Then indeed from the deep of his heart Aeneas makes loud moan as he caught sight of the spoils, sight of chariot, sight of the very | au,ró ,, cor,pús ven,débat A,chílles. Túm 485
 for gold the body was selling Achilles. Then
 ve,ro íngen,tém gemi,túm ,, dat , péctore ab ,
 indeed mighty a groan he gives his breast from
 ímo, **Út** spoli,*a*, út cur,rús, ,, ut,q*ue* 486
 bottom-most when the spoils, when the chariots, and when |

is general or indefinite. —— **corpus**, acc. sing. of *corpus, corporis*, n., 3d; direct obj. of *vendebat*. —— **vendēbat**, 3d pers. sing. imperf. ind. act. of *vendo, -ere, vendidī, venditum*, 3 (*vēnum*, = *sale*, + *dō*, = *I give*, hence *I give for sale*); agrees with the subj. *Achilles*. The passive *vendor* is used occasionally, but as a rule the passive of *vendo* is supplied by *vēneō, -īre, -īvī* or *-iī, -itum*, 4, = *I am sold;* *vēneō* is a *neutral passive* (i.e. active in form, but passive in meaning). —— **Achillēs**, nom. sing. m.; subj. of *vendebat*. The scene is the pathetic one wherein the aged Priam supplicates Achilles to give back Hector's body for a ransom; Achilles treats Priam with reverence and finally consents.

LINE 485. **Tum**, adv. of time, here connective; it is the demonstrative of the relative *ut* following, *then . . . when*. —— **vērō**, corroborative adv., strengthening *tum*. *Vero* is often used in affirmative replies, = *assuredly*, and often so with *immo* (*immo vero*); sometimes it strengthens negative words, e.g. *minime vero* = *not at all*. —— **ingentem**, acc. sing. m. of *ingens, -entis*, adj., 3d, of one termination; qualifies *gemitum*. —— **gemitum**, acc. sing. of *gemitus, -ūs*, m., 4th (from *gemō*, = *I groan*); direct obj. of *dat*. —— **dat**, 3d pers. sing. pres. ind. act. of *dō, dare, dedī, datum*, 1; the implied subj. is *Aeneas*, not *Achilles*, as the context makes it clear. —— **pectore**, abl. sing. of *pectus, pectoris*, n., 3d; governed by *ab*, expressing 'place from which.' —— **ab**, prep. with the abl.; gov. *pectore*. This word is written *a* or *ab* before consonants, *ab* before words beginning with a vowel or the letter *h*. —— **īmō**, abl. sing. n. of *imus, -a, -um*, superl. adj. (formed from the prep. *infra;* positive *inferus*, rare; comparative *inferior;* superl. *infimus* or *imus*); agrees, with partitive signification, with *pectore*.

LINE 486. **Ut**, temporal conj., followed by the indicative *conspexit*. *Ut* and *ut primum* (in temporal clauses) are followed by the indicative mood, (1) most often in the *historic* present or the perfect, but (2) occasionally in the imperfect and pluperfect: in the case of (1) the circumstances described define the time; in the case of (2) the imperfect describes a condition of affairs existing at the time of the principal verb, while the pluperfect denotes action completed in the past. A. & G. 324; B. 287; G. 561,*ff.*; H. 518. As an adverb and conjunction, *ut* has many other uses, e.g. in final and consecutive clauses. —— **spolia**, acc. plur. of *spolium, -ī*, n., 2d (akin to Greek σκύλλω = *I strip*); direct obj. of *conspexit; spolia* = *arma Hectoris*, claimed by Achilles as the prize of the victor. —— **ut**, temporal conj. (see above); *ut* is graphic and emotional in its repetition here and below (*anaphora*), and far more vivid than if its place had been taken by a copulative conjunction, for it expresses how the eye of Aeneas took in each detail in turn. —— **currūs**, acc. plur. of *currus, -ūs*, m., 4th; a direct obj. of *conspexit;* the plural is poetical, instead of the singular. Some suppose the car to be that of Achilles, to which Hector's body had been fastened, and this seems the more likely view; others think Priam's car is meant, in which he hoped to take back with him his son's corpse. —— **ut**, temporal conj., repeated by *anaphora*. —— **que**, enclitic cop. conj. —— **ipsum**, acc. sing. n. of the intensive pron. and adj. *ipse, -a, -um;* agrees with *corpus*. —— **corpus**, acc. sing. of *corpus, corporis*, n., 3d; a direct obj. of *conspexit*. —— **amīcī**, gen. sing. of *amicus*, m., 2d; poss. gen., limiting *corpus*.

487 ípsum , córpus a, míci, Ténden, témque ma, nús ,,
itself　　　*the body of his friend*　　*and stretching*　　　*hands*
488 Pria, múm con, spéxit in, érmes.　　Sé　quoque ,
Priam　　　*he beheld*　　　*unarmed.*　　*Himself*　　*also*
príncipi, bús ,, per, míxtum ag, nóvit　　A, chívis,
foremost　　　*mingled*　　*he recognized with the Achaeans,*
489 Éo, ásque aci, és ,, et , nígri , Mémnonis , árma.
and Eastern the hosts　　*and*　　*black*　　*of Memnon*　　*the arms.*

body of his friend, and Priam reaching out his unarmed hands. Himself too he recognized enclosed amid the foremost Achaeans, and the Eastern battle-host and swarthy Memnon's arms.

LINE 487. **Tendentem**, acc. sing. m. of *tendēns, -entis*, pres. part. act. of *tendō, -ere, tetendī, tensum* or *tentum*, 3 (akin to τεν, root of *τείνω*); predicate participle, agreeing with and enlarging the object *Priamum.* —— **que**, enclitic cop. conj., joining *Priamum* and *corpus.* —— **manūs**, acc. plur. of *manus, -ūs*, f., 4th; direct obj. of *tendentem ; tendentem manus*, i.e. in entreaty. —— **Priamum**, acc. sing. of *Priamus, -ī*, m., 2d (Greek Πρίαμος = ' *chief* ') ; a direct obj. of *conspexit;* the sad spectacle of the aged father beseeching Achilles is mentioned last as a climax. —— **conspēxit**, 3d pers. sing. perf. ind. act. of *conspiciō, -ere, conspēxī, conspectum*, 3 (*con = cum*, + *speciō*) ; agrees with the subj. understood, viz. a pronoun referring to Aeneas. —— **inermēs**, acc. plur. f. of *inermis, -e*, adj., 3d (for *inarmis*, from *in, = not*, + *arma ;* collateral form *inermus, -a, -um* is rare); qualifies *manus.* There are two sufficient reasons why Priam carried no weapons : the first, because he was visiting Achilles not as a foe, but as a suppliant; the second, because he was past the age of fighting.

LINE 488. **Sē**, acc. sing. of the reflexive pron. *sē*, gen. *suī ;* direct obj. of *agnovit; se* refers to *Aeneas*, the subj. of *agnovit.* Aeneas only plays a minor part in the Iliad, and for that reason Vergil refers to him so very briefly here as *one* of foremost fighters. —— **quoque**, conj.; *quoque* never stands first in a sentence, but usually second, or third if the second word is emphatic. A. & G. 151, *a*, and 345, *b*; B. 347, 1; G. 479; H. 554, I, 4. *Quoque* does not connect so forcibly as *etiam.* —— **principibus**, dat. plur. m. of *princeps, principis*, adj., 3d (for *prim-caps*, from *prīmus, = first*, + *căpiō, = I take*, hence *first, taking the first place ;* the m. is often substantival); agrees with *Achivis.* —— **permixtum**, acc. sing. m. of *permixtus, -a, -um*, perf. part. pass. of *permisceō, -ēre, -uī, permixtum* or *permistum*, 2 (*per* + *misceō*) ; agrees with *se ; principibus permixtum* is a Greek phrase, borrowed from numerous similar expressions in the Iliad, e.g. προμάχοισι μιγέντα. —— **agnovit**, 3d pers. sing. perf. ind. act. of *agnoscō, -ere, agnōvī, agnitum*, 3 (*ad* + (*g*)*noscō*) ; understand *Aeneas* as subject. The group in which Aeneas figures is, of course, a different one from the one just described, wherein Priam and Achilles are the chief figures. —— **Achīvīs**, dat. plur. of *Achīvī, -orum*, m., 2d; dat. governed by *permixtum*, instead of the usual abl. with *cum* (= *permixtum cum Achivis*) ; consult the references given in the note on *Achilli*, l. 475. Aeneas is represented as having fought his way into the front rank of the Greek warriors.

LINE 489. **Ēōās**, acc. plur. f. of *Ēōus, -a, -um* (Greek 'Ηῷος = *Eastern*, from 'Ηώς = *dawn*, hence *the East*, because day dawns in the eastern quarter of the sky); agrees with *acies ; Eoas acies* = the Aethiopians, who were led by their chief Memnon to the assistance of Priam. This army came from Aethiopia, the region now known as Abyssinia, whose inhabitants Homer honors with the mention that they were the justest of men and beloved by the gods. —— **que**, enclitic cop. conj. —— **aciēs**, acc. plur. of *aciēs, -eī*, f., 5th (from the same root as *ac-uō, = I sharpen*) ; direct obj. of *agnovit*, joined by *que* to *se* above. *Aciēs* is not complete in the plural, for *diēs* and *rēs* are the only nouns

Penthesilea, furiously raging, leads the columns of the Amazons,

Dúcit A͜,mázoni,dúm „ lu,nátis , ágmina , péltis 490

Leads   of the Amazons   crescent the columns with shields

---

of the fifth declension which are completely declined, the rest having only nom. and acc. plural as a rule. *Acies* = (1) by derivation, something *sharp*, hence *edge*, e.g. *falcis, of a sickle* (in Vergil); (2) *sharp sight*, hence *the eye* itself, or *a glance* from the eye; (3) *brightness* (derived from the notion of *flashing*) of heavenly bodies, e.g. Vergil has *stellis acies obtusa videtur;* (4) *order of battle;* (5) *an army in battle order;* (6) other figurative senses, e.g. *acuteness* of intellect, *a disputation.* Synonyms: *exercitus*, the generic word for army, denoting not one company, but all the companies of soldiers, who are trained by exercise (*exerceō*) ; *agmen* = *an army on the march, a moving column* (from *ago*, = *I drive*) ; *acies* = *an army in line of battle.* Originally *acies* may have alluded to the sharp, edge-like appearance of the front of an army; but classic writers use the word for any part, front, rear, or centre, of an army drawn up; and so we meet with such phrases as *prima acies, secunda acies*, etc. —— *et*, cop. conj. —— **nīgrī**, gen. sing. m. of *niger, nīgra, nīgrum*, adj.; qualifies *Memnonis.* Memnon is called *niger* because he was an Ethiopian, i.e. dark-skinned. Synonyms: *niger*, the generic word, and admits of comparison; *ater* is specific, and = *coal black*, i.e. the greatest possible degree of blackness. —— **Memnonis**, gen. sing. of *Memnon*, m., 3d (Greek Μέμνων = '*the steadfast one*') ; poss. gen., limiting *arma.* The story of Memnon is post-Homeric, forming part of the legends which grew round about the Iliad, and which were treated by the Cyclic poets; the lost epic " Aethiopis," composed by Arctinus of Miletus, contained the adventures of Memnon, and also of the Amazons. Memnon was a son of Tithonus and Aurora (the dawn), and ruled over a region lying east of the Troad and embracing Aethiopia. He brought 10,000 men to aid Priam, slew Nestor's son, Antilochus, and, in order not to have to fight so old a man as Nestor, he accepted a challenge to fight Achilles, by whom he was killed. Aurora prevailed upon Jupiter to grant him honors at his funeral above those of ordinary mortals, and birds fought a battle over his pyre. For further details, consult a classical dictionary. —— **arma**, gen. *armōrum*, n., 2d; acc. plur., joined by *et* to *aciēs ;* special reference is made to Memnon's arms, because they were made, at Aurora's request, by the god Hephaestus (Vulcan), as also were the arms of Achilles.

LINE 490. **Dūcit**, 3d pers. sing. pres. ind. act. of *dūcō, -ere, dūxī, ductum*, 3; agrees with the subj. *Penthesilea ; historic* present, vividly describing what Aeneas saw in the picture. —— **Amāzonidum**, gen. plur. of *Amāzonis, Amāzonidis*, f., 3d; adnominal gen. of specification, limiting *agmina.* A. & G. 214, *f;* B. 202; G. 361; H. 395. The regular word is *Amāzōn, Amāzonis*, f., 3d (Greek Ἀμαζών, and English *Amazon*, with plur. *Amāzones, -um*, = *the Amazons);* the word is probably of Scythian origin, but some derive from the Greek ἀ, = *not*, + μαζός, = *abreast*, hence *without a breast ;* the legend that the right breast was cut off in order to allow free use of weapons probably arose from this fanciful derivation. The Amazons were a nation of women, who lived near the river Thermodon in Asia Minor, and devoted themselves to warlike pursuits. Diodorus mentions a race of Amazons in Africa more ancient than those in Asia. They had at one time invaded the kingdom of Priam before the siege of Troy, and had also attacked Attica where Theseus was ruling. They assisted Priam against the Greek host.—— **lūnātīs**, abl. plur. f. of *lūnātus, -a, -um*, adj. (properly perf. part. pass. of *lūnō, -āre, -āvī, -ātum*, 1, = *I bend into the shape of a half-moon* or *crescent*, rare); qualifies *peltis.* —— **agmina**, acc. plur. of *agmen, agminis*, n., 3d (from *ago*): direct obj. of *dūcit.* —— **peltīs**, abl. plur. of *pelta, -ae*, f. (a Greek word, πέλτη = *a small, light shield;* cf. πελταστής = *a light-armed soldier*, lit. *one armed with the* πέλτη); a loose abl. of quality, describing

491	Pénthesi,léa	fu,réns, „	medi,ísque	in ,	mílibus ,	with their crescent-shields, and fights hotly amid surround-
	Penthesilea	*raging*	*and middle*	*in*	*thousands*	
492	árdet,	Aúrea, súbnec,téns „	ex,sértae ,		cíngula ,	ing thousands, clasp-
	is furious,	*golden building under*	*exposed*		*a girdle*	ing her golden girdle beneath one unbared
493	mámmae	Bélla,tríx,	au,détque		vi,rís „	breast, a warrior-
	her breast	*woman-warrior,*	*and dares*		*with men*	woman, and dares

agmina. For this ablative, see note on *velis*, l. 469. The *pelta* was crescent-shaped, and was much used by barbarian tribes, e.g. Scythians.

LINE 491. **Penthesilēa**, gen. *Penthesilēae*, f., 1st (Greek Πενθεσίλεια); nom. sing., subj. of *ducit.* Penthesilea, the queen of the Amazons, was a daughter of the god Mars. She led the Amazons to help Priam in the last year of the siege, and was slain in fight by Achilles after doing many heroic deeds. Achilles greatly admired her beauty and wept when he had killed her, whereupon Thersites (the Homeric fool) laughed and was in turn slain by Achilles. —— **furens**, gen. *furentis;* nom. sing. f. of the pres. part. act. of *furō, -ere, -uī*, no supine, 3; agrees with the subj. *Penthesilea.* —— **mediis**, abl. plur. n. of *medius, -a, -um ;* agrees partitively with *milibus.* —— **que**, enclitic cop. conj. —— **in**, prep. with the acc. or abl.; gov. the abl. *milibus.* —— **milibus**, abl. plur. of *mīlia, -ium*, n., 2d; governed by *in. Milia* is the plural of *mille*, and is akin to the Greek χίλιοι. *Mille* is indeclinable, and may be used as a noun or (more commonly) as an adjective, e.g. *mille homines* or *mille hominum ;* the plural *mīlia* (less accurately *millia*) is always a substantive and is followed by the partitive genitive, e.g. *tria milia passuum = three thousands of paces,* i.e. *three miles.* —— **ardet**, 3d pers. sing. pres. ind. act. of *ardeō, -ēre, arsī, arsum*, 2 (here figurative, = *is furious, rages*)*;* agrees with the subj. *Penthesilea,* and is joined by *que* to *ducit;* the present is *historic.*

LINE 492. **Aurea**, acc. plur. n. of *aureus, -a, -um*, adj.; qualifies *cingula.* —— **subnectēns**, gen. *subnectentis;* nom. sing. f. of the pres. part. act. of *subnectō, -ere*, no perf., *subnexum*, 3 (*sub, = under,* + *nectō, = I bind*)*;* agrees with and enlarges the subj. *Penthesilea. Subnectens* does not mean that in the picture Penthesilea was *binding the girdle*, etc., but that she was *bound with a girdle*, and = *cingula subnexa habens ;* Vergil makes frequent use of this peculiar present participle. —— **exsertae**, dat. sing. f. of *exsertus, -a, -um*, perf. part. pass. of *exserō, -ere, -uī, exsertum*, 3 (*ex, = out,* + *serō, = I connect;* hence *protruding out from*)*;* agrees with *mammam.* The belt passed over the shoulder under one breast, which was left uncovered. —— **cingula**, acc. plur. of *cingulum, -ī*, n., 2d (with collateral forms *cingulus, -ī*, m., 2d, and *cingula, -ae*, f., 1st; from *cingō, = I encircle*)*;* direct obj. of *subnectens;* the plural is a poetical variant for the singular. —— **mammae**, dat. sing. of *mamma, -ae*, f., 1st (akin to *mater*)*;* dat. of the indirect obj. governed by the compound verb *subnectens* (see the note and references to *scopulo*, l. 45). Vergil is fond of varying his constructions; a simpler construction would have been *subnectens mammam cingulā ;* cf. *onerarat vina cadis*, l. 195, for *cados vinis*, though the note on *cadis* shows the two constructions to have different grammatical explanations.

LINE 493. **Bellātrīx**, gen. *bellātrīcis*, abl. f. (f. of *bellātor*, m. adj.; rarely as noun, except as referring to Pallas); agreeing with *Penthesilēa.* —— **audet**, 3d pers. sing. pres. ind. of the semi-deponent verb *audeō, -ēre, ausus sum*, 2 (see the note on *ausus*, l. 452); joined by *que* to *ardet*, and in agreement with the same subj., *Penthesilea.* —— **que**, enclitic cop. conj. —— **virīs**, dat. plur. of *vir, virī*, m., 2d; dat. (for *cum viris*) governed by *concurrere.* For the construction, consult the note on *Achilli*, l. 475. —— **con-**

albeit a maid to clash with men. While these marvels are viewed by Dardanian Aeneas, while he is all astonished and stands rooted in one long gaze, Dido, the queen,

con,cúrrere , vírgo.   Hǽc   dum , Dárdani, *o* 494

to clash   a maiden.   These things while   Dardanian

Aéne,ǽ „ mi,ránda vi,déntur, Dúm   stupet, , 495

by Aeneas   wonderful   are seen,   while he stands amazed,

óbtu,túq*ue* „ hae,rét de,fíxus in , úno, Régi,n*a* 496

and gaze   clings   fastened   in   one;   the queen

---

currere, pres. inf. act. of *concurrō, -ere, concurrī, concursum,* 3 (*con = cum + currō*); *prolative* or *complementary* infinitive after *audet,* whose predication is incomplete. —— **virgō**, gen. *virginis,* f., 3d; nom. sing., in apposition with *Penthesilea,* the subj. of *audet.* Observe the *alliteration* in *viris* and *virgo,* which helps to bring them into contrast; also notice the emphatic position of *virgo* at the end of the line. Vergil gives a somewhat similar, though more elaborate, description of the maiden-warrior Camilla, in the last 25 lines of Aen. VII : she is also called *bellatrix,* and is said *proelia virgo dura pati.*

LINE 494. **Haec**, nom. plur. n. of the demonstr. pron. *hīc, haec, hōc;* subj. of *videntur.* —— **dum**, temporal conj. = *while,* followed by the usual present indicative (*videntur*). See the note on *dum,* l. 454. —— **Dardaniō**, dat. sing. m. of *Dardanius, -a, -um* (= *Trōiānus, -a, -um;* adj. formed from *Dardanus, -ī,* m., 2d = *Dardanus,* a son of Jupiter and Electra, the founder of the city of Dardania and of the Trojan royal house); agrees with *Aeneae.* —— **Aenēae**, dat. sing. of *Aenēās,* m., 1st decl. Greek noun (for declension, see the note on *Aeneae,* l. 92); dat. of the agent, after *videntur* (= *are seen*). A. & G. 232; B. 189; G. 354; H. 388, 1. Some regard *Aeneae* as a dative of the indirect obj. after *miranda,* = *while these things, wonderful to Aeneas, are seen.* Others again explain the dative as indirect obj. after *videntur* (= *seem*), i.e. the deponent verb, = *while these things seem wonderful to Aeneas.* —— **miranda**, nom. plur. n. of *mīrandus, -a, -um,* the gerundive of *mīror, -ārī, mīrātus sum,* 1 deponent; agrees with *haec,* which it qualifies attributively. If *videntur* be rendered *seem, miranda* must be taken as a complement in the predicate. —— **videntur**, 3d pers. plur. pres. ind. pass. of *videō, -ēre, vīdī, vīsum,* 2; agrees with the subj. *haec,* in the temporal clause introduced by *dum.* If *videntur = seem,* it is from *videor, -ērī, vīsum sum,* 2 (i.e. the passive of *videō* used as a deponent verb).

LINE 495. **Dum**, temporal conj., repeated (by *anaphora*) for effect from *dum* in the previous line, because it is more graphic than a mere copulative conjunction connecting *videntur* and *stupet.* —— **stupet**, 3d pers. sing. pres. ind. act. of *stupeō, -ēre, -uī,* no supine, 2; agrees with the subj. *Aeneas,* understood from *Aeneae* above. —— **obtūtū**, abl. sing. of *obtūtus, -ūs,* m., 4th (from *obtueor, ob + tueor*); governed by *in.* —— **que**, enclitic cop. conj. —— **haeret**, 3d pers. sing. pres. ind. act. of *haereō, -ēre, haesī, haesum,* 2; joined by *que* to *stupet,* and in the same grammatical construction. —— **dēfīxus**, nom. sing. m. of the perf. part. pass. of *dēfīgō, -ere, dēfīxī, dēfīxum,* 3 (*dē + fīgō*); agrees with the understood pronoun (referring to Aeneas) as subj. of *haeret. Defixus =* lit. *fixed down,* and exactly corresponds to the English metaphorical adjective *rooted,* used in similar connections. —— **in**, prep. with the acc. or abl.; gov. *obtutu.* For the position of *in* and other monosyllabic prepositions between the noun and the adjective which qualifies the noun, consult A. & G. 345, *a;* B. 350, 7, *b;* G. 413, REM. 1; H. 569, II, 1. The usual order is adjective, preposition, noun. —— **ūnō**, abl. sing. m. of *ūnus, -a, -um* (gen. *ūnīus*); agrees with *obtutu; obtutu in uno* signifies that Aeneas studied the pictures with *one* long gaze, being rooted to the spot and unable to transfer his gaze elsewhere.

LINE 496. **Rēgīna**, gen. *rēgīnae,* f., 1st; nom. sing., subj. of *incessit.* —— **ad**, prep. with the acc.; gov. *templum.* —— **templum**, acc. sing. of *templum, -ī,* n., 2d; governed

ád tem,plúm, „	for,má	pul,chérrima	,	Dído,
to the temple	*in figure*	*most beautiful*		*Dido*

⁴⁹⁷ Ínces,sít, mag,ná iuve,núm „ sti,pánte ca,térva.
came in,   great   of youths   escorting (her)   a troop.

⁴⁹⁸ Quális in , Eúro,tǽ ri,pís „ aut , pér   iuga ,
(Such) as on of the Eurotas the banks, or   over the hill-crests

⁴⁹⁹ Cýnthi   Éxer,cét Di,ána   cho,rós, „ quam ,
of Cynthus   keeps up   Diana   the choral dances,   whom

most excellent of beauty, stept forth towards the temple, a great company of youths escorting her. Even as on Eurotas' banks or along the heights of Cynthus Diana speeds the dance, in whose train

---

by *ad*. The expectations of Aeneas (*reginam opperiens*, l. 454) are now fulfilled by the arrival of Dido. —— **fōrmā**, abl. sing. of *forma, -ae*, f., 1st; abl. of specification, showing wherein or in regard to what Dido is said to be *pulcherrima*. The scansion proves *forma* to be the ablative case, for the final syllable is long; *pulcherrima*, on the contrary, is nom., for the last three syllables form the 5th (*dactylic*) foot. A. & G. 253; B. 226; G. 397; H. 424. —— **pulcherrima**, nom. sing. f. of *pulcherrimus, -a, -um*, the superl. of *pulcher, pulchra, pulchrum* (*poliō = I polish*); agrees with *Dido*. Adjectives in *-er* form their superlative by adding *-rimus* to the nominative singular masculine of the positive. A. & G. 89, *a*; B. 71, 3; G. 87, 1; H. 163, 1. —— **Dīdō**, gen. *Dīdōnis* or *Dīdūs*, f., 3d; nom. sing., subj. of *incessit*.

LINE 497. **Incessit**, 3d pers. sing. perf. ind. act. of *incēdō, -ere, incessī, incessum*, 3 (*in + cēdō*); agrees with the subj. *Dido*; this verb expresses majestic motion, cf. l. 405, *vera incessu patuit dea*. —— **magnā**, abl. sing. f. of *magnus, -a, -um*; agrees with *caterva*. —— **iuvenum**, gen. plur. of *iuvenis, -is*, adj., m. and f. (comparative *iunior*, superl. *natu minimus*); a sort of gen. of substance, describing *caterva*. A. & G. 214, *e*; B. 197; G. 361; H. 395. —— **stīpante**, abl. sing. f. of *stīpāns, -antis*, pres. part. act. of *stīpō, -āre, -āvī, -ātum*, 1; agrees with *caterva* in the abl. abs. construction. —— **catervā**, abl. sing. of *caterva, -ae*, f., 1st; in the abl. abs. construction with *stipante*.

LINE 498. **Quālis**, nom. sing. f. of *qualis, -e;* agrees with *Diana*. The simile introduced here is imitated by Vergil from Odyssey, VI, 102, where it is applied to Nausicaa and the maidens attending her. —— **in**, prep. with the acc. and abl.; gov. the abl. *ripis*. —— **Eurōtae**, gen. sing. of *Eurōtās*, m., 1st decl. Greek noun (Greek Εὐρώτας); poss. gen., limiting *ripis*. The Eurotas was a river of Laconia, in the Peloponnesus, flowing close by the city of Sparta ; it is now called the *Basilipotamo* (= king of rivers). It was a favorite haunt of Artemis. —— **rīpīs**, abl. plur. of *rīpa, -ae*, f., 1st; governed by *in*. —— **aut**, disjunctive conj., connecting *in ripis Eurotae* with *per iuga Cynthi*, the latter being suggested as an alternative. *Aut* is used when each alternative excludes the other ; *vel* (*ve*) offers a choice between two alternatives; *sive* gives a choice between two names of the same thing; the correlatives are *aut . . . aut, vel . . . vel, sive . . . sive.* A. & G. 156, *c*; B. 342; G. 494; H. 554, II, 2. —— **per**, prep. with the acc.; gov. *iuga*. —— **iuga**, acc. plur. of *iugum, -ī*, n., 2d (from *iungō, = I join*, hence often = *a yoke*) ; governed by *per*. *Iuga* here = *mountain-ridges*. —— **Cýnthī**, gen. sing. of *Cýnthus, -ī*, m., 2d (Greek Κύνθος); poss. gen., limiting *iuga*. Cynthus is a high mountain in Delos, where Apollo and Artemis (Diana) were born; for this reason Apollo is often called *Cynthius* and Diana *Cynthia*.

LINE 499. **Éxercet**, 3d pers. sing. pres. ind. act. of *ēxerceō, -ēre, -uī, -itum*, 2 (*ēx + arceō*); agrees with the subj. *Diana;* see *exercet*, l. 431. —— **Dīāna**, gen. *Dīānae*, f., 1st; nom. sing., subj. of *ēxercet*. Observe that the first syllable, short in all other places, is here long in quantity. Diana, the goddess of hunting, was the daughter of

a thousand Oreads	mílle	se,cútae	Hínc	at,que	hínc ,, 500
throng on this side	*a thousand*	*having followed*	*on this side*	*and*	*on that side*
and on that ; she a					
quiver bears upon	glome,rántur	O,réades: ,	ílla pha,rétram	Fért 501
her shoulder, and as	*assemble*	*mountain-Nymphs: she*	*a quiver*	*carries*
she moves towers	hume,ró, ,,	gradi,énsque	de,ás	super,éminet ,
above all the goddess-	*on her shoulder*	*and walking*	*the goddesses*	*overtowers*

Jupiter and Latona, and the sister of Apollo. —— **chorōs,** acc. plur. of *chorus, -ī,* m., 2d (Greek χόρος); direct obj. of *exercet.* —— **quam,** acc. sing. f. of the rel. pron. *quī, quae, quod;* agrees with the antecedent *Diana,* and is direct obj. of *secutae.* —— **mille,** indeclinable numeral adj.; qualifying *Oreades; mille* is not specific, but denotes a large number. —— **secūtae,** nom. plur. f. of *secūtus, -a, -um,* perf. part. of the deponent verb *sequor, sequī, secūtus sum,* 3; agrees with *Oreades.*

LINE 500. **Hīnc,** adv. of place, denoting separation. ——**atque,** cop. conjunction, joining *hinc* above to *hinc* below. —— **hīnc,** adv. of place; *hinc . . . hinc* here = *on this side . . . on that,* and the adverbs modify *glomerantur. Hinc* usually marks separation, = *from this place;* of time, = *after this;* of cause, = *from this cause, hence.* —— **glomerantur,** 3d pers. plur. pres. ind. pass. of *glomerō, -āre, -āvī, -ātum,* 1 (from the rare noun *glomus, glomeris,* n., 3d, = *a ball of yarn*); agrees with the subj. *Oreades; glomerantur* has a reflexive or deponent sense (= *congregantur*). —— **Orēades,** gen. *Orēadum,* f., 3d (sing. *Orēas, -adis,* f., = Greek 'Ορειάς, from δρος, = *mountain*); nom. plur., subj. of *glomerantur.* Observe (1) that the first *e* is long; this is because it takes the place of the Greek diphthong ει, so the Latin rule is that a vowel before another vowel is short in quantity; (2) that the final syllable is short, and not long as 3d declension nominatives are; the Greek nominative 'Ορειάδες is imitated. The Oreades were mountain-nymphs, and daughters of Phoroneus (or Jupiter) and Hecate. They generally accompanied Diana when she went on the chase. The nymphs were semi-divine beings; the chief classes are *Dryades* and *Hamadryades* (wood nymphs), *Oreades, Naiades* (spring and river nymphs), *Nereides* or *Oceanides* (sea nymphs). —— **illa,** nom. sing. f. of *ille, illa, illud* (gen. *illīus);* subj. of *fert; illa* refers to *Diana,* and the juxtaposition of *Oreades* and *illa* is intended to be emphatic, marking out Diana as beautiful beyond all the rest. —— **pharētram,** acc. sing. of *pharētra, -ae,* f., 1st (Greek φαρέτρα = *quiver;* direct obj. of *fert.* The second syllable may be either long or short in Latin verse; when a naturally short vowel precedes a mute consonant followed by *l* or *r,* the vowel may be lengthened when desired; cf. *Trīnācria.* A. & G. 347, *d;* B. 5, B, 3; G. 13; H. 578.

LINE 501. **Fert,** 3d pers. sing. pres. ind. act. of *ferō, ferre, tulī, lātum,* irreg.; graphic or *historic* present, agreeing with the subj. *illa.* —— **humerō,** abl. sing. of *humerus, -ī,* m., 2d (akin to Greek ὦμος); abl. of the instrument, with *fert.* —— **gradiēns,** gen. *gradientis;* nom. sing. f. of the pres. part. of the deponent verb *gradior, -ī, gressus sum,* 3; agrees with and enlarges the subj. of *supereminet.* —— **que,** enclitic cop. conj. —— **deās,** acc. plur. of *dea, -ae,* f., 1st; direct obj. of *supereminet.* Two MSS. read *deā,* the final syllable being long in *arsis* though the case is nominative (*dea* of course would be subject of *supereminet*) ; this is explained by supposing that those who copied the two MSS. were not aware that the nymphs could be styled goddesses (*deas*), but Propertius and others call them *deae.* —— **superēminet,** 3d pers. sing. pres. ind. act. of *superēmineō, -ēre,* no perf., no supine, 2 trans. and intrans. (*super,* = *over,* + *ēmineō,* = *I project*); agrees with the subj. *illa* and is joined by *que* to *fert.* —— **omnēs,** acc. plur. f. of *omnis, -e;* agrees with *deas.*

502 ómnes ; Láto, næ taci, tum „ per, téntant , gaúdia ,
 all ;   *of Latona*   *silent*   *thrill*   *joys*

503 péctus :   Tális   e, rát   Di, dó,   „   ta, lém   se ,
 the breast :   *such*   *was*   *Dido,*   *such*   *herself*

504 læta   fe, rébat Pér   medi, ós,   in, stáns
 gladly (lit. *glad*) *she bore through (the men's) midst, urging on*

company : joy thrills
Latona's silent heart;
such was Dido, such
she made glad prog-
ress through their
midst, urging on the

LINE 502. **Lātōnae**, gen. sing. of *Lātōna*, f., 1st (Greek Λητώ); poss. gen., limiting *pectus.* Latona was a daughter of Coeus, the Titan, and Phoebe (or of Saturn, as Homer states). Her beauty attracted Jupiter, by whom she became the mother of Apollo and Diana, giving birth to them on the island of Delos. Juno, wife of Jupiter, pursued her everywhere with her resentment, and only Neptune helped her by making the floating island of Delos stationary and giving it her for a home. Latona in course of time became a powerful deity, and her children received divine honors. —— **tacitum**, acc. sing. n. of *tacitus, -a, -um*, adj. (from *taceo, = I am silent*); qualifies *pectus. Tacitum pertentant gaudia pectus* is a Vergilian refinement on the simple Homeric γέγηθε . . . φρένα Λητώ = *Latona rejoiced at heart.* —— **pertentant** (*pertemptant*), 3d pers. sing. pres. ind. act. of *pertento (pertempto), -āre, -āvī, -ātum,* 1 (*per + tentō (temptō)*); agrees with the subj. *gaudia.* —— **gaudia**, nom. plur. of *gaudium, -ī*, n., 2d (*gaudeō*); subj. of *pertentant.* —— **pectus**, acc. sing. of *pectus, pectoris*, n., 3d; direct obj. of *pertentant.*

LINE 503. **Tālis**, nom. sing. f. of *tālis, -e ;* agrees with the subj. *Dido*, and is the complement of *erat* in the predicate *talis erat ; talis* is the demonstrative answering to the relative *qualis* which introduced the comparison in l. 498. —— **erat**, 3d pers. sing. imperf. ind. act. of *sum, esse, fuī ;* agrees with the subj. *Dido.* —— **Dīdō**, gen. *Dīdōnis* or *Dīdūs*, f., 3d; nom. sing., subj. of *talis erat.* —— **tālem**, acc. sing. f. of *tālis, -e ;* predicate adj. agreeing with the object *se.* Verbs of *making, calling, showing*, etc., may take a noun or adjective in the accusative case, referring to the direct object, but not as a mere attribute or appositive of it. A. & G. 239, 1, *a*; B. 177; G. 340; H. 373. The repetition of the adjective *talis* is vivid and emphatic; such repetitions are known by the name of *anaphora.* —— **sē**, acc. sing. of the reflexive pron. *sē ;* direct obj. of *ferebat ; se* refers to the subject *Dido.* —— **laeta**, nom. sing. f. of the adj. *laetus, -a, -um ;* agrees with the subj. of *ferebat* (*Dido* understood from the preceding sentence, or a pronoun referring to her); *laeta* has the force of an adverb. —— **ferēbat**, 3d pers. sing. imperf. ind. act. of *ferō, ferre, tulī, lātum*, irreg.; the subj. is *Dido* or a pron. *illa* understood.

LINE 504. **Per**, prep. with the acc.; gov. *mediōs.* —— **mediōs**, acc. plur. m. of *medius, -a, -um ;* agrees with *virōs* understood, and has a partitive sense as usual = *through their midst.* —— **instāns**, gen. *instantis ;* nom. sing. f. of the pres. part. act. of *instō, -āre, institī, instatum,* 1 (*in + stō*) ; agrees with and enlarges the subject of *ferebat.* —— **operī**, dat. sing. of *opus, operis*, n., 3d; dat. of the indirect obj. after the compound verb *instans* (and common after compounds of *in, con, ad, sub*, etc.). In Aen. VIII, 433, we find *instabant currum*, i.e. the accusative following *instare :* consult the note on *scopulo*, l. 45. —— **regnīs**, dat. plur. of *regnum, -ī*, n., 2d; dat. of the indirect obj., joined by *que* to *operi* and in the same construction. *Operi regnisque* is an instance of *hendiadys*, for *the work and her growing kingdom = the work of her growing kingdom*, a single idea and not two ideas. For *hendiadys*, refer to the note and references on *umbris*, l. 311. —— **que**, enclitic cop. conj. —— **futūrīs**, dat. plur. n. of *futūrus, -a, -um*, fut. part. of *sum ;* agrees with *regnis.*

toil of her rising empire. Then at the gates of the goddess, beneath the temple's central dome, set round with arms and resting high-enthroned she took her seat. Ordinances she was giving and laws to the folk, and

ope,rí	„	reg,nísque	fu,túris.	Túm	fori,bús 505
the work		*and her kingdom*	*future.*	*Then*	*in the doors*
di,væ,	„	medi,á	tes,túdine ,	témpli,	Sǽpta 506
of the goddess,		*middle*	*under the arch of the temple*		*surrounded*
ar,mís	„	soli,óque	al,té	sub,níxa	re,sédit.
by arms		*and on a throne*	*high*	*supported*	*she sat.*
Iúra		da,bát		le,gésque	vi,rís, „ 507
Enactments		*she was giving*		*and laws*	*to the men,*

LINE 505. **Tum,** adv. of time, here connective. —— **foribus,** abl. plur. of *foris, -is,* f., 3d (akin to Greek θύρα and Sanskrit *dvár*) ; abl. of 'place where.' *Foribus* clearly does not refer to the *doors* of the temple, for if it did it would be impossible to reconcile it with *mediā testudine ;* the doors are those of the sacred shrine (*cella*) at the back of the temple, and the people gathered before Dido in the large hall (under the central dome) which reached from the entrance of the temple to the shrine. One commentator mentions that there were three *cellae* in the Capitoline temple at Rome. Vergil gives a Roman touch to the description in placing the assembly in a temple hall, for the Roman Senate frequently held its meetings away from the *curia* in some temple. —— **dīvae,** gen. sing. of *dīva,* f., 1st; poss. gen., limiting *foribus.* —— **mediā,** abl. sing. f. of *medius, -a, -um ;* qualifies *testudine* partitively. —— **testūdine,** abl. sing. of *testūdō, testūdinis,* f., 3d (from *testa,* = *a shell*) ; abl. of 'place where.' *Testudo* = (1) *a tortoise,* as being a *shell-covered* animal; (2) from the shape of the tortoise arose the meaning *arch, dome ;* (3) *a tortoise,* i.e. a covering of wood or of interlocked shields under which soldiers advanced to break down the wall of a town; (4) *a lyre, lute.* —— **templī,** gen sing. of *templum,* n., 2d; poss. gen., limiting *testudine.*

LINE 506. **Saepta,** nom. sing. f. of *saeptus, -a, -um,* perf. part. pass. of *saepiō, -īre, saepsī, saeptum,* 4 (*saepēs* = *a hedge*) ; agrees with and enlarges the subj. (*Dido* understood) of *resedit.* —— **armis,** abl. plur. of *arma ;* abl. of the instrument, with *saepta.* —— **soliō,** dat. sing. of *solium, -ī,* n., 2d (probably akin to *solum*) ; dat. of the indirect obj. after the compound of *sub, subnixa.* —— **que,** enclitic cop. conj. —— **altē,** adv. (formed from the adj. *altus, -a, -um*), modifying *subnixa.* —— **subnīxa,** nom. sing. f. of *subnīxus, -a, -um,* perf. part. of the obsolete deponent verb *subnītor, -ī, subnixus sum,* 3 (*sub + nītor = I lean*) ; joined by *que* to *saepta* and in the same construction. —— **resēdit,** 3d pers. sing. perf. ind. act. of *resīdō, -ere, resēdī,* no supine, 3 intrans. (*re,* = *back,* + *sīdō,* = *I sit*) ; the implied subj. is *Dido.*

LINE 507. **Iūra,** acc. plur. of *iūs, iūris,* n., 3d; direct obj. of *dabat.* If there is any distinction at all between *iūra* and *lēges,* it is that the former = *general institutions,* i.e. the complete code of law, and the latter = *special enactments,* but probably they are identical here. *Iura dabat* must not be rendered *was dispensing justice* (which would be *ius dicebat*) ; Dido is now exercising her *legislative* function; it is in *operum . . . trahebat* that the judicial, i.e. executive, function is referred to. —— **dabat,** 3d pers. sing. imperf. ind. act. of *dō, dare, dedī, datum,* 1; agrees with a pron. understood as subj., referring to *Dido.* —— **lēgēs,** acc. plur. of *lēx, lēgis,* f., 3d (for *leg-s,* from *legō = I read,* because proposed enactments were *read* to the people to pass or condemn); direct obj. of *dabat,* joined by *que* to *iura* above. The difference between *rōgātio* (= *a bill*) and *lex* is that the former precedes the latter, and is not valid till it becomes the latter. A magistrate proposes (*rogat*) a bill, and the people *jubet* or *vetat* it. Note the following phrases : (1) *antiquare legem* = *to vote against a new law ;* (2) *abrogare legem = to rescind a*

508 ope,rúmque	la,bórem	Pártibus	,	ǽqua,bát	was apportioning by
and of the works	*the toil*	*by divisions*		*she was dividing*	just division the
509 ius,tís,	„ aut	, sórte	tra,hébat;	Cúm subi,to	work's task or was
just,	*or*	*by lot*	*was drawing;*	*when suddenly*	drawing by lot, when
					suddenly Aeneas sees
Áene,ás	„	con,cúrsu	ac,cédere	, mágno	approaching amid
Aeneas		*in a throng*	*to approach*	*great*	a great throng

law; (3) *subrogare legi = to add a clause to a law;* (4) *derogare legi = to repeal a clause in a law.* —— **que,** enclitic cop. conj. —— **virīs,** dat. plur. of *vir, virī,* m., 2d; dat. of the indirect obj. after *dabat,* or dat. of reference. —— **operum,** gen. plur. of *opus, operis,* n., 3d; poss. gen., limiting *laborem.* The meaning is that Dido was adjusting the difficulties that attended the apportionment of work on the buildings, walls, etc., of the city. —— **que,** enclitic cop. conj. —— **labōrem,** acc. sing. of *labor, labōris,* m., 3d; direct obj. of *aequabat.*

LINE 508. **Partibus,** abl. plur. of *pars, partis,* f., 3d; abl. of manner, with *aequabat.* —— **aequābat,** 3d pers. sing. imperf. ind. act. of *aequō, -āre, -āvī, -ātum,* 1 (from *aequus, -a, -um, = equal) ;* joined by *que* to *dabat.* The imperfect tense denotes continuity of action, as it does also in *dabat* above; thus *dabat* and *aequabat* are distinguished from the aorist *resedit* (l. 506), which represents a single act. *Aequābat* does not = *made equal,* but made *fair, proportionate,* for *sorte trahebat* proves that some kinds of work were more laborious than others. Nevertheless, in a new colony all classes must share in the hard work. —— **iustīs,** abl. plur. f. of *iustus, -a, -um* (akin to *ius) ;* agrees with *partibus.* —— **aut,** disjunctive conj., connecting *aequabat* and *trahebat,* and offering an alternative which excludes the one already stated. Juno either used her personal judgment, or, when it seemed advisable, allowed the lot to decide a case. —— **sorte,** abl. sing. of *sors, sortis,* f., 3d; abl. of the means or instrument, with *trahebat.* —— **trahēbat,** 3d pers. sing. imperf. ind. act. of *trahō, -ere, trāxī, tractum,* 3; joined by *aut* to *aequabat,* and in agreement with the same subj., i.e. *Dido* understood. Vergil, as usual, prefers the inversion *sorte trahebat* for the usual expression *sortem trahebat ;* it is the *lot which is drawn* that appoints some one a task, though by a similar inversion in English we speak of men *being drawn by lot* to do something.

LINE 509. **Cum,** temporal conj., followed by the pres. ind. *videt. Cum* temporal takes the indicative in the aorist and in all primary tenses, but is usually followed by the subjunctive in the imperfect and pluperfect tenses. For references and note on the other uses of *cum,* see *cum,* l. 36. —— **subitō,** adv. of time, modifying *videt accedere. Subito* is the adverbial ablative neuter of the adjective *subitus, -a, -um ;* the neuter and sometimes the feminine ablative singular of adjectives, pronouns, and nouns, may be used as adverbs, e.g. *cito = quickly, forte = by chance.* A. & G. 148, *e;* B. 77, 2; G. 91, *c, d;* H. 304, II. —— **Aeneās,** nom. sing.; subj. of *videt.* —— **concursū,** abl. sing. of *concursus, -ūs,* m., 4th (from *concurrō, con = cum, with* or *together, + currō, = I run) ;* abl. of manner, describing *accedere.* As *concursu* is modified by the adjective *magno,* the preposition *cum* (required when there is no modifying adjective) is unnecessary. A. & G. 248; B. 220; G. 399; H. 419, III. *Concursū magnō = in a vast crowd,* i.e. of the attendant Trojans. —— **accēdere,** pres. inf. act. of *accēdō, -ēre, accessī, accessum,* 3 *(ad + cēdō) ;* agrees with *Anthea (Sergestum,* etc.) in the subject-acc. and inf. construction after *videt,* which is a *verbum sentiendi.* The clause *Anthea (Sergestum, . . . Cloānthum . . . alios) accedere* is really the direct obj. of the verb *videt,* answering a possible question *quid videt? = what does he see?* Sometimes, for the sake of emphasis, the participle (e.g. *accedentes*) is used instead of the infinitive, in imitation of the Greek con-

| Antheus and Serges-tus and brave Cloan-thus, and others of the Trojans, whom the black whirlwind had scattered over sea and driven far to | Anthea , Sérges,túmque vi,dét „ for,témque 510
Antheus   *and Sergestus*   *sees*   *and brave*
Clo,ánthum Teúcro,rúm*que* ali,ós, „ a,tér quos, 511
Cloanthus,   *and of the Trojans others,*   *black*   *whom*
æquore , túrbo Díspule,rát, „ peni,túsque 512
over the sea   *a whirlwind*   *had scattered*   *and far* |

---

struction when the object-clause is a simple one, i.e. not encumbered with subordinate clauses. A. & G. 272, and REM.; B. 330, 331; G. 527; H. 534, 535. —— **magnō**, abl. sing. m. of the adj. *magnus, -a, -um ;* agrees with *concursu.*

LINE 510. **Anthea**, Greek acc. sing. of *Anthĕus*, gen. *Antheos* or *Antheī*, m., mixed 2d and 3d; subj.-acc. of *accedere*, after *videt.* For the declension of *Antheus*, consult A. & G. 43, ORPHEUS; G. 47, 6; G. ORPHEUS; H. 68, ORPHEUS. Antheus, apart from this reference, is not known. —— **Sergestum**, acc. sing. of *Sergestus, -ī*, m., 2d; subj.-acc. of *accedere*, joined by *que* to *Anthea.* Sergestus is the supposed ancestor of the Roman family of the Sergii; in the fifth book of the *Aeneid* he is mentioned as captain of the boat Centaurus. —— **que**, enclitic cop. conj. —— **videt**, 3d pers. sing. pres. ind. act. of *vidĕo, -ēre, vīdī, vīsum*, 2; agrees with the subj. *Aeneas; videt* is historic present, after the temporal conjunction *cum.* —— **fortem**, acc. sing. m. of *fortis, -e*, adj., 3d; agrees with *Cloanthum ;* in l. 222, *fortem* is an attribute of *Cloanthum*, whence we may infer that it is a fixed epithet, imitated from those used by Homer. —— **que**, enclitic cop. conj. —— **Cloanthum**, acc. sing. of *Cloanthus, -ī*, m., 2d; subj.-acc. of *accedere*, joined by *que* to *Sergestum.*

LINE 511. **Teucrōrum**, gen. plur. of *Teucrī*, m., 2d; partitive gen., limiting *alios ;* the partitive gen. represents the whole which is distributed. A. & G. 216; B. 201; G. 367, *ff.*; H. 397. —— **que**, enclitic cop. conj. —— **aliōs**, acc. plur. m. of *alius, -a, -ud ;* used substantively, and a subj.-acc. of *accedere*, joined by *que* to *Cloanthum ; alios =* *others*, not the rest (*ceteros*). —— **āter**, nom. sing. m. of the adj. *āter, ātra, ātrum ;* qualifies *turbo. Ater* is specific (= *black,* as opposed to *niger*, which is generic and admits of comparison), and sometimes has the derived sense of *gloomy*, e.g. *dies atri = unlucky days.* —— **quōs**, acc. plur. m. of the rel. pron. *quī, quae, quod ;* agrees with the antecedents *Anthea, Sergestum, Cloanthum*, and *alios*, and is the direct obj. of *dispulerat.* The relative pronoun usually stands first in the relative clause, but may be second or third in poetry. —— **aequore**, abl. sing. of *aequor, aequoris*, n., 3d (from *aequus, = level*); a locative abl. of 'place over which'; cf. *alto prospiciens*, l. 126. For synonyms of *aequor*, refer to the note on *pelago*, l. 181. —— **turbō**, gen. *turbinis*, m., 3d; nom. sing., subj. of *dispulerat.*

LINE 512. **Dispulerat**, 3d pers. sing. pluperf. ind. act. of *dispello, -ere, dispulī, dispulsum*, 3 (*dis, = in different ways, + pellō, = I drive*); agrees with the subj. *turbo* in the relative clause introduced by *quos.* —— **penitus**, adv., modifying *avexerat. Penitus* (akin to *penetro, = I penetrate*) strictly = *within*, or *from within*, but here (and in l. 536, *penitus dispulit*) has the general meaning of *far, afar.* —— **que**, enclitic cop. conj. —— **aliās**, acc. plur. f. of *alius, -a, -ud ;* agrees with *oras.* —— **āvēxerat**, 3d pers. sing. pluperf. ind. act. of *āvehō, -ere, āvēxī, āvectum*, 3 (*ā, = away from, + vehō, = I carry*); in agreement with the subj. *turbo* and joined by *que to dispulerat.* There is another reading *advexerat*, but *avexerat* is by most considered preferable. The difficulty of *oras*, the acc. without a preposition, probably gave rise to the reading *advexerat.* —— **ōrās**, acc. plur. of *ōra,-ae*, f., 1st; acc. of the limit of motion. In prose *motion to* the

513 ali,ás a,véxerat , óras.　　Óbstupu,ít　　simul ,　| other shores.　Amazed
other 　*had carried* 　*to shores.*　*He was astonished at the same time* | stood 　 the 　 hero,
514 ípse 　 ,, 　si,múl per,cússus A,chátes Lǽtiti,áque | amazed 　too 　Achates
himself, *at the same time* 　*struck* 　　*Achates* 　　*both with joy* | stricken with joy and
me,túque: 　 ,, 　avi,dí 　con,iúngere 　, 　déxtras | fear ;　 eagerly 　 they
and with fear: 　　*eager* 　　*to join* 　　*right hands* | burned to join hand

---

names of towns and small islands is expressed by the accusative alone (without a preposition *ad* or *in*); in poetry countries are often similarly treated, but the simple acc. of other nouns is not very often used without a preposition expressing motion ; cf. Aen. II, 781, *terram Hesperiam venies.* A. & G. 258, *b*, NOTE 5; B. 182, 4; G. 337; H. 380, 3.

LINE 513. **Obstupuit,** 3d pers. sing. perf. ind. act. of *obstupescō, -ere, obstupuī*, no supine, 2 (*ob* + *stupescō* = *I become amazed*); agrees with the subj. *ipse*. On the *inceptive* or *inchoative* signification of verbs in -*sco*, consult A. & G. 167, *a*; B. 155, 1; G. 133, V; H. 337.—— **simul**, adv. of time; *simul . . . simul* practically = *both . . . and*. *Simul* shows that the appearance of Antheus, etc., produced the same effect on Aeneas and Achates, a subsidiary proof that *obstupuit* is the predicate of *Achates* as well as of *ipse*. —— **ipse**, nom. sing. m. of the intensive pron. *ipse, ipsa, ipsum*; intensifies *Aeneas,* and is subj. of *obstupuit*. —— **simul**, adv. of time. —— **percussus**, nom. sing. m. of *percussus, -a, -um*, perf. part. pass. of *percutiō, -ere, percussī, percussum*, 3 (*per* + *quatiō*); agrees with *Achates*. There is another reading *perculsus*, nom. sing. m. of the perf. part. pass. of *percellō, -ere, perculī, perculsum*, 3 (*per* + *cellō*). The MSS. are very often divided over these words; both words mean much the same, but *percussus* is perhaps more suitable when the shock is of a pleasant nature. Some editors place a comma or other stop after *ipse*; in this case *percussus* is a principal verb, = *percussus est*. But most editors are agreed that the verb should be the same for *Achates* as for *ipse*, i.e. they experience the same emotion at the same time (*simul*). —— **Achātēs,** nom. sing. m., 1st decl. Greek noun; subj. of *obstupuit*, understood from *obstupuit ipse*.

LINE 514. **Laetitiā,** abl. sing. of *laetitia, -ae,* f., 1st (*laetus* = *joyful*, hence *joyfulness*); abl. of the instrument, with *perculsus,* or perhaps abl. of cause with *obstupuit.* Synonyms : *gaudium* = *the emotion of joy*, as opposed to *luctus*, i.e. the passion of grief; *laetitia* = *transport, manifested joy*, as opposed to *tristitia*, i.e. manifested sorrow. *Laetitia* is thus a much stronger word than *gaudium*. Cicero classes *laetitia* with the *appetitus vehementiores*, and says that it causes *profusam hilaritatem*, i.e. *extravagant mirth*. —— **que**, enclitic cop. conj.; *que . . . que, both . . . and.* —— **metū**, abl. sing. of *metus, -ūs,* m., 4th; abl. of the instrument (or cause), joined by *que* below to *laetitia.* —— **que**, enclitic cop. conj. —— **avidī**, nom. plur. m. of *avidus, -a, -um* (*aveō* = *I desire eagerly*); agrees with *illī* understood as subj. of *ardebant; illi* would refer to Aeneas and Achates. *Avidi* is an adverbial attribute and must be taken closely with *ardebant*, = *they burned eagerly.* —— **coniungere**, pres. inf. act. of *coniungō, -ere, coniunxī, coniunctum,* 3 (*con* = *cum* + *iungō*) ; *prolative* inf., with *ardebant* in its figurative meaning of *were desiring* (lit. *were burning*, i.e. with eagerness). In prose such verbs as *ardeo, hortor*, etc., would be followed by *ut* with the subjunctive; but the poets use the infinitive freely after verbs and adjectives. A. & G. 331, *g*; B. 326; G. 423; H. 535, IV. —— **dextrās**, acc. plur. of *dextra, -ae,* f., 1st (supply *manūs*, as *dextra* is originally the f. of *dexter*) ; direct obj. of *coniungere*.

to hand, but the | Árde,bánt;   sed , rés   ani,mós „ in,cógnita , 515
strange happening
troubles their minds. | *they were burning;   but the thing   their minds   strange*
They hide their desire | túrbat.   Díssimu,lánt;   „   et   ,   núbe 516
and shrouded in the
enwrapping cloud | *troubles.   They hide (their emotion);   and   by the cloud*
watch to learn what | ca,vá   specu,lántur   a,mícti,   Quǽ   for,túna 517
the men's lot, on what | *hollow   they watch   clothed,   what (is)   the fortune*

LINE 515. **Ardēbant**, 3d pers. plur. imperf. ind. act. of *ardeō, -ēre, arsī, arsum*, 2, intrans.; the implied subj. is *illi*, referring to *Aeneas* and *Achates*. —— **sed**, adversative conj., introducing something in opposition to *ardebant coniungere*. Of the adversative particles *sed, autem, verum, vero, at, atqui, ceterum*, and *tamen*, the only ones really adversative are *tamen* and *sed*. *Sed* is used in two ways: (1) in a strong sense, denoting a contradiction; (2) in a weaker sense, introducing a new idea. *Sed* is often strengthened by the conjunction of *tamen, autem, enim, vero. Verum* generally stands first and *vero* second in a sentence, and are practically = to *sed*. *At* introduces some new and lively objection, and so does its stronger form *atqui* (most common in argumentative sentences). *Tamen* may or may not be preceded by a concessive clause introduced by *etsi* or *etiamsi*, etc. The weakest of the adversative particles is *autem*, which is scarcely anything more than connective. A. & G. 156, *b*; B. 343, 1; G. 485; H. 554, 3. —— **rēs**, gen. *reī*, f., 5th; nom. sing., subj. of *turbat*. —— **animōs**, acc. plur. of *animus, -ī*, m., 2d; direct obj. of *turbat*. —— **incōgnita**, nom. sing. f. of *incōgnitus, -a, -um*, adj. (*in*, = *not*, + *cōgnitus*, = *known*, perf. part. pass. of *cōgnōscō, -ere, cōgnōvī, cōgnitum*, 3); agrees with *res*. *Incognitus* = (1) *unknown*, hence (2) *strange; res incognita* implies both these senses, for Aeneas and Achates were disturbed both by the *strange* event of their comrades' arrival and by the *unknown* turn their fortunes were to take, as the next two lines of the text show. —— **turbat**, 3d pers. sing. pres. ind. act. of *turbō, -āre, -āvī, -ātum*, 1 (from *turba*, = *a disturbance*, hence *turbō*, = *I move violently*); agrees with the subj. *res*.

LINE 516. **Dissimulant**, 3d pers. plur. pres. ind. act. of *dissimulō, -āre, -āvī, -ātum*, 1 (for *dissimilō*, from *dis*, denoting reversal or opposition, + *similis*, = *like*); understand *Aeneas et Achates* as subjects (or *illi* referring to them). Some think that *dissimulant*, = *they hide (their presence, se adesse)*, but this is obviously wrong, for Aeneas and Achates were still hidden in the cloud, which does not vanish till l. 587. The verb therefore refers to *laetitia* and *metus* (l. 514), i.e. *they hide (their joy and their fear). Simulo*, = *I feign, that something is which is not; dissimulo*, = *I feign, that something is not which is;* this difference is well expressed in the following hexameter : *Quae non sunt simulo, quae sunt ea dissimulantur*. —— **et**, cop. conj. —— **nūbe**, abl. sing. of *nūbēs, -is*, f., 3d; abl. of the instrument, with *amictu*. —— **cavā**, abl. sing. f. of *cavus, -a, -um*, adj.; qualifies *nube; cava* = lit. *hollow*, hence *enfolding*, as Aeneas and Achates were inside. —— **speculantur**, 3d pers. plur. pres. ind. of the deponent verb *speculōr, -ārī, -ātus sum*, 1 (from *specula* = *a look-out place*, hence *I observe, I watch*); joined by *et* to *dissimulant*. —— **amictī**, nom. plur. m. of *amictus, -a, -um*, perf. part. pass. of *amiciō, -īre, amicuī, amictum*, 4 (from *am*, = *around*, + *iaciō*, = *I throw*); agrees with and enlarges the subj. of *speculantur*.

LINE 517. **Quae**, nom. sing. f. of the interrog. adj. *quī, quae, quod;* agrees with *fortuna*, and introduces the indirect question *quae fortuna (sit) viris*. —— **fortūna**, gen. *fortūnae*, f., 1st; nom. sing., subj. of *sit* understood. The direct question which Aeneas asked himself was *quae fortuna (est) viris?* and this, put in an indirect form (after *speculantur*, = *watch to see*), has its verb in the subjunctive mood, and in a primary

518 vi, rís ; „ clas, sém quo , lítore , línquant ; Quíd | coast they leave the
  to the men,   the fleet what on shore   they leave;   why | fleet, why they are

veni, ánt : „ cun, ctís nam , lécti , návibus , | come ;   for chosen
  they come :   all   for   chosen men from the ships | men from all the

519 íbant,   Óran tés veni, am, „ ét   tem, plúm | ships were approach-
  were going   begging   favor,   and   the temple | ing, praying favor,

---

tense, as the rule of sequence of tenses requires. A. & G. 334; B. 300; G. 467; H. 528, 2, and 529, I. The relative introducing an indirect question may be a pronoun, adjective, or adverb; thus *quae* and *quo* in this line are adjectives, and *quid* in the next line is adverbial. —— **virīs**, dat. plur. of *vir, virī*, m., 2d; dat. of the possessor, after *sit* understood. —— **classem**, acc. sing. of *classis, -is*, f., 3d; direct obj. of *linquant*. Aeneas, seeing the crews safe, naturally takes it for granted that the ships were preserved also; besides, Venus (in the simile of the swans) had told him the fleet was not destroyed. —— **quō**, abl. sing. of the interrog. adj. *quī, quae, quod ;* agrees with *litore* and introduces a new indirect question, which no conjunction (*asyndeton*) joins to the preceding one. —— **lītore**, abl. sing. of *lītus, lītoris*, n., 3d; abl. of 'place where.' —— **linquant**, 3d pers. plur. pres. subjunct. act. of *linquō, -ere, līquī, līctum*, 3 (akin to Greek λείπω); the subj. implied by the personal ending is *Antheus, Sergestus*, and the rest of the Trojans. *Linquant,* = *are leaving,* not *have left* (*liquerint*, perf., as sequence requires); *linquant* practically = *dicant se reliquisse*, i.e. Aeneas *watches to see on what shore they say that they have left.* A. & G. 286; B. 267, 268; G. 509; H. 491.

LINE 518. **Quid**, adverbial acc. sing. n. of the interrog. pron. *quis, quae, quid ;* = *why,* and introduces a third indirect question *quid veniant.* —— **veniant**, 3d pers. plur. pres. subjunc. act. of *veniō, -īre, vēnī, ventum*, 4; agrees with the same subj. as *linquant* above; the mood is subjunctive because *quid veniant* is an indirect question dependent on *speculantur*, l. 516. —— **cunctīs**, abl. plur. f. of adj. *cunctus, -a, -um* (contracted from *coniunctus, -a, -um*, perf. part. pass. of *coniungō, -ere, coniunxī, coniunctum*, 3) ; agrees with *navibus ;* the sing. *cunctus* is little used, the plur. *cunctī, -ae, -a* being regularly employed. *Cunctis = omnibus* here; for *cuncti* compared with *omnes* and *universi*, refer to the note on *cunctus*, l. 154. There is another reading *cunctī*, nom. plur. m. agreeing with the subj. of *veniant ;* then the colon is placed after *cuncti ;* but there is no reason why Aeneas should wonder *why they came in a body.* —— **nam**, causal conj., introducing an explanation of *veniant.* —— **lectī**, nom. plur. m. of *lectus, -a, -um*, perf. part. pass. of *legō, -ere, lēgī, lectum*, 3; used substantively (= *chosen men*), subj. of *ibant.* —— **nāvibus**, abl. plur. of *nāvis, -is*, f., 3d; abl. of 'place from which.' The rule is that 'place from which' is expressed by the abl. case with the preposition *ab, ex,* or *de*, in conjunction with verbs compounded with these prepositions or any verb of motion; sometimes the abl. alone is regular with verbs = *to set free, to want, to deprive,* etc. But here *nāvibus* is irregular, and is one of several poetic extensions of the rule that *motion from* the names of towns or small islands is expressed by the ablative alone; cf. Aen. V, 99, *manes Acheronte remissos.* A. & G. 258, *a*, NOTE 3; B. 229, 1, *c*; G. 391, NOTE; H. 412, 2. —— **ībant**, 3d pers. plur. imperf. ind. act. of *eō, īre, īvī* or *iī, itum*, irreg. (akin to the Greek *ι-έναι*); agrees with the subj. *lecti.*

LINE 519. **Ōrantēs**, nom. plur. m. of *ōrāns, ōrāntis*, pres. part. act. of *ōrō, -āre, -āvī, -ātum*, 1 (akin to *ōs, ōris*, n., 3d, = *the mouth*) ; agrees with and enlarges the subj. *lecti ;* some think that *orantes* (*begging*) = *oraturi* (fut. part. = *about to beg*), but it is quite possible that the Trojans as they advanced made known their case (*clamore*, l. 519). —— **veniam**, acc. sing. of *venia, -ae*, f., 1st (= (1) *favor*, (2) *pardon*, a later

and with shouting | cla,móre pe,tébant. Póstquam in,trógres,si, ,, ét 520
were going towards | *with shouting were seeking.   After   they entered,   and*
the temple. After they
entered, and leave | co,rám   data   , cópia   ,   fándi,   Máximus , 521
of open speaking | *in presence was given   opportunity   of speaking,   the oldest*
was given them, aged
Ilioneus with tranquil | Ílio,neús ,, placi,dó sic , péctore , coépit :
bearing thus began : | *Ilioneus   calm   thus   with breast   began :*

meaning); direct obj. of *orantes.* The break in the sense follows *veniam,* and so it
seems better to mark the *caesura* here than after *et.* —— **et,** cop. conj. —— **templum,**
gen. *templī,* n., 2d; acc. sing., direct obj. of *petebant.* —— **clāmōre,** abl. sing. of *clāmor,*
clāmōris, m., 3d (from *clāmō,* 1, = *I cry out*); abl. of manner, with *petebant.* The omis-
sion of the preposition *cum* is poetical. A. & G. 248, at the end; B. 220; G. 399, NOTE
2; H. 419, III. —— **petēbant,** 3d pers. plur. imperf. ind. act. of *petō, -ere, petīvī* or
petiī, petītum, 3; joined by *et* to *ibant* and in agreement with the same subj. *lecti;* the
imperfects *ibant* and *petebant* are descriptive.

    LINE 520. **Postquam,** temporal conj., followed by the ind. *introgressi (sunt)* and
data (est). The construction after *postquam* is the same as after *ubi, simul ac, ut pri-
mum,* etc.; the verb is usually perf. ind. or the *historic* pres. ind., but sometimes imperf.
or pluperf. ind. (less commonly subjunctive). A. & G. 323–24; B. 287; G. 561 *ff;* H.
518. *Postquam* (cf. *ante . . . quam, prius . . . quam*) is often written in two words,
post . . . quam, which may be separated by other words or even clauses. —— **intrō-
gressi,** nom. plur. m. of *intrōgressus, -a, -um,* perf. part. of the deponent verb *intrōgre-
dior, -ī, intrōgressus sum,* 3 (for *intrōgradior,* from *intrō,* = *within,* + *gradior,* = *I step*);
agrees with *Antheus, Sergestus,* etc., understood as subjects, and forms with *sunt* under-
stood the 3d pers. plur. perf. indicative. —— **et,** cop. conj., joining the clause immedi-
ately following with the one immediately preceding. —— **cōram** (compounded of *cum*
and *ōs, ōris,* n., 3d, = *the face*), adv., modifying *fandi. Coram* is also used as a preposi-
tion, governing the ablative case, and = *in the presence of.* —— **data,** nom. sing. f. of
the perf. part. pass. of *dō, dare, dedī, datum,* 1; agrees with the subj. *copia,* and with *est*
understood forms the 3d pers. sing. perf. ind. passive. —— **cōpia** (from *co-opia,* i.e. *cum*
+ *ops,* = *means;* hence *cōpia* = (1) *plenty;* (2) *opportunity,* as here), gen. *copiae,* f.,
1st; nom. sing., subj. of *data (est).* —— **fandī,** gen. sing. of the gerund (gen. *fandī,*
and dat. and abl. *fandō* alone survive) of the defective verb *fārī,* = *to speak;* a gen. after
copia. As the gerundive is a verbal adjective, so is the gerundive a verbal noun, for as
a verb it is modified by adverbs and takes an object in the proper case, and as a noun it
is itself governed by other words, e.g. prepositions. A. & G. 295; B. 338; G. 425 *ff;*
H. 541, 542. For the parts of *fari* still in use, consult A. & G. 144, *c;* B. 136; G. 175,
3; H. 297, II, 3.

    LINE 521. **Māximus,** nom. sing. m. of *māximus, -a, -um,* superl. adj.; qualifies
Ilioneus, and = *maximus natu* (which is used as the superl. of *senex;* comparative
senior). Maximus by itself is the superlative of *magnus;* comparative *major.* We find
it applied to age in l. 654, *maxima natarum;* cf. *majores,* = *ancestors.* —— **Īlioneūs,**
gen. *Īlioneī,* m., mixed 2d and 3d Greek decl.; nom. sing., subj. of *coepit.* In l. 611,
the acc. is *Īlionea;* for declension, consult the note and references on *Anthea,* l. 510.
—— **placidō,** abl. sing. n. of *placidus, -a, -um ;* agrees with *pectore.* The Trojan crews
are excited (*clamore,* l. 519), but Ilioneus is calm and dignified. —— **sīc,** adv. of manner,
modifying *coepit.* —— **pectore,** abl. sing. of *pectus, pectoris,* n., 3d; abl. of manner, with
coepit. —— **coepit,** 3d pers. sing. perf. ind. act. of the defective verb *coepī* (perf.), inf.
coepisse, fut. part. *coeptūrus,* perf. part. pass. *coeptus;* agrees with the subj. *Ilioneus;*

522 "Ó	Re,gína,	„	no,vám	cui	,	cóndere	,	" O · Queen, whom
"O	queen,		new	to whom		to found		Jupiter has granted
523 Iúpiter	,	úrbem	Iústiti,áque			de,dít	„	it to found a new
Jupiter		a city	and with justice			has given		city and to curb
								with justice stiff-
524 gen,tés	fre,náre	su,pérbas,	Tróës	,	té			necked races, we
nations	to curb	proud,	Trojans		thee			miserable Trojans,
mise,rí,	„	ven,tís	mari,a	ómnia	,	vécti,		driven all seas
wretched		by the winds	over seas	all		carried		over by the winds,

there is an ellipse of *dicere* after *coepit*. The present tense *coepiō* is very rare; its place is taken by *incipio;* *coepiō* is derived from *co* = *cum* + the root AP in *apiscor*, = *I seize*. The perfect stem tenses are all used, and the perf. pass. *coeptus sum* is used with a passive infinitive, e.g. *coeptus sum creārī* (but *creāre coepi*). A. & G. 143, *a;* B. 133; G. 175, 5, *a;* H. 297, I.

LINE 522. **Ō**, exclamation, accompanying the voc. *rēgīna*. —— **rēgīna,** voc. sing. of *rēgīna, -ae,* f., 1st; case of the person addressed. —— **novam,** acc. sing. f. of *novus, -a, -um;* qualifies *urbem.* —— **cui,** dat. sing. f. of the rel. pron. *qui, quae, quod;* agrees with the antecedent *rēgīna* in gender and number, and is dat. of the indirect obj. after *dedit* below. —— **condere,** pres. inf. act. of *condō, -ere, condidī, conditum,* 3 (*con* = *cum* + *dō*); the inf. is direct obj. of *dedit,* and itself governs an obj., viz. *urbem.* In prose we should have had *urbem condendam* or *ut condas urbem* (*ut* with the subjunctive); but the infinitive is poetical, expressing purpose, and is borrowed from the common Greek construction, e.g. Iliad XXIII, 512, δῶκε δ᾽ ἄγειν . . . καὶ φέρειν. A. & G. 331, *g;* B. 326, NOTE; G. 421, NOTE I, *b;* H. 535, IV. —— **Iūpiter,** gen. *Iovis,* m., 3d; nom. sing., subj. of *dedit.* —— **urbem,** acc. sing. of *urbs, urbis,* f., 3d; direct obj. of *condere.*

LINE 523. **Iustitiā,** abl. sing. of *iustitia, -ae,* f., 1st (*iustus*); abl. of the means or instrument, with *frēnāre; iustitia* means more than mere *justice* here, and broadly includes all the improvements of advanced social life. —— **que,** enclitic cop. conj. —— **dedit,** 3d pers. sing. perf. ind. act. of *dō, dare, dedī, datum,* 1; agrees with the subj. *Iupiter.* This speech is cunningly constructed: the settlers are said to be humane civilizers, and Ilioneus accordingly demands that the Trojans be treated humanely. —— **gentēs,** acc. plur. of *gens, gentis,* f., 3d; direct obj. of *frēnāre.* —— **frēnāre,** pres. inf. act. of *frēnō, -āre, -āvī, -ātum,* 1 (*frēnum, -ī,* n., 2d, = *a bridle*); joined by *et* to *condere* and in exactly the same grammatical construction after *dedit.* —— **superbās,** acc. plur. f. of *superbus, -a, -um,* adj. (from *super,* = *over*); qualifies *gentes; gentes superbas* = *gentes Africas. Superbus,* = (1) *haughty;* (2) *proud* or *brave* in war.

LINE 524. **Tróës,** gen. *Trōum,* m., 3d (Greek Τρῶες, acc. Τρῶας); nom. plur., in apposition with *nos* understood as subj. of *ōrāmus.* The position of *Troes* is emphatic, and calls the attention of Dido at once to the nationality of the suppliants. —— **tē,** acc. sing. of the 2d (sing.) pers. pron. *tū;* direct obj. of *oramus.* —— **miserī,** nom. plur. m. of *miser, misera, miserum,* adj. (perhaps akin to *moereo,* = *I am sad*); qualifies *Troes.* —— **ventīs,** abl. plur. of *ventus, -ī,* m., 2d; abl. of the instrument, with *vecti.* —— **maria,** acc. plur. of *mare, maris,* n., 3d; acc. of *extension over,* a kind of cognate acc. such as is often found in poetry; e.g. l. 67, *navigat aequor,* and Aen. III, 191, *vastum- que . . . currimus aequor.* A. & G. 238; B. 176, 4; G. 333, 2; H. 371, II, and especially NOTE. —— **omnia,** acc. plur. n. of *omnis, -e,* adj., 3d; agrees with *maria.* —— **vectī,** nom. plur. m. of *vectus, -a, -um,* perf. part. pass. of *vehō, -ere, vēxī, vectum,* 3; agrees with and enlarges (in place of a relative clause, *qui vecti sumus*) *Troes.*

make entreaty, hold back the terrible fire from the ships. Spare a god-fearing race and more kindly regard our fortunes. We have not come to ravage with the sword your Libyan

Óra,mús: „ prohi,be ínfan,dós   a , návibus , 525

we pray :   *ward off*   *unutterable from*   *the ships*

ígnes;   **Párce**   pi,ó gene,rí, „ ét propi,ús res , 526

the fire;   spare (thou) *pious   a race,   and   nearer   affairs*

áspice , nóstras. **Nón** nos , aút   fer,ró „ Liby,cós 527

regard (thou) *our.   Not   we   either with steel   Libyan*

LINE 525. **Órāmus,** 1st pers. plur. pres. ind. act. of *ōrō, -āre, -āvī, -ātum,* 1 (*ōs, ōris,* n., 3d, = *mouth*) ; the subj. implied by the personal ending is *nōs.* —— **prohibē,** 2d pers. sing. imperative mood, act. of *prohibeō, -ēre, prohibuī, prohibitum,* 2 (for *prohabeō,* from *pro,* = *before,* + *habeō,* = *I hold,* hence *I ward off*) ; the implied subj. is *tu,* i.e. Dido. —— **infandōs,** acc. plur. m. of *infandus, -a, -um* (*in,* = *not,* + *fandus,* = *to be spoken of,* hence *dreadful*) ; qualifies *ignes. Infandus* is often used of things contrary to pious or civilized principles. —— **ā,** prep. with the abl.; gov. *nāvibus,* marking separation. See the note on *ab,* l. 1. —— **nāvibus,** abl. plur. of *nāvis, -is,* f., 3d; governed by *ā.* Separation is expressed by the ablative with the prepositions *a* or *ab, de, e* or *ex.* —— **ignēs,** acc. plur. of *ignis, -is,* m., 3d (akin to Sanskrit *agni,* = *fire*) ; direct obj. of *prohibē ;* the abl. sing. of *ignis* is usually *ignī,* always in the formula *aquā et ignī interdicere,* but may sometimes be *igne.*

LINE 526. **Parce,** 2d pers. sing. imperative mood, act. of *parcō, -ere, pepercī (parsī* rare), *parsum* or *parcitum,* 3 (*parcus,* = *sparing*) ; the implied subj. is *tū.* —— **piō,** dat. sing. n. of *pius, -a, -um ;* agrees with *generi ; pio,* = *god-fearing,* and perhaps has some reference to *pius* as an epithet or title of the Trojan leader Aeneas ; in any case, it implies that the Trojans have treated the Carthaginians and their city with all due respect. —— **generī,** dat. sing. of *genus, generis,* n., 3d; dat. governed by *parce.* The dative is governed by several special Latin verbs, e.g. *credere, invidere, persuadere, imperare, parere,* etc. A. & G. 227; B. 187, II; G. 346, and REM. 2; H. 385, I and II. The *caesura* is marked after *generi* instead of after *et,* because the natural pause follows *generi.* —— **et,** cop. conj. —— **propius,** comparative adv. of place, modifying *aspice ; propius* is the adverbial neuter accusative singular of the adj. *propior,* formed from the adverb and preposition *prope,* = *near ;* there is no positive; superl. of the adj. is *proximus,* of the adv. *proxime. Propius aspice,* = *regard more nearly,* i.e. more graciously, in opposition to the use of *avertor,* e.g. *aversa,* l. 482. —— **rēs,** acc. plur. of *rēs, reī,* f., 5th; direct obj. of *aspice ; res* here, as in many instances, = *fortunes, condition.* —— **aspice,** 2d pers. sing. imperative mood, act. of *aspiciō, -ere, aspēxī, aspectum,* 3 (*ad +* speciō) ; the subj. is *tu* understood ; *aspice* is joined by *et* to *parce.* —— **nostrās,** acc. plur. f. of the poss. adj. of the 1st personal pron., viz. *noster, nostra, nostrum ;* agrees with *res.*

LINE 527. **Nōn,** negative particle, limiting *vēnimus.* —— **nōs,** nom. plur. of the 1st personal pron.; subj. of *vēnimus.* The personal pronouns are not written, when they are subjects, except for emphasis or contrast; *nōs* here attracts notice to the forlorn appearance of the storm-tossed Trojans. —— **aut,** disjunctive conj., repeated correlatively below = *either . . . or ;* see note on *aut,* l. 183. —— **ferrō,** abl. sing. of *ferrum, -ī,* n., 2d; abl. of the instrument, with *populare.' Ferrum,* = lit. *iron,* hence by metonymy, = *sword,* because a sword was made of steel. A. & G. 386; B. no reference; G. no reference; H. 637, III. —— **Libycōs,** acc. plur. m. of *Libycus, -a, -um ;* qualifies *penates* —— **populāre,** pres. inf. act. of *populō, -āre, -āvī, -ātum,* 1 (with a collateral deponent form *populor, -ārī, -ātus sum,* 1) ; a free *prolative* inf., expressing purpose, after *venimus.* This use of the inf. is common in Greek, but is entirely poetic in Latin ;

528 popu, láre   pe, nátes   **Vénimus,** , aút rap, tás ,,
*to devastate penates (= homes) we have come, or	seized*
529 ad , lítora , vértere , prǽdas : **Nón** ea , vís
*to the shores to turn	booty : (is) not that violence*
ani, mó, ,, nec , tánta su, pérbia , víctis.
to our mind,   nor   so great arrogance to conquered (men).
530 **Ést**   locus, , Hésperi, ám ,, Grai, í cog, nómine ,
*There is a place, Hesperia	the Greeks	by name*

homes nor to turn
shorewards our spoils
of seizure; such vio-
lence abides not in
our hearts, nor such
pride in vanquished
men. There is a
place — the Greeks
call it Hesperia —

---

it is frequent in the comic poets (who copied Greek models) after verbs of motion, e.g. *venio, mitto, curro,* etc.; in the Augustan poets it is much less common, but there are several instances in Horace, and a considerable number in Vergil. One of the best known examples is Horace, Odes, I, ii, 8, *Proteus pecus egit altos* VISERE *montes.* In prose, the regular construction for purpose clauses after a verb of motion is the subjunctive with *ut.* A. & G. 273, *e*; B. 326, NOTE; G. 421, NOTE 1, *a*; H. 533, II. —— **penātēs,** acc. plur. of *penātēs, -ium,* m., 3d (no singular); direct obj. of *populare ; penates* (lit. *household-gods*) here stands for *domos.*

LINE 528. **Vēnimus,** 1st pers. plur. perf. ind. act. of *veniō, -īre, vēnī, ventum,* 4; agrees with the subj. *nos.* The scansion indicates that *vēnimus* must be the perfect tense, and not the present, which is *vĕnimus.* —— **aut,** disjunctive conjunction, connecting *populare* and *vertere.* —— **raptās,** acc. plur. f. of *raptus, -a, -um,* perf. part. pass. of *rapiō, -ere, rapuī, raptum,* 3 (akin to the Greek ἁρπ-άζω); predicate part., agreeing with *praedas ;* the participle takes the place of another coördinate and conjunction, e.g. *rapere et vertere.* A. & G. 292, REM.; B. 337, 2; G. 437; H. 549, 5. —— **ad,** prep. with the acc.; gov. *litora.* —— **lītora,** acc. plur. of *lītus, lītoris,* n., 3d; governed by *ad.* —— **vertere,** pres. inf. act. of *vertō, -ere, vertī, versum,* 3; poetic inf., expressing purpose, joined by *aut* to *populare,* and in the same grammatical construction. —— **praedās,** acc. plur. of *praeda, -ae,* f., 1st; direct obj. of *vertere.*

LINE 529. **Nōn,** negative adv., limiting *est* understood. —— **ea,** nom. sing. f. of the demonstr. pron. and adj. *is, ea, id,* gen. *ēius,* dat. *eī ;* agrees with *vis ; ea* is deictic, referring to the motive *populare penates,* which *Ilioneus* repudiates. —— **vīs,** gen. *vīs* (rare), acc. *vim,* dat. *vī* (rare), abl. *vī,* f., 3d; nom. sing., subj. of *est* understood. *Vis, = force, violence ; vires, -ium,* which is used as the plural, *= strength.* —— **animō,** dat. sing. of *animus, -ī,* m., 2d; dat. of the possessor, after *est* understood. —— **nec** (short form of *neque*), cop. conj., instead of *et* and the negative, *= and . . . not.* —— **tanta,** nom. sing. f. of *tantus, -a, -um,* demonstr. adj. (correlative *quantus*)*;* agrees with *superbia.* —— **superbia,** gen. *superbiae,* f., 1st (*superbus, =* (1) *overbearing,* in bad sense, as here; (2) *spirited*)*;* nom. sing., subj. of *est* understood. A. & G. 206, *c,* 2; B. 166, 3; G. 209; H. 368, 3. —— **victīs,** dat. plur. m. of *victus, -a, -um,* perf. part. pass. of *vincō, -ere, vīcī, victum,* 3; used substantively, dat. of the possessor, like *animo* above, after *est* understood. A. & G. 231; B. 190; G. 349; H. 387. *Ilioneus* explains that the Trojans have not come to ravage for two reasons: (1) they are a *genus pium,* and so have inclinations towards *vis ;* (2) they are *victi,* and so not in a position to act oppressively, even if they desired.

LINE 530. **Est,** 3d pers. sing. pres. ind. of *sum, esse, fuī ;* agrees with the subj. *locus ;* with this abrupt description compare l. 159, *est in secessu longo locus.* —— **locus,** gen. *locī,* m., 2d (plur. *locī,* m., *= topics,* or *loca,* n., *= places*)*;* nom. sing., subj. of *est ; locus* here *= regio.* —— **Hesperiam,** acc. sing. of *Hesperia, -ae,* f., 1st (a Greek word,

an ancient land, mightily blessed in arms and rich glebe land; Oenotrian men tilled it ; now the	dícunt, Térra an, tíqua, „ po, téns ar, mís at, que 531 *call* (*it*), *a land* *ancient,* *powerful* *in arms* *and* úbere , glébae ; Oéno, trí colu, ére vi, rí ; „ nunc , 532 *in richness of sod ;* *Oenotrian cultivated* (*it*) *men ;* *now*

'Εσπερία, = *western,* i.e. γῆ 'Εσπερία, = *western land ;* from "Εσπερος, = *the evening star*)*;* predicate acc. with *dicunt ;* verbs of *making, calling, appointing,* etc., take a predicate accusative. A. & G. 239, 1, *a*; B. 177; G. 340; H. 373. *Hesperiam* . . . *dicunt* is a parenthesis, explaining *locus.* *Hesperia* is the Greek name for Italy, and may only strictly be used by a writer of a nation, e.g. especially Greece, that lies east of Italy. The name *Hesperia* was also applied by the Romans to Spain, as lying *west* of Italy, e.g. Horace, Odes, I, xxxvi, 4, *Hesperia* . . . *ab ultima.* —— Graii (sometimes written *Graï*), nom. plur. of *Graiī, -ōrum,* m., 2d (properly m. of the adj. *Graius, -a, -um ; Graiï* is a dissyllable); subj. of *dicunt.* —— cognōmine, abl. sing. of *cognōmen, cognōminis,* n., 3d (*cum* + *nōmen*) *;* abl. of manner, with *dicunt.* For distinctions, etc., between *nomen, cognomen, praenomen,* etc., refer to the note on *nomen,* l. 248. —— dīcunt, 3d pers. plur. pres. ind. act. of *dīcō, -ere, dīxī, dictum,* 3; agrees with the subj. *Graii,* and governs a direct obj. *eum* understood, referring to *locus.*

LINE 531. Terra, gen. *terrae,* f., 1st; nom. sing., in apposition to *locus.* —— antīqua, nom. sing. f. of *antīquus, -a, -um* (akin to *ante*)*;* agrees with *terra ; terra antiqua* does not mean *ancient land* (which is really meaningless), but one inhabited from very early times as opposed to one newly colonized. —— potēns, nom. sing. f. of *potēns, potēntis* (originally pres. part. of *possum, posse, potuī,* but only used as an adj.); agrees with *terra.* —— armis, abl. plur. of *arma, -ōrum,* n., 2d; abl. of specification, describing *potens.* A. & G. 253; B. 226; G. 397; H. 424. —— atque, cop. conj., joining the important feature *potens ubere glebae* to *potens armis.* —— übere, abl. sing. of *über, überis,* n., 3d (= lit. *teat,* hence *fertility, fecundity ;* akin to the Greek οὖθαρ, and the English *udder*)*;* abl. of specification, with *potens ; ubere glebae* is imitated from the Homeric οὖθαρ ἀρούρης. Strictly *potens* is only applicable to *armis,* but by a kind of *zeugma* it = *powerful,* i.e. *rich,* with *ubere.* —— glēbae, gen. sing. of *glēba,* f., 1st; poss. gen., limiting *ubere.*

LINE 532. Oenōtrī, nom. plur. m. of *Oenōtrus, -a, -um* (belonging to *Oenotria, -ae,* f., 1st; Greek Οἰνωτρία, = lit. *the wine land,* from οἶνος, = *wine*)*;* agrees with *viri.* Oenotria was strictly a district of southern Italy, to which the name of Lucania was afterwards given, but Vergil uses it poetically as a name for the whole of Italy. Oenotria received its name from Oenotrus, who brought an Arcadian colony to Italy. —— coluēre, 3d pers. plur. perf. ind. act. of *colō, -ere, -uī, cultum,* 3; agrees with the subj. *viri,* and governs *eam* understood as direct object (referring to *terra*). We might have expected the imperfect tense *colebant,* = *used to till ;* but the perfect indicates that the action is past, without particularizing exactly the actual period of time; this kind of perfect is called the *historic* perfect. A. & G. 279, *a*; B. 262, B; G. 239; H. 198, 1, and esp. footnote 3. —— virī, nom. plur. of *vir, virī,* m., 2d; subj. of *coluere.* —— nunc, adv. of time. —— fāma, gen. *fāmae,* f., 1st (Greek φήμη, = lit. *that which is spoken*)*;* nom. sing., subjective complement of *est* understood in the predicate *fama* (*est*)*; fama* (*est*) introduces the acc. and inf. construction *minores dixisse,* etc., being equivalent to a *verbum declarande,* e.g. *dicunt,* = *they say.* —— minōrēs, acc. plur. m. of *minor, minus,* gen. *minōris,* comparative of the adj. *parvus, -a, -um ;* used substantively, subj.-acc. of the inf. *dixisse* in the *oratio obliqua* introduced by *fama* (*est*). In reported speech the subject is put in the accusative, and the principal verb in the infinitive; all subordinate verbs are in the subjunctive mood. *Minores* here = *posteros, descendants,* in the same

533 fáma　　　　　mi,nóres　　Ítali,ám　　di,xísse | rumor is that their
　　the rumor (is)　(that) their descendants　Italy　have called | descendants　h a v e
534 du,cís　　,,　de , nómine , géntem.　Híc cur,sús | called the nation after
　　of their leader from　the name　the nation.　This our course | their chief's name,
535 fuit ;　,　Cúm　subi,to　ássur,géns　fluc,tú　,, | Italy.　Hither our
　　was ;　　when　suddenly　rising　with a flood | course led : when on
| a　sudden,　stormy

---

way that *maiores* (comparative of *magnus*) = *ancestors.* The superlative is *minimus,*
which (like *maximus natu,* superl. of *senex*) is used with *natu,* expressed or understood,
as the superlative of *iuvenis.*

LINE 533. **Ītaliam,** acc. sing. of *Ītalia, -ae,* f., 1st; predicate acc., in the same case
as *gentem,* the obj. of *dixisse;* see the note on *Hesperiam,* l. 530. —— **dīxisse,** perf. inf.
act. of *dīcō, -ere, dīxī, dīctum,* 3; agrees with the subj.-acc. *minores* in the indirect
statement introduced by *fama (est).* A. & G. 272; B. 330, 331; G. 527; H. 534, 535.
—— **ducis,** gen. sing. of *dūx,* m. and f., 3d (for *duc-s,* from *dūcō*); poss. gen., limiting
nomine. Vergil derives the name in the popular fashion from the name of the legendary
hero *Ītalus,* who brought a colony over from Arcadia and settled in Magna Graecia.
Thucydides also mentions Italus as king of the Siculi, one of the divisions of the inhabi-
tants of Italy.　In such derivations the hero is a later invention, to explain the origin of
the name; cf. the name of the Greeks *Hellēnes,* which is similarly referred to a mythical
chief *Hellēn,* and the *Dorians* descended from *Dorus.* Some think that *Italia* really =
Vitalia (= lit. *the cattle land*), from *vitulus* (Oscan *vitlu*). But in all probability
Italia is called after the *Itali,* who inhabited the country. —— **dē,** prep. with the abl.;
gov. *nomine.* For the uses of *de,* consult A. & G. 153; B. 142; G. 417, 5; H. 434, I.
—— **nōmine,** abl. sing. of *nōmen, nōminis,* n., 3d; governed by *de.* —— **gentem,** acc.
sing. of *gens, gentis,* f., 3d; direct obj. of *dixisse.*

LINE 534. **Hīc,** nom. sing. m. of the demonstr. adj. *hīc, haec, hōc;* agrees with *cur-*
sus, and completes the predication with *fuit.* Some of the less authoritative Mss. read
huc, = *hither,* but this is probably an error or attempted emendation of an unscholarly
copyist; *hic cursus fuit,* = *this* (i.e. *hither*) *was our course,* and we may compare Aen. IV,
46, *hunc cursum.* The demonstrative adjective *hic* is often used in Latin where in
English we should use an adverb, and is very naturally used by Vergil, who is fond of
variation. —— **cursus,** gen. *cursūs,* m., 4th (from *currō*); nom. sing., subj. of *fuit.* ——
fuit, 3d pers. sing. perf. ind. of the copula *sum, esse, fuī;* agrees with the subj. *cursus.*
It is seen that this line is incomplete, only containing two feet; such unfinished lines are
called *hemistichs,* and there are nearly sixty examples in the Aeneid. Some suppose
that Vergil would have completed them if he had lived to revise the Aeneid, but this is
almost certainly a wrong view of the matter.　In only one instance is the sense left
uncertain, viz. Aen. III, l. 340, *Quem tibi iam Troia* —, and this occurs in a speech
and may well be intentional.　In nearly every other case the half-line adds force and
grandeur to the subject treated (e.g. Aen. II, 623), and the inevitable conclusion is that
hemistichs, like hypermetrical lines, are intended by the poet himself to add vigorous
variety to epic verse.　In the present example, *hic cursus fuit,* there is a long pause,
occasioned by (1) the *diaeresis* after *fuit* (see note on *fuit,* l. 17); (2) the emotion
which overcomes Ilioneus as he reaches the cause of his suppliant appearance before
Dido; (3) the pause in the sense, bringing into contrast the previous unharassed voyage
of the Trojans with the storms and disasters to which l. 535 refers.

LINE 535. **Cum,** temporal conj., followed by the ind. *tulit;* see the note and refer-
ences to *cum,* l. 36. —— **subitō,** adverbial abl. n. sing. of *subitus, -a, -um;* see *subito,*
l. 509. —— **assurgēns** (*adsurgēns*), gen. *assurgēntis;* nom. sing. m. of the pres. part.

Orion rising with the	nim , bósus O , ríon ín vada , cǽca tu , lít, „ 536
ocean's swell bore us	stormy Orion into shoals hidden carried (us),
on hidden shoals, and	
with the boisterous	peni , túsque pro , cácibus , Aústris Pérque 537
southern gales, while	and afar boisterous by south winds both through
the sea whelmed us,	
sundered us afar o'er	un , dás, super , ánte sa , ló, „ per , que invia , sáxa
waves and trackless	the waves, overcoming (us) the sea, and amid pathless rocks

---

act. of *assurgō, -ere, assurrēxī, assurrectum,* 3 (*ad + surgō*) ; agrees with and enlarges the subj. *Orion ; assurgens* has reference not merely to the rising of the constellation Orion, but also the rising of the waves (*fluctu*). —— **fluctū,** abl. sing. of *fluctus, -ūs,* m., 4th; abl. of manner, with *assurgens.* For this abl., see the note on *imperio,* l. 54. —— **nimbōsus,** nom. sing. m. of *nimbōsus, -a, -um,* adj. (from *nimbus, -ī,* m., 2d, = *a storm-cloud*) ; an attribute of *Orion.* Orion sets in winter and rises in summer; it was its setting and not its rising that heralded rough weather, but as Orion acquired the character of *nimbosus* among sailors, Vergil connects the storm that struck the Trojan fleet with the constellation. —— **Oriōn,** gen. *Oriōnis* or *Oriōnis,* m., 3d (Greek Ωρίων); nom. sing., subj. of *tulit.* Orion was a celebrated giant and hunter, and after death was changed into the constellation that bears his name.

LINE 536. **In,** prep. with the acc. or abl.; gov. the acc. *vada.* —— **vada,** acc. plur. of *vadum, -ī,* n., 2d; governed by the preposition *in.* —— **caeca,** acc. plur. n. of the adj. *caecus, -a, -um ;* agrees with *vada ; caeca,* = (1) *blind,* hence (2) *dark, hidden.* —— **tulit,** 3d pers. sing. perf. ind. act. of *ferō, ferre, tulī, lātum,* irreg.; agrees with the subj. *Orion.* —— **penitus,** adv. of place; modifies *dispulit ; penitus* here = *far,* as in l. 512. —— **que,** enclitic cop. conj., connecting *tulit* and *dispulit* below. —— **procācibus,** abl. plur. m. of *procāx,* gen. *procācis,* adj., 3d, of one termination (from the rare verb *procō,* 1, = *I ask ;* akin to *prēcēs,* hence lit. = *importunate,* and so *boisterous*) ; qualifies *Austris.* —— **Austrīs,** abl. plur. of *Auster, Austrī,* m., 2d (akin to Greek αὔω, = *I dry,* hence *the drier,* i.e. the south wind) ; abl. of the instrument, with *dispulit ;* the plural is a poetic variant for the singular, and the south wind is representative of the winds in general.

LINE 537. **Per,** prep. with the acc.; gov. *undas. Per* here may mean either *over* or *amid,* or actually *through ;* the latter is the literal meaning, and perhaps illustrates better the force of the tempest. The repetition of *perque* below is graphic, emphasizing the perils of the voyage. A. & G. 344, *f* ; B. 350, 11, *b* ; G. 682, and 636, NOTE 4 ; H. 636, III, 3. —— **que,** enclitic cop. conj.; *que . . . que,* = *both . . . and.* —— **undās,** acc. plur. of *unda, -ae,* f., 1st; governed by *per.* —— **superante,** abl. sing. n. of *superāns,* pres. part. act. of *superō, -āre, -āvī, -ātum,* 1 ; agrees with *salō* in the abl. abs. construction. This construction (i.e. a noun or pronoun in the ablative with a participle or adjective in agreement) may be used only when the noun or pronoun is not the same as the subject or object of the main sentence; it takes the place of a clause introduced by a temporal, causal, concessive, conditional, or other conjunction; thus *superante salo* = *dum salum superat.* A. & G. 255; B. 227; G. 409, 410; H. 431. —— **salō,** abl. sing. of *salum, -ī,* n., 2d (only in sing., and chiefly in the acc. and abl. cases; = Greek σάλος); in the abl. abs. construction with *superante.* —— **per,** prep. with the acc.; gov. *saxa ;* see *per* above. —— **que,** enclitic cop. conj., joining *per saxa* to *per undas.* —— **invia,** acc. plur. n. of *invius, -a, -um* (*in,* = *not, + via,* = *a way*) ; agrees with *saxa.* —— **sāxa,** acc. plur. of *sāxum, -ī,* n., 2d; governed by *per.*

538 **Díspulit.** , Húc pau,cí ,, ves,trís ad,návimus ,
    scattered.   *Hither   few   your   we have swum*

539 **óris.**   **Quód genus, hóc homi,núm? ,, quae,ve**
    to shores. *What* (*is*) *race   this   of men?   or what*

540 **húnc tam, bárbara, mórem Pérmit,tít patri, a?**
    this   so   barbarous   custom   permits   country?

rocks; to your shores hither we came by swimming. What race of men is this? what country so barbarous, that suffers such a custom? We

---

LINE 538. **Dispulit,** 3d pers. sing. perf. ind. act. of *dispellō, -ere, dispulī, dispulsum,* 3 (*dis,* = *apart,* + *pellō,* = *I drive*) ; agrees with the subj. *Orion,* and is joined by *que* (appended to *penitus*) to *tulit,* l. 536 above. —— **Hūc,** adv. of place; modifying *adnavimus.* —— **paucī,** nom. plur. m. of *paucus, -a, -um* (in sing. = *small;* mostly in plur. = *few*) ; agrees with *nos,* the implied subj. of *adnavimus.* —— **vestrīs,** dat. plur. f. of *vester, vestra, vestrum,* poss. adj. of *vōs,* the plural 2d personal pron.; agrees with *oris; vestris oris* really explains *huc.* —— **adnāvimus,** 1st pers. plur. perf. ind. act. of *adnō, -āre, -āvī, -ātum,* 1 (*ad,* = *to,* + *nō,* = *I swim,* Greek νέω); the contained subj. is *nōs.* —— **ōrīs,** dat. plur. of *ōra, -ae,* f., 1st; dat. of the indirect obj. after the compound of *ad, adnavimus;* verbs compounded with *ad, post, prae, sub, super, con, in, ante, inter, ob, pro, post,* and some with *circum,* may take this dative. A. & G. 228; B. 187, III; G. 347; H. 386.

LINE 539. **Quod,** nom. sing. n. of the interrog. adj. *quī, quae, quod;* agrees with *genus. Quod* is emphatic, and does more than merely ask for information, implying that the race, whatever it is, is barbarous and inhumane. —— **genus,** gen. *generis,* n., 3d; nom. sing., subj. of *est* understood. —— **hōc,** nom. sing. n. of the demonstr. adj. *hīc, haec, hōc;* agrees with *genus; hoc* is deictic, and suggests a gesture of Ilioneus in the direction of the Phoenicians. —— **hominum,** gen. plur. of *homō, hominis,* m., 3d; epexegetical gen. of specification, such as is common after words like *genus,* or *virtus, vitium,* etc., e.g. *virtus iustitiae.* A. & G. 214, *f*; B. 202; G. 361, 2; H. 395. *Homo,* = *a man,* as distinguished from a god on the one hand, and from other animals on the other; *vir,* = *a man,* as distinguished from a woman. —— **quae,** nom. sing. f. of the interrog. adj. *quī, quae, quod;* agrees with *patria.* —— **ve,** enclitic disjunctive conj., joining the question which *quae* introduces with the preceding one. *Vel* and *ve* (*vel* being probably the imperative of *volo,* and *ve* a weaker form of it) simply offer a choice between two alternatives, but here there is no opposition between the questions. —— **hunc,** acc. sing. m. of *hīc, haec, hōc;* agrees with *morem; hunc,* like *hoc* above, is deictic and expresses indignation. —— **tam** (probably akin to *tālis*), adv., strengthening *barbara. Tam* is not used independently like *sic,* but modifies adjectives or other adverbs, e.g. *tam diu,* = *so long;* in this way it may introduce a correlative sentence of comparison, with *quam,* e.g. *tam . . . quam,* = *so . . . as.* —— **barbara,** nom. sing. f. of *barbarus, -a, -um* (Greek βάρβαρος); agrees predicatively with *patria.* The sentence *quaeve . . . patria* is compressed, and = lit. *what country so barbarous allows,* i.e. *what is this country so barbarous as to allow. Barbarus,* properly a Greek word, was applied by the Greeks to all peoples who were other than strictly Greek in speech and customs; thus the Macedonians were called βάρβαροι, though they subjugated Greece under their kings Philip and Alexander. —— **mōrem,** acc. sing. of *mōs, mōris,* m., 3d; direct obj. of *permittit. Mōs* usually = *custom* in the singular, and *habits, character* in the plural.

LINE 540. **Permittit,** 3d pers. sing. pres. ind. act. of *permittō, -ere, permīsī, permissum,* 3 (*per* + *mittō*) ; agrees with the subj. *patria.* —— **patria,** gen. *patriae,* f., 1st (properly f. of *patrius, -a, -um,* = *native,* with *terra* supplied); nom. sing., subj. of *per-*

228　　VERGIL'S AENEID　　[LINES 541-543.

are driven from the	hóspiti,ó	„	prohi,bémur	a,rénae !
shelter of the strand.	*from the hospitality*		*we are shut out*	*of the sand !*
They rouse up war,	Bélla	ci,ént,	„	pri,máque	ve,tánt 541
and forbid us to set	*Wars*	*they stir up,*		*and first*	*forbid (us)*
foot on the very					
shore-line. If ye	con,sístere , térra.	Sí	genus ,	húma,num „ 542
reck not of the race	*to stand　on the land. If*		*the race*	*human*
of men and mortal	ét mor,tália , témnitis ,	árma,	Át	spe,ráte 543
arms, yet look for	*and　mortal　you despise*	*arms,*	*still*	*expect*

mittit. —— **hospitiō,** abl. sing. of *hospitium, -ī,* n., 2d (from *hospēs, hospitis,* m., 3d, = *a host*) ; abl. of separation, after *prohibemur.* As *prohibemur* implies the notion of *depriving,* it may govern the ablative without a preposition, though the preposition would be more usual. A. & G. 243, *a* ; B. 214, esp. 2 ; G. 390, 2, and NOTE 2 ; H. 413. —— **prohibēmur,** 1st pers. plur. pres ind. pass. of *prohibeō, -ēre, -uī, -itum,* 2 (*pro + habeō*) ; the contained subj. is *nos.* —— **arēnae,** gen. sing. of *arēna,* f., 1st (from *arēre,* = *to be dry*) ; poss. gen., limiting *hospitio.*

LINE 541. **Bella,** acc. plur. of *bellum, -ī,* n., 2d ; direct obj. of *cient.* —— **cient,** 3d pers. plur. pres. ind. act. of *cieō, -ēre, cīvī, citum,* 2 (akin to κίω, = *I go* ; hence *I make to go, rouse*) ; supply *Poenī* as the subject. —— **prīmā,** abl. sing. f. of *prīmus, -a, -um* ; agrees partitively with *terrā* ; by *prima terra* is meant the border of the country, i.e. the shore. —— **que,** enclitic cop. conj. —— **vetant,** 3d pers. plur. pres. ind. act. of *vetō, -āre, vetuī, vetitum,* 1 ; joined by *que* to *cient,* and in agreement with the same subject. The tribunes of the *plebs* were allowed the right of saying *veto,* when they disapproved of a proposed enactment, and the *veto* of even one of them was sufficient to render a measure invalid. —— **consistere,** pres. inf. act. of *consistō, -ere, constitī, constitum,* 3 (*con = cum,* + *sistō,* trans. and intrans.) ; objective complementary inf. after *vetant.* —— **terrā,** abl. sing. of *terra, -ae,* f., 1st ; abl. of 'place where.'

LINE 542. **Sī,** conditional particle, here followed by the ind. *temnitis* because the condition is represented not as ideal or purely imaginary, but as within the range of actual fact. If the verb in the *apodosis* or conclusion is in the indicative or imperative mood, or is an independent subjunctive, then the verb in the *protasis* or *if*-clause will be in the indicative. A. & G. 306, *a* ; B. 302, 4 ; G. 595 ; H. 508, 4. —— **genus,** acc. sing. of *genus, generis,* n., 3d ; direct obj. of *temnitis.* —— **hūmānum,** acc. sing. n. of *hūmānus, -a, -um* (for *homin-ānus,* from *homŏ, hominis,* 3d) ; agrees with *genus.* In spite of *ecthlipsis,* the *caesura* best follows *humanum.* —— **et,** cop. conj. —— **mortālia,** acc. plur. n. of *mortālis, -e,* adj., 3d (*mors = death*) ; agrees with *arma ; mortalia arma = arma mortalium.* —— **temnitis,** 2d pers. plur. pres. ind. act. of *temnō, -ere, tempsī,* no supine, 3 ; the contained subj. is *vōs.* —— **arma,** gen. *armōrum,* n., 2d plur. ; acc. plur., direct obj. of *temnitis ;* this clause hints that the Trojans will, if necessary, fight to save themselves, trusting that the gods, if they allowed them to be overcome, would yet punish the Carthaginians for violating the laws of hospitality.

LINE 543. **At,** adversative conj., here introducing an important argument ; refer to the note on *sed,* l. 515. —— **spērāte,** 2d pers. plur. imperative mood act. of *spērō, -āre, -āvī, -ātum,* 1 ; the contained subj. is *vōs.* Some commentators direct the student to supply *futūrōs esse,* or *fore,* after *deōs,* making an accusative and infinitive construction ; this is not obligatory, for *spero* sometimes has the rarer meaning of *I expect,* e.g. Eclogues, VIII, 26, *quid non speremus amantes ?* Others, again, mark their disapprobation of the above view by placing a comma after *deos,* but this also is unnecessary.

de, ós	„	memo, rés	fan, dí	átque	ne, fándi.	gods, mindful of the
gods		*mindful*	*of right*	*and*	*of wrong.*	lawful and unlawful.

544 Réx erat , Aéne, ás no, bís, „ quo , iústior , | Aeneas was our king, than whom no other

King was Aeneas to us, than whom more righteous | was more righteous

---

—— **deōs,** acc. plur. of *deus, -ī,* m., 2d; direct obj. of *sperate.*——**memorēs,** acc. plur. m. of *memor,* gen. *memoris,* adj., 3d, of one termination; agrees with *deōs.*——**fandī,** gen. sing. n. of *fandus, -a, -um,* the gerundive of the defective verb *fārī = to speak;* used substantively = *what must be spoken,* and is obj. gen. governed by the adj. *memores.* Adjectives expressing *power, fulness, memory,* etc., or their opposites, are followed by an objective genitive. A. & G. 218, *a;* B. 204, 1; G. 374; H. 399, I, 2. *Fandi* is used as the genitive of the indeclinable noun *fas = right divine,* and *nefandi* below is similarly used as the genitive of *nefas* (*ne + fas*).——**atque,** cop. conj., adding emphasis to the second of the words it connects, viz. *nefandi;* in this way the Carthaginians are threatened by Ilioneus with divine vengeance. ——**nefandī,** gen. sing. n. of the adj. *nefandus, -a, -um* (*ne, = not, + fandus,* as above); used substantively, and joined by *atque* to *fandi,* to which it is in grammatical construction similar. *Fandus* and. *nefandus* are specially used with regard to religion, for ill-omened words rendered a religious rite of no avail; this use was extended so that the words, which almost = *pious* (*what may be spoken*) and *impious,* came to mean *innocent* and *dreadful.*

LINE 544. **Rēx,** gen. *rēgis,* m., 3d; nom. sing., complement of *erat* in the predicate *rex erat.*——**erat,** 3d pers. sing. imperf. ind. of the copula *sum, esse, fuī,* agrees with the subj. *Aeneas.* ——**Aenēās,** nom. sing., subj. of *erat.* ——**nōbīs,** dat. plur. of *nōs ;* dat. of the possessor, after *erat.*——**quō,** abl. sing. m. of the rel. pron. *quī, quae, quod ;* agrees with the antecedent *Aeneas* in gender and number, and is the abl. of comparison after the comparative adj. *iustior.* Comparison may be expressed by the comparative degree and *quam,* the second noun being put in the same case as the first; or *quam* may be omitted, and the second noun put in the ablative instead. Thus *Caesar was braver than Crassus* may be rendered either *Caesar fortior quam Crassus erat* or *Caesar fortior Crasso erat.* A. & G. 247, and footnote; B. 217; G. 296; H. 417. ——**iustior,** nom. sing. m. of *iustior, iustius,* gen. *iustioris,* the comparative degree of the adj. *iustus, -a, -um ;* agrees with the subj. *alter,* and is complement of *fuit* in the predicate *iustior fuit.* Many commentators, following Conington, place a comma after *alter,* owing to a supposed harshness in taking *iustior pietate* (*more righteous in piety*) together; they take *pietate, bello,* and *armis* as all ablatives of specification with *maior,* and render: *than whom (neither) was there another* (lit. *a second*) *juster, nor greater in piety nor in war.* Against this there is an almost insuperable objection, viz. that as *nec . . . nec* are made in this way to connect *pietate* and *bello* (*et armis*), there is no negative with *iustior,* and so *nec* has to be supplied. There are several instances of such an omission of *nec* or *neque,* but, as Mr. Page says, "the first *nec* of two can be occasionally omitted where the sense is *perfectly clear,*" but in this passage such omission is quite inadmissible, because "the omission of *nec* is most perplexing, and rendered more perplexing by the double *nec* in the second clause." Mr. Page further points out that Aeneas is not described by Vergil as (1) just, (2) pious, (3) a warrior, but as possessing two eminent qualities, viz. dutifulness and courage (*pietate insignis et armis,* in Aen. VI, 403). Finally the harshness of *iustior pietate* is hard to discover, and though Professor Conington is a Vergilian authority of note, it is unnecessary to follow him in this, which is purely a matter of literary taste. ——**alter,** nom. sing. m. of *alter, -a, -um,* gen. *alterīus,* dat. *alterī* (fem. rarely *alterae*), regular in other cases; subj. of *fuit.* *Alter* is akin to *alius* in origin, but is quite distinct in meaning; whereas *alius . . . alius,* or *alii . . . alii* distribute any

in loyal service nor	álter	**Néc**	pie,táte	fu,ít	„	nec	,	béllo	, 545
mightier in war and	*another*	*neither*	*in piety*	*was*		*nor*		*in war*	

arms.   Whom if the | máior   et , ármis :   **Quém** si , fáta vi,rúm 546
fates preserve, if he | *greater   and   in arms :   which   if   the fates   man*

feeds   on   the   air | ser, vánt, „ si , véscitur , aúra **Aétheri**,á, ,: neque 547
of heaven,   nor | *preserve,   if   he feeds   on the air   ethereal,   and not*

---

number greater than two (whether specified or not), *alter . . . alter* distributes two only
and = *the one . . . the other*, e.g. *alter consulum hoc probat, alter illud* = one of the con-
suls approves of this, the other of that; it is used reciprocally, e.g. *fratres alter alterum
amant = the (two) brothers love one another.* As a numeral, *alter = secundus*, and has
this meaning in such phrases as *alter ego.* A. & G. 203; B. 253, 1; G. 96, 5; 221, REM. 1,
and 319; H. 459; 461, 3, and page 66, footnote 4.

LINE 545.   **Nec,** neg. cop. conj.; *nec . . . nec = neither . . . nor.* —— **pietāte,**
abl. sing. of *pietās, -ātis,* f., 3d (*pius*); abl. of specification, with *iustior.   Pietas* = not
piety, but *dutiful respect,* such as one owes to one's country, parents, and gods; the
worst kinds of *impietas* to a Roman were parricide, desecration of temples, and warfare
against Rome. —— **fuit,** 3d pers. sing. perf. ind. of *sum, esse, fuī;* agrees with the subj.
alter in the pred. *iustior fuit.* —— **nec,** neg. cop. conj.; connects *iustior* and *maior.*
The sentence may be transposed : *quo nec iustior pietate alter fuit, nec maior bello et
armis.* —— **bellō,** abl. sing. of *bellum, -ī,* n., 2d; abl. of specification, with *maior.* For
this ablative, see the references under *armis,* l. 531. —— **māior,** nom. sing. m. of *māior,
māius,* gen. *māiōris,* comparative of the adj. *magnus, -a, -um* (superl. *maximus*); agrees
with *alter,* and is a complement of *fuit* understood from *fuit* preceding, like *iustior,* with
which it is connected by *nec* just above. —— **et,** cop. conj., connecting *bello* and *armis,*
which are considered as one idea. —— **armīs,** abl. plur. of *arma, -ōrum,* n., 2d; abl. of
specification, with *maior.*

LINE 546.   **Quem,** acc. sing. m. of the rel. pron. *quī, quae, quod,* which may be pro-
noun or adjective; agrees adjectively with *virum.*   There is nothing to distinguish
quem here from the acc. of the indef. *quis* (after *si*) except the context, which makes it
clear that *quem* is the relative.   Observe that *quem* is little more than from connective here, = *et
eum.* A. & G. 180, *f*; B. 251, 6; G. 610; H. 453. —— **sī,** conditional particle, which, fol-
lowed by the pres. ind. *servant,* represents the condition as one of actual fact. —— **fāta,**
gen. *fātōrum,* n., 2d (sing. *fātum, -ī,* n., 2d = *destiny*); nom. plur., subj. of *servant; fāta*
is here personified and = *Parcae, the Fates,* the ultimate controllers of destiny, whose de-
crees even the gods themselves were powerless to alter. —— **virum,** acc. sing. of *vir, -ī,*
m., 2d; direct obj. of *servant.   Virum* is attracted into the rel. clause and so into the case
of the rel. *quem ; vir* is properly the subj. of *vescitur ;* see note on *tela,* l. 188. —— **servant,**
3d pers. plur. pres. ind. act. of *servō, -āre, -āvī, -ātum,* 1, agrees with the subj. *fāta,* in the
protasis introduced by *si.* —— **sī,** conditional particle; the repetition of *si* suggests the
rapidity of the speaker's thought, and is more emphatic than a conjunction; moreover, the
change of the subj. from *fata* to *Aeneas* is more graceful when *si* is repeated. —— **vescitur,**
3d pers. sing. pres. ind. of the deponent verb *vescor, -ī,* no perf., 3 (akin to *esca* = *food,* and
perhaps Greek βόσκω = *I feed*) ; understand *vir* (from *virum* above, i.e. Aeneas) as
subject; *vescitur* is similar in construction to *servant;* see note on *si.*   Some think *ves-
citur = utitur,* i.e. *enjoys,* but probably it = lit. *feeds upon,* which is a bold phrase imi-
tated from Lucretius. —— **aurā,** abl. sing. of *aura, -ae,* f., 1st (Greek αὖρα); abl.
governed by *vescitur.* A. & G. 249; B. 218, 1; G. 407; H. 421, I.

LINE 547.   **Aetheriā,** abl. sing. f. of *aetherius, -a, -um* (*aethēr* = *the upper air*);
agrees with *aurā.   Aetheria* is objected to by some because Aeneas, if alive on earth,

548 ad,húc cru,délibus , óccubat , úmbris,   Nón | yet lies low amid the
   as yet   *cruel*   *lies*   *in the shades*, *(there is) not* | ruthless shades, we
   | have no fear ; nor
metus; , óffici,ó „ nec , té cer,tásse pri,órem | may'st thou repent
   fear   *in service*   *nor*   *thee to have vied*   *first* | to have been first in
   | the rivalry of service.
549 Pœnite,át. „ Sunt , ét Sicu,lís regi,ónibus , | There are, too, in
   let it repent.   *There are moreover Sicilian*   *in the regions* | the regions of Sicily

could not breathe the *upper air* (*aether*), but only the lower atmosphere (*aër*) ; but
Vergil is not very precise in his use of *aether*, e.g. l. 587, where the cloud dissolves *in
aethera* (which, speaking literally, is impossible); *aetheria aura* corresponds to the
English *air of heaven.* —— **neque**, negative cop. conj., = *and* . . . *not.* —— **adhūc** (*ad*
+ *hūc*, = *to this, up to this, as yet*), adv., modifying *occubat.* *Adhuc* marks a limit, (1)
of degree, *so far ;* (2) of time, *as yet :* sometimes *adhuc* = *praeterea, besides.* —— **crū-
dēlibus**, abl. plur. f. of *crūdēlis, -e*, adj., 3d; agrees with *umbrīs.* Possibly *umbris* is
dative, in which case *crudelibus* is dative also in agreement. —— **occubat**, 3d pers. sing.
pres. ind. act. of *occubō, -āre*, no perf., no supine, 1 (*ob* + *cubō ;* akin to *occumbō*) ;
joined by *neque* to *vescitur*, in agreement with the same subj. (*Aeneas* understood) and
in the same grammatical construction. —— **umbrīs**, abl. plur. of *umbra, -ae*, f., 1st (the
plural = *Orcus, -ī*, m., 2d, *the Lower World*) ; abl. of 'place where,' = *in umbris* (i.e.
in Orco). Some, probably on the analogy of Aen. II, 62, *occumbere morti*, think *umbris*
is dat. governed by *occubat* as a compound of *ob ;* see note on *oris*, l. 377.

   LINE 548. **Nōn**, negative adv., limiting *est* understood; the *apodosis* is *non metus.*
—— **metus**, gen. *metūs*, m., 4th; nom. sing., subj. of *est* understood; the meaning is
this, *if Aeneas is alive we have no fear.* Several editors condemn *non metus*, as very
abrupt, and so change *nec* to *nē* (= *lest*), making *non metus*—*poeniteat* one sentence,
= *there is no fear that you will regret*, etc.; for the reading *ne* there is the support of
one MS. —— **officiō**, abl. sing. of *officium, -ī*, n., 2d (from *ops* + *faciō*, hence *the render-
ing of aid, a kindness*) ; abl. of specification, with *certasse.* The meanings of *officium*
are : (1) *a voluntary service, a courtesy*, as here; (2) *a ceremonial observance*, in
Tacitus; (3) *a compulsory service, a duty ;* (4) *official duty, business, office*, very common.
—— **nec** (*ne* + *que*), neg. cop. conj., here = *and* . . . *not*, connecting the sentence in
which it stands with what has gone before. —— **tē**, acc. sing. of *tū ;* the acc. of the
person affected, governed by *poeniteat.* —— **certasse** (contracted for *certavisse*), perf.
ind. act. of *certō, -āre, -āvī, -ātum*, 1 (root CER in *cernō*) ; inf. dependent on the imper-
sonal *poeniteat.* For the contraction, consult A. & G. 128, *a*, 1; B. 7, 2; G. 131, 1; H.
235. —— **priōrem**, acc. sing. f. of *prior, prius*, gen. *priōris ;* agrees with *te ;* see the
note on *prior*, l. 321.

   LINE 549. **Poeniteat**, 3d pers. sing. pres. subjunct. act. of the impersonal verb *poe-
nitet, poenitēre, poenituit*, no supine, 2 (akin to *poeniō* = *puniō, I punish*) ; hortatory
subjunct., in this instance with scarcely more force than the simple future indicative.
A. & G. 266; B. 274-276; G. 263; H. 484. The construction with impersonals, like
miseret, poenitet, pudet, piget, etc., is an infinitive, or sometimes a clause, less often a
neuter pronoun. They may also be followed by the accusative of the person affected,
and the genitive of the cause of the emotion. A. & G. 221, *b, c*; B. 138, and 11; G. 377,
and esp. REM. 3; H. 410, IV. We might have expected the impersonal to be in a past
tense, followed by the pres. inf. *certare*, but a past inf. is commonly used after a primary
tense of the impersonal. —— **sunt**, 3d pers. plur. pres. ind. of *sum, esse, fuī ;* agrees
with the subj. *urbes.* This sentence is rather abrupt, but the connecting link is *et* = *also*,
and the sequence of thought is clear, though its expression might have been improved by

cities and arms, and	úrbes, Árvaque, , Tróia,nóque ,, a , sánguine , 550
renowned Acestes, a	cities, and ploughed fields, and Trojan from blood
scion of Troy's line.	
Let leave be ours to	clárus A,céstes. Quássa,tám ven,tís ,, lice,át 551
beach our wind-shat-	famous Acestes. Shaken by the winds let it be allowed
tered fleet, to fashion	sub,dúcere , clássem, Ét sil,vís ap,táre 552
planks in the woods	to beach our fleet, and in the woods to fashion

Ilioneus; the meaning is: *if Aeneas is alive we have no fear;* (*if he is dead, and if we cannot reach Italy*), *then we have friendly, and, moreover, powerful cities in Sicily, to which we can appeal.* —— et (here = *etiam*), conj. —— Siculīs, dat. plur. f. of *Siculus,* -a, -um (from *Siculī,* -ōrum, m., 2d, = *the Siculi*) ; agrees with *regionibus.* —— regiōn- ibus, dat. plur. of *regiō,* -ōnis, f., 3d; dat. of the possessor, after *sunt;* possibly *Siculis regionibus* is a locative ablative. —— urbēs, nom. plur. of *urbs, urbis,* f., 3d; subj. of *sunt.* Vergil means the city of Acesta or Segesta, in which Acestes ruled.

LINE 550. **Arma,** gen. *armōrum,* n., 2d; nom. plur., joined by *que* to *urbes; arma* = *vīrī armati,* signifying that if the Trojans went to Sicily they would be safe among friends who could defend them, and perhaps conveying a threat that Acestes would avenge any harsh treatment. There is another reading *arvaque* = *and fields,* in allusion to the fertility of Sicily (which was the granary of Rome before Egypt) and its attrac- tions as a country in which to settle in preference to Africa; this reading is more suitable to the passage, but unfortunately its MSS. support is very inferior to that of *arma.* —— que, enclitic cop. conj., joining *urbes* and *arma.* —— Trōiānō, abl. sing. m. of *Trōiānŭs,* -a, -um ; agrees with *sanguine.* —— que, enclitic cop. conj., joining the subj. *Acestes* to the previous subjects *urbes armaque.* —— ā, prep. with the abl.; gov. *sanguine,* express- ing separation. A. & G. 152, *b,* and 153; B. 142, 1; G. 417, 1; H. 434. —— sanguine, abl. sing. of *sanguis, sanguinis,* m., 3d; governed by *a.* —— clārus, nom. sing. m. of the adj. *clārus,* -a, -um (from the root in Latin *clueō,* = *I hear,* and Greek κλύω, hence *heard*); agrees with *Acestes.* —— Acestēs, gen. *Acestae,* m., 1st decl. Greek noun; nom. sing., a subj. of *sunt.* The Trojans had previously been very hospitably received by Acestes; see l. 195.

LINE 551. **Quassātam,** acc. sing. of *quassātus,* -a, -um, perf. part. pass. of *quassō,* -āre, -āvī, -ātum, 1 intensive (for *quatsō,* from *quatiō,* = *I shake*); agrees with *classem.* —— ventīs, abl. plur. of *ventus,* -ī, m., 2d; abl. of the instrument, with *quassatam.* —— liceat, 3d pers. sing. pres. subjunct. act. of *liceō,* -ēre, -uī, -itum, 2, intrans., rarely found except impersonally in the 3d pers. sing., e.g. *licet, licuit,* or *licitum est; hortatory* sub- junct. (like *poeniteat* above, l. 549), here with the subject-inf. *subducere classem.* The constructions with *licet* are: (1) with the inf., as here, in which case the inf. is really the subject, e.g. *licet abire,* = *it is permitted to go away;* (2) with the subjunctive, after *ut* expressed or understood, e.g. *licet ut abeamus* or *licet abeamus,* = *it is allowed us to go away;* in these instances, the apparently dependent subjunctive clause is the subject. —— subdūcere, pres. inf. act. of *subdūcō,* -ere, *subdūxī, subductum,* 3 (*sub,* = *under,* i.e. from below, + *dūcō,* = *I draw,* hence *I draw up* from the water onto the land); subject- inf., with *liceat.* —— classem, acc. sing. of *classis,* -is, f., 3d; direct obj. of *subducere.* *Classis* (Greek κλᾶσις = κλῆσις, *a calling*) properly applies not only to the ships in a fleet, but to the men *summoned* to serve in them.

LINE 552. **Et,** cop. conj. —— silvīs, abl. plur. of *silva,* -ae, f., 1st; abl. of 'place where.' In prose 'place where' is denoted by the ablative with the preposition *in,* except (1) with the names of towns and small islands, and a few other nouns, which are put in the locative case, e.g. *Romae = at Rome, domi = at home;* (2) with certain indefi-

558 tra, bés   „   et   ,   stríngere   rémos,   Sí   datur ,
 beams   *and*   *to strip*   *oars,*   *if it is granted*

554 Ítali, ám,   „ soci, ís   et , rége   re, cépto,   Téndere,
 to Italy,   *comrades and king having been recovered,*   *to go,*

ut   ,   Ítali, ám   „ lae, tí   Lati, úmque   pe, támus,
 in order that   Italy   *glad*   *and Latium*   *we may seek,*

and strip (boughs for) oars, that, if it be granted us with king and comrades saved to hold our way to Italy, Italy and Latium we may gladly seek;

---

nite words, e.g. *loco, parte;* (3) with nouns qualified by adjectives, e.g. *media urbe :* in poetry the locative ablative is very freely used, not only in reference to ' place where,' e.g. *litore,* = *on the shore,* but also ' place over which ' or ' place by which,' e.g. *prospiciens pelago = looking forth over the sea.* A. & G. 258, 4, *f, g ;* B. 228; G. 385; H. 425.
——— **aptāre,** pres. inf. act. of *aptō, -āre, -āvī, -ātum,* I (*aptus = joined*); subject-inf., joined by *et* to *subducere.* ——— **trabēs,** acc. plur. of *trabs, trabis,* f., 3d; direct obj. of *aptare ;* the *trabes* (*planks*) are for making repairs in the ships. ——— **et,** cop. conj. ——— **stringere,** pres. inf. act. of *stringō, -ere, strinxī, strictum,* 3 (akin to the Greek στράγγω); subject-inf., joined by *et* to *aptare ; stringere remos =* lit. *to strip oars,* i.e. to strip branches of their leaves and shoots so as to fashion oars out of them. ——— **rēmōs,** acc. plur. of *rēmus, ī,* m., 2d (probably for *ret-mus,* akin to the Greek ἔρετμον *= an oar,* lit. the thing which one rows, from ἐρέσσειν *= to row*); direct obj. of *stringere.*
    LINE 553. **Sī,** conditional particle, followed by the ind. *datur,* which places the condition among the class of those that belong to actual fact, but in which nothing is implied as to fulfilment. Refer to the note and references under *si,* l. 18. The condition *si datur,* etc., logically follows the *ut*-clause, *in order that, if it is granted,* etc., *we may seek Italy.* ——— **datur,** 3d pers. sing. pres. ind. passive of *dō, dare, dedī, datum,* I ; the subj. is the inf.-clause *tendere Italiam.* The infinitive is really a verbal noun; as a verb it is modified by adverbs, admits of different tenses, and governs an object; as a noun, it may be the subject or object of a sentence. A. & G. 270; B. 326-328; G. 280; H. 532, and 538. ——— **Italiam,** acc. sing. of *Ítalia, -ae,* f., 1st; acc. of limit of motion, without a prep. *ad* or *in.* The names of towns and small islands are regularly put in the accusative without a preposition when ' motion to ' is to be denoted, but the extension of this rule to countries and other places is entirely poetical. A. & G. 258, *b,* NOTE 5; B. 182, 4; G. 337; H. 380, I and II, and esp. 3. ——— **sociīs,** abl. plur. of *socius, -ī,* m., 2d; abl. abs., with *receptis* understood from *rege recepto.* ——— **et,** cop. conj. ——— **rēge,** abl. sing. of *rēx, rēgis,* m., 3d; in the abl. abs. construction with *recepto ; sociis* (*receptis*) *et rege recepto =* a causal clause, *quod socii et rex recepti sunt.* ——— **receptō,** abl. sing. m. of *receptus, -a, -um,* perf. part. pass. of *recipiō, -ere, recēpī, receptum,* 3 (*re,* = *back,* + *capiō,* = *I take*); agrees with *rege* in the abl. abs. construction; from *recepto, receptis* must be understood with *sociis.* An adjective or participle frequently agrees with only *one* noun (generally the nearest), but qualifies several. A. & G. 187; B. 235, B, 2, *b*); G. 286, I; H. 439, 2.
    LINE 554. **Tendere,** pres. inf. act. of *tendō, -ere, tetendī, tensum* or *tentum,* 3 (akin to τεν, root of τείνω); the inf.-clause *tendere Italiam* is the subj. of *datur. Tendere* is used : (1) transitively, = (a) *to stretch out,* e.g. l. 487, *Tendentemque manus Priamum,* (b) *to direct,* e.g. l. 410, *gressumque ad moenia tendit,* (2) intransitively, = (a) *to strive ;* (b) *to go.* ——— **ut,** final conj., = *in order that,* followed by the subjunct. *petamus,* expressing purpose; the negative of *ut* final is *nē. Ut* sometimes introduces a consecutive clause, denoting result; the verb is then in the subjunct., and the negative is *ut non.* For other uses of *ut,* refer to the note on *ut,* l. 306. Here *ut petamus* logically follows *stringere remos ;* the sentence may be transposed as follows : *liceat . . . aptare trabes*

| but if our salvation is gone, if thou, most noble father of the Trojans, art held by the Libyan sea nor | Sín   ab, súmpta   sa, lús, „ et   té,   pater , 555
but if   has been taken away   our safety,   and   thee,   father

óptime , Teúcrum, Póntus ha, bét Liby. ǽ, „ nec , 556
excellent of the Trojans,   the sea   holds   of Libya,   nor |

---

et stringere remos, ut, si datur Italiam . . . tendere, Italiam . . . petamus; sin absumpta salus (et (si) te . . . pontus habet, nec spes iam restat Iuli) at freta . . . regemque petamus Acesten. —— Italiam, acc. sing. of *Italia, -ae,* f., 1st; direct obj. of *petamus.* —— laetī, nom. plur. m. of *laetus, -a, -um;* agrees with *nos,* the implied subj. of *petamus.* —— Latium, acc. sing. of *Latium, -ī,* n., 2d; direct obj. of *petamus,* joined by *que* to *Italiam.* Vergil, very precisely, first states the name of the *whole* country (Italy) and then the name of the particular *part* (Latium). —— que, enclitic cop. conj. —— petāmus, 1st pers. plur. pres. subjunct. act. of *petō, -ere, petīvī* or *petiī, petītum,* 3; the contained subj. is *nōs.* The mood is subjunctive, because *ut* introduces the *purpose* of *aptare trabes,* etc. A. & G. 317; B. 282; G. 545; H. 497.

LINE 555. **Sin** (shortened from *sī,* = *if,* + *ne,* = *not*), conditional conj., subject to the same constructional rules as *si ; sin* = *but if,* usually introducing a condition contrary to one previously introduced by *si. Sin* is often strengthened by *autem* or *vero* (*sin autem*). —— absumpta, nom. sing. f. of *absumptus, -a, -um,* perf. part. pass. of *absūmō, -ere, absumsī, absumptum,* 3 (*ab,* = *from,* + *sūmō,* = *I take*) ; agrees with *salus,* and with *est* understood forms the 3d pers. sing. perf. ind. passive. *Est* and not *sit* is to be supplied with *absumpta,* because the condition is exactly like *si datur,* i.e. a condition in the region of fact, without any implication respecting fulfilment. —— salūs, gen. *salutis,* f., 3d ; nom. sing., subj. of *absumpta* (*est*). *Salus* here = *hope of safety,* or perhaps simply *safety ;* in the latter case, the diction is very forcible and thoroughly Vergilian. —— et, cop. conj., here (as it usually) does joining two ideas of equal importance, for the safety of the Trojans depended on Aeneas. —— tē, acc. sing. of *tū ;* direct obj. of *habet.* —— pater, voc. sing. of *pater, patris,* m., 3d (akin to the Greek πατήρ, and Sanscrit *pitri,* from the root PÂ = *to protect* or *to nourish*) ; case of the person addressed ; Aeneas is addressed as *father,* because he was, in his position as chief, the *protector* of his subjects. The change from impersonal speech to direct address is very suitable in this passage, and illustrates the literary skill and versatility which throughout adorn the Aeneid. —— optime, voc. sing. m. of *optimus, -a, -um,* superl. of the adj. *bonus, -a, -um* (comparative *melior*) ; qualifies *pater.* —— Teucrūm (contracted for *Teucrōrum*), gen. plur. of *Teucri, -ōrum,* m., 2d ; poss. gen., limiting *pater.* For the contraction, consult A. & G. 40, *e* ; B. 25, 6; G. 33, REM. 4 ; H. 52, 3.

LINE 556. **Pontus,** gen. *pontī,* m., 2d ; nom. sing., subj. of *habet* in the conditional clause introduced by *sin.* —— habet, 3d pers. sing. pres. ind. act. of *habeō, -ēre, -uī -itum,* 2 ; agrees with the subj. *pontus; habet* = *retinet,* i.e. the dead body of Aeneas. The clause (*si*) *pontus ; habet te* is joined by *et* to the clause *sin absumpta salus.* —— Libyae, gen. sing. of *Libya,* f., 1st; adnominal gen. of specification, like *Danaum,* l. 96. —— nec (short for *neque, ne* + *que* = *and* . . . *not*) negative cop. conj., joining the clause immediately following with the one immediately preceding. —— spēs, gen. *speī,* f., 5th ; nom. sing., subj. of *restat,* in the conditional clause after *sin ;* Aeneas is the *safety* of the Trojans, and his son Iulus is their *hope.* —— iam, adv. of time, modifying *restat.* —— restat, 3d pers. sing. pres. ind. act. of *restō, -āre, restitī,* no supine, 1 (*re,* = *back,* + *stō,* = *I stand*) ; agrees with the subj. *spēs.* —— Iūlī, gen. sing. of *Iūlus,* m., 2d ; objective gen., after *spes ; spes Iuli* = *hope* IN *Iulus,* not *hope of Iulus* (poss.), for the latter would mean *the hope felt by Iulus* (subjective gen.). A. & G. 217 ; B. 200 ; G. 363, 2 ; H. 396, III. The

557	spés	iam	,	réstat	I,úli,	Át	freta	,	Sícani,æ	any more our hope in
	our hope	*now*		*remains in Iulus,*		*still*	*the straits*		*of Sicily*	Iulus survives, yet we might seek the
558	sal,tém	„	se,désque	pa,rátas,	Únde	huc	,				straits of Sicily, the
	at least		*and abodes*	*prepared*	*whence*	*hither*					homes ready built
	ádvec,tí,	„	re,gémque	pe,támus	A,césten."						whence we sailed
	we were carried,		*and the king*	*(that) we may seek*	*Acestes."*						hither, and king Aces-tes." Thus Ilioneus;
559	Tálibus	,	Ílio,neús;	„	cun,ctí	simul	,				forthright the sons of
	With such (words)		*Ilioneus;*		*all*	*at the same time*					Dardanus with one

hope which the Trojans felt respecting Iulus was that he would fulfil the prophecies and found a great empire in Italy.

LINE 557. **At,** adversative conj., marking the commencement of the *apodosis* after the *protasis* with *sin.* This use of *at* is like the Greek use of ἀλλά, and δέ ; compare l. 543, where *at* introduces the *apodosis sperate deos,* etc., after the *protasis si genus humanum temnitis.* —— **freta,** acc. plur. of *fretum, -ī,* n., 2d ; direct obj. of *petamus.* —— **Sīcaniae,** nom. sing. of *Sīcania,* f., 1st (properly f., with *terra* to be supplied, of the adj. *Sīcanius, -a, -um, = pertaining to the Sīcanī*) ; adnominal gen., after *freta ; Sīcaniae = Siciliae.* Vergil evidently identifies the two tribes, the Sicani and the Siculi, though the Greek historian Thucydides in his account of Sicily declares they are distinct in family and in the time of their settlement in Sicily. —— **saltem** (perhaps a contraction for *salutem*), adv., = *at 'least.* —— **sēdēs,** acc. plur. of *sēdēs, -is,* f., 3d ; a direct obj. of *petamus,* joined by *que* to *freta.* —— **que,** enclitic cop. conj. —— **parātās,** acc. plur. f. of *parātus, -a, -um,* perf. part. pass. of *parō, -āre, -āvī, -ātum,* I ; agrees with *sedes.*

LINE 558. **Unde,** adv. of place; refers to *Sicania.* —— **hūc,** adv. of place, = *hither.* —— **advectī,** nom. plur. m. of *advectus, -a, -um,* perf. part. pass. of *advehō, -ere, advexī, advectum,* 3 (*ad + vehō*) ; agrees with the implied subj. *nōs,* and with *sunt* understood forms the 3d pers. plur. perf. ind. passive. The passives *vehor* and *advehor* are frequently used practically as deponent verbs, e.g. *vehor = I ride* or *I sail.* —— **rēgem,** acc. sing. of *rēx, rēgis,* m., 3d; in apposition with *Acestem.* Acestes was the king of Sicily, for whom some of the followers of Aeneas eventually assisted in building the city of Acesta (i.e. Egesta, or Segesta); however, Acestes must have had a settlement built already, to which *sedes paratas* (l. 557) refers. —— **que,** enclitic cop. conj. —— **petāmus,** 1st pers. plur. pres. subjunct. act. of *petō, -ere, petīvī* or *petiī, petītum,* 3; the subject contained and indicated by the personal ending is *nōs ;* the subjunctive mood is due to the clause being one of *purpose,* after *ut* understood from *ut,* l. 554. In fact, from l. 553–558 the *purpose* clause runs on, being broken firstly by *si datur . . . tendere,* and secondly by the opposed condition *sin absumpta . . . Iuli.* —— **Acestēn,** Greek acc. sing. of *Acestēs, -ae,* m., 1st decl. Greek noun; direct obj. of *petamus,* joined by *que* (appended to *regem*) to *sedes.* Some read *Acestem,* but Vergil everywhere prefers the Greek terminations *-en* (from nouns in *-es*) and *-an* (from nouns in *-as,* e.g. *Aeneas*).

LINE 559. **Tālibus,** abl. plur. n. of *tālis, -e,* adj., 3d; used substantively (= *talibus verbis*), abl. of the means or instrument, with *dixit* understood as predicate of the subj. *Ilioneus.* —— **Ilioneūs,** gen *Īeoneī,* m., mixed 2d and 3d decl. Greek noun; nom. sing., subj. of *dixit* or some verb of *speaking* understood. For the declension, refer to the note on *Anthea,* l. 510. —— **cunctī,** nom. plur. m. of the adj. *cunctus, -a, -um* (contracted from *coniunctus ;* more common in plural than in singular); agrees with *Dardanidae,* = *all in a body.* —— **simul,** adv., modifying *fremebant.* —— **ōre,** abl. sing. of *ōs, ōris,*

voice applauded.	óre ˈfre,mébant Dárdani,dǽ. 560
Then Dído, with low-	*with mouth applauded the sons of Dardanus (= Trojans).*
ered face, makes brief	ˉTúm brevi,tér Di,dó, „ vul,túm de,míssa 561
address: "Loose fears	*Then shortly Dido, her face keeping cast down*
from your hearts, Tro-	pro,fátur: "Sólvite, córde me,túm, „ Teu,crí, 562
jans; drive care away.	*speaks forth: "Unloose from the heart fear, O Teucrians,*
Hard fortune and the	se,clúdite, cúras. Rés du,ra ét reg,ní 563
newness of my throne	*shut out cares. Fortune hard and of the kingdom*

n., 3d; abl. of the instrument, with *fremebant.* —— **fremēbant,** 3d pers. plur. imperf. ind. act. of *fremō, -ere, -uī, -itum,* 3 (Greek βρέμω); agrees with the subj. *Dardanidae.*

LINE 560. **Dardanidae,** nom. plur. of *Dardanidēs, -ae,* m., 1st decl. Greek patronymic noun, = *son* or *descendant of Dardanus,* hence *a Trojan;* subj. of *fremebant.* For declension, consult A. & G. 37; B. 21, 2, *d,* and 22, like *Cometes;* G. 65, FIRST DECLENSION ; H. 50, like *Pyrites.* This is one of the numerous incomplete lines in the Aeneid; observe, however, that the sense is quite complete, and that naturally a long pause ensues between the ending of the speech of Ilioneus and the commencement of Dido's reply. Dido could not speak until the Trojans ceased applauding (*ore fremebant*). For *hemistichs,* i.e. half-lines, refer to the note on *fuit,* l. 534.

LINE 561. **Tum,** adv. of time, here connective. —— **breviter,** adv. of degree, = *briefly.* —— **Dīdō,** gen. *Dīdōnis* or *Dīdūs,* f., 3d; nom. sing., subj. of *profatur.* —— **vultum,** acc. sing. of *vultus, -ūs,* m., 4th; acc. of the direct obj., governed by the medial use of *demissa.* —— **dēmissa,** nom. sing. f. of *dēmissus, -a, -um,* perf. part. pass. of *dēmittō, -ere, dēmīsī, dēmissum,* 3 (*dē, = down, + mittō, = I send*) ; agrees with and enlarges the subj. *Dido.* It is now recognized by all the best scholars that many participles in the perf. passive used in connection with an acc. of the past affect have an active signification, like that of the Greek middle voice, and consequently the acc. (e.g. *vultum* above) is a direct obj., and not an acc. of respect. See the notes on *sinus* and *collecta,* l. 320. —— **profātur,** 3d pers. sing. pres. ind. of the deponent verb *profor, profārī, profātus sum,* 1 (*pro, = forth, + fārī, = to speak*) ; agrees with the subj. *Dido; profatur* is a graphic *historic* present.

LINE 562. **Solvite,** 2d pers. plur. imperative mood act. of *solvō, -ere, solvī, solūtum,* 3 (for *sē-luō,* from *sē, = apart, + luō, = I loosen,* hence *I unloosen*) ; the contained subj. is *vōs.* —— **corde,** abl. sing. of *cor, cordis,* n., 3d; abl. of separation, without a prep. (*de, ex,* or *ab*) as regularly with verbs meaning *to set free, to deprive,* and the like. A. & G. 243, *a;* B. 214, esp. 2; G. 390, 2 and NOTE 2; H. 413. Perhaps the more common form of this phrase would be *solvite corda metu = free your hearts from fear,* but Vergil prefers the variation *unloosen fear from the heart.* —— **metum,** acc. sing. of *metus, -ūs,* m., 4th; direct obj. of *solvite.* —— **Teucrī,** voc. plur. of *Teucrī, -ōrum* (contracted *-ūm*), m., 2d; the case of the persons addressed. —— **sēclūdite,** 2d pers. plur. imperative mood act. of *sēclūdō, -ere, sēclūsī, sēclūsum,* 3 (*sē, = apart, + clūdō, = claudō, I shut,* hence *I shut out*) ; *vōs* is the subj. implied by the personal ending. —— **cūrās,** acc. plur. of *cūra, -ae,* f., 1st; direct obj. of *secludite.*

LINE 563. **Rēs,** gen. *reī,* f., 5th ; nom. sing., one of the subjects of *cogunt; res* has the frequent meaning of *fortune,* and *res dura = hard fortune, hard case, hardship.* —— **dūra,** nom. sing. f. of *dūrus, -a, -um ;* qualifies *res.* —— **et,** cop. conj., joining the two equally important ideas *res dura* and *novitas regni.* —— **regnī,** gen. sing. of *regnum,* n., 2d; poss. gen., limiting *novitas.* Carthage is here represented as a kingdom ruled by the monarch Dido; in historical times it was a republic, putting the chief authority in the

564 novi, tás „ me , tália , cógunt Móli, rí, ét la, té „
the newness   me   such things   compel   to contrive,   and   widely
565 fi, nés   cus, tóde   tu, éri.   Quís   genus ,
my borders   with guards   to protect.   Who   the race
Aénea, dúm,   „   quis , Tróiae , nésciat , úrbem,
of Aeneas' followers,   who   of Troy   cannot know   the city,

force me to raise these barriers, and far and wide to ward my borders with guards. Who cannot know of the race of Aeneas' company, who not know of the city Troy

---

hands of two officials who thus corresponded to the two consuls of republican Rome. —— **novitās**, gen. *novitātis*, f., 3d (*novus = new*); nom. sing., one of the subjects of *cogunt*, joined by *et* to *res*. *Novitas = newness*, referring to the very recent foundation of the city; other meanings are: (1) *the status of the novus homo*, i.e. of one standing for office at Rome whose ancestors had not held office; (2) *strangeness, unusualness;* (3) *a new* i.e. *fresh condition* of something; (4) *a novel attempt* (Ovid). —— **mē**, acc. sing. of *ego;* direct obj. of *cogunt*. —— **tālia**, acc. plur. n. of *tālis, -e*, adj. 3d; substantival, direct obj. of *moliri ; talia* refers to the threatened burning of the Trojan fleet and the inhospitable treatment in general. —— **cōgunt**, 3d pers. plur. pres. ind. act. of *cōgō, -ere, coēgī, coāctum*, 3, from (*co = cum, + agō*) ; agrees with the subjects *res* and *novitas*.

LINE 564. **Mōlīrī**, pres. inf. of the deponent verb *mōlior, -īrī, -ītus sum*, 4 (*mōlēs = a mass*) ; complimentary inf., after *cogunt. Molīrī* hints always at something laborious, a heavy task, usually in a physical sense, but here it suggests that Dido found such exclusiveness necessary but uncongenial. —— **et**, cop. conj. —— **lātē**, adv., modifying *tueri*. —— **fīnēs**, acc. plur. of *fīnis, -is*, m., 3d; direct obj. of *tueri*. The singular *finis = end*, sometimes *goal;* the plur. *fines = territory*. —— **custōde**, abl. sing. of *custōs, custōdis*, m. and f., 3d; abl. of the means or instrument, with *tueri*. Though *custode* refers to men, yet the instrumental ablative is used instead of the ablative of the agent with *a* or *ab*, because Dido refers to the guards as a *means* rather than as *agents*. Observe that the singular noun *custode* here has a collective meaning *= guards*. In Aen. III, 400, *obsedit mīlite campos, mīlite* (*= soldiery, soldiers*) is exactly similar to *custode* both as being collective and an instrumental ablative. —— **tuērī**, pres. inf. of the deponent verb *tueor, ērī, tuitus sum* and *tūtus sum*, 2 (= (1) *I behold*, (2) *I protect*) ; complimentary inf., after *cogunt*, joined by *et* to *moliri*.

LINE 565. **Quis**, nom. sing. of the interrog. pron. *quis, quae, quid;* subj. of *nesciat*, understood from *nesciat* in the clause following. This question is rhetorical, = *nemo nescit*, etc. —— **genus**, gen. *generis*, n., 3d ; acc. sing., direct obj. of *nesciat* understood. —— **Aeneadūm** (for *Aeneadārum*), gen. plur. of *Aeneadēs, -ae*, m., 1st decl. Greek patronymic noun (see *Aeneadae*, l. 157 and note); adnominal gen. of specification, describing *genus*. Observe that *e*, the second syllable, which is long in *Aenēās* (Greek Alveías), is shortened in this patronymic. The genitive plural in *-ūm* instead of *-ārum* is comparatively rare, but is fairly common with compounds of *cola* and *gena*, denoting *habitation* and *lineage*, e.g. *coelicolum*, = *of the celestials*. A. & G. 36, *d* ; B. 21, 2, *d*; G. 29, REM. 3; H. 49, 3. This genitive is not a contraction of *-ārum*, but quite a different termination, contracted from *a-um*, as the Greek ά-ων when contracted becomes ῶν. —— **quis**, nom. sing. m. (see *quis* above); subj. of *nesciat;* the repetition of *quis (anaphora*) is rhetorically effective. —— **Trōiae**, gen. sing. of *Trōia*, f., 1st ; adnominal gen. of specification, describing *urbem*. —— **nesciat**, 3d pers. sing. pres. subjunct. act. of *nesciŏ, -īre, -īvī* or *-iī, -ītum*, 4 (*nē, = not, + sciŏ, = I know*) ; agrees with the subj. *quis;* potential or deliberative subjunctive, used to imply (1) *doubt, indignation*, or (2) as here, the *impossibility* of something. A. & G. 268; B. 277; G. 265; H. 484, V. —— **urbem**, acc. sing. of *urbs, urbis,* f., 3d; direct obj. of *nesciat*.

her valor and her | Vírtu,tésque vi,rósque, ,, aut , tánti in,céndia , 566
heroes, and the blaze | *and their virtues   and men,   or   so great   the blaze*
of her glorious war? | bélli?   Nón   ob,túsa   ade,ó ,, ges,támus , 567
Not so blunt are the |
wits we of Phoenicia | *of a war?   Not   blunted   so   we carry*
wear, nor so far from | péctora   ,   Póeni;   Néc tam a,vérsus e,quós ,, 568
the Tyrian city doth | *wits (lit. breasts) Phoenicians; nor   so   averted   his horses*

LINE 566. **Virtūtēs,** acc. plur. of *virtūs, -ūtis,* f., 3d; a direct obj. of *nesciat,* joined by *que* to *urbem. Virtus,* by derivation the quality of the *vir,* = (1) *manliness;* (2) *goodness, worth;* (3) *moral perfection, virtue;* (4) *courage, valor;* (5) *Virtue,* personified as a goddess. —— **que,** enclitic cop. conj. —— **virōs,** acc. plur. of *vir, -ī,* m., 2d; a direct obj. of *nesciat,* joined by *que* enclitic below to *virtutes. Virtutes,* = *the good qualities,* and *viros,* = *the famous men,* quite separate ideas, so that the words do not form an instance of *hendiadys (the virtues of the men).* —— **que,** enclitic cop. conj. —— **aut,** disjunctive conj., presenting the following new object of knowledge, viz. the siege of Troy. —— **tantī,** gen. sing. n. of *tantus, -a, -um;* agrees with *bellī.* —— **incendia,** acc. plur. of *incendium, -ī,* 2d (from *incendo,* 3, trans. = *I burn);* a direct obj. of *nesciat,* joined by *aut* to *viros;* the *flame* of war is a metaphor common to many languages. —— **bellī,** gen. sing. of *bellum,* n., 2d; poss. gen., limiting *incendia;* of course, the reference is to the ten years' siege of Troy by the Greeks.

LINE 567. **Nōn,** negative adv., limiting *gestamus.* —— **obtūsa,** acc. plur. n. of *obtūsus, -a, -um,* adj. (properly perf. part. pass. of *obtundō, -ere, obtudī, obtunsum* and *obtūsum,* 3 (*ob* + *tundō);* predicate adj., agreeing with *pectora; non obtusa adeo gestamus pectora = pectora (quae) gestamus non (sunt) adeo obtusa. Obtusus,* = lit. *blunted,* hence figuratively, of the mind, *dull.* —— **adeō,** adv. of degree, modifying *obtusa; adeo,* = *to such a degree or result,* and is used mostly with adjectives and adverbs, but óften nevertheless with verbs. Its derivation is probably from *ad* + *eō,* the abl. n. sing. of *is,* as *ad,* etc., in an early stage of the language allowed with the ablative; some say *adeo* is from *ad* + *eom* (= *eum),* an old acc. sing. m. of *is.* —— **gestāmus,** 1st pers. plur. pres. ind. act. of *gestō, -āre, -āvī, -ātum,* 1 (akin to *gerō); nōs* implied is the subject. —— **pectora,** acc. plur. of *pectus, pectoris,* n., 3d; direct obj. of *gestamus; pectora* is poetical and = *animos* or *mentes.* —— **Poenī,** gen. *Poenōrum,* m., 2d; nom. plur., in apposition with *nōs,* the implied subj. of *gestamus.*

LINE 568. **Nec,** negative cop. conj., joining the following to the preceding sentence. —— **tam,** adv. of degree, modifying the adverbial attribute *aversus.* —— **āversus,** nom. sing. m. of *āversus, -a, -um,* perf. part. pass. of *āvertō, -ere, āvertī, āversum,* 3 (*ā,* = *from,* + *vertō,* = *I turn);* agrees with *Sol,* but really limits *iungit* with adverbial force. A. & G. 191; B. 239; G. 325, REM. 6; H. 443. —— **equōs,** acc. plur. of *equus, -ī,* m., 2d; direct obj. of *iungit. Sol* is represented as driving his fiery chariot by day through the sky; the story of Phaethon, who drove this chariot one day and was struck dead by Jove's thunderbolt for his rashness, is well known. —— **Tyriā,** abl. sing. f. of *Tyrius, -a, -um;* agrees with *urbe; Tyria urbe* probably refers to Tyre, whence Dido had only lately arrived, and not to Carthage. —— **Sōl,** gen. *Sōlis,* m., 3d (akin to Greek Ἥλιος); nom. sing., subj. of *iungit. Sol* is a deity, the sun personified; in the Odyssey he informs Hephaestus of the behavior of his wife Aphrodite. *Sol* is often identified with Phoebus and Apollo (who are also identified). —— **iungit,** 3d pers. sing. pres. ind. act. of *iungō, -ere, iunxī, iunctum,* 3 (akin to Greek ζυγ, root of ζεύγνυμι); agrees with the subj. *Sol; iungit,* = *yokes,* cf. *iugum,* = *a yoke.* Some understand this and the previous line to be a disownment of a harsh and savage disposition, from the notion that the inhabitants of a genial climate are more generous and mild than those of a cold, sunless climate. But this is probably not the meaning: *obtusa* refers to *dullness* of under-

569 Tyri,á Sol , iúngit ab , úrbe.   Seú vos ,
   Tyrian   the Sun   yokes   from   the city. Whether   you
Hésperi,ám mag,nám „ Sa,túrnia,que   árva,
   Hesperia   great   and of Saturn   the fields,
570 Síve   Ery,cís fi,nés „ re,gémque op,tátis
   or whether of Eryx the territory   and king   you choose
571 A ,césten,   Aúxili,ó   tu,tós   di,mittam, „
   Acestes,   with help   safe   I will send (you) away,

the sun yoke his
steeds. Whether ye
choose wide Hespe-
ria, the tilth of Saturn,
or the frontiers of
Eryx and Acestes for
your king, safe under
escort I will speed
your going, and help

standing, and similarly the statement "we are not so far from the sun" corresponds exactly to the expression "we are not so outlandish," i.e. so ignorant of what is going on in the civilized world. Mr. Page points out that the lands on the coast of the Mediterranean were in the eyes of the ancients the civilized parts of the world, and all lands beyond barbarous and ignorant of everything except their own affairs; Mr. Page compares Aen. VI, 797, (*iacet extra sidera tellus,*) *extra anni Solisque vias,* a land outside the sun's path and therefore wil·l.——**ab,** prep. with the abl.; gov. *urbe,* marking separation.——**urbe,** abl. sing. of *urbs, urbis,* f., 3d; governed by *ab.*

   LINE 569. **Seu** (contraction for *sīve*), disjunctive conj.; it is here used properly in a disjunctive conditional clause *sīve (seu), if either . . . sīve (seu), or if,* etc. It is also used like *aut,* and *vel* with alternative words and clauses, and particularly with two names of the same thing; refer to the note and references to *aut,* l. 183.——**vōs,** nom. plur. of *vōs,* gen. *vestrum* or *vestrī,* acc. *vōs,* dat. and abl. *vōbīs;* subj. of *optatis.*——**Hesperiam,** acc. sing. of *Hesperia, -ae,* f., 1st (consult the note, etc., on *Hesperiam,* l. 530); direct obj. of *optatis.*——**magnam,** acc. sing. f. of *magnus, -a, -um ;* qualifies *Hesperiam* and = *potentem.* Observe that the *am* of *Hesperiam* and *magnam* is accented; this would be under ordinary circumstances a blemish (viz. to accent two similar terminations in close position), but here it brings out the force of the adjective.——**Sāturnia,** acc. plur. of *Sāturnius, -a, -um,* adj. (of the noun *Sāturnus, -ī,* m., 2d, = *Saturn,* the father of Jupiter, Neptune, and Pluto); agrees with *arva.* Saturn, the king of heaven, was dethroned by his son Jupiter, but was permitted to rule in Italy, which he cultivated and civilized to such a degree that the period of his reign there was called *the golden age* and the land produced its fruits untended in abundance.——**que,** enclitic cop. conj.; observe that it joins something explanatory.——**arva,** acc. plur. of *arvum, -ī,* n., 2d (from *arō* = *I plough);* a direct obj. of *optatis,* joined by *que* to *Hesperiam ; agrī* = *fields,* without special distinction, whereas *arva* = *tilled fields.*

   LINE 570. **Sīve,** disjunctive conj., introducing an alternative condition to that of *seu Hesperiam optatis* above.——**Erycis,** gen. sing. of *Erўx,* m., 3d (Greek Ἔρυξ); adnominal gen. of specification, describing *fines.* Eryx was the name (now Giuliano) of a mountain near Drepanum in Sicily, where Venus had a celebrated temple (hence her title *Venus Erycina*). The mountain received its name from Eryx, a son of Butes and Venus, whose strength was such that he overcame all combatants in the fight with the *cestus* (loaded boxing-glove) except Hercules; he was killed by Hercules in the contest and was buried on the mountain called after him.——**fīnēs,** acc. plur. of *fīnis, -is,* m., 3d (plur. = *territory);* direct obj. of *optatis,* joined by *sive* to *Hesperiam.*——**rēgem,** acc. sing. of *rēx, rēgis,* m., 3d; in apposition with *Acesten.*——**que,** enclitic cop. conj.——**optātis,** 2d pers. plur. pres. ind. act. of *optō, -āre, -āvī, -ātum,* 1; agrees with the subj. *vōs.*——**Acestēn,** acc. sing. of *Acestēs, -ae,* m., 1st decl. Greek noun; direct obj. of *optatis,* joined by *que* to *fines.*

   LINE 571. **Auxiliō,** abl. sing. of *auxilium, -ī,* n., 2d; either abl. of manner, with *dimittam,* = *I will send you away safe (so as to be safe) with my aid (escort),* or abl. of

you from the means	opi, búsque iu, vábo. **Vúltis** et , hís 572
I have. Or would you	*and with riches I will help (you). Do you wish moreover these*
settle in this realm with me on equal	me, cúm ,, pari, tér con, sídere , régnis? **Úrbem** , 573
terms ? The city	*with me on equal terms to settle realms? The city*
which I build is	quám statu, ó, ves, tra ést: ,, sub, dúcite , náves;
yours; draw up your	*which I build yours is: draw up your ships;*

instrument, with *tutos*, = *guarded by an escort*. —— **tūtōs,** acc. plur. m. of *tūtus, -a, -nm,* adj.; predicative, agreeing with *vos* understood as the obj. of *dimittam*. *Tutos* is thus *proleptic* = *so as to be safe;* cf. *scuta latentia condunt* = *they hide their shields (so that they may be) concealed.* A. & G. 385; B. 374, 5; G. 325, *predicative attribution;* H. 636, IV, 3. Some take *tūtōs* as acc. plur. m. of *tūtus,* the perf. part. of *tueor, -ērī, tuitus* or *tūtus sum,* 2, = *I protect;* in this case the participle is used like a present participle, and is also used with passive meaning, both of which peculiarities are often found in the perfect participles of deponent verbs. A. & G. 135, *b* and *f;* B. 112, *b;* G. 167, NOTE 2; H. 231, 2. —— **dimittam,** 1st pers. sing. fut. ind. act. of *dīmittō, -ere, dīmīsī, dīmissum,* 3 (*dī* (= *dis*), *apart,* + *mittō,* = *I send*) ; the contained subj. is *ego.* —— **opibus,** abl. plur. of *ops, opis,* f., 3d (nom. *ops* only occurs as the name of a goddess; the dat. sing. *opī* is very rare; the sing. = (1) *power,* (2) *help;* the plur. = (1) *resources, riches,* (2) *help*) ; abl. of the instrument, with *iuvabo.* —— **que,** enclitic cop. conj., joining *dimittam* and *iuvabo.* —— **iuvābō,** 1st pers. sing. fut. ind. act. of *iuvō, -āre, iūvī, iūtum,* 1; the subj. is *ego* implied by the personal ending.

LINE 572. **Vultis,** 2d pers. plur. pres. ind. act. of *volō, velle, voluī,* no supine, irreg. (akin to Greek root βολ in βούλομαι); the contained subj. is *vōs.* As the sentence stands, it is a question : *do you wish moreover* (i.e. *or do you wish*) *to settle,* etc.? Some editors punctuate differently, putting a semicolon after *iuvabo* and a comma after *regnis;* thus *si* must be understood (from *seu* and *sive* above) with *vultis,* and the *apodosis* is *urbem,* etc., e.g. *or (if) you wish to settle . . . , the city which I am building is yours.* On the whole, the question-mark after *regnis* simplifies the difficulty best. For the conjugation of *volo,* consult A. & G. 138; B. 130; G. 174; H. 293. —— **et,** conj., here = *etiam, moreover ; et* is thus not very far removed from having disjunctive force, = *or.* —— **hīs,** abl. plur. n. of *hīc, haec, hōc ;* agrees with *regnis;* the accent on *his* emphasizes its deictic signification. —— **mē,** abl. sing. of *ego ;* governed by *cum ; me* refers to *Dido,* the speaker. —— **cum,** prep. with the abl.; gov. *me. Cum* is only enclitic with the personal, reflexive, and relative pronouns. A. & G. 99, *e,* and 104, *e;* B. 142, 4; G. 413, REM. 1; H. 184, 6, and 187, 2. —— **pariter,** adv. of manner (*par* = *equal*), modifies *considere; pariter* probably = here *on equal terms,* though some render *at the same time* (= *simul*). —— **considere,** pres. inf. act. of *consīdō, -ere, consēdī, consessum,* 3 (*con* = *cum, together,* + *sīdō,* = *I sit*) ; *prolative* or *complementary* inf., after *vultis.* —— **rēgnīs,** abl. plur. of *regnum, -ī,* n., 2d; abl. of ' place where '; the plur. is poetical for the singular.

LINE 573. **Urbem,** acc. sing. of *urbs, urbis,* f., 3d; *urbem* is attracted into the case of the rel. pron. *quam ;* this is called *inverse attraction.* Strictly the subj. of *vestra est* would be *urbs,* the nom. case; however, by a colloquial idiom, common in Greek and in the Roman comic poets, a noun may be put in the acc. case at the beginning of a sentence to draw attention to it, and then the sentence is carried on just as if the noun had been in the nom. as subject; Plautus has a sentence, *Istum quem quaeris ego sum.* A. & G. 200, *b;* B. 251, 4; G. 617, NOTE 2; H. 445, 9. —— **quam,** acc. sing. f. of the rel. pron. *qui, quae, quod;* agrees with *urbem,* and is direct obj. of *statuō.* —— **statuō,** 1st pers. sing. pres. ind. act. of *statuō, -ere, -uī, statūtum,* 3 (akin to *stō* through *status*) ;

574 Trós Tyri, úsque mi, hí ,, nul, ló dis, crímine | ships; Trojan and
Trojan (man) and Tyrian by me no with distinction | Tyrian by me shall be
575 a, gétur. Átque uti, nám rex , ípse, ,, | treated with no dis-
will be treated. And would that your king himself, | tinction. And would
576 No, tó com, púlsus e, ódem, Ãfforet , | that Aeneas your
by the south wind driven same, were present | king, driven by that
  same gale, were here

the implied subj. is *ego*. —— **vestra**, nom. sing. f. of *vester, vestra, vestrum*, poss. adj. of *vōs;* agrees with *urbs*, which we would expect, instead of *urbem*, for the sentence is an instance of a kind of *anacoluthon* (i.e. non-sequence); *vestra* is predicative, being the *complement* of *est*. —— **est**, 3d pers. sing. pres. ind. of the copula *sum, esse, fuī;* agrees with a supposed *urbs* as subj., though that subj. appears in the acc. case. —— **subdūcite**, 2d pers. plur. imperative mood act. of *subdūcō, -ere, subdūxī, subductum*, 3 (*sub* + *dūcō*)*;* the implied subj. is *vōs*. —— **nāvēs**, acc. plur. of *nāvis, -is*, f., 3d; direct obj. of *subducite*.

LINE 574. **Trōs**, gen. *Trōis*, m., 3d (plur. *Trōes, -um;* Greek Τρώς); nom. sing., a subject of *agetur*. —— **Tyrius**, nom. sing. m. of *Tyrius, -a, -um* (*Tyrus, -ī*, f. 2d); substantively, a subj. of *agetur*, joined by *que* to *Tros*. —— **que**, enclitic cop. conj. —— **mihī**, dat. sing. of *ego;* probably a dat. of the agent, as often in poetry. A. & G. 232; B. 189; G. 354; H. 388, 1. Some prefer to regard *mihi* as an *ethic* dative (not wishing to multiply instances of the dat. of the agent with other than the perfect tense and perf. part. passive). A. & G. 236; B. 188, 2, *b*; A. & G. 351 ; H. 389. —— **nullo**, abl. sing. n. of *nullus, -a, -um* (gen. *nullīus*, dat. *nullī*) *;* agrees with *discrīmine*. —— **discrīmine**, abl. sing. of *discrīmen, discriminis*, n., 3d (from *discernō*, = *I separate*, through the root *discre*)*;* abl. of manner, without *cum* as there is a modifying adj. *nullo*. *Discrimine* is here used in its literal and original meaning *distinction;* for other meanings, see the note on *discrimina*, l. 204. —— **agētur**, 3d pers. sing. fut. ind. pass. of *agō, -ere, ēgī, actum*, 3; agrees in the sing. with the composite subj. *Tros Tyriusque*, as forming one idea; *agetur* here = *habebitur*. The phrase *discrimine agetur* is strange but quite in Vergil's style; we find (Aen. X, 108) *discrimine habebo*, but *habebo* is quite allowable; however, Vergil is giving a mixed form of this and the phrase *agere discrimen*.

LINE 575. **Atque**, cop. conj., introducing a new and important addition; see the note and references on *que*, l. 1. —— **utinam**, adv., used in wishes, with the *optative* subjunctive; the negative is *utinam ne* or *utinam non*, or *utinam nec . . . nec*. The *optative* subjunctive is more common with *utinam* than any other word; *ut* is archaic and rare; *ō sī* is used with it, chiefly in poetry; *quī* is used in early Latin and in curses. —— **rēx**, gen. *rēgis*, m., 3d; nom. sing., in apposition with *Aeneas*. —— **ipse**, nom. sing. m. of the intensive adj. *ipse, ipsa, ipsum* (gen. *ipsīus*, dat. *ipsī*); agrees with *rex*. —— **Notō**, abl. sing. of *Notus, -ī*, m., 2d (Greek Νότος, = *the South wind*) *;* abl. of the instrument, with *compulsus;* cf. l. 536, where the Trojans are said to be driven *procacibus Austris* (*south winds*). —— **compulsus**, nom. sing. m. of the perf. part. pass. of *compellō, -ere, conpulī, compulsum*, 3 (*con* = *cum*, + *pellō*)*;* agrees with and enlarges the subj. *Aeneas* or the appositive *rex*. —— **eōdem**, abl. sing. m. of *īdem, eadem, ĭdem* (gen. *ēiusdem*, dat. *eĭdem ;* from *is* + *dem ;* see note and references on *eadem*, l. 240); agrees with *Noto*.

LINE 576. **Afforet** (*adforet*) = *adesset ;* 3d pers. sing. imperf. subjunct. of *adsum, adesse, affuī* (*adfuī*), no supine, irreg. (*ad* + *sum*) *;* agrees with the subj. *Aeneas*. The subjunctive mood is due to the sentence being a *wish* introduced by *utinam* above ; the tense is imperfect because the wish is an unfulfilled and impossible one for the present time. The *optative* subjunctive is used as follows : (1) in the pres. subjunctive, when the wish is for the future; (2) in the imperf. when the wish is for the present ; (3) in the pluperfect,

in person. At least I	Aéne,ás! „ Equi,dém per , lítora , cértos
will send trusty mes-	*Aeneas!* *Indeed* *along* *the shores* *trusty men*
sengers along the	Dímit,tam, ét Liby,æ „ lus,tráre ex,tréma 577
coasts and bid them	*I will send,* *and of Libya* *to search the uttermost parts*
search the uttermost	
parts of Libya, if per-	iu,bébo, Sí quibus , éiec,tús „ sil,vís aut , 578
chance shipwrecked	*I will order* (*them*), *if* *any* *cast ashore* *in woods* *or*
he wanders in wood	úrbibus , érrat." Hís ani,mum árrec,tí 579
or city." Cheered at	*in cities* *he is wandering."* *These* *in mind* *aroused*

when the wish refers to the past. The negative is *ne*, or (with *utinam*) *utinam non* or *utinam ne* (see *utinam* above). As we have *afforem = adessem* from the compound *adsum*, so we occasionally find *forem = essem* from *sum*. Probably *forem*, *-es, -et*, etc., was once = to *futurus essem*, as it is sometimes even in the writings of Sallust (cf. *fore*, which always = *futurus esse*). A. &. G. 119, NOTE; B. page 57, footnote 2; G. 116, and esp. NOTE 1, *c*; H. 204, and esp. 2.——— **Aenēās**, gen *Aenēae*, m., 1st decl. Greek noun; nom. sing., subj. of *afforet*.——— **Equidem**, adv.; see the note on *equidem*, l. 238.——— **per**, prep. with the acc; gov. *lītora*.——— **lītora**, acc. plur. of *lītus, litoris*, n., 3d; governed by *per*.——— **certōs**, acc. plur. m. of *certus, -a, -um*, adj.; used substantively, direct obj. of *dimittam; certos = fidos*, i.e. trusty messengers.

LINE 577. **Dīmittam**, 1st pers. sing. fut. ind. act. of *dīmittō* (see *d'mittam*, l. 571); the implied subj. is *ego*.——— **et**, cop. conj.——— **Libyae**, gen. sing. of *Libya*, f., 1st; poss. gen., limiting *extrema*.——— **lustrāre**, pres. inf. act. of *lustrō, -āre, -āvī, -ātum*, 1; complementary inf., dependent on *iubebo*.——— **extrēma**, gen. *extrēmōrum*, n., 2d = *the uttermost parts* (properly substantival neuter plural of *extrēmus, -a, -um*, adj.); acc. plur., direct obj. of *lustrāre*. *Extremus* is the superlative degree of the rare adjective *exter, extera, exterum*, = lit. *outside* (Cicero speaks of *exterae nationes*) ; the comparative is *exterior*, and there is another form of the superlative *extimus, -a, -um*. As *exter* is rare, *extremus* is usually referred back to the prep. *extra;* cf. *supremus* (*summus*) to *supra*. ——— **iubēbō**, 1st pers. sing. fut. ind. act. of *iubeō, -ēre, iussī, iussum*, 2; its subj. is *ego*, contained in the verb; *iubebo* is joined by *et* to *demittam;* understand *eos* as obj. of *iubebo*. *Iubeo* is followed by the acc. and a complementary infinitive (as above); the other common verb for *ordering*, viz. *imperō*, takes the dative of the person and *ut* with the subjunctive mood.

LINE 578. **Sī**, conditional particle, followed by the indicative *errat*, and, therefore, not introducing an indirect question. See the note on *si*, l. 18.——— **quibus**, abl. plur. f. of the indef. pron. and adj. *quis, quae, quid;* agrees with *silvis*. *Quis*, the indefinite, is rarely used except after *si* or *ne* (*if* or *lest any*).——— **ēiectus**, nom. sing. m. of the perf. part. pass. of *ēiicio, ēicere, ēiēcī, ēiectum*, 3 (*ē, = out of, + iaciō, = I throw*) ; agrees with and enlarges *Aeneas* understood as subj. of *errat; eiectus = thrown out*, i.e. from the sea onto the land. ——— **silvīs**, abl. plur. of *silva, -ae*, f., 1st; locative ablative. A. & G. 258, 4, *f* and *g*; B. 228; G. 385; H. 425.——— **aut**, disjunctive conj., joining *urbibus* as an alternative to *silvis*.——— **urbibus**, abl. plur. of *urbs, urbis*, f., 3d; abl. of 'place where,' like *silvis* above.——— **errat**, 3d pers. sing. pres. ind. act. of *errō, -āre, -āvī, -ātum*, 1; the subj. is *Aeneas* understood. The indicative mood presents the hypothesis in a matter-of-fact way, *if perchance he is wandering*. A. & G. 306, *a*; B. 302, 4; G. 595; H. 508, 4. Conington, rendering the passage freely, translates "to see if," and others have blindly followed him; this is wrong as the words are literally, for it would require *si* with the subjunctive *erret*, like *Anthea si quem . . . videat*, l. 182.

LINE 579. **Hīs**, abl. plur. n. of the demonstr. adj. *hīc, haec, hōc;* agrees with *verbis*,

580 dic, tís, „ et , fórtis A,chátes Ét pater , Aéne,ás „
by words, both　brave　Achates　and father　　Aeneas

581 iam,dúd*um* e,rúmpere , núbem Árde,bánt. „
for a long time to burst from　the cloud　were burning.

582 Prior , Aéne,án com,péllat A,chátes :　　"Náte
First　Aeneas　addresses　Achates :　" O thou born

heart by these words,
brave Achates and
father Aeneas long
since burned to burst
from the cloud. Acha-
tes first hails Aeneas
by name : "Goddess-

---

and refers to Dido's speech. —— **animum,** acc. sing. of *animus, -ī,* m., 2d; a kind of direct obj. after the medial part. *arrecti, = having their minds cheered,* and probably not an acc. of respect, *"roused as to their minds"*; see the note on *suffusa oculos,* l. 228. Vergil uses the sing. *animum,* though it refers to both Aeneas and Achates; he also uses the plur. *animos* in reference to a single individual. —— **arrectī,** nom. plur. m. of *arrectus, -a, -um,* perf. part. pass. of *arrigō, -ere, arrēxī, arrectum,* 3 (*ad + regō*); agrees with and enlarges the subjects *Achates et Aeneas.* —— **dictīs,** abl. plur. of *dictum, -ī,* n., 2d (originally perf. part. pass. neuter sing. of *dīcō*); abl. of the instrument, with *arrecti.* —— **et,** cop. conj., repeated below = *both . . . and;* refer to the note on *que,* l. 477. —— **fortis,** nom. sing. m. of *fortis, -e,* adj., 3d; qualifies *Achates.* —— **Achātēs,** gen. *Achătae,* m., 1st decl. Greek noun; nom. sing., one of the subjects of *ardebant.*

LINE 580. **Et,** cop. conj., joining *Aeneas* and *Achates.* —— **pater,** gen. *patris,* m., 3d; nom. sing., in apposition with *Aeneas.* —— **Aenēās,** nom. sing., one of the subjects of *ardebant.* —— **iamdūdum** (*iam, = already,* + *dūdum* (*diū + dum*), *not long ago*), adv. of time, modifying *ardebant. Iamdiu* and *iamdudum* always express the continuance of an action begun in the past; thus *iamdudum ardebant = they had been and were then eager,* etc. This meaning is most frequent with the present tense, e.g. *iam diu ardeo = I have for a long time been eager.* A. & G. 277, *b;* B. 260, 4; G. 234; H. 469, 2. —— **ērumpere,** pres. inf. act. of *ērumpō, -ere, ērūpī, ēruptum,* 3 (*ē, = out of,* + *rumpō,* = *I burst*); prolative inf., after *ardebant. Erumpere* is the reading of the best MSS., but some favor *abrumpere;* the former is unquestionably the correct reading, and is easily explained. *Erumpo,* which by origin is transitive, is usually intransitive, = *I burst forth,* and from the transitive *meaning* which it has (e.g. *I burst from,* i.e. *I leave the cloud*) it acquires a transitive use like that of any ordinary transitive verb. Vergil has several similar examples, e.g. Aen. V, 689, *flammam evadere.* —— **nubem,** acc. sing. of *nūbes, -is,* f., 3d; direct obj. of *erumpere* in its acquired transitive use; we should expect *nube,* abl. of separation, after *erumpere,* which is intransitive.

LINE 581. **Ardēbant,** 3d pers. plur. imperf. ind. act. of *ardeō, -ēre, arsī, arsum,* 2; agrees with the subjects *Achates et Aeneas.* —— **Prior,** nom. sing. m. of *prior, prius,* gen. *priōris,* adj.; agrees with *Achates,* and is an adverbial attribute. *Prior* is the comparative degree, formed from the adverb or preposition *prae ;* no positive; the superlative is *primus,* which is frequently used adverbially. A. & G. 191; B. 241, 2; G. 325, REM. 6; H. 443. Refer to the note on *prior,* l. 321. —— **Aenēan,** acc. sing. of *Aenēās, -ae,* m., 1st decl. Greek noun; direct obj. of *compellat; -an* is the Greek termination, preferred by Vergil in Greek nouns to the Latin *-am.* —— **compellat,** 3d pers. sing. pres. ind. act. of *compellō, -āre, -āvī, -ātum,* 1; agrees with the subj. *Achates; compellat = alloquitur,* and is a *historic* present. —— **Achātēs,** gen. *Achătae,* m., 1st decl.; nom. sing., subj. of *compellat.*

LINE 582. **Nāte,** voc. sing. m. of *nātus, -a, -um,* perf. part. of the deponent verb *nascor, -ī, nātus sum,* 3 (old form, *gnascor,* etc., root *gna = gen,* in *gens,* and Greek γεν in γέν-εσθαι, 2d aorist inf. of γίγνομαι); the case of the person addressed. For the substantival use of participles, consult A. & G. 113, *f;* B. no reference; G. 437; H. 441.

born, what thought	de, á,	quae	, núnc ani, mó	,,	sen, téntia ,
now rises in thy	*of a goddess, what*		*now in thy mind*		*thought*
heart ? Thou seest	súrgit?	Ómnia	, túta	vi, dés,	,, clas, sém 583
that all is safe, thy	*rises?*	*All things*	*safe*	*thou seest*	*the fleet*
fleet and company					
restored. One only is	soci, ósque	re, céptos.	Únus	ab, ést,	medi, o in 584
missing, whom with	*and our comrades*	*restored.*	*One*	*is absent,*	*middle in*
our own eyes we saw	fluc, tú ,,	quem ,	vídimus ,	ípsi	Súbmer, súm ; ,, 585
whelmed in mid	*the flood*	*whom*	*we saw*	*ourselves*	*overwhelmed ;*

—— **deā**, abl. sing. of *dea, -ae*, f., 1st (dat. and abl. plur. often *deābus*) ; abl. of source or origin, not often found except with participles. A. & G. 244, *a*; B. 215; G. 395, and NOTE 1; H. 415, II. —— **quae**, nom. sing. f. of the interrog. adj. *quī, quae, quod;* agrees with *sententia*. —— **nunc**, adv. of time, modifying *surgit*. —— **animō**, abl. sing. of *animus, -i*, m., 2d; abl. of 'place where.' —— **sententia**, gen. *sententiae*, f., 1st (for *sententia*, from *sentiens*, = *thinking*, prcs. part. act. of *sentiō*) ; nom. sing., subj. of *surgit*. —— **surgit**, 3d pers. sing. pres. ind. act. of *surgō, -ere, surrēxī, surrectum*, 3 (*sub* + *regō*) ; agrees with the subj. *sententia*.

LINE 583. **Omnia**, acc. plur. n. of *omnis, -e*, adj., 3d; used as a substantive = *all things*, and subj.-acc. of *esse* understood in the predicate *tuta (esse); omnia tuta esse is* the acc. and inf. construction, standing as object to the *verbum sentiendi, videt*. —— **tūta**, acc. plur. n. of *tūtus, -a, -um*, adj.; agrees with its subj.-acc. *omnia* and completes the predication *tuta (esse)*. —— **vidēs**, 2d pers. sing. pres. ind. act. of *videō, -ēre, vīdī, vīsum*, 2; the contained subj. is *tū*. For the simple acc. and inf. construction, refer to the note on *misceri*, l. 124. —— **classem**, acc. sing. of *classis, -is*, f., 3d; subj.-acc. of *receptam esse* understood from *receptos;* there is no conjunction connecting *omnia* and *classem (asyndeton)*. —— **sociōs**, acc. plur. of *socius, -ī*, m., 2d; subj.-acc. of *receptos (esse)*. —— **que**, enclitic cop. conj., joining *classem (receptam esse)* and *socios receptos (esse)*. —— **receptōs**, acc. plur. m. of *receptus, -a, -um*, perf. part. pass. of *recipiō, -ere, recēpī, receptum*, 3 (*re*, = *back*, + *capiō*, = *I take*); agrees with the subj.-acc. *socios*, and is (with *esse* understood) the perf. inf. passive of *recipio*. Observe that the *restoration* (expressed by *receptos*) applies to the fleet as well as the crews, but that the participle is only expressed with the nearest of the nouns, *socios*.

LINE 584. **Ūnus**, nom. sing. m. of *ūnus, -a, -um* (gen. *ūnīus*); subj. of *abest; unus* refers to *Orontes*, see ll. 113-117. —— **abest**, 3d pers. sing. pres. ind. act. of *absum, abesse, āfuī (ab + sum); agrees with the subj. *unus*. *Abesse* is used idiomatically in phrases = *to be so far from doing something*, e.g. *tantum abest ut* + the subjunctive. —— **mediō**, abl. sing. m. of *medius, -a, -um ; agrees with *fluctu*, which it qualifies partitively. —— **in**, prep. with the acc. and abl.; gov. the abl. *fluctū*. —— **fluctū**, abl. sing. of *fluctus, -ūs*, m., 4th (*fluō* = *I flow*); governed by preposition *in*. —— **quem**, acc. sing. m. of the rel. pron. *quī, quae, quod ;* agrees with the antecedent *unus* in gender and number, and is the obj.-acc. of *vidimus*. A. & G. 198; B. 250, 1; G. 614; H. 445. —— **vīdimus**, 1st pers. plur. perf. ind. act. of *videō, -ēre, vīdī, vīsum*, 2; the subj. is *nōs* contained in the verb. The perfect tense denotes that the action took place in the past and was instantaneous. —— **ipsī**, nom. plur. m. of the intensive pron. and adj. *ipse, -a, -um ;* agrees with and intensifies *nos*, the implied subj. of *vidimus*.

LINE 585. **Submersum**, acc. sing. m. of *submersus, -a, -um*, perf. part. pass. of *submergō, -ere, submersī, submersum*, 3 (*sub*, = *under*, + *mergō*, = *I plunge*); predicate participle, agreeing with *quem ; quem submersum vidimus* is more vivid than the

dic,tís	res,póndent	, cétera	, mátris."	flood ; all the rest
with the words	*correspond*	*the rest*	*of thy mother."*	answers to thy moth-

586 **Víx**   ea   , fátus e,rát, „cum , círcum,fúsa

Scarcely those (words) had he spoken, when   spread around

587 re,pénte **Scíndit** , sé nu,bés „et in , æthera ,

suddenly   cleaves   itself the cloud and into   air

er's words." Scarce
had he spoken, when
suddenly the mantle
of cloud parts and
melts into the bound-

---

ordinary acc. and inf. construction *quem submergī vidimus.* The participle expresses the actual condition of the object of perception; it is properly a Greek construction (after *verba sentiendi*), is very rare in early Latin, but was introduced into Latin by Cicero and others who studied Greek models. A. & G. 292, *e*; B. 336, 2; G. 536; H. 535, I, 4. —— **dictīs**, dat. plur. of *dictum, -ī*, n., 2d; dat. of the indirect obj. after *respondent; dictis matris* refers to the prophetic words of Venus disguised as a Tyrian maiden (see ll. 390 ff.). —— **respondent**, 3d pers. plur. pres. ind. act. of *respondeō, -ēre, respondī, responsum*, 2 (*re, = back* or *again, + spondeō, = I promise*, hence *I answer ;* agrees with the subj. *cetera.* *Respondeō* = (1) *I promise in return*, or *I return*, e.g. *par pari respondere,* = *to return like for like*, rare; (2) *I reply ;* (3) of lawyers, oracles, etc., = *I give an opinion* or *response ;* (4) *I answer to my name* (i.e. *appear) ;* (5) *I correspond to, answer to*, as in this passage; (6) *I prove a match for*, in Cicero; (7) *I resound, re-echo*, in Ovid and poetical. For the force of *re* and *red* in composition, refer to the notes on *repostum*, l. 26, and *remordet*, l. 261. —— **cētera**, nom. plur. n. of *cēterus, -a, -um* (= *the other, the remaining* part, in sing, which is rare); substantival, subj. of *respondent. Ceteri, -ae, -a*, the plur., is generally used, = *the rest.* —— **mātris**, gen. sing. of *māter*, f., 3d (Greek μήτηρ); poss. gen., limiting *dictis ; matris = Veneris.*

LINE 586. **Víx**, adv., modifying *fatus erat; vix* is a quasi-negative adverb used in reference to *degree* or *time.* —— **ea**, acc. plur. n. of the demonstr. pron. *is,ea, id* (gen. *ēius*, dat. *eī*, acc. *eum, eam, id*, abl. *eō, eā, eō*) ; direct obj. of *fatus erat.* A. & G. 101; B. 87; G. 103, 1 ; H. 186, IV. —— **fátus erat**, 3d pers. sing. pluperf. ind. of the defective deponent verb *fārī;* combinate tense (participle + a part of *sum*, in the perfect stem tenses passive of all verbs), agreeing with the subj. *Achates* understood. A. & G. 144 *c*; B. 136; G. 175, 3; H. 297, II, 3. —— **cum**, conj., indicating a point of time (also written *quum, quom*, rarely *qum*, originally an adverbial acc. of the rel. *qui*). Observe that *cum* is followed by the *historic* present indicative *scindit;* when *cum* is the correlative of *tum* or a phrase = to *tum* (e.g. *he had just spoken, when*), it is followed by the indicative. Usually *cum* temporal takes the imperfect and pluperfect subjunctive, and other tenses in the indicative. A. & G. 325; B. 288, 289 ; G. 580–585; H. 521. —— **circumfūsa**, nom. sing. f. of *circumfūsus, -a, -um*, perf. part. pass of *circumfundō, -ere, circumfūdī, circumfūsum,* 3 (*circum, = around, + fundō, = I pour*), agreeing with *nubes ; circumfusa nubes = nubes quae circumfusa erat.* —— **repentē**, adv., modifying *scindit se.*

LINE 587. **Scindit**, 3d pers. sing. pres. ind. act. of *scindō, -ere, scidī, scissum,* 3 (akin to Greek σχίζω = *I cleave) ;* agrees with the subj. *nubes; scindit* is a *historic* present. —— **sē**, acc. sing. of the reflexive pron. *sē* (*sēsē) ;* direct obj. of *scindit; sē* must also be supplied as obj. of the transitive verb *purgat.* Transitive verbs may acquire an intransitive sense in two ways: (1) by use with the reflexive pron. *sē* as object, e.g. *scindit se* = lit. *cleaves itself,* i.e. *parts* or *melts;* (2) by being used in the passive, e.g. *scinditur.* —— **nūbes**, gen. *nūbis*, f., 3d; nom. sing., subj. of *scindit; nubes* is the cloud of mist which Venus spread about Aeneas and Achates, see l. 411. —— **et**, cop. conj. —— **in**, prep. with the acc. and abl.; gov. the acc. *aethera.* —— **aethera**, Greek form of the acc. sing. of *aethēr, -eris*, m. 3d, (Greek αἰθήρ); governed by *in.* Strictly we ought to have l..l in

| less air. There Aeneas stood forth and shone upon them in the bright light, in face and shoulders god-like ; for herself his mother had breathed upon her son the grace of clustering hair, the bright radi- | púrgat a,pértum. Réstitit , Aéne,ás „ 588
clears (itself) open. *Stood forth* *Aeneas*

cla,ráque in , lúce re,fúlsit, Ós hume,rósque 589
and clear in the light shone out, in face and in shoulders

de,ó simi,lís: „ nam,que ípsa de,córam
to a god like: for herself beautiful

Cǽsari,ém na,tó gene,tríx, „ lu,ménque 590
hair upon her son his mother and the radiance |

aera, for the cloud melted into the atmosphere, and not into the *upper air;* this passage proves that Vergil does not always use the word strictly, cf. *aëre saepsit*, l. 411.——*pur-gat*, 3d pers. sing. pres. ind. act. of *purgō, -āre, -āvī, -ātum,* I; agrees with the subj. *nubes*, and is joined by *et* to *scindit; purgat* is not used intransitively, but *se* must be supplied as direct obj. from above.——*apertum*, acc. sing. m. of *apertus, -a, -um;* agrees with *aethera*.

LINE 588. **Rəstitit**, 3d pers. sing. perf. ind. act. of *restō, -are, restitī*, no supine, I (*re, = back, + stō, = I stand*); agrees with the subj. *Aeneas*. The force of *re* is to show that Aeneas was *left* in view as the cloud vanished.——**Aenēās**, nom. sing.; subj. of *re-stitit*. Of course Achates also *restitit*, but Vergil draws attention to the more important figure, the hero of the Aeneid.——**clārā**, abl. sing. f. of *clārus, -a, -um,* adj.; agrees with *luce.* *Clarus* = (1) *clear, bright;* (2) *renowned, famous.*——**que**, enclitic cop. conj. ——**in**, prep. with the acc. and abl.; gov. the abl. *luce.*——**lūce**, abl. sing. of *lūx, lūcis*, f., 3d (for *luc-s,* from *luc-eō, = I shine,* hence (1), *light, brightness,* (2) *daylight*) ; governed by the preposition *in.*——**refulsit**, 3d pers. sing. perf. ind. act. of *refulgeō, -ēre, refulsī*, no supine, 2 (*re, = back, + fulgeō, = I shine*) ; agrees with the subj. *Aeneas,*and is joined by *et* to *restitit.* The force of *re* in *refulsit* is the same as in *restitit* above; see the note on *refulsit*, l. 402.

LINE 589. **Ōs**, acc. sing. of *ōs, ōris,* n., 3d; acc. of respect, with *similis = like as to his face;* refer to the note on *genu*, l. 320. The following description, ll. 589-593, is a free imitation of Odyssey, XXIII, 156-162. Even the simile *quale manus*, etc., l. 592, is copied from the Homeric simile of gold and silver work.——**humerōs**, acc. plur. of *humerus, -ī,* m., 2d (akin to the Greek ὦμος) ; acc. of respect, like *os* above, to which it is joined by *que.*——**que**, enclitic cop. conj.——**deō**, dat. sing. of *deus, -ī,* m., 2d; dat. after *similis.* Adjectives expressing *likeness* may take either the genitive or the dative case; Cicero uses the genitive of living objects, the genitive or dative of inanimate objects. A. & G. 234, *d,* esp. 2; B. 204, 3; G. 359, REM. I and NOTE 4; H. 391, I, and 4, and page 205, footnotes 1, 2, 3. It is supposed that Vergil is thinking of Apollo, whose beautiful figure, hair, and shoulders are well known. But more probably he has only the passage of Homer in mind, wherein Athene *shed a wealth of beauty over the head* of the hero, and gave him οὖλας κόμας.——**similis**, nom. sing. m. of *similis, -e,* adj., 3d; agrees with *Aeneas.*——**namque** (*nam + que*), *nam,* causal conj., strength-ened by *que*, introducing an explanation.——**ipsa**, nom. sing. f. of *ipse, -a, -um;* agrees with and intensifies the subj. *genetrix.*——**decōram**, acc. sing. of *decōrus, -a, -um* (from *decor, ōris,* m., 3d), agrees with *caesariem*.

LINE 590. **Caesariem**, acc. sing. f. of *caesariēs, -ēī,* f., 5th; direct obj. of *afflārat.* Most commentators declare that *afflarat* can only be used with *caesariem* by *zeugma* (see *serenat,* l. 255), and that it is only allowed by poetic license with *lumen;* however, the whole passage is highly poetical, and if *radiance* can be *breathed* into the eyes, surely

591 iu,véntae **Púrpure,** *um,* ét lae,tós ,, ocu,lís | ance of youth, and
of youth *bright* (lit. *purple*) *and* *glad* *to his eyes* | glad glory upon his
592 af,flárat ho,nóres: **Quále** ma,nús ad,dúnt ,, | eyes, even as when
had breathed *charms:* (*such*) *as* *hands* *add* | skilled hands add

the *grace of beautiful locks* (the emphasis on *decoram*) can also be said to be divinely breathed upon Aeneas. —— **nātō**, dat. sing. m. of *natus, -a -um*, perf. part. of the deponent verb *nascor, -ī, natus sum*, 3; used substantively, dat. of the indirect obj. after *afflarat;* see note on *nate*, l. 582. —— **genetrīx**, gen. *genetrīcis*, f., 3d (from *genō*, old form of *gignō*, = *I bring forth*); nom. sing., subj. of *afflarat; genetrix = mater*, i.e. *Venus*. —— **lūmen**, acc. sing. of *lūmen, lūminis*, n., 3d (for *luc-men*, from *lūceō*, = *I shine*); a direct obj. of *afflarat*, joined by *que to caesariem*. —— **que**, enclitic cop. conj. —— **iuventae**, gen. sing. of *iuventa*, f., 1st (the state of the *iuvenis*); a sort of adnominal gen. of substance or material, the gen. being really equivalent to an adjective; *iuventae* limits *lumen*. A. & G. 214, *e*; B. 197; G. 361; H. 395.

LINE 591. **Purpureum**, acc. sing. n. of *purpureus, -a -um* (from *purpura*, = *purple*); agrees with *lumen*. The adjective *purpureus* (which = (1) *purple*, hence from the nature of this ancient dye (2) *bright, dazzling*) is used by the poets with a wide assortment of nouns, e.g. *flowers* (Aen. V, 79, *purpureos . . . flores*), light, eyes, love, swans, and snow; in all these instances the word seems to have lost its signification of colour, and to denote merely brightness. —— **et**, cop. conj. —— **laetōs**, acc. plur. of *laetus, -a, -um*, adj.; agrees with *honore*. —— **oculīs**, dat. plur. of *oculus, -ī*, m., 2d; dat. of the indirect obj. after *afflarat*. —— **afflārat**, 3d pers. sing. pluperf. ind. act. of *afflō, -āre, -āvī, -ātum*, 1 (*ad*, = *upon*, + *flō*, = *I breathe*); agrees with the subj. *genetrix;* the word is specially used here of the divine dispensation of peculiar privileges by the goddess Venus to her son. *Afflārat* is a contracted form of *afflāverat*. A. & G. 128, *a*, 1; B. 7, 2; G. 131, 1; H. 235. —— **honōrēs**, acc. plur. of *honos, -ōris*, m., 3d; a direct obj. of *afflarat*, joined by *et* to *lumen*. The plural is very rarely used meaning *beauty;* the most important meaning of the word in prose is *office, official dignity*.

LINE 592. **Quāle**, acc. sing. n. of *quālis, -e*, rel. adj.; agrees with *decus*. *Qualis* here and frequently elsewhere introduces a simile, always with the corresponding demonstrative *talis* understood before it; thus the complete logical order is: *tale decus* (in apposition with *lumen* and *honores*) *quale decus manus ebori addunt, aut* (*tale quale additur*) *ubi flavo*, etc. —— **manūs**, nom. plur. of *manus, -ūs*, f., 4th; subj. of *addunt*. A. & G. 69; B. 50; G. 62, EXCEPTIONS; H. 118. *Manus* of course = *the hands* of the workers in metal. —— **addunt**, 3d pers. plur. pres. ind. act. of *addō, -ere, addidī, additum*, 3 (*ad* + *dō*); agrees with the subj. *manus*. The comparison between the ivory in its setting, and the silver or Parian marble set in gold, is here general; the meaning is that as the setting adds peculiar beauty to ivory, etc., so the special gifts of Venus made Aeneas, regarded as a whole, beautiful. —— **eborī**, dat. sing. of *ebur, eboris*, n., 3d, = *ivory* (akin to Sanskrit *ibha* = *an elephant*); dat. of the indirect obj. after *addunt*. Vergil does not name what the setting of the ivory is, but in a like simile in Aen. X, 136, the setting is box-wood or terebinth (*inclusum buxo . . . ebur*). —— **decus**, gen. *decoris*, n., 3d; acc. sing., direct obj. of *addunt*. —— **aut**, disjunctive conj., introducing an alternative comparison; see note on *aut*, l. 183. The construction being somewhat compressed, understand after *aut, quale decus est* (or *additur*). —— **ubi**, temporal conj., followed by the ind. *circumdatur*. *Ubi* has several uses: (1) interrog. of place, = *where?* (2) of time, = *when?* (3) rel. local adv. = *where, in which place;* (4) of persons and things = *with* or *by which, whom;* (5) temporal conj. = *when*. —— **flāvō**, abl. sing. n. of *flāvus -a, -um* (probably akin to *flamma*); agrees with *auro*.

beauty to the ivory, | ebo,rí   decus,   ,   aút   ubi   ,   flávo   Árgen,túm 593
or when silver or Pa- | *to ivory   grace,   or   when   yellow   silver*
rian stone is set in | Pari,úsve   la,pís   „   cir,cúmdatur   ,   aúro.   Túm 594
yellow gold.   Then | *or Parian   stone   is encircled   with gold.   Then*
he thus addresses the |
queen, and unlooked | sic , régi,nam álloqui,túr, „ cun,ctísque re,pénte
for by all makes | *thus   the queen   he addresses,   and to all   suddenly*
speech : "Here be- | Ímpro,vísus a,ít :   " Co,rám, quem , quaéritis, , 595
fore you am I, whom | *unexpected   he says: "In presence,   whom   you seek,*

LINE 593. **Argentum**, gen. *argentī*, n., 2d (Greek ἄργυρος); nom. sing., subj. of *circumdatur.* —— **Parius**, nom. sing. m. of *Parius, -a, -um*, adj. (belonging to *Parus* or *Paros, -ī*, f., 2d); agrees with *lapis.* Paros is an island (one of the Cyclades group) in the Aegean Sea, close to Naxos and Delos, and was from early times famous for its magnificent white marble. The famous Parian marbles (inscribed) are now in the possession of the University of Oxford. —— **ve**, enclitic disjunctive conj., joining *lapis* as an alternative to *argentum.* *Vel* and its weaker form *ve* offer a choice between two alternatives; *aut* joins but excludes the two alternatives; *sive* generally gives a choice between two names of the same thing. A. & G. 156, *c*; B. 342; G. 494; H. 554, II, 2. —— **lapis**, gen. *lapidis*, m., 3d (akin to Greek λᾶας = *a stone*); nom. sing., a subj. of *circumdatur;* *lapis* is joined by *ve* to *argentum.* —— **circumdatur**, 3d pers. sing. pres. ind. pass. of *circumdō, -āre, circumdedī, circumdatum*, 1 (*circum + dō*); agrees with each of the two subjects *argentum* and *lapis* separately, as is usual when two singular subjects are connected by a disjunctive conjunction. —— **aurō**, abl. sing. of *aurum, -ī*, n., 2d (Greek αὖρον); abl. of the instrument, with *circumdatur.*

LINE 594. **Tum**, adv. of time, not so much marking the actual time when Aeneas spoke as connecting his speech with the preceding events; thus it means little more than *next.* —— **sīc**, adv. of manner, modifying *alloquitur.* —— **rēgīnam**, acc. sing. of *rēgīna, -ae*, f., 1st; direct obj. of *alloquitur.* —— **alloquitur**, 3d pers. sing. pres. ind. of the deponent verb *alloquor, -ī, allocūtus sum*, 3 (*ad + loquor*); agrees with the subj. *Aeneas* understood. Observe that, though *loquor* is intransitive, its compound *alloquitur* is transitive; a direct object may follow intransitive verbs compounded with *ad, ante, ob, trans*, etc. A. & G. 228, *a*; B. 175, 2, *a*; G. 331; 372. —— **cunctīs**, dat. plur. of *cuncti, -ae, -a* (sing. rare); probably dat. of the indirect obj. after *ait*, but perhaps an *ethic* dative, going closely with *improvisus.* —— **que**, enclitic cop. conj. —— **repentē** (from *repēns, -entis, = sudden*), adv., modifying *ait.*

LINE 595. **Improvīsus**, nom. sing. m. of the adj. *improvīsus, -a, -um* (*in, = not, + prōvīsus, = foreseen*, from *prōvideō*); agrees with *ait*, and is an adverbial attribute; *improvisus ait = suddenly says.* —— **ait**, 3d pers. sing. pres. ind. act. of the defective verb *āiō;* agrees with the subj. *Aeneas* or a pronoun understood referring to him; *ait* is joined by *que* above to *alloquitur.* For *āiō*, consult A. & G. 144, *a*; B. 135; G. 175, 1; H. 297; II, 1. —— **Cōram**, adv., strengthening *adsum.* *Coram* is sometimes used as a preposition with the ablative case, = *in the presence of.* —— **quem**, acc. sing. m. of the rel. pron. *qui, quae, quod;* agrees in gender and number with *ego*, the subject contained in the verb *adsum*, and is the direct obj. of *quaeritis* in the rel. clause. —— **quaeritis**, 2d pers. plur. pres. ind. act. of *quaerō, -ere, quaesīvī, quaesītum*, 3; the implied subj. is *vos*, referring to Dido and the Carthaginians. —— **adsum**, 1st pers. sing. pres. ind. of *adsum, adesse, adfuī* or *affuī (ad + sum);* its subj. *ego* is contained in the verb.

596 ádsum Tróïus , Aéne,ás, ,, Liby,cís e,réptus ab ,
I am here Trojan   Aeneas,   Libyan   snatched   from
597 úndis.   Ó   so,la ínfan,dós ,, Tro,iǽ mise,ráta
the waves.   O thou alone unspeakable   of Troy having pitied
598 la,bóres, Quǽ nos, , réliqui,ás   Dana,úm, ,,
the woes,   who   us,   the remnants of (= left by) the Greeks,
599 ter,rǽque ma,rísque Ómnibus , éxhaus,tós ,, iam ,
both of land   and of sea   all   worn out   now

you seek, Aeneas of Troy, snatched from out the Libyan waves. O thou that alone hast pitied Troy's agonies unutterable, who with us, the remnant left by the Greeks, worn out at last by all perils of land and sea,

---

LINE 596. **Trōius**, nom. sing. m. of *Trōius, -a, -um;* agrees with *Aeneas.* —— **Aenēās**, nom. sing. in apposition with *ego* the implied subj. of *adsum.* —— **Libycīs**, abl. plur. f. of *Libycus, -a, -um*, adj. (of nom. *Libya, -ae*, f., 1st); agrees with *undis.* —— **ēreptus**, nom. sing. m. of *ēreptus, -a, -um*, perf. part. pass. of *ēripiō, -ere, ēripuī, ēreptum*, 3 (*ē, = out of, + rapiō, = I snatch*); agrees with and enlarges *Aeneas.* —— **ab**, prep. with the abl.; gov. *undis.* —— **undīs**, abl. plur. of *unda, -ae*, f., 1st; governed by the preposition *ab; ab undis* expresses separation.

LINE 597. **Ō**, exclamation, used with the voc. *tu* understood in address. —— **sōla**, voc. sing. of *sōlus, -a, -um*, adj.; agrees with *tu* understood; *sola* is an adverbial attribute of *miserata.* —— **infandōs**, acc. plur. m. of *infandus, -a, -um*, adj. (*in, = not, + fandus, = must be spoken*); qualifies *labores.* See the note on *infandōs*, l. 525. —— **Trōiae**, gen. sing. of *Trōia*, f. 1st; poss. gen., limiting *labores.* —— **miserāta**, voc. sing. f. of *miserātus, -a, -um*, perf. part. of the deponent verb *miseror, -ārī, -ātus sum*, 1 (*miser = wretched*, hence *to be wretched about* some person or thing, *to pity*) ; agrees with *tu* understood. —— **labōrēs**, acc. sing. of *labor, -ōris*, m., 3d; direct obj. of *miserāta.*

LINE 598. **Quae**, nom. sing. f. of the rel. pron. *quī, quae, quod;* agrees with *tu* (understood) the antecedent, and is subj. of *socias*, l. 600. —— **nōs**, acc. plur. of *nōs* (gen. *nostrum* or *nostrī*, dat. and abl. *nōbīs*) ; direct obj. of *socias.* —— **rēliquiās**, acc. of the plur. nom *rēliquiae, -ārum*, f., 1st (*relinquō = I leave*, hence *the remnant*) ; acc. in apposition with *nōs; reliquias Danaum = eos qui a Danaiis relicti sunt.* —— **Danaum**, gen. plur. of *Danaī, -ōrum*, m., 2d (properly m. of the adj. *Danaus, -a, -um*, = belonging to *Danaus* (the brother of Aegyptus) who settled in Greece, hence *Danaī = the Greeks) ;* subjective gen., limiting *reliquias.* A. & G. 213, 1; B. 199; G. 363, 1; H. 396, II. *Danaūm* is contracted for *Danaōrum; cf. superum*, l. 4, and see note and references. —— **terrae**, gen. sing. of *terra*, f., 1st; subjective poss. gen., limiting *casibus.* The use of the genitive (instead of the abl. of ' place where ' = *on land and sea*) here corresponds to the English of in *perils of the land.* —— **que**, enclitic cop. conj.; *que* is repeated below, and *que . . . que = both . . . and.* —— **maris**, gen. sing. of *mare*, n., 3d; poss. gen., limiting *casibus*, and joined by *que* below to *terrae.* —— **que**, enclitic cop. conj.

LINE 599. **Omnibus**, abl. plur. m. of the adj. *omnis, -e*, 3d; agrees with *casibus.* —— **ēxhaustōs**, acc. plur. m. of *ēxhaustus, -a, -um*, perf. part. pass. of *ēxhauriō, -īre, ēxhausī, ēxhaustum*, 4 (*ēx, = out of, + hauriō, = I drain*) ; agrees with *nos.* There is another reading *ēxhaustis*, the abl. plur. m. of the participle, agreeing with *casibus* in the abl. abs. construction (*all perils having been exhausted*) ; this reading is not as well supported as *exhaustos*, nor is it so graceful. —— **iam**, adv. of time, with *exhaustos*, = *worn out at last.* —— **cāsibus**, abl. plur. of *cāsus, -ūs*, m., 4th (from *cadō, = I fall*, hence *a falling out, an event*) ; abl. of the means or instrument, with *exhaustos.* By derivation *casus* = *chance* or *fortune*, whether good or bad, but it usually stands for *misfortune.* ——

| needful of all things, | cásibus, | , | ómnium | e,génos, | Úrbe | do,mó | 600 |
| sharest thy city, thy | by misfortunes, | of all things | in need, | by city | by home |

| home! not in our | soci,ás, | „ | gra,tés per,sólvere, dígnas Nón | 601 |
| power is it to render | dost unite us (to thee) | thanks | to pay | worthy | not |

| worthy thanks, nor in | opis , ést nos,trae, „ Di,dó, nec , quídquid |
| the power of all that | of power | it is | our, | Dido, | nor (of) | whatsoever |

| yet remain of the Dar- | u,bíque est Géntis , Dárdani,æ, „ mag,núm | 602 |
| danian race that has | anywhere | there is | of the race | Dardanian, | great |

omnium, gen. plur. n. of the adj. *omnis, -e,* 3d; objective gen., dependent on the idea of *emptiness* in *egenos*. Adjectives expressing *fulness, power, knowledge,* etc., and the reverse may take this genitive. A. & G. 218, *a*; B. 204, 1; G. 374; H. 399, I, 3. *Omnium* is here used as a substantive, = *all things*. Professor Conington remarks that nowhere else has Vergil introduced this metrically awkward word into a hexameter.—— **egēnōs**, acc. plur. m. of *egēnus, -a, -um,* adj. (from *egeō,* = *I am in need*); agrees with and enlarges the object *nōs*.

LINE 600. **Urbe**, abl. sing. of *urbs, urbis,* f., 3d; abl. of the means, with *socias;* some prefer to call *urbe* and *domo* ablatives of manner.—— **domō**, abl. sing. of *domus, -ūs,* f., 4th; abl. of the means, like *urbe* above. Observe the rhetorical effect of the *asyndeton*. A. & G. 208, *b*; B. 346; G. 473, REM.; H. 636, I, 1. *Domō* is one of the 2d decl. forms of *domus*. For a full note and references on the declension of *domus,* refer to *domos,* l. 140. —— **sociās**, 2d pers. sing. pres. ind. act. of *sociō, -āre, -āvī, -ātum,* 1 (from *socius, ī-,* m., 2d); agrees with the subj. *quae* above; supply *tibi* or *tecum* (= *dost associate us with thee*). An outline of the sentence is as follows: *O tu . . . , quae nos . . .* (enlargements of *nos*) *. . . urbe domo socias, non opis nostrae est grates dignas persolvere, Dido, nec (opis est) gentis Dardaniae, quidquid ubique est, quae per magnum orbem sparsa (est).* —— **grātēs**, acc. plur. of *grātēs,* f., plur., 3d (only in nom. and acc. plur.; but Tacitus uses the abl. *gratibus*); direct obj. of *persolvere.* —— **persolvere**, pres. inf. act. of *persolvō, -ere, persolvī, persolūtum,* 3 (*per,* = *completely,* + *solvō,* = *I pay*); prolative inf., depending on *opis est* (which is the predicate of the principal sentence). —— **dignās**, acc. plur. f. of *dignus, -a, -um,* adj.; agrees with *grates*.

LINE 601. **Nōn**, negative adv., limiting the predicate *opis est.* —— **opis**, gen. sing. *ops,* f., 3d (nom. and dat. sing. are rare, and the gen. is not as common as the acc. and abl. cases); poss. gen., predicative with the copula *est.* The predicate genitive is often used with an infinitive or substantival clause as subject; it is most common in adjectives, e.g. *viri sapientis est* = *it is* (*the part* or *duty*) *of a wise man to,* etc., which practically = *it is wise to,* etc. A. & G. 214, *d*; B. 198, 3; G. 366, esp. REM. 2; H. 401-403. —— **est**, 3d pers. sing. pres. ind. of *sum, esse, fuī;* the subj. of *opis est* is *persolvere grates.* —— **nostrae**, gen. sing. f. of the poss. adj. *noster, nostra, nostrum;* agrees with *opis.* —— **Dīdō**, voc. sing. of *Dīdō, -ōnis,* or *Dīdūs,* f., 3d; the case of the person addressed. —— **nec**, negative cop. conj., joining *opis est nostrae* and *quidquid est gentis.*—— **quidquid** (*quicquid*), nom. sing. n. of the universal rel. pron. *quisquis* (see *quisquis,* l. 387); agrees with a gen. sing. n. demonstr. pron., e.g. *ēius,* understood, and is subject of *est* in the rel. clause *quidquid . . . Dardaniae; quidquid +* a gen., = *all there is of a thing.* The sentence runs, *it is not in our power nor* (*in the power of*) *all there is of the Dardanian race.* —— **ubīque** (*ubī + que*), adverb of place, indefinite. —— **est**, 3d pers. sing. pres. ind. of *sum;* agrees with *quidquid.*

LINE 602. **Gentis**, gen. sing. of *gens,* f., 3d; partitive gen., representing the whole of which a part *quidquid* is taken, though the conception is not so much partitive as

603 quae , spársa 　per , órbem.　 Dí 　tibi, ˌsí ｜ been scattered
which　was scattered　through the world.　The gods to thee, if ｜ throughout the width of the earth. The

qua　pi,ós ˌˌ res,péctant , númina, , sí 　quid ｜ gods give thee meet reward! if at all the
any　good men　regard　deities,　if anything ｜ deities regard god

---

characteristic. This kind of genitive is frequently used with the nom. and acc. neuter sing. of *quid* and *quod* and their compounds, also after such words as *satis, minus, nihil, multum*, etc. A. & G. 216, 3; B. 201, 2; G. 369; H. 397, 3. The Latin of this sentence may be thus resolved: *non opis est nostrae* (= *nostrum, of us*) *nec* (*gentis Dardaniae*), *quidquid gentis Dardaniae ubique est.*——**Dardaniae,** gen. sing. f. of the adj. *Dardanius, -a, -um* (from *Dardanus*, a son of Jupiter and ancestor of Priam); agrees with *gentis*.——**magnum,** acc. sing. m. of the adj. *magnus, -a, -um;* qualifies *orbem.*——**quae,** nom. sing. f. of the rel. pron. *qui, quae, quod;* agrees with its antecedent *gentis*, and is subj. of *sparsa* (*est*) in the rel. clause.——**sparsa,** nom. sing. f. of *sparsus, -a, -um*, perf. part. pass. of *spargō, -ere, sparsī, sparsum;* agrees with the subj. *quae*, and forms with *est* understood the 3d pers. sing. perf. ind. pass. (combinate tense) of *spargō.*——**per,** prep. with the acc.; gov. *orbem.*——**orbem,** acc. sing. of *orbis, -is*, m., 3d; governed by *per. Orbis* = lit. *a circle*, hence, with *terrarum* expressed or understood, = *circle of lands*, i.e. *the world.* It is quite needless to reject this line on the ground that Aeneas had no knowledge of any other Trojan colonies; Aeneas has in mind the Trojans whom the Greeks took prisoners, as well as those whom he himself had left in Crete and those who were ruled by Acestes in Sicily.

LINE 603. **Dī,** nom. plur. of *deus, -ī*, m., 2d (voc. sing. *deus;* plural irreg., nom. *deī, diī*, or *dī;* gen. *deōrum* or *deūm;* dat. and abl. *deīs, diīs, dīs*); subj. of *ferant*, l. 605 below.——**tibi,** dat. sing. of the 2d personal pron. *tū;* dat. of the indirect obj., after *ferant.*——**sī,** conditional conj., followed by the ind. *respectant.* When a condition is represented logically, without any implication as to possibility, fulfilment, etc., but simply stated in formula, e g. *if this is* (*not*) *so, then that is* (*not*) *so*, the verb in the *protasis* is regularly in the indicative mood, and the verb of *apodosis* is proved to be either a simple indicative, an imperative, or the subjunctive in one of its independent uses. So here *ferant* is an independent subjunctive, viz. the *optative*, and correspondingly the verbs of the *protasis* (*respectant* and *est*) are indicative. A. & G. 306, *a;* B. 302, 4; G. 595; H. 508, 4.——**qua,** nom. plur. n. of the indefinite pron. and adj. *quis, quae, quid;* agrees with *numina. Si qua*, etc., does not by any means imply that Aeneas was in doubt as to whether the gods took heed of virtue in the world; the real meaning is, *just as certainly as the gods*, etc. Nor yet does *qua* make any distinction between the gods, as though some rewarded virtue, while others did not; *qua* is virtually adverbial, and = *if the gods* AT ALL, just as in l. 181, some take *quem* adverbially (*Anthea si quem videat*, = *if he can* ANYWHERE *see Antheus*).——**piōs,** acc. plur. m. of the adj. *pius, -a, -um;* used substantively, direct obj. of *respectant.*——**respectant,** 3d pers. plur. pres. ind. act. of *respectō, -āre, -āvī, -ātum*, 1 (intensive of *respiciō*); agrees with the subj. *numina;* for the in l. mood see note on *si* above.——**nūmina,** nom. sing. of *nūmen, nūminis*, n., 3d (from *nuō*, = *I nod*); subj. of *respectant.* The meanings of *numen* are: (1) *nod;* (2) *command*, indicated by the royal nod; (3) *godhead, divine presence*, as in l. 447, *numine divae;* (4) *a god, a deity*, as in this passage.——**sī,** conditional conj., followed by the ind. *est* in logical formula; see *si* above. The repetition of *si* (*anaphora*) is rhetorical.——**quid,** nom. sing. n. of the indefinite pron. *quis, quae, quid; quid* is complement of *est* in the predicate *quid est; if justice*, etc., *is anything* (i.e. *of any account, held in esteem at all*).

| fearing folk, if any-
where justice and
conscious worth be
of account. What age
so happy gave thee
birth? What parents | Úsquam , iústiti,*a* ést „ et , méns   sibi , cónscia ,
anywhere   *justice*   *is*   *and a mind to itself*   *conscious*
récti, Præmia , dígna   fe,ránt.   „ Quae , té   tam ,
of right, rewards   *worthy*   *may bring.*   *What*   *thee*   *so*
læta   tu,lérunt   Sǽcula ?   , qui   tan,tí „
happy   *brought forth*   *ages?*   *what*   *so great* | 604

605

606 |

LINE 604. **Usquam,** adv. of place. *Usquam* = *anywhere,* like *unquam (ever)* and *quisquam (any one),* is used chiefly in negative sentences, or in quasi-negative sentences, i.e. interrogative or conditions which, apparently introducing a question or hypothesis, do so merely with the purpose of suggesting a negative. —— **iustitia,** gen. *iustitiae,* f., 1st (the quality of the *iustus*); nom. sing., subj. of *est.* Some less reliable MSS. read *iustitiae,* which is a partitive genitive after *quid* (see references on *gentis,* l. 602); *if there is any justice* (lit. *anything of justice) anywhere.* —— **est,** 3d pers. sing. pres. ind. of the copula *sum ;* agrees with the subj. *iustitia ;* the verb is singular though it has two subjects, viz. *iustitia* and *mens,* because the two nouns really represent two aspects of one idea. —— **et,** cop. conj. —— **mēns,** gen. *mentis,* f., 3d; nom. sing , a subject of *est,* joined by *et* to *iustitia.* —— **sibi,** dat. sing. of the reflexive pron. *sē ;* an *ethical* dat., after *conscia recti.* A. & G. 236; B 188, 2, *b* and *c;* G. 351–353; H. 389. It is sometimes difficult to distinguish precisely between some of the uses of a case; thus *sibi,* denoting the *mental* view of the person whose mind is *conscia recti,* may be called an ethic dative, dative of the person judging, or dative of personal interest. —— **conscia,** nom. sing. f. of *conscius, -a, -um* (from *cum* + *sciŏ*); agrees with *mens.* —— **recti,** gen. sing. n. of *rectum,* n., 2d (properly substantival n. of the adj. *rectus, -a, -um,* = *straight, upright.* hence morally = *upright, virtuous*); objective gen., dependent on *conscia.* A. & G. 218, *a;* B. 204, 1; G. 374; H. 399, I, 2 and 3.

LINE 605. **Praemia,** acc. plur. of *praemium, -ĭ,* n., 2d; direct obj. of *ferant.* —— **digna,** acc. plur. n. of *dignus, -a, -um ;* agrees with *praemia.* ——' **ferant,** 3d pers. plur. pres. subjunct. act. of *ferō, ferre, tulī, lātum,* irreg.; agrees with the subj. *di ;* the subjunctive mood is here *optative,* i.e. expresses the wish of Aeneas. The optative subjunctive is frequently introduced by *ut, utinam,* or *ō sī ;* the present tense indicates the futurity of a wish; the imperfect expresses an impossible wish for the present; the pluperfect an impossible and unrealized wish for the past. A. & G. 267; B. 279; G. 260-262; H. 483, 484. —— **quae,** nom. plur. n. of the interrog. adj. *qui, quae, quod ;* agrees with *saecula. Quae tam laeta saecula te tulerunt* (lit. *what ages so happy gave thee life*) = *what ages were so happy as to give thee life.* The question is purely rhetorical, a Vergilian variation for an exclamatory sentence, *O happy ages which,* etc., and similarly in the next line, *O noble parents,* etc. —— **tē,** acc. sing. of *tū ;* direct obj. of *tulerunt.* —— **tam,** adv., used to strengthen adjectives and adverbs; so *tam laeta* here. *Tam* is often used correlatively with *quam, tam (so)* . . . *quam (as).* —— **laeta,** nom. plur. n. of *laetus, -a, -um,* adj.; predicative, agreeing with *saecula.* —— **tulērunt,** 3d pers. plur. perf. ind. act. of *ferō* (see *ferant* above); agrees with the subj. *saecula.*

LINE 606. **Saecula,** nom. plur. of *saeculum, -ī,* n., 2d (sometimes contracted to *saeclum*) *;* subj. of *tulerunt.* —— **qui,** nom. plur. m. of the interrog. adj. *qui, quae, quod ;* agrees with *parentes.* Just as *homines* (mankind) includes men and women, but is masculine in gender, so in *parentes* the masculine predominates over the feminine; hence the masculine *qui.* —— **tanti,** nom. plur. m. of *tantus, -a, -um ;* predicative adj.,

607 ta,lém   genu,ére   pa,réntes?   Ín   freta ,
   such (a daughter)   produced   parents?   Into   the seas
   dúm fluvi,í cur,rént, „dum , móntibus , úmbrae
   while the rivers shall flow,   while on the mountains shadows
608 Lústra,búnt con,véxa, „ po,lús dum , sídera ,
   shall glide over   the hollows,   the sky   while   the stars
609 páscet : Sémper ho,nós no,ménque tu,úm, „
   shall feed :   always   thy honor   and name   thy

so mighty have thee
so good for daughter?
While to the sea the
rivers shall flow, while
on the mountains the
shadows shall move
about the hollows,
while to the stars the
sky shall give pastur-
age, ever thy honor,
thy name and merit

agreeing with *parentes.* —— **tālem,** acc. sing. f. of the adj. *tālis, -e ;* used substantively
or agreeing with *te* understood, the direct obj. of *genuere.* —— **genuēre,** 3d pers. plur.
perf. ind. act. of *gignō, -ere, genuī, genitum,* 3; agrees with the subj. *parentes.* —— **paren-
tes,** nom. plur. of *parēns, -entis,* m. and f., 3d (the plur is here m.); subj. of *genuere.*

     LINE 607. **In,** prep. with the acc. and abl.; gov. the acc. *freta.* —— **freta,** acc. plur.
of *fretum, ī-,* n., 2d; governed by *in.* *Fretum = the sea,* and specially denotes a *strait*
or *narrow sea ; aequor = the sea,* from the notion of a smooth, level surface; *pelagus =
the deep sea ; mare = the sea,* universally. —— **dum,** temporal conj , here followed by the
future simple tense, expressing continued action in future time. *Dum = while,* usually
takes the pres. ind , even in *oratio obliqua,* but may be followed by the perf. or imperf.
ind. in statements of actual fact. *Dum = until,* implying purpose or doubt, is followed
by the subjunctive. Refer to the notes on *dum,* l. 5, and *dum stetit,* l. 268. —— **fluviī,**
nom. plur. of *fluvius, -ī,* m., 2d *(fluō = I flow) ;* subj. of *current.* *Fluvius* is less com-
mon in prose than the kindred neuter noun *flumen.* —— **current,** 3d pers. plur. fut. ind.
act. of *currō, -ere, cucurrī, cursum,* 3; agrees with the subj. *fluvii ;* the fut. tense
expresses continuation of action. —— **dum,** temporal conj.; see above. This speech of
Aeneas is highly ornate and poetical; it abounds in rhetorical devices, e.g. *anaphora,* s:
. . . *si* l. 603, and *dum . . .» dum* in this passage; and also the rhetorical questions, ll
605 and 606. —— **montibus,** dat. plur. of *mons, montis,* m., 3d; dat. of reference, all th:
action of the clause bearing on and described in reference to *montibus.* The dative of
reference takes the place of a possessive genitive which may only limit a single word,
whereas the dative limits the sentence. A. & G. 235, *a;* B. 188, 1; G. 350; H. 384, 1
and 2. —— **umbrae,** nom. plur. of *umbra, -ae,* f., 1st; subj. of *lustrabunt.*

     LINE 608. **Lustrābunt,** 3d pers. plur. fut. ind. act. of *lustrō, -āre, -āvī, -ātum,* 1;
agrees with the subj. *umbrae ;* for tense, see *current* above. —— **convēxa,** acc. plur. of
convēxum, -ī, n., 2d; direct obj. of *lustrabunt.* —— **polus,** gen. *polī,* m., 2d (Greek πόλος);
nom. sing., subj. of *pascet,* in the temporal clause introduced by *dum* following. *Polus
= lit.* the end of an axis, *a pole,* but is used freely in poetry for *the sky,* as here. —— **dum,**
temporal conj. repeated by *anaphora.* A. & G. 344, *f ;* B. 350, 11, *b ;* G. 682, and
636, NOTE 4; H. 636, III, 3. —— **sīdera,** acc. plur. of *sīdus, sīderis,* n., 3d; direct obj.
of *pascet. Sidus = a constellation, a group of stars,* whereas *stella = a single star.* ——
pascet, 3d pers. sing. fut. ind. act. of *pascō, -ere, pāvī, pastum,* 3; agrees with the subj.
polus. Lucretius has *aether sidera pascit,* but presents it as a scientific theory; if Vergil
is imitating here, it is the highly imaginary and poetical comparison that he intends, and
not amateur science.

     LINE 609. **Semper,** adv. of time, extending the predicate *manebunt.* —— **honōr,**
(sometimes *honor*), gen. *honōris,* m., 3d; nom. sing., one of the subjects of *manebunt.*
—— **nōmen,** gen. *nōminis,* n., 3d; nom. sing., one of the subjects of *manebunt,* joined
by *que* to *honos.* —— **que,** enclitic cop. conj. —— **tuum,** nom. sing. n. of the poss. adj.

lau,désque ma,nébunt, Quǽ me , cúmque vo,cánt 610
and praises   will abide,   what   me   soever   call

ter,rǽ." „ Sic , fátus, a,mícum Ílio,néa 611
lands."   *Thus having spoken, his friend   Ilioneus*

pe,tít dex,trá, „ lae,váque Se,réstum ;
he seeks with his right hand, and with the left hand   Serestus ;

Póst ali,ós, for,témque Gy,án, „ for,témque 612
afterwards others, ·   and brave   Gyas   and brave

will abide, whatsoe'er the lands may be that summon me." So saying, with his right hand he greets his friend Ilioneus, with his left Serestus, then the others, brave Gyas and brave Cloanthus.

tuus, -a, -um ; agrees with *nomen.* —— **laudēs,** nom. plur. of *laus, laudis,* f., 3d ; a subject of *manebunt,* joined by *que* enclitic to *nomen.* —— **que,** enclitic cop. conj. —— **manēbunt,** 3d pers. plur. fut. ind. act. of *maneō, -ēre, mansī, mansum,* 2 (Greek μένω) ; agrees with the subjects *honos, nomen,* and *laudes.*

LINE 610. **Quae,** *quaecumque* (*quae me cumque* by *tmesis*), nom. plur. f. of *quicumque, quaecumque, quodcumque,* universal rel. pron. (declined like the rel. *qui,* + the suffix *cumque*) ; agrees with the subj. *terrae.* The adverbial suffix *cumque* may be added to any relative, making it universal, e.g. *quāliscumque,* = *of what kind soever.* A. & G. 105, *a* ; B. 91, 8 ; G. 111, 2 ; H. 187, 3, FOOTNOTE 3. *Tmesis,* i.e. the separation of the parts of a compound word, is comparatively rare in Latin, except in the case of *quicumque, post . . . quam, ante . . . quam, prius . . . quam,* and the like. The figure is common in Greek, and early Latin poets indulged in it freely, e.g. Ennius' well-known example, *saxo cere comminuit brum* (*cerebrum*). A. & G. 385 ; B. 367, 7 ; G. 726 ; H. 636, V, 3. —— **mē,** acc. sing. of *ego ;* direct obj. of *vocant.* —— **cumque,** adverbial suffix ; see *quae* above. —— **vocant,** 3d pers. plur. pres. ind. act. of *vocō, -āre, -āvī, -ātum,* 1 ; agrees with the subj. *terrae.* —— **terrae,** nom. plur. of *terra, -ae,* f., 1st ; subj. of *vocant.* —— **sīc,** adv. of manner, modifying *fatus.* —— **fātus,** nom. sing. m. of *fātus, -a, -um,* perf. part. of the defective deponent verb *fārī,* = *to speak;* agrees with and enlarges the subj. of *petit,* viz. *Aeneas* understood. Refer to the note and references to *fatur,* l. 131. —— **amīcum,** acc. sing. of *amīcus, -ī,* m., 2d ; acc. in apposition with *Ilionea.* A. & G. 184 ; B. 169 ; G. 320*ff* ; H. 359, NOTE 2.

LINE 611. **Īlionēa,** acc. sing. of *Ilioneūs,* gen. *Ilioneī* or contracted *Ilionēī* (Greek Ἰλιονεύς), m. ; direct obj. of *petit.* Refer to the note on *Achilli,* l. 30, and the references there given, for declension. The Greek accusative *Ilionea* (with the long *e*) = Ἰλιονῆα, the accusative in the Ionic dialect ; cf. the old accusative βασιλῆα of βασιλεύς. —— **petit,** 3d pers. sing. pres. ind. act. of *petō, -ere, petīvī* or *petiī, petītum,* 3 ; understand *Aeneas* as subject. —— **dextrā,** abl. sing. of *dextra, -ae,* f., 1st, = *a hand* (supply *manus,* with *dextra,* f. of adj. *dexter, dextra, dextrum,* or sometimes *dexter, -a, -um*) ; abl. of the instrument, with *petit.* —— **laevā,** abl. sing. f. of *laevus, -a, -um,* adj. (*manū* must be supplied, = *with left* (*hand*)) ; abl. of the instrument, with *petit.* —— **que,** enclitic cop. conj. —— **Serestum,** acc. sing. of *Serestus, -ī,* m., 2d ; direct obj. of *petit,* joined by *que* to *Ilionea.* Serestus is not known, except as being one of the followers of Aeneas.

LINE 612. **Post** (= *posteā*), adv., modifying *petit* understood as governing *alios* (i.e. understood from *petit* in the preceding line). *Post* is often a prep. with the acc., = *after.* —— **aliōs,** acc. plur. m. of *alius, -a, -ud* (gen. *alīus,* dat. *aliī*) ; substantival (and including *Gyan* and *Cloanthum*), direct obj. of *petit* understood from the preceding clause. —— **fortem,** acc. sing. m. of the adj. *fortis, -e,* 3d ; qualifies *Gyan.* —— **que,** enclitic cop. conj., joining *Gyan* and *alios ; que* is here explanatory, introducing *Gyan* and *Cloanthus* as most important of the *alios* mentioned. —— **Gyan,** Greek acc. sing.

613 Clo,ánthum.   Óbstupu,ít   pri,mo   áspec,tú ,,| Sidonian Dido stood
   Cloanthus.   *Was amazed*   *first*   *at the aspect* | amazed first at the
614 Si,dónia , Dído,   Cásu , deínde vi,rí   tan,to ; ,, | sight of the hero,then
   Sidonian   *Dido*   *at the lot* *then* *of the hero* *so great;* | at his exceeding
615 ét   sic , óre   lo,cúta est: "Quís te, , náte | troubles, and with her lips she spake:
   and thus with her mouth *she spoke:*   *"What thee, O born* | "What destiny, god-

---

of *Gyas*, -*ae*, m., 1st decl. Greek noun; a direct obj. of *petit* understood. —— **fortem**, acc. sing. m. of *fortis;* qualifies *Cloanthum.* —— **que**, enclitic cop. conj. —— **Cloanthum**, acc. sing. of *Cloanthus, -ī*, m., 2d; a direct obj. of *petit* understood, joined by *que* (*fortemque* immediately above) to *Gyan.* In l. 222, mention was made of *fortemque Gyan fortemque Cloanthum*, whence it appears that they are referred to together by Vergil and with the same fixed epithets *fortem*.

LINE 613. **Obstupuit**, 3d pers. sing. perf. ind. act. of *obstupescō, -ere, obstupuī*, no supine, 3 (*ob* + *stupescō*); agrees with the subj. *Dīdō.* —— **prīmō**, abl. sing. m. of *primus, -a, -um;* agrees with *aspectu*, but must be rendered as an adverb. Some prefer to take *prīmō* as an adverb, = *firstly*, but it is better to regard it as an adjective used adverbially, for it thus not merely means *firstly*, but expresses the surprise of Dido when Aeneas, glorified in beauty by Venus, *suddenly* appeared before the queen's eyes. —— **aspectū**, abl. sing. of *aspectus, -ūs*, m., 4th (akin to *aspiciō*) ; abl. of cause, with *obstupuit*. A. & G. 245; B. 219; G. 408; H. 416. —— **Sīdōnia**, nom. sing. f. of *Sīdōnius, -a, -um*, adj. (pertaining to *Sīdon, Sīdōnis*, f., 3d, = *Sidon*, the mother-city of Tyre); agrees with *Dido.* Dido really came from Tyre, but the adj. *Sidonius* is a poetic variation for *Tyrius*, etc., just as *Dardanius* is for *Troius, Troicus*, etc. —— **Dīdō**, gen. *Dīdōnis* or *Dīdūs*, f., 3d; nom. sing., subj. of *obstupuit*.

LINE 614. **Cāsū**, abl. sing. of *cāsus, -ūs*, m., 4th (*cadō*, = *I fall*, hence *a happening*, or in bad sense *a misfortune*) ; abl. of cause with *obstupuit*, joined by *deinde* to *aspectu*. —— **deīnde** (*dē*, = *from*, + *inde*, = *thence ;* cf. *dehinc*, = *from hence*), adv., used connectively to mark the order of emotions. *Dĕinde* is usually a word of three syllables, but, by *synizesis*, it is made a dissyllable, the first two vowels being contracted into a diphthong. A. & G. 347, *c*; B. 367, 1; G. 727; H. 608, III. —— **virī**, gen. sing. of *vir*, m., 2d; poss. gen., limiting *casu.* —— **tantō**, abl. sing. m. of the demonstra. adj. *tantus, -a, -um ;* agrees with *casu.* As the pause in the sentence follows *tanto*, so has the *caesura* been marked, though the final syllable of *tanto* is *elided* before *et ;* there is a strong *caesura* after *vīri* as well. —— **et**, cop. conj. —— **sīc**, adv. of manner, modifying *locuta est* and referring to the speech that follows. —— **ōre**, abl. sing. of *ōs, ōris*, n., 3d; abl. of the instrument, with *locūta est. Ore locutus* (*locuta*) *est* is a common formula preceding speeches in the Aeneid; strictly *ore* is superfluous, but Vergil uses the formula in imitation of the Homeric "spake winged words" and the like. The use of unnecessary words is called *pleonasm.* A. & G. 385 ; B. 374, 3; G. 692; H. 636, III. —— **locūta est**, 3d pers. sing. perf. ind. of the deponent verb *loquor, -ī, locūtus sum*, 3 (combinate tense); agrees with the subj. *Dido.*

LINE 615. **Quis**, nom. sing. m. of the interrog. pron. (here used adjectively) *quis, quae, quid;* agrees with *casus.* —— *Quis* is seldom used adjectively, the interrogative adjective *quī, quae, quod* (declined like the relative) being regular. —— **tē**, acc. sing. of *tū ;* direct obj. of *insequitur.* —— **nāte**, voc. sing. of *nātus, -a -um*, perf. part. of the deponent verb *nascor, -ī, nātus sum*, 3; used substantively, the case of address; *nate dea* is a frequent mode of addressing Aeneas. For the substantival use of participles, refer to

dess-born, p u r s u e s	de,á, „ per , tánta pe,rícula cásus
thee through perils so	*of a goddess, through such great dangers misfortune*
great? what violence	Ínsequi,túr? „ quae , vís im,mánibus , ápplicat, 61
brings thee to our	*pursues? what violence savage drives (thee)*
savage shores? Art	óris? Túne il,le Aéne,ás, „ quem , 617
thou that A e n e a s	*on the coasts? (Art) thou that Aeneas, whom*

the note on *nate*, l. 582.——**deā**, abl. sing. of *dea*, *-ae*, f., 1st; abl. of separation, dependent on the participle *nate*. For this ablative, refer to the note on *dea*, l. 582.——**per,** prep. with the acc.; gov. *pericula.*——**tanta,** acc. plur. n. of *tantus, -a, -um ;* agrees with *pericula.*——**perīcula,** acc. plur. of *perīculum, -ī,* n., 2d (from the obsolete verb *perior, = I try ;* cf. *ex-perior) ;* governed by the preposition *per.*——**cāsus,** gen. *cāsūs,* m., 4th (see *cāsū,* l. 614); nom. sing., subj. of *insequitur.*

LINE 616. **Insequitur,** 3d pers. sing. pres. ind. of the deponent verb *insequor, -ī, insecūtus sum,* 3 (*in, = close upon,* suggesting persistency, + *sequor, = I follow ;* cf. *in-sto, = I press upon) ;* agrees with the subj. *casus.*——**quae,** nom. sing. f. of the interrog. adj. *qui, quae, quod* (or perhaps of *quis, quae, quid,* the pron. used adjectively, see *quis* in the previous line); agrees with *vis.*——**vīs,** acc. *vim,* abl. *vī,* f., 3d (gen. *vīs,* and dat. *vī,* very rare; the sing. = *violence,* but the plur. *vīrēs, -ium, = strength) ;* nom. sing., subj. of *applicat.*——**immānibus,** dat. plur. f. of the 3d decl. adj. *immānis, -e ;* qualifies *oris.* *Immanibus* (*terrible, savage*) refers to the perilous coast and especially, by *enallage,* to the savage character of the inhabitants. A. & G. 385; B. no reference; G. 693; H. 636, IV. *Immanis* is variously derived: (1) *in, = not,* + Sanskrit root *mā, = to measure ;* hence *huge ;* (2) more probably, from *in, = not,* + an obsolete adj. *mānis, = good ;* cf. *Manes, = the Good,* a name given by euphemism to the spirits of the dead. ——**applicat** (*adplicat*), 3d pers. sing. pres. ind. act. of *applico* (*adplicō*), *-āre, -āvī* or *-uī, -ātum* or *-itum,* 1 (*ad, = upon,* + *plicō, = I fold,* hence *I force to) ;* agrees with the subj. *vis.*—— **ōrīs,** dat. plur. of *ōra, -ae,* f., 1st; dat. of the indirect obj., after *applicat,* a compound of *ad.* A. & G. 228; B. 187, III; G. 347; H. 386.

LINE 617. **Tūne** (*tū* + *ne*), *tū* is the nom. sing. of the 2d personal pron., subj. of *es* understood. The nom. case of the personal pronouns is rarely used, except for emphasis or contrast; here *tu* is very emphatic, = *art thou really,* etc.? *ne* is an enclitic interrog. particle, introducing a question and appended to the emphatic word, *tu. Ne* simply asks for information; *nonne* introduces questions expecting an affirmative answer ; *num* introduces questions where the answer is expected to be negative. A. & G. 210, *a–d ;* B. 162, 2, *c ;* G. 454; H. 351, 1 and 2. —— **ille,** nom. sing. m. of the demonstr. pron. and adj. *ille, -a, -ud ;* agrees with and emphasizes *Aeneas, = that famous Aeneas.* —— **Aenēās,** nom. sing.; complement of *es* understood in the predicate. —— **quem,** acc. sing. m. of the rel. pron. *quī ;* agrees with *Aeneas* the antecedent, and is direct obj. of *genuit.* —— **Dardaniō,** dat. sing. m. of the adj. *Dardanius, -a, -um ;* agrees with *Anchisae.* Observe that the final syllable *o* is not *elided,* though the next word *Anchisae* begins with a vowel; this is due to the *ictus* upon the final *o,* and partly also to the fact that the word refers to a proper name. For *hiatus* (i.e. non-elision), consult A. & G. 359, *e ;* B. 366, 7, *a ;* G. 720, and 784, NOTE 6; H. 608, II. It is also noteworthy that the fifth foot, which in hexameter verse is almost always a *dactyl,* is here *spondaic, Dardani*o A*nchisae.* In Homer, *hiatus* and *spondaic* lines are common, and possibly Vergil is imitating: cf. Aen. III, 74, *Neptunō Aegaeo* for *hiatus* and *spondaic* 5th foot. Many of the Vergilian instances are connected with proper names, in the form of proper nouns or adjectives derived from proper nouns. A. & G. 362, *a ;* B. 368, 2; G. 784, NOTE 11; H. 610, 3.

618 Dárdani,ó An,chísae **Álma** Ve,nús Phrygi,í „
　　Dardanian　　*to Anchises*　*kindly*　*Venus*　　*Phrygian*

619 genu,ít Simo,éntis ad , úndam ? **Át**que equi,dém
　　bare　　　*of Simois*　*at*　*the flood?*　*And*　　*indeed*

620 Teu,crúm „ memi,ní Si,dóna ve,níre, Fínibus ,
　　Teucer　　　　*I remember*　*to Sidon*　*to come,*　*from his land*

whom kindly Venus bore to Dardanian Anchises beside the wave of Phrygian Simois ? And truly I remember the coming of Teucer to Sidon, exiled from his fath-

---

—— **Anchīsae**, dat. sing. of *Anchīsēs, -ae*, m., 1st decl. Greek noun; dat. of the indirect object after *genuit*. Anchises was the son of Capys, and the father of Aeneas. When Troy was taken, Aeneas rescued him and brought him safely to Sicily, where he died. He was buried on Mount Eryx, by Aeneas and Acestes. The fifth book of the Aeneid describes the games given in honor of Anchises' funeral, when Aeneas revisited Sicily.

LINE 618. **Alma**, nom. sing. f. of the adj. *almus, -a, -um* (from *alō, = I nourish*) ; qualifies *Venus;* this adj., regularly applied to Venus, is particularly suitable to Venus in her character of Aeneas' mother. —— **Venus**, gen. *Veneris*, f., 3d; nom. sing., subj. of *genuit.* —— **Phrygiī**, gen. sing. m. of *Phrygius, -a, -um ;* agrees with *Simoëntis.* —— **genuit**, 3d pers. sing. perf. ind. act. of *gignō, -ere, genuī, genitum*, 3; agrees with the subj. *Venus.* —— **Simoëntis**, gen. sing. of *Simoīs*, m., 3d (Greek Σιμόεις); poss. gen., limiting *undam ;* refer to the note on *Simoīs*, l. 100. —— **ad**, prep. with the acc.; gov. *undam, = at the flood.* A. & G. 153; B. 182, 3; G. 416, 1; H. 433, I. —— **undam**, acc. sing. of *unda, -ae*, f., 1st; governed by the preposition *ad.*

LINE 619. **Atque**, cop. conj., here as usually introducing emphatically a new idea. —— **equidem**, adverb. This word is not derived from *ego* and *quidem*, although it is almost always used when the subject is the first personal pronoun. It is really a compound of the *e* or *ec* demonstrative, and *quidem*. —— **Teucrum**, acc. sing. of *Teucer, Teucrī*, m., 2d; subj.-acc. of *venire* in the indirect discourse introduced by *memini*. Teucer was a son of Telamon, and so a brother of the elder Ajax. Ajax committed suicide because the arms of Achilles were not awarded to him, and when Teucer returned from Troy his father Telamon banished him because he had not avenged his brother's death. Teucer then sailed for Cyprus, where, with the assistance of Belus, king of Sidon, he founded a city, which he called Salamis, after his native city. Cf. Horace, Odes, I, vii, 29, *ambiguam tellure nova Salamina.* —— **meminī**, 1st pers. sing. perf. ind. act. of *memini* (no present stem); the contained subj. is *ego*. For the conjugation of *memini*, consult A. & G. 143, *c*; B. 133; G. 175, 5, *b*; H. 297, I. —— **Sīdōna**, Greek acc. sing. of *Sīdōn, -is*, f., 3d; acc. of the end of motion, with no preposition, e.g. *ad* or *in*, because *Sidona* is the name of a town. A. & G. 258, *b*; B. 182, 1, *a*; G. 337; H. 380, II. Sidon was an ancient city of Phoenicia, and the mother-city of Tyre; it was the native place of Dido, whose father Belus ruled there as king. —— **venīre**, pres. ind. act. of *veniō, -īre, vēnī, ventum*, 4; agrees with the subj.-acc. *Teucrum* in the acc. and inf. construction following *memini*. The present infinitive (instead of the perfect) is regularly used with reference to the past when the person relating recollections was witness of the events recorded. This infinitive is sometimes called the *imperfect infinitive*, because in direct discourse its place would be filled by the descriptive imperfect indicative. A. & G. 336, A, NOTE 1; B. no reference; G. 281, 2, NOTE; H. 537, I. This infinitive is used only when the recollections are personal; otherwise the perfect infinitive is employed, as it sometimes is even when the present is admissible.

LINE 620. **Fīnibus**, abl. plur. of *fīnes, -ium*, m., 3d, = *borders, territory* (sing. *finis*, = *end*); abl. of separation, after *expulsum.* A. & G. 243; B. 214; G. 390, 1 and 2,

er's borders, seeking a new realm with Belus' aid; Belus my father was then laying waste wealthy Cyprus and held it as con- queror beneath his sway. From that time forward the Trojan	éxpul,súm　　　　patri,is, „ nova　régna pe,téntem *have been driven out*　*native,*　　*new*　　*realms*　　　*seeking*

Aúxili,ó　Be,lí : „ geni,tór tum , Bélus o,pímam 621
by the aid　*of Belus :*　*my sire*　*then*　　*Belus*　　*wealthy*

Vásta,bát　Cy,prum, „ ét　vic,tór　diti,óne 622
was laying waste　*Cyprus,*　　*and (as) conqueror*　*with sway*

te,nébat :　Témpore , iam éx il,ló „ ca,sús 623
was holding :　　*time*　　*now from*　*that*　*the fortune*

NOTE 3; H. 414, I. —— **expulsum**, acc. sing. m. of *expulsus, -a, -um*, perf. part. pass. of *expellō, -ere, expulī, expulsum*, 3 (*ex*, = *out*, + *pellō*, = *I drive*); agrees with and enlarges the object *Teucrum*. —— **patriis**, abl. plur. m. of *patrius, -a, -um* (from *pater*, gen. *patris*, m., 3d, hence *native*); agrees with *finibus*. —— **nova**, acc. plur. n. of *novus, -a, -um*, adj.; agrees with *regna ; nova* refers to the *new* settlement of Salamis in Cyprus. —— **regna**, acc. plur. of *regnum, -ī*, n., 2d; direct obj. of *petentem*. —— **petentem**, acc. sing. m. of *petēns, -entis*, prcs. part. act. of *petō, -ere, petīvī* or *petiī, petītum*, 3; agrees with and enlarges the object *Teucrum ;* observe there is no conjunction connecting the two participial enlargements, *expulsum* and *petentem*.

LINE 621. **Auxiliō**, abl. sing. of *auxilium, -ī*, n., 2d; abl. of manner, amplifying *petentem*. In poetry the abl. of manner is frequently found without the preposition *cum* which is required in prose composition; see note on *imperio*, l. 54. *Auxilio* refers to the armed assistance which Belus gave Teucer, when the inhabitants of Cyprus opposed the building of Cyprus. Belus had conquered but not yet pacified Cyprus at the time of Teucer's arrival. —— **Bēlī**, gen. sing. of *Bēlus*, m., 2d; subjective gen., limiting *auxilio*, i.e. *the assistance given by Belus*, not *to Belus* (which would be objective genitive). The name Belus (cf. the Scriptural Baal) is of Semitic origin. Belus was the father of Dido and Pygmalion. —— **genitor**, gen. *genitōris*, m., 3d (from *genō*, old form of *gignō ;* cf. *genitrix*, l. 590); nom. sing., in apposition with *Belus*. —— **tum**, adv. of time, extending *vastabat*. —— **opimam**, acc. sing. f. of *opimus, -a, -um*, adj. (= possessing *opes*, i.e. *wealthy*); qualifies *Cyprum ; opimam* refers to the fertility and general prosperity of the island.

LINE 622. **Vastābat**, 3d pers. sing. imperf. ind. act. of *vastō, -āre, -āvī, -ātum*, 1 (from *vastus*, = *waste, desolate*, hence *I lay waste*); agrees with the subj. *Belus*. —— **Cȳprum**, acc. sing. of *Cȳprus, -ī*, f., 2d (Greek Κύπρος); direct obj. of *vastabat*. Cyprus is a large island in the eastern Mediterranean, south of Cilicia; it was celebrated for its prosperity and its worship of Venus (called Cypris), who had two large temples in it. —— **et**, cop. conj., connecting the two equally important ideas, *vastabat* and *tenebat*. —— **victor**, gen. *victōris*, m., 3d (from *vincō*, through the root *vic*); nom. sing., in apposition with the subj. of *tenebat*, viz. *Belus*, or a pronoun referring to Belus, understood. —— **ditiōne** (*diciōne*), abl. sing. of *ditio* (*dicio*), *-onis*, f., 3d; abl. of the means, or perhaps abl. of manner, with *tenebat*. —— **tenēbat**, 3d pers. sing. imperf. ind. act. of *teneō, -ēre, -uī, tentum*, 2; joined by *et* to *vastabat ;* understand as subj. *Belus* or a pronoun referring to him.

LINE 623. **Tempore**, abl. sing. of *tempus, temporis*, n., 3d.; abl. of separation, governed by *ex*. —— **iam**, adverb of time; *iam ex illo tempore*, = *now from that time* is more specific than *iam pridem*, = *for a long time since*. —— **ēx**, prep. with the abl.; gov. *tempore*, denoting separation in time. The preposition *ēx* (*ē* or *ēx* before conso-nants, and *ēx* before vowels or words whose initial letter is *h*) is used to express separa-

624 mihi , cógnitus , úrbis Tróia,næ, no,ménque | city's fate has been
to me   (is) known   of the city Trojan,   and name | known to me, thy
625 tu,úm, „ re,gésque Pe,lásgi.   **Ípse** hos,tís | name too, and the
thy   and the kings Pelasgian.   He himself   a foe | Pelasgian kings.
Their very foe would

---

tion in time or place, source, origin, cause, etc. A. & G. 152; B. 142, 2; G. 417;
II. 434. —— **illō,** abl. sing. n. of the demonstr. adj. *ille, illa, illud;* agrees with *tempore; ex illo tempore* refers to Teucer's arrival at Sidon (l. 619). —— **cāsus,** gen. *cāsūs,*
m., 4th; nom. sing., subj. of *cognitus (est).* Out of consideration for Aeneas, Dido
applies the general word *casus,* = *fate* to the destruction of Troy. —— **mihi,** dat sing. of
ego; dat. of the agent, after the perfect passive *cognitus (est).* The dative of the agent
is common in poetry after perfect passive participles and the perfect passive tense. It is
usually explained as a possessive dative, owing to the presence of *sum;* e.g. *est mihi,*
= *(there is to me) I have,* and so *est mihi cognitus (there is to me known),* = *I have
known.* However, this dative is used with present and other tenses which do not admit
of such an explanation, e.g. l. 440, *neque cernitur ulli,* when some commentators regard
it as a poetic dative of the agent, while others prefer to elaborate and call it a dative of
personal interest. A. & G. 232; B. 189; G. 354; H. 388, 1. —— **cognitus,** nom. sing.
m. of the perf. part. pass. of *cognoscō, -ere, cognōvī, cognitum,* 3 (*co* = *cum,* augmentative, + *noscō,* hence *I know thoroughly*); agrees with the subj. *casus;* understand *est*
with *cognitus,* = the 3d pers. sing. perf. ind. passive. The subject of *cognitus est* is really
composite, viz. *casus, nomen,* and *reges;* but, as often, the verb is singular, agreeing only
with the nearest. A. & G. 205, *d;* B. 255, 2 and 3; G. 285, EXCEPTION 1; H. 463, I.
—— **urbis,** gen. sing. of *urbs,* f., 3d; poss. gen., limiting *casus.*
    LINE 624. **Trōiānae,** gen. sing. f. of the adj. *Trōiānus, -a, -um;* agrees with *urbis.*
—— **nōmen,** nom. sing. of *nōmen, -inis,* n., 3d; joined by *que* to *casus;* understand *cognitum est* as predicate. —— **que,** enclitic cop. conj. —— **tuum,** nom. sing. n. of the poss.
adj. *tuus, -a, -um;* agrees with *nomēn.* —— **rēgēs,** nom. sing. of *rēx, rēgis,* m., 3d; nom.
plur., subj. of *cogniti sunt* understood (from *cognitus* above); *reges* is joined by *que* below
to *nomen.* *Reges,* = *chiefs* or *kings,* especially Menelaus and Agamemnon, who were at
the head of the Greek host. There were, however, many *reges* among the Greeks, for
Homer represents as a *king* every leader of a company of men from some city in Greece.
—— **que,** enclitic cop. conj. —— **Pelasgī** (Greek Πελασγοί), nom. plur. m. of the adj.
Pelasgus, -a, -um (pertaining to the *Pelasgī, -ōrum,* m., 2d); agrees with *reges; Pelasgi*
is here equivalent to *Graeci.* The Hellenes are sometimes called *Pelasgi* in poetry, and
Greece itself *Pelasgia.* Herodotus is our chief source of information about the Pelasgians; from him it would appear that the Pelasgians were the earliest inhabitants of
Greece, who were dispersed when the Hellenes made their way from Thessaly to the
Peloponnesus and Greece proper; their language differed from the Greek. There were
very few survivals of this race in historic times, except two cities in the Chersonese, and
Argos, which is often called *Pelasgic.*
    LINE 625. **Ipse,** nom. sing. m.; agrees with and intensifies *hostis. Ipse* is by position
in the sentence and agreement with *hostis,* very emphatic. —— **hostis,** gen. *hostis,* m. and
f., 3d (lit. *the eating one,* hence (1) *stranger;* (2) *enemy;* cf. Greek ξένος, = (1) *guest,*
(2) *stranger, foreigner*); nom. sing., subj. of *ferebat.* Synonyms: *hostis,* = *a public
enemy,* i.e. the enemy of a country or state; *inimīcus,* = *a private enemy,* i.e. the enemy
of an individual. —— **Teucrōs,** acc. plur. of *Teucrī, -ōrum,* m., 2d; direct obj. of *ferebat;*
the *paronomasia* or play on the words *Teucer,* the Greek, and *Teucri,* the Trojans, is
intentional, as the next line shows. *Teucrī* is properly the m. plural of the adj. *Teucrus,
-a, -um* (collateral form *Teucrius, -a, -um,* cf. *Teucria,* f., 1st, = *Troy*); the a 'jective

with special praise ex-
tol the Teucrians, and
professed himself a
scion of the Teucri-
ans' ancient stock.
So come ye, sirs, enter
beneath our dwelling.

Teu, crós „ in, sígni , laúde   fe, rébat,   Séque 626
the Teucrians   special   with praise used to extol,   and himself

or, *tum* ánti, quá „ Teu, crórum ab , stírpe
risen   ancient   of the Teucrians from   the stock

vo, lébat.   Quáre agi, te, ó tec, tís, „ iuve, nés, 627
used to profess.   Wherefore come ye, o under roofs,   youths,

---

= *belonging to Teucer* (*Teucer, -crī*, m., 2d, or in Vergil *Teucrus, -ī*, m., 2d, cf. Greek Τεῦκρος), i.e. the Teucer who was the first king of Troy. —— **insignī**, abl. sing. f. of the 3d decl. adj. *insignis, -e* (*in*, = *on*, + *signum*, = *a mark*, hence *marked, distinguished*); agrees with *laude*. —— **laude**, abl. sing. of *laus, laudis*, f., 3d; abl. of manner, with *fere-bat;* the noun is modified by the adj. *insigni*, and therefore *cum* may be properly omitted. —— **ferēbat**, 3d pers. sing. imperf. ind. act. of *ferō, ferre, tulī, lātum*, irreg.; agrees with the subj. *hostis; ferebat*, = *used to speak about*, cf. *ferunt*, = *they say*. This meaning of *ferō* is derived from the notion of *carrying news*, hence *reporting*, hence *speaking of* some one or something.

LINE 626. **Sē**, acc. sing. of the reflexive pron. *sē*, gen *suī* (no nom.); subj.-acc. of the inf. *ortum* (*esse*), after *volebat*. The acc. and inf. construction is often used with verbs of *wishing*, especially when the subject of the infinitive is the same as the subject of the verb of wishing; however, the subjunctive is frequently used. In this passage, *volebat* does not mean *wished* so much as *boasted*, i.e. it is a kind of *verbum declarandi*, implying that Teucer *spoke in boast;* consequently the acc. and inf. construction is virtually indirect discourse. —— **que**, enclitic cop. conj. —— **ortum**, acc. sing. m. of *ortus, -a, -um*, perf. part. of the deponent verb *orior, -īrī, ortus sum*, 4; supply *esse* with *ortum*, = the perf. inf., in agreement with the subj.-acc. *se*. Teucer, the son of Telamon, traced his descent on the mother's side to Teucer, king of Troy; having been banished from Greece by Telamon, he does not pride himself on his Grecian lineage on the father's side. Telamon married Hesione, the daughter of Laomedon (Priam's father), and so his Trojan relationship extended back to Dardanus, who had married a daughter of Teucer. —— **antīquā**, abl. sing. f. of *antīquus, -a, -um;* agrees with *stirpe*. —— **Teucrōrum**, gen. plur. of *Teucrī*, m., 2d; poss. gen., limiting *stirpe*. —— **ab**, prep. with the abl. (*a* or *ab* before consonants, *ab* before vowels or *h*) ; gov. *stirpe*, denoting origin. —— **stirpe**, abl. sing. of *stirps, stirpis*, f., 3d only m. when Vergil speaks of trees or plants); governed by *ab*. —— **volēbat**, 3d pers. sing. imperf. ind. act. of *volō, velle, voluī*, no supine, irreg.; agrees with *hostis*, the subj. of *ferebat*, to which *volebat* is joined by *que*. Clearly, as Teucer *was* descended from the Trojan royal line, he cannot be said to *wish* that he was so descended; *volebat*, = *boasted*, and corresponds to the Homeric εὔχεσθαι εἶναι. *Volo* in this sense is a virtual *verbum declarandi*, and is followed by the acc. and inf. (*se ortum esse*) ; some think that *haberi* should be supplied, = *wished* (*would have*) *it believed that*, etc. For the ordinary construction of *volo*, consult A. & G. 331, *b*; B. 331, IV; G. 532; H. 498, I, and 535, II. For conjugation, A. & G. 138; B. 130; G. 174; H. 293.

LINE 627. **Quāre** (= *quā rē*), rel. adverb, originally the abl. of *rēs*, with the abl. f. of the rel. pron. *quī* in agreement; it is here connective, referring to the reasons for friend-ship enumerated. —— **agite**, 2d pers. plur. imperative mood act. of *agō, -ere, ēgī, actum*, 3; the subj. is *vos*, contained in the personal ending. An important imperative is often colloquially strengthened by the imperative *age* or *agite* preceding it immediately, often as in this passage without any conjunction to connect the two together, cf. colloquial English, *come, tell me*, and the like. —— **ō**, exclamation, with the voc. *iuvenes; o* is separated from *iuvenes* by the important word *tectis*, because Dido is in haste to assure

628 suc,cédite , nóstris. Mé quoque , pér mul,tós ,, | Me too, storm-tossed
approach ye *our.* *Me* *also* *through* *many* | through many woes,
629 simi,lís for,túna la,bóres Iácta,tam hác de,múm | a like fortune hath
similar *a fortune* *toils* *tossed* *this* *at length* | willed at length to
630 volu,ít ,, con,sístere , térra. Nón ig,nára ma,lí ,, | settle in this land.
has willed *to settle* *on land.* *Not* *ignorant* *of evil* | Not ignorant of ill do

the Trojans of *shelter* and protection. —— tectīs, dat. plur. of *tectum, -ī*, n. (from *tegō*, =
I cover); dat. of the indirect obj. after *succedite*, which as a compound of *sub* may take
this case; see the note on *oris*, l. 377. —— iuvenēs, voc. plur. of *iuvenis, -is*, m. or f.,
3d; the case of address. *Iuvenis*, = *a young man*, includes persons beyond what we call
youth; it probably applied to any age varying from 25 to 45 years of age, after which
last a man would be described as *senex*. For age gradations in Latin names, refer to the
note on *puer*, l. 267. —— succēdite, 2d pers. plur. imperative mood act. of *succēdō, -ere*,
successī, successum, 3 (*sub*, = *under*, + *cēdō*, = *I go*); understand the subj. vos. *Succedo*
governs the dative, and is used in two different senses: (1) *I go under*, e.g. a roof, as
here; (2) *I go up to*, i.e. *approach*. —— nostrīs, dat. plur. n. of the poss. adj. *noster,
nostra, nostrum;* agrees with *tectis*.

LINE 628. Mē, acc. sing. of *ego;* subj.-acc. of the inf. *consistere*, after the verb of
wishing, voluit. For the construction, refer to the notes on *se* and *volebat*, l. 626. ——
quoque, adv. and conj.; *quoque* is not quite so strong in force as *etiam ;* quoque never is
the first word in a sentence, but follows the important word, being usually second, or
even third if the second word is emphatic. A. & G. 151, *a*, and 345, *b*; B. 347, 1;
G. 479; H. 554, I, 4. —— per, prep. with the acc.; gov. *labores; per labores iactatam*,
= lit. *tossed through troubles*, i.e. (*driven*) *storm-tossed through many troubles*. ——
multōs, acc. plur. m. of *multus, -a, -um;* agrees with *labores*. —— similis, nom. sing.
f. of *similis, -e*, adj., 3d; agrees with *fortuna*. —— fortūna, gen. *fortūnae*, f., 1st (akin
to *fors*); subj. of *voluit*. —— labor, *-ōris*, m., 3d; governed by *per*.

LINE 629. Iactātam, acc. sing. f. of *iactātus, -a, -um*, perf. part. pass. of *iactō, -āre*,
-āvī, -ātum, 1 (frequentative of *iaciō*); agrees with and enlarges the subj.-acc. *me*. ——
hāc, abl. sing. f. of *hīc, haec, hōc ;* agrees with *terrā*. —— dēmum, adv. of time, modify-
ing *consistere*. *Demum* is said to be a lengthened form of the demonstrative *dem* in
īdem, tandem, etc., and related to the Greek particle δή. It is used: (1) to emphasize
or restrict, e.g. *id demum*, = *precisely that;* (2) often in conjunction with other adverbs,
e.g. *nunc demum*, = *now at last, tum demum*, = *then at length;* (3) in Suetonius, =
only, solely; (4) in late writers, e.g. Suetonius, = *at last;* (5) in Tacitus, sometimes =
finally, in short. —— voluit, 3d pers. sing. perf. ind. act. of *volō, velle, voluī*, irreg.;
agrees with the subj. *fortuna*. —— consistere, pres. inf. act. of *consistō, -ere, constitī,
constitum*, 3 (*con* = *cum* + *sistō*); complementary inf. agreeing with the subj.-acc. *me*,
after *voluit;* see note on *me*, l. 628. —— terrā, abl. sing. of *terra, -ae*, f., 1st; abl. of
'the place where,' with *consistere*.

LINE 630. Nōn, negative adv., negativing *ignara; non ignara*, = lit. *not ignorant*,
which is an understatement for *well acquainted*. The figure of understatement is called
litotes or *meiosis;* its most common form is when two negative words are used, as here,
one negativing the other, so as to make an emphatic affirmation. This is very common
in Greek, and indeed in most languages. A. & G. 386, and 209, *c*; B. 375, 1; G. 700;
H. 637, VIII. —— ignāra, nom. sing. f. of the adj. *ignārus, -a, -um* (*in*, = *not*, + *gnarus*,
= *knowing*); agrees with *ego* understood as subj. of *disco*. —— malī, gen. sing. of
malum, n., 2d (properly n. of the adj. *malus, -a, -um*); objective gen., governed by

I learn to help those in trouble." Thus she speaks, and with the words leads Aeneas within the royal palace and appoints a sacrifice for the gods' temples. Nor is she slow the while to send	mise, rís *to the wretched*	suc, cúrrere *to give help*	dísco." Síc 631 *I am learning."* Thus
	memo, rát : „ simul , *she speaks :* *at the same time*	Aéne, án in , *Aeneas* *into*	régia , dúcit *royal she leads*
	Técta ; si, múl *the palace ;* *at the same time*	di, vúm „ *of the gods*	tem, plís 632 *in the temples*
	in, dícit ho, nórem. *she appoints* *a sacrifice.*	Néc minus , *Nor less*	íntere, á „ 633 *meanwhile*

ignara ; see note and references on *fati*, l. 299. —— miserīs, dat. plur. m. of the adj. *miser, -a, -um ;* used substantively, dat. of the indirect obj. after the intransitive *succerere*, as being a compound of *sub*. —— succurrere, pres. inf. act. of *succurrō, -ere, succurrī, succursum,* 3 (*sub, = under* or *up to*, + *currō, = I run*) ; *complementary* inf. after *disco ;* this infinitive follows verbs signifying *I know how, I learn how, I dare, I am able,* and many others. A. & G. 271; B. 326; G. 423; H. 533. —— discō, 1st pers. sing. pres. ind. act. of *discō, -ere, didicī,* no supine, 3 (= lit. *to be shown* how to do anything, hence *to learn ;* akin to Greek δεικ-νυμι, = *I show*) ; the contained subj. is *ego ; disco* is more modest than *didici* (*I am learning* than *I have learnt*).

LINE 631. Síc, adv. of manner, referring to the speech just completed. —— memorat, 3d pers. sing. pres. ind. act. of *memorō, -āre, -āvī, ātum,* 1 (*memor, = mindful*) ; understand *Dido* as the subject; *memorat* is a very suitable word to apply to the personal recollections which Dido has been expressing. —— simul, adv., = *at the same time ; simul* has a very strong connective force here, joining *memorat* and *ducit* very closely together — Vergil means that as she was finishing speaking Dido began to lead Aeneas to the palace. —— Aeneān, acc. sing. of *Aeneās, -ae,* m., 1st (Greek acc. as usual); direct obj. of *ducit*. —— in, prep. with the acc. and abl.; gov. the acc. *tecta. In* with the acc. = *into*, i.e. into the interior; *ad* with the acc. = *to*, i.e. to the borders. —— rēgia, acc. plur. n. of *regius, -a, -um ;* agrees with *tecta*. —— dūcit, 3d pers. sing. pres. ind. act. of *dūcō, -ere, dūxī, ductum,* 3; understand *Dido* as subject; the present is *historic*, graphically describing a past occurrence as though it were happening in the present before the reader's eyes. A. & G. 276, *d* ; B. 259, 3; G. 229; H. 467, III.

LINE 632. Tecta, acc. plur. of *tectum, -ī,* n., 2d; governed by *in*. —— simul, adv., repeated rhetorically from *simul* above, = *at the same time leads . . . at the same time,* etc. —— dīvūm (contracted for *dīvōrum*), gen. plur. of *dīvus, -ī,* m., 2d; poss. gen., limiting *templis*. —— templīs, dat. plur. of *templum, -ī,* n., 2d; dat. of the indirect object, after *indicit*, as a compound of *in ;* cf. l. 45, *scopuloque infixit acuto ; templis* appears not to be poetical for the sing., as it is limited by the plur. *divum ;* and it was usual to dedicate a special temple to each of the chief or patron deities. —— indīcit, 3d pers. sing. pres. ind. act. of *indīcō, -ere, indīxī, indictum,* 3 (*in* + *dīcō*) ; agrees with the subj. *Dido* understood, and joined by *simul* to *indicit*. —— honōrem, acc. sing. of *honōs, -ōris,* m., 3d; direct obj. of *indicit ;* cf. Aen. III, l. 264, *indicit honores,* where *honores*, = *sacrifice,* as does *honorem* here. If this sacrifice was a thanksgiving for the safe arrival of Aeneas, Vergil is guilty of an *anachronism,* i.e. mentions a custom regular in his own day which was not observed in the heroic times of which he is writing. The host made a sacrifice and feast in his own house in Homeric days, and invited the newly arrived guest to partake of the banquet.

LINE 633. Nec (for *neque, = and . . . not*), negative cop. conj. —— minus, comparative adv. (positive *parve ;* superl. *minime*) ; *nec minus, = nor less,* i.e. *and in like*

634 soci,ís　　　ad　,　lítora　,　míttit　Vígin,tí | to the company by the
　for the companions　to　　the shore　　she sends　　twenty | shore　twenty　bulls,
635 tau,rós, ,, mag,nórum hor,réntia , céntum Térga | a hundred bristly
　bulls,　　great　　bristling　a hundred　backs | backs of huge swine,
　su,úm, ,, pin,gués cen,túm cum , mátribus , | a hundred fat lambs
　of swine,　　fat　　a hundred　with　　their dams | and their dams be-
636 ágnos, Múnera , lætiti,ámque de,í. | side, the joyous gifts
　lambs,　　the gifts　　and the joy　of the god. | of the wine-god.

manner, a common instance of *litotes;* cf. *haud aliter,* = *not otherwise.* —— **intereā,**
adv. of time; refer to *interea,* l. 124, for derivation. —— **sociīs,** dat. plur. of *socius, -ī,*
m., 2d; dat. of the indirect obj. (advantage or disadvantage), after *mittit tauros.* A. & G.
235; B. 188, 1; G. 350; H. 384, 1 and 2. —— **ad,** prep. with the acc.; gov. *litora.*
—— **lītora,** acc. plur. of *lītus, lītoris,* n., 3d; governed by *ad.* —— **mittit,** 3d pers.
sing. pres. ind. act. of *mittō, -ere, mīsī, missum,* 3; the subj. is Dido or a pronoun under-
stood referring to her; *mittit* is joined by *nec* to *indicit.*

LINE 634. **Vīgintī** (for *bī-gintī,* from *bī* (= *bis*), *twice,* + *gintī,* = *κοντα, ten*), inde-
clinable numeral adj., qualifying *tauros ; viginti* and *centum* below are really not exact,
but large numbers denoting nothing more than that the gift was generous, and illustrat-
ing the apparent but illusive exactness of facts and figures in poetry. —— **taurōs,** acc.
plur. of *taurus, -ī,* m., 2d (Greek ταῦρος; cf. Anglo-Saxon (*s*)*teor,* and English (*s*)*teer*) ;
direct obj. of *mittit.* —— **magnōrum,** gen. plur. m. of the adj. *magnus, -a, -um ;* agrees
with *suum.* —— **horrentia,** acc. plur. n. of *horrēns, -entis,* pres. part. act. of *horreō, -ēre,*
-uī, no supine, 2; agrees with *terga* attributively; *horrentia* here = *bristling,* cf. *horrenti,*
l. 165. —— **centum** (akin to Greek ἑκατόν), indeclinable numeral adj., qualifying *terga ;*
centum, = *unnumbered.*

LINE 635. **Terga,** acc. plur. of *tergum, -ī,* n., 2d (with collateral *tergus, tergoris,* n.,
3d) ; a direct obj. of *mittit;* observe the absence of a conjunction which should connect
terga and *tauros,* and of another which should join *agnos* below with *terga* (*asyndeton*).
A. & G. 208, *b;* B. 346; G. 473, REM.; H. 636, I, 1. —— **suum,** gen. plur. of *sūs, suis,*
common gender, 3d (dat. and abl. *sūbus* or *suibus ;* cf. Greek ῦς); poss. gen., or perhaps
gen. of substance or material, limiting *terga.* —— **pinguēs,** acc. plur. m. of *pinguis, -e,*
adj., 3d; qualifies *agnos.* —— **centum,** numeral adj. indecl.; qualifies *agnos.* —— **cum,**
prep. with the abl.; gov. *matribus.* —— **mātribus,** abl. plur. of *māter, mātris,* f., 3d;
governed by *cum.* —— **agnōs,** acc. plur. of *agnus, -ī,* m., 2d (akin to the Greek ἀμνος);
a direct object of *mittit;* observe the *asyndeton.* The bulls, swine, sheep, and lambs
constituted the *food* for the feast; the other very important feature of a banquet, viz. the
wine, is referred to in the next line.

LINE 636. **Mūnera,** acc. plur. of *mūnus, mūneris,* n., 3d; a direct obj. of *mittit;*
munera is described by *dei,* and *munera laetitiamque dei,* = *the gifts and gladness of the
god,* i.e. *the joyous gifts of the god* (Bacchus), by the figure known as *hendiadys.* A. & G.
385; B. 374, 4; G. 698; H. 636, III, 2. Observe that none of the objects of *mittit* are
connected by a conjunction; the *asyndeton* is rather harsh. Those who read *dii* or *die*
(instead of *dei*) regard *munera* as acc. in apposition with *tauros, terga,* and *agnos,* and
render *munera laetitiamque dii* (or *die*) = *the joyous gifts for the day.* —— **laetitiam,**
acc. sing. of *laetitia, -ae,* f., 1st (*laetus,* = *glad*); joined by *que to mūnera.* This word
is very natural if it has reference to wine; cf. l. 734, *laetitiae Bacchus dator.* —— **que,**
enclitic cop. conj., closely connecting the two nouns *munera* and *laetitiam,* which repre-
sent one idea. —— **deī,** gen. sing. of *deus,* m., 2d; poss. gen., limiting *munera.* There

But the house is being set out within in the magnificence of royal state, and midway in the palace they make ready a banquet. There are coverlets cunningly wrought	Át domus , ínteri,ór „ re,gáli , spléndida , 637		
	But the house	interior	royal	magnificent
	lúxu	Ínstrui,túr,	medi,ísque	pa,ránt „ 638
	with splendor	is being equipped,	and middle	they prepare
	con,vívia ,	téctis :	Árte	la,bóra,tǽ 639
	banquets	in the palace:	with skill	worked (there are)

are various different readings for *dei*, but *dei* is preferable for two reasons: (1) that most of the MSS. read *deī;* this is the external evidence; (2) that mention of wine is neces- sary to make the banquet complete and in character with heroic feasts. It is supported by the fact that the noun *laetitia* is elsewhere in Vergil associated with *Bacchus;* nor does the objection that *dei* is vague and does not indicate any particular god hold ground, for, in Aen. IX, 336, *multoque iacebat Membra deo victus, deo* can only = *Baccho.* Conington reads *dei*, and the sole objection is the harsh *asyndeton.* Of other readings, the chief are : (A) *diī*, an old contracted form of the gen. *diei* (*dies = a day*); the sentence then = (*bulls and lambs*) *gladsome gifts for the day*, or *gifts for the festal day.* Aulus Gellius, in the 2d century, supports *dii*, stating that an ignorant copyist, not acquainted with this gen., changed it to *dei.* *Dii* is not found anywhere else, but a few such genitives are known, e.g. *progenii* (from *progenies*) in Pacuvius; *dii* also escapes the objection of *asyndeton*, for *munera* is acc. in apposition to *agnos*, etc., but mention of wine is omitte l. (B) *diē*, another form of the gen. *diei*, cf. Georgics, I, 208, *diē som- nīque;* this gen. has in its favor that it may have originated both *dii* and *dei*, and if it is accepted the sentence must be rendered as in (A). (C) Instead of *laetitiamque dei* (*dii* or *die*), Peerlkamp suggests *laticemque Iyaeī*, = *the wine of Lyaeus;* cf. l. 686, *laticemque Lyaeum.* For the *hemistich*, cf. l. 534, *Hic cursus fuit.*

LINE 637.   **At**, adversative conj., while connecting this sentence with the preceding one, draws the attention away from the *socii* and their banquet to Aeneas himself and the preparations for his reception. —— **domus**, gen. *domūs*, f., 4th (for decl., etc., see *domos*, l. 140); nom. sing., subj. of *instruitur ; domus = regia tecta*, l. 631, i.e. the palace of Dido. —— **interior**, nom. sing. f. of the comparative adj. *interior, -ius*, gen. *interiōris*, 3d (no positive; superl. *intimus;* formed from adv. and prep. *intrā ;* cf. *superior* from *supra*); agrees partitively with *domus; domus interior =* the *atrium* or large hall of the palace. A. & G. 193; B. 241; G. 291, REM. 2; H. 440, 2, NOTE 1. —— **rēgālī**, abl. sing. m. of the 3d decl. adj. *rēgālis, -e* (from *rēx, rēgis*); agrees with *luxu.* —— **splendida**, nom. sing. f. of the adj. *splendidus, -a, -um* (from *splendeō, = I shine*, hence (1) *bright*, (2) *magnificent*); agrees with *domus*, and may be taken as an adver- bial attribute with *instruitur*, or as enlarging *domus* in the phrase *splendida regali luxu.* —— **lūxū**, abl. sing. of *lūxus, -ūs*, m., 4th; abl. of manner, with *instruitur*, = *is splen- didly set out with royal state.*

LINE 638.   **Instruitur**, 3d pers. sing. pres. ind. pass. of *instruō, -ere, instrūxī, in- structum*, 3 (*in + struō*); agrees with the subj. *domus.* —— **mediīs**, abl. plur. n. of *medius, -a, -um*, adj.; agrees with *tectis*, and is a partitive attribute, i.e. denotes the *central part* of the hall. —— **que**, enclitic cop. conj., connecting its own with the preceding sentence. —— **parant**, 3d pers. plur. pres. ind. act. of *parō, -āre, -āvī, -ātum*, 1; understand *ministri*, = *servants* or some such noun as subject. —— **convīvia**, acc. plur. of *convīvium, -ī*, n., 2d (*con = cum, with, + vīvō, = I live*, hence *a living together*, and so *a banquet*); direct obj. of *parant.* —— **tectīs**, abl. plur. of *tectum, -ī*, n., 2d; abl. of 'the place where,' with *parant.* A. & G. 258, 4, *f, g;* B. 228; G. 385; H. 425.

LINE 639.   **Arte**, abl. sing. of *ars, artis*, f., 3d (etymology doubtful); abl. of manner, with *laboratae.* —— **labōrātae**, nom. plur. f. of *labōrātus, -a, -um*, perf. part. pass. of

640 ves,tés ,, os,tróque su,pérbo, Íngens , árgen,túm *coverlets　and of purple　proud,　　huge　　silver-plate* 641men,sís, ,, cae,látaque in , aúro Fórtia , fácta *on the tables,　and engraved　in　gold　brave　the deeds* 642pa,trúm, ,, seri,és lon,gíssima , rérum,　　Pér *of ancestors,　a sequence　very long　of events,　through* tot , dúcta vi,rós ,, an,tíqua ab or,ígine , *so many traced　heroes　　ancient　from　the origin*	and of proud purple, massive silver upon the tables, and graven in gold the brave deeds of ancestral heroes, a long line of exploits traced through many a man from the early begin- ning of the race.

labōrō, -āre, -āvī, -ātum, I (from *labor*) ; agrees with *vestes; laboratae* does not = *laboratae sunt,* the perf. pass., but is purely participial, describing *vestes.* Take the sentence thus : *Sunt vestes arte laboratae ostroque superbo,* = *there are coverlets skilfully wrought and of proud purple.*——**vestēs,** nom. plur. of *vestis, -is,* f., 3d (akin to Greek ἐσθής, where the initial *digamma* has disappeared); subj. of *sunt* understood; understand *stragulae* with *vestes,* = *clothes for covering,* i.e. *coverlets.*——**ostrō,** abl. sing. of *ostrum, -ī,* n., 2d (Greek ὄστρεον = *a shell-fish, oyster) ;* abl. of quality, describing *vestes.* The Phoenicians obtained their purple from a small species of shell-fish.——**que,** enclitic cop. conj., joining *arte laboratae* and *ostro superbo.*——**superbō,** abl. sing. n. of *superbus, -a, -um ;* agrees with *ostro ;* the adj. = *regio,* for purple was the badge of royalty, and also favored by the nobles at Rome.

Line 640. **Ingēns,** nom. sing. n. of the adj. *ingēns, -entis,* 3d; qualifies *argentum.*——**argentum,** gen. *argentī,* n., 2d (akin to Greek ἀργ-υρος); nom. sing., subj. of *erat* understood. The indicative mood of *sum* is often omitted in cases when it is easily supplied or suggested by the context. A. & G. 206, *c,* 2; B. 166, 3; G. 209; H. 368, 3.——**mensīs,** abl. plur. of *mensa, -ae,* f., 1st; abl. of 'the place where.'——**caelāta,** nom. plur. n. of *caelātus, -a, -um,* perf. part. pass. of *caelō, -āre, -āvī, -ātum,* I (from *caelum,* = *a graver,* hence *to work with a caelum,* i.e. *to work in relief, to engrave) ;* agrees with and describes *facta.*——**que,** enclitic cop. conj.——**in,** prep. with the acc. and abl.; gov. *aurō.*——**auro,** abl. sing. of *aurum, -i,* n., 2d; governed by *in.* Drinking vessels of gold and silver, with scenes and figures worked in relief upon them, were highly prized by wealthy Romans, and so Vergil skilfully suggests Dido's wealth and the magnificence of her court by representing her as the owner of *massive silver* and *carved gold.*

Line 641. **Fortia,** nom. plur. n. of the adj. *fortis, -e,* 3d; agrees with *facta.*——**facta,** nom. plur. n. of *factum, -ī,* n., 2d; subj. of *sunt* understood.——**patrum,** gen. plur. of *pater, patris,* m., 3d; subjective gen., limiting *facta.*——**seriēs,** gen. *seriei,* f., 5th (from *serō,* = *I join,* hence *a joining,* i.e. *a series) ;* nom. sing., in apposition with *facta.*——**longissima,** nom. sing. f. of the superl. adj. *longissimus, -a, -um* (positive, *longus ;* comparative *longior) ;* agrees with *series.*——**rērum,** gen. plur. of *rēs, reī,* f., 5th; partitive gen. (in such instances often called *genitivus generis),* limiting *series.* This genitive is used when there is sometimes little or no partitive conception.

Line 642. **Per,** prep. with the acc.; gov. *virōs.*——**tot,** indeclinable numeral adj.; qualifies *virōs ; tot = permultos.*——**ducta,** nom. sing. f. of *ductus, -a, -um,* perf. part. pass. of *dūcō, -ere, dūxī, ductum,* 3; agrees with and enlarges *series.*——**virōs,** acc. plur. of *vir, viri,* m., 2d; governed by *per.*——**antīquā,** abl. sing. f. of *antīquus, -a, -um ;* agrees with *origine.*——**ab,** prep. with the abl.; gov. *origine,* denoting source.——**orīgine,** abl. sing. of *orīgō, -inis,* f., 3d (from *orior,* = *I rise) ;* governed by the preposition *ab.*——**gentis,** gen. sing. of *gēns,* f., 3d; poss. gen., limiting *origine.*

Aeneas—for a fa- ther's love allowed	géntis. Áene, ús — neque e, ním patri, ús ,, 643 *of the race. Aeneas — (and) not for paternal*
not his mind to rest — sends Achates speed-	con, sístere ,, méntem Pássus a, mór — ,, rapi, dum 644 *to rest his mind did allow love — swift*
ing to the ships, to bear the news to	ád na, vés prae, míttit A, cháten, Áscani, ó 645 *to the ships sends on Achates, to Ascanius*
Ascanius and bring him to the city; in	ferat , hæc, ,, ip, súmque ad , mœnia , *let him tell these things, and him himself to the city-walls*

LINE 643. **Aenēās**, nom. sing.; subj. of *praemittit.* —— **neque**, negative cop. conj., connecting the parenthetic clause *neque* . . . *amor* with the main clause *Aeneas praemittit.* —— **enim**, causal conj., here as often introducing an explanatory parenthesis; *neque enim* corresponds exactly to the Greek καὶ γάρ οὐ. —— **patrius**, nom. sing. m. of the adj. *patrius, -a, -um* (*pater*) ; agrees with *amor.* —— **consistere**, pres. inf. act. of *consistō, -ere, constitī, constitum,* 3 (*cum* + *sistō*) ; objective *complementary* inf. dependent on *passus* (*est*) ; *consistere* = lit. *to halt,* and in reference to the mind = *to rest.* —— **mentem**, acc. sing. of *mēns, mentis,* f., 3d; direct obj. of *passus* (*est*) ; *mentem* is here properly used (instead of *animus,* = *the mind,* in its emotional aspect), for Aeneas was *thinking* about Ascanius and was anxious to have him in the city.

LINE 644. **Passus**, nom. sing. m. of perf. part. of *patior, patī, passus sum,* 3 deponent; *passus* agrees with *amor,* and with *est* supplied = the 3d pers. sing. perf. indicative. —— **amor**, gen. *amōris,* m., 3d (*amō*) ; nom. sing., subj. of *passus* (*est*). *Amor* is personified in l. 689, and = *Cupīdō.* —— **rapidum**, acc. sing. m. of the adj. *rapidus, -a, -um* (from *rapiō*) ; agrees with *Achaten,* but must be rendered as = *rapidē.* Adjectives are frequently used as adverbial attributes, but *rapidum,* the adj., is preferable to the adverb here, because *rapide* would not make it clear whether the haste is displayed by Aeneas in sending or by Achates who is sent. —— **ad**, prep. with the acc.; gov. *naves.* —— **nāvēs**, acc. plur. of *nāvis, -is,* f., 3d; governed by *ad.* —— **praemittit**, 3d pers. sing. pres. ind. act. of *praemittō, -ere, praemīsī, praemissum,* 3 (*prae,* = *before,* + *mittō,* = *I send*) ; agrees with the subj. *Aeneas.* —— **Achātēn**, acc. sing. of *Achātēs, -ae* or *-ī,* m., 1st and 3d decl.; direct obj. of *praemittit;* the ending in *-en* is preferred by Vergil to *-em* in Greek nouns, just as *-an* is preferred to *-am,* e.g. *Aenean.* A. & G. 37, PERSES; B. 22, COMETES; G. 65, ANCHISES; H. 50, PYRITES.

LINE 645. **Ascaniō**, dat. sing. of *Ascanius, -ī,* m., 2d; dat. of the indirect obj. after *ferat,* = *report,* or *dativus commodī* if *ferat* be rendered *carry news.* Ascanius, the son of Aeneas and Creüsa, is variously spoken of by this name and the name Iulus. —— **ferat,** 3d pers. sing. pres. subjunct. act. of *ferō, ferre, tulī, lātum,* irreg.; agrees with a nom. sing. pron. as subj. referring to *Achates. Ferat* is not a subjunctive of purpose with *ut* or *qui* omitted, but is an oblique jussive subjunctive representing the actual command of Aeneas (*fer haec Ascanio* = *report these things to Ascanius*) in a kind of virtual *oratio obliqua,* i.e. as a quotation. For commands in indirect discourse, consult A. & G. 339; B. 316; G. 652; H. 523, III. —— **haec**, acc. plur. n. of the demonstr. pron. *hīc, haec, hōc;* direct obj. of *ferat; haec* = the glad news of Dido's warm welcome. —— **ipsum**, acc. sing. m. of *ipse, -a, -um;* intensifies *illum* understood, referring to Ascanius. —— **que**, enclitic cop. conj. —— **ad**, prep. with the acc.; gov. *moenia.* —— **moenia**, acc. plur. of *moenia, -ium,* n., 3d (no sing.); governed by *ad; moenia* = *the city-walls,* i.e. the *city* itself. —— **dūcat**, 3d pers. sing. pres. subjunct. act. of *dūcō, -ere, dūxī, ductum,* 3; joined by *que* to *ferat,* and in exactly the same grammatical construction.

646 dúcat.   Ómnis in , Áscani,ó ,, ca,rí stat ,
   let him lead.   *All*   *on*   *Ascanius*   *dear* *depends*
647 cúra   pa,réntis.   Múnera , prǽtere,*a*, ,, Ília,cís
   the care of the father.   *Gifts*   *besides,*   *of Troy*
648 e,répta   ru,ínis,   Férre   iu,bét,   ,, pal,lám
   snatched from the ruins, to bring he orders,   *a robe*
649 sig,nís   au,róque   ri,géntem,   Ét
   with figures   *and with gold*   *stiff,*   *and*
   cir,cúmtex,túm ,, croce,ó ve,lámen   a,cántho,
   woven round   *yellow*   *a veil*   *with the acanthus,*

Ascanius all the loving father's care is centred. Presents thereto, saved from the wreckage of Ilium, he bids him bring, a robe stiffly embroidered with figures of gold, and a veil woven on the border with the yellow a c a n t h u s,

LINE 646. **Omnis**, nom. sing. f. of the adj. *omnis, -e;* agrees with *cura.* —— **in**, prep. with the acc. and abl.; gov. the abl. *Ascanio.* —— **Ascaniō**, abl. sing. of *Ascanius, -ī*, m., 2d; governed by *in.* —— **cārī**, gen. sing. m. of *cārus, -a, -um*, adj. (akin to Sanskrit root KAM, = *to love*) ; agrees with *parentis ;* *cari* is active in its signification here = *loving*, rather than the more common passive = *loved, dear.* —— **stat**, 3d pers. sing. pres. ind. act. of *stō, -āre, stetī, statum*, 1; agrees with the subj. *cura ; stat = stands firm,* i.e. *is fixed in,* Ascanius. —— **cūra**, gen. *cūrae*, f., 1st; nom. sing. subj. of *stat.* —— **parentis**, gen. sing. of *parēns*, m. and f., 3d; poss. gen., limiting *cura ; parentis = patris,* i.e. *Aeneae.*

LINE 647. **Mūnera**, acc. plur. of *mūnus, mūneris*, n., 3d; direct. obj. of *ferre.* —— **praetereā**, adverb; *praeterea* is compounded of *praeter* and *ea*, cf. *postea, antea ; ea* is considered by some an abl. whose connection in one word with the prep. dates from the time when *praeter, ante,* etc., could be used with the abl., but Corrsen thinks *ea* is the neut. acc. plur. of *is, ea, id.* —— **Iliacīs**, abl. plur. f. of *Iliacus, -a, -um ;* agrees with *ruīnīs.* —— **ērepta**, acc. plur. n. of *ēreptus, -a, -um*, perf. part. pass. of *ēripiō, -ere, -uī, ēreptum*, 3 (*ē*, = *out of*, + *rapiō*, = *I snatch*) ; agrees with and enlarges the obj. *munera.* —— **ruīnīs**, abl. plur. of *ruīna, -ae*, f., 1st (*ruō = I fall down*) ; abl. of separation, after *erepta* compounded with *e.* In prose the preposition is usually repeated with the noun, e.g. *e ruinis erepta, ab urbe abire,* etc., but in poetry (and in figurative phrases in prose) the simple ablative alone is very common; see the note on *animo,* l. 26.

LINE 648. **Ferre**, pres. inf. act. of *ferō, ferre, tulī, lātum*, irreg.; objective complementary inf. after *iubet ; ferre = to bring,* i.e. from the ships as presents for Dido. —— **iubet**, 3d pers. sing. pres. ind. act. of *iubeō, -ēre, iussī, iussum*, 2; understand *Aeneas* as subj., and *Achaten* (from l. 644) as object; the pres. *iubet* is *historic.* *Iubeō* regularly governs the acc. of the person, and is followed by the inf. mood; *imperō* governs the dat. of the person, and is followed by *ut* (negative *ne*) with the subjunctive. —— **pallam**, acc. sing. of *palla, -ae*, f., 1st; acc. in apposition with *munera.* The *palla* was a long dress or robe, worn by women and high officials; it consisted of a wide piece of cloth, which was wrapped round the body, over the *tunica,* and reached from the shoulders to the feet; at the shoulder it was fastened by a *fibula* or brooch. —— **signīs**, abl. plur. of *signum, -ī*, n., 2d (here = *embroidered figures*) ; abl. of the instrument with *rigentem ;* cf. Aen. V, 267, *cymbia . . . aspera signis = drinking cups embossed with figures.* —— **aurō**, abl. sing. of *aurum, -ī*, n., 2d; abl. of the instrument, with *rigentem*, and joined by *que* to *signis.* *Signis auroque* is an instance of *hendiadys*, = *signis aureis = with figures of gold ;* cf. the stock example *pateris libamus et auro.* A. & G. 385; B. 374, 4; G. 698; H. 636, III, 2. —— **rigentem**, acc. sing. f. of *rigēns, -entis*, pres. part. act. of *rigeō, -ēre, -uī*, no supine, 2 (akin to Greek ῥιγέω); agrees with *pallam.*

LINE 649. **Et**, cop. conj. —— **circumtextum**, acc. sing. n. of *circumtextus, -a, -um*,

deckings of Argive	Órna,tús	Aɪ,gívae	Hele,næ ;	„	quos ,	ílla 650
Helen, which she had	*ornaments*	*Argive*	*of Helen;*		*which*	*she*
borne off, her mother						
Leda's wondrous gift,	My,cénis,	Pérgama	,	cúm	pete,rét „ 651
from Mycenae (what	*from Mycenae,*	*Pergamos*		*when*	*she sought*

---

adj. (*circum,* = *around,* + *texō,* = *I weave,* hence *woven round, bordered*) *;* agrees with *velamen.* —— **croceō,** abl. sing. m. of *croceus, -a, -um,* adj. (from *crocus,* = *saffron,* hence *saffron-hued, yellow*) *;* agrees with *acantho.* —— **vēlāmen,** acc. sing. of *vēlāmen, -inis,* n., 3d (from *vēlō,* = *I veil, cover*) *;* acc. in apposition with *munera,* and joined by *et* above to *pallam.* The *palla* and *velamen* are gifts highly appropriate for a woman. —— **acanthō,** abl. sing. of *acanthus, -ī,* m., 2d (Greek ἄκανθος) *;* abl. of the means or instrument with *circumtextum.* The *acanthus* or *bear's foot* had a leaf which bore some resemblance to the claw of a bear, and this plant is said to have given to the eminent sculptor Callimachus the first idea of the elaborate and intricate work of the Corinthian capital for pillars of temples and other buildings.

LINE 650. **Ornātūs,** acc. plur. of *ornātus, -ūs,* m., 4th (from *ornō,* = *I adorn*) *;* acc. in appos. to *pallam* and *velamen;* the sense is quite clear, for *munera* is described specifically by *pallam* and *velamen,* and they in turn are described as *ornatus Hellenae.* —— **Argīvae,** gen. sing. f. of *Argīvus, -a, -um,* adj. (from noun *Argī, -ōrum,* m., 2d, = *Argos;* cf. *Argīvī* = *the Argives (Greeks)*) *;* agrees with *Helenae.* Vergil is not strictly accurate in saying that Helen was an Argive or native of Argos. Her husband was Menelaus, the king of Sparta, and it was from Sparta that Helen was abducted by Paris. However, Homer calls her Ἀργείη Ἑλένη, which = *Grecian Helen,* just as Ἀργεῖοι stands for *the Greeks.* Again Vergil makes her leave *Mycenae (Mycenis* below); this is because Argos and Mycenae were not very far distant, and the poets loosely represent Agamemnon and Menelaus as ruling in Argos or Mycenae, e.g. Aeschylus makes them both kings of Argos, whereas in Homer Agamemnon is king of Mycenae, Menelaus of Sparta. —— **Helenae,** gen. sing. of *Helena,* f., 1st (Ἑλένη); poss. gen., limiting *ornatus.* Helen was the daughter of Jupiter and Leda, and the sister of Castor, Pollux, and Clytemnaestra (wife of Agamemnon); she married Menelaus, whom she chose out of many suitors, and her flight with Paris to Troy caused the Trojan War. —— **quōs,** acc. plur. of the rel. pron. *qui, quae, quod;* agrees with the antecedent *ornatus,* and is direct obj. of *extulerat.* —— **illa,** nom. sing. f. of the demonstr. pron. *ille, illa, illud;* refers emphatically to Helen, and is subj. of *extulerat.* —— **Mycēnīs,** abl. plur. of *Mycēnae, -ārum,* f., 1st plur.; abl. of 'place whence,' after *extulerat.* A. & G. 258, *a,* NOTE 3; B. 229, 1, *c;* G. 391, NOTE; H. 412, 2. Mycenae was a city of Argolis, over which Agamemnon was king. Excavations have been made there in recent years, and many valuable finds made, especially the famous lion-gates.

LINE 651. **Pergama,** acc. plur. of *Pergama, -ōrum,* n., 2d plur. (Πέργαμα); direct obj. of *peteret; Pergama* = *Troiam.* —— **cum,** temporal conj., followed by the imperfect subjunctive *peteret,* describing the time of action in the past by the circumstances. *Cum* = *when* generally takes the imperf. and pluperf. subjunctive, and the indicative of other tenses. See note on *cum,* l. 36. —— **peteret,** 3d pers. sing. imperf. subjunct. act. of *petō, -ere, petīvī* or *petiī, petītum,* 3; the subj. is a nom. f. sing. pron. referring to Helen. Observe that the final syllable should strictly be short, as the next word begins with a vowel; however, the *ictus* falls on this syllable, and the *caesural* pause follows it, and Vergil lengthens it. *Peterēt* appears to be also the old quantity of the word, and Vergil's fondness for antiquarian words, etc., further accounts for the long syllable here

652 in, cónces, sósque   hyme, náeos,   Éxtule, rát,   time she was seeking
and unlawful   *marriage,*   *had carried away,*   Pergamos and an un-
ma, trís   Le, dǽ   „   mi, rábile   dónum :   hallowed marriage);
her mother   *of Leda*   *wonderful*   *the gift :*   thereto the sceptre
653 Prǽtere, á   scep, trum,   „   Ílio, né   quod ,   which Ilione, eldest
besides   *the sceptre,*   *Ilione*   *which*   of Priam's daughters,
654 gésserat   ,   ólim,   Máxima   ,   náta, rúm   had aforetime borne,
had carried   *once,*   *eldest*   *of the daughters*

For *diastole*, consult A. & G. 359, *f*; B. 367, 2; G. 721; H. 608, V. —— inconcessōs, acc. plur. m. of *inconcessus, -a, -um*, adj. (from *in, = not, + concessus, = allowed*, perf. part. pass. of *concēdō*) ; agrees with *hymenaeos ; inconcessos* refers to the elopement with Paris. —— que, enclitic cop. conj. —— hymenaeōs, acc. plur. of *hymenaeus, -ī*, m., 2d (Greek Ὑμεναῖος = *Hymen*, the god of marriage, hence *marriage, nuptials*) ; a direct obj. of *peteret*, joined by *que* to *Pergama*. Vergil never uses a quadrisyllable to complete a *hexameter*, though it is common in Greek, except in proper names or words that are really Greek words Latinized; e.g. *hyacinthus, hymenaeus*. A *hexameter* should close : (1) with a dissyllable, preceded by a word of at least 3 syllables; (2) a trisyllable, preceded by a word of at least 2 syllables.

LINE 652. Extulerat, 3d pers. sing. pluperf. ind. act. of *efferō, efferre, extulī, ēlātum*, irreg. (*ēx, = out of, + ferō, = I carry*) ; agrees with the subj. *illa* in the rel. clause introduced by *quos*. —— mātris, gen. sing. of *māter*, f., 3d; gen. in appos. with *Ledae*. —— Lēdae, gen. sing. of *Lēda*, f., 1st (Λήδη); subjective gen. = *gift (presented by = of) Leda*. Leda was the wife of Tyndareus, and the mother of Helen by Jupiter. —— mīrābile, acc. sing. n. of the adj. *mīrābĭlis, -e*, 3d (from *mīror, = I wonder at*) ; agrees with *donum*. —— dōnum, acc. sing. of *dōnum, -ī*, n., 2d (akin to *dō, = I give*) ; acc. in appos. with and describing *ornatus*, l. 650.

LINE 653. Praetereā, adverb; see *praeterea*, l. 647. —— scēptrum, acc. sing. of *scēptrum, -ī*, n., 2d (Greek σκῆπτρον) ; joined by *praeterea* to *velamen* (l. 649), and an acc. in apposition to *munera*, l. 647. —— Īlionē, gen. *Ilionēs*, f., 1st decl. Greek noun (Ἰλιόνη) ; nom. sing., subj. of *gesserat* in the rel. clause introduced by *quod*. Ilione was the eldest daughter of the Trojan king Priam, and married Polymnestor, king of Thrace. For declension, consult A. & G. 37; B. 22; each like EPITOME; G. 65, PENELOPE; H. 50, EPITOME. —— quod, acc. sing. n. of the rel. pron. *quī, quae, quod ;* agrees with the antecedent *sceptrum*, and is the direct obj. of *gesserat*. —— gesserat, 3d pers. sing. pluperf. ind. act. of *gerō, -ere, gessī, gestum*, 3; agrees with the subj. *Ilione*. —— ōlim (for *oll-im*, from *olle*, an old form of the demonstr. pron. *ille*), adv. of time, modifying *gesserat*. *Olim* here refers to past time, = *once, formerly ;* sometimes it has reference to the future, = *one day, in time to come*.

LINE 654. māxima, nom. sing. f. of *māximus, -a, -um*, adj.; qualifies *Ilione ; maxima* here = *maxima natu, the eldest*. *Maximus* is the superl. of the adj. *magnus ;* comparative, *maior*. For its use in reference to age, cf. *minimus* (i.e. *natu*), the superl. of *parvus*. —— nātārum, gen. plur. of *nāta, -ae*, f., 1st (originally f. of *nātus, -a, -um*, perf. part. of *nascor*) ; partitive gen., after *maxima*. A. & G. 216, 2; B. 201, 1; G. 372; H. 397, 3. —— Priamī, gen. sing. of *Priamus*, m., 2d; poss. gen., limiting *natarum*. —— collō, dat. sing. of *collum, -ī*, n., 2d; this dat. is not a dat. of purpose, but a dat. of the indirect obj. (of the person or thing affected) such as frequently accompanies a dat. of purpose; thus *collo* is a dat. like *collo* in the following *monile* (*ut*

and a circlet of pearls | Pria, mí, ,, col, lóque mo, níle Báca, tum, ét 655
for the neck, and a | of Priam, and for the neck a necklace beaded, and
double diadem of | dupli, cém ,, gem, mís au, róque co, rónam.
gold and jewels.
Hasting upon this | double with jewels and with gold a crown.
errand Achates | Hæc cele, ráns, iter ád na, vés ,, 656
shaped his course | These things hastening, his way to the ships
towards the ships. But | ten, débat A, chátes. Át Cythe, réa no, vás 657
Cytherea turns over | was directing Achates. But Cytherea new

ornamento sit) collo. A. & G. 233; B. 191; G. 356; H. 390. —— que, enclitic cop.
conj. —— monīle, acc. sing. of *monīle, -is,* n., 3d; acc., joined by *que* to *sceptrum,* in
appos. with *munera,* l. 647.

LINE 655. **Bācātum,** acc. sing. n. of *bācātus, -a, -um,* adj. (from *bāca,* = *a berry*);
agrees with *monile; monile bacatum = a neckalce studded with pearls,* or if not *pearls,*
some jewels shaped like berries. —— et, cop. conj. —— duplicem, acc. sing. f. of
duplēx, -icis, adj., 3d (from *duo,* = *two,* + *plicō,* = *I fold,* hence *two-fold, double*); agrees
with *coronam.* —— gemmīs, abl. plur. of *gemma, -ae,* f., 1st; abl. of the means, or
perhaps abl. of manner, describing *duplicem. Gemma* = (1) *a jewel;* (2) *the eye,* or
bud of a plant. —— aurō, abl. sing. of *aurum, -ī,* n., 2d; abl. like *gemmis,* to which it
is joined by *que. Duplicem gemmis auroque coronam = a double circlet of jewels and
gold,* which can only mean that the crown consisted of two rings, one of gold, the other
of jewels. —— que, enclitic cop. conj. —— corōnam, acc. sing. of *corōna, -ae,* f., 1st;
acc. in appos. with *munera,* and joined by *et* above to *monile.*

LINE 656. **Haec,** acc. plur. n. of the demonstr. adj. *hīc, haec, hōc;* direct obj. of
celerans; haec celerans = hurrying these things, i.e. *hastening to perform these com-
mands.* —— celerāns, nom. sing. m. of the pres. part. act. of *celerō, -āre, -āvī, -ātum,* 1
(*celer* = *swift*); agrees with and enlarges the subj. *Achates.* —— iter, acc. sing. of
itineris, n., 3d (from *eō,* = *I go,* through the root *i*); direct obj. of *tendebat.* —— ad,
prep. with the acc.; gov. *nāvēs.* —— nāvēs, acc. plur. of *nāvis, -is,* f., 3d; governed by
the preposition *ad.* —— tendēbat, 3d pers. sing. imperf. ind. act. of *tendō, -ere, tetendī,
tensum* or *tentum,* 3; agrees with the subj. *Achates.* —— Achātēs, gen. *Achātae,* m., 1st
decl. Greek; nom. sing., subj. of *tendebat.*

LINE 657. **At,** adversative conj., introducing not an objection (as it often does),
but an important interference with the smooth course of events, as already described.
A. & G. 156, *b;* B. 343, 1; G. 485; H. 554, 3. —— Cytherēa, gen. *Cythereae,* f., 1st
(originally f. of the adj. *Cytherēus; Cytherēa, -a, -um = the goddess of Cythera,* from the noun
Cythēra, -ōrum, n., 2d); nom. sing., subj. of *versat.* Venus is called *Cytherea* because
it was on the island of Cythera that she first put foot after emerging from the sea, and
because she was especially honored there. The poets are very free with regard to the
quantity of vowels in proper names; thus the first *e* in *Cytherea* should strictly be long,
as it is in the noun *Cythēra,* cf. *Sȳchaeus* and *Sȳchaeus,* etc. The second *e* is properly
long, because it represents a diphthong in the Greek adjective. —— novās, acc. plur. of
the adj. *novus, -a, -um;* agrees with *artes.* —— artēs, acc. plur. of *ars, artis,* f., 3d;
direct obj. of *versat.* —— nova, acc. sing. n. of the adj. *novus;* agrees with *consilia.* The
asyndeton and the repetition of the same adjective are rhetorical. —— pectore, abl. sing.
of *pectus, pectoris,* n., 3d; abl. of 'the place where.' —— versat, 3d pers. sing. pres. ind.
act. of *versō, -āre, -āvī, -ātum,* 1 (intensive form of *vertō*); agrees with the subj. *Cytherea;*

658 ar‚tés‚ „ nova ‚ péctore ‚ vérsat Cónsili‚a‚ út | in her heart new
   devices,   *new in her breast turns over schemes,   how* | schemes, new plans,

659 faci‚ém „ mu‚tátus et ‚ óra Cu‚pído   Pró | how Cupid changed
   in form   *changed   and in face   Cupid   instead of* | in form and face may

dul‚ci Áscani‚ó veni‚át‚   „   do‚nísque | come in the room of
   sweet   . Ascanius   may come,   and with gifts | sweet Ascanius and

660 fu‚réntem Íncen‚dát re‚gínam‚   „   at‚que | with his gifts fire the
   frenzied   set aflame   the queen,   and | queen to frenzy and

---

versat = *turns over,* and is extended by *pectore* = *in the mind,* but often is used absolutely = *ponders* + acc. of the thing.

LINE 658. **Consilia,** acc. plur. of *consilium, -i,* n., 2d; direct obj. of *versat.* —— **ut,** final conj., denoting the *purpose* expressed in the noun *consilia.* —— **faciem,** acc. sing. of *facies, -ei,* f., 5th; acc. of specification, with the past part. *mutatus,* = *changed in shape; faciem mutatus* = *facie mutatā,* abl. abs. For this acc., refer to the note on *oculos,* l. 228. Synonyms: *facies* = *the face,* which does not change and through which one person is distinguished from another; it is often, as in this instance, used by metonymy to denote the whole form; *vultus* = *the face* or *countenance,* expressive of feeling and emotion. —— **mūtātus,** nom. sing. m. of the perf. part. pass. of *mūtō, -āre, āvī, -ātum,* 1 (akin to *moveō*) ; agrees with and enlarges *Cupido,* subj. in the final clause introduced by *ut.* *Mutatus* may be taken as *medial* = *changing his shape,* but perhaps is strictly passive; both these participles are very common in Greek with the acc. following. Refer to the note on *suffusa,* l. 228, and consult A. & G. 240, *c*; B. 180; G. 338; H. 378. —— **et,** cop. conj. —— **ōra,** acc. plur. of *ōs, ōris,* n., 3d ; synecdochical acc. of specification, with *mutatus,* like *faciem,* to which it is joined by *et ;* the plural *ora* is a poetical variation for the sing. *os.* *Os* = (1) *the mouth ;* (2) as here, *the face,* as distinguished from *faciem* (= *the form*). —— **Cupīdō,** gen. *Cupīdinis,* m., 3d (from *cupiō* = *I desire,* = *Love, Desire,* personified) ; nom. sing., subj. of *veniat.* Cupid (*Cupīdo* or *Amor*) was the son of Venus and the god of love.

LINE 659. **Prō,** prep. with the abl.; gov. *Ascanio.* A. &. G. 153; B. 142; G. 417; H. 434, I. —— **dulcī,** abl. sing. m. of the adj. *dulcis, -e,* 3d ; agrees with *Ascanio.* —— **Ascaniō,** abl. sing. of *Ascanius, -i,* m., 2d; governed by the prep. *pro.* —— **veniat,** 3d pers. sing. pres. subjunct. act. of *veniō, -īre, vēnī, ventum,* 4 irreg.; agrees with the subj. *Cupido ; veniat* is subjunct. because it expresses purpose after *ut.* A. & G. 317; B. 282; G. 545; H. 497. —— **dōnīs,** abl. plur. of *dōnum, -ī,* n., 2d; abl. of the means or instrument, with *incendat.* —— **que,** enclitic cop. conj. —— **furentem,** acc. sing. f. of *furēns, -entis,* pres. part. act. of *furō, -ere, -uī,* no supine, 3; agrees with *reginam,* but modifies the predicate *incendat,* = *fire the queen to frenzy* (i.e. so that she may be frenzied). This use of an adjective or participle is known as *prolepsis.* A. & G. 385; B. 374, 5; G. 325, *predicative attribution ;* H. 636, IV, 3.

LINE 660. **Incendat,** 3d pers. sing. pres. subjunct. act. of *incendō, -ere, incenaī, incensum,* 3 (for *incandō,* from *in,* = *into,* + root *can,* akin to Greek καίω, = *to burn*) ; agrees with the subj. *Cupido* in the final clause, and is joined by *que* above to *veniat.* —— **rēgīnam,** acc. sing. of *rēgīna, -ae,* f., 1st; direct obj. of *incendat.* —— **atque,** cop. conj., introducing a clause explaining *incendat.* —— **ossibus,** dat. plur. of *os, ossis,* n., 3d (akin to Greek ὀστέον); dat of the indirect obj. after *implicit,* which is a compound of *in ;* cf. l. 45, *scopuloque infixit acuto.* —— **implicet,** 3d pers. sing. pres. subjunct. act. of *implicō, -āre, -āvī* or *-uī, -ātum* or *-itum,* 1 (*in,* = *in,* + *plicō,* = *I fold,* hence *I enfold*) ;

twine the fire about	óssibus	,	ímplicet	,	ígnem ;	Quíppe	do,múm 661
her bones. Truly she	to her bones		apply		the fire;	because	the house
fears the doubtful							
house, the double-	timet	,	ámbigu,ám	„	Tyri,ósque	bi,língues.	
tongued Tyrians;	she fears		treacherous		and the Tyrians	double-tongued.	
cruel Juno chafes her,	Úrit		a,tróx	Iu,no,	„	ét sub	, nóctem , 662
and towards nightfall	Chafes (her)		harsh	Juno,		and towards	night
her care sweeps back.	cúra		re,cúrsat.	Érgo		his	, álige,rúm 663
Therefore with these	care		rushes back.	Therefore		these	winged

joined by *atque* to *incendat*, and in the same grammatical construction. —— **ignem**, acc. sing. of *ignis, -is*, m., 3d; direct obj. of *implicit*. The *flame* of love is a very familiar metaphor, and it is said to devour the bones, because in the marrow of the bones is said to be the seat of emotions; cf. the metaphor of *marrow freezing* under the influence of acute fear.

LINE 661.   **Quippe**, conj., conveying and emphasizing a reason for something. *Quippe* (a compound of *qui*, an old locative or abl. of the rel. pronoun, and the suffix *pte*) was originally used in interrogations, but its interrogative disappeared early. It is often used with the rel. pron. added, e.g. *quippe qui (since he . . .),* in explanations. —— **domum**, acc. sing. of *domus, -ūs*, f., 4th; direct obj. of *timet*. —— **timet**, 3d pers. sing. pres. ind. act. of *timeō, -ēre, -uī*, no supine, 2; the subj. is a pron. (*illa*) understood, referring back to *Cytherea*, l. 657; the present is the graphic *historic*, and in sequence *incendat*, etc., above in the final clauses are present. —— **ambiguam**, acc. sing. f. of the adj. *ambiguus, -a, -um* (from *ambigō, = I go round about*, hence *I doubt*); agrees with *domum;* *ambiguam = doubtful*, because the house might or might not be genuinely friendly. —— **Tyriōs**, acc. plur. m. of the adj. *Tyrius, -a, -um;* substantival, a direct obj. of *timet*, joined by *que* to *domum ;* the m. *Tyrii, -ōrum*, is used as a noun. —— **que**, enclitic cop. conj. —— **bīlinguēs**, acc. plur. m. of the adj. *bīlinguis, -e* (from *bī = bis, twice*, + *lingua, = a tongue*) ; qualifies *Tyriōs*. *Bilingues = double-tongued*, i.e. treacherous; cf. *double-faced*. This metaphor is perhaps derived from the notion that the snake had two tongues. Vergil may be thinking of the treachery of Pygmalion, but more probably, by an *anachronism*, he ascribes to Venus that distrust of the Carthaginians which was entertained by Romans of later days ; *Punica fides* was a proverb for treachery among Romans.

LINE 662.   **Ūrit**, 3d pers. sing. pres. ind. act. of *ūrō, -ere, ussī, ustum*, 3; agrees with the subj. *Iuno ;* understand *illam*, i.e. *Venerem*, as object. *Urere* does not mean *to burn* only, but may be used of various kinds of physical discomfort, e.g. *to gall* and the like; *urit* here = *troubles, chafes*, of mental worry, for the subj. *Iuno* really = *(the thought of) Juno*. —— **atrōx**, gen. *atrōcis*, 3d adj. of one termination ; nom. sing. f., agreeing with *Iuno*. —— **Iūnō**, gen. *Iūnōnis*, f., 3d; nom. sing., subj. of *urit*. Observe that the real pause follows *Iuno ;* hence the *caesural* mark is better placed here than after *et*. —— **et**, cop. conj. —— **sub**, prep. with the acc. and abl.; gov. *noctum*. *Sub* + the acc. in reference to time = *towards*. A. & G. 153; B. 143; G. 418; H. 435. —— **noctem**, acc. sing. of *nōx, noctis*, f., 3d; governed by *sub*. —— **cūra**, gen. *curae*, f., 1st; nom. sing., subj. of *recursat*. —— **recursat**, 3d pers. sing. pres. ind. act. of *recursō, -āre*, no perf., no supine, 1 intrans. (intensive of *recurrō, re*, = *back*, + *currō*) ; agrees with the subj. *cura*. Venus was anxious about Juno's schemes, fearing that if the Carthaginians were really hospitable Juno might make them otherwise, or fearing that Juno prompted Dido to welcome Aeneas with an ulterior motive.

LINE 663.   **Ergō** (*ergŏ* only rarely in Ovid, and in late Latin poets), adverb, introducing an inference from previous facts or statements, or, as here, a decision prompted

664 díc, tís   ,,   af, fátur   A, mórem :   " Náte, | words she addressed
with words   *she addresses Amor (= Cupid) :*   " *Son,* | the winged Love-god :
me, áe   vi, rés,   ,,   mea ,   mágna   po, téntia , | " Son, who alone art
my   *strength,*   *my*   *great*   *power* | my strength and my great dominion ; son,
665 sólus,   Náte,   pa, trís   sum, mí ,,   qui ,   téla | who scornest the su-
alone,   *son,*   *of the father*   *supreme*   *who*   *the darts* | preme father's Ty-

---

by that inference. *Ergo* is used sometimes like *causā*, *gratiā*, etc., with the genitive case, = *on account of, in consequence of;* it is also found (1) in questions continuing a train of thought, e.g. *ubi ergo* = *when then ? ;* (2) with the imperative or *hortatory* subjunctive, e.g. *dic ergo* = *so tell, tell now.* —— *hīs,* abl. plur. n. of *hīc, haec, hōc ;* agrees with *dictis.* —— **āligerum,** acc. sing. m. of *āliger, -a, -um,* adj. (from *āla,* = *a wing,* + *gerō,* = *I bear,* hence *winged*) ; qualifies *Amorem.* The possession of wings was ascribed to Cupid by the ancients, though not to the gods in general. —— **dictīs,** abl. plur. of *dictum, -ī,* n., 2d ; abl. of the instrument, with *affatur.* —— **affātur** (*adfātur*), 3d pers. sing. pres. ind. of the deponent verb *affor* (*adfor*), *-ārī, -ātus sum,* 1 (*ad* + obsolete *for* of *fārī* = *to speak*) ; understand *Venus* as the subject. —— **Amōrem,** acc. sing. of *Amor, -ōris,* m., 3d (*amō*) ; direct obj. of *affatur ; Amorem* (*Love* personified) = *Cupidinem.*

LINE 664. **Nāte,** voc. sing. m. of *nātus, -a, -um,* perf. part. of the deponent verb *nascor, -ī, nātus sum,* 3 ; *nate* is the m. used substantively, and is the case of the person addressed. A. & G. 113, *f ;* B. no reference ;. G. 437 ; H. 441. —— **meae,** nom. plur. f. of the poss. adj. of the 1st personal pron. sing. *meus, mea, meum ;* agrees with *vires.* —— **vīrēs,** voc. plur. of *vīrēs, -ium,* f., 3d = *strength* (the sing. *vīs,* acc. *vim,* abl. *vī,* = *violence*); voc. in apposition with *nate.* A. & G. 184 ; B. 169 ; G. 320, *ff ;* H. 359, NOTE 2. - *Meae vires* = *thou without whom I would be powerless;* an abstract noun is frequently used in poetry as a descriptive appositive of a proper name or a concrete substantive ; cf. the use of *deliciae* as an appositive in the elegiac poets, and the following lines from a familiar hymn, *O God, our strength in ages past.* —— **mea,** nom. sing. f. of *meus ;* agrees with *potentia.* —— **magna,** nom. sing. f. of the adj. *magnus, -a, -um ;* agrees with *potentia.* —— **potentia,** gen. *potentiae,* f., 1st (from *potens,* = *powerful*); nom. sing., in apposition with *solus,* which see below. Synonyms : *potentia* has been defined *in eo, quod possumus,* i.e. *power,* in reference to ability to do something ; *potestas* = *power, in eo quod licet,* i.e. in reference to permission or authority ; thus *potestas* is regularly used of *legitimate power,* and *potentia* frequently = *lawless power.* —— **sōlus,** nom. sing. m. of the adj. *solus, -a, -um* (gen. *sōlīus,* dat. *sōlī*) ; nom., used instead of the voc., in apposition with *nate.* It has been said that *solus* has no vocative, but in the grammars it is generally given or implied by the absence of any statement to the contrary ; Priscian has denied that there is no vocative. Here *sōlus* = *O tu solus,* and *mea . . . solus* is best rendered by a rel. clause, e.g. *O thou who art alone my great might.* If it were not evident from the context that *solus* must be taken with *potentia,* it would be simple to regard *mea magna potentia* as vocatives, and take *solus* with *qui,* (= *qui solus . . . temnis*). For the use of the nominative instead of the vocative case in apposition, cf. Aen. VIII, 77, and consult A. & G. 241, *a ;* B. 171, 2 ; G. 321, NOTE 1 ; H. 369, 2. This use of the nom. for the voc. is a strange kind of attraction, and occurs chiefly when the nom. is in apposition with the subject of an imperative, e.g. *audi tu, populus Albanus,* = *hear, O thou Alban people.*

LINE 665. **Nāte,** voc. sing. m. of *nātus, -a, -um* (see above) ; the case of address. *Nate* is repeated for emphasis and effect ; this figure is called *anaphora,* viz. the repetition of the same word at the beginning of different clauses. —— **patris,** gen. sing. of

274　　　　　　　VERGIL'S AENEID　　　　　[LINES 666–668.

phoian bolts, to thee	Ty,phóïa ,	témnis,	Ád	te ,	cónfugi,o,	ét 666
I flee and bending	*Typhoian*	*dost despise*	*to*	*thee*	*I flee,*	*and*
supplicate thy divin-	sup,pléx „	tua ,	númina ,		pósco.	Fráter 667
ity. How Aeneas, thy	*suppliant*	*thy*	*divinity*		*entreat.*	*Brother*
brother, is driven o'er	ut ,	Aéne,ás „	pela,gó	tuus ,	ómnia ,	
the deep about every	*how*	*Aeneas*	*over the sea*	*thy*	*all*	
coast through the hate	círcum	Lítora ,	iácte,túr „	odi,ís	Iu,nónis 668	
of angry Juno thou	*around*	*shores*	*is being tossed*	*by the hate*	*of Juno*	

---

pater, m., 3d; poss. gen., limiting *tela; patris* here = *Iovis.* The father of Cupid was Jupiter; but some describe Cupid as the son of Mars and Venus, and others of Mercury and Venus. Here *patris summi* = *the most mighty sire* or *the sire on high,* i.e. *the father* of men and gods; cf. *pater omnipotens.* —— **summī**, gen. sing. m. of *summus, -a, -um,* superl. adj.; agrees with *patris.* —— **quī**, nom. sing. m. of the rel. pron.; agrees with the antecedent *nate,* and is subj. of *temnis.* —— **tēla**, acc. plur. n. of *tēlum, -ī,* n., 2d; direct obj. of *temnis.* —— **Typhōia**, acc. plur. n. of *Typhōius, -a, -um,* adj. (= *of* or *pertaining to Typhoeus;* Greek Τυφωεύς, = *one sending forth smoke);* agrees with *tela; Typhoïa tela,* = *weapons,* i.e. *bolts which slew Typhoeus.* Typhoeus was the son of Tartarus and Terra, and was a fearful giant with 100 heads. He set out to punish the gods for the destruction of his brother-giants, the Titans (who vainly invaded Olympus); the gods changed to different animals to escape him, e.g. Venus became a fish, Jupiter a ram, but finally Jupiter slew him with a thunderbolt and buried him under Mount Aetna in Sicily. —— **temnis**, 2d pers. sing. pres. ind. act. of *temnō, -ere, tempsī,* no supine, 3; agrees with the subj. *qui,* and is 2d pers. because the voc. *nate = tu nate.* Love is often described as supreme, and the vanquisher of gods and mortals.

LINE 666. **Ad**, prep. with the acc.; gov. *te.* —— **tē**, acc. sing. of the 2d personal pron. *tū* (plur. *vōs*) ; governed by *ad.* —— **confugiō**, 1st pers. sing. pres. ind. act. of *confugiō, -ere, confūgī, confugitum,* 3 *(con = cum + fugiō)* ; the subj. implied by the personal ending is *ego.* The metaphor conveyed by the words *confugio* and *supplex* is taken from the custom of divine supplication among mortal men. —— **et**, cop. conj. —— **supplēx**, nom. sing. f. of the adj. *supplēx, -icis,* 3d; agrees with *ego* understood as subj. of *posco;* refer to the note on *supplex,* l. 49. —— **tua**, acc. plur. n. of the poss. adj. *tuus, -a, -um ;* agrees with *numina.* —— **nūmina**, acc. plur. n. of *nūmen, nŭminis,* n., 3d (from *nuō,* = *I nod) ;* direct obj. of *posco.* —— **poscō**, 1st pers. sing. pres. ind. act. of *poscō, -ere, poposcī,* no supine, 3; the contained subj. is *ego; posco* is joined by *et* to *confugio.*

LINE 667. **Frāter**, gen. *frātris,* m., 3d; nom. sing., in appos. with *Aeneas.* —— **ut**, adv. and conj. (old form *utī*) ; here = *how,* introducing an indirect exclamation. For the various uses of *ut* as an adverb, and as a temporal, final, and consecutive conjunction, refer to the note on *ut,* l. 306. —— **Aeneās**, nom. sing.; subj. of *iactetur* in the subordinate clause introduced by *ut.* —— **pelagō**, abl. sing. of *pelagus, -ī,* n., 2d; abl. of 'the place over which,' a special kind of locative ablative. For synonyms, refer to the note on *aequore,* l. 29. A. & G. 39, *b,* and 258, 4, *f, g* ; B. 26, 2, and 228; G. 34, EXCEPTIONS, and 385; H. 51, 7, and 425. —— **tuus**, nom. sing. m. of the poss. adj. of the 2d personal pron.; agrees with *frater.* —— **omnia**, acc. plur. n. of the adj. *omnis, -e,* 3d; agrees with *litora.* —— **circum**, prep. with the acc.; gov. *litora.*

LINE 668. **Lītora**, acc. plur. n. of *lītus, lītoris,* n., 3d; governed by *circum.* —— **iac-tētūr**, 3d pers. sing. pres. subjunct. pass. of *iactō, -āre, -āvī, -ātum,* 1; agrees with the subj. *Aeneas* in the indirect exclamation; the verb is subjunctive because *ut* introduces

669 a, cérbae	**Nóta**	ti, bi ;	ét	nos, tró ,,	knowest well, and cft
angry	*(are things) known to thee;*	*and*	*our*		hast thou sorrowed
670 dolu, ísti	, sǽpe	do, lóre.	**Húnc**	Phoe, níssa	with our sorrow. Him
thou hast grieved often	*with grief.*	*Him*	*Phoenician*		Phoenician Dido
te, nét	Di, dó,	,, blan, dísque		mo, rátur	holds, and stays him
holds	*Dido,*	*and smooth*		*delays (him)*	with smooth words;

an indirect exclamation. Many of the grammars only mention indirect questions, but in several cases the direct speech would be an exclamation and not a question. The present tense *iactetur* is in sequence with the present tense in the main clause, *nota (sunt)*. A. & G. 334; B. 300; G. 467; H. 528, 2, and 529, I. For tense-sequence, consult A. & G. 286; B. 267, 268; G. 509; H. 491. Observe that the final syllable *ur* is lengthened, partly because it is accented and partly because of the strong *caesura* after it ; cf. *peterēt*, l. 651, and see the note and references. The original quantity appears to have been short, so *iactētūr* is not an archaism. Many MSS. read *iacteturque*, but this is meaningless and obviously wrong. —— **odiis**, abl. plur. of *odium*, *-ī*, n., 2d; abl. of cause, explaining *iactetur*. A. & G. 245, and 2, *b*; B. 219; G. 408, and NOTE 2; H. 416. The plural, instead of the singular, is merely poetic. —— **Iūnōnis**, gen. sing. of *Iūnō*, f., 3d; subjective poss. gen., limiting *odiis*. —— **acerbae**, gen. sing. f. of the adj. *acerbus*, *-a, -um ;* qualifies *Iunonis*. *Acerbus* = *bitter, sour,* both literally and figuratively, hence *violent, hostile.* Some MSS. read *inīquae* (*unfriendly,* hence *hostile*), but most editors reject it.

LINE 669. **Nōta**, nom. plur. n. of *nōtus*, *-a, -um,* adj. (properly perf. part. pass. of *noscō, = I know*) ; agrees with the substantival clause *ut Aeneas . . . iactetur* as subj., *nota* being the *complement* of *sunt* understood. We should have expected *notum est,* for the plural in such cases is very rare; it is copied from the Greek, where the neuter plur. of an adjective is often used in phrases like *it is well known, it is impossible,* etc., e.g. ἀδύνατά ἐστιν. —— **tibī**, dat. sing. of *tū ;* dat. of the agent, with *nota (sunt) ;* this dat. is explained as a poss. dat. due to the presence of a part of *sum* expressed or understood; refer to the note on *mihi,* l. 326. Observe that the final syllable of *tibi* is long here; it is often short, for the final syllable of *mihi, tibi, sibi, ubi,* etc., are called common. A. & G. 348, 6; B. 363, 3; G. 707, 4, EXCEPTION 4; H. 581, I. —— **et**, cop. conj. —— **nostrō**, abl. sing. of the poss. adj. *noster, nostra, nostrum ;* agrees with *dolore. Nostro* = *meo,* cf. the use of ' we ' in royal declarations and commands. —— **doluistī**, 2d pers. sing. perf. ind. act. of *doleō, -ēre, -uī,* no supine, 2; the subj. *tu* is contained in the verb. —— **saepe** (comparative *saepius ;* superl. *saepissime*), adv. = *often,* with *doluisti.* —— **dolōre**, abl. sing. of *dolor, -ōris,* m., 3d (from *doleō*) ; abl. of cause, with *doluisti.*

LINE 670. **Hunc**, acc. sing. m. of the demonstr. pron. *hĭc, haec, hŏc ;* direct obj. of *tenet ; hunc* refers to Aeneas. As the first word in the sentence it is very emphatic. ——. **Phoenissa**, nom. sing. f. of the adj. *Phoenissus, -a, -um* (collateral forms *Phoenīceus, -a, -um,* and *Phoenīcius, -a, -um ;* Greek Φοίνισσα); agrees with *Dido.* —— **tenet**, 3d pers. sing. pres. ind. act. of *teneō, -ēre, -uī, tentum,* 2; agrees with the subj. *Dido.* The verbs *tenet* and *moratur* imply that Dido not merely gives Aeneas the hospitality which he requested, but purposely *detains* him, with the object (as Venus thinks) of doing him some mischief at Juno's bidding. As Juno was the patron deity of the new settlement (see l. 446), Venus had some reason to fear. —— **Dīdō**, gen. *Dīdōnis* and *Dīdūs,* f., 3d; nom. sing., subj. of *tenet.* —— **blandīs**, abl. plur. f. of the adj. *blandus, -a, -um ;* agrees with *vocibus.* —— **que**, enclitic cop. conj. —— **morātur**, 3d pers. sing. pres. ind. of the deponent verb *moror, -ārī, -ātus sum,* I (*mora = delay*); agrees with the subj. *Dido,* and is joined by *que* to *tenet. Moror* is used both transitively and intransitively.

and I shrink from the
thought how Juno's
welcome is to issue;
at this crisis in his for-
tunes she will not be
idle. Wherefore I
have in mind to fore-
stall the queen by
craft and wrap her

Vócibus ; , ét vere,ór, „ quo , sé 67ɪ
with words; *and* *I fear* *whither themselves*

Iu,nónia , vértant Hóspiti,a ; haúd tan,tó „ 67ᴈ
Juno's • *are to turn hospitalities;* *not* *so great*

ces,sábit , cárdine , rérum. Quócir,cá 67ᴈ
she will be idle *at a crisis* *of affairs.* *Wherefore*

cape,re ánte do,lís „ et , cíngere ,
to take (her) before with craft *and* *to surround*

LINE 671. **Vócibus**, abl. plur. of *vōx, vōcis*, f., 3d; abl. of the instrument, with *mora-tur*. —— **et**, cop. conj., connecting its own with the preceding sentence. —— **vereor**, 1st pers. sing. pres. ind. of the deponent verb *vereor, -ērī, veritus sum*, 2; the subj. is *ego* contained in the verb. —— **quō**, adverbial abl. of the rel. *quī*, = *whither*, here introducing the indirect subjunct. *vertant*. *Quō* = (1) interrog. *whither ? for what reason ?* (2) relative, *for which reason, wherefore ; quo* is used rather than *ut* in final clauses, where the emphatic word is an adverb or adjective in the comparative degree, e.g. *quo celerius hoc faceret, Romam venit*, = *in order to accomplish this more quickly he came to Rome*. —— **sē**, acc. plur. of the reflexive pron., acc. and abl. *sē (sēsē)*, dat. *sibi*, gen. *suī*, no nom. or voc.; direct obj. of *vertant; se* refers back to the subj. *hospitia*. —— **Iūnōnia**, nom. plur. n. of the adj. *Iūnōnius, -a, -um* (= *of* or *belonging to Iūnō*)*;* qualifies *hospitia*. Venus, in describing the welcome given to the Trojans as *Juno's*, clearly shows how perilous she thought was the position of her son Aeneas. —— **vertant**, 3d pers. plur. pres. subjunct. act. of *vertō, -ere, vertī, versum*, 3, agrees with the subj. *hospitia*. *Vertant* may be considered simply an ordinary subjunctive, required in the indirect question introduced by *quo, = I fear how Juno's welcome will turn out;* but more probably it is the *deliberative* subjunctive in an indirect clause after *quo, = I fear how Juno's welcome is to turn out*, i.e. the direct would be the deliberative subjunctive *quo se vertant ?* = *how is (the welcome) to turn out ?* A. & G. 268; B. 277; G. 265; H. 484, V.

LINE 672. **Hospitia**, nom. plur. of *hospitium, -ī*, n., 2d (from *hospes, -itis,* = *a host*, hence *hospitality*, shown by a host); subj. of *vertant*. —— **haud**, negative adv., limiting *tanto*. *Haud* negatives adjectives or adverbs, rarely verbs (except a very few, e.g. *haud scio an, haud ignoro*, in Cicero); *non* negatives verbs, and also adjectives and adverbs. —— **tantō**, abl. sing. m. of the demonstr. adj. *tantus, -a, -um* (correlative *quantus;* cf. *tot . . . quot*, etc.); agrees with *cardine*, and is emphatic. —— **cessābit**, 3d pers. sing. fut. ind. act. of *cessō, -āre, -āvī, -ātum*, 1 (for *cedso*, intensive of *cēdō*, = *I yield*)*;* understand the subj. *Iūnō*, from the adj. *Iunonia* in the sentence above. —— **cardine**, abl. sing. of *cardō, -inis*, m., 3d; a figurative abl. of ' time when.' A. & G. 256; B. 230; G. 393; H. 429. *Cardō*, = lit. *the pivot*, which was used to fasten a door, also = *the socket* in which the pivot turned, the word being usually rendered freely as *hinge;* hence it is used by metonymy in the sense of *crisis, hinge* of events, *turning-point*. —— **rērum**, gen. plur. of *rēs, reī*, f., 5th; poss. gen., limiting *cardine*. *Res* is a vague word, = *thing, affair, circumstance*, and is very widely used in Latin, especially in connection with other words, e.g. *res publica*, = lit. *the public affair (welfare)*, hence *commonwealth, state*.

LINE 673. **Quōcircā** (*quō + circā*), adv., = *wherefore, for which reasons*, summing up arguments already given and leading up to a conclusion. *Quocirca* is derived from *quō*, the abl. of *qui*, and the prep. *circā*, = *round, round about*, and originally the two words were probably separate, becoming united in process of time as they acquired together a special meaning; cf. *antea*, etc. —— **capere**, pres. inf. act. of *capiō, -ere, cēpī, captum*, 3; *prolative* inf., dependent on *meditor;* governs *reginam. Capere . . . ante*

674 flámma   Régi,nám   medi,tór, „ ne , quó se , round with flame, lest
  with flame   *the queen*   *I design,*   *lest*   *any herself* through some deity

675 númine ,   mútet ;   Séd   mag ,no she change, but that
  by god   *she may change; but (in order that)*   *great* rather she may be kept

Aéne ,aë „ me ,cúm   tene ,átur   a ,móre. on my side by mighty
  of Aeneas   *with me*   *she may be possessed*   *by love.* love   for   Aeneas.

= *antecapere*, = *to take beforehand ;* the metaphor is taken from operations in besieging an enemy's stronghold. —— **ante**, adv., with *capere*. *Ante* in prose is a preposition, but in poetry it is also occasionally used as an adverb, = *anteā*. —— **dolīs**, abl. plur. of *dolus, -ī*, m., 2d (Greek δόλος); abl. of the means or instrument, extending *capere*. —— **et**, cop. conj. —— **cingere**, pres. inf. act. of *cingō, -ere, cinxī, cinctum*, 3; *prolative* inf., joined by *et* to *capere*, and dependent on *meditor ;* gov. *reginam. Cingere flamma* is another military metaphor, for a besieged town was often surrounded by fires to prevent escape; cf. Aen. X, 119, *moenia cingere flammis.* —— **flammā**, abl. sing. of *flamma, -ae*, f., 1st (akin to *flāgrō*, and Greek φλέγω); abl. of the means or instrument, extending *cingere. Flamma* goes with *cingere* in the metaphor, but it has special reference to the *flame* of love, love being the *doli* by which Dido was to be stormed.

LINE 674. **Rēgīnam**, acc. sing. of *rēgīna, -ae*, f., 1st; direct obj. of *capere* and of *cingere.* —— **meditor**, 1st pers. sing. pres. ind. of the deponent verb *meditor, -ārī, -ātus sum ;* the implied subj. is *ego*, i.e. Venus. *Meditor*, = (1) *I ponder, I reflect upon*, hence as the result of reflection; (2) *I purpose, I prepare.* —— **nē**, negative final conj., = *lest, in order that not ;* it is followed by the subjunctive in purpose clauses, as *mutet* below. For the other uses of *ne*, refer to the note on *ne*, l. 299. A. & G. 331, *f* ; B. 296, 2; G. 550; H. 498, III. —— **quō**, abl. sing. n. of the indef. pron. and adj. *quis, quae, quid ;* agrees with *numine. Quis* is rarely used except with *ne* and *se.* —— **sē**, acc. sing. of the reflexive pron.; direct obj. of *mutet ; se* refers to the subj. of *mutet*, viz. Dido. —— **nūmine**, abl. sing. of *nūmen, nūminis*, n., 3d; abl. of cause, extending *mutet ;* the vague *quo numine* refers to Juno. —— **mūtet**, 3d pers. sing. pres. subjunct. act. of *mūtō, -āre, -āvī, -ātum*, 1; the subj. is a pron. understood (*illa*), referring to *reginam* above. *Se mutare* or *mutari* practically = intransitive verbs.

LINE 675. **Sed**, adversative conj., joining *mutet* in one final clause to *teneatur* in the other; see note on *sed*, l. 515. —— **magnō**, abl. sing. m. of the adj. *magnus, -a, -um ;* agrees with *amore.* —— **Aenēae**, gen. sing. of *Aenēās*, m., 1st decl. Greek; objective gen., dependent on *amore.* A. & G. 217; B. 200; G. 363, 2; H. 396, III. *Amore Aeneae*, = *love for Aeneas ;* only the context can in some cases decide whether a genitive is subjective or objective; as far as the grammar is concerned, *Aeneae* might be subjective, = *the love of* (i.e. *felt by*) *Aeneas*, but the sense proves that it must be objective here. —— **mēcum** (*mē* + *cum*), *mē* is the abl. sing. of the 1st personal pron. *ego ;* governed by *cum. Cum* is a prep. with the abl.; gov. *me.* A. & G. 153; B. 142; G. 417, 4; H. 434. For the enclitic use of *cum*, refer to the note on *cum*, l. 37. *Mecum* probably = *like me ;* but some render *with me*, i.e. *on my side*, supposing that Aeneas could not be loved by Dido in the same sense that he was loved by his mother. —— **teneātur**, 3d pers. sing. pres. subjunct. pass. of *teneō, -ēre, -uī, tentum*, 2; the subj. is a pron. understood referring to Dido; *teneatur* is joined by *sed* to *mutet*, but *ut* must be understood with it from *ne* in l. 674, = *in order that . . .* she may *not* change, but *in order that* she may be held, etc. The subjunctive mood is due to the final (purpose) nature of the clause; see note on *ne* above. —— **amōre**, abl. sing. of *amor, -ōris*, m., 3d; abl. of manner, modified by *magno*, and hence dispensing with the prep. *cum.*

Now hear our thought	Quá	face,re	íd	pos,sís, ,,	nos trám 676
how thou may'st avail	By what means to do		that thou may'st be able,		our
to do this. The young	nunc ,	áccipe ,	méntem :	Régius , 677
prince, my special	now	receive (= hear)	mind:	royal
care, makes ready at	ácci,tú ,,	ca,rí	geni,tóris ad	úrbem
his dear father's	at the summons	dear	of his sire to	the city
summons to go to	Sídoni,ám	puer ,	íre pa,rát, ,,	mea , 678
the Sidonian city,	Sidonian	the boy	to go is preparing,	my

LINE 676. **Quā**, adv. = *how* (originally abl. fem. sing. of the rel. *quī*) ; introduces the indirect question after *accipe mentem.* —— **facere**, pres. inf. act. of *faciō, -ere, fēcī, factum*, 3 (*fīō* is used as the passive); *prolative* inf., completing the predication with *possis.* —— **id**, acc. sing. n. of the demonstr. pron. *is, ea, id* (gen. *ēius*, dat. *eī*, abl. *eō, eā, eō*) ; direct obj. of *facere; id* refers to the motives explained in ll. 674, 675, viz. (1) that Dido should not be changed by Juno; (2) that she should love Aeneas like Venus. —— **possis**, 2d pers. sing. pres. subjunct. of *possum, posse, potuī*, no supine, irreg. ; the subj. *tu* is contained in the verb; the mood is subjunctive, because *possis* is a subordinate verb, standing in the clause of the indirect question introduced by *qua.* A. & G. 334 ; B. 300; G. 467; H. 528, 2, and 529, I. —— **nostram**, acc. sing. f. of the poss. adj. *noster, nostra, nostrum ;* agrees with *mentem ; nostram = meam*, cf. *nostro* and note, l. 669. —— **nunc**, adv. of time. —— **accipe**, 2d pers. sing. imperative mood act. of *accipiō, -ere, accēpī, acceptum*, 3 (*ad + capiō*) ; the subj. *tu* is implied by the ending of the verb. —— **mentem**, acc. sing. of *mens, mentis*, f., 3d; direct obj. of *accipe. Mens, = mind*, as the seat of the intellect, but sometimes = *thought;* cf. the similar use of *mind* in the English phrase, *to speak one's mind.*

LINE 677. **Rēgius**, nom. sing. m. of the adj. *rēgius, -a, -um* (from *rēx, rēgis*) ; agrees with *puer ; regius puer*, = Ascanius, the son of Aeneas (cf. l. 544, *rex erat Aeneas nobis*). —— **accītū**, abl. sing. of *accītus, -ūs*, m., 4th (*ad + cieō*) ; abl. of cause, extending *parat ire. Accitu* and other similar ablatives of cause, e.g. *iussu, rogatu*, etc., are adverbial. A. & G. 245; B. 219; G. 408; H. 416. —— **cārī**, gen. sing. of the adj. *cārus, -a, -um* (see *cari*, l. 646); agrees with *genitoris.* —— **genitōris**, gen. sing. of *genitor*, m., 3d (from *genō*, old form of *gignō*) ; subjective gen., limiting *accitu ; accitu genitoris, = at the summoning of his sire* (i.e. his sire having summoned him). Venus refers to the dispatch of Achates to the ships, to bring Iulus to the city and presents for Dido. —— **ad**, prep. with the acc.; gov. *urbem.* —— **urbem**, acc. sing. of *urbs, urbis*, f., 3d; governed by the preposition *ad*.

LINE 678. **Sīdoniam**, acc. sing. f. of the adj. *Sīdonius, -a, -um* (= *of* or *belonging to Sidon, Sidonian*, from the noun *Sidōn, -ōnis* or *-ŏnis*, f., 3d); agrees with *urbem.* Carthage is called *the Sidonian city*, because Dido and her subjects came from Tyre, which was a colony of Sidon. —— **puer**, gen. *puerī*, m., 2d; nom. sing., subj. of *parat.* See *puer*, l. 267, for the limit of age which it denotes. —— **īre**, pres. inf. act. of *eō, īre, īvī* or *iī, itum*, irreg.; *prolative* or *complementary* inf. after *parat.* —— **parat**, 3d pers. ind. act. of *parō, -āre, -āvī, -ātum*, 1 ; agrees with the subj. *puer.* —— **mea**, nom. sing. f. of the poss. adj. *meus, -a, -um ;* agrees with *cura.* —— **māximā**, nom. sing. f. of the superl. adj. *māximus, -a, -um* (superl. of *magnus ;* comparative *māior*). —— **cūra**, gen. *cūrae*, f., 1st; nom. sing., in apposition with *puer.* Venus displays her particular affection for the young Iulus by taking him with her out of harm's way to Idalia, in Cyprus, her own special haunt.

679 máxima　,　cúra,　Dóna　fe,réns,　,,　pela,go | bearing gifts, relics
greatest　　　care,　　gifts　bearing,　　to the sea | of the sea and the
680 ét　flam,mís　res,tántia　,　Tróiae :　Húnc | flames of Troy; him,
and to the flames remaining over　　of Troy :　　him | lulled to slumber, I
ego　,　sópi,túm　som,nó　,,　super　,　álta | shall hide away on
I　　　lulled　with sleep　　over　　high |
681 Cy,théra　Aút　super　,　Ídali,úm　,,　sa,cráta　, | high Cythera or in Ida-
Cythera　　or　over　　Idalium　　consecrated | lium in my hallowed

LINE 679. **Dōna**, acc. plur. of *dōnum, -ī,* n., 2d; direct obj. of *ferens.* The *dona* are specified in lines 647-655. —— **ferēns**, nom. sing. m. of the pres. part. act. of *ferō, ferre, tulī, lātum,* irreg.; agrees with and enlarges the subj. *puer.* —— **pelagō**, dat. sing. of *pelagus, -ī,* n., 2d; a dat. of relation, denoting a person or object from whom (or which) something has been taken, and in reference to whom (or which) the remainder may be said to be left over. The most authoritative commentators regard *pelago* as such a dative, like the dative with *superstes, superesse,* and the like. A. & G. 229; B. 188, 1 and 2, *d*; G. 347, 2 (for *superesse*), and 5; H. 385, 4, 2. In prose we should expect *de pelago,* and some consider *pelago* and *flammis* as ablatives of separation with the preposition omitted. —— **et**, cop. conj. —— **flammīs**, dat. plur. of *flamma, -ae,* f., 1st; a dat. of relation, like *pelago,* to which it is joined by *et.* —— **restantia**, acc. plur. n. of *restāns, -antis,* pres. part. act. of *restō, -āre, restitī,* no supine, 1 (*re, = back,* i.e. *behind,* + *stō, = I stand,* hence *I stand behind, remain over*)*;* agrees with *dona. Re* has a separative force in this word. —— **Trōiae**, gen. sing. of *Trōia, f.,* 1st; poss. gen., limiting *flammis.*

LINE 680. **Hunc**, acc. sing. m. of the demonstr. pron. *hīc, haec, hōc;* direct obj. of *recondam; hunc* refers to Ascanius. —— **ego**, nom. sing.; subj. of *recondam.* Observe that *ego* is emphatic; the close position of *hunc* and *ego* marks the particular care which Venus intends to take of Ascanius. —— **sōpītum**, acc. sing. m. of *sōpītus, -a, -um,* perf. part. pass. of *sōpiō, -īre, -īvī* or *-iī, -ītum,* 4; agrees with and enlarges the obj. *hunc.* The noun *sōpor* is generally used for *deep sleep,* but etymologically there is no difference in meaning between *somnus* and *sopor,* for *somnus = sopnus;* from the same root is the Greek noun for *sleep,* ὕπνος. *Sopitum* is a predicate participle, and *sopitum recondam* takes the place of two coördinate clauses, *sopiam et recondam.* A. & G. 292, REM.; B. 337, 2; G. 437; H. 549, 5. —— **somnō**, abl. sing. of *somnus, -ī,* m., 2d (= *sopnus;* akin to *sōpor*)*;* abl. of manner or abl. of the means with *sopitum.* —— **super**, prep. with the acc. and abl.; gov. the acc. *Cythera. Super* with the abl. denotes *rest above,* with the acc. *motion over;* here the implied notion of *carrying* in *recondam* accounts for the acc. with *super.* A. & G. 153, and 260; B. 143; G. 418, 4; H. 435. —— **alta**, acc. plur. n. of the adj. *altus, -a, -um;* qualifies *Cythera.* —— **Cythēra**, gen. *Cythērōrum,* n., 2d (Greek Κύθηρα); acc. plur., governed by *super.* Cythera (Cerigo) is an island rising high out of the Aegean Sea to the south of Laconia.

LINE 681. **Aut**, disjunctive conj., connecting *super Cythera* and *super Idalium,* each alternative excluding the other; refer to the note on *aut,* l. 183. —— **super**, prep.; gov. the acc. *Idalium; super* here and in the line above means little more than *on high to.* —— **Idalium**, acc. sing. of *Idalium, -ī,* 2d (collateral 1st decl. form *Idalia, -ae,* f.); governed by *super.* Idalium was the name of a city and grove in Cyprus sacred to Venus. —— **sācrātā**, abl. sing. f. of *sācrātus, -a, -um,* perf. part. pass. of *sācrō, -āre, -āvī, -ātum,* 1 (from *sacer, sācra, sācrum,* adj., = *sacred*)*;* agrees with *sede. Sacratus, =* (1) *consecrated, hallowed,* as here; (2) in bad sense, *accursed.* —— **sēde**, abl. sing. of

abode, that he may	séde	re,cóndam,	Né	qua	,	scíre 682
know nought of	in my abode	I will hide,	lest	anyhow to know of		
the trick nor inter-	do,lós	, medi,úsve	oc,cúrrere	,	póssit.	
pose therein. Do	the tricks	or midway	to intervene he may be able.			
thou for one single	Tú faci,em	illi,ús	,,	noc,tém	non	, 683
night feign his form,	Thou the form	of him		for night	not	

---

sēdēs, -is, f., 3d; abl. of 'the place where,' with *recondam.* —— **recondam,** 1st pers. sing. fut. ind. act. of *recondō, -ere, recondidī, reconditum,* 3 (*re, = back,* + *condō, = I hide,* hence *I hide away);* the subj. *ego* is implied by the personal ending.

LINE 682. **Nē,** negative final conj., taking the subjunct. *possit;* refer to the note on *ne,* l. 674. —— **quā,** adverbial abl. sing. f. of the rel. *quī,* or perhaps of the indefinite *quis; ne qua, = lest in any way.* —— **scīre,** pres. inf. act. of *sciō, -īre, scīvī* or *sciī, scītum,* 4; *prolative* inf., with *possit.* Synonyms: *scire, = to know* facts or truths as objects of conviction, e.g. *scio* (neg. *nescio*) *quis sit, = I know who he is; noscere, = to know* things or persons as the objects of perception, e.g. *novi hominem, = I know the man.* —— **dolōs,** acc. plur. of *dolus, -ī,* m., 2d; direct obj. of *scire.* —— **medius,** nom. sing. m. of the adj. *medius, -a, -um;* agrees with the subj. *ille* (viz. *ille* understood, referring to Ascanius), but really modifies the inf. *occurrere* like an adverb (e.g. *obviam*). A. & G. 191; B. 239; G. 325, REM. 6; H. 443. —— **ve** (shortened form of *vel,* which is probably an imperative of *volo*), enclitic disjunctive conj., usually offering a choice between two alternatives, but here with scarcely any more force than a copulative conjunction. See the note on *ve,* l. 9, where *sive, ve, aut* are compared. —— **occurrere,** pres. inf. act. of *occurrō, -ere, occurrī, occursum,* 3 (*ob* + *currō*), *prolative* inf., with *possit; medius occurrere, = to run in the way between,* i.e. to interfere. —— **possit,** 3d pers. sing. pres. subjunct. act. of *possum, posse, potuī,* no supine, irreg.; the subj. is a pron. (*ille*) understood, referring to Ascanius. A. & G. 137, *b;* B. 126; G. 119; H. 290. The subjunctive is due to the purpose denoted by *ne,* and the tense is present in primary sequence after the principal future *recondam.* A. & G. 286; B. 267, 268; G. 509; H. 491.

LINE 683. **Tū,** nom. sing. of the 2d personal pron.; subj. of *falle.* The nominative of the personal pronouns is not found in Latin except when emphasis or contrast is aimed at; here *tu* is very emphatic, and also stands in contrast with the first word of l. 680, *hunc,* and with *illius* below. —— **faciem,** acc. sing. of *faciēs, -ieī,* f., 5th; direct obj. of *falle;* as in l. 658, *faciem* refers to the whole *form,* for the *face* is referred to below in *indue vultus.* —— **illīus,** gen. sing. m. of the demonstr. pron. *ille, illa, illud;* poss. gen., limiting *faciem; illius = Ascanī.* The genitive singular in *-ius* usually has the *i* long, except *alterius,* which is always short; in poetry, however, metrical needs require the *i* short. A. & G. 347, *a,* EXCEPTION; B. 362, 1, *a;* G. 706, EXCEPTION 4; H. 577, I, 3 (3). —— **noctem,** acc. sing. of *nōx, noctis,* f., 3d (Greek *νύξ*); acc. of duration of time, answering a possible question, *how long?* A. & G. 256; B. 181; G. 336; H. 379. —— **nōn,** negative adv., limiting *amplius.* —— **amplius,** adv. in the comparative degree (positive, *ampliter,* superl. *amplissime;* from the adj. *amplus, -a, -um*)*;* modifies *unam; non amplius noctem unam, = not more (than) one night.* A. & G. 92; B. 76, 2, and 77, 1; G. 93; H. 306. *Amplius, = more, further,* in reference to time, number, and sometimes distance. Synonyms: *amplius,* as above; *potius, = more, rather,* of preference; *magis, = more,* in regard to action or quality ; *plus, = more,* of number or degree. Comparison is usually expressed by a comparative adj. or adv. followed by *quam,* or by the abl. case without *quam ;* but *plus, amplius, minus,* and *longius,* without *quam,* frequently modify a word of measure or number (no matter what its case may be) without affecting its case

684 ámplius   ,   únam   Fálle   do,lo,   ét   no,tós
    more (than)   *one*   *feign*   *by guile, and well-known*

pue,rí   „   puer   ,   índue   ,   vúltus :
of the boy   *a boy*   *put on*   *the countenance:*

685 Út   cum   ,   té   gremi,o   „   áccipi,ét
    in order that when   *thee   in her bosom*   *shall receive*

686 lae,tíssima , Dído Réga,lés in,tér   men,sás „
    most joyful   *Dido*   *royal*   *amid the tables (= feast)*

and wear, thyself a
boy, the boy's familiar
face, so that when
with full-filled joy,
amid the royal ban-
quet and the flow of
wine, Dido shall take
thee to her bosom,

---

in any way; e.g. *plus trecenti interfecti sunt,* = *more than three hundred were killed* (the case being that of the subj. of the sentence, with *plus* as a kind of appositive, e.g. *three hundred, (and) more, were killed*). A. & G. 247, *c*; B. 217, 3; G. 296, REM. 4; H. 417, I, NOTE 2. —— **ūnam,** acc. sing. f. of the numeral adj. *ūnus, -a, -um* (gen. *ūnīus,* dat. *ūnī*) ; agrees with *noctem.*

LINE 684. **Falle,** 2d pers. sing. imperative mood act. of *fallō, -ere, fefellī, falsum,* 3; agrees with the subj. *tu; falle dolo,* = lit. *trick by guile, counterfeit. Fallere,* = (1) *to deceive, to dupe;* (2) *to beguile, to make to pass unnoticed,* e.g. time, trouble, etc.; (3) impersonally, *fallit,* = *it escapes notice,* with the acc., e.g. *me fallit,* = *it escapes my notice. Falle* here, in the sense of *imitate,* is unexampled; but most editors so render it. Deuticke, to escape the difficulty, takes *noctem . . . dolo* as a parenthesis, and reads *tu faciem illius . . . et notos pueri puer indue vultus* as the principal sentence, in which *faciem* is (like *vultus*) a direct object of *indue.* However, such a parenthesis is very harsh, and poets are never very stringent in regard to the accurate use of words. —— **dolō,** abl. sing. of *dolus, -ī,* m., 2d; abl. of manner, with *falle.* —— **et,** cop. conj. —— **nōtōs,** acc. plur. m. of the adj. *nōtus, -a, -um ;* agrees with *vultus.* —— **puerī,** gen. sing. of *puer,* m., 2d; poss. gen., limiting *vultus.* —— **puer,** nom. sing.; in apposition with *tu* understood as subj. of *indue.* —— **indue,** 2d pers. sing. imperative mood act. of *induō, -ere, induī, indūtum,* 3 (Greek ἐνδύω); understand *tu* as subj.; *indue* is joined by *et* to *falle. In-duo,* = *I put on,* is opposed to *exuo,* = *I put off.* —— **vultūs,** acc. plur. of *vultus, -ūs,* m., 4th; direct obj. of *indue ;* the plur. *vultus,* instead of the sing. *vultum,* is a poetic variation.

LINE 685. **Ut,** final conj.; it is separated from the verb of purpose *inspires* by the temporal clauses introduced by *cum,* l. 685 and l. 687. —— **cum,** temporal conj., with the future simple *accipiet. Cum* temporal takes the imperfect and pluperfect subjunctive, but the indicative in other tenses. A. & G. 325; B. 288, 289; G. 580-585; H. 521. —— **tē,** acc. sing. of *tū ;* direct obj. of *accipiet.* —— **gremiō,** abl. sing. of *gremium, -ī,* n., 2d; abl. of 'the place where,' extending *accipiet* adverbially. —— **accipiet,** 3d pers. sing. fut. ind. act. of *accipiō, -ere, accēpī, acceptum,* 3 (*ad + capiō*); agrees with the subj. *Dido.* The future tense is properly used of an act in the future; the English 'when she receives' is grammatically loose, referring to the future. —— **laetissima,** nom. sing. f. of the adj. *laetissimus, -a, -um* (superl. of *laetus, -a, -um*); agrees with *Dido,* and is probably an adverbial attribute, = *in her exceeding joy.* —— **Didō,** nom. sing.; subj. of *accipiet* in the clause introduced by *cum.*

LINE 686. **Rēgālēs,** acc. plur. f. of the adj. *rēgālis, -e,* 3d (*rēx, rēgis*) ; agrees with *mensas.* —— **inter,** prep. with the acc.; gov. *mensas.* —— **mensās,** acc. plur. of *mensa, -ae,* f., 1st; governed by *inter. Mensa,* = lit. *a table,* and as the tables were small and often carried away as each course was ended, *mensa* comes itself to = *a course ;* thus *regales inter mensas,* = *at the royal banquet,* and modifies *accipiet* with the adverbial force

shall clasp thee in	lati,cémque	Ly,æum,	Cúm	dabit , 687
embrace and print	*and wine*	*Lyaean,*	*when*	*she shall give*
sweet kisses on thee,	ámplex,ús „	at,que	óscula ,	dúlcia ,
thou may'st breathe	*embraces*	*and*	*kisses*	*sweet*
within her the secret	fíget,	Óccul,tum	ínspi,rés	ig,ném, „ 688
flame and instil thy	*shall imprint,*	*hidden*	*thou may'st inspire*	*a fire,*
poison unawares."	fal,lásque	ve,néno."	Páret	A,mór 689
The Love-god obeys	*and deceive her*	*with poison."*	*Obeys*	*Love*

of a phrase denoting time or place. —— **laticem**, acc. sing. of *latex, laticis,* m., 3d (= lit. *a liquid,* hence *wine*) ; governed by *inter,* and joined by *que* to *mensas.* —— **que**, enclitic cop. conj. —— **Lyaeum**, acc. sing. m. of the adj. *Lyaeus, -a, -um* (= *of* or *belonging to Lyaeus,* i.e. Bacchus; cf. the Greek Λυαῖος = lit. *the Releaser,* from λύω = *I release,* i.e. from care, etc.) ; agrees with *laticem. Lyaeus* is properly a substantive, and *laticem Lyaeum = laticem Lyaei.* The poets often use a noun as an adjective; cf. Aen. VI, 877, *Romula . . . tellus = tellus Romuli.*

Line 687. **Cum,** temporal conj., taking the future simple *dabit;* see *cum* above. —— **dabit,** 3d pers. sing. fut. ind. act. of *do, dare, dedī, datum;* agrees with a pron. understood as subj., referring to *Dido.* —— **amplexūs,** acc. plur. of *amplexus, -ūs,* m., 4th (from *amplector = I embrace*) ; direct obj. of *dabit; dare amplexus* is a periphrasis for *amplecti* used absolutely, and with it may be compared many other periphrastic combinations, e.g. *dare laxas habenas,* = *to loosen the reins.* —— **atque,** cop. conj., joining a third member to the series and emphasizing it; the first action is *cum gremio accipiet,* the second *cum dabit amplexus,* and the third (*cum*) *oscula figet* represents the complete abandonment of Juno to joy. —— **oscula,** acc. plur. of *osculum, -ī,* n., 2d; direct obj. of *figet; osculum,* being a diminutive of *ōs, ōris,* = lit. *a little mouth,* but is nearly always used with the meaning *a kiss.* —— **dulcia,** acc. plur. n. of the adj. *dulcis, -e,* 3d; qualifies *oscula.* —— **figet,** 3d pers. sing. fut. ind. act. of *fīgō, -ere, fīxī, fīxum,* 3; joined by *atque* to *dabit,* and in agreement with the same subject.

Line 688. **Occultum,** acc. sing. m. of *occultus, -a, -um,* perf. part. pass. of *occulō, -ere, -uī, occultum,* 3 (*ob* + root CUL, akin to *cēlō,* hence *I cover over, conceal*) ; attributive part., agreeing with *ignem.* —— **inspīrēs,** 2d pers. sing. pres. subjunct. act. of *inspīrō, -āre, -āvī, -ātum,* 1 (*in,* = *into,* + *spīrō,* = *I breathe*) ; the subj. *tu* is contained in the verb, and refers to Cupid. *Inspirare* is regularly used of divine *inspiration;* and ' the divine afflatus ' of the poets is the *breathing in* of the poetic spirit by the muses. —— **ignem,** acc. sing. of *ignis, -is,* m., 3d ; direct obj. of *inspires;* the metaphor of the *secret flame* of love is familiar in our own poetry. —— **fallās,** 2d pers. sing. pres. subjunct. act. of *fallō, -ere, fefellī, falsum,* 3; joined by *que* to *inspires,* and in agreement with the same subject. *Fallo* is regularly used of various kinds of *unseen* action; here *fallas* hardly = *decipias* (*deceive*), but rather *take unawares.* —— **que**, enclitic cop. conj. —— **venēnō,** abl. sing. of *venēnum, -ī,* n., 2d; abl. of the means or instrument, extending *fallas; poison* is metaphorically used for *love,* because they both often work insidiously, and sometimes (as in Dido's case) fatally.

Line 689. **Pāret,** 3d pers. sing. pres. ind. act. of *pāreō, -ēre, -uī, -itum,* 2; agrees with the subj. *Amor.* —— **Amor,** gen. *Amōris,* m., 3d (personified, = *Cupidō*) ; nom. sing., subj. of *paret.* —— **dictīs,** dat. plur. of *dictum, -ī,* n., 2d (properly perf. part. pass. n. sing. of *dīcō*) ; dat. of the indirect obj. after *paret.* Many special verbs, e.g. *invideo, parco, credo, persuadeo, pareo,* etc., govern the dative case. A. & G. 227; B. 187, II;

dic,tís	„	ca,rǽ	gene,trícis,	et	,	álas	his dear mother's be-
the words		*dear*	*of his mother,*	*and*		*his wings*	hests, lays aside his
690 Éxuit,	,	ét	gres,sú	„	gau,déns	in,cédit	wings, and walks ex-
puts off,		*and with the step*			*rejoicing*	*walks*	ulting with Iulus'
691 I,úli.	Át	Venus	,	Áscani,ó	„	placi,dám	step. But Venus
of Iulus.	*But*	*Venus*		*to Ascanius*		*gentle*	sheds the dew of
692 per	,	mémbra	qui,étem	Írrigat,	,	ét	peaceful sleep upon
through		*his limbs*	*slumber*	*diffuses,*		*and*	Ascanius' limbs, and

G. 346, and REM. 2; H. 385, I and II.—— **cārae**, gen. sing. f. of the adj. *cārus, -a, -um;* agrees with *genetrīcis.* —— **genetrīcis**, gen. sing. of *genetrīx*, f., 3d (from *genō*, old form of *gigno;* cf. the corresponding m. *genitor*) ; poss. gen., limiting *dictis; genetricis = Veneris.* —— **et**, cop. conj. —— **ālās**, acc. plur. of *āla, -ae*, f., 1st; direct obj. of *exuit.*

LINE 690. **Éxuit**, 3d pers. sing. pres. ind. act. of *ēxuō, -ere, ēxuī, ēxūtum*, 3 (the opposite of *induo*) ; agrees with a pron. understood as subj. referring to *Amor; exuit* is joined by *et* to *paret.* —— **et**, cop. conj. —— **gressū**, abl. sing. of *gressus, -ūs*, m., 4th (from *gradior, -ī, gressus sum*, 3); abl. of manner, describing *incedit.* When the ablative of the noun expressing manner is not modified, it should be preceded by the preposition *cum ;* but in poetry the preposition is frequently omitted. A. & G. 248, at the end; B. 220; G. 399, NOTE 2; H. 419, III. *Gressu* is here emphatic, signifying that Cupid is now *walking* (not *flying*) and that the wings have been laid aside for the occasion. —— **gaudēns**, nom. sing. m. of the pres. part. of the semi-deponent verb *gaudeō, -ēre, gavīsus sum*, 2; agrees with *Amor* (understood from above) as the subj. of *incedit.* The picture of Cupid is the conventional one of a boy *exulting* in the mischievous but doubtless entertaining work of inflaming mortal men and women with love. —— **incēdit**, 3d pers. sing. pres. ind. act. of *incēdō, -ere, incessī, incessum*, 3 (*in + cēdō*) ; understand *Amor* from above as subject; *incedit* is joined by *et* to *exuit.* The present tense is *historic* (as also in *paret* and *exuit* above), representing past action more graphically and rapidly than a past tense would. *Incedit* expresses *graceful* or *majestic motion.* —— **Iūlī**, gen. sing. of *Iūlus*, m., 2d; poss. gen., limiting *gressu.*

LINE 691. **At**, adversative conj., here drawing the attention away to a short digression connected with the plot of Venus. —— **Venus**, gen. *Veneris*, f., 3d; nom. sing., subj. of *irrigat.*—— **Ascaniō**, dat. sing. of *Ascanius, -ī*, m., 2d; dat. of the indirect obj. after *irrigat*, which is a compound of *in.* A. & G. 228; B. 187, III; ·G. 347; H. 386. Observe the poetic skill of Vergil in bringing into close juxtaposition in the verse Venus, the plotter, and Ascanius, the object of the plot. —— **placidam**, acc. sing. f. of the adj. *placidus, -a, -um* (from *placeō*) ; agrees with *quietem.* —— **per**, prep. with the acc.; gov. *membra.* —— **membra**, acc. plur. of *membrum, -ī*, n., 2d; governed by the preposition *per.* —— **quiētem**, acc. sing. of *quiēs, -ētis*, f., 3d (akin to Greek κεῖμαι = *I lie down*) ; direct obj. of *irrigat.*

LINE 692. **Irrigat** (*inrigat*), 3d pers. sing. pres. ind. act. of *irrigō, -āre, -āvī, -ātum*, 1 (*in, + rigō = I moisten*) ; agrees with the subj. *Venus;* the present is *historic.* The metaphor of being *bathed* or *drowned* in sleep is seen to be common to both English and Latin; sleep is supposed to creep over a person as silently and steadily as water advances in channels over the land. The phrase Vergil uses here is Lucretian, for Lucretius has, *somnus per membra quietem irrigat.* Mr. Page compares another but not dissimilar metaphor in Keble's 'Evening Hymn' ; "When the soft *dews* of kindly sleep My

fondled on her bosom	fo,túm	gremi,ó	„	dea	,	tóllit	in,
raises him by power	(him) fondled	in her bosom		she		a goddess	bears
divine to the lofty	áltos	Ídali,æ	lu,cós,	„	ubi	,	móllis 693
groves of Idalia, where	to high	of Idalia	the groves		where		soft
soft amaracus cradles	a,máracus	,	íllum	Flóribus	,	ét	dul,ci 694
him with flowers and	the marjoram		him	with flowers		and	sweet
the sweet breath of	áspi,ráns	„	com,pléctitur		,		úmbra.
its fragrant shade.	breathing upon (him)		enfolds				with shade.

weary eyelids gently steep." —— et, cop. conj. —— fōtum, acc. sing. m. of *fōtus, -a, -um*, perf. part. pass. of *foveō, -ēre, fōvī, fōtum*, 2; predicate part., agreeing with *eum* understood (from *Ascanio*) as the direct obj. of *tollit; fotum tollit = eum fovet et tollit*. A. & G. 292, REM.; B. 337, 2; G. 437; H. 549, 5. *Fotum* expresses a notion of *nursing;* perhaps it is best rendered *fondled.* —— gremiō, abl. sing. of *gremium, -ī*, n., 2d; abl. of ' the place where.' —— dea, gen. *deae*, f., 1st; nom. sing., in apposition with *Venus* understood from above as the subj. of *tollit.* Some take *dea* as the subj. of *tollit*, but the word would be needless and inartistic after *Venus* mentioned above; clearly it has a special force here and = *by her divine power*. —— tollit, 3d. pers. sing. pres. of *tollō, -ere, sustulī, sublātum*, 3 (the perf. and supine are borrowed from *sufferō*) ; understand *Venus* as subject; *tollit* is joined by *et* to *irrigat*, and is a *historic* present. —— in, prep. with the acc. and abl.; gov. the acc. *lucos.* —— altōs, acc. plur. m. of the adj. *altus, -a, -um;* agrees with *lucos. Altus = high*, as viewed from below; *deep*, as viewed from above.

LINE 693. **Idaliae**, gen. sing. of *Īdalia*, f., 1st (also *Īdalium, -ī*, n., 2d); poss. gen., limiting *lucos.* Refer to the note on *Idalium*, l. 681. —— lūcōs, acc. plur. of *lūcus, -ī*, m., 2d; governed by *in. Lucus = a grove*, especially one set apart for the worship of some deity. —— ubi, adverb of place, = *where. Ubi* has several uses: (1) interrog., of place = *where ?*, of time, *when ?;* (2) relative adv. = *where, in which place*, often with a preceding demonstrative adv. *ibi ;* it often refers to persons or things, = *with* or *by whom, which* (cf. *unde* in the sense *a quo*). (2) *Ubi* is further used as a particle in temporal clauses = *when*, and its syntax is similar to that of *postquam*, and *simul ac.* —— mollis, nom. sing., m. or f., of the adj. *mollis, -e*, 3d; qualifies *amaracus.* —— amāracus, gen. *amāracī*, m. or f., 2d (Greek ἀμάρακος); nom. sing., subj. of *complectitur.* —— illum, acc. sing. m. of the demonstr. pron. *ille, illa, illud;* direct obj. of *complectitur.*

LINE 694. **Flōribus**, abl. plur. of *flōs, flōris*, m., 3d; abl. of the instrument, with *complectitur.* A. & G. 248, *c*; B. 218; G. 401; H. 420. —— dulcī, abl. sing. f. of the adj. *dulcis, -e*, 3d; qualifies *umbra.* —— aspīrāns (*adspīrāns*), nom. sing., m. or f., of the pres. part. act. of *aspīrō* (*adspīrō*), *-āre, -āvī, -ātum*, 1 (*ad, = upon,* + *spīrō, = I breathe*); agrees with *amaracus.* The hive = *the marjoram cradles him with flowers and the fragrance of its sweet shade* (lit. *and breathing upon him with sweet shade*). We should have expected *et* to connect another instrumental ablative with *floribus*, but Vergil's love of variety leads him to use a participial clause instead, *umbra* being an ablative of manner with *aspirans* and not (as some take it) an ablative of the instrument with *complectitur.* —— complectitur, 3d pers. sing. pres. ind. of the deponent verb *complector, -ī, complexus sum*, 3 (*cum, + plectō, = I entwine*, hence medial *I entwine myself with, embrace*); agrees with the subj. *amaracus.* —— umbrā, abl. sing. of *umbra, -ae*, f., 1st; abl. of manner, with *aspirans.*

695 Iámqu*e*　　i,bát　　dic,tó　　pa,réns,　　,,　　et ,
And now　　was going　to the word　obedient　　　　　and
696 dóna　Cu,pído　Régia ,　pórta,bát　Tyri,ís, ,,
the gifts　Cupid　　royal　　was carrying for the Tyrians,
697 duce ,　　létus　A,cháte.　Cúm　venit, ,
(as) guide　rejoicing　with Achates.　When　he comes,
aúlae,ís　,,　iam ,　sé　re,gína　su,pérbis
amid tapestries　already　herself　the queen　　　　proud

And now joyously
going in Achates'
guidance Cupid, obe-
dient to her word,
went and bore the
royal presents for the
Tyrians. As he draws
near, the queen has
already taken her seat

LINE 695. **Iam,** adverb of time, used connectively as often in the Aeneid; it resumes the narrative where the side-description of Venus hiding the real Ascanius interrupted it. —— **que,** enclitic cop. conj., connecting its own sentence with what has preceded. —— **ībat,** 3d pers. sing. imperf. ind. act. of *eō, īre, īvī* or *iī, itum,* irreg.; agrees with the subj. *Cupido;* the imperfect tense is used in continued description. —— **dictō,** dat. sing. of *dictum, -ī,* n., 2d (or the dat. sing. n. of *dictus, -a, -um,* perf. part. pass. of *dīcō, -ere, dīxī, dictum,* 3, = lit. *the thing told,* i.e. *what he was ordered*); dat. of the indirect obj. governed by *parens* (for case, see note on *dictis,* l. 689 above). —— **pārēns,** nom. sing. m. of the pres. part. act. of *pāreō, -ēre, -uī, -itum,* 2; agrees with and enlarges the subj. *Cupido.* —— **et,** cop. conj. —— **dōna,** acc. plur. of *dōnum, -ī,* n., 2d; direct obj. of *portabat.* The *gifts* are those which Aeneas had instructed Achates to bring when he brought Ascanius to the city; the disguised god, true to his assumed character, omits no detail which Ascanius would have observed. —— **Cupīdō,** gen. *Cupīdinis,* m., 3d (per-sonified; from *cupiō = I desire*); nom. sing., subj. of *ibat* and *portabat.* *Cupido* is subj. of *ibat,* but for metrical reasons stands in the sentence with *portabat.*

LINE 696. **Rēgia,** acc. plur. n. of the adj. *rēgius, -a, -um;* agrees with *dona.* —— **portābat,** 3d pers. sing. imperf. ind. act. of *portō, -āre, -āvī, -ātum,* 1; agrees with the subj. *Cupido; portabat* is joined by *et* to *ibat,* and the two verbs = *ibat portans,* which further accounts for the position of *Cupido* in the sentence. —— **Tyriīs,** dat. plur. of *Tyriī, -ōrum,* m., 2d (substantival m. plur. of the adj. *Tyrius, -a, -um);* dat. of the indirect obj., denoting the persons interested or affected by the phrase *dona portabat.* —— **duce,** abl. sing. of *dūx, ducis,* common gender, 3d (from *dūcō = I lead);* either in appos. with *Achate* as an abl. of cause, with *laetus,* or in the abl. abs. construction with *Achate.* In either case the sense is practically the same, *rejoicing in the leadership of Achates.* The most common form of the *ablative absolute* is when a noun or pronoun is modified by a participle in agreement; but the noun is frequently modified by an adjec-tive or by another noun in the same case, and if there were a present participle of *sum,* that participle would be in the ablative as a copula. A. & G. 255; B. 227; G. 409, 410; H. 431. —— **laetus,** nom. sing. m. of the adj. *laetus, -a, -um;* agrees with *Cupido.* —— **Achātē,** abl. sing. of *Achātēs,* gen. *Achat-ae* or *-ī,* m. (cf. *Achate,* l. 312); either an abl. of cause, with *laetus,* or abl. abs. with *duce.*

LINE 697. **Cum,** temporal conj., followed by the graphic *historic* present, *venit.* Refer to the note on *cum,* l. 36. —— **venit,** 3d pers. sing. pres. ind. act. of *veniō, -īre, vēnī, ventum,* 4 irreg.; understand *Cupido* as subject. —— **aulaeīs,** abl. plur. of *aulaeum, -ī,* n., 2d (Greek αὐλαία); this abl. is called the *abl. of attendant circumstances,* chiefly used in locative connections, and an extension of the locative ablative. *Aulaea* are the *tapestries* hung in a hall (*aula,* Greek αὐλή), and not the tapestries on the couches. —— **iam,** adv. of time, really the antecedent of *cum,* as *iam* (= *tum*) *regina se composuit . . . cum venit.* —— **sē,** acc. sing. of the reflexive pron. *sē,* gen. *suī;* direct obj. of *composuit.* —— **rēgīna,** nom. sing.; subj. of *composuit; regina* of course = *Dido.* —— **superbīs,** abl

on a golden couch	Aúrea ,	cómposu,ít	spon,dá, „ 698
amid proud awnings	*golden*	*has settled*	*on a couch,*
and sat with the guests	medi,ámque	lo,cávit : Iám	pater , 699
around her. Now	*and in the middle*	*has set (herself): now*	*father*
father Aeneas and	Aéne,ás, „ et ,	iám Tro,iána	iu,véntus
	Aeneas and	*now Trojan*	*the youth*
now the Trojan youth	Cónveni,únt, ,	stra,tóque	su,pér 700
gather together and	*assemble,*	*and strewn*	*upon*

plur. of the adj. *superbus, -a, -um,* agrees with *aulaeis.* *Superbus = proud* is properly an epithet of persons, but is often used with things which belong to and illustrate the power of royal or noble personages.

LINE 698. **Aurēā,** abl. sing. f. of the adj. *aureus, -a, -um ;* agrees with *sponda. Aurea* is here a dissyllable, for *ĕă* by *synizesis* becomes *ēā ;* cf. l. 726, *aurēis.* A. & G. 347, *c* ; B. 367, 1 ; G. 727 ; H. 608, III. —— **composuit,** 3d pers. sing. perf. ind. act. of *compōnō, -ere, composuī, compositum,* 3 (*cum* + *pōnō*) ; agrees with the subj. *regina.* —— **spondā,** abl. sing. of *sponda, -ae,* f., 1st ; abl. of ' the place where,' with *composuit.* A. & G. 258, 4, *f, g* ; B. 228 ; G. 385 ; H. 425. —— **mediam,** acc. sing. f. of the adj. *medius, -a, -um ;* agrees with *se* understood from the preceding clause as obj. of *locavit.* Some refine upon this passage and describe Dido as seated in the centre of the *triclinium,* between Aeneas and Ascanius ; but probably *mediam* simply = *in the midst* of the assembled guests. —— **que,** enclitic cop. conj. —— **locāvit,** 3d pers. sing. perf. ind. act. of *locō, -āre, -āvī, -ātum,* 1 (*locus = a place*) ; joined by *que* to *composuit* and in agreement with the same subject.

LINE 699. **Iam,** adv. of time; *iam* above and *iam* here are emphatic, and indicate the actual state of affairs at the time of Cupid's arrival ; *now the queen has seated herself . . . now Aeneas and the Trojans are assembling.* —— **pater,** gen. *patris,* m., 3d ; nom. sing., in apposition with *Aeneas.* —— **Aenēās,** nom. sing., one of the subjects of *conveniunt.* —— **et,** cop. conj. —— **iam,** adv. of time; see note above. —— **Trōiāna,** nom. sing. f. of the adj. *Trōiānus, -a, -um ;* agrees with *inventus.* —— **iuventus,** gen. *iuventūtis,* f., 3d ; nom. sing., a subj. of *conveniunt; iuventus,* which is strictly an abstract = *youth* (the state of a *iuvenis*), is here collective and = *iuvenes.*

LINE 700. **Conveniunt,** 3d pers. plur. pres. ind. act. of *conveniō, -īre, convēnī, conventum,* 4 (*con = cum, together,* + *veniō, = I come*); agrees with the composite subj., *Aeneas* and *iuventus.* —— **strātō,** abl. sing. n. of *strātus, -a, -um,* perf. part. pass. of *sternō, -ere, strāvī, strātum,* 3 (akin to the Greek στορέννμι); agrees with *ostro. Strato = spread,* i.e. spread upon the couches. —— **que,** enclitic cop. conj. —— **super,** prep. with the acc. and abl.; gov. the abl. *ostro.* Some take *super* as an adverb, modifying *strato = spread over,* i.e. he couches ; but *ostro* by itself is an awkward ablative, and to take *ostro strato* as an ablative absolute would be very harsh. —— **discumbitur,** 3d pers. sing. pres. ind. pass. of *discumbō, -ere, discubuī, discubitum,* 3 (*dis,* expressing laxness, + *cumbō, = I lie down,* hence *I recline*) ; used impersonally, = lit. *it is lain down,* i.e. *they lie down* or *recline ;* cf. *itur = it is gone* (some one goes), and *pugnatum est = it was fought* (fighting was going on). The passive of intransitive verbs is frequently used impersonally, and the passive of verbs which govern the dative case can be used in no other way, e.g. *parcitur mihi = I am spared.* A. & G. 146, *c* ; B. 256, 3 ; G. 208, 2 ; H. 301, 1. Some take *discumbitur* to mean *they take each his place,* supposing that *dis* marks the *separa-*

701 dis,cúmbitur　　　　，　　　óstro.　　　　　Dánt | the guests recline
they recline (lit. it is reclined)　on the purple.　　　Give | upon the strewn pur-

famu,lí　　mani,bús　lym,phás, „ Cere,rémque | ple. Servants give
men-servants for the hands　water,　　　and bread | water for the hands,
　　　　　　　　　　　　　　　　　　　　　　　　　　　　　| and serve out bread
702 ca,nístris　Éxpedi,únt,　„ ton,sísque　fe,rúnt | from baskets, and
in baskets　　prepare,　　　and shorn　　carry | bring napkins with

703 man,télia　　，　víllis.　Quínqua,gínta　in,tús | close-shorn pile.
napkins　　with wool.　Fifty (there are)　within | Within are fifty maid-

tion of the guests as they take their couches. But *discumbere* is the regular word for *to recline*, and is found in passages in reference to a single person only. The ancient Romans did not sit down to eat, but reclined at length on a couch with a raised border, on which one elbow was rested. For the *triclinium* (dining couches arranged in the form of three sides of a square), refer to Smith's or some other good dictionary of antiquities, or to Becker's Gallus. —— **ostrō**, abl. sing. of *ostrum, -ī*, n., 2d; governed by *super.* *Ostro* refers to the purple *stragulae vestes* or *coverlets* which were laid over the couches. Those who take *aulaeis* above as referring to the tapestries of the couches identify *aulaeis* and *ostro ;* but the words almost certainly refer to different things; see note on *aulaeis*, l. 697.

LINE 701. **Dant**, 3d pers. plur. pres. ind. act. of *dō, dare, dedī, datum*, 1; agree? with the subj. *famuli*. —— **famulī**, nom. plur. of *famulus, -ī*, m., 2d (collateral f. noun *famula, -ae*, 1st); subj. of *dant*. —— **manibus**, dat. plur. of *manus, -ūs*, f., 4th; a dat. of purpose, like *tecto*, l. 425. —— **lymphās**, acc. plur. of *lympha, -ae*, f., 1st (*nympha* and *lympha* are really the same word); direct obj. of *dant*. —— **Cererem**, acc. sing. of *Cerēs, Cereris*, f., 3d; direct obj. of *expediunt; Cererem* is used by the figure *metonymy* for *panem = bread*, as Ceres was the goddess of agriculture. A. & G. 386; B. no reference; G. no reference; H. 637, III. —— **que**, enclitic cop. conj. —— **canistrīs**, abl. plur. of *canistra, -ōrum*, n., 2d (Greek κάναστρα); abl. of manner, with *expediunt.* The singular of *canistra* is not used in classical Latin; *canistra = a basket*, woven with reeds.

LINE 702. **Expediunt**, 3d pers. plur. pres. ind. act. of *expediō, -īre, -īvī* or *-iī, -ītum*, 4 (*ex, = from*, + *pēs, = the foot, = to extricate*, originally the foot from a snare); joined by *que* to *dant*, and in agreement with the same subject. —— **tonsīs**, abl. plur. m. of *tonsus, -a, -um*, perf. part. pass. of *tondeō, -ēre, totondī, tonsum*, 2; agrees with *villis; tonsis villis = with shorn nap*, i.e. soft and smooth napkins. —— **que**, enclitic cop. conj. —— **ferunt**, 3d pers. plur. pres. ind. act. of *ferō, ferre, tulī, lātum*, irreg.; joined by *que* to *expediunt*, and in agreement with the same subj., viz. *famuli*. —— **mantēlia**, acc. plur. of *mantēle, -is*, n., 3d (connected with *manus, the hand); direct* obj. of *ferunt*. —— **villīs**, abl. plur. of *villus, -ī*, m., 2d; abl. of quality, describing *mantelia*. A. & G. 251; B. 224; G. 400; H. 419, II. *Villus* is etymologically related to the Greek οὖλος and ἔριον (at one time ϝεριον, with the *digamma*), and to the English *wool*.

LINE 703. **Quinquāgintā** (*quinque, + gintā, = κοντα, ten*, hence *five tens*), indeclinable numeral adj., qualifying *famulae*. —— **intus** (akin to Greek ἐντός), adv., = *within*, i.e. in an inner room or kitchen. —— **famulae**, nom. plur. of *famula, -ae*, f., 1st; subj. of *sunt* understood. The duties of the *famuli* or men-servants are in the immediate neighborhood of the guests; those of the *famulae* or women-servants are in the kitchen, in cooking the various foods and arranging them in such a way that the *famuli* may receive them and set them before the banqueters. —— **quibus**, dat. plur. f.

| servants, whose care it is to array in long line the food-store and to kindle the hearth with flames. | famu,læ,
maid-servants,
Cúra   pe,núm
(it is) the care food | ,,   quibus
to whom
strue,re
to arrange | ,   órdine
in line
ét
and | ,   lóngo
long
flam,mís ,, 704
with flames |

of the rel. pron, *quī, quae, quod;* agrees with the antecedent *famulae*, and is the dat. of the possessor after *est* understood with *cura (quibus cura est struere,* etc.). A. & G. 231; B. 190; G. 349; H. 387. For the omission of the copula, refer to the note on *irae*, l. 11. —— **ordine**, abl. sing. of *ordō, -inis*, m., 3d; abl. of manner, with *struere*. —— **longō**, abl. sing. m. of the adj. *longus, -a, -um;* agrees with *ordine; ordine longo struere = to array in long line*, a very natural, if prosaic, description of the preparations in the kitchen. There is another reading *longam* which several editors adopt. The arguments in favor of each are as follows: (A) *Longo*. This is the reading of all the MSS., except the Palatine MS., and it should be read unless the evidence against it is convincing. The phrase is quite Vergilian, and occurs in several different places; moreover. the sense is perfectly clear. (B) *Longam*. Gellius (A.D. 150, about) mentions this reading, as well as *longo*, and the most ancient grammarian Charisius supports it. Moreover, the poet Ausonius appears to have this line in mind (with *longam* read), as the *pentameter* "*cui non* LONGA PENUS, *huic quoque prompta fames*" seems to show. The main objection against *longam* is the strange meaning which it acquires, viz. *struere longam penum = to arrange provisions for a long time* (to last a long time), or perhaps *provisions in long succession*. If the MSS. were not almost unanimous in reading *longo*, the law of textual criticism that a difficult reading is more likely to be right than an easy one might be urged in favor of *longam:* on the whole, it is safer to read *longo*.

LINE 704. **Cūra**, gen. *curae*, f., 1st; nom. sing., predicative with *est* understood; *cura est* agrees with the subject-inf. *struere;* the predicative dat. *curae* would be more idiomatic. —— **penum**, acc. sing. of *penus*, gen. *-ūs* or *-ī*, m. and f. (with collateral forms *penum, -ī*, n. and *penus, -oris*, n.); direct obj. of *struere*. *Penus* is used of a plentiful supply of provisions, and from this word *Penates* is most probably derived: they are the *gods of the household*, and particularly the *larder (penus)*. —— **struere**, pres. inf. act. of *struō, -ere, struxī, structum*, 3; subj.-inf. of *cura (est)*. For the use of this inf. as a verbal noun, both subject and object, consult A. & G. 270; B. 326-328; G. 280; H. 532, and 538. *Struere* does not = *to pile up*, as some suppose (who add "in the store-house"), for this would be out of place here where a special feast is being described; it = *to arrange*, referring to the *arraying* of the different courses on the *fercula* or trays (so Servius, quoted by Mr. Page, defines *struere*). —— **et**, cop. conj. —— **flammīs**, abl. plur. of *flamma, -ae*, f., 1st; abl. of the means or instrument, with *adolere*. —— **adolēre**, pres. inf. act. of *adoleō, -ēre, -uī, adultum*, 2 (kindred inceptive form *adolescō;* both from *ad +* root OL = *to grow*, hence *I make to grow);* a subj.-inf., joined by *et* to *struere*, and a subj. of *cura (est)*. *Adolere Penates = to make the hearths blaze*, for *famulae* would scarcely have *to sacrifice to the household gods ; Penates* may poetically = *hearths*, as their images were kept near the hearth, and elsewhere *Penates* is used poetically as an equivalent for *domos*, l. 527. *Adolere* is used in various curious ways: e.g. *adolere verbenas = to* BURN *branches, adolere honores = to* OFFER *sacrifices*. Of its two regular meanings, (1) *to make to grow, to increase* (cf. *adolescens*), (2) *to honor, to magnify*, i.e. the gods, only the first is possible here, for it is expected of cooks to build up big fires but not to offer sacrifices in the name of the master of the house. —— **penātēs**, gen. *penātium*, m. plur., 3d (from *penus = provisions);* direct obj. of *adolere; penates* here stands for the *hearth-fire*, over which the household gods watched, as also over the whole house.

705	ado,lére	pe,nátes ;	Céntum	ali,æ, ,,	There are an hundred
	to magnify	the penates;	(there are) a hundred	others,	other handmaidens
706	toti,démque	pa,rés	ae,táte	mi,nístri,	Quí	and as many pages
	and as many	equal	in age	pages,	who	like in age, to load
	dapi,bús	men,sás	one,rént,	,,	et ,	the board with viands
	with viands	the tables	are to load,		and	
707	pócula ,	pónant. Néc	non ,	ét Tyri,í ,,	and set out the cups.
	the cups	are to set. Nor	not	also the Tyrians	And the Tyrians too

LINE 705. **Centum**, indecl. numeral adj., qualifying *aliae*. —— **aliae**, nom. plur. f. of
alius, -a, -ud (gen. *alīus*, dat. *aliī*) ; substantival, or agreeing with *famulae* understood,
subj. of *sunt* to be supplied. —— **totidem** (*tot* + the pronominal suffix *dem*), indecl.
numeral adj. = *just so many*, qualifying *ministri*. —— **que**, enclitic cop. conj. —— **parēs**,
nom. plur. m. of the adj. *pār*, gen. *paris*, 3d (gen. plur. usually *parium*. *Par* is found
with the gen. and dat. cases, like *similis*, etc.; in Vergil it is used with the inf., and in
the best prose is followed by *atque, ac,* or *quam,* e.g. *parem numerum ac = a like num-
ber as . . . . Par* is also used in phrases, e.g. *par est = it is fit,* or *suitable that . . . .*
Occasionally *par* is a substantive, = *an equal, a fellow, a match,* etc. Synonyms: *similis
= like,* expressing resemblance; *aequalis = equal,* mutually and absolutely; *par = like,
equal,* in mutual and proportionate congruity. Thus two gloves may be *similes,* e.g. in
color, but not for that reason *pares;* they may also be *aequales,* e.g. of the same size,
but not *pares;* when they are *similes* in color and make, and *aequales* in size, then they
are *pares.* —— **aetate**, abl. sing. of *aetās, -ātis,* f., 3d; abl. of specification, denoting
in what respect the *ministri* are *pares.* A. & G. 253; B. 226; G. 397; H. 424. ——
ministrī, nom. plur. of *minister, ministrī,* m., 2d; subj. of *sunt* which must be supplied.
    LINE 706. **Quī**, nom. plur. m. of the rel. pron. *quī, quae, quod;* subj. of *onerent ;
qui* here = *ut ei,* introducing a final or purpose clause, and so followed by the subjunc-
tive *onerent* and *ponant.* For final clauses introduced by *qui* or *ut,* consult A.&. G. 317;
B. 282; G. 545; H. 497. —— **dapibus**, abl. plur. of *daps, dapis,* f., 3d (usually in the
plural); abl. of the means or instrument with *onerent.* The construction might have
been acc. and dat. (reversed from dat. and acc. as here), e.g. *dapes mensis onerent.* A.
& G. 225, *d;* B. 187, I, *a;* G. 348; H. 384, 2, and *footnote* 1. —— **mensās**, acc. plur. of
mensa,-ae, f., 1st; direct obj. of *onerent.* —— **onerent**, 3d pers. pres. plur. subjunct. act. of
onerō, -āre, -āvī, -ātum, 1 (from *onus, oneris,* n., 3d = *a burden*) ; agrees with the subj.
qui ; the subjunctive mood expresses intention or purpose after *qui.* —— **et**, cop. conj.
—— **pōcula**, acc. plur. of *pōculum, -ī,* n., 2d (rarely syncopated, *poclum*) ; direct obj. of
ponant. —— **pōnant**, 3d pers. plur. pres. subjunct. act. of *pōnō, -ere, posuī, positum,* 3;
joined by *et* to *onerent,* and in precisely the same grammatical construction. The best
MSS. read *onerent* and *ponant ;* but a few have *onerant* and *ponunt,* the present indica-
tive. The indicative, describing the actual scene, is not so good as the subjunctive which
defines the duties; the feast would be already set out when the guests arrived.
    LINE 707. **nec** (shortened form of *neque = and . . . not*), negative cop. conj., con-
necting the sentence in which it stands with what has preceded. *Nec non = nor not
(and not npt)* is strongly asseverative, for two negatives make an emphatic affirmative.
—— **nōn**, neg. adv., going closely with *nec.* —— **et**, conj., here = *etiam, also ;* the Tro-
jan guests have been mentioned, and here *et Tyrii = the Tyrians also* claim the poet's
attention. —— **Tyriī**, gen. *Tyriōrum,* m., 2d; nom. plur., subj. of *convenere.* —— **per**,
prep. with the acc.; gov. *limina.* —— **limina**, acc. plur. of *līmen, līminis,* n., 3d (for
lig-men from *ligō = I fasten*) ; governed by *per ; per limina = over the threshold,* i.e.
into the *atrium* or hall, where the feast would have to be held owing to the large

| came thronging o'er the festal threshold to the gathering, reclining at the bidding on embroidered couches. They marvel at Aeneas' gifts, marvel at Iulus, at the god's glowing | per   ,   límina   ,
across   *the threshold*
Cónve,nére,   to,rís ,,
came together, on the couches
píctis.   Míran,túr
embroidered.   *They marvel at*
mi,rántur   I,úlum,
they marvel at   *Iulus,* | lǽta
festal
ius,sí
invited
do,na
the gifts
Flágran,tésque
and burning | fre,quéntes
thronging
dis,cúmbere , 708
to recline
Aéne,ǽ ; ,, 709
of Aeneas;
de,í 710
of the god |

number of guests. —— **laeta**, acc. plur. n. of *laetus, -a, -um*, adj. ; agrees with *limina ;* the attribute of the guests is transferred to the house where the banquet is given; cf. *crudeles aras.* A. & G. 385; B. no reference; G. 693; H. 636, IV. —— **frequentēs**, nom. plur. m. of *frequēns, -entis*, adj. 3d; agrees with *Tyrii ; frequentes = thronging, in large numbers,* cf. *frequens senatus = the crowded Senate. Frequens* is sometimes an adverbial attribute, and = *often,* e.g. *frequens ibam = I used to go frequently.*

LINE 708. **Convenēre,** 3d pers. plur. perf. ind. act. of *conveniō, -īre, convēnī, conventum,* 4 (*con = cum, together,* + *veniō, I come*) *;* agrees with the subj. *Tyrii.* Of the two 3d per. plur. perf. ind. act. endings, *-ērunt* and *-ēre,* the former is met more often in prose, while the latter, a popular form, is much favored by poets for metrical reasons. —— **torīs,** abl. plur. of *torus, -ī,* m., 2d; abl. of 'the place where,' with *discumbere.* —— **iussī,** nom. plur. m. of *iussus, -a, -um,* perf. part. pass. of *iubeō, -ēre, iussī, iussum,* 2; agrees with and enlarges the subj. *Tyrii ; iussi = invited.* —— **discumbere,** pres. inf. act. of *discumbō, -ere, discubuī, discubitum,* 3 (*dis, = freely, loosely,* + *cumbō, = I lie*) *; prolative* or *complementary* inf., completing the predication of *iussi.* —— **pictīs,** abl. plur. m. of *pictus, -a, -um,* perf. part. pass. of *pingō, -ere, pinxī, pictum,* 3; agrees with *toris ; pictis acū* (*painted* or represented pictorially *with a needle,* i.e. *embroidered*) would be the complete phrase; cf. *toga picta.*

LINE 709. **Mīrantur,** 3d pers. plur. pres. ind. of the deponent verb *mīror, -ārī, -ātus sum,* 1; understand *Tyrii,* from the preceding sentence, as the subject. —— **dōna,** acc. plur. of *dōnum, -ī,* n., 2d; direct obj. of *mirantur.* —— **Aenēae,** gen. sing. of *Aenēās ;* subjective poss. gen., limiting *dona ; dona Aeneae = the presents given by Aeneas* (not *to Aeneas,* which would be objective possessive). —— **mīrantur,** 3d pers. plur. pres. ind. (see above); understand *Tyrii* as subject. Observe the *asyndeton ;* the absence of the conjunction and the rhetorical repetition of *mirantur* well express the admiring wonder with which the Tyrians viewed Aeneas' gifts and the glorified beauty of Iulus (personated by Cupid). A. & G. 208, *b* ; B. 346; G. 473, REM.; H. 636, I. For the *anaphora,* refer to the note and references on *hic,* l. 17. —— **Iūlum,** acc. sing. of *Iūlus, -ī,* m., 2d; direct obj. of *mirantur.*

LINE 710. **Flāgrantēs,** acc. plur. of *flăgrāns, -antis,* pres. part. act. of *flăgrō, -āre, -āvī, -ātum,* 1 (akin to Greek φλέγω); agrees attributively with *vultus. Flagrantes* is a very suitable epithet to apply to the features of the god of love, and the verb *flagro* is constantly used in the poets with the sense of *burning with love.* —— **que,** enclitic cop. conj.; *que . . . que = both . . . and.* For *que . . . que, et . . . et, et . . . que,* and *que . . . et* refer to the note on *et,* l. 63, and to the references on *et,* l. 3. —— **deī,** gen. sing. of *deus,* m., 2d; poss. gen., limiting *vultus. Deī* is very skilfully introduced, reminding us that *Iulum* and *dei* are the same person, viz. Cupid masquerading as the son of Aeneas. —— **vultūs,** acc. plur. of *vultus, -ūs,* m., 4th; direct obj. of *mirantur.* The *que* appended to *flagrantes* does not = *and* (as if connecting *Iulum* and *vultus*)

vul,tús,	„	simu,látaque	,	vérba,	face and feigned
the countenance,		*and feigned*		*(his) words,*	words, at the robe
711 Pállam,que	ét	pic,túm	croce,ó „	ve,lámen	and the veil em-
and the robe	*and*	*embroidered*	*yellow*	*the veil*	broidered with the
					yellow acanthus. In
712 a,cántho.	Præcipu,e	ínfe,líx,	,	pes,tí	chief the hapless
with acanthus.	*Especially*	*unhappy,*		*to ruin*	Phoenician, doomed
713 de,vóta	fu,túrae,	Éxple,rí	men,tém „		to future ruin, cannot
doomed	*future,*	*to satisfy*	*her soul*		sate her soul and

but = *both;* thus *flagrantes* . . . *verba* is a particular description of *Iulum,* and *pallam* . . . *acantho* is a particular reference to *dona.* *Vultus = the countenance,* as the means of expressing thought or emotion; the divinity of Cupid was possibly partly discernible in the expression. —— simulāta, acc. plur. of *simulātus, -a, -um,* perf. part. pass. of *simulō, -āre, -āvī, -ātum,* 1; agrees with *verba; simulata verba = feigned words,* i.e. feigned to be the utterances of the real *Iulus.* —— que, enclitic cop. conj. —— verba, acc. plur. of *verbum, -ī,* n., 2d; joined closely by *que* just above to *vultus.*

LINE 711. Pallam, acc. sing. of *palla, -ae,* f., 1st; joined by *que* enclitic to *vultus;* refer to l. 648, *pallam signis auroque rigentem.* —— que, enclitic cop. the correlative of *que* appended to *flagrantes; que . . . que* corresponds here to the Greek τε . . . καί. —— et, cop. conj. —— pictum, acc. sing. n. of *pictus, -a, -um* (see *pictis,* l. 708); agrees with *velamen; pictum = pictum acu, embroidered.* —— croceō, abl. sing. m. of the adj. *croceus, -a, -um;* agrees with *acantho.* —— vēlāmen, acc. sing. of *vēlāmen, -inis,* n., 3d (from *vēlō = I cover, I veil);* one of the direct objects of *mirantur,* and joined by *et* to *pallam.* —— acanthō, abl. sing. of *acanthus, -ī,* m., 2d (Greek ἄκανθος = *thorn-flower);* abl. of manner, with *pictum.*

LINE 712. Praecipuē, adv., formed from the adj. *praecipuus, -a, -um.* —— infēlīx, nom. sing. f. of the adj. *infēlīx, -īcis,* 3d (*in, = not, + fēlīx, =* actively *propitious,* passively as here *fortunate);* qualifies *Phoenissa; infelix* and *devota pesti,* while being attributes of Dido, also refer to *nequit expleri mentem,* etc. —— pestī, dat. sing. of *pestis, -is,* f., 3d (akin to *perdō = I destroy;* hence (1) *plague,* or infectious *disease;* (2) *ruin, destruction);* dat. of the indirect obj., after *devota.* *Pesti* refers to the *destruction* of Dido, who killed herself on a funeral pyre when Aeneas sailed away from Carthage. —— dēvōta, nom. sing. f. of *dēvōtus, -a, -um,* perf. part. pass. of *dēvoveō, -ēre, aēvōvī, dēvōtum,* 2 (*dē, = from, + voveō, = I vow,* hence *I transfer by a vow* something from myself to someone else, *I devote);* agrees with *Phoenissa.* —— futūrae, dat. sing. f. of *futūrus, -a, -um,* fut. part. of *sum, esse, fuī;* agrees with *pestī.* For the death of Dido, refer to Aen. IV, ll. 650–666.

LINE 713. Explērī, pres. inf. pass. of *expleō, -ēre, -ēvī, -ētum,* 2 (*ex,* intensive, + *pleō, = I fill,* hence *I fill up, I sate); prolative* inf. depending on *nequit.* Some few render *cannot be sated as to her soul* (acc. of respect), but *expleri* is undoubtedly medial and a good example of a Latin imitation of the Greek middle voice, if not of an obsolete middle voice in Latin itself; *expleri mentem = to sate her soul,* or *to have her soul sated.* —— mentem, acc. sing. of *mens, mentis,* f., 3d; direct obj. of the medial inf. *explerī,* and not an acc. of respect. —— nequit, 3d pers. sing. pres. ind. act. of *nequeō, -īre, nequīvī* or *iī, nequitum,* irreg. and intrans. (*ne, = not, + queō, = I am able);* agrees with the subj. *Phoenissa.* The present tense of *nequeo* is as follows: *nequeo, nonquis, nequit, nequimus, nequitis, nequeunt;* the pres. subjunct. is *nequeam,* etc.; the imperfect is *nequibam,* etc.; the future is missing except *nequībunt.* *Nequeo* and *queo* are rarely

burns afire with	nequit,	árdes,cítque	tu,éndo
gazing and is moved	*is unable,*	*and glows*	*with gazing*
in like degree by the	Phœnis,sa,	ét pari,tér ,,	pue,ró 714
boy and his gifts.	*the Phoenician (Dido),*	*and equally*	*by the boy*
He, when he had	do,nísque	mo,vétur. Ílle	ubi , 715
hung in Aeneas' arms	*and by the gifts*	*is moved. He*	*when*
and about his neck	cómplex,u Aéne,áe ,,	col,lóque	pe,péndit,
and had filled to the	*in the embrace of Aeneas*	*and on the neck*	*has hung,*
full his false father's	Ét mag,núm fal,si	ímple,vít ,,	geni,tóris 716
	and great false	*has fulfilled*	*of his sire*

used except in the present, and *queo* is not used at all by Caesar. A. & G. 144, *g*; B. 137, 1; G. 170, *a*, *b*; H. 296. —— **ardescit,** 3d pers. sing. pres. ind. act. of *ardescō, -ere, arsī,* no supine, 3 (*inceptive* or *inchoative* form of *ardeō*); joined by *que* to *nequit,* and in agreement with the same subj. *Phoenissa.* For *inceptives,* consult A. & G. 167, *a*; B. 155, 1; G. 133, V; H. 337. —— **que,** enclitic cop. conj. —— **tuendō,** abl. of *tuendum,* gen. *-ī,* dat. and abl. *-ō* (no nom.), the gerundive of *tueor, -ērī, tuitus* or *tūtus sum,* 2; abl. of cause, or rather an abl. of the attendant circumstances (= *dum tuitur*), with *ardescit.* The inf. may stand as subj. or obj. of a sentence; its other cases are supplied by the gerund; e.g. acc. *propensus ad legendum;* gen. *ars amandi;* dat. *operam quaerendo dabo;* abl. *discimus legendo.* A. & G. 295; B. 338; G. 425, *ff,* esp. 431; H. 541, 542.

LINE 714. **Phoenissa,** gen. *Phoenissae,* f. adj. and, as here, substantive, 1st (Greek Φοίνισσα; from *Phoenīx, -īcis,* m., 3d, = *a Phoenician,* Φοῖνιξ); nom. sing., subj. of *nequit* and *ardescit; Phoenissa = the Phoenician* woman, i.e. Dido. —— **et,** cop. conj. —— **pariter** (from *par = equal*), adverb of time or degree, modifying *movetur.* —— **puerō,** abl. sing. of *puer, -ī,* m., 2d; abl. of cause, with *movetur.* A. & G. 245; B. 219; G. 408; H. 416. —— **dōnīs,** abl. plur. of *dōnum, -ī,* n., 2d; abl. of cause, joined by *que* to *puero.* —— **que,** enclitic cop. conj. —— **movētur,** 3d pers. sing. pres. ind. pass. of *moveō, -ēre, mōvī, mōtum,* 2; joined by *et* above to *ardescit,* and in agreement with the same subj. *Phoenissa.*

LINE 715. **Ille,** nom. sing. m. of the demonstr. pron. *ille, illa, illud;* subj. of *petit; ille* is emphatic, and refers to the supposed Iulus, *as for him, he,* etc. —— **ubi,** temporal conj., followed by the perf. ind. *pependit. Ubi* takes the perfect and *historic* present in the indicative; less commonly it is followed by the imperfect or pluperfect indicative (occasionally but rarely subjunctive). The mood of the verb largely depends on whether the particle itself marks the time of the main clause or whether the time of the main clause is described by the details. A. & G. 323–334; B. 287; G. 561, *ff;* H. 518. —— **complēxū,** abl. sing. of *complēxus, -ūs,* m., 4th (*complector*); a loose locative•abl., with *pependit; complexu = in the embrace* of Aeneas, i.e. in his arms. —— **Aenēae,** gen. sing. of *Aenēās,* m., 1st decl. Greek; subjective poss. gen., limiting both *complexu* and *collo.* —— **collō,** abl. sing. of *collum, -ī,* n., 2d; abl. of 'the place where,' with *pependit. Complexu* and *collo* are poetical ablatives of 'place where' and would be impossible in prose. A. & G. 258, 4, *f, g;* B. 228; G. 385; H. 425. —— **que,** enclitic cop. conj. —— **pependit,** 3d pers. sing. perf. ind. act. of *pendeō, -ēre, pependī,* no supine, 2; the subj. is a pron. understood referring to *Iulus (Cupido).*

LINE 716. **Et,** cop. conj., joining two ideas of equal importance. —— **magnum,** acc. sing. m. of the adj. *magnus, -a, -um;* qualifies *amorem.* —— **falsī,** gen. sing. m. of the adj. *falsus, -a, -um* (from *fallō = I deceive);* agrees with *genitoris; falsi genitoris = of*

717 a, mórem,   Régi, nám   petit. , Hǽc   ocu, lís, ,,| love, proceeds to the
    the love,   *the queen*   *seeks.*   *She with her eyes,*| queen. She clings to
718 haec   ,   péctore   ,   tóto   Hǽret ;   et ,| him with her eyes,
    she   *with her heart*   *whole*   *clings ;*   *and*| with all her heart, and
ínter, dúm gremi, ó ,, fovet, , ínscia , Dído| anon caresses him at
at times *on her bosom* *fondles (him),* *unaware* *Dido*| her bosom, nothing
| knowing, poor Dido!

---

his false (pretended) father, i.e. *genitoris qui fallebatur.* If *falsi* be regarded as the adjective and not the participle, it should really be used of Cupid, but Vergil means that, as the son was *false,* the relationship between the false son and the father was also *false.* —— **implēvit**, 3d pers. perf. ind. act. of *impleō, -ēre, -ēvī, -ētum,* 2 (*in,* = *into,* + *pleō,* = *I fill,* hence *I satisfy) ;* joined by *et* to *pependit,* and in agreement with the same subj.; *pependit* and *implevit* are perfects dependent on *ubi.* —— **genitōris,** gen. sing. of *genitor,* m., 3d; pos. gen., limiting *amorem.* —— **amōrem,** acc. sing. of *amor, amōris,* m., 3d; direct obj. of *implevit; implevit amorem = satisfied his father's affection,* i.e. the active tokens of affection.

LINE 717. **Rēgīnam,** acc. sing. of *rēgīna, -ae,* f., 1st; direct obj. of *petit.* Cupid loses very little time in commencing what he and Venus had designed; cf. l. 720. —— **petit,** 3d pers. sing. pres. ind. act. of *petō, -ere, petīvī* or *-iī, petītum,* 3; agrees with the subj. *ille.* The present tense here and in the verbs following is *historic ;* as the perfect, used to describe single acts, and the imperfect, used to describe continued acts, would be monotonous, Vergil makes very free use of the *historic* present, which brings the action before the reader's mind vividly, as if it were taking place as he reads. —— **Haec,** nom. sing. f. of the demonstr. pron. *hīc, haec, hōc ;* subj. of *haeret.* Observe the *anaphora,* i.e. the rhetorical repetition of *haec* below; we may express this by the same figure in English thus, *with her eyes, with her whole heart she clings.* *Anaphora* is very expressive of emotion; the repeated word frequently takes the place of an ordinary, commonplace conjunction, whereby much of the effect would be lost, e.g. *haec oculis et pectore toto haeret.* A. & G. 344, *f ;* B. 350, 11, *b ;* G. 636, NOTE 4, and 682; H. 636, III, 3. —— **oculīs,** abl. plur. of *oculus, -ī,* m., 2d; a free and poetic abl. of the means, with *haeret.* —— **haec,** nom. sing. f.; repeated by *anaphora* from *haec* above. —— **pectore,** abl. sing. of *pectus, pectoris,* n., 3d; abl. of the means, like *oculis* above. —— **tōtō,** abl. sing. n. of the adj. *tōtus, -a, -um* (gen. *tōtīus,* dat. *tōtī) ;* agrees with *pectore.*

LINE 718. **Haeret,** 3d. pers. sing. pres. ind. act. of *haereō, -ēre, haesī, haesum,* 2; agrees with the subj. *haec.* —— **et,** cop. conj. —— **interdum** (perhaps *inter* + *dum* = *dium,* old acc. of *dies,* hence *at intervals in a day,* i.e. *occasionally),* adv., modifying *fovet.* —— **gremiō,** abl. sing. of *gremium, -ī,* n., 2d; locative abl., with *fovet.* Some editors enter on an amusing discussion of *gremio fovet = fondles o (in) her bosom ;* one side urges that Ascanius was rather an old boy to fondle in such an affectionate way, and so thinks there must be a reference to Dido's near position to Ascanius at the *triclinium ;* the other side sensibly urges that the scene is a poetical one, and that Vergil gives his imagination wings. —— **fovet,** 3d pers. sing. pres. ind. act. of *foveō, -ēre, fōvī, fōtum,* 2; joined by *que* to *haeret,* and in agreement with the same subject. —— **inscia,** nom. sing. f. of the adj. *inscius, -a, -um (in,* = *not,* + *sciō,* = *I know) ;* agrees with *Dido.* —— **Dīdō,** nom. sing.; in appos. with the subj. *haec.* *Inscia Dido,* placed as it is in the sentence, is pathetic : we might imitate it thus, *and fondles him in her bosom, nothing knowing, hapless Dido, how great,* etc.

how great a god is	Ínsi,dát	quan,tús	,,	mise,rǽ 719
settling deep in her	*is settling*	*how great*		*within her unhappy (self)*
soul. But he, mind-	deus !	,	Át memor	,	ílle Mátris 720
ful of his Acidalian	*a god!*		*But mindful*		*he of his mother*
mother's wish, begins	A,cídali,ǽ	,,	pau,látim	abo,lére	Sy,chǽum
by slow feints to drive	*Acidalian*		*little by little*	*to make fade*	*Sychaeus*
Sychaeus out and	Íncipit,	,	ét vi,vó	,,	ten,tát prae,vértere 721
works to surprise with	*begins,*		*and living*		*strives to anticipate*

LINE 719. **Insīdat**, 3d pers. sing. pres. subjunct. act. of *insīdō, -ere, insēdī, insessum,* 3 (*in* + *sīdō; insideō* from *in* and *sedeō*) ; agrees with the subj. *deus; insidat* is subjunctive in the indirect exclamation introduced by the relative adj. *quantus.* The direct would obviously be exclamatory (*how powerful a god,* etc.), not interrog. (*how powerful is the god who,* etc. ?). Refer to the note and references on *sit,* l. 454. There is another but not so authoritative reading *insideat,* from *insideō.* —— **quantus,** nom. sing. m. of the rel. adj. *quantus, -a, -um* (*tantus* is the corresponding demonstr. adj.); agrees with *deus,* and introduces the indirect exclamation dependent on *inscia.* —— **miserae,** dat. sing. f. of the adj. *miser, -a, -um;* agrees with *sibi,* which must be supplied; *miserae sibi* is the dat. of the indirect obj. governed by *insidat* (a compound of *in*). —— **deus,** nom. sing.; subj. of *insidat.* —— **At,** adversative conj., often used to bring in an objection in an argument; so here *at* introduces the aspect in which Cupid views the matter, as opposed to the human view which Vergil has just mentioned so pathetically. —— **memor,** gen. *memoris,* adj. 3d of one termination; nom. sing. m., agreeing with *ille.* —— **ille,** nom. sing.; subj. of *incipit; ille* is emphatic, and contrasts the heartless god of love with the ill-fated and affectionate queen.

LINE 720. **Mātris,** gen. sing. of *mater,* f., 3d (Greek μήτηρ); objective gen., dependent on *memor.* A. & G. 218, *a*; B. 204, 1; G. 374; H. 399, I, 2. —— **Acīdaliae,** gen. sing. of the adj. *Acīdalius, -a, -um* (*of* or *belonging to* (*the fountain*) *Acidalius* or *Acidalia* in Boeotia); agrees with *matris.* Venus is called *Acidalian,* because she and the Graces used to bathe in the Acidalian fountain in Boeotia. —— **paulātim** (from *paulus,* = *little*), adv., modifying *abolere.* —— **abolēre,** pres. inf. act. of *aboleō, -ēre, -ēvī* or *-uī, -itum,* 2 (*ab,* = *away,* denoting reversal, + root OL, = *to grow,* hence *to cause to fade; prolative* inf., completing the meaning of *incipit.* *Abolere* is the opposite of *adolere* (= *to make to grow);* observe that the opposition is obtained by means of the prepositions in the composition. —— **Sychaeum,** acc. sing. of *Sўchaeus, -ī,* m., 2d; direct obj. of *abolere; abolere Sychaeum = to obliterate* (Dido's memory of) *Sychaeus.* It will be remembered that Sychaeus, whom Pygmalion slew, had been the husband of Dido. Vergil treats the quantities of vowels in proper names freely; thus the *y* in *Sychaeus* is usually short (as here), but in l. 343 it is long.

LINE 721. **Incipit,** 3d pers. sing. pres. ind. act. of *incipiō, -ere, incēpī, inceptum,* 3 (*in,* = *in,* + *capiō,* = *I take,* hence *I take in hand, I begin);* agrees with the subj. *ille.* —— **et,** cop. conj. —— **vīvō,** abl. sing. m. of the adj. *vīvus, -a, -um;* agrees with *amore.* The phrase *vivo amore* (*with a living love*) is another instance of Vergil's use of an adjective strictly only applicable to persons (or animate beings) as an attribute of a thing or abstract word; cf. *crudeles aras.* The meaning is that Cupid intends Dido to love the *live* Aeneas, instead of the *dead* Sychaeus. —— **tentat** (*temptat*), 3d pers. sing. pres. ind. act. of *tentō* (*temptō*), *-āre, -āvī, -ātum,* 1 ; joined by *et* to *incipit* and in agreement with the same subject. —— **praevertere,** pres. inf. act. of *praevertō, -ere, praevertī, praeversum,* 3 (*prae* + *vertō*); *prolative* inf., dependent on *tentat; praevertere = to surprise*

722 a,móre　　Iám　　pri,dém　　resi,dés　　ani,mós ,,　　a life-full love her
　　with love　　*already for a long time inactive*　　*her mind*　　long-calm spirit and

723 de,suétaque　　,　córda.　　Póstquam　　,　príma　　heart long-unused.
　　and unaccustomed　　*her heart.*　　*After*　　*(there was) first*　　At the feast's first

qui,és　　epu,lís,　　,,　　men,sǽque　　re,mótae,　　lull, when the boards
the lull　　*to the feast,*　　　　*and the tables*　　*were removed,*　　were cleared, they set

724 Cráte,rás　　mag,nós　　statu,únt,　　,,　　et　,　vína　　out the great mixing-
　　mixing-bowls　　*great*　　*they place,*　　　　*and*　*the wine*　　bowls and crown the

---

or *to anticipate* Dido, *before* (*prae*) she notices the design or *before* her old passion for Sychaeus is awakened. —— amōre, abl. sing. of *amor, -ōris*, m., 3d; abl. of the means, with *praevertere.*

LINE 722. **Iam,** adv. of time, strengthened by *pridem,* and modifying *resides* and *desueta.* —— prīdem (*pri,* as in *pri-or, pri-mus,* + the demonstr. suffix *dem*), adv., = *a long time ago. Iam pridem = for a long time since,* and is often employed like *iam dudum* (*iamdudum*) with the present and imperfect, denoting that the action begun in the past has been continued to the present or to the time indicated by the imperfect. For *iamdudum* (or *iam pridem*) with the present tense, refer to the note and references on *gero,* l. 48; for its use with the imperfect, to the note on *iamdudum,* l. 580. —— resĭdēs, acc. plur. m. of the adj. (*reses*), *residis,* 3d of one termination (from *resideō,* = *I remain behind,* hence *I am inactive;* nom. sing. *reses* is very rare); agrees with *animos.* —— animōs, acc. plur. of *animus, -ī,* m., 2d; direct obj. of *praevertere;* the plural is poetic (for *animum;* cf. l. 710, *vultus* for *vultum*). —— dēsuēta, acc. plur. n. of *dēsuētus, -a, -um,* perf. part. pass. of *dēsuescō, -ere, dēsuēvī, dēsuētum,* 3 (*dē,* = *from,* + *suescō,* = *I accustom,* hence *I disaccustom*); agrees with *corda. Desueta* is a trisyllable, the *ue* being treated as a diphthong in poetry. —— que, enclitic cop. conj. —— corda, acc. plur. of *cor, cordis,* n., 3d (akin to Greek κῆρ and καρδία); a direct obj. of *praevertere,* joined by *que* to *animos;* the plural is poetic.

LINE 723. **Postquam,** temporal conj., followed either by the *historic* present *est* or the perfect *fuit* understood. *Postquam* is often found separated as two words *post . . . quam,* cf. *prius . . . quam,* etc. For the syntax of *postquam,* see the references under *ubi,* l. 715. —— prīma, nom. sing. f. of the superl. adj. *prīmus, -a, -um* (from *prae;* no positive; comparative, *prior, -us*); agrees with *quies.* —— quiēs, gen. *quiētis,* f., 3d; nom. sing., subj. of *fuit* or *est* (*historic* pres.) understood. *Quies* refers to the pause in the banquet, after the feasting was done and before the regular *symposium* (wine-drinking) commenced. It was the custom to prolong a banquet by drinking wine, in the course of which music was played and dances danced, and various amusements (e.g. conundrums and the wine game of *kottabos*) indulged in. Consult a dictionary of antiquities (*symposium*) or Becker's 'Charicles.' —— epulīs, dat. plur. of *epulae, -ārum,* f., 1st; poss. dat., after *est* or *fuit* understood. —— mensae, nom. plur. of *mensa, -ae,* f., 1st; subj. of *remotae* (*sunt*); *mensae* = the small *tables* on which each course was brought in; these tables were removed with each course, hence *mensae* often = *courses.* —— que, enclitic cop. conj., joining *quies fuit* and *mensae remotae sunt.* —— remōtae, nom. plur. f. of *remōtus, -a, -um,* perf. part. pass. of *removeō, -ēre, remōvī, remōtum,* 2 (*re,* = *back,* + *moveō,* = *I move*); supply *sunt,* = the 3d pers. plur. perf. ind. pass. agreeing with the subj. *mensae.*

LINE 724. **Crātērās,** acc. plur. of *crātēr, -ēris,* m., 3d (Greek κρατήρ, = *a mixing-bowl,* from κεράννυμι, = *I mix*); direct obj. of *statuunt.* —— magnōs, acc. plur. m.; agrees with *crateras.* —— statuunt, 3d pers. plur. pres. ind. act. of *statuō, -ere, -uī, -ūtum,* 3; understand *ministri* (see ll. 705–706) as subject. —— et, cop. conj. ——vīna,

wine. The noise of the folk grows loud in the palace and they raise their echoing voices amid the hall. Lamps newlighted hang from gilded network of	co,rónant.	Fít	strepi,tús	tec,tís, ,, 725
	they crown.	Is made	a din	in the palace,
	vo,cémque	per ,	ámpla vo,lútant	Átria ; , 726
	and their voice through	spacious	they roll	halls ;
	dépen,dént	lych,ní ,,	laque,áribus ,	aúreis
	hang down	lamps	from the chainwork	golden

acc. plur. of *vīnum, -ī,* n., 2d (Greek οἶνος, originally ϝοῖνος); direct obj. of *coronant.* ——**corōnant,** 3d pers. plur. pres. ind. act. of *coronō, -āre, -āvī, -ātum,* 1 (*corōna,* f., 1st = *a garland, wreath*) ; joined by *et* to *statuunt. Vina coronant* is explained in two different ways : (1) *wreathe the wine-cups,* i.e. *coronis = with garlands.* This was a common Roman custom at banquets, cf. Aen. III, 525, *magnum cratera* CORONĀ INDUIT *implevitque mero.* (2) *crown the cups with wine* (lit. *the wine-cups*), or *fill the cups to the brim,* literally *wreathing them with the wine* that overflowed. This is the meaning of the Homeric phrase κρητῆρας ἐπεστέψαντο ποτοῖο (Iliad I, 470, and other places in the Iliad and Odyssey). Vergil doubtless had Homer's phrase in mind, but in all probability varied it to suit Roman customs; thus (1) is to be preferred.

LINE 725. **Fit,** 3d pers. sing. pres. ind. of *fīō, fīerī, factus sum,* irreg. (used as pass. of *faciō*) ; agrees with the subj. *strepitus.* Some MSS. read *it,* 3d pers. sing. pres. ind. of *eō, īre, īvī,* or *iī, itum,* irreg. ——**strepitus,** gen. *strepitūs,* m., 4th (from *strepō = I make a noise*) ; nom. sing., subj. of *fit. Strepitus = the din* and shouting of the revellers. ——**tectīs,** abl. plur. of *tectum, -ī,* n., 2d; abl. of 'the place where.' ——**vōcem,** acc. sing. of *vōx, vōcis,* f., 3d; direct obj. of *volutant. Vox =* (1) *voice,* (2) *speech,* (3) *a word* or *a name;* here *vocem = voces.* ——**que,** enclitic cop. conj., joining its own to the preceding sentence. ——**per,** prep. with the acc.; gov. *atria.* ——**ampla,** acc. plur. n. of *amplus, -a, -um ;* agrees with *atria.* ——**volūtant,** 3d pers. plur. pres. ind. act. of *volūtō, -āre, -āvī, -ātum,* 1 (for *volv-tō,* frequentative of *volvō = I roll;* cf. *canō* and *cantō, clamo* and *clamito*) ; agrees with *illi* (i.e. the guests) understood as subject. *Volutant* well expresses the rolling and reverberation of sound in a lofty hall.

LINE 726. **Ātria,** acc. plur. of *ātrium, -ī,* n., 2d (*āter*) ; governed by *per.* The *atrium* or hall of a Roman house was a large room into which one passed after entering through the vestibule; round it were kept in cupboards the waxen images of famous ancestors. ——**dēpendent,** 3d pers. plur. pres. ind. act. of *dēpendeō, -ēre,* no perf., no supine, 2 (*dē, = down from, + pendeō, = I hang*) ; agrees with the subj. *lychni.* ——**lȳchnī,** nom. plur. of *lychnus, -ī,* m., 2d (Greek λυχνός); subj. of *dependent.* The *lychni* in a Roman house were often beautiful and very costly works of art. ——**laqueāribus,** abl. plur. of *laqueāre, -is,* n., 3d (collateral form *laquear, -āris,* N., 3d); abl. of 'place from which,' governed by *de* compounded with *pendeo* (*dependent*) ; in prose the prep. *de* would be repeated with the ablative. There is a spelling *lacunāribus,* from the noun *lacuāre, -is,* etc. It is apparent from a comment made by Servius on Aen. VIII, 25 (*laquearia*), that the form *laquear* is derived from *laqueus* (= *a noose* or *net*) and so means *chain* or *net-work,* while *lacuāre* (*lacunar*) is derived from *lacus* and refers to something *hollowed out,* viz., *sunk-panel work.* The noun *lacunar* (= *ceiling*) is also derived from *lacus.* The ceilings of fine houses were usually made with a framework of crossed beams, and the panels in the hollows between the beams were often richly carved or painted. ——**aurēis,** abl. plur. n. of the adj. *aureus, -a, -um ;* agrees with *laquearibus.* Notice that *aureis* is a dissyllable, as *eis* is compressed by *synizesis* into a single syllable. A. & G. 347, *c;* B. 367, 1; G. 727; H. 608, III.

727 **Íncen,si, ét noc,tém ,, flam,mís fu,nália ,** | chains and the flames
lighted, and the night by their flames torches | of torches overmaster
728 **víncunt. Híc re,gína gra,vém ,, gem,mís** | the night. Here at the
conquer. Here (= then) the queen heavy with jewels | queen called for a
729 **au,róque po,póscit Ímple,vítque me,ró** | heavy jewelled cup of
and with gold 'called for and filled with pure wine | gold and filled it with
pate,rám, ,, quam , Bélus et , ómnes | pure wine — a cup
a bowl, which Belus and all (descended) | which Belus and all

LINE 727. **Incensī,** nom. plur. m. of *incensus, -a, -um,* perf. part. pass. of *incendō, -ere, incendī, incensum,* 3 (*in, = into,* + root KAN, = *to burn*); agrees with *lychni; incensi* is emphatic, denoting that the lamps are only now being lighted. —— **et,** cop. conj. —— **noctem,** acc. sing. of *nŏx, noctis,* f., 3d; direct obj. of *vincunt.* —— **flammīs,** abl. plur. of *flamma, -ae,* f., 1st; abl. of the means or instrument, with *vincunt.* —— **fūnālia,** nom. plur. of *fūnāle, -is,* n., 3d (*fūnis = a rope*); subj. of *vincunt; funalia* are torches made of twisted fibre or rope, covered with pitch or wax. —— **vincunt,** 3d pers. plur. pres. ind. act. of *vincō, -ere, vīcī, victum,* 3 ; agrees with the subj. *funalia.*

LINE 728. **Hīc,** adv. of place. *Hic* in this instance refers to time rather than place, and = *at this stage* of the feast, *then.* —— **rēgīna,** nom. sing., subj. of *poposcit.* —— **gravem,** acc. sing. f. of the adj. *gravis, -e,* 3d (probably akin to Greek βαρύς); agrees with *pateram.* —— **gemmīs,** abl. plur. of *gemma, -ae,* f., 1st (= lit. *a bud,* hence from the resemblance *a jewel*); abl. of specification, explaining *gravem.* A. & G. 253; B. 226; G. 397; H. 424. —— **aurō,** abl. sing. of *aurum, -ī,* n., 2d; abl. of specification, joined by *que* to *gemmis ; pateram gravem gemmis auroque = a goblet heavy with jewels and gold,* i.e. a heavy golden goblet encrusted with jewels. This is not an instance of *hendiadys,* as some say, for *gemmis* and *auro* go closely with *gravem,* and together make the bowl heavy. —— **que,** enclitic cop. conj. —— **poposcit,** 3d pers. sing. perf. ind. act. of *poscō, -ere, poposcī,* no supine, 3; agrees with the subj. *regina.* The perfect tense describes the single action of Dido in calling for the goblet.

LINE 729. **Implēvit,** 3d pers. sing. perf. ind. act. of *impleō, -ēre, -ēvī, -ētum,* 2 (*in, = into,* + *pleō, = I fill*); joined by *que* closely to *poposcit,* and in agreement with the same subject *regina.* —— **que,** enclitic cop. conj. —— **merō,** abl. sing. of *merum, -ī,* n., 2d (from the adj. *merus, -a, -um, = pure,* supply *vinum*); abl. of the instrument, with *implevit. Merum =* the strong, undiluted wine. The wine of the ancient Romans was thick and usually required a large admixture of water before it was fit for drinking. —— **pateram,** acc. sing. of *patera, -ae,* f., 1st (from *pateō = I lie open*); direct obj. of *poposcit implevitque.* The *patera* was a large and shallow open bowl, generally used in making libations; cf. *pateris libamus et auro.* —— **quam,** acc. sing. f. of the rel. *quī;* agrees with the antecedent *pateram,* and direct obj. of *implēre* understood as the *complement* of *soliti (sunt).* —— **Bēlus,** gen. *Bēlī,* m., 2d; one of the subjects of *soliti (sunt).* Belus was the king of Tyre and the father of Dido and Pygmalion. If this Belus be meant, Vergil makes him the founder of the Tyrian dynasty, but probably the word is a title here (= *Lord;* cf. *Baal*), and is used in much the same way as *Caesar* was by the Roman emperors. —— **et,** cop. conj. —— **omnēs,** nom. plur. m. substantival of the adj. *omnis, -e,* 3d; joined by *et* to *Belus,* and a subj. of *soliti (sunt).*

of Belus' line were wont to fill. Then silence fell within the hall. "Jupiter, for men say that thou dost set the laws 'twixt host and guest, be it thy will that this day be one of joy to the Tyrians and the	Á Be,ló soli,tí ; tum , fácta 730			
	from Belus were wont (to fill); then was made			
	si,léntia , téctis : "Iúpiter, , hóspiti,bús ,, 731			
	silence in the building: "Jupiter, to guests (and hosts)			
	nam , té dare , iúra lo,quúntur,			
	for (that) thou givest the laws they say,			
	Húnc lae,túm Tyri,ísque di,ém ,, Tro,iáque 732			
	this joyful both to Tyrians day and from Troy			

LINE 730. **Ā**, prep. with the abl.; gov. *Belo*, denoting origin. *A* or *ab* (*ab* before vowels and *h*, *ab* or *a* before consonants) expresses with the abl. : (1) *the agent;* (2) *place whence;* (3) *cause;* (4) *origin;* (5) *time from which.* A. & G. 152, *b*, and 153; B. 142, 1; G. 417, 1; H. 434. —— **Bēlō**, abl. sing. of *Bēlus;* governed by the prep. *a; omnes a Belo = all* (*orti = descended*) *from Belus.* —— **solitī**, nom plur. m. of *solitus, -a, -um*, perf. part. of the semi-deponent *soleō, -ēre, solitus sum*, 2; supply *sunt* with *soliti*, = the 3d pers. plur. perf. ind., in agreement with the composite subj. *Belus et omnes;* the predication is grammatically incomplete (though clear from the context) and the *prolative* inf. *implere* must be understood (from *implevit* above). Semi-deponent verbs are those which are active in meaning, but owing to the absence of perfect-stem active tenses supply them in the passive form. There are very few in use, viz. *gaudeo, audeo*, and *soleo*. A. & G. 136; B. 114, 1; G. 167, 1; H. 268, 3, and 465, 2, NOTE 2. —— **tum**, adv. of time, here connective. —— **facta**, nom. plur. n. of *factus, -a, -um*, perf. part. of *fīō, fierī, factus sum*, irreg. (used as the pass. of *faciō*); supply *sunt* with *facta*, = the 3d pers. plur. perf. ind. pass. of *facio*, agreeing with the subj. *silentia*. —— **silentia**, nom. plur. of *silentium, -ī*, n., 2d (*sileō = I am silent;* pres. part. *silens*); subj. of *facta* (*sunt*); the plural is poetic for singular. —— **tectīs**, abl. plur. of *tectum, -ī*, n., 2d; abl. of 'the place where.'

LINE 731. **Iūpiter**, voc. sing. of *Iūpiter*, gen. *Iovis*, m., 3d (= *Dies . . . piter;* cf. Greek Ζεύς, gen. Διός, and the Sanskrit *dju = light*, and *dyu = heaven);* the case of address. Lines 731–735 are spoken by Dido, though the verb of saying does not appear until the end (*dixit*, l. 736). Jupiter is addressed, because he was the *god of strangers* or *hospitality*, with the title in Greek of Ζεὺς Ξένιος (ξένος = *a stranger*). —— **hospitibus**, dat. plur. of *hospes, hospitis*, common gender, 3d (= (1) *a host*, (2) *a guest);* dat. of the indirect obj. of *dare.* —— **nam**, causal conj., introducing in parenthesis a reason for addressing Jupiter; cf. *nam*, l. 65. *Nam* usually stands first and *enim* second in a sentence. —— **tē**, acc. sing. of *tū ;* subj.-acc. of *dare* in the indirect discourse after *loquuntur.* —— **dare**, pres. inf. act. of *dō, dare, dedī, datum*, 1; agrees with the subj.-acc. *te.* A. & G. 272, and REM.; B. 330, 331; G. 527; H. 534, 535. —— **iūra**, acc. plur. of *iūs, iūris*, n., 3d ; direct obj. of *dare. Ius* is used of *law*, both human and divine, written and unwritten; cf. *ius gentium ;* here it refers to the divinely prompted, unwritten moral principle of hospitality. —— **loquuntur**, 3d pers. plur. pres. ind. of the deponent verb *loquor, -ī, locūtus sum*, 3; the subj. is indefinite, = *they say* (French *on dit*). *Loquor* is seldom found introducing the acc. and inf. construction, though other verbs of *saying*, e.g. *narrant, dicunt, ferunt*, etc., are regularly followed by that construction.

LINE 732. **Hunc**, acc. sing. m. of *hīc, haec, hōc ;* agrees with *diem.* —— **laetum**, acc. sing. m. of the adj. *laetus, -a, -um ; laetum* is predicative, being the *complement* of the copula *esse* in the acc. and inf. construction *velis hunc diem laetum esse.* —— **Tyriīs**, dat. plur. of *Tyrii, -ōrum*, m., 2d; dat. of the indirect obj., dependent on *laetum.* —— **que**, enclitic cop. conj.; here *que . . . que* (τε . . . καί) = *both . . .*

733 pro, féctis	Ésse	ve, lís,	„	nos, trósque	farers from Troy, and
(to those who) set out to be	may'st thou will,			and our	that our children's
734 hu, iús	memi, nísse	mi, nóres.		Ádsit ,	children may keep it
of this (day)	to be mindful	descendants.		May be present	in mind. May Bac-
létiti, æ	„ Bac, chús	dator,	,	ét bona ,	chus, giver of joy, be
of joy	Bacchus	giver,		and kind	with us, and gracious

---

and; refer to the note on *que*, l. 332. —— **diem,** acc. sing. of *diēs, diēī,* 5th, m. (always in plur.; sometimes f. in sing.); subj.-acc. of *esse laetum* in the acc. and inf. construction dependent on *velis.* —— **Trōiā,** abl. sing. of *Trōia, -ae,* f., 1st; abl. of 'the place from which'; a preposition is not used when the 'place from which' is the name of a town or small island, but if *urbe* had been added in apposition, a preposition (*a* or *ab, ex*) would have been necessary. —— que, enclitic cop. conj.; see *que* above. —— **profectis,** dat. plur. m. of *profectus, -a, -um,* perf. part. of the deponent verb *proficiscor, -ī, profectus sum,* 3; dat. of the indirect obj., joined by *que* to *Tyriis; profectis* is substantival, = *those who set out.* A. & G. 113, *f*; B. no reference; G. 437; H. 441. *Profectis Troia* = *Troianis,* and is a Vergilian variation from what would be simple and expected.

LINE 733. **Esse,** pres. inf. of *sum;* agrees with the subj.-acc. *diem* in the acc. and inf. construction introduced by *velis.* —— velis, 2d pers. sing. pres. subjunct. of the irreg. verb *volō, velle, voluī* (akin to Greek βούλομαι): the subj. *tu* is contained in the verb. The subjunctive mood is *hortatory,* expressing Dido's entreaty. The *hortatory* subjunctive covers entreaties, mild orders, commands, and concessions. A. & G. 266; B. 274-276; G. 263; H. 484. —— nostrōs, acc. plur. m. of *noster, nostra, nostrum;* agrees with *minores.* —— que, enclitic cop. conj., joining the subordinate *minores meminisse* with *diem laetum esse* above. —— hūius, gen. sing. m. of *hīc, haec, hōc;* agrees with *diēī,* which must be supplied from *diem* above. *Huius* is emphatic, and so is *hunc* in the preceding verse. Verbs which express remembrance or the reverse may govern the genitive case; they appear in most cases to govern the acc. of things, e.g. *haec memini,* and the genitive of persons, e.g. *fratris memini,* but this rule has many exceptions. A. & G. 219; B. 206; G. 376; H. 406, 2, and 407. —— meminisse, perf. inf. act. of *meminī* (perf.), *memineram* (pluperf.), no present stem tenses; agrees with the subj.-acc. *minores* in the acc. and inf. construction dependent on *velis.* A. & G. 143, *c*; B. 133; G. 175, 5, *b*; H. 297, I. —— minōrēs, acc. plur. m. of the comparative adj. *minor, minus,* gen. *minōris,* 3d (pos. *parvus;* superl. *minimus*) ; substantival, the subj.-acc. of *meminisse.* *Minores* (i.e. *natu*) = *descendants;* cf. *maiores* = *ancestors,* and *minimus* (*natu*) and *maximus* (*natu*), superlatives of *iuvenis* and *senex* respectively.

LINE 734. **Adsit,** 3d pers. sing. pres. subjunct. of *adsum, adesse, affuī (adfuī),* a compound of *ad* and *sum;* agrees with the subj. *Bacchus;* the subjunctive mood is *optative,* expressing a wish for the immediate future. A. & G. 267; B. 279; G. 260-262; H. 483, 484. —— laetitiae, gen. sing. of *laetitia,* f., 1st (from *laetus*) ; objective gen., dependent on the idea of agency expressed in *dator.* A. & G. 217; B. 200; G. 363, 2; H. 396, III. With *laetitiae dator,* cf. l. 636, *laetitiam dei.* —— Bacchus, gen. *Bacchī,* m., 2d (Greek Βάκχος); nom. sing., subj. of *adsit.* Bacchus, the son of Jupiter and Semele, was the god of wine and a patron of erotic poets. He was worshipped in Greece and especially Athens under the name of Dionysus, and his festivals were observed with much mingled solemnity and revelry. His worship, as imported from Greece to Rome, was marred by so much licentiousness that it was repeatedly forbidden by law. —— dator, gen. *datōris,* m., 3d (*dō = I give*) ; nom. sing., in appos. with *Bacchus.* —— et, cop. conj., connecting *Bacchus* and *Iuno.* —— bona, nom. sing. f.; agrees with *Iuno.*

Juno : and do ye,	Iúno ;	Ét	vos,	ó	coe,túm,	,	Tyri,í, 735
Tyrians, honor our	*Juno;*	*and*	*you,*	*o*	*the gathering,*		*Tyrians,*
gathering with good	cele,bráte		fa,véntes."		Díxit,	et	, in 736
accord." She spake,	*honor*		*showing favor."*		*She spoke,*	*and*	*onto*
and poured libation-	men,sám	„	lati,cúm	li,bávit		ho,nórem,
offering of wine upon	*the table*		*of wine*	*poured as libation*		*the. offering,*
the board, and after	Prímaque,	,	líba,tó,	„	sum,mó	tenus , 737
the libation first	*and first,*		*libation being made,*		*outside*	*as far as*

——Iúnō, nom. sing.; joined by *et* to *Bacchus.* Observe that the singular verb *adsit* agrees only with the nearest subject *Bacchus,* and that it must be understood with *Iuno.* ——
LINE 735. **Et,** cop. conj., connecting this sentence with the one preceding.——
vōs, nom. plur.; subj. of *celebrate.* *Vōs* is very emphatic; Dido has entreated the gods, and directly addresses the Tyrians. ——ō, exclamation, with the voc. *Tyrii.* When the main verb is an imperative, *o* is occasionally separated from the voc. by an important word. ——coetum, acc. sing. of *coetus, -ūs,* m., 4th (a collateral form of *coitus,* from *co* = *cum* + *eō*): direct obj. of *celebrate.*——Tyriī, voc. plur. of *Tyriī, -ōrum,* m., 2d; the case of address. ——celebrāte, 2d pers. plur. imperative mood act. of *celebrō, -āre, -āvī, -ātum,* I (from adj. *celeber,* = *much frequented*): agrees with the subj. *vos.* *Celebrate* = *honor, celebrate.* ——faventēs, nom. plur. m. of *faveⁿs, -entis,* pres. part. act. of *faveō, -ēre, fāvī, fautum,* 2; predicate part., agreeing with the subj. *vos.* *Celebrate faventes* = *celebrate et favete,* i.e. *honor our gathering with all good will.* Sometimes *favere* is used in the special religious phrase *favete linguis* = lit. *be favorable with your tongues,* i.e. *be silent,* so as to avoid the chance of saying anything of ill omen. *Faventes* means something very different here, and may perhaps be rendered *applauding.* ——
LINE 736. **Dīxit,** 3d pers. sing. perf. ind. act. of *dīcō, -ere, dīxī, dictum,* 3; understand *Dido* or *regina* as subject. The abrupt departure from the description into the direct speech of Dido, without any verb of *saying* except *dixit* at the end, is very effective, and is one of the many examples of Vergil's appreciation of variety and mastery of literary devices. ——et, cop. conj. ——in, prep.; gov. the acc. *mensam.* —— mensam, acc. sing.; governed by the prep. *in.*——laticum, gen. plur. of *lātex, laticis,* m., 3d; gen. of the substance or material. A. & G. 214, *e*; B. 197; G. 361; H. 395. *Laticum explains honorem* = *the offering of the flowing wine.* *Latex* is usually modified by an adj. = e.g. *Lyaeus,* l. 686, or by a genitive, e.g. *latex Lyaei*; but here it is used absolutely with the meaning of *wine.* ——lībāvit, 3d pers. sing. perf. ind. act. of *libō, -āre, -āvī, -ātum,* I (akin probably to Greek λείβω = *I pour*): joined by *et* to *dixit,* and in agreement with the same subject. *Libavit* = *poured as a libation;* it was customary at all heroic banquets to pour some wine as a thank-offering to the gods; at sacrifices milk was sometimes substituted for wine. —— honōrem, acc. sing. of *hŏnos, -ōris,* m., 3d; direct obj. of *libavit.* We should expect *laticem* or *vinum* as object, but Vergil for variety has *honorem laticum* = *the offering* (special sense) *of wine.*
LINE 737. **Prīma,** nom. sing. f. of the adj. *prīmus, -a, -um;* agrees with the subj. of *attigit* (i.e. *Dido*). *Prima* is an adverbial attribute. A. & G. 191; B. 241, 2; G. 325, REM. 6; H. 443. —— que, enclitic cop. conj. —— lībātō, abl. sing. n. of *lībātus, -a, -um,* perf. part. pass. of *lībō* (see *libavit* above); adverbial abl. abs. standing alone and impersonally, i.e. without a substantive. *Libato* = *quum libavisset, when she had made a libation.* Some think that *honore* should be supplied with *libato* in the abl. abs. (in which case *libato* is a masculine abl., not neuter), as the phrase *libavit honorem* occurs

738 áttigit   ,   óre ;   Túm   Biti, ié   dedit ,   touched the cup with
touched (the bowl)   her mouth;   then   to Bitias she gave (it)   her lips, then passed

íncrepi, táns :   ,,   il, le   ímpiger   ,   haúsit   it to Bitias with a
challenging: he   not slow   drained   challenge. Nothing

739 Spúman, tém   pate, *ram*,   ,,   ét   ple, nó   se ,   loath he drained the
foaming   the bowl,   and   brimful   himself   foaming bowl, and

---

just above; then (*honore*) *libato = when the libation-offering had been poured.* But probably *libato* is impersonal; cf. other adverbial ablatives, e.g. *auspicato, consulto, audito, optato,* etc., found in Cicero. A. & G. 255, *c*; B. 227, 3; G. 410, NOTE 4; H. 431, NOTE 2. —— summō, abl. sing. n. of *summus, -a, um;* partitive adj., agreeing with *ore.* A. & G. 193; B. 241; G. 291, REM. 2; II. 440, 2, NOTE 1. —— tenus, prep. with the abl.; gov. *ore. Summo tenus ore =* lit. *as far as the surface of her mouth,* i.e. *with the lips.* A. & G. 152, *b*; B. 142, 3; G. 417, 14; H. 434, NOTE 4.   *Tenus* (from the root *ten* or *tan,* as in *ten-do = I stretch,* and in Greek τείνω) is in origin the accusative case of a noun, and so sometimes takes the genitive, e.g. *lumborum tenus = as far as the loins.* But *tenus* almost always in prose governs the ablative; in late Latin, it is found with the accusative. *Tenus* always follows the noun which it governs. —— attigit, 3d pers. sing. perf. ind. act. of *attingō, -ere, attigī, attactum,* 3 (*ad + tangō*); joined by *que* to *libavit,* and in agreement with the same subject. —— ōre, abl. sing. of *ōs, ōris,* n., 3d; governed by *tenus.* Dido just sipped the wine, for it would have been indecorous for her as queen and a woman to do as Bitias did.

LINE 738. Tum, adv. of time. —— Bitiae, dat. sing. of *Bitiās, -ae,* m., 1st decl. Greek noun; dat. of the indirect obj., dependent on *dedit.* Bitias was one of Dido's courtiers; his name is Phoenician, and occurs in other places in the Aeneid. —— dedit, 3d pers. sing. perf. ind. act. of *dō, dare, dedī, datum,* 1; understand Dido as subject. —— increpitāns, nom. sing. f. of the pres. part. act. of *increpitō, -āre, -āvī, ātum,* 1; predicate part., agreeing with the subj. of *dedit; dedit increpitans = dedit (et increpita-vit* or *et, dum dat, increpitavit).* There is no notion of *chiding* in *increpitans;* it may be rendered *challenging.* —— ille, nom. sing.; subj. of *hausit; ille* is emphatic. —— impiger, nom. sing. m. of the adj. *impiger, impigra, impigrum (in, = not, + piger, = indolent,* hence *quick);* agrees with *ille; impiger* is an adverbial attribute, = *briskly.* Vergil undoubtedly intends a humorous contrast between the dainty sip of Dido and the deep draught of Bitias. —— hausit, 3d pers. sing. perf. ind. act. of *hauriō, -īre, hausī, haustum,* 4; agrees with the subj. *ille.*

LINE 739. Spūmantem, acc. sing. f. of *spūmāns, -antis,* pres. part. act. of *spūmō, -āre, -āvī, -ātum,* 1; agrees with *pateram* attributively. —— pateram, acc. sing. of *patera, -ae,* f., 1st; direct obj. of *hausit.* —— et, cop. conj. —— plēnō, abl. sing. of the adj. *plēnus, -a, -um (pleō = I fill) ;* qualifies *auro.* —— sē, acc. sing. of the reflexive pron. *sē,* gen. *suī,* dat. *sibi,* abl. *sē;* direct obj. of *proluit.* —— prōluit, 3d pers. sing. perf. ind. act. of *prōluō, -ere, prōluī, prōlūtum,* 3 (*prō + luō) ;* joined by *et* to *hausit* and in agreement with the same subject. *Se proluit = drenched himself in the brimming gold;* cf. Horace, speaking of a sailor *multā prolutus vappa* (Mr. Page renders "a sailor soaked in swipes"). There is one of the very few passages in Vergil where we get a glimpse of that heroic humor which is so abundant in Homer. —— aurō, abl. sing. of *aurum, -ī,* n., 2d; abl. of the means, with *proluit. Auro = aureā paterā, gold* standing by *metonymy* for *the golden bowl.* A. & G. 386; B. no reference; G. no reference; H. 637, III.

drenched him in the	próluit	,	aúro ;	Póst	ali, í	proce, rés. ,, 740
brimming gold :	drenched		in the gold;	afterwards	other	chiefs.
thereafter other chiefs partook. Long-haired	Citha, rá		cri, nítus	I, ópas		Pérsonat , 741
Iopas, whom mighty	On the lyre		long-haired	Iopas		plays loudly
Atlas taught, made	aúra, tá,	,,	docu, it	quem	,	máximus ,
the hall resound with	gilded,		taught	whom		most mighty
his gilded lyre. He	Atlas.	Híc	canit	, érran, tém		lu, nám ,, 742
sings of the wandering	Atlas.	He	sings of	wandering		the moon

LINE 740. **Post,** adv. = *posteā* ; *post* is rarely used as an adverb, being a preposition with the accusative; but cf. *ante* used adverbially. —— **aliī,** nom. plur. m. of *alius, alia, aliud* ; agrees with *proceres.* —— **procerēs,** nom. plur. of *procer, -is,* m., 3d (*prō,* = *before,* + CER, root akin to Greek κάρα = the *head*), subj. of *hauserunt* understood (from *hausit* above). —— **Citharā,** abl. sing. of *cithara, -ae,* f., 1st (Greek κιθάρα); abl. of the means or instrument, with *personat.* —— **crīnītus,** nom. sing. m. of the adj. *crīnītus, -a, -um* (from *crīnis* = *hair,* hence here *with long hair*) ; agrees with *Iopas.* The custom of wearing long hair was followed by ancient bards, because their patron Apollo was represented with flowing hair. —— **Iōpās,** gen. *Iōpae,* m., 1st decl. Greek; nom. sing., subj. of *personat.* The introduction of a bard at the feast is consistent with the customs of heroic times; cf. Phemius and Demodocus in the Odyssey. It was a common custom also in Scotland ; cf. Sir Walter Scott's " Lay of the Last Minstrel," etc.

LINE 741. **Personat,** 3d pers. sing. pres. ind. act. of *personō, -āre, -uī, -itum,* 1 (*per* + *sonō*) ; agrees with the subj. *Iopas.* —— **aurātā,** abl. sing. f. of the adj. *aurātus, -a, -um* (from *aurum* = *gold*) ; agrees with *cithara.* —— **docuit,** 3d pers. sing. perf. ind. act. of *doceō, -ēre, -uī, doctum,* 2 ; agrees with the subj. *Atlas* in the relative clause introduced by *quem.* —— **quem,** acc. sing. m. of the rel. pron. *quī;* agrees with the antecedent *Iopas,* and is the direct obj. of *docuit.* There is another reading *quae; ea* must in this case be understood as direct object of *personat,* and *quae* is acc. n. plur. governed by *docuit* (*personat ea quae Atlas docuit*). But *quem* is generally preferred, both because *persono* is often used absolutely, i.e. without an object, = *accompanies himself* or *fills* (*the hall*) *with music.* —— **máximus,** nom. sing. m. of the superl. adj. *máximus, -a, -um* (pos. *magnus ;* comparative *māior*) ; agrees with *Atlas ; maximus* refers to the stature and strength of Atlas. —— **Atlās,** gen. *Atlantis,* m., 3d (Greek "Ατλας); nom. sing., subj. of *docuit* in the relative clause. In mythology, Atlas was one of the giants known as Titans, who, for his part in the rebellion against the gods, was forced to bear the world on his shoulders. In Homer he is so described, and is, moreover, called ὀλοόφρων, i.e. the possessor of strange and wonderful knowledge. The stories that connect Atlas with Africa are later; in these we find him as a Mauritanian king, very learned in astronomy (from which fact some derive the legend that he supported the world), who, having refused Perseus hospitality, was changed by means of Medusa's head into the mountain bearing his name. Vergil selects Atlas here because of his supposed connection with Africa.

LINE 742. **Hīc,** nom. sing. m. of the demonstr. pron. *hīc, haec, hōc ;* subj. of *canit; hic* is deictic and emphatic, distinguishing Iopas from Atlas. —— **canit,** 3d pers. sing. pres. ind. act. of *canō, -ere, cecinī, cantum,* 3; agrees with the subj. *hic ; canit* is active and = *sings of* or *celebrates in song.* —— **errantem,** acc. sing. f. of *errāns, -antis,* pres. part. act. of *errō, -āre, -āvī, -ātum,* 1; agrees with *lunam ; errantem lunam = lunae*

743 so,lísque	la,bóres ;	**Ǔ**nde	homi,núm	moon and the suffer-
and of the sun	*the toils;*	*whence*	*of men*	ings of the sun;
genus ,	ét pecu,dés ;	,, un,de	ímber et ,	whence comes the
the race	*and cattle;*	*whence*	*rain and*	race of men and
				beasts; whence rain
744 ígnes,	**Á**rctu,rúm	pluvi,ásqu*e*	Hya,dás ,,	and fire; of Arcturus,
fires,	*(he sings of) Arcturus*	*and rainy*	*the Hyades*	the rainy Hyades,and

errores, the wanderings of the moon. The reference is to the constant change in the moon's position, which is more noticeable as the moon is nearer the earth than any other heavenly body. —— **lūnam,** acc. sing. of *lūna, -ae,* f., 1st (= *lucna,* from *luceō,* = *I shine*) ; direct obj. of *canit.* Whereas Homeric and Scottish bards sing songs of the deeds of brave men, Vergil's bard sings of the wonders of the physical world and astronomy. Vergil was evidently attracted to natural philosophy, as we see from his frequent imitation of Lucretius (the author of *De rerum natura*). —— **sōlis,** gen. sing. of *sōl,* m., 3d (Greek ἥλιος); poss. gen., limiting *labores.* —— **que,** enclitic cop. conj. —— **labōrēs,** acc. plur. of *labor, labōris,* m., 3d; direct obj. of *canit,* joined by *que* to *lunam.* In Georgics, II, 478, *lunae labores* = *the travails of the moon,* a poetic way of referring to its *eclipses ;* and in the same passage the *defectus solis* are mentioned (*the eclipses of the sun*). So here *labores* possibly = *eclipses* (*defectus,* the proper word), and suggests also the great tasks which the sun has to perform in following its course in the heavens.

LINE 743. **Unde,** adv. of 'place from which,' here introducing the indirect question (*canit, unde sit hominum genus*). A. & G. 334; B. 300; G. 467; H. 528, 2, and 529, I. —— **hominum,** gen. plur. of *homŏ, -inis,* m., 3d; adnominal gen. of specification, describing *genus.* —— **genus,** gen.*generis,* n., 3d; nom. sing., subj. of *sit* understood in the indirect question. —— **et,** cop. conj. —— **pecudēs,** nom. plur. of *pecus, pecudis,* f., 3d (sing. = a single head of cattle; the plur. = *cattle* in general; collateral form *pecus, pecoris,* n., 3d, = *a herd,* usually *of cattle*) ; subj. of *sint* understood in the indirect question introduced by *unde.* —— **unde,** adv., repeated rhetorically from *unde* above. —— **imber,** gen. *imbris,* m., 3d (akin to Greek ὄμβρος); nom. sing., one of the subjects of *sint* understood (*unde imber et ignes sint*). —— **et,** cop. conj. —— **ignēs,** nom. plur. of *ignis, -is,* m., 3d; joined by *et* to *imber,* and one of the subjects of *sint* understood. All these subjects had been discussed by the Ionic philosophers in Asia Minor; some held water to be the primal element, others the air, others fire, etc.; they greatly advanced natural philosophy, and by setting men's mind at work paved the way for mental and moral philosophy.

LINE 744. **Arctūrum,** acc. sing. of *Arctūrus, -ī,* m., 2d (Greek Ἀρκτοῦρος = *the Bear-Keeper*) ; direct obj. of *canit.* This star, near the tail of the Bear (hence its name), is the brightest star in Boötes; its rising and setting were said to be accompanied by storms. —— **pluviās,** acc. plur. f. of the adj. *pluvius, -a, -um* (from *pluit,* = *it rains*) ; qualifies *Hyadas ;* observe that the Latin exactly translates the Greek word *Hyadas* (from ὕειν, = *to rain*). —— **que,** enclitic cop. conj. —— **Hyadās,** acc. plur. of *Hyades, -um,* f., plur. 3d (Greek Ὑάδες, from ὕειν, = *to rain*) ; Greek acc. (Ὑάδας), joined by *que* to *Arcturum ;* a direct obj. of *canit.* The Hyades are seven stars in Taurus, and their rising in the spring brought rain (whence their name). Mythology makes them daughters of Atlas, who made such lament for their brother Hyas, killed by a boar, that Jupiter changed them to stars. The *Hyades* are known in Latin as *Suculae* (= *Little Pigs*), which word illustrates the popular derivation from ὗς, gen. ὑός, = *a pig.* —— **geminōs,** acc. plur. m. of *geminus, -a, -um ;* agrees with *Triones.* —— **que,** enclitic cop. conj. —— **Triōnēs,** acc. plur. of *Triōnes, -um,* m., plur. 3d (from *triō,* originally *ter-iŏ,* = *a plough-*

the twin Bears; why	gemi,nósque	Tri,ónes ;	Qúid	tan,tum 748
winter suns so haste	*and twin*	*the Wains (Bears) ;*	*(sings) why*	*so much*
to dip in ocean, and	ócea,nó	prope,rént	„ se , tíngere	, sóles
what delay checks the	*in the ocean*	*hasten*	*themselves to dip*	*the suns*
slow-gliding nights.	Híber,ní,	vel ,	quǽ tar,dís „	mora , 746
	wintry,	*or*	*what lingering*	*delay*
The Tyrians redouble	nóctibus	, óbstet.	Íngemi,nánt	plau,sú 747
with applause, and	*the nights*	*hinders.*	*Redouble*	*with applause*

ing ox) ; direct obj. of *canit,* joined by *que* to *Hyadas ; geminos Triones* = lit. *the twin oxen,* i.e. *the twin Bears* (Greater and Lesser). The regular Latin word for the north is *septentriones* (*septem triones* = *seven oxen*). Both the Greater and Lesser Bear consist of seven stars. Their regular names are *Ursa Maior* and *Ursa Minor.*

LINE 745. **Quid,** adverbial n. acc. sing. of the interrog. pron. *quis, quae, quid;* introduces the indirect question *quid soles properent,* dependent on the principal verb *canit,* l. 742. —— **tantum,** adv. of degree, extending *properent.* For the adverbial use of the acc. sing. n. of adjectives, consult the references under *multum,* l. 3. —— **ōceanō,** abl. sing. of *ōceanus, -ī,* m., 2d (Greek ὠκεανός); abl. of 'the place where' with *tingere.* —— **properent,** 3d pers. plur. pres. subjunct. act. of *properō, -āre, -āvī, -ātum,* 1 (from *properus* = *hastening*); agrees with the subj. *soles;* the mood is subjunctive because *quid* (after *canit* understood from above) introduces an indirect question. —— **sē,** acc. plur. of the reflexive pron.; direct obj. of *tingere.* —— **tingere,** pres. inf. act, of *tingō, -ere, tinxī, tinctum,* 3 (Greek τέγγω); poetic *prolative* inf., dependent on *properent;* in prose we should require *ut* with the subjunctive, expressing purpose, e.g. *properent ut se tingant.* A. & G. 273, *e;* B. 326, NOTE; G. 421, NOTE 1, *a;* H. 533, II. —— **sōlēs,** nom. plur. of *sōl, sōlis,* m., 3d; subj. of *properent* in the indirect question. This line and the one following are repeated word for word from Georgics, II, 481, 482.

LINE 746. **Hībernī,** nom. plur. m. of the adj. *hibernus, -a, -um* (for *hiem-ernus,* from *hiemps,* gen. *hiemis,* = *winter*); agrees with *soles.* —— **vel** (probably old imperative of *volō*), enclitic disjunctive conj., joining the alternative theme *quae mora obstet* with *quid soles properent.* A. & G. 156, *c;* B. 342; G. 494; H. 554, II, 2. —— **quae,** nom. sing. f. of the interrog. adj. *quī, quae, quod;* agrees with *mora,* and is followed by the subjunct. *obstet* in indirect question. —— **tardīs,** dat. plur. f. of the adj. *tardus, -a, -um;* agrees with *noctibus. Tardis* is contrasted with *properent;* the sun sinks swiftly in winter, while in summer the nights are long in coming on. —— **mora,** gen. *morae,* f., 1st; nom. sing., subj. of *obstet.* —— **noctibus,** dat. plur. of *nōx, noctis,* f., 3d (Greek νύξ); governed by *obstet.* —— **obstet,** 3d pers. sing. pres. subjunct. act. of *obstō, -āre, obstitī, obstātum,* 1 (*ob,* = *in the way,* + *stō,* = *I stand*); agrees with the subj. *mora,* and, being a compound of *ob,* governs the dat. *noctibus;* the indirect question (*canit*) *quae mora* requires the subjunct. *obstet.*

LINE 747. **Ingeminant,** 3d pers. plur. pres. ind. act. of *ingeminō, -āre, -āvī, -ātum,* 1 (*in,* = *upon,* intensive, + *geminō,* = *I double*), hence *I redouble);* agrees with the subj. *Tyrii.* —— **plausū,** abl. sing. of *plausus, -ūs,* m., 4th (from *plaudō,* = *I clap*); abl. of manner, with *ingeminant.* Some MSS. read *plausum,* direct obj., = *they redouble their applause,* but *plausu* is more in Vergil's style; cf. Aen. IX, 811, *ingeminant hastis* = *they redouble* (i.e. their blows) *with their spears,* and Georgics, I, 333, *ingeminant Austri,* where *ingemino* is used absolutely. —— **Tyrii,** nom. plur.; subj. of *ingeminant.* —— **Trōes** (Greek Τρῶες), nom. plur.; subj. of *sequuntur.* Observe the juxtaposition of the two subjects *Tyrii* and *Troes;* this is intended to give a distributive effect such as in

748 Tyri,í, „ Tro,ésque se,quúntur. Néc non , the Trojans follow.
the Tyrians, and the Trojans follow. Nor not Thereto besides with
ét vari,ó „ noc,tém ser,móne tra,hébat changing talk hapless
also changing the night with talk was protracting Dido drew out the
749 Ínfe,líx Di,dó, „ lon,gúmque bi,bébat night, and drank in
unhappy Dido, and lasting was drinking in lasting love, asking
750 a,mórem, Múlta su,pér Pria,mó rogi,táns, „ many a question of
love, many things about Priam asking, Priam, many of Hec-
751 super , Héctore , múlta ; Núnc, quibus , tor ; now in what
about Hector many things; now what

Greek would be attained by μέν . . . δέ. —— que, enclitic cop. conj., joining its own
to the preceding clause. —— sequuntur, 3d pers. plur. pres. ind. of the deponent verb
sequor, -ī, secūtus sum, 3; agrees with the subj. *Troes.*
  LINE 748. Nec (= *neque, nor, and . . . not*), negative cop. conj.; joins this sen-
tence to the one above, and with *non* (*nec non = nor . . . not*) makes an emphatic
assertion. —— nōn, negative adv. —— et, cop. conj., here = *etiam, moreover.* ——
variō, abl. sing. m. of the adj. *varius, -a, -um;* agrees with *sermone.* —— noctem, acc.
sing. of *nōx, nōctis,* f., 3d; direct obj. of *trahebat.* —— sermōne, abl. sing. of *sermō,
-ōnis,* m., 3d; abl. of the means, or abl. of manner, with *trahebat.* —— trahēbat, 3d
pers. sing. imperf. ind. act. of *trahō, -ere, trāxī, tractum,* 3; agrees with the subj. *Dido.*
  LINE 749. Infēlīx (*in, = not, + fēlīx, = fortunate*), adj. nom. sing. f.; agrees with
Dido. Infelix is attributive, but by its emphatic position suggests that Dido was doom-
ing herself by protracting the night with talk. —— Dīdō, gen. *Dīdōnis or Dīdūs,* f., 3d;
nom. sing., subj. of *trahebat.* —— longum, acc. sing. m. of the adj. *longus, -a, -um;*
agrees with *amorem; lōngum* is very forcible, and = *unceasing.* Cf. *longa oblivia =
endless forgetfulness.* —— que, enclitic cop. conj. —— bibēbat, 3d pers. sing. imperf. ind.
act. of *bibō, -ere, bibī, bibitum,* 3 (root BI = πι, in πίνω = *I drink*); joined by *que* to
trahebat, and in agreement with the same subj. *Dido.* —— amōrem, acc. sing. of *amor,
-ōris,* m., 3d; direct obj. of *bibebat.*
  LINE 750. Multa, acc. plur. of the adj. *multus, -a, -um;* substantival, and direct
obj. of *rogitans.* —— super, prep. with the acc. and abl.; gov. the abl. *Priamo. Super*
usually = *over,* of place, denoting *motion over* with the acc., and *rest over* with the abla-
tive. Here *super = de, over, touching, concerning.* A. & G. 153, and 260; B. 143; G.
418, 4; H. 435. —— Priamō, abl. sing. of *Priamus, -ī,* m., 2d; governed by *super.*
Dido makes eager inquiries respecting the principal figures and events connected with
the siege of Troy. —— rogitāns, nom. sing. f. of the pres. part. act. of *rogitō, -āre, -āvī,
-ātum,* 1 (frequentative of *rogo;* cf. *clāmō,* and *clāmitō*); predicate part., agreeing with
Dido; rogitans = dum rogitat. —— super, (see above); gov. *Hectore.* The repe-
tition *multa super . . . super . . . multa* expresses the eager interest which Dido takes
in her distinguished guest and the heroes whom he had personally known. —— Hectore,
abl. sing. of *Hector, -is,* m., 3d; governed by *super.* —— multa, acc. plur. n.; direct obj.
of *rogitans; multa* is repeated from above, and expresses great excitement.
  LINE 751. Nunc, adv. of time, with *rogitans* understood. Observe the *anaphora,
nunc . . . nunc, now . . . now,* and the skill with which Vergil breathes the spirit of
reality into his picture of Dido's increasing eagerness to hear of Troy. *Nunc . . . nunc*
suggests that Aeneas no sooner answers one question than Dido asks another. —— qui-
bus, abl. plur. n. of the interrog. adj. *quī, quae, quod;* agrees with *armis.* —— Aurōrae,

armor the son of the Dawn had come; now of what sort were the steeds of Diomedes; now how mighty was Achilles. "Nay come, guest," she sayeth, "and from the earliest beginning tell

Aúro,ræ „ ve,nísset , fílius , ármis ;
of Aurora had come the son with arms;
Núnc, qua,lés Dio,médis e,quí ; „ nunc, ,
now of what sort of Diomedes the horses (were); now
quántus A,chílles. "Ímmo age, et , á
how mighty (was) Achilles. "Nay come, and from
pri,má „ dic, , hóspes, o,rígine , nóbis
first tell, o guest, the origin to us

---

gen. sing. of *Aurōra*, f., 1st (akin to Greek αὐ-ώς, = ἠ-ώς, *the Dawn*); poss. gen., limiting *filius*. Aurora was the wife of Tithonus, and the mother of Memnon. —— **vēnisset**, 3d pers. sing. pluperf. subjunct. act. of *veniō, -īre, vēnī, ventum*, 4; agrees with the subj. *filius;* the mood is subjunct. in the indirect question introduced by (*rogitans*) *quibus . . . armis.* —— **fīlius** (voc. *fīlī*), nom. sing. m.; subj. of *venisset; filius = Memnon.* Memnon is probably called the son of Aurora because he came from the east. —— **armīs**, abl. plur.; abl. of manner, with *cum* omitted. With this passage cf. l. 489, *nigri Memnonis arma.* The arms of Memnon were made by Vulcan.

LINE 752. **Nunc**, adv., repeated rhetorically from the verse above. —— **quālēs**, nom. plur. m. of the interrog. adj. *quālis, -e* (= *of what kind?*); agrees with *equi.* —— **Diomēdis**, gen. sing. of *Diomēdēs*, m., 3d (Greek Διομήδης = *Zeus-counselled*); poss. gen., limiting *equi.* Diomedes was the son of Tydeus, hence often called *Tydides. The horses of Diomedes* here mentioned are those which took part in the chariot race (Iliad, XXIII, 377 ff.). It was an unfortunate question on Dido's part, for Diomede had captured these horses from Aeneas. For this reason, some suppose that other horses of Diomedes are meant, for he both bred and captured others; but there are none sufficiently famous, except the horses which Diomedes and Ulysses took from the camp of Rhesus. As this latter incident was painted on the temple walls, perhaps the horses of Rhesus are referred to (see lines 469–473). —— **equī**, nom. plur.; subj. of *essent* understood in the predicate *quales essent; essent* is the subjunct. due to the indirect question with *quales.* —— **nunc**, adv., repeated by *anaphora* for effect; see *nunc* above. —— **quantus**, nom. sing. m. of the interrog. adj. *quantus, -a, -um;* agrees with *Achilles.* —— **Achillēs** (for decl. see *Achilli*, l. 30), nom. sing., subj. of *esset* in the indirect question (*rogitans*) *quantus esset Achilles.*

LINE 753. **Immō** (perhaps = *ipsimō*, from *ipse*), adv., used both affirmatively and negatively; it heightens a previous statement when affirmative (*yes indeed*), and makes a correction or removes some doubt when negative (*nay rather*). *Immo age et dic = nay rather, come tell us,* etc. —— **age**, 2d pers. sing. imperative mood act. of *agō, -ere, ēgī, actum*, 3; the subj. *tu* is contained in the verb. *Age*, as often, precedes and makes emphatic a second imperative *dic.* —— **et**, cop. conj. —— **ā**, prep. with the abl.; gov. *origine*, denoting source. —— **prīmā**, abl. sing. f. of the adj. *prīmus, -a, -um;* agrees with *origine*, and exercises a partitive force. A. & G. 193; B. 241; G. 291, REM. 2; H. 440, 2, NOTE 1. —— **dīc**, 2d pers. sing. imperative mood act. of *dīcō, -ere, dīxī, dictum*, 3; the subj. *tu* is implied; *dic* is joined by *et* to *age.* As *dic* (for *dice*) from *dico*, so is the imperative *fer* from *fero*, and *fac* from *facio;* A. & G. 128, *c*; B. 116, 3; G. 130, 5; H. 238. —— **hospes**, gen. *hospitis*, m., 3d (= (1) *host*, (2) as here, *guest*); voc. sing.; the case of address. —— **orīgine**, abl. sing. of *origō, -inis*, f., 3d (*orior = I rise*); governed by the prep. *ā.* —— **nōbīs**, dat. plur.; dat. of the indirect obj. governed by *dic.*

754 **Insidi,ás,"**　in,quít,　"Dana,úm,　,, ca,súsque | to us the treachery of
the ambush,"　*she says,*　*"of the Greeks,*　*and the fortunes* | the Greeks, thy peo-
755 **tu,órum,**　　**Érro,résque**　**tu,ós ;**　,, nam , té | ple's fate, and thine
of thy (people),　*and wanderings*　*thy ;*　*for*　*thee* | own wanderings; for
756 **iam , séptima , pórtat Ómnibus , érran,tém ,,** | 'tis now the seventh
now　*seventh*　*carries*　*all*　*wandering* | summer that carries
ter,rís　et　,　**flúctibus ,**　**ǽstas."** | thee a wanderer over
over lands　*and*　*over seas (waves)*　*the summer."* | all lands and seas."

LINE 754. **Insidiās**, acc. plur. of *insidiae, -ārum*, f., plur., 1st (from *insido;* cf. *incidat*, l. 719); direct obj. of *dic*. *Insidias* refers to the wooden horse, filled with armed men, which the Trojans are induced by Sinon's guileful tale to take within the city walls, and to the sack of Troy; this forms the subject-matter of the second book of the Aeneid.——**inquit**, 3d pers.. sing. pres. ind. act. of the defective verb *inquam ;* agrees with the understood subj. *Dido; inquit*, as it regularly does, is included in the quotation to which it refers. A. & G. 144, *b*; B. 134; G. 175, 2; H. 297, II, 2.—— **Danaüm,** contracted gen. plur. (for *Danaōrum ;* cf. *Teucrūm*, l. 555); subjective gen., limiting *insidias.*——**cāsūs**, acc. plur.; direct obj. of *dic*, joined by *que* to *insidias.*—— **que,** enclitic cop. conj.——**tuōrum,** gen. plur. m. of *tuus, -a, -um ;* substantival, and poss. gen., limiting *casus*.

LINE 755. **Errōrēs,** acc. plur. of *error, -ōris*, m., 3d (from *errō, = I wander*) ; direct obj. of *dic*, joined by *que* to *casus*. The wanderings of Aeneas are related in the third book of the Aeneid. —— **que,** enclitic cop. conj.——**tuōs**, acc. plur. m. of *tuus;* agrees with *errores*.——**nam,** causal conj., introducing an explanation of *errores*.——**iam,** acc. sing. of *tū ;* direct obj. of *portat*.——**iam,** adv. of time, extending *portat*.——**septima**, nom. sing. f. of the adj. *septimus, -a, -um* (ordinal of *septem*) ; agrees with *aestas*. The wanderings of Aeneas are apportioned as follows : (1st year) After the fall of Troy, Aeneas spends the winter in preparing a fleet; (2d) sails in the spring to Thrace, and tries to settle, but is deterred by the omen of Polydorus, and leaves in the next spring; (3d, 4th, and part of the 5th year) Aeneas sails to Delos, and thence, as advised by Anchises, to Crete, where they attempt to found Pergameum, but owing to plague and blighted crops they sail away, and as directed by the *penates* (and Anchises, who remembers Cassandra's prophecy) make for Italy; they encounter the Harpies and a storm, and reach Actium; (winter of 5th year) they spend the winter at Actium, and celebrate games; (6th year) Aeneas sails along the coast of Epirus to Buthrotum, meeting Helenus and Andromache; Helenus foretells their visit to Sicily, and warns them to sail round Sicily, and escape Scylla and Charybdis; the Trojans sail on and anchor in a port near Mount Aetna in Sicily; they meet Achaemenides, who had been left behind by Odysseus' company among the Cyclopes, and also see Polyphemus, but escape him by sailing away with Achaemenides; they coast along Sicily, passing many towns, to Drepanum, where Anchises dies; (7th year) early in the summer, Aeneas sails to Carthage. —— **portat,** 3d pers. sing. pres. ind. act. of *portō, -āre, āvī, -ātum,* 1; agrees with the subject. *aestas.*

LINE 756. **Omnibus**, abl. plur. f. of *omnis, -e,* adj., 3d; agrees with *terris.*—— **errantem,** acc. sing. m. of *errāns, -antis,* pres. part. act. of *errō, -āre, -āvī, -ātum,* 1; predicate part., agreeing with *te ; errantem* practically = *qui erravisti omnibus terris et fluctibus, et nunc erras.*——**terrīs,** abl. plur.; abl. of 'place over which' (locative). —— **et,** cop. conj.——**fluctibus,** abl. plur. of *fluctus, -ūs*, m., 4th; abl. of 'place over which,' joined by *et* to *terrīs.*—— **aestās,** gen. *aestātis,* f., 3d; nom. sing., subj. of *portat.*

VERGIL'S AENEID, BOOK I.

COMPLETELY SCANNED

VERGIL'S AENEID, BOOK I.

PREFACE AND INVOCATION

Árma vi‚rúmque ca‚nó ‖ Tro‚iáe qui ‚ prímus ab ‚ óris
Ítali‚ám, ‖ fa‚tó profu‚gús, ‖ La‚víniaque ‚ vénit
lítora, ‚ múlt*um* il‚*le* ét ter‚rís ‖ iac‚tátus et ‚ álto
ví supe‚rúm sae‚váe ‖ memo‚rém Iu‚nónis ob ‚ íram,
múlta quo‚q*ue* ét bel‚ló pas‚sús ‖ dum ‚ cónderet ‚ úrbem, 5
ínfer‚rétque de‚ós Lati‚ó, ‖ genus ‚ únde La‚tínum
Alba‚níque pa‚trés ‚ at‚q*ue* áltae ‚ móenia . Rómae.

Músa, mi‚hí cau‚sás memo‚rá, ‖ qao ‚ númine ‚ láeso,
quídve do‚léns, re‚gína de‚úm ‖ tot   vólvere ‚ cásus
ínsig‚ném pie‚táte vi‚rúm, ‖ tot ad‚íre la‚bóres   10
ímpule‚rít.   Tan‚táen*e* ‖ àni‚mís coe‚léstibus ‚ írae?

THE WRATH OF JUNO

Úrbs an‚tíqua fu‚ít, ‖ Tyri‚í tenu‚ére co‚lóni,
Cártha‚g*o*, Ítali‚ám con‚trá ‖ Tibe‚rínaque ‚ lónge
óstia, ‚ díves o‚púm ‖ studi‚ísq*ue* as‚pérrima ‚ bélli;
quám Iu‚nó fer‚túr ‖ ter‚rís magis ‚ ómnibus ‚ únam   15
pósthabi‚tá colu‚ísse Sa‚mó; ‖ hic ‚ íllius ‚ árma,

311

híc cur₁rús fuit; ₁ hóc ‖ reg₁núm dea ₁ géntibus ₁ ésse,
sí qua ₁ fáta si₁nánt, ‖ iam ₁ túm ten₁dítque fo₁vétque.
Prógeni₁ém sed e₁ním ‖ Tro₁iáno a ₁ sánguine ₁ dúci
aúdie₁rát, Tyri₁ás ‖ o₁lím quae ₁ vérteret ₁ árces;   20
hínc popu₁lúm la₁té re₁gém ‖ bel₁lóque su₁pérbum
véntu₁rum éxcidi₁ó Lib₁yáe; ‖ sic ₁ vólvere ₁ Párcas.
Íd metu₁éns vete₁rísque me₁mór ‖ Sa₁túrnia ₁ bélli,
príma quod ₁ ád Tro₁iám ‖ pro ₁ cáris ₁ gésserat ₁ Árgis:
nécdum eti₁ám cau₁sae íra₁rúm ‖ sae₁víque do₁lóres   25
éxcide₁ránt ani₁mó: ‖ manet ₁ álta ₁ ménte re₁póstum
iúdici₁úm Pari₁dís ‖ spre₁táeque in₁iúria ₁ fórmae,
ét genus ₁ ínvi₁sum, ‖ ét rap₁tí Gany₁médis ho₁nóres:
hís ac₁cénsa su₁pér ‖ iac₁tátos ₁ áequore ₁ tóto
Tróas, ₁ réliqui₁ás ‖ Dana₁um átque im₁mítis A₁chílli,   30
árce₁bát lon₁gé Lati₁ó, ‖ mul₁tósque per ₁ ánnos
érra₁bánt ac₁tí fatís ‖ mari₁a ómnia ₁ círcum.
Tántae ₁ mólis e₁rát ‖ Ro₁mánam ₁ cóndere ₁ géntem.
Víx e ₁ cónspec₁tú ‖ Sicu₁láe tel₁lúris in ₁ áltum
véla da₁bánt lae₁ti ‖ ét spu₁más salis ₁ áere ru₁ébant,   35
cúm Iu₁no áeter₁núm ⁎ ser₁váns sub ₁ péctore ₁ vúlnus
háec se₁cúm: "Me₁ne íncep₁tó ‖ de₁sístere ₁ víctam,
néc pos₁se Ítali₁á ‖ Teu₁crórum a₁vértere ₁ régem?
qúippe ve₁tór fa₁tís. ‖ Pal₁lásne ex₁úrere ₁ clássem
Árgi₁vum átque ip₁sós ‖ potu₁ít sub₁mérgere , pónto,   40
únius ₁ ób no₁xam ét furi₁ás ‖ A₁iácis O₁íli?

Ípsa, Io,vís rapi,dúm ‖ iacu,láta e , núbibus , ígnem,

dísie,cítque ra,tés ‖ e,vértit,que áequora , véntis;

íllum ex,spíran,tém ‖ trans,fíxo , péctore , flámmas

túrbine , córripu,ít ‖ scopu,lóque in,fíxit a,cúto; 45

ást ego, , quáe di,vum ‖ ínce,dó re,gína, Io,vísque

ét soror , ét con,iúnx, ‖ u,ná cum , génte tot , ánnos

bélla ge,ro. Ét quis,quám ‖ nu,men Iu,nónis a,dórat

práetere,a aút sup,pléx ‖ a,rís im,pónet ho,nórem?"

SHE CONFERS WITH AEOLUS

Tália , flámma,tó ‖ se,cúm dea , córde vo,lútans 50

nímbo,rum ín patri,ám, ‖ loca , féta fu,réntibus , aústris,

Áeoli,ám venit. , Híc ‖ vas,tó rex , Áeolus , ántro

lúctan,tés ven,tós ‖ tem,pésta,tésque so,nóras

ímperi,ó premit, , ác vin,clís ‖ et , cárcere , frénat.

Ílli in,dígnan,tés ‖ mag,nó cum , múrmure , móntis 55

círcum , cláustra fre,múnt; ‖ cel,sá sedet , Áeolus , árce

scéptra te,néns, mol,lítque ani,mós ‖ et , témperat , íras :

ní faci,át, mari,a ác ter,rás ‖ coe,lúmque pro,fúndum

qúippe fe,ránt rapi,dí se,cúm ‖ ver,rántque per , áuras :

séd Pater , ómnipo,téns ‖ spe,lúncis , ábdidit , átris, 60

hóc metu,éns, ‖ mo,lémque et , móntes , ínsuper , áltos

ímposu,ít, re,gémque de,dít, ‖ qui , fóedere , cérto

ét preme,re ét la,xás ‖ sci,rét darè , iússus ha,bénas.

Ád quem , túm Iu,nó ‖ sup,pléx his , vócibus , úsa est :

"Áeole, ͺ námque tiͺbí ‖ diͺvúm pater ͺ átque homiͺnúm rex ₆₅
ét mulͺcére deͺdít flucͺtús ‖ et ͺ tóllere ͺ vénto,
géns iniͺmíca mīͺhí ‖ Tyrͺrhénum ͺ návigat ͺ áequor,
Ílium in ͺ Ítaliͺám porͺtáns ‖ vicͺtósque peͺnátes :
íncute ͺ vím venͺtís ‖ subͺmérsasͺque óbrue ͺ púppes,
aút age ͺ díverͺsós ‖ et ͺ dísiice ͺ córpora ͺ pónto.   ₇₀
Súnt mīhi ͺ bís sepͺtém ‖ praeͺstánti ͺ córpore ͺ nýmphae,
quárum ͺ quáe forͺmá ‖ pulͺchérrima ͺ Déioͺpéia,
cónnubiͺó iunͺgám stabiͺlí ‖ propriͺámque diͺcábo,
ómnes ͺ út teͺcúm ‖ meriͺtís pro ͺ tálibus ͺ ánnos
éxigat ͺ ét pulͺchrá ‖ faciͺát te ͺ próle paͺréntem."   ₇₅
Áeolus ͺ haec conͺtrá : ‖ "Tuus, ͺ Ó reͺgína, quid ͺ óptes,
éxploͺráre laͺbór ; ‖ mihi ͺ iússa caͺpéssere ͺ fás est.
Tú mihi ͺ quódcumͺque hóc regͺní, ‖ tu ͺ scéptra Ioͺvémque
cónciliͺás, tu ͺ dás epuͺlís ‖ acͺcúmbere ͺ dívum,
nímboͺrúmque faͺcís ‖ temͺpéstaͺtúmque poͺténtem."   ₈₀

A STORM THREATENS THE FLEET

Háec ubi ͺ dícta, ‖ caͺvúm conͺvérsa ͺ cúspide ͺ móntem
ímpulit ͺ ín latus : ͺ ác venͺtí, ‖ velut ͺ ágmine ͺ fácto,
qúa data ͺ pórta, ruͺúnt ‖ et ͺ térras ͺ túrbine ͺ pérflant.
Íncubuͺére maͺrí, ‖ toͺtúmque a ͺ sédibus ͺ ímis
úna Euͺrúsque Noͺtúsque ruͺúnt ‖ creͺbérque proͺcéllis   ₈₅
Áfricus, ͺ ét vasͺtós ‖ volͺvúnt ad ͺ lítora ͺ flúctus.
Ínsequiͺtúr claͺmórque viͺrúm ‖ striͺdórque ruͺréntum.

Éripi₁únt subi₁tó nu₁bés ‖ coe₁lúmque di₁émque

Téucro₁rum éx ocu₁lís ; ‖ pon₁tó nox ₁ íncubat ₁ átra.

Íntonu₁ére po₁li ét cre₁brís ‖ micat ₁ ígnibus ₁ áether,   90

práesen₁témque vi₁rís ‖ in₁téntant ₁ ómnia ₁ mórtem.

Éxtem₁plo Áene₁áe ‖ sol₁vúntur ₁ frígore ₁ mémbra ;

íngemit, ₁ ét dupli₁cés ‖ ţen₁déns ad ₁ sídera ₁ pálmas

tália ₁ vóce re₁fért : ‖ "O ₁ térque qua₁térque be₁áti,

quéis an₁te óra pa₁trúm ‖ Tro₁iáe sub ₁ móenibus ₁ áltis   95

cóntigit ₁ óppete₁re ! ‖ Ó Dana₁úm for₁tíssime ₁ géntis

Týdi₁dé, me₁ne Ília₁cís ‖ oc₁cúmbere ₁ cámpis

nón potu₁ísse tu₁áque ani₁mam. ‖ hánc ef₁fúndere ₁ déxtra,

sáevus u₁bi Áeaci₁dáe ‖ te₁ló iacet Héctor, u₁bi íngens

Sárpe₁dón, ubi ₁ tót Simo₁ís ‖ cor₁répta sub ₁ úndis   100

scúta vi₁rúm gale₁ásque ‖ et ₁ fórtia   córpora ₁ vólvit ? "

SHIPWRECK

Tália ₁ iáctan₁tí ‖ stri₁déns Aqui₁lóne pro₁célla

vélum ad₁vérsa fe₁rít, ‖ fluc₁túsque ad ₁ sídera ₁ tóllit.

Frángun₁túr re₁mí ; ‖ tum ₁ próra a₁vértit et ₁ úndis

dát latus ; ₁ ínsequi₁túr cumu₁ló ‖ prae₁rúptus a₁quáe mons.   105

Hí sum₁mo ín fluc₁tú pen₁dént, ‖ his ₁ únda de₁híscens

térram in₁tér fluc₁tús ape₁rít, ‖ furit ₁ áestus a₁rénis.

Trés Notus ₁ ábrep₁tás ‖ in ₁ sáxa la₁téntia ₁ tórquet ;

sáxa vo₁cánt Ita₁lí ‖ medi₁ís quae in ₁ flúctibus ₁ áras,

dórsum im₁máne ma₁rí sum₁mó ; ‖ tres ₁ Éurus ab ₁ álto   110

ín brevi*a* ₁ ét syr₁tés ur₁guét, ‖ mise₁rábile ₁ vísu,

ílli₁dítque va₁dís ‖ at₁q*ue* ággere ₁ cíngit a₁rénae.

Únam, ₁ quáe Lyci₁ós ‖ fi₁dúmque ve₁hébat O₁rónten,

ípsius ₁ ánte ocu₁lós ‖ in₁géns a ₁ vértice ₁ póntus

ín pup₁pím ferit : ₁ éxcuti₁túr ‖ pro₁núsque má₁gister   115

vólvitur ₁ ín caput ; ₁ ást il₁lám ‖ ter ₁ flúctus i₁bídem

tórquet a₁géns cir₁c*um*, ‖ ét rapi₁dús vorat ₁ áequore ₁ vértex.

Áppa₁rént ra₁rí ‖ nan₁tés in ₁ gúrgite ₁ vásto,

árma vi₁rúm tabu₁láeq*ue* ‖ et ₁ Tróïa ₁ gáza per ₁ úndas.

Iám vali₁d*am* Ílio₁neí na₁vém, ‖ iam ₁ fórtis A₁chátae,   120

ét qua ₁ véctus A₁bás, ‖ et ₁ q*uá* gran₁dáevus A₁létes,

vícit hi₁émps ; ‖ la₁xís late₁rúm com₁págibus ₁ ómnes

áccipi₁únt ini₁míc*um* im₁brém ‖ ri₁mísque fa₁tíscunt.

INTERVENTION OF NEPTUNE

Íntere₁*á* mag₁nó ‖ mis₁céri ₁ múrmure ₁ póntum,

émis₁sámq*ue* hie₁mém ‖ sen₁sít Nep₁túnus et ₁ ímis   125

.stágna re₁fúsa va₁dís, ‖ gravi₁tér com₁mótus ; et ₁ álto

próspici₁éns sum₁má ‖ placi₁dúm caput ₁ éxtulit ₁ únda.

Dísiec₁t*am* Áene₁áe ‖ to₁tó videt ₁ áequore ₁ clássem,

flúctibus ₁ óppres₁sós Tro₁ás ‖ coe₁líque ru₁ína.

Néc latu₁ére do₁lí ‖ fra₁trém Iu₁nónis et ₁ írae.   130

Eúr*um* ad ₁ sé Zephy₁rúmque vo₁cát, ‖ dehinc ₁ tália ₁ fátur :

"tántane ₁ vós gene₁rís ‖ tenu₁ít fi₁dúcia ₁ véstri ?

Iám coe₁lúm ter₁rámque ‖ me₁ó sine ₁ númine, ₁ vénti,

mísce,re, ét tan,tás ‖ au,détis , tóllere , móles?

quós ego , —séd mo,tós ‖ prae,stát com,pónere , flúctus: 135

póst mihi , nón simi,lí ‖ poe,ná com,míssa lu,etis.

Mátu,ráte fu,gám, ‖ re,gíque haec , dícite , véstro:

nón il,lí ímperi,úm pela,gí ‖ sae,vúmque tri,déntem,

séd mihi , sórte da,túm. ‖ Te̜net , ílle im,mánia , sáxa,

véstras, , Eúre, do,mós; ‖ il,lá se , iáctet in , aúla   140

Aéolus , ét clau,só ‖ ven,tórum , cárcere , régnet."

Síc ait, , ét dic,tó citi,ús ‖ tumi,da áequora , plácat,

cóllec,tásque fu,gát nu,bés ‖ so,lémque re,dúcit.

Cýmotho,ë̈ simul , ét Tri,tón ‖ an,níxus a,cúto

détru,dúnt na,vés scopu,ló; ‖ levat , ípse tri,dénti,   145

ét vas,tás ape,rít syr,tés ‖ et , témperat , áequor,

átque ro,tís sum,más ‖ levi,bús per,lábitur , úndas.

Ác velu,tí mag,no ín popu,ló ‖ cum , sáepe co,órta est

séditi,ó, sae,vítque ani,mís ‖ ig,nóbile , vúlgus,

iámque fa,cés et , sáxa vo,lánt, ‖ furor , árma min,ístrat: 150

túm pie,táte gra,vem ác meri,tís ‖ si , fórte vi,rúm quem

cónspex,ére, si,lént ‖ ar,réctis,que aúribus , ádstant;

ílle re,gít dic,tís ani,mós, ‖ et , péctora , múlcet:

síc cun,ctús pela,gí ‖ ceci,dít fragor, , áequora , póstquam

próspici,éns geni,tor ‖ coe,lóque in,véctus a,pérto   155

fléctit e,quós cur,rúque vo,láns̄ ‖ dat , lóra se,cúndo.

THE TROJANS LAND IN AFRICA

Défes₁sí Aénea₁dǽ ‖ quae ₁ próxima ₁ lítora cúrsu

cónten₁dúnt pete₁re, ét Liby₁ǽ ‖ ver₁túntur ad ₁ óras.

Ést in ₁ séces₁sú ‖ lon₁gó locus: ₁ ínsula ₁ pórtum

éfficit ₁ óbiec₁tú late₁rúm, ‖ quibus ₁ ómnis ab ₁ álto 160

frángitur ₁ ínque si₁nús ‖ scin₁dít se₁se únda re₁dúctos.

Hínc at₁*que* hínc vas₁tǽ ru₁pés ‖ gemi₁níque mi₁nántur

ín coe₁lúm scopu₁lí, ‖ quo₁rúm sub ₁ vértice ₁ láte

ǽquora ₁ túta si₁lént: ‖ tum ₁ sílvis ₁ scǽna co₁rúscis

désuper ₁ hórren₁tí*que* ‖ a₁trúm nemus ₁ ímminet ₁ úmbra; 165

frónte sub ₁ ádver₁sá ‖ scopu₁lís pen₁déntibus ₁ ántrum,

íntus a₁quǽ dul₁cés ‖ vi₁vóque se₁dília ₁ sáxo,

Nýmpha₁rúm domus. ₁ Híc ‖ fes₁sás non ₁ víncula ₁ náves

úlla te₁nént, un₁có ‖ non ₁ álligat ₁ áncora ₁ mórsu.

Húc sep₁*tem* Aéne₁ás ‖ col₁léctis ₁ návibus ₁ ómni 170

éx nume₁ró subit; ‖ ác mag₁nó tel₁lúris a₁móre

égres₁sí ópta₁tá ‖ poti₁úntur ₁ Tróes a₁réna,

ét· sale ₁ tában₁tés ar₁tús ‖ in ₁ lítore ₁ pónunt.

Ac pri₁múm sili₁cí ‖ scin₁tíll*am* ex₁cúdit A₁chátes

súsce₁pít*que* ig₁ném foli₁ís ‖ at₁*que* árida ₁ círcum 175

nútri₁ménta de₁dít ‖ rapu₁ít*que* in ₁ fómite ₁ flámmam.

Túm Cere₁rém cor₁rúpt*am* un₁dís ‖ Cere₁ália₁*que* árma

éxpedi₁únt, fes₁sí re₁rúm; ‖ fru₁gésque re₁céptas

ét tor₁rére pa₁ránt flam₁mís ‖ et ₊ frángere ₁ sáxo.

THE FEAST ON THE SHORE

Aéne₍ás scopu₍lum ‖ íntere₍á con₍scéndit, et ₍ ómnem   180

próspec₍túm la₍té ‖ pela₍gó petit, ₍ Ánthea ₍ sí quem

iácta₍túm ven₍tó vide₍át, ‖ Phrygi₍ásque bi₍rémes,

aút Capyn, ₍ aút cel₍sís ‖ in ₍ púppibus ₍ árma Ca₍ici.

Návem in ₍ cónspec₍tú nul₍lám, ‖ tres ₍ lítore ₍ cérvos

próspicit ₍ érran₍tés; ‖ hos ₍ tóta ar₍ménta se₍quúntur   185

á ter₍go, ét lon₍gúm ‖ per ₍ válles ₍ páscitur ₍ ágmen.

Cónstitit ₍ híc, ‖ ar₍cúmque ma₍nú cele₍résque sa₍gíttas

córripu₍ít, ‖ fi₍dús quae ₍ téla ge₍rébat A₍chátes;

dúcto₍résque ip₍sós pri₍múm, ‖ capi₍ta álta fe₍réntes

córnibus ₍ árbore₍ís, ster₍nít, ‖ tum ₍ vúlgus; et ₍ ómnem 190

míscet a₍géns te₍lís ‖ nemo₍ra ínter ₍ fróndea ₍ túrbam.

Néc prius ₍ ábsis₍tít, ‖ quam ₍ séptem in₍géntia ₍ víctor

córpora ₍ fúndat hu₍mo, ‖ ét nume₍rúm cum ₍ návibus ₍ æquet.

Hínc por₍túm petit, ₍ ét soci₍ós ‖ par₍títur in ₍ ómnes.

Vína bo₍nús quae ₍ déinde ca₍dís ‖ one₍rárat A₍céstes   195

lítore ₍ Trínacri₍ó ‖ dede₍rátque abe₍úntibus ₍ héros,

dívidit, ₍ ét dic₍tís ‖ mae₍réntia péctora ₍ múlcet:

"Ó soci₍í, neque en₍im ígna₍rí ‖ sumus ₍ ánte ma₍lórum,

ó pas₍sí gravi₍óra, ‖ da₍bít deus ₍ hís quoque ₍ fínem.

Vós et ₍ Scýllae₍ám rabi₍ém ‖ peni₍túsque so₍nántes   200

ácces₍tís scopu₍lós; ‖ vos ₍ ét Cy₍clópea ₍ sáxa

éxper₍tí. Revo₍cáte ani₍mós, ‖ maes₍túmque ti₍mórem

míttite. ˌ Fórsan et ˌ hǽc ‖ oˌlím memiˌnísse iuˌvábit.

Pér variˌós caˌsús, ‖ per ˌ tót disˌcrímina ˌ rérum

téndimus ˌ ín Latiˌúm, ‖ seˌdés ubi ˌ fáta quiˌétas   205

óstenˌdúnt : ilˌlíc ‖ fas ˌ régna reˌsúrgere ˌ Tróiae.

Dúraˌte, ét vosˌmét ‖ reˌbús serˌváte seˌcúndis."

Tália ˌ vóce reˌfért; ‖ cuˌrísque inˌgéntibus ˌ ǽger

spém vulˌtú simuˌlát, ‖ premit ˌ áltum ˌ córde doˌlórem.

Ílli ˌ sé praeˌdae áccinˌgúnt ‖ dapiˌbúsque fuˌtúris :   210

térgora ˌ déripiˌúnt cosˌtís, ‖ et ˌ víscera ˌ núdant;

párs in ˌ frústa seˌcánt, ‖ veriˌbúsque treˌméntia ˌ fígunt;

lítore aˌéna loˌcánt aliˌí, ‖ flamˌmásque miˌnístrant.

Túm vicˌtú revoˌcánt viˌrés, ‖ fuˌsíque per ˌ hérbam

ímplenˌtúr veteˌrís Bacˌchí ‖ pinˌguísque feˌrínae.   215

Póstquam exˌémpta faˌmés epuˌlis, ‖ menˌsǽque reˌmótae,

ámisˌsós lonˌgó ‖ sociˌós serˌmóne reˌquírunt,

spémque meˌtúmque inˌtér dubiˌí, ‖ seu ˌ vívere ˌ crédant,

síve exˌtréma paˌtí ‖ nec ˌ iam éxauˌdíre voˌcátos.

Prǽcipuˌé pius ˌ Aéneˌás ‖ nunc ˌ ácris Oˌrónti   220

núnc Amyˌcí caˌsúm ‖ gemit ˌ ét cruˌdélia ˌ sécum

fáta Lyˌcí, forˌtémque Gyˌán, ‖ forˌtémque Cloˌánthum.

VENUS APPEALS TO JUPITER

Ét iam ˌ fínis eˌrát : ‖ cum ˌ Iúpiter ˌ ǽthere ˌ súmmo

déspiciˌéns mare ˌ vélivoˌlúm ‖ terˌrásque iaˌcéntes,

lítoraˌque ét laˌtós popuˌlós, ‖ sic ˌ vértice ˌ cœli   225

cónstitit, ǀ ét Liby͵ǽ ‖ de͵fíxit ǀ lúmina ǀ régnis.

Átque il͵lúm ta͵lés ‖ iac͵tántem ǀ péctore ǀ cúras

trístior ǀ ét lacri͵mís ‖ ocu͵lós suf͵fúsa ni͵téntes

álloqui͵túr Venus: ǀ "Ó ‖ qui ǀ rés homi͵númque de͵úmque

æter͵nís regis ǀ ímperi͵ís, ‖ et ǀ fúlmine ǀ térres,   230

qúid meus ǀ Áene͵ás ‖ in ǀ té com͵míttere ǀ tántum,

qúid Tro͵és potu͵ére, ‖ qui͵bús, tot ǀ fúnera ǀ pássis,

cúnctus ob ǀ Ítali͵ám ‖ ter͵rárum ǀ claúditur ǀ órbis?

Cérte hinc ǀ Róma͵nós o͵lím, ‖ vol͵véntibus ǀ ánnis,

hínc fore ǀ dúcto͵rés ‖ revo͵cáto a ǀ sánguine ǀ Teúcri   235

qúi mare, ǀ quí ter͵rás ‖ om͵ní diti͵óne te͵nérent,

póllici͵tús: ‖ quae ǀ té, geni͵tór, sen͵téntia ǀ vértit?

Hóc equi͵dem ócca͵súm Tro͵iǽ ‖ tris͵tésque ru͵ínas

sóla͵bár, fa͵tís ‖ con͵trária ǀ fáta re͵péndens.

Núnc ea͵dém for͵túna vi͵rós ‖ tot ǀ cásibus ǀ áctos   240

ínsequi͵túr. Quem ǀ dás fi͵ném, ‖ rex ǀ mágne, la͵bórum?

Ánte͵nór potu͵ít, ‖ medi͵ís e͵lápsus A͵chívis,

Íllyri͵cós pene͵tráre si͵nús ‖ at͵que íntima ǀ tútus

régna Li͵búrno͵rum, ‖ ét fon͵tém supe͵ráre Ti͵mávi,

únde per ǀ óra no͵vém ‖ vas͵tó cum ǀ múrmure ǀ móntis   245

ít mare ǀ prórup͵tum ‖ ét pela͵gó premit ǀ árva so͵nánti.

Híc tamen ǀ ille ur͵bém Pata͵ví ‖ se͵désque lo͵cávit

Teúcro͵rum, ét gen͵tí ‖ no͵mén dedit, ǀ ármaque ǀ fíxit

Tróïa; ǀ núnc placi͵dá ‖ com͵póstus ǀ páce qui͵éscit:

nós, tua ǀ prógeni͵és, ‖ coe͵lí quibus ǀ ánnuis ǀ árcem,   250

návibus ┊ ínfan┊d*um*! ámis┊sís, ‖ u┊níus ob ┊ íram
pŕódimur, ┊ átq*ue* Ita┊lís ‖ lon┊gé dis┊iúngimur ┊ óris.
Híc pie┊tátis ho┊nós? ‖ sic ┊ nós in ┊ scéptra ┊re┊pónis?"

PROPHECY OF ROMAN GREATNESS

Ólli ┊ súbri┊déns ‖ homi┊núm sator ┊ átque de┊órum
vúltu, ┊ quó coe┊lúm ‖ tem┊pésta┊tésque se┊rénat,   255
óscula ┊ líba┊vít na┊tǽ, ‖ dehinc ┊ tália ┊ fátur:
"Párce me┊tú, Cythe┊réa; ‖ ma┊nént im┊móta tu┊órum
fáta ti┊bí; ‖ cer┊nés ur┊b*em* ét pro┊míssa La┊víni
mœ́nia, ┊ súbli┊mémque ‖ fe┊rés ad ┊ sídera ┊ cœli
mágnani┊m*um* Aéne┊án; ‖ neque ┊ mé sen┊téntia ┊ vértit.   260
Híc — tibi ┊ fábor e┊ním, ‖ quan┊d*o* hǽc te ┊ cúra re┊mórdet,
lóngius ┊ ét vol┊véns ‖ fa┊tór*um* ar┊cána mo┊vébo —
béll*um* in┊géns geret ┊ Ítali┊á, ‖ popu┊lósque fe┊róces
cóntun┊dét; ‖ mo┊résque vi┊rís et ┊ mœnia ┊ pónet,
tértia ┊ dúm Lati┊ó ‖ reg┊nántem ┊ víderit ┊ ǽstas,   265
térnaque ┊ tránsie┊rínt ‖ Rutu┊lís hi┊bérna sub┊áctis.
Át puer ┊ Áscani┊ús, ‖ cui ┊ núnc cog┊nómen I┊úlo
ádditur, ┊ — Ílus e┊rát, ‖ dum ┊ rés stetit ┊ Ília ┊ régno, —
trígin┊tá mag┊nós ‖ vol┊véndis ┊ ménsibus ┊ órbes
ímperi┊*o* éxple┊bít, ‖ reg┊númq*ue* ab ┊ séde La┊víni   270
tránsferet, ┊ ét lon┊gám ‖ mul┊tá vi ┊ múniet ┊ Álbam.
Híc iam ┊ tér cen┊túm ‖ to┊tós reg┊nábitur ┊ ánnos
génte sub ┊ Héctore┊á, ‖ do┊néc re┊gína sa┊cérdoṣ

Márte gra₁vís gemi₁nám ‖ par₁tú dabit ₁ Ília ₁ prólem.

Índe lu₁pǽ ful₁vó ‖ nu₁trícis ₁ tégmine ₁ lǽtus   275

Rómulus ₁ éxcipi₁ét gen₁*tem,* ‖ ét Ma₁vórtia ₁ cóndet

mœnia, ₁ Róma₁nósque ‖ su₁ó de ₁ nómine ₁ dícet.

Hís ego ₁ néc me₁tás re₁rúm ‖ nec ₁ témpora ₁ póno;

ímperi₁úm sine ₁ fíne de₁dí. ‖ Quin ₁ áspera ₁ Iúno,

quǽ mare ₁ núnc ter₁rásque me₁tú ‖ coe₁lúmque fa₁tígat,   280

cónsili₁*a* ín meli₁ús refe₁rét, ‖ me₁cúmque fo₁vébit

Róma₁nós, re₁rúm domi₁nós, ‖ gen₁témque to₁gátam.

Síc placi₁túm. ‖ Veni₁ét lus₁trís la₁béntibus ₁ ǽtas,

cúm domus ₁ Ássara₁cí ‖ Phthi₁ám cla₁rásque My₁cénas

sérviti₁ó premet, ₁ ác vic₁tís ‖ domi₁nábitur ₁ Árgis.   285

Násce₁túr pul₁chrá ‖ Tro₁iánus o₁rígine ₁ Cǽsar,

ímperi₁*um* ócea₁nó, ‖ fa₁mám qui ₁ términet ₁ ástris,

Iúlius, ₁ á mag₁nó ‖ de₁míssum ₁ nómen I₁úlo.

Húnc *tu* o₁lím coe₁ló, ‖ spoli₁ís Ori₁éntis o₁nústum,

áccipi₁és se₁cúra; ‖ vo₁cábitur ₁ híc quoque ₁ vótis.   290

Áspera ₁ túm posi₁tís ‖ mi₁téscent ₁ sǽcula ₁ béllis;

cána Fi₁dés et ₁ Vésta, ‖ Re₁mó cum ₁ frátre Qui₁rínus

iúra da₁búnt; ‖ di₁rǽ fer₁*ro* ét com₁págibus ₁ ártis

claúden₁túr bel₁lí por₁tǽ; ‖ Furor ₁ ímpius ₁ íntus,

sǽva se₁déns super ₁ árm*a,* ‖ et ₁ céntum ₁ vínctus a₁énis 295

póst ter₁gúm no₁dís, ‖ fremet ₁ hórridus ₁ óre cru₁énto."

MEETING OF VENUS AND ÆNEAS

Hǽc ait: ǀ ét Mai¡á geni¡túm ‖ de¡míttit ab ǀ álto,
út ter̦¡rae, útque no¡vǽ ‖ pate¡ánt Car¡tháginis ǀ árces
hóspiti¡ó Teu¡crís, ‖ ne ǀ fáti ǀ néscia ǀ Dído
fínibus ǀ árce¡rét. ‖ Volat ǀ ílle per ǀ áëra ǀ mágnum   300
rémigi¡o ála¡rum, ‖ ác Liby¡ǽ citus ǀ ádstitit ǀ óris.
Ét iam ǀ iússa fa¡cít; ‖ po¡núntque fe¡rócia ǀ Pœni
córda, vo¡lénte de¡o; ‖ ín pri¡mís re¡gína qui¡étum
áccipit ǀ ín Teu¡crós ‖ ani¡múm men¡témque be¡nígnam.
Át pius ǀ Aéne¡ás ‖ per ǀ nóctem ǀ plúrima ǀ vólvens,   305
út pri¡múm lux ǀ álma da¡ta ést, ‖ ex¡íre loc¡ósque
éxplo¡ráre nov¡ós, ‖ quas ǀ vénto ac¡césserit ǀ óras,
qui tene¡ánt, nam in¡cúlta vi¡dét, ‖ homi¡nésne fe¡rǽne,
quǽrere ǀ cónstitu¡ít, ‖ soci¡ísque ex¡ácta re¡férre.
Clássem in ǀ cónvex¡ó ‖ nemo¡rúm sub ǀ rúpe . ca¡váta   310
árbori¡bús clau¡sám cir¡cum ‖ átque hor¡réntibus ǀ úmbris
ócculit: ǀ ípse u¡nó ‖ gradi¡túr comi¡tátus A¡cháte,
bína ma¡nú la¡tó ‖ cris¡páns has¡tília ǀ férro.
Cuí ma¡tér medi¡á ‖ se¡sé tulit ǀ óbvia ǀ sílva,
vírginis ǀ ós habi¡túmque ge¡réns ‖ et ǀ vírginis ǀ árma   315
Spárta¡nǽ, vel ǀ quális e¡quós ‖ Thre¡íssa fa¡tígat
Hárpaly¡cé, volu¡crémque fu¡gá ‖ prae¡vértitur ǀ Hébrum.
Námque hume¡rís de ǀ móre habi¡lém ‖ sus¡pénderat ǀ árcum
véna¡tríx, dede¡rátque co¡mám ‖ dif¡fúndere véntis,

núda ge₁nú, ‖ no₁dóque si₁nús col₁lécta flu₁éntes.   820

Ác prior, ₁ "Heús," in₁quít, "iuve₁nés, ‖ mon₁stráte me₁árum

vídis₁tís si ₁ quam híc ‖ er₁rántem ₁ fórte so₁rórum,

súccinc₁tám phare₁tra ‖ ét macu₁lósae ₁ tégmine ₁ lýncis,

aút spu₁mántis a₁prí cur₁súm ‖ cla₁móre pre₁méntem."

Síc Venus; ₁ ét Vene₁rís con₁trá ‖ sic ₁ fílius ₁ órsus: 825

"Núlla tu₁árum au₁díta mi₁hí ‖ neque ₁ vísa so₁rórum,

Ó—quam ₁ té memo₁rém, vir₁gó? ‖ nam₁que haúd tibi ₁ vúltus

mórta₁lís, ‖ nec ₁ vóx homi₁ném sonat. ₁ Ó dea ₁ cérte:

án Phoe₁bí ‖ soror? ₁ án nym₁phárum ₁ sánguinis ₁ úna?

Sís fe₁líx, nos₁trúmque le₁vés, ‖ quae₁cúmque, la₁bórem,   830

ét quo ₁ súb coe₁ló tan₁dém, ‖ quibus ₁ órbis in ₁ óris

iácte₁múr, doce₁ás. ‖ Ig₁nári homi₁númque lo₁córumque

érra₁mús, ven₁to ‖ húc et ₁ vástis ₁ flúctibus ₁ ácti.

Múlta ti₁bi ánte a₁rás ‖ nos₁trá cadet ₁ hóstia ₁ déxtra."

THE TALE OF DIDO'S FLIGHT

Túm Venus: ₁ "Haúd equi₁dém ‖ ta₁lí me ₁ dígnor ho₁nóre;   835

vírgini₁bús Tyri₁ís ‖ mos ₁ ést ges₁táre pha₁rétram,

púrpure₁óque al₁té ‖ su₁rás vin₁círe co₁thúrno.

Púnica ₁ régna vi₁dés, ‖ Tyri₁ós et A₁génoris ₁ úrbem;

séd fi₁nés Liby₁cí, ‖ genus ₁ íntrac₁tábile ₁ béllo.

Ímperi₁úm Di₁dó ‖ Tyri₁á regit ₁ úrbe pro₁fécta,   840

gérma₁núm fugi₁éns. ‖ Lon₁ga ést in₁iúria, ₁ lóngae

ámba₁gés; sed ₁ súmma se₁quár ‖ fas₁tígia   rérum.

Huíc con¡iúnx Sy¡chǽus e¡rát, ‖ di¡tíssimus ¡ ágri

Phǿni¡*cum*, ét mag¡nó ‖ mise¡rǽ di¡léctus a¡móre,

cuí pater ¡ íntac¡tám dede¡rát, ‖ pri¡mísque iu¡gárat   845

ómini¡bús. Sed ¡ régna Ty¡rí ‖ ger¡mánus .ha¡bébat

Pýgmali¡ón, ¡ scele¡*re* ánte ali¡ós im¡mánior ¡ ómnes.

Quós in¡tér medi¡ús ‖ ve¡nít furor. ¡ Ílle Sy¡chǽum

ímpius ¡ ánte a¡rás ‖ at¡*que* aúri ¡ cǽcus a¡móre

clǽm fer¡*ro* íncau¡túm supe¡rát, ‖ se¡cúrus a¡mórum   850

gérma¡nǽ; fac¡túmque ‖ di¡ú ce¡lávit, et ¡ ǽgram,

múlta ma¡lús simu¡láns, ‖ va¡ná spe ¡ lúsit a¡mántem.

Ípsa sed ¡ ín som¡nís ‖ inhu¡máti ¡ vénit i¡mágo

cóniugis; ¡ óra mo¡dís ‖ at¡tóllens ¡ pállida ¡ míris,

crúde¡lés a¡rás ‖ tra¡iéctaque ¡ péctora ¡ férro   855

núda¡vít, cae¡cúmque do¡mús ‖ scelus ¡ ómne re¡téxit.

Túm cele¡ráre fu¡gám ‖ patri¡á*que* ex¡cédere ¡ suádet,

aúxili¡úmque vi¡ǽ ‖ vete¡rés tel¡lúre re¡clúdit

thésau¡rós, ‖ ig¡nótum ar¡génti ¡ póndus et ¡ aúri.

Hís com¡móta fu¡gám ‖ Di¡dó soci¡ósque pa¡rábat.   860

Cónveni¡únt, quibus ¡ aút odi¡úm ‖ cru¡déle ty¡ránni

aút metus ¡ ácer e¡rát; ‖ na¡vés, quae ¡ fórte pa¡rátae,

córripi¡únt, one¡rántq*ue* au¡ró. ‖ Por¡tántur a¡vári

Pýgmali¡ónis o¡pés pela¡gó; ‖ dux ¡ fémina ¡ fácti.

Déve¡nére lo¡cós, ‖ ubi ¡ núnc in¡géntia ¡ cérnis   865

mǿnia ¡ súrgen¡témque ‖ no¡vǽ Car¡tháginis ¡ árcem,

mérca¡tíque so¡lúm, ‖ fac¡tí de ¡ nómine ¡ Býrsam,

taúri₁nó quan₁túm ‖ pos₁sént cir₁cúmdare ₁ térgo.

Séd vos ₁ quí tan₁dém, ‖ quibus ₁ aút ve₁nístis ab ₁ óris,

quóve te₁nétis i₁tér?" ‖ Quae₁rénti ₁ tálibus ₁ ílle   870

súspi₁ráns, i₁móque tra₁héns ‖ a ₁ péctore ₁ vócem:

REPLY OF ÆNEAS

"Ó dea, ₁ sí pri₁má ‖ repe₁téns ab o₁rígine ₁ pérgam,

ét vacet ₁ ánna₁lés ‖ nos₁trórum au₁díre la₁bórum,

ánte di₁ém clau₁só ‖ com₁pónat ₁ vésper O₁lýmpo.

Nós Tro₁ia ánti₁quá, ‖ si ₁ véstras ₁ fórte per ₁ aúres   875

Tróiae ₁ nómen i₁ít, ‖ di₁vérsa per ₁ ǽquora ₁ véctos

fórte su₁á Liby₁cís ‖ tem₁péstas ₁ áppulit ₁ óris.

Súm pius ₁ Aéne₁ás, ‖ rap₁tós qui ex ₁ hóste pe₁nátes

clásse ve₁hó me₁cúm, ‖ fa₁má super ₁ ǽthera ₁ nótus.

Ítali₁ám quae₁ró ‖ patri₁am, ét genus ₁ áb Iove ₁ súmmo.   880

Bís de₁nís Phrygi₁úm ‖ con₁scéndi ₁ návibus ₁ ǽquor,

mátre de₁á mon₁stránte vi₁ám, ‖ data ₁ fáta se₁cútus.

Víx sep₁tém con₁vúlsae un₁dís ‖ Eu₁róque su₁pérsunt.

Ípse ig₁nótus, e₁géns, ‖ Liby₁ǽ de₁sérta per₁ágro,

Eúro₁pa átque Asi₁á pul₁sús." ‖ Nec ₁ plúra que₁réntem   885

pássa Ve₁nús medi₁ó ‖ sic ₁ inter₁fáta do₁lóre est:

VENUS REASSURES HIM BY AN OMEN

"Quísquis es, ₁ haúd, cre₁do, ‖ ínvi₁sús coe₁léstibus ₁ aúras

víta₁lés car₁pís, ‖ Tyri₁ám qui ad₁véneris ₁ úrbem.

Pérge mo₁do, átque hinc ₁ té re₁ginae ‖ ad ₁ límina ₁ pérfer.

Námque ti¡bí redu¡cés soci¡ós ‖ clas¡sémque re¡látam   890

núntio, et ¡ ín tu¡túm ‖ ver¡sís aqui¡lónibus ¡ áctam,

ní frus¡tra aúguri¡úm ‖ va¡ní docu¡ére pa¡réntes.

Áspice ¡ bís se¡nós ‖ lae¡tántes ¡ ágmine ¡ cýcnos,

aétheri¡á quos ¡ lápsa pla¡gá ‖ Iovis ¡ áles a¡pérto

túrba¡bát coe¡ló ; ‖ nunc ¡ térras ¡ órdine ¡ lóngo   895

aút cape¡re, aút cap¡tás ‖ iam ¡ déspec¡táre vi¡déntur :

út redu¡cés il¡lí lu¡dúnt ‖ stri¡déntibus ¡ ális,

ét coe¡tú cin¡xére po¡lúm, ‖ can¡túsque de¡dére,

haúd ali¡tér pup¡pésque tu¡æ ‖ pu¡bésque tu¡órum

aút por¡túm tenet, ¡ aút ple¡nó ‖ subit ¡ óstia ¡ vélo.   400

Pérge mo¡do, ét, ‖ qua ¡ té du¡cít. via, ¡ dírige ¡ gréssum."

Díxit ; et ¡ áver¡téns ‖ rose¡á cer¡více re¡fúlsit,

ámbrosi¡æque co¡mæ ‖ di¡vínum ¡ vértice o¡dórem

spíra¡vére : ‖ pe¡dés ves¡tís de¡flúxit ad ¡ ímos ;

ét ve¡ra ínces¡sú ‖ patu¡ít dea. ¡ Ílle ubi ¡ mátrem   405

ágno¡vít, ta¡lí ‖ fugi¡éntem est ¡ vóce se¡cútus :

" Quíd na¡túm toti¡és ‖ cru¡délis ¡ tú quoque ¡ fálsis

lúdis i¡mágini¡bús ? ‖ cur ¡ déxtrae ¡ iúngere ¡ déxtram

nón datur, ¡ ác ve¡rás ‖ au¡díre et ¡ réddere ¡ vóces ? "

VEILED IN A CLOUD ÆNEAS AND ACHATES VIEW THE CITY

Tálibus ¡ íncu¡sát, ‖ gres¡súmque ad ¡ mœnia ¡ téndit.   410

Át Venus ¡ óbscu¡ró ‖ gradi¡éntes ¡ áëre ¡ sæpsit,

ét mul¡tó nebu¡læ ‖ cir¡cúm dea ¡ fúdit a¡míctu,

cérnere ǀ né quis e,ós, ǀǀ neu ǀ quís con,tíngere ǀ pósset.
Móli,ríve mo,ram, ǀǀ aút veni,éndi ǀ póscere ǀ caúsas.
Ipsa Pa,phúm sub,límis ab,ít, ǀǀ se,désque re,vísit   415
læta su,ás, ubi ǀ témpl*um* il,lí, ǀǀ cen,túmque Sa,bǽo
thúre ca,lént a,ræ ǀǀ ser,tísque re,céntibus ǀ hálant.
Córripu,ére vi,*am* ínvere,á, ǀǀ qua ǀ sémita ǀ mónstrat.
Iámq*ue* as,cénde,bánt col,lém, ǀǀ qui ǀ plúrimus ǀ úrbi
ímminet, ǀ ádver,sásq*ue* ǀǀ as,péctat ǀ désuper ǀ árces.   420
Míra,túr mo,l*em* Aéne,ás, ǀǀ ma,gália ǀ quóndam ;
míra,túr por,tás, ǀǀ strepi,túmq*ue* et ǀ stráta vi,árum.
Ínstant ǀ árden,tés Tyri,í ǀǀ pars ǀ dúcere ǀ múros,
móli,ríq*ue* ar,c*em,* ǀǀ ét mani,bús sub,vólvere ǀ sáxa ;
párs op,táre lo,cúm ǀǀ tec,to, ét con,clúdere ǀ súlco ;   425
iúra ma,gístra,túsque le,gúnt, ǀǀ sanc,túmque se,nátum ;
hic por,tús ali,*i* éffodi,únt ; ǀǀ hic ǀ álta the,átris
fúnda,ménta lo,cánt ali,*i,* ǀǀ ímma,nésque co,lúmnas
rúpibus ǀ éxci,dúnt, ǀǀ sce,nís deco,*ra* álta fu,túris :
quális a,pés aes,táte no,vá ǀǀ per ǀ flórea ǀ rúra   430
éxer,cét sub ǀ sóle la,bór, ǀǀ cum ǀ géntis a,dúltos
édu,cúnt fe,tús, ǀǀ aut ǀ cúm li,quéntia ǀ mélla
stípant, ǀ ét dul,cí ǀǀ dis,téndunt ǀ néctare ǀ céllas ;
aút one,*ra* áccipi,únt ǀǀ veni,ént*um,* aut ǀ ágmine ǀ fácto
ígna,vúm fu,cós ǀǀ pecus ǀ á prae,sépibus ǀ árcent :   435
férvet o,pús, redo,léntque thy,mó ǀǀ fra,grántia ǀ mélla.
"Ó for,túna,tí, ǀǀ quo,rúm iam ǀ mœnia ǀ súrgunt ! "

Aéne_|ás ait, _| ét, ‖ fas_|tígia _| súspicit _| úrbis.

Ínfert _| sé saep_|tús nebu_|lá, ‖ mi_|rábile _| díctu,

pér medi_|ós, mis_|cétque vi_|rís ; ‖ neque _| cérnitur _| úlli.   440

THE TEMPLE OF JUNO

Lúcus in _| úrbẹ fu_|ít medi_|á, ‖ lae_|tíssimus _| úmbrae,

quó pri_|múm iac_|táti un_|dís ‖ et _| túrbine _| Pœni

éffo_|dére lo_|có sig_|núm, ‖ quod _| régia _| Iúno

mónstra_|rát, caput _| ácris e_|quí ; ‖ sic _| nám fore _| béllo

égregi_|am ét faci_|lém vic_|tú ‖ per _| sǽcula _| géntem.   445

Híc tem_|plúm Iu_|nóni in_|géns ‖ Si_|dónia _| Dído

cónde_|bát, do_|nís ‖ opu_|léntum et _| númine _| dívae ;

aérea _| cuí gradi_|bús ‖ sur_|gébant _| límina, _| níxaeque

aére tra_|bés : ‖ fori_|bús car_|dó stri_|débat a_|ēnis.

Hóc pri_|mum ín lu_|có ‖ nova _| rés ob_|láta ti_|mórem   450

léniit, _| híc pri_|mum Aéne_|ás ‖ spe_|ráre sal_|útem

aúsus et _| áfflic_|tís ‖ meli_|ús con_|fídere _| rébus.

Námque sub _| íngen_|tí ‖ lus_|trát dum _| síngula _| témplo

régi_|nam ópperi_|éns, ‖ dum, _| quǽ for_|túna sit _| úrbi,

ártifi_|cúmque ma_|nús ‖ in_|tér se ope_|rúmque la_|bórem   455

míra_|túr, videt _| Ília_|cás ‖ ex _| órdine _| púgnas,

béllaque _| iám fa_|má ‖ to_|túm vul_|gáta per _| órbem,

Átri_|dás, Pria_|múmque, ‖ et _| sǽvum am_|bóbus A_|chíllen.

Cónstitit, _| ét lacri_|máns, ‖ " Quis _| iám locus," _| ínquit, " A_|cháte,

quǽ regi_|o ín ter_|rís ‖ nos_|trí non _| pléna la_|bóris?   460

Én Pria₁mús ! ‖ Sunt ₁ híc eti₁ám sua ₁ præmia ₁ laúdi ;
súnt . lacri₁mǽ re₁rum, ‖ ét men₁tém mor₁tália ₁ tángunt.
Sólve me₁tús ; feret ₁ hǽc ali₁quám ‖ tibi ₁ fáma sa₁lútem."
Síc ait, ₁ átque ani₁múm ‖ pic₁túra ₁ páscit i₁náni,
múlta ge₁méns, ‖ lar₁góque hu₁méctat ₁ flúmine ₁ vúltum.   465

THE PICTURED WALLS

Námque vi₁débat, u₁tí ‖ bel₁lántes ₁ Pérgama ₁ círcum
hác fuge₁rént Grai₁í, ‖ preme₁rét Tro₁iána iu₁véntus ;
hác Phryges ; ₁ ínsta₁rét cur₁rú ‖ cris₁tátus A₁chílles.
Néc procul ₁ hínc Rhe₁sí ‖ nive₁ís ten₁tória ₁ vélis
ágnos₁cit lacri₁máns, ‖ pri₁mó quae ₁ pródita ₁ sómno   470
Týdi₁dés mul₁tá ‖ vas₁tábat ₁ cǽde cru₁éntus,
árden₁tésque ·a₁vértit e₁quós ‖ in ₁ cástra, pri₁úsquam
pábula ₁ gústas₁sént Tro₁iǽ ‖ Xan₁thúmque bi₁bíssent.
Párte ali₁á fugi₁éns ‖ a₁míssis ₁ Tróilus ₁ ármis,
ínfe₁líx puer, ₁ átque im₁pár ‖ con₁gréssus A₁chílli,   475
fértur e₁quís, cur₁rúque hae₁rét ‖ resu₁pínus i₁náni,
lóra te₁néns ₁ tamen : ₁ huíc cer₁víxque co₁mǽque tra₁húntur
pér ter₁ram, ét ver₁sá ‖ pul₁vís in₁scríbitur ₁ hásta.
Íntere₁a ád tem₁plúm ‖ non ₁ ǽquae ₁ Pálladis ₁ íbant
crínibus ₁ Ília₁dés pas₁sís, ‖ pep₁lúmque fe₁rébant   480
súpplici₁tér tris₁tés ‖ et ₁ túnsae ₁ péctora ₁ pálmis ;
díva so₁ló fi₁xós ocu₁lós ‖ a₁vérsa te₁nébat.
Tér cir₁cum Ília₁cós ‖ rap₁táverat ₁ Héctora ₁ múros,

éxani₁múmqu*e* au₁ró ‖ cor₁pús ven₁débat A₁chílles.

Túm ve₁r*o* íngen₁tém gemi₁túm ‖ dat péctore ab ₁ ímo,   485
út spoli₁*a*, út cur rús, ‖ ut₁qu*e* ípsum ₁ córpus a₁míci,
ténden₁témque ma₁nús ‖ Pria₁múm con₁spéxit in₁érmes.

Sé quoque ₁ príncipi₁bús ‖ per₁míxt*um* ag₁nóvit A₁chívis,
Éo₁ásqu*e* aci₁és ‖ et ₁ nígri ₁ Mémnonis ₁ árma.

Dúcit A₁mázoni₁dúm ‖ lu₁nátis ₁ ágmina ₁ péltis   490
Pénthesi₁léa fu₁réns, ‖ medi₁ísqu*e* in ₁ mílibus ₁ árdet,
aúrea ₁ súbnec₁téns ‖ ex₁sértae ₁ cíngula ₁ mámmae
bélla₁tríx, au₁détque vi₁rís ‖ con₁cúrrere ₁ vírgo.

DIDO

Hǽc dum ₁ Dárdani₁*o* Áéne₁ǽ ‖ mi₁ránda vi₁déntur,
dúm stupet, ₁ óbtu₁túqu*e* ‖ hae₁rét de₁fíxus in ₁ úno,   495
régi₁n*a* ád tem₁plúm, ‖ for₁má pul₁chérrima ₁ Dído,
ínces₁sít, mag₁ná iuve₁núm ‖ sti₁pánte ca₁térva.

Quális in ₁ Eúro₁tǽ ri₁pís ‖ aut ₁ pér iuga ₁ Cýnthi
éxer₁cét Di₁ána cho₁rós, ‖ quam ₁ mílle se₁cútae
hínc at₁qu*e* hínc ‖ glome₁rántur o₁réades : ₁ ílla pha₁rétram 500
fért hume₁ró, ‖ gradi₁énsque de₁ás super₁éminet ₁ ómnes ;
Láto₁nǽ taci₁túm ‖ per₁téntant ₁ gaúdia ₁ péctus :
tális e₁rát Di₁dó, ‖ ta₁lém se ₁ lǽta fe₁rébat
pér medi₁ós, in₁stáns ope₁rí ‖ reg₁nísque fu₁túris.

Túm fori₁bús di₁vǽ, ‖ medi₁á tes₁túdine ₁ témpli,   505
sǽpt*a* ar₁mís ‖ soli₁óqu*e* al₁té sub₁níxa re₁sédit.

Iúra da₁bát le₁gésque vi₁rís, ‖ ope₁rúmque la₁bórem
pártibus ₁ æqua₁bát ius₁tís, ‖ aut ₁ sórte tra₁hébat ;
cúm subi₁to Aéne₁ás ‖ con₁cúrsu ac₁cédere ₁ mágno
Ánthea ₁ Sérges₁túmque vi₁dét ‖ for₁témque Clo₁ánthum   510
Teúcro₁rúmque ali₁ós, ‖ a₁tér quos ₁ æquore ₁ túrbo
díspule₁rát, ‖ peni₁túsque ali₁ás a₁véxerat ₁ óras.
Óbstupu₁ít simul ₁ ípse ‖ si₁múl per₁cússus A₁chátes
lætiti₁áque me₁túque : ‖ avi₁dí con₁iúngere ₁ déxtras
árde₁bánt ; sed ₁ rés ani₁mós ‖ in₁cógnita ₁ túrbat.   515
Díssimu₁lánt ; ‖ et ₁ núbe ca₁vá specu₁lántur a₁mícti,
quæ for₁túna vi₁rís ; ‖ clas₁sém quo ₁ lítore ₁ línquant ;
quíd veni₁ánt : ‖ cun₁ctís nam ₁ lécti ₁ návibus ₁ íbant,
óran₁tés veni₁am, ‖ ét tem₁plúm cla₁móre pe₁tébant.

THE TROJANS TELL THEIR STORY

Póstquam in₁trógres₁si, ‖ ét co₁rám data ₁ cópia ₁ fándi,   520
máximus ₁ Ílio₁neús ‖ placi₁dó sic ₁ péctore ₁ cœpit :
" Ó re₁gína, ‖ no₁vám cui ¡ cóndere ₁ Iúpiter ₁ úrbem
iústiti₁áque de₁dít ‖ gen₁tés fre₁náre su₁pérbas,
Tróës ₁ té mise₁rí, ‖ ven₁tís mari₁a ómnia ₁ vécti,
óra₁mús : ‖ prohi₁be ínfan₁dós a ₁ návibus ₁ ígnes ;   525
párce pi₁ó gene₁ri, ‖ ét propi₁ús res ˙₁ áspice ₁ nóstras.
Nón nos ₁ aút fer₁ró ‖ Liby₁cós popu₁láre pe₁nátes
vénimus, ₁ aút rap₁tás ‖ ad ₁ lítora ₁ vértere ₁ prædas :
nón ea ₁ vís ani₁mó, ‖ nec ₁ tánta su₁pérbia ₁ víctis.

Ést locus, ‚ Hésperi‚ám ‖ Grai‚í cog‚nómine ‚ dícunt,   530

térr*a* an‚tíqua, ‖ po‚téns ar‚mís · at‚q*ue* úbere ‚ glébae ;

Oéno‚trí colu‚ére vi‚rí ; ‖ nunc ‚ fáma mi‚nóres

Ítali‚ám di‚xísse du‚cís ‖ de ‚ nómine ‚ géntem.

Híc cur‚sús fuit ;

cúm subi‚*to* ássur‚géns fluc‚tú ‖ nim‚bósus O‚ríon   535

ín vada ‚ cæca tu‚lít, ‖ peni‚túsque pro‚cácibus ‚ aústris

pérq*ue* un‚dás, super‚ánte sa‚ló, ‖ per‚q*ue* ínvia ‚ sáxa

díspulit. ‚ Húc pau‚cí ‖ ves‚trís ad‚návimus ‚ óris.

Quód genus ‚ hóc homi‚núm ? ‖ quae‚*ve* húnc tam ‚ bárbara ‚ mórem

pérmit‚tít patri‚*a* ? hóspiti‚ó ‖ prohi‚bémur a‚rénae !   540

Bélla ci‚ént, ‖ pri‚máque ve‚tánt con‚sístere ‚ térra.

Sí genus ‚ húma‚n*um* ‖ ét mor‚tália ‚ témnitis ‚ árma,

át spe‚ráte de‚ós ‖ memo‚rés fan‚d*i* átque ne‚fándi.

Réx erat ‚ Aéne‚ás no‚bís, ‖ quo ‚ iústior ‚ álter

néc pie‚táte fu‚ít ‖ nec ‚ béllo ‚ máior et ‚ ármis :   545

quém si ‚ fáta vi‚rúm ser‚vánt, ‖ si ‚ véscitur ‚ aúra

aétheri‚á, ‖ neq*ue* ad‚húc cru‚délibus ‚ óccubat ‚ úmbris,

nón metus ; ‚ óffici‚ó ‖ nec ‚ té cer‚tásse pri‚órem

pœnite‚át. ‖ Sunt   ét Sicu‚lís regi‚ónibus ‚ úrbes,

árvaque, ‚ Tróia‚nóq*ue* ‖ a ‚ sánguine ‚ clárus A‚céstes.   550

Quássa‚tám ven‚tís ‖ lice‚át sub‚dúcere ‚ clássem,

ét sil‚vís ap‚táre tra‚bés ‖ et ‚ stríngere ‚ rémos,

sí datur ‚ Ítali‚ám, ‖ soci‚ís et ‚ rége re‚cépto,

téndere, ut ‚ Ítali‚ám ‖ lae‚tí Lati‚úmque pe‚támus,

sín ab¡súmpta sa¡lús, ‖ et ¡ té, pater ¡ óptime ¡ Teúcrum, 555

póntus ha¡bét Liby¡ǽ, ‖ nec ¡ spés iam ¡ réstat I¡úli,

át freta ¡ Sícani¡ǽ sal¡tém ‖ se¡désque pa¡rátas,

únde huc ¡ ádvec¡tí, ‖ re¡gémque pe¡támus A¡césten."

Tálibus ¡ Ílio¡neús; ‖ cun¡ctí simul ¡ óre fre¡mébant

Dárdani¡dǽ.   560

DIDO'S WELCOME AND GENEROUS OFFER

Túm brevi¡tér Di¡dó, ‖ vul¡túm de¡míssa pro¡fátur:

"Sólvite ¡ córde me¡túm, ‖ Teu¡crí, se¡clúdite ¡ cúras.

Rés du¡ra ét reg¡ní novi¡tás ‖ me ¡ tália ¡ cógunt

móli¡ri, ét la¡té ‖ fi¡nés cus¡tóde tu¡éri.

Quís genus ¡ Aénea¡dúm, ‖ quis ¡ Tróiae ¡ nésciat ¡ úrbem, 565

vírtu¡tésque vi¡rósque, ‖ aut ¡ tánti in¡céndia ¡ bélli?

Nón ob¡túsa ade¡ó ‖ ges¡támus ¡ péctora ¡ Pœni;

néc tam a¡vérsus e¡quós ‖ Tyri¡á Sol ¡ iúngit ab ¡ úrbe.

Seú vos ¡ Hésperi¡ám mag¡nám ‖ Sa¡túrnia¡que árva,

síve Ery¡cís fi¡nés ‖ re¡gémque op¡tátis A¡césten,   570

aúxili¡ó tu¡tós di¡míttam, ‖ opi¡búsque iu¡vábo.

Vúltis et ¡ hís me¡cúm ‖ pari¡tér con¡sídere ¡ régnis?

Úrbem ¡ quám statu¡ó, ves¡tra ést: ‖ sub¡dúcite ¡ náves;

Trós Tyri¡úsque mi¡hí ‖ nul¡ló dis¡crímine a¡gétur.

Átque uti¡nám rex ¡ ípse, ‖ No¡tó com¡púlsus e¡ódem, 575

áfforet ¡ Aéne¡ás! ‖ Equi¡dém per ¡ lítora ¡ cértos

dímit¡tam, ét Liby¡ǽ ‖ lus¡tráre ex¡tréma iu¡bébo,

sí quibus ¡ éiec¡tús ‖ sil¡vís aut ¡ úrbibus ¡ érrat."

ÆNEAS DISCLOSED

Hís ani₁m*um* árrec₁tí dic₁tís, ‖ et ₁ fórtis A₁chátes

ét pater ₁ Aéne₁ás ‖ iam₁dúd*um* e₁rúmpere ₁ núbem   580

árde₁bánt. ‖ Prior ₁ Aéne₁án com₁péllat A₁chátes:

"Náte de₁á, quae ₁ núnc ani₁mó ‖ sen₁téntia ₁ súrgit?

Ómnia ₁ túta vi₁dés, ‖ clas₁sém soci₁ósque ‸re₁céptos.

Únus ab₁ést, medi₁*o* ín fluc₁tú ‖ quem ₁ vídimus ₁ ípsi

súbmer₁súm; ‖ dic₁tís res₁póndent ₁ cétera ₁ mátris."   585

Víx ea ₁ fátus e₁rát, ‖ cum ₁ círcum₁fúsa re₁pénte

scíndit ₁ sé nu₁bés ‖ et in ₁ æthera ₁ púrgat a₁pértum.

Réstitit ₁ Aéne₁ás ‖ cla₁ráq*ue* in ₁ lúce re₁fúlsit,

ós hume₁rósque de₁ó simi₁lís: ‖ nam₁q*ue* ípsa de₁córam

cǽsari₁ém na₁tó gene₁tríx ‖ lu₁ménque iu₁véntae   590

púrpure₁*um* ét lae₁tós ‖ ocu₁lís af₁flárat ho₁nóres:

quále ma₁nús ad₁dúnt ‖ ebo₁rí decus, ₁ aút ubi ₁ flávo

árgen₁túm Pari₁úsve la₁pís ‖ cir₁cúmdatur ₁ aúro.

Túm sic ₁ régi₁n*am* álloqui₁túr, ‖ cun₁ctísque re₁pénte

ímpro₁vísus a₁it: "Co₁rám, quem ₁ quǽritis, ₁ ádsum   595

Tróïus ₁ Aéne₁ás, ‖ Liby₁cís e₁réptus ab ₁ úndis.

Ó so₁la ínfan₁dós ‖ Tro₁iæ mise₁ráta la₁bóres,

quæ nos, ₁ réliqui₁ás Dana₁úm, ‖ ter₁ræque ma₁rísque

ómnibus ₁ éxhaus₁tós ‖ iam ₁ cásibus, ₁ ómni*um* e₁génos,

úrbe do₁mó soci₁ás, ‖ gra₁tés per₁sólvere ‸ dígnas   600

nón opis ₁ ést nos₁trae, ‖ Di₁dó, nec ₁ quídquid u₁bíq*ue* est

géntis ₁ Dárdani₁æ, ‖ mag₁núm quae ₁ spársa per ₁ órbem.

Dí tibi, ₁ sí qua pi₁ós ‖ res₁péctant ₁ númina, ₁ sí quid

úsquam ₁ iústiti₁a ést ‖ et ₁ méns sibi ₁ cónscia ₁ récti,

præmia ₁ dígna fe₁ránt. ‖ Quae ₁ té tam ₁ læta tu₁lérunt 605

sæcula? ₁ quí tan₁tí ‖ ta₁lém genu₁ére pa₁réntes?

Ín freta ₁ dúm fluvi₁í cur₁rént, ‖ dum ₁ móntibus ₁ úmbrae

lústra₁búnt con₁véxa, ‖ po₁lús dum ₁ sídera ₁ páscet:

sémper ho₁nós no₁ménque tu₁úm, ‖ lau₁désque ma₁nébunt,

quǽ me ₁ cúmque vo₁cánt ter₁ræ." ‖ Sic ₁ fátus, a₁mícum 610

Ílio₁néa pe₁tít dex₁trá, ‖ lae₁váque Se₁réstum;

póst ali₁ós, for₁témque Gy₁án, ‖ for₁témque Clo₁ánthum.

RECEPTION OF ÆNEAS — A HOSPITABLE QUEEN

Óbstupu₁ít pri₁mo áspec₁tú ‖ Si₁dónia ₁ Dído,

cásu ₁ deínde vi₁rí tan₁to; ‖ ét sic ₁ óre lo₁cúta est:

" Quís te, ₁ náte de₁á, ‖ per ₁ tánta pe₁rícula ₁ cásus   615

ínsequi₁túr? ‖ quae ₁ vís im₁mánibus ₁ ápplicat ₁ óris?

Túne il₁le Aéne₁ás, ‖ quem ₁ Dárdani₁ó An₁chísae

álma Ve₁nús Phrygi₁í ‖ genu₁ít Simo₁éntis ad ₁ úndam?

Átque equi₁dém Teu₁crúm ‖ memi₁ní Si₁dóna ve₁níre,

fínibus ₁ éxpul₁súm patri₁ís, ‖ nova ₁ régna pe₁téntem   620

aúxili₁ó Be₁lí: ‖ geni₁tór tum ₁ Bélus o₁pímam

vásta₁bát Cy₁prum, ‖ ét vic₁tór diti₁óne te₁nébat:

témpore ₁ iam éx il₁ló ‖ ca₁sús mihi ₁ cógnitus ₁ úrbis

Tróia₁næ, no₁ménque tu₁úm, ‖ re₁gésque Pe₁lásgi.

Ípse hos,tís Teu,crós ‖ in,sígni ، laúde fe,rébat,   625

séque or,tum ánti,quá ‖ Teu,crórum ab ، stírpe vo,lébat.

Quáre agi,te, ó tec,tís, ‖ iuve,nés, suc,cédite ، nóstris.

Mé quoque ، pér mul,tós ‖ simi,lís for,túna la,bóres

iácta,tam hác de,múm volu,ít ‖ con,sístere ، térra.

Nón ig,nára ma,lí ‖ mise,rís suc,cúrrere ، dísco."   630

Síc memo,rát: ‖ simul ، Aéne,án in ، régia ، dúcit

técta; si,múl di,vúm ‖ tem,plís in,dícit ho,nórem.

Néc minus   ínter,eá ‖ soci,ís ad ، lítora ، míttit

vígin,tí tau,rós, ‖ mag,nórum hor,réntia ، céntum

térga su,úm, ‖ pin,gués cen,túm cum ، mátribus ، ágnos,   635

múnera ، lætiti,ámque de,í.

At domus ، ínteri,ór ‖ re,gáli ، spléndida ، lúxu

ínstrui,túr, medi,ísque pa,ránt ‖ con,vívia ، téctis:

árte la,bóra,tæ ves,tés ‖ os,tróque su,pérbo,

íngens ، árgen,túm men,sís, ، cae,látaque in ، aúro   640

fórtia ، fácta pa,trúm, ‖ seri,és lon,gíssima ، rérum,

pér tot ، dúcta vi,rós ‖ an,tíqua ab o,rígine ، géntis.

TROJAN GIFTS TO DIDO

Aéne,ás — neque e,ním patri,ús ‖ con,sístere ، méntem

pássus a,mór — ‖ rapi,dum ád na,vés prae,míttit A,cháten,

Áscani,ó ferat ، hæc, ‖ ip,súmque ad ، mœnia ، dúcat.   645

Ómnis in ، Áscani,ó ‖ ca,rí stat ، cúra pa,réntis.

Múnera ، prætere,a, ‖ Ília,cís e,répta ru,ínis,

férre iu₁bét, ‖ pal₁lám sig₁nís au₁róque ri₁géntem,

ét cir₁cúmtex₁túm ‖ croce₁ó ve₁lámen a₁cántho,

órna₁tús Ar₁gívae Hele₁næ ; ‖ quos ₁ ílla My₁cénis,   650

Pérgama ₁ cúm pete₁rét ‖ in₁cónces₁sósque hyme₁næos,

éxtule₁rát, ma₁trís Le₁dæ ‖ mi₁rábile ₁ dónum :

prætere₁á scep₁trum, ‖ Ílio₁né quod ₁ gésserat ₁ ólim,

máxima ‖ náta₁rúm Pria₁mí, ‖ col₁lóque mo níle

báca₁tum, ét dupli₁cém ‖ gem₁mís au₁róque co₁rónam.   655

Hæc cele₁ráns, iter ₁ ád na₁vés ‖ ten₁débat A₁chátes.

VENUS SUMMONS CUPID TO HER AID

Át Cythe₁réa no₁vás ar₁tés, ‖ nova ₁ péctore ₁ vérsat

cónsili₁a, út faci₁ém ‖ mu₁tátus et ₁ óra Cu₁pído

pró dul₁ci Áscani₁ó veni₁át, ‖ do₁nísque fu₁réntem

íncen₁dát re₁gínam, ‖ at₁que óssibus ₁ ímplicet ₁ ígnem ;   660

quíppe do₁múm timet ₁ ámbigu₁ám ‖ Tyri₁ósque bi₁língues.

Úrit a₁tróx Iu₁no, ‖ ét sub ₁ nóctem ₁ cúra re₁cúrsat.

Érgo his ₁ álige₁rúm dic₁tís ‖ af₁fátur A₁mórem :

"Náte, me æ vi₁rés, ‖ mea ₁ mágna po₁téntia ₁ sólus,

náte, pa₁trís sum₁mí ‖ qui ₁ téla Ty₁phóïa ₁ témnis,   665

ád te ₁ cónfugi₁o; ét sup₁pléx ‖ tua ₁ númina ₁ pósco.

Fráter ut ₁ Aéne₁ás ‖ pela₁gó tuus ₁ ómnia ₁ círcum

lítora ₁ iácte túr ‖ odi₁ís Iu₁nónis a₁cérbae

nóta ti₁bi ; ét nos₁tró ‖ dolu₁ísti ₁ sæpe do₁lóre.

Húnc Phoe₁níssa te₁nét Di₁dó, ‖ blan₁dísque mo₁rátur   670

vócibus; ǀ ét vereǀór, ǁ quo ǀ sé Iuǀnónia ǀ vértant

hóspitiǀa; haúd tanǀtó ǁ cesǀsábit ǀ cárdine ǀ rérum.

Quócirǀcá capeǀre ánte doǀlís ǁ et ǀ cíngere ǀ flámma

régiǀnám mediǀtór, ǁ ne ǀ quó se ǀ númine ǀ mútet,

séd magǀno Áéneǀǽ ǁ meǀcúm teneǀátur aǀmóre.   675

Quá faceǀre íd posǀsís, ǁ nosǀtrám nunc ǀ áccipe ǀ méntem:

régius ǀ ácciǀtú ǁ caǀrí geniǀtóris ad ǀ úrbem

Sídoniǀám puer ǀ íre paǀrát, ǁ mea ǀ máxima ǀ cúra,

dóna feǀréns, ǁ pelaǀgo ét flamǀmís resǀtántia ǀ Tróiae:

húnc ego ǀ sópiǀtúm somǀnó ǁ super ǀ álta Cyǀthéra   680

aút super ǀ Ídaliǀúm ǁ saǀcráta ǀ séde reǀcóndam,

né qua ǀ scíre doǀlós ǁ mediǀúsve ocǀcúrrere ǀ póssit.

Tú faciǀem illiǀús ǁ nocǀtém non ǀ ámplius ǀ únam

fálle doǀlo, ét noǀtós pueǀrí ǁ puer ǀ índue ǀ vúltus:

út cum ǀ té gremiǀo ǁ áccipiǀét laeǀtíssima ǀ Dído   685

régaǀlés inǀtér menǀsás ǁ latiǀcémque Lyǀǽum,

cúm dabit ǀ ámplexǀús ǁ atǀque óscula ǀ dúlcia ǀ fíget,

ócculǀtum ínspiǀrés igǀném, ǁ falǀlásque veǀnéno."

Páret Aǀmór dicǀtís ǁ caǀrǽ geneǀtrícis, et ǀ álas

éxuit, ǀ ét gresǀsú ǁ gauǀdéns inǀcédit Iǀúli.   690

Át Venus ǀ Áscaniǀó ǁ placiǀdám per ǀ mémbra quiǀétem

irrigat, ǀ ét foǀtúm gremiǀó ǁ dea ǀ tóllit in ǀ áltos

Ídaliǀǽ lu cós, ǁ ubi ǀ móllis aǀmáracus ǀ illum

flóribus ǀ ét dulǀci áspiǀráns ǁ comǀpléctitur ǀ úmbra.

THE BANQUET IN HONOR OF THE TROJANS

Iámqu*e* i_ibát dic_itó pa_iréns, ‖ et ، dóna Cu_ipído   695
régia ، pórta_ibát Tyri_iís, ‖ duce ، lǽtus A_icháte.
Cúm venit, ، aúlae_iís ‖ iam ، sé re_igína su_ipérbis
aúrea ، cómposu_iít spon_idá, ‖ medi_iámque lo_icávit :
iám pater ، Aéne_iás, ‖ et ، iám Tro_iiána iu_ivéntus
cónveni_iúnt, ‖ stra_itóque su_ipér dis_icúmbitur ، óstro.   700
Dánt famu_ilí mani_ibús lym_iphás, ‖ Cere_irémque ca_inístris
éxpedi_iúnt, ‖ ton_isísque fe_irúnt man_itélia ، víllis.
Quínqua_igínt*a* in_itús famu_ilǽ, ‖ quibus ، órdine ، lóngo
cúra pe_inúm strue_ire ét flam_imís ‖ ado_ilére pe_inátes ;
cént*um* ali_iǽ, ‖ toti_idémque pa_irés ae_itáte mi_inístri,   705
quí dapi_ibús men_isás one_irént, ‖ et ، pócula ، pónant.
Néc non ، ét Tyri_ií ‖ per ، límina ، lǽta fre_iquéntes
cónve_inére, to_irís ‖ ius_isí dis_icúmbere ، píctis.
Míran_itúr do_in*a* Aéne_iǽ ; ‖ mi_irántur I_iúlum,
flágran_itésque de_ií vul_itús, ‖ simu_ilátaque ، vérba,   710
pállam_iqu*e* ét pic_itúm croce_ió ‖ ve_ilámen a_icántho.
Prǽcipu_ie ínfe_ilíx, ‖ pes_ití de_ivóta fu_itúrae,
éxple_irí men_itém ‖ nequit, ، árdes_icítque tu_iéndo
Phœnis_is*a* ét pari_itér ‖ pue_iró do_inísque mo_ivétur.
Íll*e* ubi ، cómplex_i*u* Aéne_iǽ ‖ col_ilóque pe_ipéndit,   715
ét mag_inúm fal_is*i* ímple_ivít ‖ geni_itóris a_imórem,
régi_inám petit. ، Hǽc ocu_ilís, ‖ haec ، péctore ، tóto

hǽret; et ǀ ínterǀdúm gremiǀó ‖ fovet, ǀ ínscia ǀ Dído

ínsiǀdát quanǀtús ‖ miseǀrǽ deus! ǀ Át memor ǀ ílle

mátris Aǀcídaliǀǽ ‖ pauǀlátim aboǀlére Syǀchǽum   720

íncipit, ǀ ét viǀvó ‖ tenǀtát praeǀvértere aǀmóre

iám priǀdém resiǀdés aniǀmós ‖ deǀsuétaque ǀ córda.

FESTIVITIES FOLLOW THE FEAST

Póstquam ǀ príma quiǀés epuǀlís, ‖ menǀsǽque reǀmótae,

cráteǀrás magǀnós statuǀúnt, ‖ et ǀ vína coǀrónant.

Fít strepiǀtús tecǀtís, ‖ voǀcémque per ǀ ámpla voǀlútant   725

átria; ǀ dépenǀdént lychǀní ‖ laqueǀáribus ǀ aúreis

íncenǀsi, ét nocǀtém ‖ flamǀmís fuǀnália ǀ víncunt.

Híc reǀgína graǀvém ‖ gemǀmís auǀróque poǀpóscit

ímpleǀvítque meǀró pateǀrám, ‖ quam ǀ Bélus et ǀ ómnes

á Beǀló soliǀtí; ‖ tum ǀ fácta siǀléntia ǀ téctis: 730

"Iúpiter, ǀ hóspitiǀbús ‖ nam ǀ té dare ǀ iúra loǀquúntur,

húnc laeǀtúm Tyriǀísque diǀém ‖ Troǀiáque proǀféctis

ésse veǀlís, ‖ nosǀtrósque huǀiús memiǀnísse miǀnóres.

Ádsit ǀ lǽtitiǀǽ ‖ Bacǀchús dator, ǀ ét bona ǀ Iúno;

ét vos, ǀ ó coeǀtúm, ‖ Tyriǀí, celeǀbráte faǀvéntes."   735

Díxit, et ǀ ín menǀsám ‖ latiǀcúm liǀbávit hoǀnórem,

prímaque, ǀ líbaǀtó, ‖ sumǀmó tenus ǀ áttigit ǀ óre;

túm Bitiǀǽ dedit ǀ íncrepiǀtáns: ‖ ilǀle ímpiger ǀ haúsit

spúmanǀtém pateǀram, ‖ ét pleǀnó se ǀ próluit ǀ aúro;

póst aliǀí proceǀrés. ‖ Cithaǀrá criǀnítus Iǀópas   740

pérsonat ₁ aúra₁tá, ‖ docu₁ít quem ₁ máximus ₁ Átlas.

Híc canit ₁ érran₁tém lu₁nám ‖ so₁lísque la₁bóres ;

únde homi₁núm genus ₁ ét pecu₁dés ; ‖ un₁de ímber et ₁ ígnes,

Árctu₁rúm pluvi₁ásque Hya₁dás ‖ gemi₁nósque Tri₁ónes ;

qúid tan₁tum ócea₁nó prope₁rént ‖ se ₁ tíngere   sóles   745

híber₁ní, vel ₁ quæ tar₁dís ‖ mora ₁ nóctibus ₁ óbstet.

Íngemi₁nánt plau₁sú Tyri₁í, ‖ Tro₁ésque se₁quúntur.

Néc non ₁ ét vari₁ó ‖ noc₁tém ser₁móne tra₁hébat

ínfe₁líx Di₁dó, ‖ lon₁gúmque bi₁bébat a₁mórem,

múlta su₁pér Pria₁mó rogi₁táns, ‖ super ₁ Héctore ₁ múlta ; 750

núnc, quibus ₁ Aúro₁ræ ‖ ve₁nísset ₁ fílius ₁ ármis ;

núnc, qua₁lés Dio₁médis e₁quí ; ‖ nunc, ₁ quántus A₁chílles.

"Ímmo age, et ₁ á pri₁má ‖ dic, ₁ hóspes, o₁rígine ₁ nóbis

ínsidi₁ás," in₁quít, " Dana₁úm, ‖ ca₁súsque tu₁órum,

érro₁résque tu₁ós ; ‖ nam ₁ té iam ₁ séptima ₁ pórtat   755

ómnibus ₁ érran₁tém ‖ ter₁rís et ₁ flúctibus ₁ æstas."

Vergil Titles Published by Bolchazy-Carducci

A Digital Tutor for the AP* Selections from Vergil's *Aeneid*
Anthony Hollingsworth
(Forthcoming)

Vergil's *Aeneid*
Selections from Books 1, 2, 4, 6, 10, and 12, 2ND EDITION
Barbara Weiden Boyd
Student Text: (2004, 2nd edition)
Paperback, ISBN 0-86516-584-X Hardbound, ISBN 0-86516-583-1,
Teacher's Guide: (2002) Paperback, ISBN 0-86516-481-9

Vergil's *Aeneid*, 10 & 12: Pallas & Turnus
Barbara Weiden Boyd
Student Text: xii + 44 pp. (1998) Paperback, ISBN 0-86516-415-0
Teacher's Guide: vi + 13 pp. (1998) Paperback, ISBN 0-86516-428-2

Vergil's *Aeneid:* BOOKS I–VI
Clyde Pharr
Illus., xvii + 518 pp. + fold-out (1964, Reprint 1998) Paperback, ISBN 086516-421-5,
Hardbound, ISBN 086516-433-9

Vergil Vocabulary Cards for AP* Selections
Dennis De Young
184 pp. (2005) 8½" x 11" Paperback 0-86516-610-2

A Vergil Workbook
Latin Literature Workbook Series (LLWS)
Katherine Bradley and Barbara Weiden Boyd
x + 260 pp. (2006) 8½" x 11" Paperback 0-86516-614-5

Poet & Artist: Imaging the *Aeneid*
Henry V. Bender and David Califf
xvi + 88 pp., 2 Illustrations, (2004) 8 ½" x 11" Paperback + CD-ROM 0-86516-585-8

Why Vergil?
A Collection of Interpretations
43 essays plus bibliography (2000) Paperback, ISBN 0-86516-418-5
Hardbound, ISBN 0-86516-435-5

The Art of the *Aeneid*, 2ND EDITION
William A. Anderson
vi + 138 pp. 2005 (2nd Ed., 1989 reprint of the 1969 Prentice-Hall edition)
6" x 9" Paperback 0-86516-598-X

Vergil: A Legamus Transitional Reader
Thomas J. Sienkewicz and LeaAnn A. Osburn
xxiv + 136 pp, Line Drawings (2004) 8 ½" x 11" Paperback 0-86516-578-5

The Labors of Aeneas
What A Pain It Was to Found the Roman Race
vi + 108 pp. (2003) 6" x 9" Paperback, ISBN 0-86516-556-4

Vergil's *Aeneid*
Hero • War • Humanity
G. B. Cobbold, translator
xviii + 366 pp. (2005) 5" x 7 ¾" Paperback 0-86516-596-3

Vergil for Beginners: A Dual Approach to Early Vergil Study
Rose Williams
(Forthcoming)